MISS DJUNA BARNES i... ...an life as a singer, but because no voice ca... ...life without breaking, turned to quill and p... ...e necessary silence, the abundant inadequacie... ... Has been called eccentric, mad, inc... ...ne wonders why, thinking what a fine lyric be... *Ulysses* had, with impartial addenda for folia... ...*mber Music*, the casual inevitability of *Dubliners*, the passion and prayer of Stephen Dedalus. . . One wonders if at last Ireland has created her man.

MR. MATTHEW JOSEPHSON in **BROOM** (Rome): May be summed up as the work of a man who possesses an amazing sensibility for physical qualities, an extraordinary knowledge of English, and an inferior intellect. . . . There is a madness in him for *the word*: the play of it, the colour, the tempo of a handful of them. . . . Fragments of astonishing poetry. . . . Perhaps the sternest charge against *Ulysses* is its sinful length.

DOMINI CANIS in **THE DUBLIN REVIEW**: . . . A fearful travesty on persons happenings and intimate life of the most morbid and sickening description. . . . We are prepared to do justice to the power and litheness of the style, when intelligible, to the occasional beauty of a paragraph, and to the adventurous headlong experiments in new literary form, but as a whole we regard it as the screed of one possessed. . . . In this work the spiritually offensive and the physically unclean are united . . . in its reading lies not only the description but the commission of sin against the Holy Ghost. Having tasted and rejected the devilish drench, we most earnestly hope that this book be not only placed on the Index Expurgatorius, but that its reading and communication be made a reserved case. . . . A great Jesuit-trained talent has gone over malignantly and mockingly to the powers of evil.

THE SPORTING TIMES (THE " PINK'UN "): The main contents of the book are enough to make a Hottentot sick . . . not alone sordidly pornographic, but it is intensely dull.

MR. JAMES DOUGLAS in **THE SUNDAY EXPRESS**: I say deliberately that it is the most infamously obscene book in ancient or modern literature. The obscenity of Rabelais is innocent compared with its leprous and scabrous horrors. All the secret sewers of vice are canalised in its flood of unimaginable thoughts, images and pornographic words. And its unclean lunacies are larded with appalling and revolting blasphemies directed against the Christian religion and against the name of Christ. . . . The book is already the bible of beings who are exiles and outcasts in this and in every civilised country. It is also adopted by the Freudians as the supreme glory of their dirty and degraded cult.

MR. S. B. P. MAIS in **THE DAILY EXPRESS**: . . . From his pages there leap out at us all our most secret and most unsavoury private thoughts. Our first impression is that of sheer disgust, our second of irritability because we never know whether a character is speaking or merely thinking, our third of boredom at the continual harping on obscenities; our fourth, of real interest at watching the vagaries of a mind sensitive to all scents and sounds and colours. But art (if this is art) consists no longer in selection.

THE SPHERE: . . . The maddest, muddiest, most loathsome book issued in our own or any other time—inartistic, incoherent, unquotably nasty—a book that one would have thought could only emanate from a criminal lunatic asylum.

GLASGOW HERALD: Truthful, frank, insparing, and so it is bound to shock most people . . . a work of genius. . . .

DAILY MAIL: . . . Is being much discussed by those interested in the new Irish literature. . . . The book will cause mixed sensations in Dublin. Actual places and living persons are freely introduced into the pages, which are like uncensored photographs of Dubliners' doings and Dubliners' souls.

YORKSHIRE POST: An extremely interesting experiment in technique, large parts of the book being an absolutely candid record of the flow of consciousness and semi-consciousness in one mind. . . . with the last reticence, the last barrier which has hitherto divided Art and Life, burst down. . . . Ireland is the only country we can understand producing a brain so hardily callous in its clarity allied with an imagination so intense as to project *Ulysses*.

NEW YORK HERALD: There is to be found in *Ulysses* some of the finest English that has been written. . . . To Mr. Joyce the inexpressible does not exist. He proves the suppleness, the flexibility of English. . . . The record is monumental, almost staggering and incontestably true to life . . . of an almost diabolic clairvoyance.

SCOTS PICTORIAL: . . . Extraordinary, monstrous essay. . . Nothing like *Ulysses* has ever met the face of type.

LIVERPOOL DAILY COURIER: A freak production apart from its deliberate indecency, and it represents the newest school at its newest.

TEACHERS' WORLD: . . . Amazing work of madness and scatology which is causing such excitement among the " advanced " critics in London and Paris . . . immense mass of clotted nonsense.

IRISH INDEPENDENT: *Ulysses* has come in for some severe criticisms.

Leveridge & Co., Harlesden. N.W.

DEAR MISS WEAVER

DEAR MISS WEAVER

Harriet Shaw Weaver 1876–1961

JANE LIDDERDALE
& MARY NICHOLSON

THE VIKING PRESS
New York

Published in 1970 by The Viking Press, Inc.
625 Madison Avenue, New York, N.Y. 10022

SBN 670-26084-3

Library of Congress catalog card number: 70-124320

Printed in Great Britain

ACKNOWLEDGMENTS

HUMILITY, shyness and love of privacy made Harriet Weaver hard to know. The writers who saw her in her Egoist days knew little more about her than 'her great goodness', as one of them put it; most of her friends in the Communist Party learned of the help she gave James Joyce only from the obituaries; her family heard little about her literary or her political life. Fortunately, as I discovered after undertaking this biography, there was a remarkable amount of material, published and unpublished, to draw on; and the recollections given me were of the greatest help in bringing to light hidden pieces of the mosaic. When I had taken the work some way, however, I realized I could not finish it within a reasonable number of years single-handed. I asked a friend, Mary Nicholson, to help me, and later invited her to be joint author. We worked together very happily, and I am greatly indebted to her. But as it was to me that people lent material, gave their recollections and granted permission to quote, it falls to me to thank them.

Three people, whose help has been especially valuable, must be thanked first. Frank Budgen knew James Joyce well; and he knew and understood his feelings about women and about Harriet Weaver, both as a benefactress and as a friend. I am grateful to him and his wife for many invitations to Belsize Square, where I listened with profit and delight to his reminiscences. He was also good enough to read a number of chapters in draft and to allow me to quote from his *James Joyce and the Making of Ulysses*. Richard Ellmann gave me constant encouragement from the start; and he read, and gave me a string of detailed comments on, the (appallingly long) first draft. He also allowed me to quote as much as I liked from his superlative life of

7

ACKNOWLEDGMENTS

James Joyce and from a number of letters he lent me. From the nineteen-thirties, Miss Edith Walker probably saw more of Harriet Weaver than did any other friend. She was endlessly kind in drawing on her phenomenal memory; and without her help some important episodes would have gone unrecorded. She also kindly checked a number of drafts.

I owe a particular debt of gratitude to Harriet Weaver's sister Maude (the late Mrs Campbell Hone) and her sister-in-law—and my maternal aunt—Muriel (the late Mrs Alfred Weaver). They were unstinting in their help with the first two chapters (Part I), which they both read and corrected. Muriel Weaver knew a good deal about Harriet's life at Seldom Seen and also gave me detailed information on the last years, when they lived together at Castle End. The late Bishop Hone enlarged my understanding of the family's attitude to Harriet's literary and political pursuits. Several Hampstead contemporaries gave me many valuable reminiscences: two of Muriel Weaver's younger sisters, Miss Winnifred Adair-Roberts and Mrs Aileen Collison; and Mrs C. P. Barlow, Lady Floud and the late F. R. D'O. Monro, a life-long friend who became Harriet's solicitor —and James Joyce's. The late Miss Helen Saunders, who met Harriet during the First World War, gave me some notes on her recollections of that period and of the years Harriet spent at Oxford under the Saunders' roof. She wrote as well as she painted.

Harriet's eldest nephew, John Weaver, was good enough to lend some useful family papers; and her nieces Margaret Bruce Lockhart, Rosemary Cockle, Elizabeth Lovett Cameron, Katharine Mills, Mercy Olivier and Rosamond Snow, and her two other nephews R. M. (Robin) Hone and Anthony Weaver and his wife Alla gave me many recollections of their 'Aunt Hat'. The family was not given to keeping letters from her (or from anyone else); but Mercy Olivier and Anthony Weaver kept some, lent them and allowed me to quote from them. Margaret Bruce Lockhart and Anthony Weaver were good enough to read the final draft and suggested some amendments.

When he heard that this biography had been embarked upon, T. S. Eliot invited me to come to see him. But ill-health forced him first to postpone and eventually to abandon the meeting. Five other people who saw something of Harriet Weaver when she was running *The New Freewoman*, and then *The Egoist* and The Egoist Press were the greatest help in throwing light on the large but uneven mass of published and unpublished material bearing on this period: Miss Iris

8

ACKNOWLEDGMENTS

Barry, who met her during the First World War and who helped get out *Ulysses* for The Egoist Press; Miss Grace Jardine, who worked closely for several years with Dora Marsden; Miss Storm Jameson, Ezra Pound and Dame Rebecca West. Ezra Pound, though recovering from an operation—'I only came out of fog 5 days ago'—wrote twice and at length, his regard for Harriet Weaver still unswerving. He also kindly agreed to my quoting excerpts from a number of published and unpublished letters, a poem and three articles. Dame Rebecca met Harriet Weaver only once but she knew Dora Marsden well and introduced Ezra Pound to *The New Freewoman*, of which she was Assistant Editor. She generously gave a great deal of time to making suggestions for chapters 3, 4 and 5, and to reading and correcting the first draft of them. I am grateful to her also for giving permission to quote excerpts from several unpublished letters and from an article.

Patricia Hutchins met Harriet Weaver in the nineteen-forties, talked to her about *The Egoist* and later wrote about what she had learned. She kindly put together some useful notes, lent some unpublished drafts of her own, and agreed to my quoting from several letters from Harriet Weaver and one from T. S. Eliot, which she also lent me. The Home Office and the Commissioners of Customs and Excise took endless pains in helping me to piece together the history of the seizure of the second Egoist edition of *Ulysses*.

Mrs Maria Jolas was tireless in answering questions about the Joyce family and their troubles in the nineteen-thirties. She was also good enough to lend a number of letters and to allow me to quote extracts from some of them. The late Stuart Gilbert's views on some aspects of James Joyce's relations with Harriet Weaver were most valuable; and he read and commented on the passages dealing with his discussions with her about the first volume of *Letters*. George D. Painter and Professor T. J. Brown gave me vivid accounts of her visits to the British Museum before and after her gift to it of the *Finnegans Wake* manuscript. Professor Clive Hart kindly identified for me the early drafts from the *Wake* that she typed and commented upon; and J. S. Atherton was the greatest help in plotting the development of her views on it. A number of other Joyceans assisted in other ways. Among them, I would particularly like to thank Professor Walton Litz, whose description of the sort of help Harriet Weaver gave Joyce scholars was enlightening.

Geoffrey de Ste Croix, Mrs Maire Gaster, A. T. K. Grant, Miss

ACKNOWLEDGMENTS

Lucile Hyneman, Dr Elizabeth Jacobs, my brother Halliday Lidderdale, and Miss Helen Roeder all gave me their recollections of Harriet Weaver's political work in Marylebone; and Mrs Winifred Carritt, Mrs Isabel M. Cooper, Mrs M. Cortesio, Bridget and Christopher Hill, Ernie Keeling and Mick Leahy were equally kind in giving theirs of her political work in Oxford.

F. Lionel Monro, Executor with me of Harriet Weaver's Estate, kindly agreed to my housing her papers while I was working on them, and to my quoting from them and from her letters—mostly unpublished—and articles. As Administrator of the Estate of James Joyce, he was good enough to allow me to quote extensively from James Joyce's letters and excerpts from *A Portrait of the Artist as a Young Man* and from other writings. He also read the final draft and made some valuable corrections. Miss Elaine Dyson generously put at my disposal the papers left by her aunt Dora Marsden, and gave permission to quote from Miss Marsden's articles and (unpublished) letters. Her father, the late Reverend James Dyson, and her uncle, the late Ewart Marsden, were also most helpful in recalling details of Miss Marsden's experiences as a suffragette and her life at Seldom Seen. Mrs F. J. Dennis was most kind in allowing me to quote from letters (unpublished) from her sister, Sylvia Beach, to her family and to Harriet Weaver. Mrs T. S. Eliot was equally kind in giving permission to quote from some published and unpublished letters of her husband and from his article in the *Mercure de France* on Sylvia Beach.

For permission to quote excerpts from the *Letters of James Joyce* I must thank Faber and Faber and The Viking Press, as the publishers; from *A Portrait of the Artist as a Young Man*, Jonathan Cape, The Viking Press and the Society of Authors; from *James Joyce* by Richard Ellmann, the Oxford University Press; from *James Joyce and the Making of Ulysses* by Frank Budgen, the Indiana University Press; from *The Letters of Ezra Pound*, edited by D. D. Paige, Harcourt, Brace & World, Inc. and Faber and Faber; from *Being Geniuses Together* by Robert McAlmon, Michael Joseph, Ltd. and Doubleday & Co. (copyright © 1967 by Kay Boyle); from *Beginning Again* by Leonard Woolf and from *A Writer's Diary*, Being Extracts from the Diary of Virginia Woolf, edited by Leonard Woolf, the Literary Executor of the late Leonard and Virginia Woolf, The Hogarth Press, and Harcourt, Brace & World, Inc.; from the eight o'clock News Bulletin for 13th January 1941, the British Broadcasting Corporation.

ACKNOWLEDGMENTS

By the time this book is published, a passage from chapter 10 will have appeared in *The James Joyce Quarterly*.

For permission to quote unpublished letters, I am grateful to Samuel Beckett, Herbert Cahoon, the late Stuart Gilbert, Dr R. J. Hayes, then Director of the National Library of Ireland, Mrs B. W. Huebsch, Miss Storm Jameson, Mrs Stanislaus Joyce, Madame Paul Léon and John J. Slocum.

The Trustees of the British Museum were good enough to allow me to quote some passages from early drafts of *Finnegans Wake*. The Lockwood Memorial Library of the State University of New York at Buffalo gave permission to quote from letters in their Beach Collection from James Joyce to Sylvia Beach; and Oscar A. Silverman, the Director of Libraries, showed me a number of kindnesses. Cornell University Library gave permission to quote from their collection of letters from Harriet Weaver to James Joyce. Faber and Faber put all their 'Weaver' files at my disposal. They also lent me advance copies of Volumes II and III of the *Letters of James Joyce*—a great boon. (Harriet Weaver allowed some two hundred and sixty of his letters to her to be published in the *Letters* in whole or in part. Nearly half appeared in Volumes II and III, eventually published in 1966. It was not possible to study the originals as all his letters to her were bequeathed to the British Museum under a ten-year seal.)

The National Library of Ireland allowed me to use the correspondence between Harriet Weaver and their then Director, Dr R. J. Hayes; and to quote from a letter from her to James Joyce. Princeton University Library, as owners of the manuscripts, kindly gave permission to quote from their Beach Collection, which has two hundred and forty-five letters from Harriet to Sylvia Beach. The letters are not intimate but proved an invaluable source of information on many aspects of Harriet's life between 1920 and 1960. I owe a special debt of gratitude to Howard C. Rice Jnr, the Assistant University Librarian for Rare Books & Special Collections, whose interest and help was a great encouragement. The Society of Authors generously put at my disposal all their files of the James Joyce Estate, which throw much light on Harriet's work as Literary Executrix and as an Administrator of the Estate. Miss Anne Munro-Kerr, the Society's official in charge of the Estate, was a constant help and read in draft the passages on this work, which spanned twenty years. Yale University's Beinecke Rare Books and Manuscript Library kindly agreed to my quoting from the large correspondence between Harriet Weaver

ACKNOWLEDGMENTS

and John J. Slocum and Herbert Cahoon; and Miss Marjorie G. Wynne, their Research Librarian, took a great deal of trouble in answering numerous questions.

Miss Lucia Joyce was good enough to allow me to use an unpublished letter to her from her father and another from her mother; and to give me some recollections. J. S. Atherton, J. B. Bamborough, Bryher, Professor David Hayman, Professor Matthew Hodgart, the late B. W. Huebsch and Bjørn Rasmussen lent letters to them from Harriet Weaver; and Mrs T. S. Eliot, letters to her husband. The National Book League gave permission to quote inscriptions by James Joyce in books given by him to Harriet Weaver and also lent me their correspondence with her about her gift of the books to the League. New York Public Library allowed me to quote from a letter to John Quinn from Ezra Pound; and Texas University Library, a letter from her to J. Schwartz.

Many other people and bodies kindly provided information: the Librarian, Royal Astronomical Society; J. B. Bamborough; the Registrar, Bedford College (University of London); the Assistant Librarian, Department of Printed Books, Bodleian Library; F. H. Boland; the Keeper of Manuscripts, British Museum; Brown Knight & Truscott Ltd.; the General Secretary, Cambridge University Settlement; the Librarian, Carlisle Public Libraries; the General Secretary, Children's Country Holiday Fund; Miss Evelyn Cotton; Mrs Edna Cox; Constantine Curran; the Information Officer, Family Welfare Association; the Librarian, the Fawcett Library; the Clerk, Frodsham Parish Council; Donald C. Gallup; Miss Mary Gawthorpe; the late Miss Katie Gliddon; the General Secretary, Invalid Children's Aid Association; George Joyce; James (Stanislaus) Joyce; Alister Kershaw; Eustace H. Lidderdale; the London Master Printers Association; the Secretary, London School of Economics and Political Science; A. Lowy; the Registrar, University of Manchester; the Librarian, Royal Society of Medicine; Andrew Mellor; the Librarian, *The Morning Star*; Miss Iris Murdoch; Miss Barbara Niven; Partridge & Cooper (Westminster) Ltd.; Professor Norman Holmes Pearson; Arthur Power; Professor Joseph Prescott; the Federation of Master Process Engravers; the late Sir Herbert Read; Professor Ben L. Reid; Mrs Marianne Rodker; the late W. R. Rodgers; Anthony Rota; the Clerk, Rural District Council of Runcorn; the Honorary Secretary, St Hilda's East Settlement; the Town Clerk, former Metropolitan Borough of St Marylebone; the Honorary Secretary, St Marylebone

ACKNOWLEDGMENTS

Labour Party; the Librarian, former Metropolitan Borough of St Pancras; Miss Ethel Saunders; Mrs Elizabeth Solterer; J. V. Somers-Cocks; the Hospital Secretary, South London Hospital for Women and Children; A. F. Stephenson (*The Southport Visiter*); Professor W. Y. Tindall; Tinlings of Liverpool Ltd.; the Secretary, Toynbee Hall; F. H. Truslove; Miss Angela Tuckett; Dr Bertha Turner; Dr W. von Leyden; P. Beaumont Wadsworth; Michael Weaver (no relation).

For help in collating and checking texts, in collecting material and in other work, I am grateful to Mrs Enid Adelson, Miss Julia Bellord, Miss Barbara Cagby, Dennis Cole, Mrs Cynthia Clark, Miss F. N. Donnelly, Madame Marie-Laure Duchemin, Miss Dorothy Ethelston, my nieces Sarah Gretton and Hester Hawkes, my nephews Thomas and Edward Gretton, Nigel Lewis, Miss Marjorie Massey and Harriet's great-nephew Nicholas Weaver.

J. H. L.

Campden Hill,
September 1969

CONTENTS

15

CONTENTS

PART IV   1941–1961

ILLUSTRATIONS

ILLUSTRATIONS

ILLUSTRATIONS

Plates 2–6, 9, 19, 21, 25, 28, 33, 37, 39 and 43, and the end-papers (extracts from press notices issued by The Egoist Press) are reproduced by courtesy of the Executors of the Estate of the late Harriet Shaw Weaver.

PART I

1876—1912

I

EARLY YEARS

HARRIET SHAW WEAVER was born at Frodsham, a small country town in Cheshire, where her father was a doctor, on 1st September 1876. The four-square, late Georgian family house, on an abrupt bluff overlooking the river Weaver, winding its way to the Mersey, already housed five children—Mary, Edward, Annie, Kearsley and Alfred—besides a cook, a housemaid and Hannah their beloved nurse. Two more children, Harold and Maude, arrived later.

Dr Weaver and his wife were very loving parents and liked to have their family with them. The children came to dining-room meals as soon as they were old enough to sit at table and, unlike some 'nursery children', they grew up in a secure world of family affection. But the discipline was strict. The Weavers, staunch members of the Church of England, in its most evangelical form, believed that their upbringing should be carefully controlled, that their reading should be supervised and that all worldly pleasures—such as dances and theatres—must be banned. Every day, Dr Weaver read family prayers, not once but twice—in the dining-room before eight o'clock breakfast, and in the drawing-room at ten o'clock in the evening. When the gong sounded, the servants and then all the family (except the youngest) and visitors, trooped in. On Sundays, the younger children went to Sunday school, and the older ones went to church with their parents in the morning and in the evening. For the rest of the day, in their Sunday clothes, they were allowed to play only Sunday games and read Sunday books.

In her early childhood, when she knew no other way of life, Harriet was undoubtedly happy. She, Harold and Maude formed a little group on their own, occasionally joined by Alfred. In the garden and orchard there were many places to play. The field behind the house was good for rounders and cricket; and the room, with its great ox-eye window, in the coach house behind their father's surgery, was splendid for developing photographs, besides being the place where their elder brothers were, in due course, allowed to smoke. Harriet particularly loved climbing trees, walls and cliffs and used to 'give people fits' by her recklessness.

A joint enterprise of these younger members of the family was the East Bank Hen Company Limited, founded in 1886. Alfred was President, Harriet Treasurer, Harold Manager. Maude, then aged five, was called the 'sleeping partner . As it was she who fed the hens every morning before breakfast, she very understandably resented this and was mollified only when promoted to the post of Sub-Manager. The Company had 'about a dozen head of bird'—all called after medicines—and sold eggs and old hens for the table to their mother. Every year, Harriet distributed a dividend to the partners— her first, and successful, initiation into company business. The prime object of the enterprise was to make some pocket-money, not provided by their parents. But the takings from eggs laid on the sabbath were put into the missionary box.[1]

The children's education was moulded by Victorian conventions. Mary, gentle and retiring, had been sent to Cheltenham Ladies College, where she had done well but had not been happy and had suffered from headaches. She had been taken away after a year and none of the other girls was sent to boarding school. Harriet had a governess for the whole of her schooling. The education of the boys, too, was typical. They all went to Uppingham, (chosen because of the reforms in the old, hide-bound curriculum introduced there by its great headmaster, Edward Thring) and thence to Trinity College, Cambridge. If it be asked how a country doctor with a practice that was not very extensive (Frodsham then had a population of less than four thousand) could afford to educate four sons in this way, the answer is that he could not. He was helped.

A twenty-minute walk down the hill from East Bank and through Frodsham leads to Castle Park, a large and heavy-looking Georgian house spoilt by Victorian additions, built on the site of Frodsham Castle, a twelfth-century fortified manor that guarded the road to Chester. Here lived Edward Abbott Wright, Harriet's grandfather. He had been a cotton spinner in Oldham and had made a great deal of money by a great deal of hard work and exceptional foresight and drive. He had, no doubt, driven his work people at least as hard as himself; but he was, at least, the first to draw up and get accepted a standard list of wages for hand mule spinning and was recognized for his work in reducing friction between masters and men.[2] He had bought Castle Park in 1861, when still in his early fifties; and when Harriet grew up was living there, a widower, with two unmarried daughters, her aunts Harriet and Emily. His only son, through whom he had hoped to found a county family, had died when a schoolboy.

His relations with his eldest daughter Mary and her husband were never straightforward. He had opposed their marriage and had hoped, by delaying tactics pursued for three years, to get it called off. Dr Weaver, although of rather better social standing than the Wrights, was not a man of means, and, as a country doctor newly settled in Frodsham, could not be expected to become one. Mr Wright could not bring himself to welcome a son-in-law whose social suitability was not matched by the appropriate promise of success. He adopted and maintained until his death an attitude of reserve towards him and his growing family and did nothing directly to ease his decidedly limited circumstances. This was why, among other things, the younger children depended on the Hen Company for pocket money. Mr Wright was prepared, however, to educate the boys.

Harriet's own education at home owed much to her father. Dr Weaver loved poetry and had an immense capacity for learning it by heart and a fondness for reciting it. He expected the same of his children. On any suitable occasion, in the evening and particularly on walks, he would recite to them and get them to recite to him. The language of the great English poets was familiar to Harriet from her earliest years, as a language to be spoken and remembered.*

Her education owed much also to the governess who came when she was ten and remained until she was eighteen and her formal schooling was brought to an end. Miss Marion Spooner was a young gentlewoman of decided powers. She was a good linguist and very musical, though these were qualities to which Harriet and the others,

---

* Years later, when Harriet Weaver was thirty-three, the memories of the four Weaver daughters were put to a remarkable test. The family was at Worthing, where Mrs Weaver was recovering from an illness. Nearby was a series of roads called after poets—Wordsworth, Byron, Shelley, Southey, Tennyson, Shakespeare, Cowper. Dr Weaver took his daughters along them and required each to repeat something different by the poet after whom the road in which they were at that moment was called.

25

who all had no ear, could not respond. She had a vivid interest in history and in current affairs and pronounced Liberal views. To these Harriet warmed. Under Miss Spooner's tutelage she probably received as broad an education as any single-handed teacher could have given her.

Harriet very soon became a great reader, partly for the love of reading and partly in reaction against her mother's rigid views of what was and what was not appropriate to her education. Reading became a refuge and secret reading an act of defiance. She was already seeking moral freedom, and she was acutely sensitive to any restrictions imposed on conduct or thought. Her sisters were less troubled by them.

A large family of boys and girls creates its own society and cannot altogether be run by rule. Differing attitudes and aims and principles can develop almost unseen, and there are many occasions, however strict the rule, when happy children do not ask themselves if what they are doing is right or wrong. Harriet was not this kind of buoyant, unquestioning child; she wanted to rebel. But she could not be the kind of child who gains, by rebelling openly, a reassuring measure of tolerance. Her love for her family and for good order and good manners, strong through life, divided her will and forced her to notice, and suffer some anxiety, when she ventured even in thought outside the approved terrain. She kept her own counsel, but she was recognized as tense and nervous. Her sisters began to find her difficult to talk to and, although it was a period when highly-strung children were not indulged, they sometimes wondered if she was happy.

Walt Whitman was one of the authors she discovered and loved without the guidance of her parents or her governess:

I had a narrow upbringing in a small provincial town but somehow or other came across a pocket edition of *Leaves of Grass*—though in what edition I cannot be sure and found it a liberating influence and even could discreetly read it on Sundays as it wasn't a novel![3]

In 1892 the family moved from Frodsham. Harriet's grandfather had died and her mother had inherited her share of a very considerable fortune. The decision was made to move to London. There were strong reasons for it. Edward was already established there, a gay young bachelor reading for the Bar, and Kearsley was studying medicine and was to go to Barts.* It would be far better for them to live at home than in lodgings. Besides, the Frodsham Parish Church services, influenced by the Oxford Movement, had become altogether too 'High'.

The choice of Hampstead appears to have been determined, at any rate in part, by Mrs Weaver's regard for Christ Church, a Gothic Revival edifice which then seated one thousand four hundred and had a thriving and suitably 'Low' congregation which supported twenty-five missionaries. Hampstead itself, at that time on the edge of open country, had much else to offer a family of young people devoted to walks and to outdoor games of all sorts and with developing interests—professional, social, charitable—of various kinds.

Cedar Lawn, the house to which they moved, stood at the summit of the hill just beyond the Whitestone Pond. It had grounds of more than two acres giving on to the West Heath and had a splendid view over to the Harrow Ridge and Berkshire and Buckinghamshire hills. It was a long, straggling house, partly Georgian, partly Victorian, largely covered with Virginia creeper and of no architectural pretensions. Its glory was its garden and its great cedars. For the next twenty-two years it was Harriet's home, a home which, in its essentials, differed not at all from the old one at Frodsham. There were now, it is true, six inside servants, including their dear Hannah, who had come with them, a coachman, a gardener, who lived in the lodge, and a boy. Miss Spooner had also come with them and lived in, by then a fast friend of the family and known as Birdie. Life was comfortable, but it remained simple and unworldly. Family prayers continued to be said twice every day. Theatres were still not allowed. Luxuries, whether in food or in dress, were unknown. There is a story of Harriet's brother Alfred lunching with his tutor at Cambridge and being confronted for the first time with asparagus. Some quick thinking brought him to the conclusion that it most resembled celery. He proceeded to eat the white, not the green, part to the astonishment of his tutor who, when luncheon was over, could contain himself no longer. 'Mr Weaver, please forgive me, but may I enquire why it is that you eat the stalk and not the tip of asparagus?' Alfred felt that he had let not so much himself as the family down: its honour must be defended. 'Oh,' he said, with as much nonchalance as he could muster, 'we always eat it like that at home. We prefer it.'

* St Bartholomew's Hospital, London.

A strong sense of family solidarity is no doubt characteristic of the period; but the Weaver family seems to have been, even for the period, exceptionally close-knit. Because of their evangelical upbringing, the children were dependent to an unusual degree on their own and their relations' social resources though the move to Hampstead soon brought a wider circle of acquaintances, some of them interesting and distinguished people. Sir Samuel Hoare, for instance, who lived next door in the house later owned by Lord Leverhulme, was an early member of this wider circle.

The presiding spirits of the household—Dr and Mrs Weaver— were both, in their different ways, pervasive influences. Harriet was fifteen when the family moved to Hampstead. This is about the age when children recognize that the father and mother they know and love, in relation to themselves, exist also as independent human beings with distinct views and temperaments and histories.

John Weaver, her paternal grandfather, came of a long line of Cheshire yeoman farmers—farmers who owned their land but had no tenants. He became a successful doctor in Chester and was known at the Infirmary as the 'dandy' doctor. He married Anne Davies, the daughter of a surgeon who had practised in London but had by then returned to his native Cheshire to remove his daughters from its temptations. Harriet's father, Frederic Poynton Weaver, was the seventh of their twelve children. At the age of fifteen he was 'apprenticed' to his father as 'Surgeon and Apothecary'. After qualifying at Guy's Hospital, London, he returned to Cheshire, worked for a time with his father, and in 1863 went to Frodsham to look after the practice of a sick colleague, who died within the month. He took over his practice and his house and the same year met and fell in love with Mary Wright.

Harriet's father became a good doctor, particularly with babies and young children. But he was never a very successful one, even within the limitations of a country practice. One reason for this was undoubtedly the wide range of his interests: travel, walking, poetry and, as an unswerving Conservative, politics and local government. When he left Frodsham, he gave up regular practice and devoted himself to his many interests. He was soon a Justice of the Peace, a churchwarden at Christ Church, and, perhaps more important to him than anything else, a member of the board of numerous medical missionary societies. To these societies, he also gave practical help, examining their candidates for service abroad, and holding a Thursday surgery at the Kentish Town Medical Mission. The care of those who were poor, as well as sick, had been a lifelong concern; and he worked at Kentish Town for fifteen years, until he was well over seventy.

His good works were inspired by an exacting faith. When he was twenty, and in doubt about his career, he had suffered also from a 'deep sense of sin' until he had been led, one Sunday in April, 'by the mercy of God to accept Jesus Christ as a Sacrifice for sin and to resolve with God's help henceforth to live to His glory'. In old age, he looked back on this event 'as the most important of his life'.[4] But his style, as visitors to the house saw it, was not conscience-ridden. He was always hospitable, made whimsical jokes which they did not always grasp, and kept up a number of old-fashioned traditions, as for instance reciting Grace after meat *before* the dessert came round. Dr Weaver, everyone agreed, was 'a dear'.

He and his wife were devoted, they shared many interests and, as he put it, 'were agreed in principles' but in many ways they were unlike. She was a more complicated person, harder to get to know. He was a good height, pleasant looking, neat looking, rather polished. She was short, rather plain and had a protruding lower lip. When she spoke she used the clipped north country 'a' (as Gladstone did) and she was always dressed very simply. Behind this rather severe appearance lay a very clear mind. She was an exceptionally intelligent woman and had inherited something of her father's mathematical brain. She had followed closely her children's early education, and had taught them Scripture. She read to them in the evening, from their earliest days until long after they were grown up. She had a very sweet voice and read aloud well and felt that everyone should be taught to do so. She was very much loved. All her children loved her. Their friends loved her and they never forgot her or her hospitality, especially the supper parties she gave after tennis at which she would quietly preside, looking rather small and dumpy, at the end of the huge, long dining-room table.

The inheritance of wealth made not a jot of difference to her mode of life. Except that entertaining of family and friends was undertaken on a larger scale, her daily round continued at Cedar Lawn exactly as it had done at East Bank. She continued to rise in the winter at six o'clock and in the summer at half past five, to dress and to go to her sitting-room to read her Bible and then to make tea, when she would sometimes be joined by a son after an early morning walk or ride.

She retired to bed every night as soon as prayers were over—that is, shortly after ten o'clock. These habits she considered good ones and she had very firm and long-held views on the importance of acquiring good habits. 'It is much more difficult,' she had written in a school-girl essay, 'to overcome a bad Habit, than it is to form a new one; for this reason, the Grecian flute-players were accustomed to charge double fees to those pupils who had been taught by inferior masters. . . .'[5]

Mrs Weaver was a person not only of fixed habits but of fixed views. It would not be right to call her prejudiced. Before making a decision on any action or before making up her mind about any issue, she would consider it carefully and objectively but once her mind was made up she was inflexible—nothing could move her. For instance, in November, 1880, her husband had a bad fall from a shying horse and fractured a bone in his back. She decided to nurse him herself and continued to do so for six months—until brought to bed of her eighth child. She did not have her husband's imaginative quality or range of interest but she was admirably suited to ruling a large household and, at the age of fifty-two, rose quietly to the challenge of inherited wealth.

When the family moved to Hampstead, and for some years after, there was nothing about Harriet's everyday behaviour or about her interests to suggest that she would not continue indefinitely to share their outlook and views. The most striking thing about her was her love of games. Hockey was her first love. The youngest Weavers, very soon after their arrival, started a mixed hockey team, first play-ing on the Heath and later hiring a field for the winter. Harriet played an 'unflinching' game, sometimes as a back but more often in goal. She very soon established herself as outstanding and became known throughout their acquaintance as 'the bold Harriet'. Hockey gradually gave way to lawn tennis. A Hampstead friend recalled: 'Harriet played a very good and steady game, back line only of course for women in those days. She was nice to watch, being so lithe, but perhaps too serious. I cannot remember her smiling when playing'. 'We had a pretty high standard of tennis and H.S.W. was as good as any of us. I can see her bashing away at the ball, standing behind the back line and doing long sweeping drives across the court, wearing her usual determined expression.'*[6]

* In fact, Phyllis Ford (now Lady Floud), was generally admitted to be the best woman player, and Harriet second only to her.

In 1894, Birdie Spooner left, though she was to remain a lifelong friend. Harriet was eighteen. She would have liked to go to a university and even put out a tentative feeler. Her parents' response was practical and negative: 'What would be the use of such a course?' None of their daughters would ever need to earn her living and the pursuit of a profession for its own sake was not for them. The same answer had been given to Annie. She would have liked to be a doctor but never got nearer to medicine than dispensing at the Kentish Town Medical Mission—and a very good dispenser she was.

There was nothing out of the ordinary in Dr and Mrs Weaver's attitude: most parents of their day and in their position would have given the same answer. But it was perhaps Mrs Weaver's influence that was decisive. Contemporaries of her children who remembered her attitude considered that she was stricter than most with her daughters, was more concerned to protect them from worldly influences. Besides, though she was intelligent, she was not an intellectual.

Harriet's next years, therefore, were given to following short courses of various sorts, to reading on her own and, generally, to living the life of a daughter at home. She had drawing lessons at the Hampstead Conservatoire and French lessons with a Mademoiselle Marcelle Couton, to whom 'everyone' in Hampstead then went. Soon she joined seven others as a teacher at the Infants' Sunday School at Christ Church. Mary, already very experienced, had been teaching the older children since the Weavers' arrival in Hampstead and Annie had joined her the following year. They both taught at the parish mission house at North End, the hamlet north of Cedar Lawn. It was clearly expected of Harriet that she should follow in their footsteps; and she taught for six years, from 1896 to 1901.*[7]

It is not difficult to guess her reason for choosing the Infants' class. Her doubts about her faith were already beginning to trouble her and she would have chosen the infants, those aged three to seven, because they would not be expected to address their minds to questions of doctrine.

Harriet's early reading was what would be expected of a young person of her generation and background: Scott, Dickens, Thackeray, George Meredith, Jane Austen, the Brontës. But this phase was not to

* One of Harriet Weaver's later, and very junior, charges was christened Albert Diamond Jubilee, a singular tribute to the sixtieth anniversary of the accession of Her Majesty Queen Victoria!

last long. With some notable exceptions, novels ceased to attract her. Essayists interested her: Emerson, Oliver Wendell Holmes. Love of poetry, inherited from her father and encouraged by him, and a thorough-going and meticulous approach to study inherited from her mother, led to the development of a more personal taste. Coleridge she loved, particularly *Christabel* and *Kubla Khan*. Milton, Wordsworth, Shelley, Keats, Browning she knew well and enjoyed. If she could not sleep at night she would repeat to herself Shelley's *Ode to the West Wind*:

> ... *Wild Spirit, which art moving everywhere;*
> *Destroyer and preserver; hear, oh, hear! ...*

Tennyson she was not fond of, except for the *Lotus Eaters*—very different from another *Lotus Eaters* she was to discover later on. But first and always there was Shakespeare. Much she learned by heart. She and Maude used to repeat the dialogue 'On such a night . . .' from *The Merchant of Venice*, saying the parts in turn.

Birdie Spooner's main influence had been towards politics and economics. Harriet became a frequent borrower from the Hampstead Public Library and was soon a disciple of John Stuart Mill. Her desire for independence of mind, for freedom of thought (if not of action) for herself, manifested in small, hardly detectable ways from her early years, was maturing and becoming more articulate and she found in *Liberty* a philosophic justification, a sanction, for championing individualism: 'We can never be sure that the opinion we are endeavouring to stifle is a false opinion; and if we were sure, stifling it would still be an evil'. 'All good things that exist are the fruits of originality.' Such statements strike a youthful, groping mind with a double force. They seem at once to give form to unformed thoughts and to come as a revelation. Mill's liberal, radical political philosophy gave her a framework within which to develop her own thoughts on social progress and his work on *The Subjection of Women* gave her support for her own personal and growing preoccupation with this issue.

About the reading Harriet was known to have achieved there is nothing remarkable. But, never content to allow her reading to be directed or inspired solely by her seniors, she had continued to read on her own and had refrained from drawing attention to or discussing an author that might not be acceptable. This early habit, in which self-assertion, discretion, and consideration for others were nicely

1 Harriet aged four

2 Three members of the Board of the East Bank Hen Company—Harriet, Harold, and Maude—in 1886

3 Harriet aged about fourteen

4 A house party at Ballater, about 1897. Harriet is standing between her father and Harold and behind Annie and her mother, who has Maude beside her, on the rug. Alfred is standing on the right behind Mary

blended, had become entrenched. On one never-to-be-forgotten occasion, however, her discretion failed her.

One day at Cedar Lawn her mother came into the room in which Harriet was sitting reading and enquired what it was that was absorbing her. Harriet held up the book she had just begun: it was *Adam Bede*. This was not one, she felt, that might be frowned upon. But she was wrong. Her mother was horrified, aghast. To her, and to countless others of her generation and outlook, novel reading by young women was a pastime, to be indulged only with restraint; and, far more important, it had to be rigorously limited to works innocent of ideas or events or characters likely in any way to distress or to harm their daughters. *Adam Bede* was well known to be the story of a girl who had brought into the world an illegitimate child. And this was not all. It was written by a woman who had lived for over twenty years with a man who was not her husband. Mrs Weaver told Harriet that she had better go up to her room until she was called. She felt unable to speak to her herself and so begged the Vicar, Canon Head, to come at once, to explain why the book could not be countenanced. The Vicar came. Harriet was called down from her room and heard what he had to say. The book was taken from her.*

Whatever the rights and wrongs of this incident, it was to remain branded on her mind for the rest of her life. Fifty years later she was to speak of it, to a sympathetic niece, in a low voice and with pain. It epitomized for her the coming conflict between her loyalty to her family and her championing of freedom of thought and the rights of the individual. Its immediate effect must have been to encourage further clandestine reading. What she read secretly in the years that followed will never be known, but, together with what she read openly, it unquestionably deepened her sympathy with advanced views, and advanced movements, whether social, political or literary, and helped her to be ready to identify herself with them when the time came.

---

* Harriet Weaver confided this story to Robert McAlmon, the American writer whose work she was to publish in the early 1920's. His account of it in his autobiography, in which he describes her as a Quaker and as having been 'reprimanded from the pulpit by the village minister' is not altogether accurate if only because the Society of Friends has no ministers and no pulpits.

2

SOCIAL WORK

AFTER TWO or three years given to private reading and the round of lessons and lectures thought appropriate for her, Harriet needed some wider activity, and it was natural that her thoughts should turn towards social work. Both family tradition and her own budding interest in political and social problems inclined her in this direction. But what should she do?

The answer was suggested, one day at Cedar Lawn, by a young man just down from Cambridge with a First in History: Frederick Waldegrave Head, the Vicar's son.* He was talking about his work in Bermondsey for the Children's Country Holiday Fund, when he turned to Harriet and said: 'Why don't you come and I'll give you a job?'

The Holiday Fund, founded by Canon Barnett, had grown rapidly from small beginnings. He and his wife had taken a few ailing children from their East End parish down to a house in Cornwall they had for the summer of 1877. By the time Harriet was roped in, the Fund had sent away over thirty thousand children for a holiday. There were thirty local committees engaged throughout the year in sorting out applications: not more than one child in forty could be accepted.[1]

Harriet's regular job was to collect pennies at a school in Bermondsey from the children fortunate enough to have been chosen. If parents could not afford to give anything, that was no bar; but, if they could, they were asked to do so. A very usual assessment for the fortnight was 3s. 6d., which was collected from the children, penny by penny, before the time for the holiday came. Harriet also visited

* Later Archbishop of Melbourne.

34

parents of children not yet chosen and of those who had been chosen, and kept in touch with them at every stage. She soon established a reputation for remembering accurately and at once the address of and details about any child whose name came up for discussion. But, though she liked the work well enough, it was not suited to her interests because it offered only fleeting contact with multitudinous ailing children. As she gradually came to realize, her interests lay in giving sustained support to a small number of protégés chosen for their promise.

This first, tentative step beyond the family circle, however, led to more than ten years of voluntary work largely inspired by two remarkable people: her cousin, Eleanor Davies-Colley, and the political philosopher E. J. Urwick.

After two or three years working for the Holiday Fund, Harriet received an invitation from her cousin to help her in her work for invalid and other children in a district north of the Thames. '. . . how can I persuade you of the greater attractions of St George's in the East as a district to work in?', she wrote. '. . . I have found no one to take over some of my work for me . . . I wish you could come, not really so much on account of my present distress, as because I should like to have you working with me . . .'.[2]

Eleanor Davies-Colley, Harriet's cousin on her father's side, was two years her senior. She came of a long line of doctors: one, in the eighteenth century, had been Apothecary to three King Georges; her father was a distinguished surgeon. She was able, brilliant and beautiful, with a smile that lit up her rather austere face. On leaving school, she had plunged into work in the East End, and was soon living, on a very small income, in a 'people's dwelling' in Wapping, one of the poorest and roughest districts on the north bank.

Elly, as she was known to Harriet, felt passionately about social conditions and particularly about inequality of opportunity for children. Her breadth of view, her vision and her reforming zeal raised Harriet's conception of social work to a new level.

The Invalid Children's Aid Association became Harriet's prime concern.* Because of shortage of funds, it could help only those who were 'seriously invalided' and whose condition gave promise of at least some improvement. For such children the society tried to obtain the best possible medical treatment and, if necessary, training for

* The Association was founded in 1888.

earning a livelihood. It worked chiefly through 'visitors', who were voluntary. Visitors were grouped under 'representatives' and they, in turn, under local committees.

Harriet began as a visitor, working under her cousin, and before long had got to know Wapping and the many agencies from which help might be sought. Then Elly came to the conclusion that she could help her fellow human beings in a more definite and satisfactory way if she were a doctor. She worked in the evening for the examinations that would qualify her to enter the London School of Medicine for Women and, when she had passed them, she handed over her work for the invalid children to Harriet.

Harriet took over from her cousin in 1902 both as honorary secretary of the East End branch of the Association and as representative for St George's-in-the-East, the riverside slum of mean streets, warehouses and wharfs dominated by its magnificent early eighteenth-century church (by Hawksmoor), built when the sea captains and merchants had houses there. For trees, there were masts of ships tied up or nosing their way alongside the streets to their berths in the docks.

The office of the East End branch had recently moved to a club room put at its disposal by Toynbee Hall, in Commercial Street, about a mile from St George's.* Toynbee provided Harriet not only with an office but with a stable base, always manned, from which to pursue her case work; and with a circle of like-minded young people.

Her first undertaking was an examination of all the cases on the books, in order to establish exactly what the current position was. She finished the year with three hundred and seventy-five 'live' cases, of which one hundred and twenty-three were new. Three years later, she had five hundred and seven cases and she had four visitors under her in her own St George's district, a great improvement on the single visitor of the previous years.

Most of the diseases from which the children suffered were those to be expected from the conditions in which they lived—tuberculosis and rickets, for example. Here is a report of a typical case dealt with at this period:

* Toynbee Hall, founded in 1884, was the first settlement and the prototype of others in England and overseas. It was built by Canon Barnett next his St Jude's rectory and named by him after Arnold Toynbee, the social reformer and economist, who had had many ties with Whitechapel.

Johnnie W., a little Jewish boy, aged four years. In September, 1902, this child's parents applied to us for help to keep him at a Nursing Home in South London, in which he had been for the previous three months. He was suffering from severe rickets, and was unable to speak or to walk. It was feared, indeed, that he was mentally deficient. We gave the parents some help in co-operation with the Jewish Board of Guardians. In March, 1903, the child was transferred to a cottage near Southend. He returned home the following September wonderfully improved and able to run about. In December 1903, having become weak again, Johnnie was sent back to Essex for another long stay. He has been at home now for five months, and appears to be quite cured. . . .[3]

The East End Branch Committee was a strong one. It included in its membership R. C. K. Ensor, the writer and historian, later to be knighted, whose *Modern Socialism* had recently appeared; and its honorary treasurer was E. J. Urwick, then at the beginning of a long and distinguished career as an economist and political philosopher.

In 1905, however, Harriet resigned. The Committee were sorry to lose her and recorded in their annual report:

. . . Her loss was a very serious one, for her long connection with the Association had given her a thorough grasp of all branches of the work.[4]

The honorary treasurer's regret was more formal than real. He had influenced her to take up, instead, a special course of study. She had decided she wanted to delve more deeply into problems of social justice and later, perhaps, to become a professional social worker; and she was going to the London School of Sociology and Social Economics, founded two years previously by the Charity Organization Society.* Mr Urwick was its director. She was also to attend a course of lectures he was to give that autumn on 'Social Relations at the Present Day: the Economic Basis of Social Relations' at the London School of Economics, then a small institution ten years old with a part-time staff and open only to adult students.

E. J. Urwick was a great teacher. Behind his piercing eye, walrus

* This School was pioneering a course that included training in methods of administration and the study of underlying subjects—industrial history, economic theory, sociology—as well as practical work.

moustache and courtly manner lay a passionate desire to help his students to develop a capacity to relate the knowledge they derived from books and courses to the problems of contemporary civilizations and culture; and a critical attitude to Western civilization that had slowly taken form in the years he had given to work in the East End, notably as sub-warden of Toynbee, since he went down from Oxford with a First in Lit. Hum. in 1890.

It is not difficult to understand the admiration that Harriet came to have for him. His philosophy had obvious affinities with Mill's, particularly its emphasis on the individual, but it was perhaps at once more coherent and more pragmatic. His concern as a philosopher with social justice was matched by his insistence on the primacy of the individual over the state and by his readiness to grapple with the daily frustrations of 'slumming': a combination of qualities which Harriet herself was already developing.

The students following the course were required to do their practical work with an approved voluntary organization and Harriet, like most of her fellows, was assigned to an office of the Charity Organization Society. She joined the Whitechapel Committee of the C.O.S. (the Society for Organizing Charitable Relief and Repressing Mendicity) of which E. J. Urwick was a member; and she was appointed immediately to its Sub-committee on Skilled Employment. Here, at last, she found scope for the interests and talents that had gradually become articulated: helping underdogs—or underpuppies—with brains to get the chance they deserved.

The Society's prime object was to improve the condition of the poor by enabling them to become independent. In an area in which something like a third of the child and adult labour was casual, this was particularly difficult. Though some progress had been made in the previous decade in helping selected children to be apprenticed or to undergo some training, the Society was still at a pioneer stage—an additional attraction to its new recruit.

In order to get to know her new East End district, Harriet went into residence for a year, 1905–1906, at the nearest settlement, St Hilda's East, in Bethnal Green. Her work entailed getting lists of school leavers and reports on their aptitudes and abilities, visiting the children and their parents, negotiating apprenticeships with employers and appealing for help in paying premiums from such bodies as the East London Apprenticeship Fund, the Metropolitan Association for Befriending Young Servants, City Companies and local charities. Money had also to be raised to maintain the children while they were being trained.

In her first year on the committee, Harriet helped to sort out applications from seventy-two boys and seventy girls. The work soon snowballed and it claimed her for six years. She was joined, shortly after her own appointment, by another honorary secretary who was assigned to the boys so that she could concentrate on the girls. Dressmaking, box-making, feather-curling, upholstery and millinery were the sort of trades in which she would find them work where they would be given some training—apprenticeship was not very usual for girls. If she could, she would get them into the new local Trade School, where the training was more thorough. Her work did not end with a successful placing: she kept in touch with the children and made them feel that she was behind them and following their progress. This more sustained contact was just what she wanted and needed. A post-card to one of them, Edith Walker, who was sent by her to a Trade School, with a grant from a local charity, was later to lead to an enduring friendship.

Harriet became honorary secretary of the Whitechapel Skilled Employment Sub-Committee, under the chairmanship of the Rt Hon W. Ellison Macartney, Deputy Master of the Mint, in 1906 and continued in this post until 1912, when she was thirty-six. By that time, the Board of Trade had set up Labour Exchanges, with Juvenile Advisory Committees. These eventually took over the work pioneered by the voluntary agencies, a development of which Harriet approved.[5] By now a confirmed socialist, she could welcome the transfer of responsibility to a public body; and, as an amateur of sound administration, she could be assured that the new service would be wisely directed: it was headed by William Beveridge, who had been subwarden of Toynbee when Harriet was running the East End Branch of the Invalid Children's Aid Association.*

Harriet's social work was an important and regular commitment but it did not take up all her time; and as 1912 was a fateful year for her, this is perhaps the moment to look at other aspects of her life and to take stock.

She was a little above middle height, slim and straight. Her eyes were small, round and a clear blue. Her brown hair, taken back into a bun, made only a slight concession to the 'bouffant' fashion of the

---

* In the 1940's, William Beveridge made history as the 'architect' of 'social security' and later became a peer.

day. Contemporaries remembered her as 'very neat, very austere,
like a beautiful nun: she had a precise mouth'. She was 'a very calm
person, more reserved than shy'; she 'always looked at you straight,
taking everything in. She just didn't want to talk—she had no urge.
Her urge was to listen'.[6] She made few friends outside her family
until she was well on in her twenties, when (their respective mothers
having called upon one another) she got to know and to like three of
the eight daughters of a Protestant Irish family newly installed in
another large Hampstead house, Oak Hill Lodge. They were Norah,
Naomi and Muriel Adair Roberts. A little later, she made great
friends with an American girl resident with her at St Hilda's East
Settlement—and, with Alfred and Maude, went to stay with her in
Baltimore.

More formal social life did not appeal to Harriet at all, so that some
of the restrictions of life at home, such as the ban on dancing, were
not, in practice, irksome to her. Though she looked lovely in evening
dress, she did not look at ease in it, and, at least on one occasion when
she arrived for a big dinner party, was seized with sudden panic. She
and Maude were announced: 'Miss Harriet Weaver, Miss Maude
Weaver'. But Harriet remained rooted to the spot and Maude saved
the day by going in first.*[7] Perhaps her hesitancy sprang in part from
what appeared to be a total lack of interest in the other sex, except as
human beings. Such an attitude was by no means uncommon among
young women of her generation, class and interests. It was enough,
for them, to be free to choose not to marry. Though men liked her, if
they persevered sufficiently to break through her reserve, and she
enjoyed their company and their brains, 'there was never a flicker of
a flirtation with anyone'.[8]

Harriet, however, had genuine feminine qualities but they were displayed only in her private, family life. She was good with her needle,
not creative at all, but an excellent plain sewer and darner. Whenever
one of her parents was ill, Mary would help with or take over the
management of the household, Annie took on the nursing or super-
vized it; and Harriet sat in the sick room. It was she more than anyone
else that her father and her mother liked to have with them when
they were ill. She was quick to notice their wants but what she was
most liked for was the quietness of her presence.[9] With children also
she had a delicate and unerring touch that was immediately recog-

---

* Mrs Campbell Hone (Maude) protested that this story is apocryphal.

nized and appreciated. Her god-daughter still remembers the occasion when her godmother took her up to rest after lunch: the tenderness with which she settled the pillow, spread a rug and lowered the Venetian blind; and her soft, companionable voice that wafted her half way to sleep before the door had closed. What struck her first niece, Edward's daughter Rosamond, while still in her nursery, and was to strike all her nieces and nephews later, was the 'glorious fact' that she would always treat them as equals.[10] She had shrewd insight into character, and, feeling less inhibited with members of the younger generation, she was very soon on terms with them.

Though her relations with her family were complex, there was much in family life at home that she immensely enjoyed. The quiet, well-ordered everyday life appealed to her; the politenesses of every-day life, particularly at table; the chance to play billiards or bridge. She and other members of the family also took up golf and Harriet became a good player.*

Though even a straightforward railway journey always made her nervous, there were, every year, holidays and tours at home or abroad, always with at least one member of the family and sometimes with one or two friends also. There were holidays in Switzerland, Italy (never to be forgotten) and France; bicycling tours in Cornwall and Scotland; walking tours in the Cheviots, on Dartmoor, in Switzerland or on the Sussex Downs. When she and Maude went walking together, they would take their beloved collie Wolf and would stay at whatever inn turned out to be most convenient when night fell.

Walking Harriet always loved. She, Alfred and Maude would often go to the Lakes at Easter, and were sometimes joined by Edward or by his brother-in-law Fred Monro, later Harriet's solicitor, or by Fred's brother-in-law Percy Hone and his brother Campbell

---

* A glimpse of Harriet Weaver on the Hampstead links is afforded by a triolet written by a neighbour, Mr E. M. Beach, with a graceful apology for its inadequacy to the occasion:

> *When we last played in 'foursomes' keen,*
> *And won that black umbrella prize,*
> *Our 'putts' were 'holed' on many a 'green'*
> *When we last played in 'foursomes' keen;*
> *Ah! may that gamp but seldom screen*
> *The lurking laughter in those eyes—*
> *When we last played in 'foursomes' keen*
> *And won the black umbrella prize.*

Hone. They walked fifteen or twenty miles almost every day, sometimes starting by waggonette or by pony cart as far as the road would take them.

Fred Monro considered Harriet 'a wonderful walker'. 'I was a bit of an athlete myself', he said, 'and used to boast that I was never tired. I remember one walk Harriet and I had together, when we were all at Lodore Hotel, at the end of Derwentwater. We started from the hotel and went towards Styhead Pass, then over Greenup Edge (that must be a bit over two thousand feet) and from there down to Grasmere. Then we went on by road from Grasmere, leaving Helvellyn on our right, to Thirlmere. Then back, over the fells, to Lodore. We started at nine o'clock and got in at seven. We didn't stop for a meal. We had a few sandwiches and chocolate with us and ate them as we went. We walked for ten hours. Harriet showed no signs of tiredness. She had a good stride, very even. Maude was an exceptional walker; Harriet was quite extraordinary. She walked like an athlete.'*[11]

Though her private life was still lived very much within the home circle, her relations with her parents and with her brothers and sisters were not intimate. Not only was she by nature reserved—'a person alone', as one of her contemporaries put it—and undemonstrative but she was also finding it increasingly difficult to carry her brothers and sisters with her in her thinking on social and political questions. Of all of them, Harold was perhaps the closest and might have given her some support and encouragement. His sudden, tragic death in 1905 robbed her of this hope.

On his return from the Boer War, Harold had resumed his medical studies and was working for his final examination much handicapped by insomnia when he accidentally took an overdose of sleeping tablets. His mother called him as usual in the morning and found him unconscious. He died four days later.

At the end of her own life, Harriet was able to write: 'What comforted me most when [he] died . . . was the thought that it was better to have had him as a dear brother for his short life than not to have had him . . .'.[12] But, at the time, she was distraught, frantic. How much she was devoted to Harold her friends knew and they tried to comfort her. '. . . I can't keep silent any longer and my heart bleeds dear brave friend for the anguish you are suffering, a whole world of

* Fred Monro was certainly an athlete himself. In his first term at Oxford, in 1896, he broke the quarter-mile record. But cricket was his chief interest.

misery and anguish crowded into these few terrible days', Fred's sister Edith wrote the day he died; and a few days later: 'I know that the light seems to have gone out of your life and nothing seems worth doing or thinking of any more. . . . Couldn't we go out for a long long walk. I needn't speak at all if you would rather not. If you knew how I longed to be with you. I have loved you so much for so many years and now that you are in trouble I seem quite useless'.*[13]

After Harold's death, Harriet was exhausted and unwell and for long afterwards felt his loss acutely. The loss of her mother four years later was of a different kind. Mrs Weaver had reached the end of the biblical span of years: her death was not tragic, but for Harriet it must have had a particular poignancy. Mother and daughter, both determined women, were at once too like and too unlike to make possible the development of an easy relationship, devoted as they undoubtedly were to one another. Harriet, indeed, treasured a letter of condolence that ended: '. . . what in her character might have been harsh and severe because of its strength and firmness was softened by her wonderful humility and her tender lovingness; and her simple dear way with every one seems to me to have been the fragrance arising from her beautiful inward life of consecration'.[14]

Harriet became financially independent on her mother's death and could have launched out on her own—she could have set up house for herself. She chose instead a middle course to which, in one form or another, she kept for the rest of her life. She remained at Cedar Lawn, now with Mary and Annie as joint chatelaines, and gave more time to her outside interests. More important, she threw over some of the restrictions to which she had until then submitted. It was a great day when she felt able to accept an invitation to go to a theatre —though her host's choice, *Peter Pan*, might not have been hers!

But her life became departmentalized. In one compartment was her private reading and speculation; in another, her family life and interests; and in another, her voluntary work and sponsorship of causes. Each compartment was kept as separate as possible from the others, though she was still able to be open with her family circle about her voluntary work and open enough about politics. For instance, in the Lakes one Easter, Fred Monro ordered all the left-wing and working-class papers to be delivered to her at breakfast one morning. In came salver after salver laden with them, among them

* Harriet Weaver kept all her letters of condolence on Harold's death.

even the sporting paper the *Pink 'Un*. Harriet could enjoy the joke and greeted it all with 'a little shy smile'.[15]

About religion, she was unable to be open at all. The faith in which she had been brought up she had rejected by the turn of the century— long before her political views had formed. She did not know how to tell her parents for fear of hurting them and continued to go to church with them and, after their death, with Mary and Annie or any other relative.[16] 'I shrank—and have always shrunk—from discussing [religious questions] with my family, excusing myself to myself on the ground of not doing anything to disturb another's comforting faith . . .', she wrote fifty years later.[17]

Harriet had, in fact, evolved a mode of existence which served her well, though it was hardly that of most rebels. Behind her tenderness for the feelings of others, genuine though it was, lay a squeamishness about slipping her moorings; and behind the squeamishness, a sense of guilt at failing to be entirely at one with those she loved. Her self-imposed silence on religion pointed to an imperfect resolution of the conflicting loyalties that claimed her. But she had moved farther from her nearest and dearest than either she or they realized. This was to become manifest quite soon. In 1912, two new claims were to be made on her time, one congenial to her family, the other wholly uncongenial; and it was the second which was to carry her away and beyond the farthest reach of their sympathy and understanding.

Elly Davies-Colley again looked to her for help. She knew, perhaps, that Harriet found it almost impossible to refuse a plea from her. By this time, she was an established surgeon and she had just made history by becoming the first woman FRCS. She had been giving a good deal of time for over a year to helping her friend, Miss Chadburn, an even more distinguished surgeon, with whom she shared a house in Harley Street, to found another general hospital for and staffed by women.

Not all women wanted a woman doctor but many more did so than could be treated by one: in the previous year, for example, over two thousand women who applied for out-patient treatment at the only hospital staffed by women, the New, in the Euston Road, had to be turned away. A woman of seventy-two who came up from the country was more fortunate. She had had an injury from which she had suffered for more than twenty years without being able to bring herself to take her doctor into her confidence. 'Please, mum', she said, when she arrived at Euston Road, 'I've only just heard of the ladies.' For her, the 'ladies' managed to find room.

Another hospital was urgently needed; and it had been decided that South London, at the opposite pole from the Euston Road, would be the right locality for it. By September 1911, two large houses on the south side of Clapham Common had been found; and a year later both had been bought. But the purchase had exhausted the generosity of Miss Chadburn's friends and subscribers. She recognized that an appeal to the public would have to be launched.

Harriet was brought in to act, at the start, as joint honorary secretary, with her cousin, of the Executive Committee for the appeal. After a few meetings, she became sole honorary secretary and was soon caught up in a series of drawing-room meetings, held by society hostesses, and the organizing of a wide appeal through the press for £20,000. People having weight with the main national and more specialized papers were enlisted to write to them. Harriet herself wrote to journals in which she had an interest such as the *Anti-Suffrage Review* and *Women's Employment*.

A letter to *The Times* from Lady Robert Cecil drew a reply from a medical man who argued that the needs of women patients were already adequately catered for and that women doctors were merely seeking to stimulate a demand for their services that did not exist. Miss Chadburn's reply and the subsequent correspondence caught the eye of some wealthy supporters of the cause of medical women. A spokesman called on Miss Chadburn and went away with the assurances they wanted: the proposed new hospital would always be officered by women doctors; it would admit only women patients (and boys up to the age of six). A dumbfounded Executive Committee then received from these well-wishers £53,000 for the building of the hospital—far more than they had asked for—and an additional £40,000 for endowment, on the one further condition that the donors were to remain anonymous for ever.[18]

The Committee moved into action but they soon found that even £53,000 was not going to be enough. A further appeal was launched, with another series of drawing-room meetings stretching into 1914. But by the spring of 1913 they could see their way ahead. Harriet was appointed honorary secretary of a Board of Management, set up in April, with Lady Castlereagh as chairman; and, three weeks later, she was appointed to a sub-committee charged with the task of planning the laying of the foundation stone of the in-patient department.

On 1st July 1913, Princess Louise, Duchess of Argyll, wearing black

merve* and a black chiffon blouse over pearl-grey satin, and a white
hat trimmed with tulle and mauve wisteria, arrived for the ceremony. Harriet read the address to Her Royal Highness. The Bishop
of Southwark then offered prayer, the assembly, accompanied by the
band of the Scots Guards, sang 'Now thank we all our God', and the
Princess laid the foundation stone, saying: 'I declare this stone to be
well and truly laid in the name of the Father, the Son and the Holy
Ghost. May God's blessing rest on this work'.[19]

For her service to the hospital, Harriet was that year made a Life
Governor; and she continued to be honorary secretary to the Board
until 1916, when she resigned. But her main work for the hospital
was done.

It was while she was working for the hospital appeal that she became increasingly interested in a new cause: the suffrage movement.
Not only sick women, but her East End girls and their mothers—all
women—were an underprivileged group, and she believed they
should be freed. Several of her friends, among them some of the
Adair Robertses, were already working for the Women's Social and
Political Union, and encouraged her to join them. Characteristically,
she gave her help in unassuming ways; paid a subscription, made a
collection and occasionally distributed pamphlets. But she never took
part in any sensational exploit.

Harriet was accustomed to read round subjects that interested her
and certainly kept up with feminist literature. But the W.S.P.U.
journal, *Votes for Women*, was too narrowly propagandist for her
taste. In her social work, she had learned a great deal about women's
practical difficulties, and she knew that a vote was not the only thing
they wanted and needed. She became a subscriber to a new independent periodical which appeared in the winter of 1911.

It was called *The Freewoman* and sub-titled 'A Weekly Feminist
Review'. An editorial statement in the first number announced that,
while other journals 'deal with something that women may acquire
. . . We find our chief concern in what they may become'. More
generally, the paper stood for freedom of thought and of speech, and
aimed to interest men and women, as well as feminists. In May 1912
the sub-title was changed to 'A Weekly Humanist Review'. The
editorial policy was 'To show that the two causes, man's and
woman's, are one'.[20]

* Merve is a short term for 'satin merveilleux', a sumptuous fabric in high fashion
in the later nineteenth and early twentieth centuries.

These good principles attracted contributions of varying standard. Indeed, some of the articles seem to have been accepted only because they were about subjects not then mentioned in drawing-rooms. Yet it remained an achievement to establish, at that date, that they could be discussed in print.

Harriet had strong, personal reasons for affirming that no subject should be forbidden. Though some of the topics (lust, masturbation, homosexuality) must have seemed remote, she was well equipped to understand the emotional relief that free discussion can give, to people who have suffered in secret. The sense of relief was particularly evident in the contributions from homosexuals, and letters signed with the current pseudonym 'Uranian'.*

The paper fought for the oppressed and unfortunate, whoever they might be. But the editor, in a series of forceful leaders, made it very plain that they must also fight for themselves:

The person who is responsible for the tyrant is the slave; the person who is responsible for the selfish man is the unselfish man. It is indecent for the slavish man to make tyrants and then whine about the result.[21]

The enfranchisement of women, too, was presented as a human achievement rather than a human right:

There comes a cry that woman is an individual, and that because she is an individual she must be set free. It would be nearer the truth to say that if she is an individual she *is* free, and will act like those who are free.[22]

These thoughts had a bearing on Harriet's personal problems. Her belief in freedom was at odds with her chosen role as a daughter-at-home in a conventional, affectionate family; and since her mother's death she had had occasion to re-examine her life and responsibilities. One responsibility, in particular, was weighing on her. She doubted her right to an unearned income.

A series of articles, by Arthur Kitson of the Banking and Currency Reform League, reinforced her doubts:

* There was also frustration, behind the scenes, if contributions failed to appear. A telegram in Dora Marsden's files reads, 'Return love child and Uranian immediately messenger'.

What is usury? It is the exaction of payment for the use of things, and particularly for the use of money. Our ancestors were probably more honest than we are, for they regarded the exaction of three per cent as much a violation of the moral law as the imposition of 100 per cent.[23]

Harriet made no immediate decision; but the idea that she was living on usury took root. It was not an unwelcome idea. Though she loved the kindness and comfort of her family home, she was ready to seek elsewhere for enlightenment and truth.

The Freewoman met her need, and she was tolerant of its weaknesses. In the early issues, the editor gave too much space to personal quarrels with the Pankhursts and too little space to subjects of general or literary interest. But as time went on, the balance improved. There was an interesting article by J. J. Mallon on an industrial dispute.* H. G. Wells, who approved of the paper's 'breakaway from the monomania for the vote', made several witty contributions. A correspondent, Muriel Ciolkowska, sent occasional discerning articles on events in Paris and Rebecca West, at that time nineteen years old, contributed a series of thoroughly professional reviews.

Harriet pursued her new interests further by becoming a member of the Freewoman Discussion Circle. It was a successful group, inaugurated at a meeting of more than eighty people. The numbers increased so fast that its first meeting-room, at the Suffragette shop, was too small. So was its second, at the Eustace Miles vegetarian restaurant; and its final home was at the Chandos Hall. The programme for the session July to October 1912 included talks on Eugenics by Mrs Havelock Ellis and on Divorce Reform by E. S. P. Haynes. Other subjects were Sex Oppression and the Way Out, Celibacy, Prostitution, and the Abolition of Domestic Drudgery.

The speakers opened the meeting but the debate, described on one occasion as 'ardent', was perhaps the main attraction; and the debaters often pursued their theme down The Freewoman's correspondence columns. For instance, when the proprietor, Charles Granville, speaking on 'Thought-Mists', used the words 'Soul', 'Spirit' and 'Salvation', a correspondent objected that religion was discussed enough in church. She recommended to the discussion circle 'the questions of love, passion and sex'.[24]

* J. J. Mallon was later the distinguished warden of Toynbee Hall.

5 Cedar Lawn, Hampstead

6 Harriet with her father and Cicely Mander, a
cousin's daughter, in about 1909

7 Eleanor Davies-Colley

Harriet probably came and went unnoticed by the ardent talkers. Not a talker herself, her gifts as an attentive listener must have served her well; and she was quite capable of appreciating the comedy which zealous and high-minded groups so often generate. Rebecca West has given a description of it:

Everyone behaved beautifully—it's like being in Church, except Miss [Rona] Robinson & myself. Barbara Low has spoken very seriously to me about it.* [25]

Miss West's sense of fun must have cheered things up, whatever the secretary said. It was allied to a refreshing sense of proportion. In the background, she was working hard to make the paper more of a literary review. She was frankly bored by prolonged attacks on the Pankhursts.

Among the subscribers were a number of Pankhurst supporters. The attacks which bored Miss West infuriated them. They stopped their subscriptions. Another group were put off by love, passion and sex.

At the end of July, the *Morning Post* carried a letter from Lord Percy condemning *The Freewoman* as an immoral paper. Charles Granville wrote to defend it, and hastened round to deliver his defence by hand. It was never printed although, as he pointed out, he had explained that 'THE FREEWOMAN's work was to cleanse the gutters of our national existence, gutters which, at present, are an offensive stench in the nostrils of God'.[26]

The hostility of the *Morning Post* was irritating but not lethal; the two papers were hardly likely to reach many of the same readers. A more serious blow was a boycott by W. H. Smith, the countrywide booksellers and newsagents. The final blow came on 10th October 1912 when the editor announced that the proprietors (that is, Charles Granville) had decided to withdraw their support. The paper must cease publication unless or until new financial backing was found. Readers were asked to send in their names if they wished to support its 'financial re-establishment'. Harriet responded. The formal acknowledgment she received is signed by the Editor, Dora Marsden.

This exchange marks the opening of a new period in Harriet's life, with new responsibilities, new and extraordinary friends, and far wider horizons.

* Barbara Low, the Circle's secretary, was a psychoanalyst and writer.

PART II

1912—1924

3

'THE SPIRIT OF FREEDOM'

DORA MARSDEN, founder, editor and leader-writer of *The Free-woman*, became one of Harriet's lifelong friends. Harriet later described her as 'a remarkable person, a genius and also very beautiful to look upon. She had had a hard bringing up, had won a scholarship for Manchester University, taken a degree in arts, been a teacher for a few years, thrown that up in order to join the Woman's Militant Suffrage Society; had thrown that up too before long, finding the leaders too autocratic, in order to start a paper, The Freewoman'.*[1]

Harriet was not alone in her admiration. Mrs Pethick Lawrence, who knew her well when she was working for the W.S.P.U., regarded her as a 'brave and beautiful spirit'.[2] Throughout the movement, many people heard of her 'courage and capacity'.[3] And later, as an editor, she was praised by Rebecca West, whose critical judgment was rarely at fault, for writing 'wonderful front-pages' and inspiring 'other people to write wonderfully'.[4]

Unhappily, events showed that Dora was one of those ill-fated people whose achievements always fall short of their friends' expectations. Dora had already suffered—and she was due to suffer—repeated disappointments. But as a young woman she undoubtedly looked, talked and acted in a way that gave her friends a sense of extraordinary power and promise.

Harriet was prepared, by zealous reading of *The Freewoman*, for a personality of this high order. 'It must have been edited on a mountain-top,' she wrote, 'it breathed so deeply of the spirit of freedom—a wide, deep freedom, not the noisy counterfeit which will clamour

* Dora Marsden, born in 1882, the same year as James Joyce, was Harriet Weaver's junior by five years.

for advantage and shy at responsibilities, but the genuine sort which is prepared to count the costs, and, finding them heavy, agree to pay.'[5]

A passion for freedom and justice, powerful in both women, gave them a common aim; but temperamentally they could hardly have been more different. The natural sympathy of like with like seems to have been strengthened by its opposite—the paradoxical sympathy of unlike with unlike. Dora, who had been to prison for her militant convictions, was a symbol of a life Harriet could never lead, and of an attitude to life she could share only in imagination. It was not in her nature to give public testimony or engage in open controversy, but she loved those who did. She wanted to help them, unostentatiously, whenever help was needed. For herself, she sought to enlarge her experience by listening, and to protect her integrity by silence.

Dora Marsden, a fighter and visionary, believed in speaking out. Her dedication to the light that was in her was imperious and un-compromising. She influenced, over-worked and often infuriated her friends. Harriet brought to friendship an entirely different style, rooted in the family tradition of good nursery manners. In that calm air, it was difficult for Dora to create a personal crisis.

In her previous work, for the suffragettes, Dora had passed from one crisis to another. She was a compelling speaker and a very successful demonstrator—but she was not an accomplished organizer. As district organizer in Southport for the W.S.P.U., she could not be persuaded to wait for proper authorizations or to submit proper estimates. Nothing, she felt, should stand in the way of plans she had formed for a Great Exhibition and Pageant, with paid stars and side shows where, among other amusements, the enemies of the suffra-gettes (notably Mr Asquith) could be shot down, for prizes. After several admonitory letters from the Pankhursts, she received the final blow from Mrs Pethick Lawrence. The Pageant must be dropped and the Great Exhibition converted into 'a little Bazaar held in a provincial watering place'.[6]

Dora resigned at once. But within a very few days she had been given a job by the other militant organization, the Women's Freedom League. There, events took much the same course, but they moved faster. She was beginning to think of editing a paper of her own, and she wanted the League to finance it. But her insistence on editorial independence—and the fact that the League already had an official journal—made her proposals entirely unacceptable. She resigned again; and the treasurer, harassed by requests for expenses that were not regularly returned, fired a parting shot:

I see that you knew nothing about the spirit of the League but you never had the least intention of adapting yourself to it. Your account partly shows this, no true Freedom Leaguer would ever spend 2/6 on lunch.[7]

Dora still had friends, however, in the W.S.P.U. Her particular ally and supporter was Mary Gawthorpe, the intelligent and witty Yorkshire girl who was one of the star speakers at outdoor meetings. Mary had confidence in her, and was ready, although she was still very ill after rough handling by the police, to work hard on her behalf. They found their backer, Charles Granville. His firm, Stephen Swift, published in the main unorthodox writers, free-thinkers and mystics, but their list also included Katherine Mansfield.

Rona Robinson, her suffragette friend from their university days, joined in the enterprise, and dealt capably with a great deal of the work. Mary Gawthorpe, persuaded against her will and against her best interests, became joint editor. From the first, she urged that the paper should carry more literary work and less criticism of Pankhursts. But ill health forced her to retire, within a few weeks, long before this object was achieved.

Her last contribution was a calm, good-natured reply to Pankhurst supporters who felt that subscriptions had been sold to them on false pretences. The attacks continued sporadically, but the paper survived for eleven months. Then, the editor received a note from the printers. They were not able to set up the next issue, because there was no money in the kitty, and the backer had withdrawn.

Dora made her appeal to her readers, and went home to her mother in Southport, to await results. She was joined there by her friend Grace Jardine. They had first met, some years before, at a bus-stop, where Grace, instantly impressed, had agreed to join her in her work. They had worked together, in politics and journalism, ever since. The three women made up 'a happy household'.[8] Hannah Marsden, quiet, kind and capable, gave her blessing to their work and encouraged their more feminine interests by making up clothes to their own, highly original, designs.

Dora needed a little time to recover and collect her thoughts. In London, the Discussion Circle were still meeting, but they were disappointed that the editor had not come in person to explain what she had in mind. Rebecca West wrote to Dora to suggest that, although they were 'quite excited' about the paper's re-establishment, she could not expect them to support her proposals without knowing quite what they were. 'Do send a statement of the prospects which can be read aloud to the assembled multitude.'[9]

Rebecca West knew how she herself wanted the paper to develop. She had been studying the files and found 'no literary side to it at all. Visiak and my still small voice were the only notes of dissent in a storm of purely moral and intellectual enthusiasm'.[10] She recommended short stories, literary essays, poetry. 'I don't see why a movement towards freedom of expression in literature should not be associated with and inspired by your gospel.'[11]

Besides mediating between the editor designate and the Discussion Circle, Rebecca West was looking for new writers and investigating possible printers. She also offered to type the appeal, when it was drafted, and send it to all the people she could think of. In her letters to Dora, urgent requests arrived in quick succession; but she also passed on a compliment: 'Wells expatiated at length the other day on your sweetness and brilliance. I think he misses *The Freewoman* very much.'[12]

Dora's letter to the Discussion Circle came at last. Rebecca West reported that she had read it out, evidently 'with deep expression, for subsequently Mrs Macdonald rose from her seat and congratulated me on my lovely voice, and kissed me. There is an epidemic of kissing in the Freewoman discussion circle'. She had been kissed also by the secretary, by three other women she knew by name, and by 'a lady in deep mourning with an interest in Eugenics who gives away leaflets on proportional representation'.[13]

Harriet was not among the kissers. Her enthusiasm had taken a more practical turn. She had offered £200, for shares in the new enterprise.

The target was £5,000, but only twenty other offers were made, and the largest of them was £75. Harriet's offer, as it turned out, gave her a controlling interest. Dora wrote to her at the beginning of December to suggest that, if a publishing company were formed, she should be chairman of the board.

Harriet did not accept. She knew nothing about publishing and did not want a position of command. She had not yet met Dora, or seen detailed proposals, but she must have felt (even when the proposed capital issue was reduced to two thousand shares) that she was hardly likely to remain the largest shareholder.

In the new year, 1913, Dora heard that an influential group in America were forming a 'Thousand Club', to secure one thousand long-term subscribers and so give the new paper some initial security. She wrote to Harriet to suggest a Thousand Club in England. By this time, their correspondence included some personal exchanges, and Harriet, always so very reserved in conversation, had lately felt able to confide to paper a haunting problem of her own. Dora responded warmly: 'I should like very much to have a talk with you. I was extremely interested to read of your personal attitude in connection with "usury". It made me think that the New Era—the Free Era—is nearer than most of us imagine.' [14]

In February they met at last, and took an instant liking to each other. Harriet had expected genius, but nothing had prepared her for Miss Marsden's beauty: the small, light frame, and the face of 'a Florentine angel'.[15] Though their friendship was expressed in an entirely formal manner—Harriet did not permit her Christian name to be used outside the family circle—the ties of friendship were established from the first.

Miss Marsden had come to London for a quiet afternoon's talk with Miss Weaver. In fact, they spent their time 'running round' together, dealing with all sorts of odd jobs, and by the end of the afternoon Harriet was deeply committed. Miss Marsden, writing to thank her for her great kindness, listed her immediate tasks: to write to prospective subscribers, to sort out the duplications in two subscription lists, to open a bank account and think of a name for it, and to see that a prospective printer was put in touch with the prospective honorary secretary of the Thousand Club. A stream of similar requests followed. Dora told Harriet that nothing would ever get done unless they did it themselves.

Her other supporters were not, in fact, idle. Grace Jardine was acting as her personal assistant and secretary; Mary Gawthorpe was sending out circulars; Edwin Herrin, a member of the Discussion Circle, was giving free legal advice; Barbara Low, as secretary, was keeping it together; and Rebecca West was still mediating between it and the editor designate. She read out another letter from Dora, but this time there was no kissing. No one wanted to pay £1 for Thousand Club membership unless it carried a shareholder's vote; and everyone was waiting impatiently for a statement of policy.[16]

A Thousand Club committee had now been formed: chairman, Dora Marsden; secretary, Mrs Leisenring, secretary of the Blavatsky Institute;* treasurer, Harriet Shaw Weaver. Harriet immediately started to keep meticulous accounts; but she was obliged to record that nine subscriptions had 'got lost', presumably at the stage when several people were collecting them, and the paper had no official existence.

Now, the Blavatsky Institute had provided a London address for the editorial offices, and a room in their publishing offices at Oakley House, Bloomsbury, round the corner from the British Museum. Dora, like many of the suffragettes, was interested in esoteric cults, particularly in the Theosophists; she had already agreed to speak at their Summer School. The Bloomsbury office, therefore, gave her journal an appropriate home, among friends. The neighbours in the block were a mixed collection, spiritual and commercial. Among them were solicitors and Swedenborgians, a milliner and a missionary society, a firm of reinforced concrete engineers, and Christopher Louis Pelman, Teacher of Memory.

Harriet went to Bloomsbury for Thousand Club committee meetings, and Mrs Leisenring was on the spot. But the chairman, Miss Marsden, remained in the north and her letters, though frequent, still failed to satisfy prospective members. In the end, Rebecca West and the secretary prepared a draft and so elicited the first formal statement of policy. It went out as a circular, appealing, in the name of 'The New Freewoman', for members willing to finance the paper 'by taking out *forthwith* a full-length subscription of eighteen months'. The policy statement was less explicit. Miss Rebecca West was joining the staff as assistant editor and there were some 'new contributors to be announced later'. But, since Miss Marsden's other associates were well known to *Freewoman* readers:

It appears unnecessary to attempt a lengthy explanation of the policy and character of the new paper. It will be sufficient to say that *The New Freewoman* will be the only journal of recognised standing expounding a doctrine of philosophic individualism either in England or America. Editorially, it will endeavour to lay bare the individualist basis of all that is most significant in modern movements including feminism. It will continue *The Freewoman*'s policy of ignoring in its discussions all existing tabus in the realms of morality and religion. . . .[17]

* Helena Petrovna Blavatsky, founder of the Theosophical Society, established its European headquarters in London in 1885.

Although the criticisms made at the Discussion Circle were never answered, Rebecca West's final, and spirited, appeal had some success: '. . . The "tried friends of the Cause" *did* give me the hell of a time at the D.C. But all the same these names marked T.C.M. have promised to give the £1. I had on a new hat with 5 pink ostrich feathers & I caught them at the door as they went'.[18]

The fact remained that money was not coming in as fast as the promoters hoped. Publication day was deferred and there was talk, first, of making the paper a fortnightly instead of a weekly, and then of making it a monthly instead of a fortnightly. Rebecca West characteristically recommended the editor to adopt the form which ensured the best possible content. 'In a monthly,' she observed, 'you could do without padding.'[19]

The effort put into securing subscriptions began to show results in April, and there was a further advance in May. By the end of May, one hundred and eighty people had subscribed, sixteen of them through the Thousand Club 'branches' in New York City and Evanston, Illinois.*

The treasurership of the Thousand Club was Harriet's formal responsibility, but from February onwards she was dealing also with the paper's 'preliminary expenses' as well as with all receipts. She bought stationery, paid bills, gave out petty cash to Dora Marsden and kept careful accounts in a Day Book.

Dora, who could never interest herself in petty cash, took this side of Harriet's work very much for granted; but she was delighted to have found a friend and colleague who could always be trusted to carry out her instructions and make contacts on her behalf in the same reliable way. Harriet was consistently reliable, not only in character but also in health and was a great asset to a group of people who seem to have been unusually prone to illness. That spring and summer, Grace Jardine was off sick several times, Dora Marsden had recurrent attacks of what she describes as 'neurasthenia', and Rebecca West, the youngest and the most robust, had repeated attacks of influenza and inflammation of the eyes. Harriet, never on the sick list till she was eighty, remained in good health; also, she lived in London and was prepared, among other things, to write a great many letters.

Since the editor came to London rarely, and then only for a few hours, the difficulties of floating the new periodical were vastly increased. Harriet had at times to write daily to Dora Marsden.† In

* Later, the figures for these two months appear as an isolated peak.
† Only a few of Harriet Weaver's letters to Dora Marsden have survived.

these letters, mainly concerned with work, she sometimes also relieved her mind. One such occasion arose when her father died, suddenly, at Cedar Lawn, on 27th February 1913.

Even before the twelve carriages moved off from the house to Christ Church, headed by a detachment of the Hampstead police, as befitted the funeral of a Justice of the Peace, Harriet must have been wondering how to resolve the problem of living an independent life on inherited money. She confided in Dora and received a prompt reply: 'It must be very awe-inspiring breaking such close family ties in rapid succession. It seems to throw all the emphasis suddenly on one's own personal destiny. What are you going to do with life now? Perhaps it will not involve any great changes. I should be very interested to hear if you cared to tell me'.[20]

What was Harriet going to do with her life? The question now sounds senseless, because she had already made the decision to support *The Freewoman* and, in so doing, had taken the first step to meet an exceptional 'destiny'. For the time being, however, her way of life was hardly altered. She continued to live with her sisters, to spend holidays with relations, and, within the family circle, she was finding great happiness in the role of a beloved aunt: Alfred had married Muriel Adair Roberts and was living, with their two sons, nearby in Hampstead.

Outside her family, Harriet retained all her old interests, but her new concern, so different in its aims and supported by people so unlike the social workers and fashionable hostesses of the South London Hospital appeal, was occupying her thoughts and taking up an increasing amount of her time.

She was now treasurer of the 'Establishment Fund', responsible for raising capital. It was not a comfortable position. Well-wishers with money were scarce, and those who had already put in for shares were getting restive, because the paper had not yet appeared, because the company was not yet formally constituted, and because it was beginning to look as if it would never be properly financed. Some demanded a directorship; others, wounded that a seat on the board was not offered, refused to accept it when it was. Harriet was expected to smooth things over, and generally succeeded. But the subscriber who had offered £75 withdrew, and added insult to injury by buying eighteen shares in someone else's name.

Rebecca West, meanwhile, had been combing London for a printer who was cheap as well as reliable; and, against all the odds,

believed she had found one. He was A. G. Fifield, a publisher and
printer whose list included theosophical and anarchist books, and he
was very much interested in Miss Marsden's concept of individualism.
He put in an offer for ten shares and addressed himself to the practical
problems.

Dora Marsden negotiated with him herself, by letter, and evidently
reached the conclusion that he was the answer to all her financial
problems. She asked Harriet—as Hon. Treasurer (pro. tem.) of 'The
NEW FREEWOMAN'—to sign and send out to supporters an optimistic
statement:

The promises of Capital and Support justify the immediate formation
of a Company to be called 'The New Freewoman Limited' the
Capital of which will be in £1 shares.

Miss Marsden has concluded arrangements with Mr A. G. Fifield...
on the favourable terms of £1 a week and 5% on Sales to publish the
paper for the Company as a 6d fortnightly. . . .[21]

The terms were indeed favourable, even assuming that Miss Marsden, who expected a circulation of about two thousand, had judged
her public correctly. Harriet obeyed instructions and sent the circular
out, under her own name. Mr Fifield, she said, had agreed to be
'Managing Director of the New Company'.

Mr Fifield himself was not happy. Rebecca West dropped in on
him and reported that, though still 'anxious to publish it', he was
worried about crowding extra staff into his establishment. Soon after,
he tried to withdraw, because he had suffered a serious injury to his
back; but he could not resist Miss Marsden's strength of purpose. He
agreed to struggle on, while Edwin Herrin began drafting the articles
of association for the new company, and Harriet was asked to form a
London committee to deal with company affairs.

At the beginning of May, Dora Marsden and Grace Jardine came
to London for a meeting with Harriet, Mr Fifield and others; and the
three women went on afterwards to give Mr Herrin his final instructions. The draft which emerged was a complete surprise to Mr
Fifield. Unexpected names were on the list of directors, there was no
mention of a registered address, and the proposed capital had shrunk
to £1,000.

Mr Fifield wrote to Mr Herrin on these points, and added: 'I am
getting more sick than ever of the whole affair and wish I had never

heard of the paper. I only agreed at Miss Marsden's urgent request because she said that my withdrawal now would injure whatever chances the paper had. But as I told you all the other day, I think its possibilities are almost nil. . . .' [22]

After receiving a long, pacifying letter from Mr Herrin, he explained himself more calmly to Miss Marsden. He was concerned because the policy and control of the paper were to be in her hands, and the compositor would be the 'only censor of libellous or seditious statements'. [23] He did not like the prospect of being arrested and imprisoned for statements he had never seen, and might not approve.

Mr Herrin had soothed his temper, but he had also introduced a new anxiety. He had remarked that Miss Marsden advocated physical violence. Mr Fifield himself was 'violently opposed to physical violence of any sort'. When Miss Marsden sent him the article in question, he read:

The first duty of a wage-man is to join his regiment, his Union; and the first duty of the Regiment is to provide its members with arms and see that they can use them. [24]

He was terrified. But Dora, reluctant to let him go, urged him to remain as publisher and farm out the printing. He yielded to the extent of getting some printers' estimates; and then learned, with relief, that she had found another publisher and printer. He withdrew his name; and with it, his bid for ten shares. 'All told,' he wrote regretfully, 'you are well rid of me.' [25]

Dora complained about the last-minute blow. But she admitted to Harriet that *The Freewoman* could endanger the mind and health of a man so nerve-stricken and sensitive. [26] Her new printer, F. C. Charles, of the International Publishing Company, Oxford, impressed her as 'an extremely nice man, enthusiastic in his quiet way for what the paper stands for, & I think, just the man for us'. [27]

Mr Charles had been summoned, by telegram, to call on her in Southport, and his visit had been a success. She had just heard from Mr Herrin that the London Committee had melted away and that, in his opinion, the prospects of forming a company had melted away with it. But Mr Charles said that forming a company was easy. She sent Mr Herrin a stern note: 'People have bought shares. Can you have shares and not have a company?' [28]

Mr Charles, immediately involved in the rush of assembling copy and settling the technicalities of printing and layout, became also her legal and financial adviser. His letters, to her and Grace Jardine, through the first half of June, make up thirty quarto pages of type-script, and a good deal of the space is given to advice on companies.

He laid in stocks of paper and received £30 on account. A warm friendship had developed. He invited Miss Marsden and Miss Jardine to stay. They would like the place and he hoped they might decide to move the editorial offices to Oxford. As for the paper, due for delivery on the following Sunday, he expected them to find it 'fairly satisfactory'. In any case, he concluded, 'I doubt if anything is worth worrying about.' [29]

In London, Harriet and Mr Herrin were taking life more seriously, with practical results. On 13th June 1913, Harriet presented an application to the Board of Trade and the New Freewoman Company was registered. The nominal capital was £1,000, and the fifteen registered shareholders had taken up three hundred and fifty-nine £1 shares. The largest block of shares, after Harriet's, was thirty, bought by Miss Bessie Heyes. She became a director, with three others: Harriet, Dora and Grace Jardine.

The company was registered three days before the first issue was due to come out. The copy was ready in Oxford for Mr Charles to run off, and it was beginning to emerge that Mr Fifield's resignation had been a real misfortune. However nerve-stricken, he never scamped work or wasted money; but Mr Charles, pleasant as he was, did not aspire to the same high standard. Rebecca West reacted violently to her proofs: 'This will never do.' [30] She found over thirty 'gross and confusing errors in three columns' and despaired of getting anyone to write for them, unpaid, if they saw work like this. 'My Lord, what printing,' she exclaimed. 'The carelessness, the dirt, the shakiness. . . .'

Publication day, 16th June—later to have happier associations for Harriet as Bloomsday—was a Saturday. Dora went to Oxford a day or two before and stayed, not with the Charles family but out at Witney, where Harriet joined her. They hoped to spend Friday to-gether, seeing the paper to bed, but the final galleys were not ready. Harriet left on Friday evening, after a frustrating day.

The dire events of Saturday were reported to her by Dora, from a lurching north-bound train on a very hot day. The proofs had reached her late on Friday night, and she had to take them into Oxford first thing in the morning, only to find that the paper could not possibly be printed that day, even if the men stayed all afternoon.

She told Mr Charles that she was not going to leave until she saw the copy ready for the machines. After a heated argument, everyone stayed 'until seven in the evening, with one man working their *one* machine, & the manager Mr Braque setting up by hand. They were *fuming*. . . .' [31]

Mr Charles should have known that he was not equipped to do more than miscellaneous work. 'He cannot print the N.F.', Dora concluded, with love to Miss Weaver, and 'very real appreciation of your great kindness'. On the following day, Harriet received a note from Grace Jardine, summing up the views of the editorial staff: 'The paper looks horrible.' [32]

It consisted of twenty pages, large and soft, with a heavy title riding like a thunder-cloud across the front page; and the body of the text showed that poor Mr Braque had been using odds and ends from a very mixed collection of founts. The content, too, was makeshift. The editor, distracted by problems of printing and finance, had put in far too much padding from the old *Freewoman* files. 'Art and the soul', a contributor observed, 'are one'.

Rebecca West immediately put in a detailed criticism, and a plea that Dora should stop attacking the Pankhursts. She was interested in gaining new readers, and this production had a very limited appeal— to like-minded and constant readers of the old paper. No concessions were made to the propaganda needs of a new paper, on its first appearance.

The editorial too suffered from this defect. But the editor did make a constructive point that champions of the oppressed often overlook. Because they feel like victims, they attract victimization; and their struggle for freedom must be against forces within as well as forces without. The down-trodden, Dora announced, must 'GET UP'. She was already thinking of the egoist as the moral opposite of the slave. In her third issue, the egoist was introduced, by name, as the free man or woman, unamenable to pressures directing him towards what he ought to be, but fully alive to what he is, and ready to take responsibility for what he does and thinks.

It was a powerful image, suited to a time when traditional faith was under attack from all sides, and it had a special appeal for Harriet. In one of her favourite books, Walt Whitman's *Leaves of Grass*, she had read: 'I celebrate myself, I sing myself'. Although she was determined to remain uncelebrated, she loved and admired people whose gifts were, in some sense or other, for self-celebration; and, in her

8 Harriet skating at Montana in 1905

9 Harriet with Harold and their niece, Rosamond,
at St. Ives in 1905

10 Harriet in 1907

own, very different, way, she was working to free herself further from the condition of mental, moral, and financial dependence in which she had been brought up.

The first meeting of the directors was held at Dora's home in Ainsdale, Southport, and Harriet made her first visit there. She was appointed honorary secretary to the company, and wrote the minutes. Dora Marsden, editor; Rebecca West, assistant editor; and Grace Jardine, sub-editor and editorial secretary, were formally appointed, each with a salary of £52 a year. A new printer was appointed, Messrs Robert Johnson and Co., who printed the local paper in Southport; and it was decided that Mr Charles should be asked to revise his bill.

The second number of *The New Freewoman* looked much better than the first. The titling had a certain elegance, the spacing was improved, and the type was no longer clumsy and ink-laden. The paper was now in the hands of people who had printed a paper before. The company headquarters, too, was fortunately placed, in publishing offices that distributed the theosophists' journal, *The Path*. It seemed only a minor inconvenience that correspondents had to send their letters, addressed to Miss Marsden by name, to Ainsdale, England.

The New Freewoman was floated, insecurely, tentatively, only temporarily financed, with no solid body of good contributors, and a policy which was arbitrary, obsessive and badly explained—but it had made a start. Though it was involved with many difficulties, and some absurdities, this was still an achievement. Whatever Dora Marsden's mistakes, she had brought it off. She had provided a platform where freedom could be discussed in terms of individuality.

Harriet was given the task of sorting things out with Mr Charles, and of prevailing upon him to send the stocks of paper to Southport. In the role of willing helper she was accepted and appreciated—and given the unrewarding jobs that no one else wanted to do. Nobody yet realized that this quiet and capable woman, who was giving the paper her time as well as her money, was also getting the experience which later equipped her to edit it.

4

THE NEW FREEWOMAN

WHILE HARRIET and Dora Marsden were pre-occupied with organization and finance, Rebecca West was looking for new contributors, particularly for writers who could help to develop *The New Freewoman* as a literary journal. She was now reviewing regularly for the *Daily News* and, as she was well-versed in contemporary English literature and knew personally a number of writers, she was well-equipped to find useful people. But it was not easy at first to persuade them to contribute to the revived version of a paper, founded for feminists and free-thinkers, which was hardly known in literary circles and never paid for contributions. She was, however, persistent and resourceful, and her growing reputation as a writer carried some weight. By the time the first issue of *The New Freewoman* appeared, she was hopeful of securing some of the writers she wanted. One of them was the young American poet, Ezra Pound.

He was living in London and working, with generous enthusiasm, to promote a group of young and struggling poets. They were already known in America as the Imagist (or Imagiste) group; and he hoped to establish Imagism in England as the leading literary movement of the time. He had contributed to *The English Review*, and had been recommended to Rebecca West, as a literary editor for *The New Freewoman*, by Ford Madox Hueffer and his friend Violet Hunt.* The introduction was made, early in the summer of 1913, at one of Violet Hunt's literary parties in her house on Campden Hill; and Rebecca West, after discussing her plans with Ezra Pound, decided that he

* Ford Madox Hueffer, later Ford Madox Ford, was the founder and editor of *The English Review*.

would do well.* ¹ Soon after, she wrote to ask him to submit something in writing. He was ready with a number of proposals. When Dora saw them, she asked for more details, and he replied to her:†

I can not make out from your not[e] just what Miss West had written to you. She wrote requesting contribution and I made the following offer. (The only offer I can make unless I am to be paid) A. That I fill a page per number, for, say, six months tho' I might be quite willing to go on after that. As follows.

> 1st of each month. verse, selected by me. Including my own stuff and other work which I should be able, probably, to pay for and thus to spare the authors the disgrace of printing creative stuff without being paid. 15th. of each month. prose article. critique presumably of current books, especially poetry. here, and possibly in france.

Miss West accepted this suggestion.²

Rebecca West had also approved his offer to get a translation of Remy de Gourmont's *Chevaux de Diomedes*, and he had now succeeded, after telling de Gourmont: 'I thought sufficiently well of the Freewoman [sic] to be willing to give it my verse free, which I would not do for any other periodical.' ³ In addition, he had submitted a note on the possibility of having a regular column (or a page) of extracts from French periodicals; his friend W. B. Yeats had just been complaining that 'there was no way of keeping in touch with european criticism'.⁴

He explained to Dora that, as collector for two of the best paying U.S. magazines, he saw a lot of good and promising work; and he enclosed a cutting about his 'literary sect'. He wanted an answer soon, as the 'Sanctus Patronus' who had offered the money to pay his contributors, might change his mind.‡

---

* This is Rebecca West's account. Ezra Pound's memory, given to Patricia Hutchins, of a heroine of the suffragette movement who called upon him in Church Walk must refer to some other event. None of the editorial staff paid calls to ask for contributions.

† Ezra Pound's letters are reproduced as written with emendations in square brackets, or annotations where the meaning needs clarifying.

‡ The Sanctus Patronus cannot have been Ezra Pound's later patron John Quinn. Charles Norman in *Ezra Pound* identifies *The New Freewoman*'s backer as John Gould Fletcher. He does not make clear, however, that the backing was for Ezra Pound's 'section' only, not for the paper as a whole.

Only a few days had passed since Ezra Pound first heard of *The New Freewoman*, and Dora was certainly impressed by his extraordinary capacity for producing, at short notice, a lavish flow of ideas. But unlike Rebecca West, who was prepared to pass on to him all the useful literary contacts she had made already, Dora was very uneasy about yielding territory. Mr Pound was clearly determined to command his own territory, and she would be in no position to argue if *his* contributors to *her* paper were supported by his unnamed patron.

Ezra Pound had remarked to Rebecca West that he was all ready to promote the paper as soon as it was ascertained that he was the 'Literchure Dept'. But Dora still had some questions to ask. He replied in haste:

The seven minutes at my instant disposal is hardly enough to define my philosophical credentials adequately.
I suppose I'm an individualist. . . .
I don't suppose a literary page will queer the editorial columns. Miss West has inspected the data of our particular sect, and has not been alarmed unduly. I am probably amenable to reason (?????, !??). . . .
I don't want to 'boss' but if I am to make the page efficient, I must follow my own scheme. . . .[5]

Dora was not entirely satisfied. Mr Pound was asking for a free hand, with insistence that was very like her own; and she found it very hard to make a decision. Mr Pound would obviously bring to the paper just what it needed, particularly as she herself was uninterested in the arts, and was already finding her editorial duties extremely taxing. But she foresaw alarming consequences.

Her anxieties were fostered by ill-health and overwork. She had started writing an ambitious philosophical book and, at times when all her energies were engaged on it, she found any decision so painful that she put off opening the letters from her London office. Mr Pound had now evoked a conflict of emotion. She wanted the paper's scope to be extended; but she dreaded any influence that was likely to change its character.

Ezra Pound's position, in charge of at least one page, and organizing several more, was not immediately ratified, but he did get some assurance that he would be in complete control for a trial run of six months. By 1st August, he had arranged the next 'verse number' and delivered four chapters of *Diomedes*. He had also written some reviews and, as the first article could not come out for a fortnight, felt at leisure.

Harriet was not, at this stage, involved in Ezra Pound's plans. She was dealing with business, keeping the records, paying the bills and doing the accounts.* At the beginning of August, six short-term subscriptions lapsed, and were not renewed, but seventy-two new subscriptions had come in; the guaranteed circulation was now two hundred and sixty-six copies per issue, twenty-four of them to America and one to France. Sales of single copies came to about a hundred and twenty per issue.† A few of these copies were ordered by post, and a few were taken by half-a-dozen shops, including the Suffragette shop, at various trade discounts; but the best sales were made from the Blavatsky bookstall at Oakley House. As a tenant there, *The New Freewoman* received the full price, 6d.; and these sixpences provided the company with ready money.

Dora had had a success at the International Summer School. She had not only 'demolished most of the arguments of the Theosophists'; she had also sold all the copies of the paper that she had with her.[6] Her hopes were high, and she held to her original printing order of two thousand copies. The new printers, though they sometimes complained about her lavish proof-corrections, were doing a reasonable job, at about £14 a run.

Harriet was still trying to get back some of the £30 given to Mr Charles, and reminding him that he had not yet sent on their stocks of newsprint, or the 'list of wholesalers from whom he had orders'.[7] She was very persistent with this problem, as she was with larger problems later, but she was by no means committed to perpetual meekness. 'I am sick of Mr Charles!' she cried.[8] Mr Fifield, who had quickly recovered his sweet temper, finally came to her aid and worked out what the stocks were worth. But it was some months before a final settlement was reached.

During the summer, she spent some time with her family, but her

---

* Harriet Weaver's account books give a full and fascinating picture of the affairs of *The New Freewoman*. Her task as book-keeper was complicated by the system of marginal debits and credits used on occasions when ready cash was used to pay bills; but she made very few mistakes. See Appendix.

† Harriet Weaver's Day Book shows receipts on sales. The numbers sold are calculated at fifty to the £1, and receipts are spread to allow for credit terms.

problems followed her round. One letter from Dora caught up with her on Dartmoor, and she wrote from the hotel at Two Bridges: '. . . the three of us—my youngest sister, our dog & myself, are thoroughly enjoying our walking tour. The weather is glorious. We have walked into the heart of Dartmoor & are two or three days here, then moving on West and North. . . . It has been a delightful holiday & quite new ground to both (or rather the three) of us. The collie is supremely happy & was evidently intended to be a country dog.' [9]

They were out of doors all day and very sleepy in the evenings. But in spite of her sleepiness, Harriet dealt briskly with several queries and reported on progress: 'Subscribers dribble in very slowly now'.

Back in London, she addressed herself to the unfamiliar duties of running a company. Mr Herrin's clerk broke the news that she must 'make out a formal statement of accounts for the shareholders meeting, & that the wretched thing must afterwards have a five shilling stamp affixed to it'.[10] She agreed it must be as correct and up-to-date as possible, but feared 'they will not think us brilliant business people'. She was also caught by the difficulties of fixing a shareholders' meeting, at a time when most of them were on holiday, and the gap between the required notice and the latest permissible date was closing in. It was already only three weeks.

She was not yet concerned with editorial problems, and fully occupied with her own. But Ezra Pound had grasped that Miss Weaver was of some importance in the *New Freewoman* set-up, and had written to Dora: 'Re/Miss Weaver will she be bored if [I] go to see her. Not that she asked me. Still you might make enquiries in such a way that she needn't feel obliged to.' [11]

Before this visit took place, Harriet had seen the issue of 15th August, and read:

An image is that which presents an intellectual and emotional complex in an instant of time. . . . It is the presentation of such a 'complex' instantaneously which gives that sense of sudden liberation; that sense of freedom from time limits and space limits: that sense of sudden growth, which we experience in the presence of the greatest works of art.*

Harriet, who believed that original writing had a liberating in-

* Signed by F. S. Flint but known to be written by Ezra Pound.

fluence, was well able to appreciate this statement. It came from an article explaining the Imagist creed. With it, were 'A few don'ts by an Imagiste' by Ezra Pound, and seven poems written by him 'since he became an Imagiste'. Rebecca West had written an introductory paragraph:

Because the public will not pay for poetry it has become the occupation of learned persons, given to soft living among veiled things and unaccustomed to being sacked for talking too much. This is why from the beautiful stark bride of Blake, it has become the idle hussy hung with ornaments kept by Lord Tennyson, handed on to Stephen Phillips and now supported at Devonshire Street by the Georgian Group. But there has arisen a little band who desire the poet to be as disciplined and efficient at this job as the stevedore. Just as Taylor and Gilbreth want to introduce scientific management into industry so the *imagistes* want to discover the most puissant way of whirling the scattered star dust of words into a new star of passion. . . .

The first contribution from Ezra Pound was largely made up of two long extracts from the March issue of *Poetry*, Chicago. Rebecca West was not very happy, because the editor of *Poetry* had not yet given permission to reprint. But she let it pass, partly because she was suffering from headaches and eye trouble, and had no copy of her own to send in. She was disturbed, too, by the first instalment of *Diomedes*. She had reviewed another book of de Gourmont's for *The Freewoman*, and had thought him an exquisite writer. But this translation was very poor:

She would enter like a glance, as if gliding through the chink of the door, and would move with no more noise than was made by her moving grace in the mirror. Neither love, nor slight disrobings— whether by his hand or by his look, nor his apparent kisses upon her throat, nor the ambiguous prayers—no—nothing of these re-assured and nothing troubled the clearness of her wondering eyes, eyes like those which hailed the angelic visitation, but without faith, and passive.

Ezra Pound's poems were in a more robust tradition, and still have a more contemporary ring:

I have seen the fishermen picknicking in the sun,
I have seen them with untidy families,
I have seen their smiles full of teeth
And heard ungainly laughter.

It was probably an advance copy of this issue that he sent, on
Rebecca West's request, to Amy Lowell in Boston, suggesting that
'a dmd. low rate' might be 'worth while as a supplement to some of
your darlings', and that it would sometimes be convenient to secure
the English copyright.[12] Space was opening before him, because
Rebecca West had become too unwell to contribute regularly: '... I
simply cannot write . . . I suppose Pound's stuff will prevent you
being short.' [13] She was correct. His one-page territory had spread to
five, and was still extending.

Dora had allowed things to take their own course. She aimed to
set out, in the book she was writing, the whole of her philosophy, and
it was a struggle to turn her mind from fundamental ideas. Even her
own editorials, though she attached great importance to them, were
at times too mundane to manage, particularly if they involved some
popularization of the book's philosophic themes. For various reasons
—incapacitating headaches, trouble with her book, trouble with her
subject—her copy generally arrived late.

Dora's main concern was in 'Linguistic Philosophy', and the nature
of thought; and neither of these subjects lends itself to brief, popular
exposition. In addition, though Miss Weaver was able to send her
large consignments of books, she had cut herself off from the give and
take of discussion with her intellectual equals, and isolation was beginning to make communication difficult. She was becoming more
and more preoccupied with the aim of constructing a self-supporting
philosophical system and presenting it in 'assertive' terms.

The Theosophist Summer School was her last recorded appearance
at an intellectual gathering. There, though she had triumphed over
criticism, she had not liked it. She had retired to read and think,
sometimes with joy and energy, and sometimes in a mood of bitter
frustration. These moods, certainly, were natural to her cast of mind
but it was also an unlucky accident of history that she came to seman-
tic studies at that early stage, when many of the important books
were not yet written.

It is a measure of her growing isolation that the interest she took in
Ezra Pound's activities did not include an interest in his work. He had

been writing for the paper for three months when she remarked to Miss Weaver: '. . . As for E.P.'s poems, I haven't read 'em. Speak it not. He is a nice old thing.' [14]

Harriet willingly took on the role of confidante and mediator. But it was a different matter when the editor asked her to become a contributor, and suggested several subjects. She refused, very reasonably, to undertake a series on the English Individualists since Spencer. She had 'read nothing at all of the writing of Auberon Herbert, nor the later individualists . . . and only a few of Herbert Spencer's books';[15] but she did, with great diffidence, embark on a review of *The Science of Society* by Reginald Wright Kauffman: 'My review has made a lame & dull start. It seems as though it will be a string of quotations from the book. When you get it you will either send it back by return or burn it.' [16]

The review survived, to appear in October. It reveals her as an inexperienced, but very conscientious writer, with a strong preference for letting her author speak for himself. It was a fault on the right side, and Dora, who liked her unadorned style, persisted. Under her influence, Harriet's writing did gain in freedom of expression, but she never wrote very much.

Her first contribution cost her a great deal of time and effort. Arranging the statutory shareholders' meeting, in London on 11th September, was more straightforward. Dora came up for it and stayed at Cedar Lawn. This was her first introduction to Harriet's family, and Harriet had written to warn her that she would find them assembled in force: 'The thing is my youngest sister has lately become engaged (to my brother's sister-in-law's brother-in-law! making a circle or triangle of families), & as several members of the three families are staying in Hampstead that night we are arranging to have them for a family dinner here at 7.30.' [17]

Harriet was not free to meet Dora at the station, nor was she free to run round with her. Dora paid several visits by herself. She had come to the conclusion that she should strengthen her own position, *vis-à-vis* Mr Pound, by bringing in supporters of her own, and she was particularly looking forward to a meeting with the socialist writer, Allen Upward, who was a friend of Mary Gawthorpe's, had contributed to the paper, and had sent her some suggestions for improving its management and finance. She had been a little unnerved when Mr Upward addressed her as 'High Priestess', but Harriet had reminded her, 'We do seem to need a business manager to push the paper'.[18]

Harriet went to Oakley House for the shareholders' meeting, and presented her financial statement to an unusually large assembly—Miss Marsden, Miss Bessie Heyes and four other shareholders. The receipts, in round figures, were £592, including the 'capital' raised by the sale of shares; and £237 had been spent. Now, 'the secretary reckoned that the balance [of £355] was sufficient to cover expenses for a further six months'.[19]

Harriet had felt encouraged by the money that came in during August: 'Between £9 & £10 . . . not bad for a holiday month.'[20] But the financial statement showed that the working capital was melting away before its work was done. Immediately after the shareholders' meeting, a directors' meeting was held, where it was decided to send out a batch of sample copies and to spend £10 on advertising. The circulation must be increased. In the expectation that it would be increased, the editor kept the printing order at two thousand.

Soon after Dora went home, Harriet, at her suggestion, invited Mr Pound to visit her at Cedar Lawn. Of this first meeting, he retained a visionary memory of quietness and calm: on the 'perfect' summer lawn, shaded by great trees, the collie was 'languidly consenting to gather a languidly thrown ball'. And 'the stillness of the first encounter' with Harriet was never forgotten. 'Certainly no one has left an image more definite in outline than H.S.W.', he recalled half a century later. 'H.S.W. in whatever group—not like silence, come gradually, but like a sudden stopping of all noise.'[21]

Her family were a little uneasy about Harriet's new friends. The household was not one where visitors could ever be given a poor welcome, but it was noticed that these visitors were very different from the usual circle of friends and relatives. They were described, later, as 'scruffy'; and although the family said little at the time, criticism was implied in what they did. From her large family circle, Harriet collected only three short-term subscriptions—from her brother Kearsley, whose subscription was never renewed, and from her two suffragette sisters-in-law. Months later, her cousin and friend, Eleanor Davies-Colley, expressed the feelings that the rest of the family certainly shared: 'I am afraid I must confess to not liking the paper very much.'[22]

When Harriet realized that her family did not approve she responded in her own way, paradoxically, by keeping her various interests even more firmly apart. It was as if she had decided to avoid the risk of distressing overlaps by extending the range of subjects that

74

were closed by her own choice. She let her family know what she was doing, in a general way, but she took them into her confidence on one subject only—the South London Hospital for Women—where her work could be accepted as 'normal'. The same habit persisted in later life, when she took up new interests. Her friends and colleagues in one sphere were often quite unaware that she was deeply involved in another.

There is nothing unusual about moving in circles that never comfortably meet, but Harriet's reaction was most unusual. Because she could not compromise with her convictions, and because she suffered so intensely when people she loved thought her misguided or stubborn, she was forced to intensify her natural reserve, to a pitch that most people, and certainly most women, would find intolerable.

The cost was heavy. Though she never asked for sympathy, and never wanted the easy sympathy that weaker characters demand whenever life is difficult, she did have a need for sympathy of another kind—a whole-hearted understanding and acceptance of the ideals and loyalties which guided her conduct. This is much more difficult for a family to provide, especially to a reserved person whose independence of mind is taken for granted. Although it is obvious that independent people must be, in some sense, lonely, it is not obvious that they must sometimes find their loneliness hard to bear. Harriet certainly suffered, though she could not conceivably have said so, when the kind of sympathy she needed was not forthcoming. Harold, who had been particularly close to her, was dead; and the rest of the family were not open to the new influences which had seized her imagination.

The Gap, as the family called it, was treated with affectionate good humour by everyone except Harriet. She took it more hardly. But her decision was unaffected. She was committed to *The New Freewoman*, and to Dora, who was beginning to seek her advice on important editorial decisions, as well as on practical matters.

In September, she was asked what she thought about changing *The New Freewoman*'s name. Ezra Pound had protested against its present name, and Dora had proposed the name and image which already had some importance in her thought and her writing. It had not, evidently, been well received, as Harriet wrote emphatically, '*I* quite like your suggestion of "The Egoist" '.[23]

It was some weeks before agreement was reached between the directors and the contributors. In the meantime, one problem still loomed large in Dora's mind. How could she keep Mr Pound and his friends under control?

Harriet was more inclined to take him as he was. His youthfulness, his kindness, his talents—even his awkwardness—appealed to her. It was a mixture that made her feel a little less shy than usual. But she understood Dora's anxiety. The paper was her brain-child; and Mr Pound seemed to think it was his. This was not so. He had spoken with confidence of securing American capital and selling the paper to a large circle of literary friends, but the capital had not materialized and circulation had not increased. The literary section, good as it was, had brought no practical benefits to the paper as a whole.*

Rebecca West, as assistant editor, found herself in a particularly frustrating situation. She was anxious to support Dora's authority as editor, but it was hard to see how. The literary contributors, several of whom had been introduced by her, were now paid by Ezra Pound and sometimes seemed to think that he was in charge of the paper. In the hope of strengthening Dora's position, she kept up her efforts to find new finance, but here again she was plunged into a conflict of loyalties. There was some money about, but the offers she received were made by people who took no interest in Dora's political and philosophic aims. They were prepared to back the paper only if she herself, or Ezra Pound, or both, consented to take it over.

These proposals did not interest her. She still believed, as before, that Ezra Pound had the right gifts for editing a literary journal; but she had no intention of providing him with the opportunity of squeezing Dora out.

Dora's attempts to find new money had also failed. Allen Upward never took over her business problems, though he moved to London and became an occasional contributor. Harriet was asked to find him lodgings where 'he could take his meals with a family of children', and spent a morning searching in vain. She could only find 'something that may do temporarily'.[24]

Ezra Pound's reaction to Allen Upward's arrival was complex. In a short letter to Dora he suggests that the newcomer should become one of 'his' contributors, and rather unkindly rubs in that there is some doubt about who actually finances, or manages, *The New Free-*

* Among the new contributors were Ford Madox Hueffer, Richard Aldington, H.D. (Hilda Doolittle), F. S. Flint and William Carlos Williams; and poems by D. H. Lawrence, Robert Frost, Walter de la Mare, and John Gould Fletcher had been reviewed.

woman: 'Allen Upward's translations from the Chinese (vid. "Poetry" for Sept.*) are, well its no use scrabbling for adjectives. Will he let me have them for the poetry page in his very own weekly, or your weekly or whose ever it is.' [25]

The uncertainty about who was managing the paper was more than Rebecca West could tolerate. She had other, more rewarding, work to do; and she resigned in October. Harriet sent her a month's salary, which she refused: 'As Miss Marsden has let me go, I think the least I can do is to go without looting the till'.[26]

Richard Aldington, now a regular contributor, rallied round and helped to make up the issue of 1st November. Soon after, Dora offered him Rebecca West's job and, after some delay, wrote to tell Harriet what she had done.

Will you please get ready for a shock: though possibly rumour will have made it into no shock but ancient history: *This* half of the directors has appointed Mr. Richard Aldington as sub-editor in place of Miss Rebecca West, departed.† Mr. Pound was very keen about the appointment: he says it will do the paper a great deal of good in many ways—in particular—because of his connections. I had by a half-suggestion given Mr. Pound the chance of saying whether he would care to take it up: he does so much for the paper—so much more than Rebecca could have done in a literary way—that I thought I ought to sound him.‡ His reply was as I have said—that Mr. Aldington was the person who wd. do the paper most good considering our shaky financial basis. Well, I agreed, & said I would inform you & get your consent.[27]

Harriet readily gave her consent to the new appointment. Ezra Pound, however, although he had recommended it, was not entirely happy after it was made. Dora soon noticed 'the way he and the new "sub" spit and scratch at each other'.[28]

Richard Aldington had brought to *The New Freewoman* his great gifts as a scholar and a remarkable knowledge of French and English literature; and had settled in with amazing speed. Perhaps he had

---

* *Sayings of K'ung. The New Freewoman* 1st December 1913 et seq.

† 'Sub-editor' and 'assistant editor' were used by Dora Marsden as synonyms. Rebecca West was assistant editor, never sub-editor.

‡ Dora Marsden had unfortunately lost sight of all that Rebecca West had done for her and for the paper.

already shown too much independence for Ezra Pound's taste, and resented his attempts to tell him how to do his job.* Richard Aldington was often touchy and Ezra Pound, who was happiest in a master-pupil or patron-protégé relationship, was apt to be irascible or bored when he felt that his authority was waning. Though he still made suggestions, and introduced new authors, he no longer paid the contributors.†

Dora came to London at the end of November, accompanied by Grace Jardine; and Harriet recorded in the minute book that a directors' meeting was held. In fact, the arrangements for meeting had miscarried, and she had learned of the resolutions from Grace Jardine. She wrote in some agitation: 'I made up minutes of a Directors' Meeting from our conversation of November 25th. Will you please tell me (by Thursday) if you or Miss Marsden think there is too much cooking about this? . . . I can easily tear the page out of the minute book'.[29]

The page was not torn out. It records the decision to change the paper's name 'if a suitable one can be found', and lists the names suggested: The Egoist, The Free Voice, The Prophet, The Revealer, and Tomorrow. The change was to be made gradually, 'The new name to appear first in small type as a sub-title, & in larger and larger type in succeeding issues, & the present title to become correspondingly smaller until it shall be entirely superseded by the new title'.[30]

Within a day or two, the new name was chosen. *The New Freewoman* was to become *The Egoist*. Harriet, determined to have a real directors' meeting, asked Miss Heyes to attend and pass the formal resolution. Miss Heyes dismayed her by objecting that the name was foolish and conveyed nothing to the 'ordinary practical person'. She herself was interested in Miss Marsden's 'gospel' and felt that the paper was not accomplishing what they had all intended. 'Some of the articles begin about nothing, twist and turn through a maze of

* In *Richard Aldington An Intimate Portrait*, Southern Illinois University Press, 1965, his friends freely admit that he was 'cantankerous' but remember him as a good friend, and as a man who, when he in his turn became an established writer, did a great deal to help other young writers. With Dora Marsden, Richard Aldington had occasional 'tiffs' but there is no suggestion that he ever quarrelled with Harriet Weaver. She must have known how to help him to forget the chip on his shoulder.

† In November, *The New Freewoman* made a payment (the first, and the last for three years) of ten shillings to F. S. Flint for an article on Le Théâtre du Vieux Colombier.

words, and when I come to the end, I wonder for what purpose it was written. Then the poetry, pages upon pages of it . . .'.[31]

In the event, Miss Heyes voted as required; and Dora, now that the men had come round to the name she first thought of, gave up the idea of making the change secretively. The new title, *The Egoist*, was proposed in the issue of 15th December. The editor explains that:

> . . . the old title has become a handicap . . . the critics who accuse us of selling "Aeolian harps under the name of tin whistles" indicate the positive element from which the paper suffers.

The contributors' point of view was stated in a letter, drafted by Allen Upward and signed also by Richard Aldington, now appearing on the masthead as assistant editor, Ezra Pound, Huntly Carter and Reginald Wright Kauffman:

> We, the undersigned men of letters who are grateful to you for establishing an organ in which men and women of intelligence can express themselves without regard to the public, venture to suggest to you that the present title of the paper causes it to be confounded with organs devoted solely to the advocacy of an unimportant reform in an obsolete political institution.
>
> We therefore ask with great respect that you should consider the advisability of adopting another title which will mark the character of your paper as an organ of individualists of both sexes, and of the individualist principal in every department of life.

Harriet, with some difficulty, assembled two of the shareholders to confirm the decision. On 23rd December 1913, *The New Freewoman* completed its 13-issue span of life and was transformed into its better-known successor *The Egoist*.*

The new 'sub-editor', Richard Aldington, had made a good impression on Harriet. She met him at the office, collecting specimen copies to distribute to his friends, and she felt he was 'trying actively to push the paper'.[32] In spite of all efforts, however, circulation did not improve. Although the printing order was reduced to one thousand copies, there were still large piles of remainders. Out of

---

* The company, however, kept its original title.

ninety lapsed subscriptions, only six had been renewed; and new subscriptions were not filling the gap.

The underlying trouble was that the paper could not afford to pay contributors.[33] This meant, on Miss Marsden's side, that experienced writers rarely contributed and the manuscripts from which she selected were often written with more passion than talent. It also meant, on Mr Aldington's side, that a large proportion of the contributions, though new to English readers, were translations or reprints of work that had already been published elsewhere. Unless more money came in, there was no way of paying for original work of high quality.

Miss Marsden still hoped to solve this problem by raising more capital. Miss Weaver, who had more experience in handling money, was more concerned with increasing the returns. On her own authority, she arranged with a publisher's traveller to 'get the paper round to booksellers'. She wrote to Dora 'in haste. In the middle of a wedding fuss!'. Her sister Maude was married on New Year's Day 1914, at Christ Church, to Campbell Hone, then Vicar of Mount Pellon, Halifax. This wedding was the last of the big occasions at Cedar Lawn. The house was to be sold.

Her elder sisters, Mary and Annie, were preparing to move to a large house, Westwick, on the outskirts of Guildford, not far from where Kearsley was in practice, and hoped that Harriet would make her home with them. She was drawn, however, to a life of her own and was looking for a flat near the centre of London. It was a break with the traditions of the family home, but Harriet and her sisters maintained the old ties. She was always able to stay at Westwick, not as a guest but as a member of the household, with a room of her own.

It was on New Year's Day too that the first number of *The Egoist* came out—with an unexpected addition to the staff. The name of Leonard Compton-Rickett appeared on the front page as assistant editor, jointly with Richard Aldington. Harriet had heard of Mr Compton-Rickett, because Dora had been trying to persuade him to put up some money; but his appointment was news. Dora wrote a few days later to say that she hoped, by doing him this favour, to bring him up to scratch. She did not want to be 'at the mercy of Mr Pound and Mr Aldington', who were still talking about raising some money themselves. 'The appointment,' she said, 'will doubtless annoy them considerably but I will just slur the matter over. They have already more side than there is justification for.'[34]

11 A Whitechapel street in 1911

12 The South London Hospital for Women

13 Dora Marsden

Harriet was the only one of her colleagues who had earned her full confidence. The letter ended warmly: 'I hope you will have a very happy new year. You have been a perfect treasure to me and to the paper. It seems odd that a year ago we did not know you'.

5

EDITOR OF *THE EGOIST*

IN MID-DECEMBER 1913, Harriet noticed that it was some time since she had seen or heard of Mr Pound. He was not, however, inactive. He was working as hard as usual on behalf of the writers he admired, and although he was no longer formally connected with *The Egoist*, he still counted on making good use of it. Negotiations with publishers went better when some of the author's work could be shown in print.* Over a period, he achieved many successes; but at the time he was often exasperated because the achievement, which cost so much effort, was so far short of all he meant to achieve. He desired, and had described, a society inspired by art, science and philosophy: and the actual world was very different.[1]

D. H. Lawrence gave him this advice: 'You sound a little bit at odds with the world. Why don't you take it more calmly?'[2] He was replying to a request for contributions and, although he had never heard of *The Egoist*, he suggested a short story, and promised to 'try and look up some poetry'. In due course, five poems appeared, but no story. He had already published four works of fiction and could expect to sell his short stories. The publishing situation was distinctly worse for a young Irish writer, James Joyce, at that time earning a precarious living by teaching in Trieste.

Ezra Pound learned of his predicament from W. B. Yeats and wrote to Trieste shortly before Christmas 1913. He introduced himself and asked for any manuscript he would like to send. 'Mr. Yeats has been

* Ezra Pound told James Joyce that it had been 'much easier' to place *The Horses of Diomedes* because it had already been serialized. (Ezra Pound to James Joyce, 4th January 1914. *Pound/Joyce*. Edited and with a commentary by Forrest Read. New York. New Directions, 1967. London. Faber and Faber, 1968, p. 19)

speaking to me of your writing. I am informally connected with a couple of new and impecunious papers (The Egoist . . . and the Cerebrilist [sic])* . . . The latter can pay a little, the former can not pay at all, we do it for larks and to have a place for markedly modern stuff. . . . Appearance in the Egoist may have a slight advertising value if you want to keep your name familiar.' [3]

James Joyce (according to Forrest Read) sent Ezra Pound the first chapter of *A Portrait of the Artist as a Young Man*, with *Dubliners*.† Ezra Pound pronounced 'the novel' 'damn fine stuff' and sent it off at once to *The Egoist*, though not without misgivings. He was quite sure *The Egoist* was the right place for it—publication in book form seemed out of the question—but he was afraid that even it, or, rather the two ladies behind it, might 'jibe' at one or two of the phrases.[4] His fear proved groundless. The first instalment of *A Portrait* appeared in *The Egoist* a fortnight later.

It was Miss Marsden, as editor, to whom he sent the chapter; it was she who accepted it and saw it through the press. As events showed later, however, she did no more at this stage than satisfy herself that the work was acceptable; and of course the current shortage of good copy made it very acceptable. It was not until *A Portrait* was published in book form that she read it.

Harriet first became aware of the author on opening her copy of *The Egoist* for 15th January 1914. Under the title *A Curious History*, she read a 'statement' Ezra Pound had received from James Joyce intended as a preface to his 'luckless book', *Dubliners*, a collection of stories still unpublished after eight years' frustration. The 'statement', with a few sentences by Ezra Pound at the beginning and end, served to introduce the new author, whose first instalment was appearing in the following issue.

Harriet learned that Mr Grant Richards, in London, had signed a contract to publish the book but ten months later had asked for various passages and one whole story to be omitted, as they were not

---

* *The Cerebralist*, as it turned out, achieved only one issue. Cerebralism was presented as 'an intellectual ocean whose waves touch all shores of thought'.

† Harriet Weaver, however, recollected that it was Arthur Symons, who had arranged for the publication of *Chamber Music*, who sent Ezra Pound the manuscript. (Her letter of 28th March 1961 to Bjørn Rasmussen; also her letter of 25th February 1947 to John Slocum.) Before Ezra Pound appeared on the scene, it was to Arthur Symons that James Joyce would most naturally have sent it. Perhaps he had already sent him a copy, or sent him a copy when Ezra Pound wrote. Arthur Symons may then have got into touch with Ezra Pound and with Harriet Weaver.

acceptable to his printers. Mr Joyce had refused and after further correspondence, during which he consulted an international jurist, had had his manuscript returned to him. Later, Dublin publishers, Messrs Maunsel, to whom he was introduced in 1908, had also signed a contract to publish the book, though only after a year's delay, and, unlike their London predecessor, had then raised objection to a passage in one of the stories, 'Ivy Day in the Committee Room', relating to King Edward VII. Upon this objection Mr Joyce had then endeavoured, but failed, to obtain a ruling from his successor, King George V. The Private Secretary at Buckingham Palace had informed him that it was 'inconsistent with rule for His Majesty to express his opinion in such cases'. Mr Joyce had then sent an open letter to the Press of the United Kingdom in which he had rehearsed his difficulties up to that point and had given Messrs Maunsel permission to publish the story 'with what changes or deletions they may please to make'. By then it was the summer of 1911. Only two papers had published the letter, both of them Irish. Messrs Maunsel had ignored it. After waiting nine months, Mr Joyce had gone to Ireland in the hope of coming to terms. Instead, he had been confronted not only with a much longer list of proposed deletions but a demand that all references to places in Dublin, even to railway stations, should be changed. Yet, after giving his despairing consent to all these demands, he had received from Messrs Maunsel a refusal to publish the book altered or unaltered and a threat to sue him if he did not make them an offer to cover their printing losses. Mr Joyce had then agreed to pay 60 per cent of these costs if he could acquire a thousand copies of the book and himself arrange publication. To this Messrs Maunsel had consented. But, on the very day on which the agreement was to be signed, the printers had refused to hand over the copies and they had destroyed them all, save one which the author had managed to obtain for himself, and they had broken up the type.

It is not difficult to imagine the effect on Harriet of this 'statement'. Here, clearly, was an author to whom the right of publication had been denied. Although, for the time being, she was not personally involved in redressing the injustice, her imagination and her sympathies were engaged on his behalf and prepared her for taking up his cause as soon as the opportunity for action came.

The *Egoist* printers, Robert Johnson and Co., like the editor, saw nothing objectionable in the text for this issue for 2nd February. Certainly it opened innocently enough:

Once upon a time and a very good time it was, there was a moo-cow
coming down along the road . . .*

The instalment took up five and a half columns. It was enough to
show that Mr Joyce, whose misfortunes invited help, deserved also
admiration as an original and powerful writer.

The de Gourmont serial was still drifting and floating from issue to
issue, and had reached its penultimate instalment:

The limbs were those of Neo, her white knees dimpled all round with
pretty holes filled with shadows, knees like those of a plump strong
child. At that moment, had he been a woman, he would have been
conquered by the slightest touching; he would have closed his eyes
but to reopen them in harmony with the lips and hands. . . .

The new serial was very different:

Night prayers and then bed: he shivered and wanted to yawn. It
would be lovely in a few minutes. He felt a warm glow creeping up
from the cold shivering sheets, warmer and warmer till he felt warm
all over, ever so warm and yet he shivered a little and still wanted to
yawn.

The appearance of the new serial was by far the most important
event in *The Egoist*'s history, but James Joyce was not the only contributor who was worth reading. Richard Aldington was a conscientious and sensitive literary editor, and Dora's section of the paper was
now enlivened by regular, topical dispatches from Madame Ciolkowska in Paris. On the business side, however, the difficulties had
not abated; and Harriet was beset by unexpected problems. The lease
of the office fell in, and it seemed for a while that there was no space
for them in Oakley House; Grace Jardine was ill and off work for
nearly three months, and Dora was suffering attacks of some un-
defined illness. Harriet, in need of counsel, looked forward to a
promised visit from Dora, but it was deferred week after week.

Dora craved uninterrupted time for her own writing and finally
proposed that she should give up her administrative position as
editor and as a 'Contributing Editor' concentrate on her regular

* This and the following quotations from *A Portrait of the Artist as a Young Man* are
taken from the *Egoist* text.

articles. Ezra Pound, she told Harriet, held out hopes that he could find a new editor, as well as new finance. She asked Harriet's advice; were these hopes likely to be realized? Harriet made the dry comment: 'His lady certainly does sound a last plank'.

The 'lady' was the American, Amy Lowell, poet and patron of poets. She was in sympathy with the Imagist group and happy to spend her time and her money advancing their cause.* It was, therefore, a logical idea that she should take over the English paper in which their work was appearing. But Harriet's scepticism was well-founded; Amy Lowell herself had not yet heard of the proposed rescue operation. She had taken an interest in the idea that *The Egoist* should have an American correspondent, and she had sent in five poems of her own, but it was later on that Ezra Pound put to her the crucial question: '*Do you want to edit The Egoist?*'[5]

He gave his views on the present state of the paper. The directors had been timid and trusted too much to voluntary work. At least two of the contributors would have to be fired, and the sex problem must be dropped, but his conclusion was that 'a clever manager could make it a property (perhaps)'.[6] Amy Lowell already knew that he had, as he put it, given up direct control, and she showed no eagerness to take it over herself. Meanwhile Dora, awaiting her response, sometimes hoped she would accept and sometimes hoped she would refuse. She had never met Miss Lowell but she had seen a photograph, and the stately figure had intimidated her.

She came to London on 4th March for a directors' meeting. The meeting, attended only by herself and Harriet, was as usual formally recorded. Harriet wrote:

Miss Marsden stated that she wished to resign her post as editor of "The Egoist" after June 1st, but that she would continue to write as much for the paper as she had done hitherto.[7]

It was a notice of intention, known and approved by Harriet. But she was taken by surprise when Dora delivered a message from Grace Jardine. She, too, wished to resign. Her loyalty had always been to Dora and she did not want to be involved in a re-organization.

Harriet's own report, as treasurer, was not cheerful either. Her traveller had introduced the paper to several new shops, but their

* Amy Lowell published the three Imagist Anthologies, 1915, 1916 and 1917.

orders were small and money was running out. Rent, wages, and printing could be met only until the end of May, when the financial year ended. She had, however, arranged to lease a new office, in a large front room at Oakley House, for £40 a year.

She had evidently given Dora, off the record, her personal guarantee that the money would be found. She had financed *The Egoist*, at the start, so that original writing could have its chance of publication, and she could not allow it to founder when only eight short instalments of *A Portrait* had come out. A month later, she put £100 into the bank account of The New Freewoman Ltd. It was her first decisive move in her long, determined and ultimately successful effort to bring James Joyce to his public.

She entered the gift in her account book as an anonymous 'Donation', and later destroyed any letters that referred to it. She had long believed that her money, tainted by usury, was hers in trust, and she consistently suppressed anything that might draw attention to her gifts, or suggest that they were acts of generosity.*

For this reason, very few of the letters Dora wrote her at this period escaped destruction, and it is not known when the thought first arose that some of their problems could be solved by making Harriet editor of *The Egoist*. Nor is it known how Harriet responded to a prospect that must have startled her. She had had time to get used to the idea when Dora wrote: 'Agreeing with me as I think you will that the Egoist spark of intelligence is not to be extinguished under Miss Lowell's respectable bulk, I propose that we decide finally (decision to be confirmed whenever we meet) that you become sole editor on and after June 15th.'[8]

Dora had seen an 'epistle' from Miss Lowell—'exactly what I expected'—and she had observed, and always remembered, Mr Pound's air of 'vacant bewilderment' when she finally asked him to 'make good his general promises' about 'money in the spring'.[9] She was disappointed in Mr Pound; nonetheless, by securing Miss Weaver as editor, she had successfully applied his formula for an editor-backer but in a context that promised her the independence that could not be assured under Pound/Lowell management.

Miss Weaver, scrupulously aware of her own inexperience, seems to have accepted the appointment as a temporary one. Once she had

* There is a note in Harriet Weaver's hand, in her folder of Dora Marsden's earlier letters: 'I destroyed the bulk of Dora Marsden's letters—and in particular, the more personal ones. March 1944. H.S.W.'

accepted it, however, Miss Marsden preferred to think of it as permanent. She decided that negotiations with Amy Lowell, still vaguely open, must be definitely closed, and that the joint assistant editor, Mr Compton-Rickett, should be told that the reorganized editorial staff would not include him.

Harriet was apprehensive about her new duties in prospect. Dora and Grace Jardine had always seen the paper to press, and she was going to be in charge with a new printer in London. Dora invited her to come and stay, so that she could meet the Southport printers, and see how the editorial work was done: 'It would be so much better if you could become familiar with the working before you felt any grounds for "nerves" on account of responsibility. I am certain you will manage the thing with ease once you feel accustomed to it.'[10]

Dora was still doing all she could to encourage Harriet to write more. She had given her a novel to review, *The Spider's Web* by Reginald Wright Kauffman, and asked her to think about starting her own column on Topics of the Day. Harriet had submitted her review in draft, and Dora commented 'I think you will write very well indeed when you get on to "Topics". You use words very tersely & well!'[11]

Harriet's doubts about her own capacities were certainly not shared by anyone else. Dora was delighted that Richard Aldington had written 'so charmingly' to his future chief, and that Ezra Pound was 'likewise very amiable'. She herself felt sure that they were 'doing the very best thing for the paper in changing matters as we are doing now'.

She had intended to give Harriet three months to learn the trade, but she was again very unwell, and it was not long before some of the editorial responsibilities were shifted to London. In particular, since her leader of 8th March was the last for four months, Harriet and Richard Aldington had to work out how to fill the gap. They solved this problem by using, instead of leaders, four literary articles and one set of poems by Richard Aldington himself; a collection of Chinese anecdotes by Allen Upward; the first of a series on contemporary music by Leigh Henry; and the last of three articles which Dora had reluctantly accepted from Leonard Compton-Rickett. His style, condemned by Dora as unformed, explains her reluctance: 'One feels that such poems [Byron's] are flung off like foam from the tossing head of a charger suddenly brought to a stop by the curb.'[12]

James Joyce's work had certainly been placed in mixed company.

It was not the first time, or the last, that the editors were obliged to fill up with work none of them liked. This was one of the problems Harriet was taking over.

A new phase was opening in her private life too; she was moving to a home of her own.* It was a service flat in Gloucester Place, Marylebone, a quiet residential street of terrace houses, brick and stucco, built in 1810. Her three-room flat on the second floor, was in a block of two converted houses, where her neighbours were professional people, out at work all day. Excellent service was given by a couple, a cook-housekeeper and a caretaker-valet, who sometimes also acted as butler—for the other tenants. Harriet did not give formal dinner parties. She was served by the parlourmaid, who unloaded meals from the rumbling hand-drawn lift on the landing, and laid and cleared the table. These arrangements were not, at that date, luxuries. They represented just what Harriet wanted—a simplified way of life.

Her sitting-room, with two windows looking east, served as dining-room, drawing-room, study and, very occasionally, as a second spare room. Her Victorian knee-hole desk, with knob handles on the drawers, became a side-board when she had visitors to meals; the large sofa, with a let-down end, could be made into an emergency bed; and there was a gas-ring for making tea. But the room was large enough to accommodate all these purposes without crowding. It was a comfortable, pleasant room, a reflection of Harriet's calm, individual style. The books along one wall, the chairs round the fire, with covers of clear blue and soft gold, the two Georgian pieces, a small dining-table and an inlaid chest of drawers, lived in harmony. And there were always flowers, lovingly arranged by Harriet to look natural.

Other domestic tasks did not come naturally to her. She had never done any cooking at home, and, as week-day lunches were not provided, she was puzzled at first about how to make them for herself. Then she discovered, in a health food shop nearby, food that needed no cooking. She became a mid-day vegetarian. Young nephews and nieces, fed on nut cutlets and salad, cheese and fruit, were sometimes left 'hungry but elated'.[13] She loved the young, and they in turn responded to the charm of a place, and a person, where simplicity and warmth were combined in an unusual way.

Her concern for the young was evident also outside the family

* 74 (later renumbered 101) Gloucester Place was her home until 1941.

circle. Margaret Storm Jameson, who had contributed to *The Egoist* several shrewd and vivid reviews, while she was still a research student at King's College, was pleased and touched by an invitation to join the staff. 'Even at that age' she said later, 'I had the wit to realise that she was only inventing a way to pay me £2 a week while I established myself as a writer, if I could.'[14]

Harriet's offer was no doubt partly inspired by a wish to help Miss Jameson; but it also shows that she could choose, then as later, people who were worth helping. There was now no one on the paper with a journalist's flair for topical treatment of topical subjects, and Storm Jameson could have filled this gap. Unfortunately, the offer could not be accepted. Storm Jameson was needed at home, and could only contribute occasionally. Later, when she met Harriet, she still regretted that she had missed the chance of working with her. She could recognize the resolute, fighting spirit behind her undemanding manner and retained 'a clear image of that deceptively serene face of hers, and of the kindness of her look and voice'.[15]

Harriet's serenity was severely tested through the early summer of 1914. She was taking over a penniless paper, at a time when the main contributor was in an unproductive phase; and, while she struggled with the accounts and with an editor who was often inaccessible, she was also under great pressure to write for the paper herself.

It was the writing which seems to have given her most anxiety. The first draft of her review was submitted in March, and it had taken her some weeks to re-cast in a form that met Dora's criticism without doing violence to her own very strong views. The author, she said, had 'dished up round a hero' a tract that would have been 'less unpalatable in plain form'.[16] The hero himself, in conflict with the spider's web of high finance in America, was described in the author's preface as a man who came to believe in a 'life-augmenting' philosophy akin to Dora Marsden's. Harriet, after conscientiously summarizing the story, could not agree. The hero, whose reflections she quoted, had a morality; *The Egoist* had none. He aspired 'to do the decent thing because it *is* the decent thing'; while Miss Marsden 'insists on doing her own thing—what it pleases her or suits her to do'. The story ended with the hero's death. Harriet concluded her review with the hope that 'Miss Marsden's lack of any species of conscience will preserve her from a like untimely end'.

In principle, Dora's contempt for the decent thing made a strong appeal to her. In practice, however, it often turned out that her own thing *was* the decent thing: an uncalculated response to the demands of a situation.

In early June, at a shareholder's meeting Harriet announced that an anonymous donor (in fact herself) had promised a further £250. On 15th June, she took up her appointment as editor. She had completed arrangements for moving to a London printer—Partridge and Cooper Ltd, a subsidiary of James Truscott and Son—and her first issue was in preparation. At this critical moment, Grace Jardine called on her, and resigned, firmly and finally, from the staff of *The Egoist*. This was one of many occasions where Harriet showed herself both kind and resourceful. She wrote at once to Dora: 'I have a suggestion to make. As Miss Jardine has resigned & won't be having her salary after this, we shall have to think how to use this money. My proposal is that you have £2 a week now instead of £1. You may find you need a private secretary. If so and if you happened to engage Miss Jardine for the post, it would be no concern of the New Freewoman Ltd. Nor of any shareholder, nor director (as such) thereof.'[17]

She was very busy, but she still had time to work out how Miss Jardine, who was taking up a job in publishing, could be paid for any work she still did for Dora. And she was not too preoccupied to enjoy her first meeting—a chance encounter—with one of her contributors, Hilda Doolittle, 'tall, thin, pale, rather handsome, dreamy-eyed, pleasant-mannered. . . .' But she was writing on the day, 1st July, when her name appeared for the first time as editor of *The Egoist* and she had also another story to tell, of rage and frustration: 'We have been fuming and swearing for the last three days & are still doing it! for the papers which were due at 9.30 have not yet arrived (11.15) & won't be here for another hour or so, we hear by telephone, & here we are with nothing to do waiting to wrap them up'.[18]

Ezra Pound was well aware of the difficulties she was likely to encounter; and sent a note: 'Permit me to sympathise with you in your new and painful position as editor.'[19]

The inevitable pains did not, however, destroy her pleasure in a satisfactory issue. She observed that 'it looks very well'.[20] Moreover, fifty years later, it reads well. Dora Marsden, under the heading *Just and Moral*—'not justice and morality be it noted'—develops her descriptive philosophy crisply and cogently; Richard Aldington reviews the June number of *Poetry*, and a collection of poems by Robert Frost: there is an article on music, a review of the Futurist exhibition in London, and a review of exhibitions, plays and publications in

Paris: and an entertaining set of cuttings from the *Times Literary Supplement* which reads like a rehearsal for *This England*. The only reference to the suffragettes was playfully made by one Bastien von Helmholtz—Ezra Pound in disguise.

The paper had made a real break with the past; and the new serial was establishing its future:

Stephen was once again seated beside his father in the corner of a railway carriage at Kingsbridge. He was travelling with his father by the night mail to Cork. . . .

It was here, at the start of a journey, that *A Portrait* came into Harriet's care. Dora had seen through ten instalments and the manager at her Southport printers, Samuel Wilkinson, an enlightened man, had followed the text assiduously. Though he had raised objections to certain words and phrases, she or Grace had always succeeded in talking him round.* 21 Harriet's new printers set up her first instalment without complaint, but they substituted inverted commas for the dashes the author used to introduce speech. She had this put right in the next instalment. Again, it went through without trouble, although it ended with Stephen's first Nighttown adventure, where he was accosted by a prostitute 'in a long pink gown'. But when the next instalment was in galleys and the whole issue ready for the press, the printers telephoned: Would she come over and discuss a passage they felt they could not print? It was the second paragraph of Chapter III, where Stephen, sitting over his algebra, daydreams about Nighttown—the 'gloomy secret night', his own 'tremor of fear and joy', and the whores' 'soft perfumed flesh'. Then greetings:

— Hello, Bertie, any good in your mind?
— Is that you, pigeon?
— Number ten. Fresh Nelly is waiting on you.
— Good night, husband! Coming in to have a short time?

Harriet had learned from *A Curious History* that Mr Joyce abhorred any changes in his text. She made a strong protest, but the printers were adamant. She felt it was out of the question to hold up the issue while she sought the author's advice; and *The Egoist* appeared on its due date, 1st August, without the offending paragraph. This was the first reverse in her long up-and-down campaign. It had no effect on

* In England, the printers, as well as the publishers, are liable to prosecution if published material printed by them is considered pornographic.

her conviction that James Joyce's text should be printed exactly as he had written it. Although she had been editor only for six weeks, and had assumed, as Dora did, that she had everything to learn, she had already decided to fight for a policy entirely her own. The previous editor had nothing to teach her about the scrupulous treatment of a text.

Dora had been a merciless editor. She corrected grammar, re-slanted arguments, and dropped out passages which bored her. Even when she made some attempt to placate infuriated contributors, she never admitted that they had any right on their side. Harriet handled *A Portrait* in a very different spirit. She dedicated herself, from the very beginning, to 'protecting' the text against anyone who threatened, by chance or by choice, to corrupt it.[22]

At this stage, when all she knew of James Joyce was his 'curious history', her dedication was to the principle rather than the person. Indeed, just before her first engagement in the long fight to defend his writing, she had had some practice in defending her own. Some weeks after her review appeared, the author attacked it in a letter to the editor. Her reply was spirited, and unyielding. Dora wrote to congratulate her: 'You have handled [Mr Kauffman] in a most finished manner. . . . Why don't you open up a tirade of your own— 'Notes of the Week'? *I am sure* you could do them in just the way we have been wanting them done for so long.'[23]

She was all the more eager to use Miss Weaver's talent for tirade because Richard Aldington was, in her view, far too ready with praise. The Imagists were all committed to commending each other, and the mutual admiration system had lately been extended to the Vorticists, who had come before the public in the first issue of Wyndham Lewis's *Blast*.

On this occasion, Dora was happy to note that Richard Aldington's review (of *Poetry* and *Blast*) was not quite so bland as usual. But she still wanted writers with more bite. In her next letter, she tried another argument with Harriet: 'It is *your duty* to start those Notes of the Week'.[24]

Harriet had other things to think about. She had sent out an appeal to shareholders, with no result. The £250 she had donated was melting away. There was a crisis every fortnight because Dora's leaders came late; and because she could never let a proof alone the printers sent in big bills for corrections. Harriet argued with the printers and remonstrated with Dora. Dora promised amendment, and suggested also that she should deal with any letters concerning her leaders. 'I prefer', she said crisply, 'to answer them on the spot.'[25]

She was working at the time on an exceptionally long leader, analyzing her own reactions to the threat of war, and Harriet, who did not believe she would find time to attend to anything else, replied to Grace Jardine: 'I don't suppose that at this stage Miss Marsden would open the letter if I wrote to her! . . . What should the procedure be . . . if Miss Marsden delays—and delays—answering [the letters to the editor] they may never get put in, but we have to pay for the setting up.'[26]

It was a frustrating situation. In Harriet's letters to Dora and Grace, she made her appeal to reason, but she let off steam in verse:

With apologies to Caliban

You made me edit, and my profit on't
Is, I know how to curse. May headaches never quit you
For learning me to edit! When first thou cam'st
Thou talkedst smooth, and madest light of it; wouldst tell me
No need to worry so. And I believed you.
Cursed be I that did so! All the charms
Of Ainsdale, sands, winds, rabbits, light on you!
For I am all the editors you have
(Until your book is published), which was first
But mine own happy self. And now you stie me
In a vile office, whiles you do keep from me
The whole o' your article. Sometimes am I
So short of copy that I'm driven to make
A leader out of Carter's trash. Shrugs't thou, Malice?
If thou neglectst or dost unwillingly
What I command, I'll pester thee with postcards,
Fill all thy house with swearing telegrams
Thou'lt blush to meet the postman in the street.
As wicked words, as e'er Miss Jardine swore
At stupid printers in her hottest mood.
I'll wire you every day. Your conscience † hears me
And yet I needs must curse.

> † Note to the 400th edition: This is an error. Recent researches have shown she never had one.[27]

Dora delivered in good time a challenging editorial for the issue of 1st August. She was still attracted and stimulated, as in her suffragette days, by the idea of force, and disgusted by the leisurely pace of constitutional procedures. She preferred, she said, 'the spirited risks of war' to 'the placid joys of peace' and she condemned democracy as 'the idealization of stick-in-the-mud'. She was exhilarated, too, by a rumour that *The New Age* (where a skit on *The Egoist* had recently appeared) was in financial difficulties: 'If it were to go down it certainly wd be an opportunity. If we could get Bechhofer & Rebecca West we could make things go—especially in an empty field.'* [28]

For the moment, she forgot that *The Egoist* was in a similar plight. Ezra Pound, unwilling to conclude his negotiations, had suggested introducing Harriet to Amy Lowell, who was paying a visit to London; and there was talk of giving her four pages an issue, for a rent of £250 a year. Amy Lowell, however, was less interested in *The Egoist* than Ezra Pound, in his enthusiasm, liked to think. She was occupied with other things, particularly with her plan for assembling and publishing the imagist poets as a recognizable group. She had already issued one anthology, *Des Imagistes*, and she was spending much of her time in London entertaining, encouraging and getting to know the young Imagist writers.

On 4th August, England declared war on Germany. Now, when more than half a century has passed, the date marks a profound change in the forms of human existence and the goals of human effort; but at the time, when a world war had never been experienced, there seemed no reason to doubt that creative work, like business, would go on as usual.

Amy Lowell gathered her friends round her, to read poetry aloud. They met in her sitting-room at the Berkeley, described in retrospect by F. S. Flint:

Through the long French window open in the corner could be seen the length of Piccadilly, its great electric globes, its shiny roadway, and, on the left, the tops of the trees of Green Park, dark grey in the moonlight; the noise of the motor-buses and of the taxis reached us in a muted murmur, and at the corner of the park opposite, beneath the street lamp, stood a newsboy, whose headlines we strained our

* The skit was written by Bechhofer.

eyes from time to time to catch. It was in this tenseness created by the expectation of news that Miss Lowell read Paul Fort or Henri de Regnier (she reads French beautifully). . . .[29]

Harriet, meanwhile, went doggedly on with her chosen work. From the Kent coast, where she was having a holiday with her brother Alfred's family, she wrote to Dora on 5th August about her troubles with the printers. Because of the dispute over the Joyce text, and over charges for corrections, she had written to tell them: 'We must make other arrangements . . . meantime we will try to send in only the most "proper" matter'.[30]

War had been declared, but it was yet to be experienced. Across the channel, the general mobilization was a brutal reality. Muriel Ciolkowska, travelling into Paris from the country, watched the troop-trains going past:

A few men, just a small minority of the very lowest class, look glum; one feels they would not have gone had they not known what would have happened to them for refusing. But the general tone is not one merely of resignation but of real determination; a wise enthusiasm without fanfaronade. "We are wanted," it seems to say, "we must go." Men past the age-limit have re-enlisted or proposed to re-enlist. At the Gare Montparnasse, guarded by police and soldiery, the tickets are collected by young boys. . . .[31]

In Paris, she saw, with 'hideous perplexity' how the preparations for war challenged her habitual beliefs:

. . . The concierge is up nursing a baby; her eyes are red; her brother left yesterday, her husband goes in a few days. On every doorstep are whispering, softly weeping women. Never did I imagine such a sight would come within my experience. I have not believed in the possibility of universal peace, but unfamiliarity with warfare has blunted the edge of whatever one's anticipations might be. Verily, when we spoke so glibly of the advantages of war—we who are not pacifists, for how can we be?—how little we realised what it meant, how its effects entirely surpass every possible notion which is not founded on experience.[32]

The dispatch from Paris arrived in London towards the end of the month; but nothing came through from Trieste. The issues of 15th

15 99 and 101 Gloucester Place, St. Marylebone.
Harriet lived in the second-floor flat at 101 (formerly
74) from 1914 to 1941

14 Rebecca West in about 1935

16 Ezra Pound drawn in 1914 by Henri Gaudier-
Brzeska, some of whose work was reproduced in
The Egoist

August and 1st September brought the Joyce serial to the end of Chapter III—and to the end of the text in Harriet's hand. It was a satisfaction to her that these two instalments went through unscathed: the printers were not alarmed by Stephen's 'agony of shame', by the school sermon on hell, or by his confession. But it was a grievous disappointment that the story could not be continued.

The series of articles on music, by Leigh Henry, was also interrupted, and Harriet's immediate problem was to fill up the next issue. Ezra Pound, thoroughly discouraged, made a suggestion: 'Do, if possible, get Mrs Ciolkowska to fill *all* the paper as long as the war lasts.'[33] Fortunately, Harriet received, in time, another dispatch from Paris, but she had to use also a lot of 'padding' rescued from among the manuscripts that Dora had never accepted—but never returned. She explained the position in a *Notice to Readers*:

We regret being obliged to suspend publication of the concluding chapters of the serial story 'A Portrait of the Artist as a Young Man' by Mr. James Joyce, and the series 'Liberations: Studies of Individuality in Contemporary Music', by Mr. Leigh Henry. The writers are in Austria and Germany respectively, and unable to send the MSS.[34]

The issue was, as usual, twenty pages. At the last minute, confronted by some empty space, Harriet had overcome her reluctance to write, and contributed a snatch of light verse and a two column review signed Josephine Wright.* She had been reading 'after long abstinence' three suffragette papers, and she condemned them as small-minded and muddle-headed. At a time of national crisis, there was little force in the old cry 'get the vote and all will be well'. It sounded in her ears like the 'bleating of sheep'.

Dora was surprised and pleased. 'I suppose you are Miss Josephine Wright? Very hearty congratulations on the acidity of the comment: & the Song of the Sock. . . . The paper needs lightening: obviously to lighten it is your destiny.'[35] But Harriet, though she was ready to rally round in a crisis, could not write regularly. Her destiny—to publish James Joyce in England—was served by keeping *The Egoist* alive, against all the odds and against a barrage of very sensible advice. Ezra Pound put to her a 'practical point of view'. Since there was no

---

* Harriet Weaver's maternal grandfather's father, Joseph Wright, died as a young man. She took the pseudonym Josephine Wright to give him a new lease of life.

chance, now, of increasing sales—and therefore no chance of attract-
ing good writers by paying them—he recommended that *The Egoist*
'suspend publication during duration of the war'.[36] He did, however,
send in a contribution—the first for some weeks—for the issue of 2nd
November.

It was a new version of a cherished dream. A year before, he had
announced the Angel Club, a world-wide association of creative
people, to be given a home by 'the purchase or seizure of an island or
oasis'.[37] Now, he presented the 'prospectus' of a College of Arts,
whose aim was 'an intellectual status no lower than that attained by
the courts of the Italian Renaissance'.[38]

Ezra Pound, disillusioned with the world as it existed, took refuge
in his own Utopia. Harriet was undeterred. She made a small concession to the forces of circumstance by reducing the paper to sixteen
pages, but she still hoped to increase the circulation. With Richard
Aldington's help, she drafted a new appeal, to be sent out before
Christmas to potential subscribers.

As Ezra Pound had forecast, the appeal failed; but Harriet's other
efforts met with success. It was a minor success that she pacified the
printers, when they objected to a statement that war was a malignant
disease; and a major success that she found a way of getting James
Joyce's text from Trieste to London. She had appealed to Muriel
Ciolkowska, whose sister, living in neutral Switzerland, had agreed
to act as go-between.

She wrote to James Joyce, for the first time in her life, to give him
the good news. He replied on 11th November 1914:

Dear Miss Weaver:
Many thanks for your kind letter of 21 ult which reached me on
the 7 inst.
I have now sent on . . . the fourth and also the fifth (and last)
chapters of *A Portrait of the Artist as a Young Man.** I hope you will
receive them safely. It is very kind of you to take so much trouble in
the matter.
Any letter forwarded to me should be in Italian or German and
preferably in open envelope and quite formal.[39]

The two chapters arrived safely—through Italy and Switzerland—

* After the package was sent off, James Joyce went on working on Chapter V, and
it was his final draft, sent later, that appeared in *The Egoist*.

late in November; and Harriet immediately sent Chapter IV to the printers. They were prepared to set up two instalments, but the third and last was unacceptable. Dora commiserated with Harriet: 'I am afraid Truscott's have far too naughty minds for us.'[40]

When Harriet submitted Chapter V, they raised more objections; and she decided to make the change to another printer as soon as she could.[41] From a short-list of three, she chose Ballantyne, Hanson & Co., of Tavistock Street, Covent Garden. Then she wrote to Truscotts:

I regret to say that as we are never sure what you will be willing to print and knowing that you are not willing to print the rest of the story: *A Portrait of the Artist as a Young Man* as it stands, we have decided to leave you after the issue of January 1st. We are very well satisfied with the way in which you have done the work and are very sorry to have to leave.[42]

If it had been possible to give the month's notice at the end of November, there would have been no more trouble. The two December instalments, as agreed, were printed intact. Stephen, in a state of grace, mortified the flesh; but the call to the priesthood did not touch him. He remained 'elusive'.

There was nothing here to disturb a Protestant compositor, but the next instalment was deeply disturbing. Stephen, strolling on the seashore, was reborn of the earth.[43] He watched his schoolfellows bathing and parried their banter with easy words. Yet 'it was a pain to see them, and a swordlike pain to see the signs of adolescence that made repellent their pitiable nakedness'. A girl, standing in midstream, was beautiful. Her legs were delicate as a crane's, and 'her thighs, fuller and soft hued as ivory, were bared almost to the hips, where the white fringes of her drawers were like featherings of soft white down'. These two eloquent sentences were slashed by the printer's bluepencil. In spite of Harriet's protests, the instalment of 1st January 1915 appeared in a mutilated form.

This issue was the first number of *The Egoist*'s second volume and Harriet, at a recent directors' meeting, had proposed some changes. Over the last six months, sales and subscriptions had brought in £37 and the paper had cost £337. In effect, she had carried the entire wages and printing bill and, though she was happy to go on doing it, she felt that it was prudent to make some economies. *The Egoist* became a monthly instead of a fortnightly; the editorial salaries were reduced; and the printing order was cut from one thousand to seven hundred and fifty. The margin was still generous—very few of the original subscribers had become faithful readers—and occasional entries in the Day Book record, with a certain pathos, a few shillings credit for waste paper.

During the spring, she put in £80, and there were two other, exceptional, donations: £10 from May Sinclair and £10 from Amy Lowell. Harriet did a calculation of costs per issue and forecast, with remarkable accuracy, the financial needs of the future. But she was not inclined to formalize the position by providing a regular income. She preferred to feel that each one of her donations was a personal matter, made in her own time. She arranged them, for the next two years, comfortably ahead of demand, and kept a small but respectable balance at the bank. She also decided to open a ledger.* She saw no hope of making the paper solvent, but at least she could keep track of where the money went.

The economy drive had drastically reduced the space that had to be filled; but there was still a shortage of copy to fill it. Several of the well-established contributors had dropped out, and one of the most valuable, Ezra Pound, had lost his first enthusiasm. His contributions now came in at very long intervals.

During the spring, Harriet's difficulties increased. Dora was planning a series of editorials on Truth and Reality, and her anxiety to make them of permanent value conflicted with her solemn undertaking to get them to Harriet on press day. In February, Grace Jardine appealed to Harriet to hold up the issue: 'Dora has worked and worked on [her editorial] but as it stands just now it *isn't clear*. . . . Dora says that if these psychological and metaphysical articles have any value at all it will be a permanent one so it is really more to the point to have them in readable form—even a day or so late—than to prejudice acceptance of their meaning by putting in statements which may be true but which are open to question on the surface. . . . We recommend ourselves for mercy'.[44]

Grace Jardine still addressed Harriet as Miss Weaver; but it was about this time that Harriet and Dora rather tardily became less formal. Harriet had not lost her fastidious distaste for any general use of

* The ledger was later destroyed, but Harriet Weaver tore out and kept the pages recording most of the later publications, which have proved invaluable. She did not, of course, keep the pages which recorded her own donations.

the name given her at baptism, but she had acquired a pseudonym, Josephine. It served, paradoxically, as a protection and as a mark of intimacy. It was also perhaps a sign that her new role, outside the family circle, corresponded to a real personality.

Dora's leader, when it appeared in the March issue, still had a great deal in it to prejudice acceptance. Indeed, it shows why she failed, in spite of her native intellectual gifts, to make her philosophy acceptable as a whole. She argues, very reasonably, that people can communicate only when they have a common understanding of linguistic procedure, and compares these procedures to the rules of a game. But then she immediately restricts the play of thought by pursuing the notion of agreed rules, and neglecting everything else that contributes to a good game. Worse still, she insists that words should have absolute and invariable 'meanings', established by definition.

The ambition to define everything is easy to understand in someone who shows, in thought as in life, very little appreciation of context and relevance. This was Miss Marsden's great weakness, and the attempt to offset it by constructing a self-supporting intellectual system led her into further difficulties. Her philosophy had to be, as she herself described it, 'assertive'; and the more assertive it became, the more distant it was from the realities of human discourse. It became progressively more difficult to write and much more difficult to read.

James Joyce, in the same issue, happens to touch on the same theme:

—One difficulty—said Stephen—in aesthetic discussion is to know whether words are being used according to the literary tradition or according to the tradition of the market-place. I remember a sentence of Newman's, in which he says of the Blessed Virgin that she was detained in the full company of the saints. The use of the word in the market-place is quite different. *I hope I am not detaining you.*—
—Not in the least—said the dean politely.
—No, no—said Stephen smiling—I mean. . . .[45]

For the time being, *A Portrait* was having a smooth passage; the printers raised no objection to the instalments of Chapter V. Mr Joyce was now seeking a publisher for it and Harriet, who had known of this for some time, was concerning herself with his difficulties. She had sensed the urgency of his desire to see *A Portrait* published, as he put it, 'in book'.

The previous summer, Grant Richards had, after all, published

Dubliners.* To his surprise and relief he had not found himself faced either with prosecution or with actions for libel, and he had asked James Joyce if he had any other manuscripts to submit. James Joyce replied: 'Have you not seen my novel *A Portrait of the Artist as a Young Man?*'[46] He confirmed that Grant Richards had an option on it, and suggested that he should see the instalments already published in *The Egoist*.

It was six months before Grant Richards responded to this offer. Then he was immediately sent the *Egoist* printed text, as far as it went, and the remainder of the book in typescript.[47] James Joyce made these arrangements through Ezra Pound, but he wrote to Harriet, too, to ask if the type was still standing.[48] She had to give the disappointing answer that this was an expense *The Egoist* could never afford. She asked anxiously if Grant Richards had already contracted to publish; and suffered a second disappointment when James Joyce wrote to explain that the option, which gave the publisher the right of first refusal, did not put him under any obligation to accept the book.[49]

Grant Richards let the weeks go by without giving a decision. In May, when Harriet asked him for the typescript back, in order to set up the remaining instalments, he returned it without comment.[50] Though he had in fact decided to reject it, because he thought any possible public had been dispersed by the war, it was some time before he said so.

Harriet's correspondence was heavy, but it did not prevent her leaving London. A family holiday at the seaside was planned for August, and in June she went to stay with her sister Maude, who was awaiting her first child. The two sisters made the trimmings for the baby's cot, which looked 'absolutely sweet', Maude said, when it was put up. Harriet had left before the confinement, and Maude was writing to her soon after: 'Thank you very much for your letters both to me & to Katharine, the one to her made us laugh so much that it hurt me. . . . I think you will like her.'[51]

During this pleasant domestic interlude, Harriet remained hopeful that 'Mr Joyce's tale' (as Dora called it) was on its way to publication. She also had reason to think that the worst of his troubles were over. H. G. Wells, staunch supporter and lively critic of *The Egoist*, had read and liked *A Portrait*, and persuaded his own agent, James Pinker, to take on the author.

* Under the contract for *Dubliners*, Grant Richards had the right of refusal of the next work and the same right for any other book, for the following four years.

Harriet was planning to complete the serial in four instalments, when James Joyce wrote to her from a new address, in Zurich, to say he supposed his novel had now come to an end.[52] She had, of course, sent him copies of every issue, but some had miscarried, so that his supposition was a shot in the dark. Harriet interpreted it, rightly, as a wish; she asked if he would like it finished sooner, ready for publication in book form.[53] He welcomed this suggestion, and she arranged to complete in two instalments, with the final instalment on 1st September 1915, which happened to be her birthday. When he wrote to thank her, he reminded her that the first instalment had appeared in 1914, on 2nd February, 'which, strange to say, is also my birthday'.[54] It seemed a good augury. Conjunctions of this kind held for him a magical importance and Harriet, in an unmagical way, was deeply interested too. As he learned later, she was second to none, and his match, in remembering anniversaries.

Now that he was settled in Zurich, he felt able to accept an offer she had made to replace the lost *Egoists*. They arrived safely, and he looked carefully through them. 'I am glad you have changed your printer,' he wrote. He was shocked to find that the last of the instalments printed by Partridge and Cooper had 'whole sentences' left out, but he also noted that 'the instalments printed by Ballantyne, Hanson and Co (February to July) are of course carefully done'.[55]

Unhappily, while Mr Joyce in Zurich was commending the printers, they were giving Miss Weaver in London a good deal of trouble; they had refused to print the August instalment as it stood. Two words, not familiar to her, *fart* and *ballocks*, were unacceptable to them. The sentence in which the first appeared was to be deleted—making nonsense of the passage which followed—and the second was to be replaced by asterisks. Again, she could do nothing to reverse these decisions. She could only write to Mr Joyce to convey to him how sorry she was.

She explained that she had left Partridge and Cooper because of their 'stupid censoring of your novel' and that Ballantyne's were now acting in the same way. 'I can but apologise to you. . . . I hope you will not have this annoyance when the novel comes to be printed in book form'.[56]

James Joyce was the most important, but not the only, contributor whose work she hoped to see published, and she herself was now planning to bring out, with Richard Aldington's help, a number of pamphlets under the title *The Poets' Translation Series*. Each number was to be a reprint from *The Egoist*, priced at not more than sixpence, and the first number was announced, in August, for September. The announcement said:

The translators will take no concern with glosses, notes, or any of the apparatus with which learning smothers beauty . . . The first six pamphlets, when bound together, will form a small collection of unhackneyed poetry, too long buried under the dust of pedantic scholarship. . . .[57]

This marked the first entry into publishing, on a small scale with very moderate risks.* It was regarded as a trial run and a more ambitious list was promised, if the venture proved a success. In the event, only one other title was added during the year—*Et J'ai Voulu la Paix*, poems by André Spire, who had failed to find a publisher in France.

The last instalment of *A Portrait* was about to appear, and James Joyce wrote twice during August to thank Harriet for her 'defence' of his text, for the interest she had shown and the trouble she had taken. She protested that it was the least she could do, when he had 'given' the novel and allowed it to make its first appearance in *The Egoist*. It had been 'a pleasure' too.[58] But, as later events proved, her conscience was uneasy. She did not feel that her warm thanks repaid him for his gift.

She was a little embarrassed, also, because he had sent his thanks and good wishes to her and to her 'staff'.[59] It was a natural thing to do, as she was still, to James Joyce, a shadowy figure at the head of some enigmatic enterprise obscured by the energetic presence of Ezra Pound. Harriet was tempted to disclose the real situation: her staff numbered exactly one, the assistant editor Richard Aldington. But she decided it was better to tell a white lie, and politely ended: 'With very grateful thanks from all our staff. . . .'

Meanwhile, J. B. Pinker had discovered that his new author's book was not placed with Grant Richards. He had expected to negotiate the contract; now he had to find another publisher. He offered it first to Martin Secker, who turned it down promptly, and then to Duckworth. Harriet, fearing lest Mr Pinker had submitted the ex-

* Richard Aldington was in charge of the pamphlets, and looked after sales and accounts. Someone, perhaps Harriet Weaver, paid for the printing. Her accounts have no record of how they fared, until years later when a little money was paid in.

purgated text, wrote to him—from the seaside—for reassurance.[60] This he could give—he had sent the unexpurgated galleys—but the rest of his news was bad: Duckworth wanted some revision made before coming to a decision.

For a while, James Joyce believed that Duckworth, like other publishers, were taking an inordinately long time to make up their minds. Then he began to lose hope. He had experienced years of frustration before *Dubliners* was published, and it seemed that the same incubus was upon him again.

Harriet replied to a melancholy letter:

I am much obliged to you for your kind promise of a copy of your book (which of course I shall be very glad to accept) "when and if" it is published. From this "if" I take it you must be having difficulties with publishers again and I am very sorry to hear it. I hope indeed they will not all prove so stupid as to decline to bring out your novel.[61]

Harriet's confidence in James Joyce's work was not shaken, but she suffered vicariously from his frustrations. She had, too, frustrations of her own. She had been editor of *The Egoist* for fifteen months and the strain had been continuous. Although, as secretary of the company, she was able to put in money without any of the usual formalities, it was dreary work priming a pump that was going to need priming for ever. As editor, too, although she had reason to take pride in some of her contributors, she had others whose work was only good for padding. Yet she had to have padding. Although Dora had produced all but one of this year's leaders, there was the haunting doubt whether her copy, often late, was going to arrive at all; and the James Joyce serial—not only a great work but also an admirable space-filler—had now come to a finish.

It was the moment when sensible people ask themselves if it is worth it. How Harriet put this question to herself is not known. Nor is it known what particular incident raised the subject with such urgency that she sent Dora a telegram. Dora replied promptly, and at great length. She began with a realistic assessment of the situation: 'The paper is slowly but surely fizzling out'. It had no united purpose which could be made to grow 'increasingly attractive and intelligible to the readers. . . . What should be the yeast to lighten the heaviness of Egoism is the equally unleavened heaviness of Imagism'.

As chairman of the board, Dora felt she must point out that 'we are not merely risking failure, but are actively chasing it, & as you were munificent enough to say that you would "foot the bills" until you were bored with the business I think it is the least I can do to tell you my plain opinion about the paper you are financing'. Having relieved her conscience, she set out three possibilities: suspending the paper, giving the war as a plausible excuse; handing it over to Richard Aldington and the Imagists, in the hope that they would win 'a modest success' and perhaps secure Amy Lowell's support once Dora herself had gone; suspending it for three months, while there was 'a nucleus of circulation left', and using the interval to save money and to advertise that things were going to be changed.

The nucleus of circulation was, at that date, about one hundred and sixty copies of each issue. Dora blamed herself for 'being an absentee'. Harriet, she felt, had been put in an impossible situation. At this point in her argument she suddenly reached the conclusion that the paper could be rescued, and that she could rescue it. She proposed coming to London in the new year and instituting a new order, with new writers and new poets 'of a different brand from Imagists'. Richard Aldington would remain a contributor, but not assistant editor.[62]

These suggestions did not go very far in showing Harriet how the 'new order' would come about: the paper was almost entirely dependent on Ezra Pound and Richard Aldington for securing new contributors. But Dora saw herself as the paper's only possible guiding spirit. She made no reference to Harriet's real achievement, the completion of the James Joyce serial. She had still not read it: she was mainly, perhaps exclusively, interested in writing that was aimed at changing people's ideas. She could not recognize Harriet's strength as an editor—her determination to look after her authors.

The *Poets' Translation Series*, with two numbers now on sale, at least enabled Harriet to provide young poets with a generous allowance of free copies.* It was a practical way of giving them a little help, but of no interest to Dora. Preoccupied with her own plan, she asked Harriet to announce a three-month suspension with the disingenuous explanation that 'our prospects are so bright' and 'financially we were never so secure'.

---

* The record in the accounts for many books gives a combined figure for press and author's copies, in some cases over a hundred. As this is well above the number likely to be sent out for review, it suggests that authors could, in effect, have what they wanted.

She had worked out her arrangements without reference to the war. A sharp reminder came when Harriet wrote to describe her first 'zeppelin experience'. London was quite unprepared. Black-out regulations on the roads were not enforced, and the underground trains came to the surface with their windows blazing. The early anti-aircraft guns had proved useless, and there was only one effective weapon, brought over with difficulty from France, garaged in Ladbroke Grove. The crew's first duty in a raid was to drive it across London to a carefully chosen site in Finsbury Park.

At seven o'clock on Wednesday evening, 13th October 1915, a report came in that zeppelins had crossed the coast. The gun-crew had dispersed, after a long exercise, and it took two hours to collect them. By that time, one zeppelin had reached London, but the most obvious menace was the gun-carriage. It raced through the streets forcing the buses, just in time, up on to the pavement, and it rammed straight through a road-block in Holborn. At half-past nine it was installed, and the first shot was fired.

The sky was clear, but a light ground mist lay in places, and only three aeroplanes were able to get off the ground. The enemy, meanwhile, was visible from Trafalgar Square—a zeppelin hanging above the east wing of the National Gallery. Its target was the Admiralty, but height and wind-drift had been miscalculated and the first string of bombs fell along the Strand and Kingsway. Some of the bombs were high explosives, some incendiaries.[63]

There were some casualties, but the list was not published. Harriet, like most of the other interested spectators, felt no alarm. But her letter frightened Dora. 'Do please seek refuge in the country . . . and if you like it, I'll come and settle the other side of the village pump sometime in January,' she wrote. 'Can't you? Won't you??'[64]

Harriet would not. She had no intention of reducing her commitment to *The Egoist*. On the contrary, she was about to extend it.

6

PUBLISHING *A PORTRAIT*

The Egoist was not suspended. There was even a slight improvement in circulation, and a useful demand for complete files of *A Portrait*. The November 1915 issue carried H.D's translation, *Choruses from Iphigenia* (issued also as a pamphlet) and Harriet herself contributed, at last, a front-page article. It was the first of a series headed—since she did not presume to think of herself as a leader-writer—*Views and Comments*. Ezra Pound thought it 'a blessing' that Harriet was standing in for Dora. Her articles, he said, 'made sense'.[1]

James Joyce, meanwhile, though gloomy about the prospects of publication in book form—Duckworth's answer was still awaited—urged his friends to do what they could. Ezra Pound, as it happened, was having a memoir published by John Lane and took advantage of this link to interest them in *A Portrait*. Violet Hunt, whom he may have introduced to it as it appeared in *The Egoist*, tried to interest a publisher she knew, T. Werner Laurie. Arthur Symons, for once, could offer no suggestions.[2] James Joyce then turned to an idea he had been entertaining for some weeks: to find a French publisher. Harriet, asked whether her Paris correspondent could help, replied at once that she felt sure Madame Ciolkowska would gladly do what she could; and then went on to make a diffident proposal of her own:

> ... But I am afraid it is a bad time to hope to get a book published in Paris. Most publishers there seem either to be closed or to be under-taking very little ordinary work just now—very little besides war books I mean.
>
> I have been wondering whether *The Egoist* could do it. Of course this would be nothing like so satisfactory as if the book were brought

out by a proper book-publisher in London with his regular machinery for advertisement etc. but it might perhaps be just better than having it published in Paris.

If you like I will speak to Mr Pinker & see what he thinks about it. If he thought the scheme at all practicable I would then consult the other members of our staff and the directors of our small publishing company (The New Freewoman Ltd.) whose consent would have to be obtained.

We are bringing out a small pamphlet of poems by a French poet who has not been able to get them printed in Paris at this time.*

The December Egoist is late again.†

With kind regards

Yours sincerely

Harriet Weaver[3]

'I am writing from the station to save time', wrote James Joyce from Zurich six days later—on a postcard, which would pass through the censorship more quickly. 'Sincerest thanks for your kind proposal. By all means telephone to Mr Pinker and also lay the matter before your staff and company. . . . Is not part of the type still set up? As for the advantages of a regular publisher I have not seen them till now. 26 (twenty-six) copies of my book *Dubliners* were sold in the United Kingdom during the last six months. I have never received any money from either of my two publishers: and I dislike the prospect of waiting another nine years for the same result. I am writing a book *Ulysses* and want the other published and out of the way once and for all. . . .'[4]

On the same day he wrote also to his agent, twice, to say he himself wished to take up Miss Weaver's proposal, but urging on him to try first every publisher to whom any approach had been made and to give them not more than three weeks in which to make a decision. 'All these schemes can be worked simultaneously one against the other, can they not?'[5] But J. B. Pinker, like any other agent who values the publisher's good will, was not prepared to approach several at once. He was also reluctant to hurry them. He

---

* André Spire's poems, *Et j'ai voulu la Paix*, were published in December 1915; also Richard Aldington's *Latin Poetry of the Italian Renaissance* (number four of the *Poets' Translation Series*).

† James Joyce was still seeing *The Egoist*, as he had accepted Harriet Weaver's offer to go on sending him copies after the conclusion of the serial.

went on waiting for some weeks for a definite answer from Duckworth.

Harriet, meanwhile, was occupied with *The Egoist* and the new year 1916 opened well with a good issue leading off with her *Views and Comments*. Dora wrote enthusiastically: '. . . consider yourself established & an institution henceforth!'[6] This first leader, though inspired by the theme Dora had introduced in November, was certainly, as she herself put it, reflections of her own. Dora, contrasting journalism and literature, had observed that journalism had an overriding interest in presenting theories and doctrines as eternal truths; Harriet takes a less abstract view and begins by describing the condition of a person who is first enslaved to doctrine and then liberated from it:

. . . We are all . . . so much, and in so long a line, the children of propagandists, we are born and bred into spheres where the atmosphere is charged with honour and respect for the perpetuated Theory —that it is with a feeling of surprise and relatively late in life, if at all, that one realizes that theories not only may be, but advisedly should be treated with coldness and caution. Oddly enough, however, when once it is apprehended this attitude takes on the appearance of the most obviously commonplace. . . .[7]

In science, she says, theories are rightly used as hypotheses to be tested, and possibly discarded; elsewhere, a theory is likely to become a pet or hobby, carefully sheltered from all discordant facts. It is only in literature, as distinct from journalism, that the facts have absolute precedence over the theories. The writer of genuine literature is 'content to enquire what men *are*, without hampering himself overmuch with foregone conclusions as to what they *should* be'. And *The Egoist* had a similar aim: 'To probe to the depths of human nature, to keep its curiosity in it fresh and alert, to regard nothing in human nature as foreign to it'.

Harriet's independence of mind had now reached the point where she could speak, as editor, with force and authority—though, in the event, she did so rarely. This leader was clearly written from the heart and, by implication, proclaimed her conviction that *The Egoist*'s aims were not unworthy of the author she now hoped to publish. Meantime, she remained vigilant over practical matters. Dora was again unwell, and short of money, so Harriet restored her salary from £6 a month to the original £8 13s. 4d. This was un-expected and Dora wrote that the 'fabulous sum' had plunged her into dreams of splendour where she saw herself 'clothed in—a tailor-made costume at least!'[8]

Dora delayed another week before commenting on Harriet's pro-posal that *The Egoist* should become book publishers, and then admitted that the prospect terrified her. She consented to it with reservations, on the understanding that it was Harriet's affair. This was probably what Harriet expected, and may well have been exactly what she wanted. Although she had made sure that the formalities had been correctly observed, she still saw the arrangement primarily as a matter between herself and Mr Joyce. There is a suggestion, for instance, in Dora's letters, that Harriet had not been quite plain about who was to pay for publication. Mr Joyce, it appeared, had a friend who would guarantee *The Egoist* against loss; and although Dora may have suspected that his friend was Harriet herself, she was evidently not in a position to say so. 'About the embarking upon a full-blown publishing business,' she wrote, 'you know how timorous I am: though if our clients (?) always guarantee us against loss it is difficult to point out where disaster is to come from—though one might suggest Work & Worry'.[9]

Harriet was already considering a new manuscript, Wyndham Lewis's *Tarr*, which had been refused by publishers and had been offered to her. She thought it 'a conglomeration of smart views';[10] and did not admire it 'in the way she admired *A Portrait*' though it was 'clever and interesting and unusual'.[11] But then she met Wynd-ham Lewis, and liked him, and was persuaded by Ezra Pound to accept the book first as a serial and not, for the moment, as the second title on her book list.* [12] Her immediate need was for copy to fill *The Egoist*.

Number five of the *Poets' Translations*, *The Poems of Leonidas of Tarentum* by James Whitall, was now on sale; and the last title, *The Mosella of Ausonius* by F. S. Flint, was ready for February. Ezra Pound, who had sent in nothing for some months, liked the idea of reprinting

---

* Wyndham Lewis had contributed several articles to *The Egoist* in its early days, and still occasionally saw it. He was then a member of the group he called Ezra Pound's 'youth racket'. 'He never got us under canvas it is true—we were not the most promising material for Ezra's boy-scoutery'; but he 'organized us willynilly'. (*Blasting and Bombardiering*, p. 254) Ezra Pound also gave Wyndham Lewis's own group its name—the Vorticists.

contributions as pamphlets and his interest revived. He wrote to offer Harriet a minor work of his own:

I think to keep my work from being too disjointed. & also for the sake of the announcement of the new years work that you had better announce.

"The Dialogues of Fontenelle"
Translated by Ezra Pound.

I will do a dialogue each month and also a very brief article as I feel moved. . . .[13]

It is understandable that Richard Aldington sometimes found his position uncomfortable. Although it was more than two years since he had taken over, he found Ezra Pound still regarded *The Egoist* as his own domain. Harriet was not sensitive on this score. She never lost sight of the fact that she owed Mr Pound a great deal, though she did not always carry out his brisk instruction. She accepted *Fontenelle* for *The Egoist* but left in abeyance for some time the question of reprinting it. The publication of *A Portrait* was her first interest.

When she knew that Dora did not positively object to it, she wrote immediately to make her offer a firm one. 'I have the necessary permission', she wrote to Zurich; and then went on to make another offer, which was to constitute another important precedent.

. . . Meantime, as our journal, after stringent economies, is now in a better financial position that it was when your novel was running through it, we think it only fair to make you some payment for the past serial rights, and we could now pay you £50. For safety, lest the letter should by any chance go wrong, I am writing from my flat and avoiding our official paper, so that the name of the sender may not appear. . . . And for safety also I am sending half the amount now & when I hear that this has reached you I will send the other half.[14]

Harriet had an additional reason for keeping the record of this transaction out of the office files; it does not appear in the accounts. She herself put up the money, without consulting anyone; and it suited her to write as a private person. At the same time, so that Mr Joyce could feel he was being paid for his work in the conventional way, she had to tell him that *The Egoist* was now able to afford it,

17 Richard Aldington

18 Hilda Doolittle

19 James Joyce in 1916—the photograph used
for the woodcut in *The Egoist*

20 Ben Huebsch

though this was not true. Its whole earned income came to less than £50 in a year. But it was true that the 'stringent economies' had reduced outgoings—by half—so that her losses were lower than they were.

A telegram announced the safe arrival of the first £25 and was followed by a letter. 'I have no words to thank you for your generosity and kindness. It comes at a moment when it is much needed by me.' And he was very glad indeed to hear that the company had given 'the necessary permission'. He was writing to his agent at once. 'This news gave me great joy as I foresaw many years of useless waiting.'[15]

Harriet was quick to disclaim any idea that she had been kind. She insisted that the payment was a debt owed to him. And she had just heard from Ezra Pound something of the author's difficulties in Zurich and that he was 'in need of money'.* 'I felt wretched & ashamed,' she went on, 'to think we had had your wonderful book and made you no return whatever. The kindness is entirely yours in never having drawn attention to the fact. . . . May I send you good wishes for your birthday?'[16]

Here was another reason why *A Portrait* should be published in book form: Mr Joyce's need of money. But Harriet's chief reasons were undoubtedly her admiration for its 'beauty' and her conviction that it deserved to be read by a wider public than that of *The Egoist*. Ezra Pound did not 'thrust' James Joyce 'down her throat', as Wyndham Lewis suggests.[17] He had no need to do so. Indeed, *A Portrait* must have had a personal as well as a literary appeal for her. She, like its hero Stephen Dedalus, had gradually come to recognize herself to be 'different' from the other members of her family and from their circle; she, like him, had rejected the religion in which she had been brought up and in spite of 'habits of quiet obedience' to superiors. She also was 'as formal in speech' with others as they were with her. These similarities must have touched her. Stephen's courage must have affected her more deeply. 'I will not serve that in which I no longer believe, whether it call itself my home, my fatherland, or my church,' he declares, and carries his defiance to a point far beyond any reached by her. She still felt acutely that she lacked the courage to go as far as she thought she should in breaking away; and would tax herself on this count throughout her life.

---

* James Joyce had arrived in Zurich almost penniless and at a time, the summer vacation, when there was no teaching to be had. He unburdened himself to Ezra Pound.

J. B. Pinker rated Harriet's offer as an unlikely last resort if all else failed. It was a severe disappointment to him, therefore, when Duckworth announced that they would not publish the book and returned the text. He sent it to T. Werner Laurie, who refused it also. He turned again to Duckworth, hoping against hope that they would change their mind. For answer, they sent him their reader's report—pronounced by Ezra Pound 'the insults of an imbecile': there were 'longueurs' —much pruning was needed; 'ugly things, ugly words' were too prominent; the entire book needed revision and 'time and trouble spent on it to make it a more finished piece of work'.[18]

Harriet, undeterred, started to look for a printer willing to print the book entire so that, if Mr Pinker eventually agreed to *The Egoist* as publisher, no time would have been lost. Her first choice was The Complete Press (of West Norwood) and she delivered it herself to their Strand office, conscious that she was handling a valuable document. She was already apprehensive about the outcome and wrote to Dora for counsel.

Dora was more interested in other subjects: Ezra Pound and his friends, with *Tarr* as a bridgehead, seemed ready to occupy almost all of the paper. After urging resistance, she refers casually to Harriet's biggest problem. 'Re Joyce: suppose we see the estimates first: then pass them on to Joyce's friend guarantor & get his opinion of their "highness".'[19]

The Complete Press, however, wrote:

We are much obliged to you for the MS of "A Portrait of the Artist as a Young Man" which you handed to our Mr Pentland.* Our reader has carefully gone through same and has drawn our attention to several paragraphs which we regret we do not see our way to pass. If you could get the Author to delete or modify these paragraphs, we shall be only too pleased to submit you an estimate. . . .[20]

Harriet immediately approached a second firm, Richard Clay & Sons, who saw no difficulties. She discussed details with them while

---

* Mr Pentland had an unusual gift. Although he was one of the people responsible for requiring deletions in the text, his relations with Harriet Weaver, who valued every word, remained friendly and dignified. The next issue of *The Egoist* was the second, and last, printed by Spottiswoode, to whom she had recently gone after dropping Ballantyne, Hanson. In April 1916, The Complete Press took over, and printed the paper for three years.

she was sending to press the issue of *The Egoist* for 1st March. Her second leader followed logically on her first. She attacked the dishonesty of appealing to man's 'higher nature' in order to rouse his 'lower nature', so-called; and scathingly denounced concerts of patriotic music in aid of army recruiting. But her object was to announce the coming publication of *A Portrait* 'not because we desire to saddle ourselves with fresh responsibilities in this difficult time, but in order to save a work of exceedingly high merit from oblivion'; and their success in 'happily' finding a printer who would print without deletions. Mr Joyce was to be congratulated upon 'his tenacity and courage in holding to what he knows his own work should be' and on 'having won for the critical understanding intellect standing-room on a portion of the territory now held specially sacred to exhibitions of a vapid sentimentality trapped out with a furtive salaciousness'.* [21]

But at the eleventh hour, just as the issue was being put to bed, Richard Clay & Sons withdrew; and Harriet had to add a footnote:

Since the above was written we are informed that, on reflection and on the same grounds as other printers, the printer here referred to declines to print. We shall not, however, relax our efforts in the matter.—Ed.

This was a major reverse and, throughout the spring, she was so much beset by work, worry and frustration it is hardly surprising that she resigned as honorary secretary of the South London Hospital for Women. During March, she went on approaching printers, one after the other; she opened negotiations with American publishers; she consulted James Joyce at ever step; she dealt with Ezra Pound's letters, sometimes at the rate of two a day, about Joyce's affairs; and acted, as usual, as a buffer state between him and Dora in his newest attempt to take over. Her enterprise did not go unnoticed, at least by Ezra Pound who saw with admiration that she was 'showing the curious vitality of this Island which people always say is on its last legs'.[22]

Harriet was also busy with the usual work of making up the April issue. She was not short of copy—she had allowed *Tarr* nine of the sixteen pages—but she had somehow to find time for doing the work she found hardest of all: writing a leader.

* The subject of the article had been suggested to Harriet Weaver by Dora Marsden, who also worked on and added to it. (To James Joyce, 15th April 1916)

Other work had the first claim. By the time her announcement of one refusal was in print, she had received another. William Clowes returned the text on the day they received it. Percy Lund, Humphries were the next to decline. Because the chance of finding a printer seemed poor, she did not press Mr Pinker for a contract. But James Joyce, when he heard of the delay, was up in arms:

I have written to Mr Pinker instructing him to draw up the agreement without further delay and to accept unconditionally, subject to his commission of 10%, whatever terms you propose. . . . If Mr Pinker does not send you his agreement at once I shall send you a blank agreement with my signature so that he can fill it in at your dictation. . . .[23]

As for binding and other details, he left them all in her hands. But if she decided to send him proofs, instead of having them read in England, to save time, he undertook (if the attack of rheumatism from which he was suffering did not go to his eyes) to return them corrected within one day after receipt of them.[24]

Finding a printer still remained the first task. Harriet, in her old tennis-playing style, shot off the manuscript at once each time it was returned to her and was ready to shoot it off again and again. Ezra Pound, 'much pleased with [*The Egoist's*] sporting intention of publishing Joyce's novel in despite of all fools, printers, censors, etc., whatsoever', was diligently seeking some way of helping her to get it printed.[25] He was also maintaining his revived interest in it as he was hoping to raise some money for developing it in his own way. The money, this time, was to come from John Quinn, the New York Irish lawyer and collector of manuscripts and pictures, who was already interested in James Joyce. As often happened, Ezra Pound identified himself so closely with the object of his interest that he immediately saw himself as the paper's directing influence (which had never been more than half-true) and he could not resist representing himself as having a controlling interest (which had never been true). He wrote to Kate Buss, 'Re *Egoist*: Am trying to put a little life into it again. If I succeed in getting a little cash I shall properly revive it'.[26]

Harriet, who actually had a controlling interest, did not hear of his plans for a week or two. To her, he sent a suggestion for ending the deadlock over the publication of *A Portrait*: 'If all printers refuse

(I have written this also to Joyce) I suggest that largish blank spaces be left where passages are cut out. Then the excisions can be manifolded (not carbon copies, but another process) by typewriter on good paper, and if necessary I will paste them in myself'.[27]

The idea did not attract Harriet but she felt differently when three more firms had refused and one of them, Billing and Sons of Guild-ford, particularly brusquely:

We . . . beg to say that we could not for one moment entertain any idea of printing such a production. We are convinced that you would run very great risk in putting such a book on the market, and would advise, if you still think of publishing it, to have it gone over very carefully, and all objectionable passages expunged.[28]

She was becoming 'fairly hopeless' but sent the manuscript to Turnbull and Spears, the Edinburgh firm who printed the Temple edition of Shakespeare. If they refused, that was probably that. All the printers, she thought, had been frightened by the recent prosecu-tion of D. H. Lawrence's book *The Rainbow*.[29]

Perhaps she was right. Whatever the reason, she now felt that Ezra Pound's plan might well be the only solution. The solution of other difficulties was not yet in sight. A clerk at Oakley House, whose services Harriet was proposing to borrow, and who was the only per-son there who knew anything about publishing (curiously enough he had worked for Maunsel in Dublin and remembered the dispute over *Dubliners*) was expecting to be called up. Without him, Harriet would have no one to help her.[30] The draft agreement, received at last from J. B. Pinker, stipulated publication that year. 'I hope it may be done,' she wrote to Zurich, 'but owing to all these difficulties there is of course some doubt. I should have no hesitation in signing it if we had only you to deal with, but it is a different matter to be in Mr Pinker's hands & he appoints himself your representative on all questions concerning the carrying out of the agreement.'[31]

Relations with Mr Joyce's agent were becoming a little strained. But Mr Joyce himself had no hesitation in signing the agreement and did so on 31st March. Under it, he was to receive a royalty of 25 per cent on the published price—6s.—of each and every copy; and his agent's formal status was confirmed.[32] J. B. Pinker, however, by this time was just as discouraged as Harriet and far less active. A literary agent, like other agents, works hardest on the products which sell well, and J. B. Pinker, besides having the burden of a very slow seller, also had the excuse that the author's honorary agents were doing a great deal of work. But Ezra Pound, ironically calling him 'the practical Pinker', had lost all patience with him and had come to the conclusion that the best hope now lay in publication in the United States. His own book, *This Generation*, was with John Marshall in New York, and he wrote him a 'very strong letter' advising him to publish *A Portrait* instead. 'I can't go further than that,' he told Harriet. 'I advise you to send him . . . at once the leaves of *The Egoist* containing the novel *and also* the bits the printer cut out'.[33] Not content with this splendid gesture—as Harriet used to say, 'Mr Pound was always so kind'—he wrote also to another American contact, Byrne Hackett, an Irishman running The Brick Row Print and Book Shop at New Haven, with useful connections with the Yale University Press and publishers in New York; and asked Harriet to send a text to him too.

Harriet was very ready to fall in with these suggestions: she did not mind who published *A Portrait*, as long as it was published entire. She was less enthusiastic about Ezra Pound's newest plans for reorganization. He now had John Quinn's promise of '£120 a year for myself in connection with *The Egoist*';[34] and expounded them in a talk with her. They were based on the curious idea he had put forward before, that *The Egoist* should lease space to him at some agreed rate per page.

His proposals, which probably looked to him as if he was offering money to the paper, in fact meant that the paper would be subsidizing him and his contributors. The arrangement required also a very peculiar division of editorial responsibility and made no allowance for the fact that there was an assistant editor, Richard Aldington, in charge of the section he had his eye on.

Dora, when Ezra Pound submitted the proposals to her, as chairman of the board, saw their absurdity but was undecided about how to respond. She unburdened herself at length to Harriet. '. . . it is a question of E.P. & his friends against R.A. & his friends. . . . Well, of course, which gang do we prefer? . . . Say not a word—not even in hint—but *I think very little* of Pound's supposed big sums. . . . He doesn't propose putting £800 into the N.F.W. Ltd. He asks for anything from ½ to ⅔ of the paper—wh: the N.F.W. Ltd. pays for. . . . He reduces *our* editorial powers to zero. Fixed items allowed for—he bags the rest. He really is ingenious. *On the other hand* . . . Pound is more *entertaining* than R.A. except when the latter chooses: & he hasn't chosen very often lately. . . . Be sweet and gracious and say nothing for a while. . . . I would never cede any rights over the space of the paper, formally, if I were you.'[35]

On one count, Dora failed to do justice to Ezra Pound: this time, the money was real. But she was right in thinking that he wanted more space than he could pay for. A proportion of the £120 was going to pay his contributors and the remainder was unlikely to cover a half, and much less two-thirds, of the outgoings and over-heads of a paper which cost at least £240 a year. Even if the directors axed Richard Aldington, the prospects of making a new literary section self-supporting were not bright. Ezra Pound had been very successful in securing contributors, but his influence had never halted the steady decline in circulation; and his practice of placing manu-scripts simultaneously in England and America hardly helped to gain American subscribers.

The plan had, however, one great attraction for Harriet: under it, James Joyce was to be invited to contribute regularly. She had other reasons, too, for accepting, in a genuine spirit, Dora's tactical advice to be 'sweet and gracious'. Mr Pound was a friend. Unlike Dora, she had no real difficulty in working with him and she was getting to know him personally. They sometimes took tea together (he had introduced her to his wife, Dorothy) and she started to go to the Monday suppers in Soho, often at Gennaro's, where Imagists and Vorticists and other writers, painters and critics met each week to talk about literature and art.

Ezra Pound brought the Imagists and sometimes his wife; Wynd-ham Lewis brought the Vorticists. Harriet still liked Mr Lewis, although he alarmed her rather and brought out her nervous habit of tugging her collar up and her skirt down. To Gennaro's there came also, from time to time, Ford Madox Hueffer, T. S. Eliot, John Rodker, Eugene Goossens, Arthur Waley, Violet Hunt and many others. As no introductions were made, some of the occasional visitors may have remained faces without names.

One of the few people Harriet got to know and like was the painter Helen Saunders, a friend of Walter Sickert and Fred Etchells and, at that time, honorary secretary of the Vorticist Group. She often went to Gloucester Place, generally for tea. She shared with Harriet a gift for silent attention to the talk at Gennaro's and certainly noticed her for this reason. '. . . She was as silent in "company" as I was myself and I can't remember anything that either of us said! She was noticeably plainly dressed—so plainly as to be distinguishable from the rest—tweed country style coat and plain felt hat. . . .'[36]

Harriet knew Mr Pound quite well by now and she understood what Dora meant when she spoke of his playing 'the little god' among his friends.[37] She would never have expressed it so brutally, but she had pondered over the whole question of leaders and masters, and made her own comment in the April issue. Meanwhile, she sent a note to Ezra Pound saying that Miss Marsden wanted a little time to think over his proposals 'before deciding on any drastic changes, & it *would* be rather drastic to shunt off Mr Aldington at once . . .'. She would herself, however, welcome Mr Joyce being offered 'one definite "job" in his very difficult time'; and 'definite, regular & good contributors'. Among them Mr Eliot had been recommended and she asked: 'What was his line?'[38]

It was a kindly if somewhat ambivalent note. Her leader, by contrast, was severe. It was on the subject of 'Wonder' and the danger of 'school-forming' in the arts and sciences, whenever unoriginal minds found 'masters' to admire. She particularly condemned the effect on the 'masters': 'Vanity and worshipping followers will combine to make many a man of genuine parts a charlatan'.[39] Harriet evidently meant exactly what she said, as a warning to anyone, known or unknown to her, who ran any risk of becoming a master. One passage, deleted from an earlier draft, must have been more pointed, since Dora remarked: 'In view of the new developments I could wish that you had put in the whole by way of defining the editorial attitude'.[40] But Harriet did not care to particularize at the expense of her young friend.

In any case, her note distressed him acutely. 'I *DONT WANT* ALDINGTON FIRED. I must have been very stupid and ambiguous,' he wrote, by return. 'I particularly dont want him fired. If he goes off to fight I don't see why his job shouldn't be kept open for him. . . . I thought I distinctly said there would be room for him in the new scheme.' The directors had, perhaps failed to understand his intentions on this score. He himself was still convinced that his offer would help *The Egoist* financially and he was baffled and hurt by their hesitancy in accepting it. 'You said you "hoped somebody would put some money into the paper",' he reminded Harriet, '(it was a vague general wish—but I went ahead on it. I can't expect another offer. . . .' He went farther: the paper 'should be made to pay its own way from now on' if his offer were accepted.* He ended a little more calmly:

Eliot is very intelligent. He has a large education, writes a little very intelligent verse. (vide Catholic Anthology). His prose seems very good, though he has not yet had a chance to write it unhampered. Next to Lewis and Joyce he seems to me the best of the younger men. NOT weedy.

I am still rather weak from sciatica. Can you come to tea on Saturday? And can Miss Marsden let me have some sort of an answer fairly soon?

If you don't want the arrangement, I have two courses open, I can either chuck the thing, or I can hunt around for some other paper to take it on. I don't know of any other paper that I want to mix up with, but it seems rather too good an offer to throw back in Mr . . . . .'s teeth.[41]

The *Egoist* directors failed to respond. Ezra Pound went on hoping that his friend Miss Weaver would prevail over Miss Marsden. His hopes were not realized but he bore no malice and remained a regular contributor—his *Dialogues of Fontenelle* ran from April to the following January—and the paper remained under one editor, Harriet Weaver.

At the end of April 1916, Dora came to London for a directors' meeting at Harriet's flat. The decision to publish *A Portrait* 'was confirmed—subject to the obtaining of confirmation of the undertaking that "The Egoist" would be guaranteed against loss'. Since Harriet was the 'friend guarantor', she could easily have told Dora on the spot that all was in order, but she preferred to keep up the fiction that someone else had still to be consulted.

The book was held up for other reasons. She still could not find a printer. Turnbull and Spears had refused it within two days, and although she had felt at the time that they were a last hope, she had tried again, driven on, perhaps, by James Joyce's cry of despair: 'I am so nervous about it that I cannot write any more but if it were published it would make my way clearer'.[42]

* Current circulation of *The Egoist* was about two hundred copies an issue—at least a thousand short of paying its way. At the time, Ezra Pound does not seem to have pressed for a realistic statement on circulation, although he complained later that the editors were secretive about it. (Ezra Pound to John Drummond, 30th May 1934. *The Letters of Ezra Pound*, p. 344)

In the meantime, a few fitful rays of hope came from America. She had sent Byrne Hackett the *Egoist* text, with the deleted passages written out by hand, and a covering note. If he would undertake publication in America, *The Egoist* would like unbound copies for publication in England. Would he cable his reply?[43]

Byrne Hackett, unfortunately, read the deleted passages first and immediately concluded that it would not be possible for the Yale University Press to publish the novel. But he wrote: '. . . in your interest, I have talked to B. W. Huebsch, the New York publisher, and I am sending him a portion of the manuscript this week. I have asked Mr Huebsch to write directly to you concerning it, and I would consider both you and Mr Joyce fortunate, were you to be able to make arrangements for its publication through Mr Huebsch who has made an enviable name for himself as a highly intelligent and success-ful young publisher'. All this sounded encouraging. But what followed must have pleased Harriet particularly: Mr Hackett went on to say that he had been at Clongowes with Mr Joyce.* 'I can bear testimony to the reality of his description, and I admire his book as an extraordinarily interesting piece of work. You can be assured of my hearty interest in bringing about its publication if I may be able to do so.'[44]

Byrne Hackett's response struck a new note. But in England the printers were maintaining a rigid attitude. By the second week of May, three more had declined with varying degrees of abruptness.[45] Harriet, in despair, asked *The Egoist* printers, The Complete Press, whether they would be prepared to print with gaps for duplicated inserts to be added later. The answer, again, was No, though their Mr Pentland 'considered the matter carefully' and they regretted they were 'compelled to take this attitude as their business relation-ship has been so pleasant'.[46]

But now things were really beginning to move in America. One of Ezra Pound's contacts, John Marshall, offered to publish without excisions and proposed 'very fair' terms, which James Joyce accepted.[47] The simultaneous approach to a number of publishers, however, soon brought complications. While details were being discussed with John Marshall, Ben Huebsch, apparently unaware of them, made an offer to J. B. Pinker. He had been impressed by *Dubliners* and, as he had already told the author, wanted to publish its successor. 'I expect

* James Joyce was unable to recall that Byrne Hackett (his junior) was at school with him.

to write to you very soon in regard to the offer,' he told Harriet.[48]

This was news. She was James Joyce's appointed English publisher, and so had a status in negotiations for his foreign rights; but she was only one member of his team of unofficial agents and, although she was always careful to report her own moves, at least to James Joyce, she could not be sure of hearing what moves were being made elsewhere.* Meantime, while she awaited Ben Huebsch's next letter, there was one thing at least she could do on her side of the Atlantic.

The paper's title, *The Egoist*, was of course intended to be of undetermined sex. The company's name, The New Freewoman Limited, however, had remained feminine. Harriet discussed with Mr Herrin the possibility of changing it; and, at the annual general meeting on 7th June 1916, she set in motion the formal arrangements for renaming the company The Egoist Limited, so securing an acceptable imprint in England for Mr Joyce's books.

Ben Huebsch's offer to publish 'absolutely' in accordance with the author's wishes arrived soon after the meeting. He was inclined to believe that such success as the novel might attain would be 'artistic rather than popular'. Nevertheless, publication would 'afford a foundation for Mr Joyce's other works on this side' and he would supply 'imprints' at such rate as might seem fair to her. (He was offering a royalty of 10 per cent, as against her 25 per cent.) He was anxious, indeed, 'to get all of his works so that by concentration of interest and economy of effort, he may be properly introduced on this side'. Ben Huebsch added a postscript in his own hand: 'I ought to hear from you immediately to get the best results as my Fall List is in preparation'.† [49]

Harriet, however, though she replied 'immediately', and was impressed by his eagerness, could give him no overt encouragement. She had to remind him that it would be Mr Pinker with whom he would have to deal, not herself, if his offer was entertained at all. Mr Marshall still apparently intended to publish the novel, though he had failed to reply to letters for several weeks.[50] She went, however, that same day, to see J. B. Pinker, showed him Ben Huebsch's letter and got him to promise to write to Zurich 'at once'.[51]

---

* Ben Huebsch, too, was uninformed on one point. He wrote under the impression that 'H. S. Weaver' was a man, as did Byrne Hackett, until undeceived.

† 'Immediately' was to become the key word in Ben Huebsch's correspondence with Harriet Weaver in the months that followed. He realized rather slowly that she was as keen as he was to see *A Portrait* published without more delay.

A fortnight later, John Marshall briefly announced that he could not, after all, publish *A Portrait*. While the terms of a contract were being discussed with Ben Huebsch, Richard Aldington went off to the war and Harriet gave his job to his wife, Hilda Doolittle. She also watched, from a distance, one last fruitless effort to persuade an established English publisher to take the novel. Ezra Pound, who swore her to secrecy, was behind the move but did not want to be known as its instigator.[52] He had persuaded one of his London society contacts, Lady Cunard, to persuade William Heinemann to read the book.

But Harriet did not share his hopes. 'I think it unlikely that [Mr Heinemann] will agree to publish without deletions and it will probably remain for us to do it', she told Ben Huebsch and asked him to let her know the cost of '750 and 1,000' unbound copies. But she did not want to publish an edition that did not exactly reflect Mr Joyce's wishes and she went on: 'Meantime I have written to ask Mr Marshall to send on to you his copy of the text which contains Mr Joyce's corrections (chiefly the deletion of unnecessary commas and capitals put in by the printer). Mr Joyce would like the book printed exactly according to this corrected text . . .'.[53]

William Heinemann took some weeks to make up his mind and it was only on 19th August that Harriet heard he had refused and knew finally that it would be for The Egoist Limited to publish the book in England. That same day, she cabled to New York ordering seven hundred and fifty copies in sheets.[54]

It was no use now to press for an estimate: it would only hold things up; and, acutely conscious of being 'an utter novice at book publishing', she did not 'venture' to order more.[55] After all, the freight charges would be very high and she did not expect a large demand for the successor to *Dubliners* which had sold only seven copies in the first six months of the year.[56] To save time, too, she would not offer to read the proofs, as she had done in May, when the negotiations with John Marshall were going so smoothly.

'I hope nothing will go wrong now,' she wrote to James Joyce. But more difficulties cropped up. Ben Huebsch tried to retrieve the corrected text from John Marshall but found that he could not be reached;* and he wanted to propose some modifications of the contract J. B. Pinker had sent him. 'If he accepts these and cables me to

---

* John Marshall's wife had fallen ill and he had gone to Quebec to be with her.

that effect, I shall proceed at once with the setting up of the book,' he told Harriet. 'I think you had better send me immediately the copy for the title-page* . . . [and] it would be a good thing for you to see Mr Pinker to urge him to give my letter immediate attention. . . .'[57]

Here, at any rate, was a publisher who meant business. Harriet went after lunch to see J. B. Pinker and found he had already accepted the amendments to the contract. He cabled New York there and then. She herself wrote to New York on returning to Gloucester Place and, perhaps to show her appreciation, ventured to dispense with 'Dear Sir' and to begin 'Dear Mr Huebsch'. The all-important question now was how to secure for him most expeditiously all the corrections to the text: the only other completely corrected text was still in William Heinemann's hands. Those for Chapters III and IV she had, and would send the next day; those for the other three chapters, she would ask Mr Joyce to provide. 'And I shall not be able to insert the deleted passages but I will mark the places where they come and perhaps you will kindly see that they are inserted from the copy you already have', she went on. 'If you are not able to wait until these corrections arrive perhaps you could have them made in the proofs . . . .'[58]

Having posted the letter, her conscience smote her: she could do a little better. That evening, she went through Chapters III and IV, added Mr Joyce's corrections and posted them by the late night post. Next day, she went through Chapters I, II and V, added the corrections as far as she could from memory and sent them off to New York. Then she cabled: 'Joyce corrections coming. Egoist'.[59] To Zurich, she sent off, by express post, cuttings of I, II and V and explained what she had done in a separate letter. '. . . Mr Huebsch is anxious to hurry the affair on in order to include the book in his autumn list but your corrections of these chapters would no doubt reach him in time for the reader to use them when correcting the proofs. Many thanks for your letter. It pleased me greatly that you should have remembered my birthday: please accept my best thanks for your very kind wishes.'[60]

But Ben Huebsch, probably rightly, would have nothing of Harriet's plan to print from her corrections and insisted on waiting on the author's. In fact, only a fortnight was lost. James Joyce made his corrections (adding some) and returned them to Harriet without

---

* She had already done so.

the loss of a day and she sent them on, the day she received them. As he explained to her, he did not send them to Ben Huebsch for two reasons:

first, I think the post between this country and the United States is at present very slow and it might not arrive in time: secondly, I know absolutely nothing about Mr Huebsch or the contract for the publication of my book or the date of publication. . . . May I ask you . . . to let me know as soon as you have any other definite news. It is really a dreadfully troublesome book. . . .[61]

As for her edition, 'In order to save time I think it better to say that I leave all the details of publication absolutely in your hands: I mean binding, etc.'. But he had two suggestions to make. A few extracts from the reviews of *Dubliners* might be inserted in the copies for the press; and he would like to buy ten copies, if possible before publication, to send to writers and critics who had befriended him. 'Possibly they might write something about it and no doubt that would be an advantage: but even if they do not I feel that I ought to make some return for their kindness.'[62]

Whatever J. B. Pinker may or may not have done to keep James Joyce currently informed of what was going on, he would hardly have found it easy to outdo Harriet's promptitude and assiduity. She was, after all, brought up to answer letters if possible by return of post, to take all the points raised in letters to which she was replying and to keep everyone concerned posted on common interests. And her upbringing was backed by her own natural gift for unflagging attention to detail, and by her experience, gained in her social work in the East End, of dealing with a variety of agencies. James Joyce, accorded the attention enjoyed by all Harriet's correspondents, found it increasingly worthwhile to look to her to sort out the hundred and one detailed points that seemed to him to need attention as publication day approached. But he was not unmindful of her work on his behalf. He ended his long letter: 'I thank you again and very gratefully for all the trouble you have taken and hope it will be rewarded in every way'.[63]

There was one duty, however, that she failed to discharge—the duty to do more original work herself. In her four leaders, she had made a first attempt to describe a conceptual world where every feature was provisional, and the success of any intellectual enterprise was proved not by the discovery of a final truth, but by the ability to re-shape, in the light of experience, the assumptions that had served so far. This was her standpoint—though it was to change later. With it, she held strong views on a number of subjects, but found it hard to put them into words. Besides, she was burdened, as always, by an inhibiting sense that she lacked the courage to express her views—let alone act on them.

During the summer, she attempted to sort out some ideas and put them down on paper; but she failed. Dora was furious: '*Where* are those moral discourses??! You've burnt them—wretch!'[64] It was a lost cause. Harriet had made her last contribution to *The Egoist*. She had chosen to devote herself to other people who could speak for her.

Anyone who furthered their cause earned her gratitude. Byrne Hackett, touched by her letter of thanks, wrote: 'The courtesy of your note . . . pleased me since it is seldom that one receives acknowledgement of service rendered. . . . I am tremendously glad that you for Mr James Joyce and my friend B. W. Huebsch have come together, since he is in my judgement the best of the younger publishers in this country by "best" I mean most imaginative honourable and resourceful'.[65]

Harriet was glad of this confirmation of her own hunch that the right American publisher had been found. But his resourcefulness soon put her on the spot. He asked for 'a portrait' of Mr Joyce and 'as much biographical material and items of interest concerning him as possible', for handouts to the press both before and after publication. She had no 'biographical material': she knew not much more of the author than that he was hard up, had just had trouble with rheumatism, and was engaged on another book about which she knew nothing except its title. Nor had she so much as seen a photograph of him. Ben Huebsch also wanted to have a look at *Chamber Music*. Could she procure him a copy?[66]

Her first job was to send on to Zurich, by express post, the letter from New York and then to go to Cork Street to see Mr Mathews. He said he would print sheets of *Chamber Music* for 8d a copy (a third of the published price of the book) or sell the American copyright for, he thought, £10. Harriet reported this to New York and added: 'I suppose it would be proper for you to communicate also with Mr Pinker', another hint that she was not Mr Joyce's official agent.[67] But the role Ben Huebsch thrust on her was not uncongenial; and, one way and another, she was gradually being caught up in all the convolutions of James Joyce's literary life.

She had, for example, recently sent to Zurich a copy of Ezra Pound's long and helpful review of *Exiles* that had appeared in the spring in the Chicago journal *Drama*. The play interested her very much. And James Joyce now excited her curiosity in the book on which he was currently at work: '. . . the action takes place in Dublin in 1904. I have almost finished the first part and have written out part of the middle and end. I hope to finish it in 1918'.[68]

Because of 'nervous breakdown', it was not until 8th November that he sent her, for New York, some notes on himself and on all his writings, published and unpublished, even including a pamphlet on Parnell written when he was nine. There was a graceful allusion to 'Mr Pound's' 'friendly help' and to 'the enterprise of Miss Weaver'.[69] Some photographs came later.

There was no time to be lost. Neither Ben Huebsch nor Harriet wanted to lose a day if they could help it; and James Joyce had made it known, rather belatedly, that he was particularly anxious that the book should bear the date '1916'. Harriet copied the notes, chose one of the photographs and shot them off to New York, where they arrived as the book was 'just off press'. On 30th December, she received a cable: 'Published Huebsch'; and she, in turn, cabled Zurich. 'As a matter of fact,' Ben Huebsch wrote a few days later, 'I got just enough copies from the bindery to make it possible for me truthfully to say that the book was published. The distribution to the bookshops and to the reviewers will be made this month.'* [70]

Meanwhile Harriet had been suffering unexpected delay over changing the name of her firm. Although the rules for a quorum were not now strictly kept, it was still difficult to get people to come to the required meetings, and it was not until January 1917 that *The Egoist* appeared with new proprietors: The Egoist Limited.

On 22nd January, seven hundred and sixty-eight sets of sheets, in three cases, arrived at Harriet's forwarding agents.† Ben Huebsch had lost no time: he had sent them off the day the book came 'off press' and Harriet, too, lost no time getting them to her binders, already alerted. For insertion in review copies, which she hoped to send out in the first week of February, she had ready a short list

---

* A copy of *The Egoist* for 15th January 1914, that James Joyce also wanted used, was still wending its way through submarines in the Atlantic in December. In the event, it may have arrived just in time.

† Harriet Weaver sent Ben Huebsch a draft for 214.50 dollars for the sheets on 23rd January 1917, the day after they arrived.

A Portrait of the Artist as a

2.

Young Man

<table>
<tr><td>1917</td><td>Expenditure</td><td>W. Joyce's Royalties</td><td colspan="2">Publication Expenses</td></tr>
<tr><td>Jan. 19</td><td>To Leighton, Son & Hodge for freight & charges of Davies, Turner & Co. 3 cases from America</td><td></td><td>12</td><td>11</td><td>0</td></tr>
<tr><td>» 23</td><td>W. B. W. Huebsch for 968/950 sets of sheets $211.00
3 cases
per Thomas Cook & Son $ 214.50 =</td><td></td><td>45</td><td>8</td><td>2</td></tr>
<tr><td>» »</td><td>Cash book</td><td></td><td></td><td>2</td><td>0</td></tr>
<tr><td>» »</td><td>Stamps for 97 notices</td><td></td><td></td><td>8</td><td>1</td></tr>
<tr><td>» »</td><td>Envelopes</td><td></td><td></td><td>2</td><td>3</td></tr>
<tr><td>» 25</td><td>Durrants' Press Cuttings (125)</td><td></td><td>1</td><td>1</td><td>0</td></tr>
<tr><td>Feb. 7</td><td>Postage of 23 review copies</td><td></td><td></td><td>7</td><td>8</td></tr>
<tr><td>» »</td><td>String</td><td></td><td></td><td></td><td>10</td></tr>
<tr><td>» 8</td><td>1000 printed labels (Coffin & Budd)</td><td></td><td></td><td>14</td><td>0</td></tr>
<tr><td>» »</td><td>500 Press notices "Dubliners" » »</td><td></td><td>2</td><td>0</td><td>0</td></tr>
<tr><td>» »</td><td>100 Review slips » »</td><td></td><td></td><td>8</td><td>0</td></tr>
<tr><td>» »</td><td>750 Book wrappers » »</td><td></td><td>1</td><td>5</td><td>0</td></tr>
<tr><td>» 23</td><td>To Mr Pinker, advanced on Mr. Joyce's a/c</td><td>25 0 0</td><td></td><td>0</td><td>0</td></tr>
<tr><td>» 23</td><td>Postage of 3 copies (2 review copies)</td><td></td><td></td><td>1</td><td>1</td></tr>
<tr><td>» 26</td><td>» to H. Read ~ E. R. Brown</td><td></td><td></td><td></td><td>8</td></tr>
<tr><td>» »</td><td>» » Cambridge, Dublin (4 copies)</td><td></td><td></td><td>1</td><td>0</td></tr>
<tr><td>» 28</td><td>» » W. Haldron</td><td></td><td></td><td></td><td>5</td></tr>
<tr><td>March 3</td><td>» » Mr. Frank Swinnerton (review copy)</td><td></td><td></td><td></td><td>4</td></tr>
<tr><td></td><td></td><td>25 0 0</td><td>64</td><td>11</td><td>6</td></tr>
</table>

21 First right-hand page of the Egoist accounts for
A Portrait of the Artist as a Young Man

22 Helen Saunders. A snapshot taken by Fred Etchells in
about 1916

23 (*Below, left*) Seldom Seen

24 (*Below, right*) Ullswater
from Seldom Seen. There
was no telegraph pole in
Harriet's day

of notices of *Dubliners*, taken from a list given her by J. B. Pinker.

Ben Huebsch's plans for publicizing the novel in the United States had, however, brought home to her that she ought to do something of the sort for the English edition, though 'promotion' did not come naturally to her. 'I am afraid I am not an imaginative enterprising and resourceful publisher but merely imitative,' she wrote to Zurich. 'The request of the American publisher has suggested to me that it would be useful to print in *The Egoist* before the publication of your novel an article on you which perhaps Mr Pound would be good enough to write. If you agree to this I will ask him. Would you be willing for it to be accompanied by a woodcut of yourself which I would get the young Norwegian, Mr Kristian, to do. . . ?'[71] James Joyce suggested that *The Egoist* must have had enough of him, but fell in with Harriet's proposals. When the photographs arrived—first two sets of two, which the sitter thought 'very bad', and then two different poses, by C. Ruf—Harriet chose one of the second batch, in profile, for Mr Kristian to work on.

Ezra Pound, on the other hand, was not at all clear that an article by him would be the best policy. He thought he had written so much already that other people should be tried before the reader of *The Egoist* was required 'to hear any more Me on Joyce'. He suggested Edward Marsh could do much more than he.* Or, if Edward Marsh would not write, a 'set of testimonials' might be attempted. 'From H. G. Wells, me, Marsh, George Moore (if he will), Martin Secker(??), anyone else you can. I can hardly add anything to what I said in *Drama*. It was about the strongest kind of statement one could make. . . .'[72]

His letter was forwarded to Harriet in Yorkshire, where she was staying with her sister Maude and her parson husband at the Vicarage, Brighouse, after visiting her two old maiden aunts, Harriet and Emily Wright, at Castle Park, Frodsham. It did not dissuade her. She wanted reviews from the friendly critics on Ezra Pound's list, and the article from him. On her return to London she won her point.

Having taken on the job, Ezra Pound decided to seize the opportunity to pour scorn on other periodicals and critics likely to be antipathetic to the novel and, by anticipating their tone, to forestall them. Harriet did not think this wise and told him so. He replied, at length. '. . . I don't think you are right about *The Nation* and *Athenaeum*. . . .

---

* Edward Marsh, 1872–1953, a Civil Servant, founded *Georgian Poetry* in 1915 and was a friend of many writers and painters.

If, however, you don't want to name names, I could consent to "attacks from a few sheltered, and therefore courageous anonymities". It is well to forestall attack, and the nasty Catholics like the M—and T—stye are bound to attack because Joyce so allmightily wipes the floor with the "Whore of Babylon" in that chapter on the long sermon. . . .'[73] And so Harriet had her way: no naming of names.

By the end of January, much had been done to ensure that the novel would be given wide notice and here Ezra Pound had been most helpful: he had been taking soundings for weeks past and Harriet was tolerably certain of full-length reviews by William Archer, Arthur Clutton Brock, for the *Times Literary Supplement*, and two or three others.* But Mr Wells had disappointed her. 'Life is short,' he wrote. '*The Nation* is sure to give Joyce a thumping review. Still I will ask Massingham about it when I see him. I've already sent for two copies of the book.'[74] A week later there came a postcard from him on which were written two words: 'Nous verrons'.[75]

Everything was now set. James Joyce had asked for a few more copies for presentation including 'one for myself and two for you and Mr Pound. In these latter I should like to write a few words if you will allow me to do so'.[76] And Harriet had replied that she was 'very much obliged' to him and, if he would accept it from her, she would like to give him his own copy.[77]

The binders, Leighton Son and Hodge, were even better than their word and delivered the books in the afternoon of 6th February. James Joyce's presentation copies, now twelve in number as he had added his Dublin friend Constantine Curran, went off the same afternoon.† The copies for review outside London went off by post the next day, and those for review in London were delivered by hand—no doubt by Harriet—on the day after.[78]

The group that met for the Monday evening dinners was beginning to recognize that an unusual strength of purpose informed the mysteriously silent Miss Weaver. Among her newer friends and admirers there were T. S. Eliot, 'generally silent but with a smile that was as

* In the event, William Archer did not review *A Portrait*.

† The other people to receive copies were the author's father John Joyce, his wife's uncle Michael Healy, his aunt by marriage Mrs Murray, W. B. Yeats, Arthur Symons, William Archer, H. G. Wells, Lady Cunard, Edmund Gosse, George Moore and Edward Marsh.

shy as it was friendly', John Rodker, poet, printer and conscientious objector, thin and pale after a period in prison; and Iris Barry, the young poet (and one-time suffragette) lately introduced to the circle by Ezra Pound.* It was Iris Barry who put into words the impression Harriet made:

Who was the lady sitting up so very straight with her severe hat and nervous air—she might have been a bishop's daughter, perhaps? *That* was the lion-hearted Miss Weaver who printed Joyce when nobody else would. . . .[79]

On 12th February 1917, The Egoist Limited published the first English edition of *A Portrait of the Artist as a Young Man*; and, in Ezra Pound's words, *The Egoist* 'was' Harriet Shaw Weaver.[80]

---

* Iris Barry later became a film critic for the *Daily Mail* and, in 1933, the first curator of what is now the Film Department of the Museum of Modern Art, New York. Her work for film archives has been acknowledged by her appointment as Founder-President of the International Federation of Film Archives.

7

MORE PUBLISHING

PUBLISHING *A Portrait* was its own reward but Harriet no doubt enjoyed Ezra Pound's congratulations: '. . . you are to be very much complimented on sticking to the job until you got it done.'[1] And Dora wrote: 'It looks exceedingly well, & the novel is really tip-top. I've just glanced through it in parts: the four sermons & the Parnell passage are unsurpassable . . .'.[2] From the family there was silence.* 'The Gap' was widening.

But publication also had its anxieties. A police raid on the office was a real risk. Harriet decided not to keep all the stock there and was commended by Dora: 'The passage about the relative merits of Christ and Tzar as icons will give them plenty of ground to move on without counting the fruity "langwidge"'.[3] Trouble came almost at once. Some libraries that bought copies took fright and asked for their money back. One or other of them might feel obliged to draw the book to the attention of the police. Harriet was rattled in spite of reassurance from Dora. 'Let them send the book to the police by all means and we'll have a *cause célèbre* with H. G. Wells and Mr Clutton Brock and other pillars of respectability in as witnesses . . . a blessed police court trial would be worth a £1000 of advertising!'[4]

Nothing came of the alarm, however, and Harriet could turn to working out how to arrange her accounts. Dora knew that The Egoist Press was 'guaranteed against loss' on the book but did not know, and never learnt, that Harriet was paying the production costs.

---

* Alfred Weaver, the most likely member of the family to show some interest, did indeed read the book but confided to his diary his conclusion that it was squalid and obscure. The 'artist' rebels against the R.C. priesthood but 'in quite repulsive and blasphemous language'. (J. H. Weaver.)

James Joyce, on the other hand, had been led to believe that the costs were being met in the normal way by the firm. It was essential that his royalty cheques should be drawn on the *Egoist* account, but it was also important that there should be no permanent record of the transactions in the accounts. Her solution to this problem appears, rather indistinctly, in the Day Book, where she made a pencil note of the royalty payments, which were off-set by payments from her private account. Thus she provided herself with entries that could be checked against bank statements but did not appear as debits and credits.* In her *Portrait* account book, opened in February 1917, she kept a complete record of earnings and expenditure, with royalty payments shown in a separate column from the other expenditure.†
Nor did she show where the money for initial expenses came from (sheets and freight cost £58 and binding £12) but carried forward a diminishing deficit as the earnings gradually moved up towards the costs. It was not in Harriet's nature, however, to pay herself back the money she had given away. The receipts on *A Portrait* were, it appears, immediately given to *The Egoist*.

Ezra Pound's cyclical affection for *The Egoist* was again at a spring peak. The January issue had carried the first of three articles on his development and achievements as 'a great scholar' and 'a very good poet', by the French writer de Bosschère and probably translated by the 'great scholar' himself. He made some proposals which, though not entirely clear, seemed to suggest that what he wanted was the Contributing Editorship; and that he had £400 somewhere in the background for paying his contributors.[5] Dora, as usual, was sceptical and concluded that what he really wanted was power to keep out articles like one in the January issue by John Cournos pronouncing Vorticism and Futurism dead. But Harriet considered, as usual, that *The Egoist* could not afford to lose him and his influence entirely. Dora agreed.[6] But when Harriet offered him the Contributing Editorship and a minimum of four pages an issue, she discovered he wanted to defer his decision: he was negotiating also with *The Little Review*. 'I am sorry that I can't send you a definite answer until I get an answer from America. Heaven only knows how long that will

---

* The first of these entries shows a payment made on 23rd February 1917: 'Cheque £25 to Mr Pinker on Mr Joyce's a/c—not to be entered'. Later entries, corresponding to the royalty payments noted in her personal record of *A Portrait*, have sometimes been rubbed out.

† This account book records the three editions of *A Portrait*; and *Ulysses*.

take under present conditions. I'm sorry for the delay, but I am afraid you'd better not put my name on the paper until I do hear.'[7]

James Joyce had become even more elusive. Harriet had had no word from him on the publication of *A Portrait*, indeed since Christmas; and had had no reply to two letters. She became apprehensive lest there had been a return of illness—perhaps of the 'collapses' that were 'due to nervous breakdown' that he had suffered in the autumn.[8] So she wrote once more, giving him again some details he wanted on the published and the trade price of the book and on the arrangements for sending him the American reviews. She ended, 'I asked [in my earlier letter] whether you would accept your own copy from me. . . . Though I have not heard from you I shall venture to send it now without waiting any longer. I have wondered whether you were ill again or whether I had annoyed you. . . . In the one I wrote more than a month ago I sent my best wishes for your birthday and am sorry if the message did not reach you on the day'.[9]

It was natural that Harriet should wish to hear from him when his novel had at last been published in England. She could not tell him another reason for wishing to do so: the chance to infer from his letters whether he was in better spirits. A few days before, she had instructed Fred Monro, now her solicitor, and a member of the firm Slack Monro Saw & Co., to send him some money in instalments, but not to mention her name.* She had learnt from Ezra Pound that James Joyce was endeavouring to support a family by giving English lessons and, in such time as remained to him, to write his next book. But Ezra Pound, though convinced that the income from lessons was inadequate, had not been able to raise any regular funds from his own literary circle.

No combination of circumstances was more likely to give Harriet concern: the wellbeing of a family at stake, the father, a writer of great power, beset by worry and ill-health. Perhaps also the profile photograph that she had kept for the Egoist publicizing of the book —so punctilious yet with a hint of the forlorn—had touched her? But this time, she could not pretend that it was *The Egoist* that was sending the money. She had to adopt another ruse, faithfully reflected in Fred's formal letter:

We are instructed to write to you on behalf of an admirer of your

---

* The firm was later, in turn, Monro Saw & Co. and Monro Pennefather & Co.

writing, who desires to be anonymous, to say that we are to forward you a cheque for £50 on the 1st May, August, November and February next, making a total of £200, which we hope you will accept without any enquiry as to the source of the gift.

We trust that this letter will reach you, the address having been taken by our client from 'Who's Who' for 1917.* [10]

The ruse succeeded: Fred reported that Mr Joyce, in a letter of gratitude which accompanied copies of his books for his unknown benefactor, clearly had no idea that it was to his London publisher of *A Portrait* that he was indebted.† In a copy of *Chamber Music*, of *Dubliners* and of the Egoist edition of *A Portrait* he had written: 'To an unknown and generous friend in gratitude for a munificent gift'.[11]

But he was in trouble again. 'My sight is still weak but I hope out of danger. I have been ill for four weeks,' he wrote. He sent a money order for £2 6s. 4d. for a dozen copies of *A Portrait* at the trade price of 3s 6d. and 4s. 4d. for postage of thirteen at 4d. a copy.[12] Harriet's fears had been justified. His assiduity, however, in discharging a small debt at the first opportunity must have pleased her: here, it seemed, was someone who looked after the pence.

Harriet agreed to act as a clearing house for reviews. On James Joyce's suggestion, Ben Huebsch was to send her American reviews for sending on, with English ones, to Zurich; and she was to send English reviews to New York. She took out a subscription to a press cutting service and decided to buy all periodicals with articles on the author. She was determined to miss nothing. So began her collection of cuttings and articles which was gradually to achieve alpine proportions.

* A second letter to James Joyce announced the continuance of the quarterly payments while the war lasted. (Ellmann, p. 427) The copies of these letters, and other correspondence with James Joyce, were lost when the solicitor's office was bombed in the blitz on London in the spring of 1941.

† Harriet Weaver would have been pleased to know, what she was to learn years later from Herbert Gorman's biography, how the news of her help reached James Joyce. He was lying in a darkened room, talking to a Zurich friend, Felix Beran, when there was a ring at the door. Felix Beran took from the postman a registered letter with an English postmark and, on returning to the room, was begged to open it and read it aloud. He always retained 'an extraordinarily beautiful remembrance' of the occasion, for 'Joyce was in sore financial straits and here came real help in need'. (*James Joyce*, by Herbert Gorman. New York. Rinehart, 1940. London. The Bodley Head, 1941, p. 244)

The first notice to appear was Ezra Pound's article in the February *Egoist*. He praised the 'hard, clear-cut, writing', 'the nearest thing to Flaubertian prose that we have now in English'. 'It is very important that there should be good prose. The hell of contemporary Europe is caused by the lack of representative government in Germany, *and* by the non-existence of decent prose in the German language. . . .'

The first review proper appeared in *The Nation* for 24th February. What was Harriet's surprise when she saw that it was by 'Mr Wells'! So that was what he had meant by 'Nous verrons'! And he was unreserved in his praise. 'The writing is great writing. . . . The technique is startling but on the whole it succeeds. . . . The interest of the book depends entirely upon its quintessential and unfailing reality. . . . One believes in Stephen Dedalus as one believes in few characters in fiction . . . A most memorable novel.' In Harriet's opinion this review did more than any other to help sales. It was followed a few days later by another in the *Times Literary Supplement*, 'a special review in the body of the paper, not in the ordinary review column,' as she reported immediately to Zurich.[13] It was by Arthur Clutton Brock but, in accordance with the paper's practice, not signed by him; and it also was highly appreciative. 'Like all good fiction, it is as particular as it is universal. . . . Mr Joyce can present the external world excellently. . . . His mind is a mirror in which beauty and ugliness are intensified. . . . It is wild youth, as wild as Hamlet's, and as full of music.'[14]

'The news about the *Times* review is almost anticlimax!,' Dora wrote. 'Talk of virtue rewarded! The Sunday School story-books are beaten hollow. Well, I congratulate you. You will have established a little niche for yourself in literary history.'[15]

By the middle of April, Harriet had twenty-three English notices, not all of them favourable—*Everyman*, for example, dismissed the book as 'garbage'—and nine American, including one in the New York *Sun* by James Huneker, 'one of the best critics we have in America,' Ben Huebsch told her. He too was in buoyant mood. 'That the book will meet with at least a succès d'estime there is no doubt.'[16] Harriet sent the lot to Zurich though only after getting round difficulties raised by the censor about the American cuttings.[17]

James Joyce was pleased with the press in general and with The Egoist Limited in particular. He told Harriet how glad he was that *The Sphere* had mentioned her 'publishing house' favourably and that

Mr John Quinn, in a review in *Vanity Fair*, New York, had spoken highly of her 'enterprise' in publishing the novel.[18] 'How nice of J.J.,' wrote Dora, to whom Harriet relayed the compliment, 'to think that the "firm" should have feelings and receive patting on the head. I think he must be a nice man in spite of his reputation for quarrelling with all the world.'[19] She had already given more warm praise on her own account. 'How exceedingly well things have gone with the Portrait. Does it dawn on you that you have published the "Book of the Season"?'[20]

But selling the book was now Harriet's prime concern. Orders had come in well at first—by the middle of March nearly two hundred copies were earmarked, a few of them for two Dublin bookshops—and then had flagged as the number of new reviews fell off. Most of the papers, as she reported to Zurich, were devoting very little space to book reviews at that grave period of the war.[21] She felt very much at a disadvantage in having no agents or travellers, in fact no business staff at all.[22] She concluded that the book would 'have to make its way gradually now'.[23] But before even three hundred copies were sold she had decided on her own next step in helping it on its way: a second edition.

Harriet discovered, however, that the Board of Trade were unlikely to grant a licence for importing 'non-essential' sheets as long as the enemy submarines were taking a heavy toll of shipping. Still, she wrote to Ben Huebsch to find out what he would charge for another lot of sheets and enclosed a money order for 3s. so that he might cable his estimate.[24] His offer—sheets in lots of five hundred at 25 cents or in lots of a thousand at 21 cents a copy, flat, f.o.b. New York, if The Egoist Press would pay for the cases—she did not pursue.[25] Instead, she asked whether he could send moulds from the type set up.[26]

Ezra Pound, meantime, announced the completion of his arrangements with *The Little Review* but said nothing about *The Egoist*'s offer of an editorship. Dora thought this odd. She was 'not keen on running an identical crowd';[27] and was furious that he wanted an announcement in *The Egoist* of his *Little Review* appointment.[28]

But there was no cause for alarm. Ezra Pound at this point dropped his plan to get 'a position' for himself on the paper and suggested instead the appointment of his friend T. S. Eliot as assistant editor. He had met him in 1914 at Oxford, and recognized him as a writer worth promoting; and now, acting as his agent, he offered Harriet his first book of poems—rescued from Elkin Mathews, who was making difficulties—*Prufrock and Other Observations*. He liked the idea of keeping arrangements in his own hands, and proposed to contribute to the cost of publication and to pay a part of his salary.

Dora liked the poems for their 'pervasive freshness' and 'subtle observation'. She told Harriet: 'The book is good: I'm glad you laid hold on it'. She was less happy about the assistant editorship—for the usual reasons: '. . . it should be an arrangement made between us & Eliot. We have no place for a nominee of Mr Pound's in the position of an independent editor & paid only or mysteriously (very!) by the latter . . .'.[29]

Harriet had just learnt that it was John Quinn who was providing Ezra Pound with some money for his literary enterprises and she had had a letter from him himself.* Dora wondered whether he had been persuaded to back *The Egoist* or would merely 'emulate the large lady Miss Lowell'.[30] In the event, he did not make any direct grant to *The Egoist* but he did buy five files of the paper and take out five subscriptions, at a cost of £10 2s. od., nearly a quarter of its annual income. He also bought three copies of *A Portrait*.

Though she would have enjoyed having Mr Pound on her staff, Harriet fell in with his new proposals and discussed them with Hilda Doolittle, who agreed to them in a very friendly way. H.D. had no particular interest in journalism, and evidently felt that she and Richard had been treated perfectly fairly. 'I think the new plan really very good!' she wrote. 'You are very thoughtful too, to call it "temporary" as, of course, I feel it would be jolly for Richard to go back to this old post on his return.'[31]

T. S. Eliot was, therefore, appointed as assistant editor from June 1917, at a salary of £9 a quarter, to which Ezra Pound contributed £5, and later another £7. But he did not attain, as Dora had feared he might, 'a proprietary position'. His contribution to *Prufrock* was £5 'towards expenses', later repaid.† Some, or all, of these arrangements were kept a dead secret from T. S. Eliot.

* John Quinn sent Harriet Weaver £30. There is no indication what this was for. As James Joyce's publisher, however, she might have been asked to pass on the money to him.

† Ezra Pound's generosity is unquestioned; but his 'proprietary' air was sometimes misleading. The impression he gave his friends, that he was responsible, single-handed, for publishing *Prufrock*, was the natural effect of his enthusiasm and high spirits.

Prufrock was the first of a series of publications.* By the end of the financial year, in May, *The Egoist* had earned £46 and cost Harriet £250; *A Portrait*, with the last two hundred and fifty sheets on the way to the binders, had earned £75 and had recovered two-thirds of its costs. Although these costs were a little unreal, because most of the overheads were carried by *The Egoist*, the book had undoubtedly done much better than the periodical. This was solid achievement. Harriet and Dora were now prepared to develop The Egoist Press as a modest publishing house. For their third title they chose Ezra Pound's *Dialogues of Fontenelle*, currently appearing in the paper.

This decision led Harriet to another: to put *The Egoist* on a more business-like footing. For some years, she had realized that no one except herself was going to provide capital and she had put up money from month to month. Now, she decided to make a larger donation of £400, made up of £285 for a new Development Fund, to finance publications, and £115 for a General Fund to finance the paper. She also provided for closer control of the money through the ledger.†

Then came Ben Huebsch's reply to her enquiry about importing moulds for a second Egoist Press edition of *A Portrait*. It brought a surprise: he had just printed a second edition and immediately afterwards had received from J. B. Pinker a long list of corrections. 'If you are going to have an edition in England,' he wrote, 'you will want to have it in accordance with Mr Joyce's recently expressed desires.'[32] The surprise was the greater because their correspondence had been brisk and there had been no hint of a possible second American edition. Indeed, Harriet had, about a fortnight before, sent to New York a list of corrections compiled by her, as a first step towards one. She had realized that the printers had not understood James Joyce's directions regarding words normally hyphenated. He had wanted them run on but the printers had separated them.[33]

There was now nothing for it but to find a printer in the United Kingdom willing to print *A Portrait* entire. She had already put out a few feelers, against the probability that the Board of Trade would

---

* *Prufrock* was published in June 1917. For the time being, no royalties were paid, and the arrangement between author and publisher evidently was that profits should be shared after costs had been covered. But, judging by Harriet Weaver's usual practice, T. S. Eliot was probably given a very generous allowance of press and complimentary copies, which are always of use to a young writer whose work is not yet well known.

† The two funds were not banked separately and the accounts become more complex at this stage.

not grant a licence for the importing of the moulds, but without success. Even *The Egoist*'s own printers, The Complete Press, after raising her hopes, refused.[34] But, a few days after the news from New York, she found printers, Pike's Fine Art Press, at Brighton, who had been impressed by the reviews and looked as though they were going to agree. The one snag now was that, as far as she was aware, the only authorized list of corrections was on the other side of the Atlantic and James Joyce was ill again and should not be asked to make another.* 'Could you therefore,' she wrote to Ben Huebsch, 'be so kind as to have the corrections he sent you copied out and sent to me—as soon as possible? I should be very much obliged. Or, if you were to send the original corrections (for the second edition) I would afterwards return them to you; but, owing to risk of loss in transit, the former course would be safer—if not too much trouble.'[35]

As Harriet had recently learned from Ezra Pound, James Joyce had glaucoma, a disease of the eye which, she discovered, was 'very serious and dangerous'. 'If it would not hurt you to send me a card,' she wrote, 'I would like to know how you are now and what the prospects are.'[36] Then he had tonsilitis. 'You are indeed unfortunate in being troubled with such a number of illnesses: they seem to have a conspiracy not to let you alone. I suppose there are not many people who have the good fortune to be always well like me.'[37]

Her increasing concern for James Joyce as an ailing man and regard for him as a writer did not prevent her, however, from telling him the bald truth, as she saw it, about sales of *A Portrait*. 'I am sorry to hear the sales are so poor,' he wrote. 'My book of stories had a good press also yet my royalties after three years came to 2/6.'[38] Harriet forbore to point out that royalties on *A Portrait* had already exceeded £30; nor did she give him news of her second edition until she was sure Pike's Fine Art Press were going to print it. An opportunity to tell him came at the end of June when Grant Richards had disposed of the rest of his edition of *Dubliners* to Ben Huebsch as remainders; and the author had given her permission to do the same with *A Portrait* 'whenever the sales reach an unprofitable point. I think you have had quite enough unrewarded trouble till now'.[39] 'But I hope

---

* James Joyce was rather put out by Ben Huebsch's omitting to tell him that a second edition had been decided on and wrote, disgruntled, to Ezra Pound that there were 'nearly four hundred misprints'—no doubt most of them the mistaken treatment of hyphenated words. Harriet Weaver thought the text 'very carefully set up' except for this.

there will be no necessity for this,' Harriet replied. 'In fact we are arranging to bring out another edition in September when someone who has been with a large publisher is coming to us and shall be able to push the sales.* Owing to recent restrictions on the import of books the new edition is to be printed in England.'[40]

'I am glad you are bringing out a second issue of the book,' James Joyce wrote, by return and in spite of fever. 'It would be well to have it set up at once so that I could read the full proof. My agent has my corrections for it.'[41] So there was another copy, after all, and in London! Harriet obtained it from J. B. Pinker, though by then she was expecting Ben Huebsch's copy daily.† She transferred the corrections to a copy of her first edition, and sent it off to Pike's.

Everything was now set. Even Ben Huebsch wrote in a vein less matter-of-fact than usual, though still not clear who she was, except that she was not a man. 'I am glad to learn . . . that the difficulty with regard to printing . . . has been overcome. Some day you will look back on these refusals of printers to print and censors to approve as bad dreams. Or, perhaps, our great-grandchildren will.'[42] James Joyce, contrite at the thought of the extra cost of setting up the type, and sure that her 'slender margin of profit' would be reduced to little or none, suggested that she introduced some modification in her favour in their contract. He would agree in advance to anything she proposed.[43]

His letter came just as Harriet was making up the *Portrait* accounts at the end of July. Four hundred and eighty-two copies had earned (in round figures) £91, against a cost of £89 for production and distribution and £40 for royalties. It was rather a worry that the royalty was calculated on all copies invoiced, fifty-four of which had not been paid for. Mr Joyce had guessed right: there was no margin of profit. The book had been priced too low.‡ She was not inclined,

---

* This appointment was not made, in the event. Grace Jardine, who was working as a traveller for Hodder & Stoughton, had been asked to come and help; but she turned the suggestion down.

† Ben Huebsch's copy arrived, in the end, nearly a fortnight later, perhaps from a ship in a convoy that had had to zigzag to evade submarines. So she had saved time by using J. B. Pinker's copy.

‡ At 5s. net there had never been any real possibility that the account for *A Portrait* would balance, for various reasons. Only forty-seven of the copies sold brought in 5s. The rest were sold at various discounts to the trade or overseas. The royalty, however, was calculated at 1s. 6d. on all copies sold, including the export sales at 3s. 9d. and sales to the author at 3s. 6d. Since the cost of each book was about 2s. 4d. many of the sales were made at a loss.

however, to withdraw the royalties on copies he bought for himself or to follow the usual practice of reducing the royalty on export sales. She decided to put up the price of the book to 6s. net. To James Joyce she wrote simply '. . . as the book is to be charged at 6/– net—most of the novels published in London now are to be charged at 6/– net I am told —the increased expense with the English printing should be met in this way unless the increased price proves a hindrance to the sales'.[44]

Harriet was working at the office a fortnight later when the telephone rang. It was a trunk call from Brighton. The manage of Pike's Fine Art Press wished to speak to her. He said it was his predecessor, now called up, who had agreed to print without deletions, and that he himself could not do so.[45] In the post the next morning was the book and a note regretting 'we cannot proceed to set same unless the passages marked in blue pencil are modified or removed'.[46]

Harriet broke the news at once to New York, Zurich and Southport: 'a catastrophe has occurred'.[47] 'It would be a waste of words to characterize the attitude of your printer. I sympathize with you completely,' wrote Ben Huebsch.[48] James Joyce had had an iridectomy on his right eye only four days before and replied through his wife. He suggested, if Pike's were adamant, seeking the assistance of Edward Marsh at the Colonial Office in getting permission to import sheets, for which he offered to pay.[49] Dora's first thought was also to put pressure on the Board of Trade. 'It is wretched about the "Portrait": you *are* being given a time with it. . . . It is too bad. . . . If it becomes a matter for the *Board of Trade* we must really endeavour to liquidate our assets & turn that loud applause to some business account.' She then returned to an idea she had put up before—trying Johnsons, *The Egoist*'s old printers at Southport: Harriet had evidently not been attracted by it, for Dora goes on to say that she felt she had been scarcely fair to them. '[Johnsons] would produce quite as decent looking an affair as the first edition was—given normal conditions. . . . I should send Grace over to interview their manager and let her point out all the difficulties of the situation—including your fears as to their capacity.'[50]

Harriet's own instinct was to go on trying for an English printer. As Johnsons, or rather, their manager Sammy Wilkinson, had on earlier occasions always in the end agreed to print matter he considered 'objectionable', she got Grace to see him.* If Johnsons would

* When in Southport and when her work as a traveller permitted, Grace Jardine was very willing to lend a hand. She did go and talk to the manager of Johnsons.

not print the book, nobody would. 'By fairy godmother good luck', they agreed.* [51] By the end of September, everything was in train; and the proofs, which James Joyce agreed that Harriet should read for him, were promised for the third or fourth week in October.[52]

Through the summer and autumn of 1917, Harriet was drawn into helping him in other directions also. His play, *Exiles*, written several years before, was not yet published, let alone performed. A year before, when it was being looked at on both sides of the Atlantic, he had written, 'My manuscripts are dispersed like Little Bo-Peep's sheep but I hope they will come home as safely as hers did'.[53] He was increasingly irked by its non-appearance and wanted it published and out of the way, to 'set his mind at rest'. He would have 'much preferred' Harriet as its English publisher, but by mid-July 1917 he had it accepted by Grant Richards, who had the right of refusal. He thereupon suggested, 'if you and Mr Richards approve', the insertion in all the copies of some English press notices he had had printed.[54] Having established at the General Post Office that such an import would be legal, Harriet 'approved'—though she had no standing in the matter. And she went one better by offering to distribute a thousand leaflets through *The Egoist*.† [55]

While the negotiations with Johnsons were going through, Harriet undertook to publish *Ulysses* as a serial in *The Egoist*, and, since the £50 'advance' she was giving him would not be enough, sought help in meeting the expenses of his eye operation, which had left him without reserves. She was moved by his predicament and perhaps also by the fact that he had written only a few days after the operation, and in the dark, to remember her birthday.[56]

Urged on by Ezra Pound, she made an approach to two men who

---

* Robert Johnson founded the firm in 1844, when he established the *Southport Visiter*, which carried the names of 'visiters' to the various hotels and boarding houses —hence the *Visiter* Printing Works, to appear on the imprint of *A Portrait*. (The firm always maintains that this is the correct spelling.) In 1917, the board of six directors, all Southport people, included a solicitor (chairman), two barristers, one of whom later became a High Court judge, a Justice of the Peace, and a knight. The surviving records of the company, however, show that the decision to print *A Portrait* was taken by Sammy Wilkinson without reference to his highly-respectable board.

† James Joyce, after correcting the proofs of *Exiles*, decided to give them to his unknown benefactor. He wrote to his agent to get them from Grant Richards and send them to Slack Monro Saw & Co. for their client. (*Letters* II, 410) The whereabouts of these proofs is not known and there is no evidence that Harriet Weaver ever received them.

had both helped on an earlier occasion. Edmund Gosse in 1915 had prevailed on the Royal Literary Fund to make James Joyce a grant of £75; and a year later Edward Marsh, then Assistant Private Secretary to the Prime Minister, had obtained for him a Civil List grant of £100. Edmund Gosse proved a non-starter. He regretted to hear that Mr Joyce was again in so much trouble but could not help as his 'influence with the Privy Purse ceased when Mr Asquith ceased to be the Prime Minister'.[57] Edward Marsh looked at first as though he was to prove a non-starter also, for no reply came from him for over a week. He had been promoted, in fact, and was in France in attendance, as Private Secretary, on the Minister of Munitions, Mr Winston Churchill. Harriet had written: '. . . I do not know whether you have heard of the very serious and dangerous disease of the eyes . . . from which [Mr Joyce] has been suffering for the last seven months. . . . The constant illness is of course a great expense and Mr Joyce is again in distressing financial difficulties. . . . Would you be kind enough to allow me to see you and talk the matter over with you? It seems lamentable that a writer of such power and talents should be so handicapped by constant financial worry—added to the burden of ill health'.[58]

Edward Marsh, when he read Harriet's letter on his return from France, decided that he himself would help. He no doubt considered out of the question a further application for a Civil List grant only a year after the first. But he had resources of his own. He had inherited a sixth of the income from a sum of £50,000 granted by Parliament to the twelve surviving children of Spencer Perceval, his great-grandfather, who, in 1812, when he was Prime Minister, as he entered the lobby of the House of Commons, was shot by a man with a grievance. Edward Marsh used the 'murder money', as he called it, to help artists and out of it he paid for the operation.[59]

In November Ezra Pound's *The Dialogues of Fontenelle* came out. Harriet had six hundred copies printed and sold them at 1s. 3d. each, though she raised the price later to 1s. 6d. *Prufrock*, with its price raised from 1s. to 1s. 3d. and later to 1s. 6d., was selling steadily though slowly, but *Fontenelle* was a disappointment. Perhaps most people who wanted to read it had read it already in *The Egoist*. These productions had not made much of a hole in the Development Fund, but *The Egoist* had eaten away at the usual rate into the General Fund. The new system did, however, allow for one unusual item of expenditure—for the second time in its history, the paper paid

25 Harriet in 1919

26 James Joyce and
Sylvia Beach
under the
Pink 'Un poster

a contributor. Arthur Symons was given £4 4s. od. for two articles.

It was only at the end of November that the last batch of proofs arrived from Southport. Harriet had been afraid to hurry Johnsons lest they should do the work badly. She ventured to have bound only five hundred copies, as before, and had to wait until the end of February before the binders, again Leighton, Son and Hodge, could get the books to her. Her second edition, this time of a thousand copies, was out.[60] A third was not to be needed until the summer of 1921.

In appearance the book was disappointing. The dark green cloth binding, chosen by her for Egoist Press publications, was decent looking, but the paper was, perhaps inevitably, of poor, wartime quality, the ink pale and the margins mean. 'Poorly produced', 'provincial looking', she thought.[61] Ben Huebsch thought so too: 'The shrunken appearance of the book confirms all that I hear about the difficulties that you labor under', he wrote, though he added, handsomely, 'I presume that we will soon approach similar conditions'.* [62] But Harriet was glad to see that Johnsons had done a careful job on what mattered most—the text.

* America had by then entered the war.

8

EDITOR OR PUBLISHER?

'We should be very glad indeed to have it', Harriet had written, when James Joyce suggested the simultaneous appearance of *Ulysses* as a serial in *The Egoist* and in *The Little Review*, a Chicago 'magazine of the Arts making no compromise with the public taste', apparently recommended by Ezra Pound. She knew no more about the book than the odd scraps gleaned from letters: that Mr Joyce had begun it in Rome in 1909 or 1910; that he was expecting to finish it in 1918; and that 'the action takes place in Dublin in 1904'.[1] But she assumed from the first that it would be as troublesome as *A Portrait*. 'I hope you would understand that if by any unfortunate chance the printers should insist on making any deletions we should be powerless to do anything. I have sufficient experience now of London printers to feel convinced it would be useless to try a change of firm.'[2]

His first instalment was, however, overtaken by a translation he had done of a review of *A Portrait* by Diego Angeli, the Tuscan novelist and critic of English literature. Harriet had asked him to translate it for *The Egoist* because it had pleased her and she put the translation in the issue for February 1918. It ends: 'He is a new writer in the glorious company of English literature. . . . We must welcome him with joy'.*

It was in this spirit that she welcomed the first three episodes of *Ulysses* that arrived, via Ezra Pound, a little later; and, though her praise of them was not effusive—'bitter reading' to her, 'difficult too, the third section—but of vital interest'[3]—her determination to do for the book everything that was in her power was instant.

* The review appeared originally in the Florentine journal *Il Marzocco* on 12th August 1917, one of a number of papers in Italy, Switzerland and France to which Harriet Weaver sent review copies.

That the book was likely to prove more troublesome than *A Portrait* soon became clear. *The Egoist*'s usually co-operative printers, The Complete Press, got cold feet after setting up the first episode, the *Telemachus*, for the March 1918 issue and refused to print it even with deletions. 'I am trying to find another firm,' Harriet wrote to Zurich, 'but it will be difficult I know. I have tried the printers of the Rationalist Press Association whom you suggested some time ago but they have already as much work as they can cope with at this time. I daresay the Southport printer would do it but it would be extremely inconvenient, almost impossible, to have the *Egoist* printed so far away from London.'[4] In an attempt to break the deadlock, James Joyce persuaded a Paris firm, Georges Crès, to place their printer at her disposal. But, to Harriet, Paris was even more out of the question than Southport. Had she been able to foresee events, she might have decided otherwise and the history of the publication of *Ulysses* would have taken a different course.

But she had already decided that she would like to publish 'the novel' in book form and had written to J. B. Pinker to put the proposal to him. James Joyce, writing direct to Harriet, ceded the rights 'gladly', though he was sure it was 'in more senses than one a Greek gift'. Grant Richards had the right of refusal for another fifteen months but was unlikely to want the book 'at any time'. 'Moreover,' he went on, 'if, in view of the increased price of production, you wish to modify in any way the terms of our existing contract I beg you to notify my agent of the fact. . . . Allow me to thank you once more for your most generous enterprise and also for the kind words of appreciation of my book. I am very grateful for them.'[5]

For better or for worse, Harriet was committed; and, this time, the decisions were hers alone. Dora Marsden looked on from the sidelines, interested enough in a detached way in the first episodes, which Harriet sent her. 'I have just re-read Episode III of "Ulysses",' she wrote. 'My dear editor go down on your knees & thank your stars for possessing *one* writer of metaphysics who is CLEAR! That's *ME*!! Joyce is . . . my word! He's appalling! If the British public will struggle with this production it is equal to anything Fate could have in store for it. . . . Shouldn't the 1st word, 2nd line be 'no more:'—this punctuation rather than a comma? It seemed to me it might help.'*[6]

* Dora Marsden was criticizing the punctuation of the opening sentence of the *Proteus* (third) episode: 'Ineluctable modality of the visible: at least that if no more, thought through my eyes'.

Harriet, for her part, was intent on finding a solution to her immediate problem: how to find a printer to print the episodes as the author had written them, down to the last comma; and she came to the conclusion that she would have to abandon all hope of serializing in the normal way: the serial would have to be printed separately and privately and would have to be published as a supplement to *The Egoist*. The type could be left standing and used when publication in book form became possible when the book was finished. But where to find a private press equal to the task?

T. S. Eliot had read the text and shared his editor's regard for it. He made a suggestion. He had just made the acquaintance of Leonard and Virginia Woolf, who had recently learnt to print and had acquired a press of their own. Why did she not go to Richmond and have a talk with them? '. . . on Sunday, April 14, 1918, Miss Weaver came to tea, bringing with her a large brown paper parcel containing the MS.,' Leonard Woolf wrote later. '. . . we put this remarkable piece of dynamite into the top drawer of a cabinet in the sitting-room . . .'.[7] To him, Harriet seemed merely 'a very mild blueeyed advanced spinster'; but to his wife she seemed impossible. Harriet, on the defensive, was no doubt at her most silent and intractable. 'I did my best,' Mrs Woolf confided to her diary, 'to make her reveal herself in spite of her appearance, all that the editress of the Egoist ought to be, but she remained unalterably modest, judicious and decorous. Her neat mauve suit fitted both soul and body; her grey gloves laid straight by her plate symbolized domestic rectitude; her table manners were those of a well bred hen. We could get no talk to go. Possibly the poor woman was impeded by her sense that what she had in the brown paper parcel was quite out of keeping with her own contents. But then how did she ever come in contact with Joyce and the rest? Why does their filth seek exit from her mouth? Heaven knows. She is incompetent from the business point of view and was uncertain what arrangements to make. . . . And so she went.'[8]

The encounter had been neither happy nor fruitful. Much of the discussion was, perhaps, at cross purposes—the Woolfs interested in printing *Ulysses* only if they published it themselves, Harriet in her scheme to find a private printer? And perhaps Virginia Woolf, unable to credit their visitor with any business, literary, fashion or social sense, failed to disguise her contempt?*

* Harriet Weaver did not live to see Virginia Woolf's diary entry. But she read another, published in 1953: '1941 . . . Wednesday, January 15th. Then Joyce is dead:

A month later, she wrote, from their country house in Sussex and in a tone more suited to correspondence, to announce 'with very much regret' that the length of Mr Joyce's novel was an insuperable difficulty: a book of '300 pages' would take them at least two years to produce, 'which is, of course, out of the question for you or Mr Joyce'. She had told her servants at Richmond to send the manuscript back.[9]

Harriet waited until the manuscript arrived from Mrs Woolf's servants and then sent a bare acknowledgment. That was that. But she wondered whether she would ever achieve the tasks she had set herself and was worried by her lack of professional expertise. Although the professionals had mostly failed Mr Joyce, she still had a high regard for professional excellence and, as it happened, her young friend Mr Eliot, just before her visit to the Woolfs, had written a severe article for *The Egoist* castigating 'non-professionalism' in writing. Here was a painful reminder that, as a writer and as a publisher, she was an amateur. And her literary friends, who shared her admiration for James Joyce, had no idea of the other responsibilities she had taken on. James Joyce's work was one of them; another, of little interest to these friends, was Dora Marsden's.

James Joyce and Dora Marsden were very different people, yet they made the same sort of claim on Harriet. She believed then that Dora was going to reveal new vistas in philosophy, as James Joyce did in literature. There were similar problems, too, bedevilling both writers. They both welcomed, as a first approach to their public, the chance to appear in a journal, but book publication was their aim. James Joyce was ahead of Dora in producing full-length books, but she had assembled a great deal of material, much of it already printed as *Egoist* leaders, and she was busy re-writing and extending it for publication. For the present, therefore, while *Ulysses* was serialized and while Dora still had passages that could stand separately as leaders, the journal was serving Harriet's purpose; but it was doubtful how long this could go on. Her time was not infinitely extendable,

Joyce about a fortnight younger than I am. I remember Miss Weaver, in wool gloves, bringing *Ulysses* in typescript to our tea table at Hogarth House. . . . Would we devote our lives to printing it? The indecent pages looked so incongruous: she was spinsterly, buttoned up. . . .' (*A Writer's Diary Being Extracts from the Diary of Virginia Woolf*, edited by Leonard Woolf. London. The Hogarth Press, 1953, p. 363. Harcourt, Brace & World, Inc., 1954) This hurt and angered Harriet Weaver. 'What is wrong with woollen gloves?' she would ask with acerbity whenever this was quoted, as it not infrequently was.

nor was her money; and at some point her authors were very likely to need a publisher more than they needed an editor.

It is impossible to tell when Harriet was first conscious of this stress in her double role as editor and publisher but by April 1918 she was already conducting the journal into a steady decline. Twice she had cancelled an issue and she had just decided to reduce the paper's size from sixteen pages to twelve or fourteen. This decision, suggested by the prospect, however dim, of running *Ulysses* as a supplement, was implemented in May, although the supplement did not appear. From then on Harriet was relieved of one long-standing problem. She had copy, a great deal of it good copy, to fill the space, and most of it came from regular contributors. She was prepared also, if at any time the regular contributors had better things to do, to combine two issues in one.

The make-up of the May 1918 issue illustrates how the new editorial policy worked out. Dora Marsden's leader (four pages) *Our Philosophy of the 'Real'* was section XVI of her series on the science of signs. T. S. Eliot, under the pseudonym of T. S. Apteryx, reviewed an American anthology *Others* and two books of literary criticism (one page); and probably also wrote the column of shorter notices. Muriel Ciolkowska, in her regular feature *Passing Paris* (one page) discussed among other things a new book by Colette and some of the paintings and drawings collected by Degas and lately put on sale after his death; and she contributed also an article on Jean Giraudoux (one page)—the tenth in a series on *The French Word in Modern Prose*. Ezra Pound, writing on *The Anglo-French Society and M. Davray* (one page) reproached the *Mercure de France*, in the person of Monsieur Davray, its editor, for a recent recommendation of 'Gosse' and 'Colvin' and recommended to him 'Mr Joyce', 'Mr Lewis' and 'Mr Eliot'. Huntly Carter, now writing much less than he did for *The Egoist*, contributed the first of a short series on *The Theatre of Peace* (one page); and there were three poems, *A Celebration* by William Carlos Williams, *Psittacus eois Imitatrix Ales ab Indis* by Sacheverell Sitwell and *Virginity* a short and rather spiteful epigram by John Rodker.*

* The back page was taken up by advertisements of Egoist publications and of three American journals, Harriet Monroe's *Poetry*, Margaret Anderson's *Little Review*, and *The Eagle and the Serpent*, published by J. B. Barnhill in Washington, which offered 'the boiled-down wit and wisdom and wickedness of Stirner, Nietzsche, Montaigne, Rochefoucauld, Chamfort, Emerson, Thoreau, saving the earnest inquirer after forbidden truth a thousand hours of wearying research'. These American

Harriet's policy was, therefore, to fill at least nine pages with contributions from her regulars, now strengthened by T. S. Eliot, who had contributed a signed article to each issue but one. As Dora had feared, he gave a lot of attention to the Imagists, and he had reviewed, in his first article, *Passages from the Letters of William Butler Yeats*, her bugbear; but he had reviewed other writers, too, and had introduced some cogent thoughts on the theory of criticism. He was already formulating the principles, and developing the style, which later served him well as a mature literary critic.

Richard Aldington, still in the army, had contributed six poems in 1917, but he had not, understandably enough, produced the material for the second set of *Poets' Translation Series* which Harriet had hope-fully announced, from time to time, ever since 1915. Her next publi-cation was Wyndham Lewis' *Tarr*, completed as a serial in the pre-vious November, and due to come out in July. *Tarr* was more ex-pensive to produce than *A Portrait*; it cost nearly £160. But the Development Fund was still well in credit. The General Fund was in far worse case. Against an expenditure of £260, the paper had earned from sales and subscriptions less than £60.

Harriet was prepared to lose money in a good cause and she still hoped to find a way of publishing episodes of *Ulysses* in *The Egoist*. But it was now falling behind *The Little Review*, which was publishing an instalment a month. Its editor, Margaret Anderson, however, was better placed than she was. Printers in the United States, unlike their English counterparts, are not liable to prosecution for setting matter judged pornographic; and Margaret Anderson's printer was pre-pared to print anything. But *The Little Review* was being too slow for Ben Huebsch. He wanted to publish the book before the end of the year—before the completion of the serial. The first thing he wanted established was when the book would be finished. Once again, he looked to Harriet to act as a clearinghouse and general fac-totum-cum-unofficial-agent. He thought it would be 'simpler for Mr Joyce' if he were to take up with her the question of publication in both countries.[10]

'It is impossible to say how much of the book is really written,' James Joyce told her, in a buoyant, five-hundred-word letter. He had so far delivered six of the seventeen episodes planned. 'Several other episodes have been drafted for the second time but that means nothing

advertisements were not money-earners; they earned advertising space for *The Egoist* in them.

because although the third episode of the *Telemachia* has been a long time in the second draft I spent about 200 hours over it before I wrote it out finally. I fear I have little imagination. This subject I am sure must be rather tiresome to you. However, if all goes well the book should be finished by the summer of 1919.' As for her own efforts, he feared she had lost a great deal of money on his 'wretched book' and proposed that the sums advanced already for the serial rights be considered as an advance on royalties, to be written off eventually in two or three deductions. 'I think I ought to say in conclusion that if you wish to print any other book as a serial story in the place of *Ulysses* I beg you not to consider any imaginary claims of mine. . . .'[11]

Such ideas Harriet could not entertain for a moment. She wrote to reassure him '. . . there will be no loss on the book because the extra expense of the supplement will be offset by the fact that the type will have been set up and therefore your very kind proposal . . . is not one that could with any fairness be taken advantage of. And there is no other novel that we would like to print as a serial in place ot yours . . .'.[12]

But however optimistic and openhanded she was inclined to be about *Ulysses*, she had to face the fact that she had lost £15 on the first edition of *A Portrait*, whose account she had just closed. This discovery perhaps influenced her in making a different kind of contract with Wyndham Lewis. No royalties were to be paid on *Tarr*, also priced at 6s., until her costs had been covered. And she recalled that James Joyce, a year ago, had told her she might modify his contract in her own favour if she thought proper; and she asked him if he would agree that royalties should be paid only on the copies for which payment had been received—not, as hitherto, on those invoiced.*[13] He was happy about this arrangement, and she ordered her accounts accordingly. It was a serious attempt to make her publications more of a business proposition, but it was short-lived. She preferred dealing with him informally and personally; and soon went back to the original arrangement.

The Egoist meanwhile, although its most distinguished contributor

* Harriet Weaver had been accustomed to pay royalties on the first edition of *A Portrait* on copies invoiced, without waiting for payment to come in; and now that the account was completed she was reluctant to pay a royalty on the bad debts. She was also reluctant to pay out, for the second edition, a royalty of £8 10s. od. on the one hundred and thirteen copies invoiced, when the forty-seven copies sold had brought in only £9.

was absent, had been making very creditable appearances. The elimination of padding was an advantage; Dora Marsden, in one of her happier phases, was vigorously organizing her philosophical speculations and setting them out in the forceful, well-articulated prose that Harriet so much admired; and the other regular contributors combined to give the paper a merit it had lacked in the past—the authority of a professional production.

Dora was particularly pleased with the August issue and told Harriet 'how nice the Egoist looks this month. . . . Everybody seems to have done his very best'. And she asked Harriet to send Richard Aldington a postcard 'to say how delightfully vigorous his little sketch is. . . . You ought to be very pleased with yourself & the behaviour of your troupe'.[14]

The 'great' war was drawing to its ambiguous conclusion and people were beginning to understand that the peace they were hoping for would not be the peace they had known in the past. Richard Aldington, brooding over the cratered, rutted road leading from the battle-front, concluded:

And just before dawn when the last limber rattles away and the last stretcher has gone back to the line, then the ghosts of the dead armies march down, heroic in their silence, battalion after battalion, brigade after brigade, division after division; the immeasurable forces of the dead youth of Europe march down the road past the silent sentry by the ruined house, march back, march home.

Muriel Ciolkowska, whose column since 1915 had been called *Passing Paris*, reverted to her earlier title *Fighting Paris* because 'the events of 1914 finding an echo at the present time, the heading which this chronicle then assumed becomes once again more appropriate than the one, now of all too ominous augury, which followed and has endured since'.*

T. S. Eliot, who contributed only shorter notices to this number,

* The August 1918 issue of *The Egoist* had Dora Marsden's sixteenth extract from *Our Philosophy of the 'Real'*, the third of three articles by Arthur Symons on Debussy, a poem *The Fish*, by Marianne Moore, *Early Translators of Homer* by Ezra Pound, *The Road*, by Richard Aldington, *Fighting Paris* and *The French Word in Modern Prose: XI Alain-Fournier*, [one of the first gifted young writers to be killed in the war] by Muriel Ciolkowska, *The Japanese Noh Play* by Yone Noguchi, and some *Short Notices* by T. S. Eliot.

had not proved, as Dora had feared he would, a dedicated disciple of Ezra Pound's. But he had taken on one of his more awkward roles—promoter of a series of proposals for putting *The Egoist* under new management. These proposals, which always came to nothing, took up an inordinate amount of everyone's time, and involved Harriet and Dora in endless, fruitless correspondence.

The first round had opened in January, when T. S. Eliot had submitted a proposal that a publisher, Mr Hutchinson, prevented by war-time restrictions from starting a paper of his own, should run an *Egoist* supplement. But when Harriet pressed Mr Hutchinson to disclose what he was prepared to pay for the association, the negotiations foundered. Then, in October, an entirely new proposal was made, involving almost all of the old *Egoist* well-wishers, and some new ones. A Captain Read* came to call on Harriet to suggest combining *The Egoist* and other literary groups with a shop or exhibition gallery. 'It is very odd your letter coming just now,' Dora wrote. 'It has been running in my head for days past that the "hardy annual" offer of amalgamation was overdue. And here it is! I take it that it emanates from the same group: "cubist tendencies" means Wyndham Lewis; W.L. means E.P., and also Ford Madox Hueffer. They evidently are the "Blast" crowd who are settling in for "after the war".... Their offer is a tribute to our staying power and solidity.... Let us crow!'[15]

Harriet, though she recognized that the offer differed from the others in proposing an amalgamation with *The Egoist*, thought the whole thing an illusion. The young poets, pleased with their invention of a bigger and better circus, had not made any proper preparations for running it. She had had enough experience of running a mixed circus to feel sure that the thirty-two pages they proposed to publish every month would be difficult to fill and difficult to sell; and she was glad when Captain Read, perhaps put off by her stonewalling, did not pursue the negotiations.

Her own instinct, now, was that the time had come to cut down *The Egoist* once again. She decided that, whether or not she was able to print *Ulysses*, she could manage a sixteen-page issue possibly every other month provided she put up the price from 6d. to 9d. in the new year. She ran her November and December 1918 issues into one and announced in it the new rate; the abandonment of the plan to publish *Ulysses* as a supplement; and a new series from Dora, who

---

* Later Sir Herbert Read, poet and art critic.

saw the country 'on the verge of social political & economic events of the first magnitude'[16] and hoped to influence them.*

Harriet did not announce her alternative plan for *Ulysses*. She had been working on it, but experience had shown how rash it was to attempt to publish any plan at that stage. Johnsons in Southport, her last hope, had refused to print it as a supplement and she had returned to her original plan, though in a modified form. She now had in her hands the first seven episodes—*Telemachus*, *Nestor*, *Proteus*, *Calypso*, *Lotus-eaters*, *Hades* and *Aeolus*—and it had occurred to her that the manager of the Complete Press, presumably Mr Pentland, although he had let her down over the first episode, might consent to print some of the others in the body of the paper.

The refusal of The Complete Press a year before to allow her to publish the *Telemachus*, after setting it up, had led 'to a quarrel which grieved both our hearts—mine and the printers' manager's—but he was adamant'. He had decided the episode did not 'keep up the character' of her 'respectable and high-minded journal' and that was the end of it.[17] But he still seemed to her to be a liberally-minded man, well enough disposed to people ready to take risks and she was now on good enough terms with him to ask him to look at the other episodes. He agreed to set up the second and third.

Nestor appeared in the first issue of 1919, dated January–February, and, apart from another outbreak of inverted commas to introduce speech (Harriet must have omitted to pass on the author's views) the instalment was printed as it stood and with only one typographical slip—*amor mortis* for *amor matris*. *Proteus* appeared in the issue for March–April but not entire. The manager insisted on cutting out the misbirth in a bag; Stephen's near-blasphemous ruminating on the doctrine of consubstantiation and on his own conception; and his picking of his nose. Harriet hoped the manager would agree to print another episode for her next issue. But the prospect was too much for him: other matter had given rise to difficulties and this new serial was the last straw. He gave notice that the Press could not continue as *The Egoist*'s printers.

It was a severe blow. Harriet's admiration for the book had been growing with the arrival of each new episode. *Scylla and Charybdis* had enthralled her so much that she could not sleep after reading it.[18] But her disappointment on James Joyce's behalf was as keen, more

---

* This series was eventually dropped in favour of more philosophy.

particularly as he had been ill again. 'This time the attack was in my "good?" eye so that the decisive symptoms of iritis never really set in,' he told her. 'It has been light but intermittent so that for five weeks I could do little or nothing except lie constantly near a stove like a chimpanzee whom in many things I resemble.'[19]

Harriet was disappointed too in the sluggish reception that her second edition of *A Portrait* had been given. In fourteen months, she had sold only three hundred and fourteen copies, less than the first edition had earned in six months. *Tarr* had made a much better start, over four hundred copies had been sold; and the *Prufrock* account, almost within sight of breaking even, had repaid Mr Pound £1 15s. 0d. on account of his £5 loan. In his usual generous way, he had asked her to give Mr Eliot, as a royalty, the balance of £3 5s. 0d., but she decided to defer any payments, except on loans, until there was a real credit balance.

She found, when she made up the year's accounts at the end of May 1919, that the paper had cost her almost as much as usual; although it had sometimes been smaller than before, and come out less often, prices had gone up. But she was prepared to go on losing money on it as long as it could be of use to Mr Joyce and to Dora.

As Dora wrote more of her book, however, the prospects of her completing it seemed to recede. As Harriet knew, it can take a very long time to write a book; but Dora's was unusually subject to sudden and violent extensions of scale. The current sub-section (on *Truth*) was to have finished in the new year but was now to run till December. No firm date was in sight for the finish of *Ulysses* either. Harriet had never planned to be a publisher for life, but it was beginning to appear that, in order to publish the two books she felt responsible for, she might have to stick to the job for a very long time.

Meanwhile, she had two other books on the stocks, both announced in July, *Quia Pauper Amavi*, poems by Ezra Pound, and *Images*, poems by Richard Aldington, most of them already published in Imagist collections. *Images* was a slim volume which Harriet priced at 3s. 6d.; *Quia Pauper Amavi* she was able to treat more lavishly.* Besides the five hundred copies to sell at 6s., she ordered one hundred on hand-made paper to sell at 10s. 6d. She was planning also to publish in the autumn Wyndham Lewis' *The Caliph's Design. Architects!*

* See Appendix.

Where is your Vortex? and to introduce, at last, the second set of *Poets' Translations* with Richard Aldington's *Greek Songs in the Manner of Anacreon.*

Through the spring and the early summer, however, her over-riding concern was undoubtedly for James Joyce. She was now over-whelmingly convinced of his genius. He deserved substantial help but there was little prospect of help from any quarter, let alone royalties. She decided, however, against further remittances: he should not be regarded as, should not be turned into, 'a remittance man'. She decided, if he would accept the gift, to settle on him, again anonymously, £5,000 worth of 5 per cent War Loan.* This would yield £250 a year as against the total of £200 a year to which the remittances had added up. She went to see Fred Monro in his office in the City. 'She simply told me what to do,' he recalled. 'There was not a single word of any sort about her attitude.'[20]

Monro Saw's letter came while James Joyce was away. Nora Joyce opened it and, as she read it, Lucia, her daughter, 'peeped over her shoulder' at the 'big letter with such good news'. She told Lucia that the money would help to educate her and her brother;[21] and then ran out to send a telegram to Locarno where her husband had taken his friend Frank Budgen for a holiday in part payment for a portrait he had just painted of her: 'Hope you are well letter from Monro client wishes to settle 5000 pounds 5% war loan upon you hearty congratulations letter following'.[22]

When the telegram arrived early the next morning, James Joyce did not wait for the letter. Without even a word to his friend, he hurried back to Zurich, where his wife, overflowing with joy and relief, had just danced a jig on the steps of a tram.[23] Composing his reply to Monro Saw took longer. He wanted to draw them out on the identity of their client. Was it indeed John Quinn, as Ezra Pound had surmised?[24] But why should he use a London firm of solicitors? Or perhaps this was deliberate—a smokescreen? He wrote, eventually, hinting merely, not stating, that he was aware of the identity of their client and would be glad if he might be relieved of the obligation imposed on him to respect the anonymity of the gift.

But Harriet was not to be drawn. Though her main object in

---

* The settlement was made between Fred Monro and the Public Trustee. Under it, James Joyce was entitled to the income during his life. On his death, the trust fund passed as he by Will or Codicil should appoint. The capital could be used during his life only with the consent of the Public Trustee; and, in effect, could not be touched.

offering the gift anonymously had been to make easier its acceptance, and this object had now been achieved, she still preferred to remain anonymous. So, on her instructions, Fred wrote:

We are asked to express our Client's thanks to you for your letter of May 20th and to say that though the way in which you have accepted the gift is an honour in itself, rendering further acknowledgment superfluous, our Client nevertheless will feel it a privilege to read anything else you care to send.

We are desired to say also that . . . as the matter is now settled the anonymity is of less importance than before and that you may therefore take which course you prefer in regard to it—if it is really the fact that you have the power which your words imply.[25]

Though his bluff had not succeeded, James Joyce did not give up. He obviously wanted even more keenly to know who the client was and, equally obviously, was determined not to risk himself naming John Quinn. He asked for information that would help him decide whether his supposition was right. In particular, what was it in his writing that most interested the client? Harriet was now a good deal puzzled. She was fairly sure that Ezra Pound had recently 'twigged' that it was she who had been sending the quarterly remittances and that he had told Mr Joyce. How was it, therefore, that Mr Joyce was still so much at sea? Fred Monro, after hearing the whole story and learning her reasons for admiring his work wrote:

. . . Our Client had known for some time of your circumstances from a mutual friend who had bestirred himself in your interest until finally he appeared to have exhausted all likely channels to which he could look for help. When this seemingly hopeless point was reached our client felt it necessary to take action, and was afterwards duly informed by this friend of the anonymous gift received by you. It was obvious that the source of it was at that time a mystery to him, but later on our Client, for various reasons, was led to believe that he had since arrived at a correct surmise as to its origin, and could not but be conscious of the likelihood of his acquainting you with such surmise. That he had done so seemed to be corroborated afterwards unwittingly by an elderly Italian lady who had been in Zurich and who called once last year at your suggestion to make an enquiry at an office managed by our client. She said she had known you for ten years and mentioned the gift you had had 'from some lady'.*

When therefore in your letter of May 20th you appeared to suggest that you were aware of the identity of the supposedly anonymous person and spoke of respecting the condition 'imposed' seeming to imply a wish that it had not been imposed, our client thought it rather foolish and perhaps unfriendly—in particular after your allusions to your state of depression—to persist in a course whose main object has been achieved. Otherwise had you not dwelt on the subject of the anonymity, she (we can now use the pronoun) would have let the matter remain as it has been up to the present.

Briefly, the qualities in your writing that most interest her are your searching piercing spirit, your scorching truth, the power and startling penetration of your 'intense instants of imagination'. As such qualities are greatly lacking in most writers of the day, when they do show themselves, and especially when accompanied as in your case by a very unusual and astonishing power of expression, our client counts it a misfortune that they should not be given as free scope as is possible in the circumstances and therefore has done what she can to further this end.[26]

Harriet had now given James Joyce quite enough information to enable him to tumble to the identity of his benefactor and she clearly expected him to reveal that he had done so. Instead, he wrote to Monro Saw to say only that he appreciated the delicacy and self-effacement that dictated the donor's continued desire to remain anonymous. It was most vexing. His next letter to her, all about *Ulysses*, tempted her to put an end to the confusion. She wanted to write to him in any case because she had a lot of news:

Dear Mr Joyce,
. . . After the last number of the *Egoist* came out (in April) our printers gave us notice, chiefly, though not entirely, on account of *Ulysses*. I have since made arrangements with another firm and they are bringing out the next number this week. Half of the sixth episode will appear in it; the other half in the following number. After that the paper is probably to be suspended for a time, partly in order to

* Unknown to Harriet Weaver, James Joyce had been receiving, since March 1918, a thousand Swiss francs a month from Mrs McCormick, *née* Rockefeller, who was living in Zurich.

allow Miss Marsden some free time in which to prepare her philosophical series for publication in book form, and partly in order to develop our book publishing venture. I remember mentioning this new firm in a previous letter: the manager, a Roman Catholic Irishman, had been much interested in your first novel. He has now seen the first ten chapters of *Ulysses* and so far as he can judge from these will be willing to print the complete text.*

It is difficult to know what to say about your suggestion that the book when it is finished be issued in a paper cover at a price equivalent to that current in France† . . . perhaps this matter could be decided near the time of publication when the expenses of publication may have altered. . . .

Mr Pound sent me the Sirens episode a little time ago. I think I can see that your writing has been affected to some extent by your worries; I mean that this episode seems to me not quite to reach your usual pitch of intensity. I hope you are able to make progress now with the Cyclops episode. I hope too that your health will improve when you leave what is to you the unhealthy climate of Zurich and that you will have less trouble with your eyes.

An inch and a half of writing paper remained. Here was her opportunity to reveal her now awkward secret with the least possible ceremony.

Perhaps I had better add that it was I who sent the message through Messrs Monro Saw and Co and that I am sorry I sent it in the way and in the form I did. It is rather paralysing to communicate through solicitors. I fear you will have to withdraw all words about delicacy and self effacement: I can only beg you to forgive my lack of them.

With kind regards
Yours sincerely
Harriet Weaver[27]

It was done. She and the client had become one and the same person.

James Joyce reacted by becoming very much more sensitive to her views on his current work. Her doubts about the *Sirens* worried him

---

* This was the Pelican Press, 2 Carmelite Street, London, E.C. It has not proved possible to discover more about it; and Harriet Weaver's previous letter has not come to light.

† About 3s.

particularly because Ezra Pound and Arthur Clutton Brock had both found themselves in difficulties over it. 'It took me five months to write it . . . The elements needed will only fuse after a prolonged existence together. I confess that it is an extremely tiresome book but it is the only book which I am able to write at present,' he wrote in the first of two long letters on the subject.[28] '. . . the passages . . . were not intended by me as recitative. There is in the episode only one example of recitative on page 12 in preface to the song. They are all the eight parts of a *fuga per canonem*: and I did not know in what other way to describe the seductions of music beyond which Ulysses travels. I understand that you may begin to regard the various styles of the episodes with dismay and prefer the initial style much as the wanderer did who longed for the rock of Ithaca. But in the compass of one day to compress all these wanderings and clothe them in the form of this day is for me only possible by such variation which, I beg you to believe, is not capricious. . . .'[29]

As Frank Budgen has pointed out, 'The beauty of *The Sirens* episode lies in this: that Joyce has mimicked all the musician's mannerisms and rhythmical devices with so much fantastical humour. . . .'[30] But Harriet had no ear and the beauty of the *Sirens* was lost on her. There were, however, compensations. James Joyce wrote also:

As you are the person who introduced my book *A Portrait of the Artist as a Young Man* to the 'notice' of the public I shall feel very thankful to you if you will accept from me the MS of that book. It is in Trieste and, as soon as circumstances there are more favourable, I shall get it and forward it to you. . . .[31]

And, because he had been pleased and surprised by a message 'of very appreciative praise' from her, on the publication of *Exiles*, he sent her a copy of the German translation on the eve of its production at the Munich Schauspielhaus.[32] He knew too little of her to realize that the subject of *Exiles*—behaviour when all moral conventions are rejected—was one that made a profound appeal to her, if only because she knew that she could not adopt such behaviour for herself. The play interested her for another reason also: she felt sure that it had 'something of autobiography in it'.[33] It might help to shed light on the man, as distinct from the author, whom she was helping to support. She carried off the German edition to Totland Bay, where Edward and his wife had taken a house for the summer, perhaps in the hope that it would vouchsafe something more than the English edition. But she wrote merely 'I do not know why you should have been surprised that it interested me—though I think you have more scope in a novel with its freer form—in spite of the difficulties you have set yourself in *Ulysses*: the necessity of compressing all the wanderings into the compass of one day'.[34]

Harriet Weaver and James Joyce had now been corresponding for nearly five years. His letters, at first studded with the *ults* and *insts* he judged appropriate to business, had soon begun to touch on matters not strictly germane: his birthday, his health, his aspirations and frustrations, his current work, and now were devoted almost entirely to them. He dwelt on them not only because he needed to do so, and because he had discovered that they were of more than passing interest to her. Harriet had become for him much more than a sympathetic ear.

From his boyhood, James Joyce had been convinced that he was one of the elect—indeed, the only one of his kind; and he needed, from time to time, the reassurance of the power that had elected him. Unlike the religious elect, however, he did not look to that power for guidance. As alone as the Creator, he wrote what he chose to write. Having thus arrogated to himself one of the prerogatives of his elective power, his attitude to it was ambivalent. That power was, nevertheless, important to him; and Harriet was there to personify the myth. She had singled him out. That in itself was enough. But, being extremely superstitious, he probably saw in this singling out something, if not mystical, certainly supernatural. She possessed, furthermore, an essential characteristic of an elective power: impartial judgment. Her obvious sincerity in commenting on his work had an immense appeal for him. She could not, would not, flatter. To Harriet, needless to say, it would have been inconceivable that she was performing an important symbolic function in lightening for him his double burden as Creator and Creature. But, for instance, his motive in giving her presents of books, proofs and manuscripts is most easily understood in the light of such an interpretation.

When, in October 1919, his wealthy American acquaintance, Mrs McCormick, with a capriciousness to which she became increasingly prone, cut off, just before his return to Trieste, the monthly allowance she had been giving him, he clearly hoped to win her over to resuming it when he hastily despatched to her the manuscript of what was already written of *Ulysses*.* For him, she was no more than a

* Mrs McCormick did not accept the *Ulysses* manuscript and eventually returned it.

grant-aiding body. Though his presents to Harriet may have been motivated in some degree by a desire to repay and by hope of further help, they should be regarded, rather, as first-fruits.

The *Cyclops* episode, the tale told by a nameless and far from mealy-mouthed narrator, arrived, via Ezra Pound, by a late post on 1st November. 'I have read it through,' Harriet wrote the next day, 'but too hastily to venture on any comment—except the passing remark that on finishing the chapter it was difficult to speak straight and to avoid interlarding one's words with the favourite and quite unlady-like adjective employed so constantly by the figure who is the narrator. . . .'[35] The episode had been typed (by a colleague of Frank Budgen's at the British Consulate) just before the Joyces left Zurich for Trieste and there had been no time to revise it. Harriet promised to read it carefully and make what corrections she could.

She was having a busy and rather difficult time both as publisher and editor. *Images* and *The Caliph's Design* had come out as planned and the first *Poets' Translation Series* had covered its costs and was now earning small sums such as 25s. But the second series was proving rather embarrassing. Subscriptions, at £2, were coming in well but she had not succeeded in finding new material to print; and, in order to give the series a quick start, she had been forced to use, for three of the four numbers now ready, reprints of the first four in the earlier series. Except for numbers 5 and 6 of that series, she had no material, new or old, for the next six issues of the new.

This was a problem, however, that could be shelved. One that could not be shelved was the future of *The Egoist*. She confirmed her decision to suspend it. With the first part of the *Wandering Rocks* episode, she had reached the limit of what the paper could print. Now that she had a printer, she must concentrate her energies on seeing *Ulysses* through in book form as soon as it was ready. Moreover, Dora had reached the end of a long section and felt that the time had come to contemplate her projected book as a whole, without the distraction of writing for a periodical. Her final leader, in the last issue, dated December 1919, summed up the work of six years. It opens:

This is the closing chapter in our long series of studies, and we shall use our remaining opportunity for exposition to harmonise our conception of the future and destiny of (human) life with our basic egoistic positions.

Harriet's final editorial statement followed immediately. After announcing that there would be 'no issues of THE EGOIST in journalistic form in 1920', she allowed herself a thrust at the general run of printers:

> . . . we have in working practice in England a printer's censorship much more drastic than that of the official censorship itself. So it comes about that an intelligence abnormally acute and observant, an accomplished literary craftsman who sets down no phrase or line without its meaning for the creation as a whole, is faced with a situation in which the very possibility of existence for his work lies at the mercy and limitations of intelligence of—let us say—the printing-works foreman! . . .

She went on to an exposition of her policy as a publisher, riding a favourite hobbyhorse. *The Egoist* had gone into publishing solely 'to give existence in book form to Mr Joyce's novel *A Portrait of the Artist as a Young Man*, and only after it had been proved impossible to find for that book any other English publisher willing to risk prosecution . . . we then came to realise how urgent was the need for a publishing concern animated neither on the one hand by desire for financial gain, nor on the other by propagandist aims of a limitedly partisan kind. . . .'

The editorial ends with an argument, clearly elaborated, or written, by Dora Marsden, leading to the conclusion that only artists and writers who can 'explain' their work are worth backing: '. . . *brains* would become an absolute necessity in an artist, a positively revolutionary thought indeed':

> It has been uphill work, but we are confident that before very long the note of genuineness and authenticity in the work made current must find its response in the unprecedented interest in such matters among the general public. . . .

Harriet must have felt at the end of a chapter and the beginning of a new one. Perhaps it was on this account that she decided to mark Christmas by sending to Trieste some photographs of herself: two new ones and two old ones. One old one, a snapshot taken in 1905 at St Ives, shows her on the beach with Harold and her eldest niece, Rosamond.* Of the others, she wrote:

* See plate 9, facing page 64.

. . . The new ones are said to be good likenesses of what I am now; but they are deceptive in a way—though not, I believe, so very much more than I am myself and have been at all ages—for in reality I am old.* To be precise, I was forty three on September 1st and am therefore just five years and five months older than yourself. I fancy that Mr Pound and the rest of them except Miss Marsden imagine me to be several years younger than I am and I do not disillusion them, for, though not to bear the traces of all one's years upon one's face is scarcely a feat to be proud of, I am so weak as to allow myself the pleasure of being credited still with something of youth.

In connection with this matter of age I may say that I saw your verses in the August number of the Anglo-French Review and find them very apt for myself in certain moods, especially in moods in which the thought of my great age weighs upon me and depresses me. . . .† [36]

James Joyce thought the letter 'melancholy' but was pleased with the photograph taken at St Ives: he liked the Cornish. And here at last was something definite about Miss Weaver. 'By the way,' he asked Frank Budgen, whom he always insisted was a Cornishman, though only his mother had been Cornish, 'do you or did you know any Weavers in St Ives?'[37] It must have been a disappointment when Harriet wrote, '. . . I do not come from any so fascinating spot . . . I am afraid I am hopelessly English, unadulterated Saxon'.[38]

She suggested that he might venture, if the posts were now reliable enough, to send her the manuscript of A Portrait. 'I think I have expressed very little appreciation of the gift of it that you are making me: please understand that I shall value it very highly indeed. . . .'[39] Posts to and from Trieste James Joyce had not found reliable. To lessen the risk of loss, he sent off the manuscript in four parcels and promised to copy out anything that was lost. 'The "original" original,' he explained,

I tore up and threw into the stove about eight years ago in a fit of rage on account of the trouble over Dubliners. The charred remains of the MS were rescued by a family fire brigade and tied up in an old sheet where they remained for some months. I then sorted them out

* See plate 25, facing page 144.

† James Joyce's poem in The Anglo-French Review (sandwiched between two articles, La Pêche à la Mouche en France and The Perils of Bureaucracy) was Bahnhofstrasse.

and pieced them together as best I could and the present MS is the result. . . . Unfortunately I have not yet found a flat and have not as much quiet and freedom as I should like. I am working at the *Nausikaa* episode. It is very consoling to me that you consider me a writer because every time I sit down with a pen in my hand I have to persuade myself (and others) of the fact. However, I hope to finish this episode during January . . . and hope to complete my book during the year.[40]

How many times did Harriet walk down to the head of the stair-case leading to the hall, to see whether a parcel for her lay on the big mahogany table by the front door? One came, then a second, then a third, following one another closely. She feared the fourth had gone astray but it arrived at last. 'I am doubly glad the whole manuscript has arrived intact,' she wrote, 'because, though I am touched that you should suggest copying out for me any or all of it that might fail to reach me, I should have been very sorry for you to waste your time in such a way and strain your eyes unnecessarily on my account. In view of what happened to the "original" original it is fortunate that the chapters of *Ulysses* are typed out as soon as they are written and the typescript dispatched to safe keeping in England and America!'[41]

The suspension of *The Egoist*, described as 'temporary', was in fact permanent. The publishing business was on its own. There was still some money in the kitty and her expenses were reduced as she was doing all the work herself, and had no regular salaries to pay. For a while, also, there were no printing bills, as T. S. Eliot's *Art of Poetry*, announced in the final issue, was placed elsewhere in the end.* But rent was still a standing charge and, as she did not expect any of her titles to contribute to the overheads of publishing, she went on putting in donations to a general fund.

Harriet was now set to publish, in due course, the two big books which she particularly valued—Mr Joyce's new novel and Dora's philosophy. She had provided him with money to live on meanwhile, and now did the same for Dora, though on a smaller scale. Dora's way of life was very modest; she had never had, or wanted, more than a bare subsistence income. But she did need, in order to do her creative work, a great deal of personal support; and Harriet was increasingly troubled about where it was to be found.

*With the title *The Sacred Wood*.

9

STORM CAPES

The Little Review soon ran into trouble in publishing episodes of *Ulysses*. The United States Post Office, the department responsible for prosecuting publishers of obscene works sent through the post, had confiscated two issues in 1919 and now, in January 1920, they confiscated the last of the four instalments of *Cyclops*. Confiscation meant burning. 'It was like a burning at the stake as far as I was concerned,' Margaret Anderson said.[1]

Harriet was amused by James Joyce's remark that this was the second time that he had had the pleasure of being burned while on earth.* [2] But she realized, perhaps better than he did, that the chances of publication anywhere in book form were getting dimmer. John Quinn was even more pessimistic. He had been convinced from the start that *The Little Review* was doing *Ulysses* a disservice by publishing it in serial form: only in book form, when obscene passages would fall into place, could it be properly judged; and even in book form he was certain prosecution would follow publication. After the confiscations of 1919, he sent a protesting brief to the solicitor to the Post Office Department, though he considered the published episodes guilty within the meaning of the American statute.[3] A copy of this defence of the book reached Harriet through T. S. Eliot. She was impressed by it and in sending it on to Trieste she stressed that 'it would be well to preserve the document in case of future trouble over *Ulysses* on its publication in book form in this country'.† [4]

James Joyce, in the middle of writing *Nausikaa*, went doggedly on.

* Maunsel destroyed their edition of *Dubliners* by cutting it into pieces; but James Joyce believed that they had burnt it.

† The 'protesting brief' has not come to light.

The episode, which reached Harriet in March 1920, only added to her admiration for the book and her determination to back it. She thought *Nausikaa* very good for the soul, 'medicinal'. 'You are so unflattering to our human nature,' she wrote, 'I think you have something of both—the Reverend James Joyce, S.J., M.D.'[5]

He, meantime, was instructing J. B. Pinker—after a curt reminder to him that his address was Via Sanita, not Via Vanita—to draw up a contract for the publication of *Ulysses* in England and America: 'I shall feel obliged if you will see to this matter at once'.[6] But with the end of *Ulysses* not yet in sight and *The Egoist* 'suspended', Harriet was freer. In the past four years, though she had always managed to get down to Guildford to Mary and Annie for an occasional night or two and for a walk with Wolf on the Downs, she had been able to join her family only for infrequent short holidays. This went against the grain. The Edwardian habit of paying family visits for weeks at a time had suited her, and had given her fine opportunities for enjoying country pleasures and finding, in her love and understanding of natural beauty, a solace for the doubts and difficulties that attended her chosen role on the human scene as an independent, freedom-loving spirit.

Now, her morning visit to the office no longer necessary, she was able to see more of her family and of the rising generation. Her nieces were getting to know her as 'the young aunt'.[7] She was young in her physical strength, in her lively interests and, above all, in her gift for treating children as people, sharing their interests and inviting them to share hers. She delighted them by pointing to a star and remarking on the exact number of years that its light, now visible on earth, had travelled through space; she never lost her way, because she always knew how the hills and streams lay; and she understood the weather and the clouds.[8]

Her first spring visit, and the first extended visit of her life outside the family circle, was to Dora Marsden. Dora and her mother had now moved from their house in Southport, in search of the peace Dora needed for undisturbed work on her book, to what Harriet described as 'a primitive cottage on the lower slopes of Helvellyn, one of the highest mountains in the lake district of northern England with Lake Ullswater at its foot, a very beautiful lake'.[9]

Harriet was accustomed to exploring the countryside from the well-appointed base of a middle-class country house, where clothes could conveniently be dried and where the regular appearance of meals could be taken for granted. Dora's cottage had no such pretensions. It was one of a row of ten, built for lead miners employed in the pit beyond the hill. An earlier generation of miners had deserted the cottages for the softer life of the lakeside village, Glenridding, two miles away; and the cottages were now owned by Miss Allsop, who lived in one at the end of the row and let the others, if she could, mostly to summer visitors.

The small, lonely settlement was called Seldom Seen. From the lakeside, a steep, rough track led up to it. The coal store and earth closets were out at the back, and all water had to be fetched in buckets and cans from an open pipe that led from the spring up the hill. Old Mrs. Marsden, a selfless—even saintly—woman who had always been much loved by Dora's friends, managed the housekeeping bravely, and Dora was more or less indifferent to creature comforts: but Harriet was shocked by the conditions in which her friends were living.

One of the objects of the visit was to find out how Dora's work was going and to give her an opportunity for developing her ideas in discussion. Dora, committed for many years to solitary reading and reflection, had a great need to talk to an intelligent listener; but, as her aim was to 'assert', the dialogue was often one-sided. She was still in the preliminary stages of establishing a new method and defining terms for 'the long-drawn-out but incalculably valuable process of assimilating one's own conclusions'.[10] Harriet, who had always admired her insistence on a strict linguistic discipline, was well able to act as her sounding-board. But she must have been disappointed to find that less than a couple of chapters were in final draft, and that Dora's headaches and general malaise sometimes prevented her working for two days out of three.

In one way, however, the holiday was an undoubted success. Harriet had brought Wolf with her and the wild, beautiful fells pleased them both. Though the weather was bad that Easter, with rain often blotting out the lake, they were able to get out of doors and enjoy the solitude and freedom of mountain country. But in spite of its beauty, there was something weird about the place, especially on misty days. Then, in the early morning when the miners climbed the hill to work, Harriet could hear their footsteps—and their singing, for they often sang as they went—while they remained hidden; and Miss Allsop's two animals—a very large dog and a very small donkey—loomed out of the mist looking like fabulous cross-

breeds. Dora, who did not share Harriet's love of walking, sometimes felt she was confined in 'a benighted spot'.

From this strange place, Harriet went on to Maude and Campbell's wholly conventional vicarage at Brighouse, Yorkshire, to the
sort of hospitality she had always known and the delightful company
of their two small daughters, her nieces Katharine and Margaret.
There she received, forwarded from London, a letter from James
Joyce. Tauchnitz were interested in publishing a continental edition
of *A Portrait*. If they did so, it would sell, he thought, at about
a tenth of the current price on the Continent of the English edition,
because of the depreciation of currencies. Would she send Tauchnitz
a copy by express registered post? 'Of course I mention this as a
suggestion and subject to your approval of such a cession of continental rights,' he added.[11]

Harriet wrote to Katie Gliddon, a painter friend of Helen Saunders,
who had bravely agreed to mind the office, to find a copy of *A
Portrait* and to send it, by express registered post, to Tauchnitz; and
to James Joyce she wrote: 'I do not think that *The Egoist* has any
continental rights over the book, but in any case, of course, we would
not exercise them under present conditions when the rate of exchange
makes the price of English books prohibitive to continental buyers'.[12]

More immediate was the arrival of the contract for *Ulysses*. It
provided, as arranged, for a royalty of 25 per cent, an advance of £25
and publication at 6s. unless otherwise agreed.[13] Harriet signed it,
though she added a note of warning, both to J. B. Pinker and to the
author, about the price at which the book might have to be published. To the latter, she added:

English readers do not now expect to obtain a new novel for 6/–:
indeed the mind of the British public appears to be such that the
higher the price of an article the greater the value attached to it.
There could perhaps be a Tauchnitz edition of this book also afterwards so that your desire for a low-priced book for the continent
could be met. . . .[14]

In maintaining her view about the likely price at which it would
be possible to publish a novel as long as *Ulysses* promised to be,
Harriet was sure of her ground. She was less sure of her ground on
the question whether it was going to be possible to publish at all. She
continued to assume, or to appear to assume, that it would prove

possible. Looking back on the contract many years later, however, with the advantage of hindsight, it seemed to have an air of fantasy. She concluded that Mr Joyce must have 'signed it without reading it, as his custom was'.[15] And that the operative clause in Mr Pinker's eyes was the final one empowering him to collect the 25 per cent royalties and so to deduct 'his own heavy percentage on them'; or that he had drawn it up 'more for his own edification than for anything else'.[16]

Whether or not she was being fair to James Joyce, she was scarcely fair to his agent. It is perhaps difficult for anybody who has never had to earn a living to appreciate that most people need to be paid for their work. Harriet did not find it difficult unless the work seemed to her usurious or to be exploiting others. She seems to have thought that the work of literary agents had something of both these faults— though she can have had very little idea of the work done by them for authors, successful or otherwise.

Harriet left Yorkshire for Cheshire towards the end of May 1920 to make the last of her round of visits, a stay of several weeks at Castle Park with her two old maiden aunts, who were as fond of her as she was of them and who, like Maude, gave her the family welcome and family life that she had always loved. They took the opportunity of her visit to tell her that they were settling some money on her. Harriet was privately rather embarrassed by this announcement, but touched by it also, as she was by the forlorn state of her elder aunt, Harriet, who had recently had an iridectomy. In reply to James Joyce's enquiries, she was able to assure him that the operation had been without complications and successful. But this first experience of watching recovery from an eye operation brought home to her how much more he must have suffered, and to less purpose.[17]

On returning to Gloucester Place, Harriet closed the company accounts for the year and wound up the journal. She repaid unexpired subscriptions (mostly in the form of Egoist Press publications) and opened the new year with a balance of just over £130, about half from the General Fund and half from the Development Fund. She now merged them but evidently still made in her own mind a distinction between the overheads, which she expected to subsidize herself, and the individual titles which she hoped to see through with the money already available, and from further sales. In the event, these hopes were fulfilled for all the books financed through the account.

In the meantime, most of her titles were selling slowly. Less than two-thirds of her second edition, of a thousand, of *A Portrait*, had been sold since its appearance more than two years before. The second set of the *Poets' Translation Series* was still in the doldrums; Ezra Pound's *Dialogues of Fontenelle* and *Quia Pauper Amavi* and Richard Aldington's *Images* had all done poorly. But Wyndham Lewis' *Tarr* was still doing well (nearly six hundred copies sold), and his new book *The Caliph's Design* had made a very good start. Wyndham Lewis' two books had so far earned £170, against a cost of £246; and all the other titles had earned in all £114 and had cost £264.

The *Oxen of the Sun* episode arrived as Harriet was completing this work. 'Scene: Lying-in-hospital. Technique: a ninepart episode without divisions. . . . Bloom is the spermatozoon, the hospital the womb, the nurse the ovum, Stephen the embryo,' as James Joyce explained to Frank Budgen, who had returned to London from Switzerland and whose company and critical mind he continued to miss acutely.[18] Harriet thought the episode 'might also have been called *Hades* for the reading of it is like being taken the rounds of hell'.[19] This remark touched too closely on the subject of scorching to be agreeable to James Joyce. He had already lamented to her, when she had praised the 'scorching truth' of his writing, that the word had a peculiar significance for his 'superstitious mind not so much because of any quality or merit in the writing itself as for the fact that the progress of the book is in fact like the progress of some sandblast. As soon as I mention or include any person in it I hear of his or her death or departure or misfortune: and each successive episode . . . leaves behind it a burnt up field. . . .'[20] 'Do you mean,' he asked her now, 'that the *Oxen of the Sun* episode resembles *Hades* because the nine circles of development . . . seem to you to be peopled by extinct beings?'[21] Harriet, vexed to find herself caught up again in speculations she had not intended, replied that this was not what she meant: 'I must ask you once more not to pay the slightest attention to any foolish remark I may make—which really I must give up making—if I can'.[22]

James Joyce wrote from Paris, where he intended to stay for three months, as he explained, 'to write the last adventure *Circe* in peace(?) and also the first episode of the close. . . . Mr Pound wrote to me so urgently from Sirmione (lake of Garda) that in spite of my dread of thunderstorms and detestation of travelling I went there bringing my son with me to act as a lightning conductor. I remained two days there and it was arranged when I explained my general position and wishes that I should follow him on to Paris'.[23] He was to remain there for twenty years—at some seventeen different addresses. The move ushered in a new phase in Harriet's relations with him.

Shortly after his arrival, he met John Rodker, the young English poet whom Harriet knew as a contributor to *The Egoist* and a member of the restaurant supper meetings of 1916 and 1917. John Rodker was now living in Paris and had begun to publish books on his own small handpress. He already knew about the difficulties *Ulysses* had been running into. He suggested printing it in France and publishing it under his own imprint—if The Egoist Press would finance the scheme!

How this idea originated is not known.* Harriet probably heard about it from Ezra Pound, who was, however, unlikely to have started it as he currently preferred another of his own—printing in America.[24] He returned to England a few days later, when he probably also gave Harriet his impression of James Joyce. Both at Sirmione and in Paris he had been able to see for himself, for the first time, how pressed for money his protégé appeared to be—in spite of the help he was receiving. At Sirmione, indeed, he was so much touched by his lack of clothing that he handed over a suit and some boots of his own —though too small. As for the man himself, he probably told Harriet what he wrote at the time to John Quinn: '. . . the real man is the author of *Chamber Music*, the sensitive. The rest is the genius; the registration of realities on the temperament, the delicate temperament, of the early poems. . . . He is, of course, as stubborn as a mule or an Irishman, but I failed to find him at all *unreasonable*. Thank God, he had been stubborn enough to know his job and stick to it'.[25]

Harriet soon had further evidence of James Joyce's sticking to his job: she received an enquiry from him whether it would be possible to get from the printer she had 'alluded to' confirmation that he would still be prepared to print *Ulysses*. Mr Rodker's proposals were worth considering seriously only if printing in England had to be ruled out.[26] This printer, it is assumed, was the Irish Roman Catholic running The Pelican Press, who printed the last three issues of *The Egoist*. He had told Harriet that, so far as he could judge from the first ten episodes, he would be willing to print the complete text.†

* John Rodker's papers were lost in an aerial bombardment of Paris in the Second World War. They might have thrown light on this idea.

† There is no evidence that Harriet Weaver made approaches to any printer other than The Pelican Press. A letter to Sylvia Beach (of 21st March 1950) appears to bear this out.

The enquiry from Paris forced the issue. Harriet was not surprised when she heard his decision, which she passed on at once. He now reluctantly but definitely declined to print the book; and she felt sure it would be utterly useless to try any other English firm. Should it prove too much for John Rodker's handpress, as she feared, it could perhaps be printed in Paris, if Mr Huebsch failed, as now looked likely. Two years before, she had asked him whether he would be willing, if he published *Ulysses*, to let her have sheets, as he had done for *A Portrait*. But now that the book had run into difficulties in *The Little Review*, she knew that he was in two minds whether he could run the risk of publishing it.

But Harriet had sugar for the pill. She had probably decided very quickly that the money her aunts were settling on her, £100 a year, should be handed on to Mr Joyce, and she felt that this was the moment to tell him. He was, she believed, in his most powerful and creative years and ought not to be handicapped by any mundane anxieties.* Two months later, touched by the Joyce family's difficulties in finding quarters in Paris, she backed up this settlement with a cheque for £200.

Harriet felt strongly that she had no need for and no use for more money than she had already inherited. She intensely disliked the idea of possessing any more than she required for the simple life and the interests she had chosen for herself; and she disapproved, on grounds of her socialist principles, of wealth not proportionate to personal need. It must have seemed providential to her that only a few weeks after learning of her aunts' gift she learned of Mr Joyce's manifest need for help in achieving in Paris a mode of life settled enough in which to write.

In correspondence, and now by report, she was gradually getting to know him better, though her knowledge of him was still fragmentary and she was unacquainted with the darker side of his genius. Meanwhile, her spring visit to Dora—the first occasion when they had spent some while together—had given her a new insight into the troubles that beset her other 'genius'. Dora was living uncomfortably, her health was wretched and she was suffering, personally and intellectually, from the isolation that her way of life entailed.

In the old days, although Dora had often rebelled against the disci-

* This gift, and subsequent ones, Harriet Weaver did not put into the hands of the Public Trustee as she felt that James Joyce might need to draw on capital from time to time until he had an adequate income from royalties.

pline of press day, she had at least been linked by it to an exterior world; and its demands, in general and in detail, had been the subject of a vast correspondence. This exchange had enabled her to resist the temptation to withdraw into a life of concepts and images. But her present way of life gave her no way out from the prison of an excessively introverted disposition.

Harriet, even if she was not fully aware of these tensions, could see that the demise of *The Egoist* was bound to leave a gap in Dora's interests and contacts. Through the summer, she made a point of writing often, whether or not there was any business to discuss. In fact there was very little. Mr Lewis had had plans for launching a new periodical, *Tyro*. She had agreed to publish though not to subsidize it; and Mr Sidney Schiff had put up £50.* But the plans were hanging fire. She had in preparation two more reprints for the second *Poets' Translation Series—Poseidippos and Askleiades* by Edward Storer and *Meleager of Gadara* by Richard Aldington. And so on. 'You are a dear to write to this benighted spot as regularly as if it were a Xtian land,' Dora wrote.[27]

Harriet's chief concern, however, was how to publish *Ulysses*. The chances of doing so began to look slighter. In the autumn, John Rodker had to decline to publish it—as she half expected; and the New York Society for the Suppression of Vice instituted court proceedings against *The Little Review* for the issue of July–August, devoted to the last part of *Nausikaa*. In his sworn deposition, the secretary of the society alleged that the issue 'represents and is descriptive of scenes of lewdness and of obscenity'; and that 'a minute description of the same would be offensive to the Court and improper to be placed upon the record thereof'.[28]

This turn of events was exactly what John Quinn had feared. He was doing his best to have the trial postponed in the hope that it might be possible to get *Ulysses* published in book form, in a private edition, before the case came on, when Ben Huebsch crossed the Atlantic to discuss things first with the author and then with Miss Weaver.

The meeting in Paris was not a success. *Ulysses* was still far from

* Sidney Schiff, the writer Stephen Hudson, was a good friend to many younger writers. The first number of *Tyro* came out the following year and earned for The Egoist Press less than £15. Wyndham Lewis's friend Edward Wadsworth, the Vorticist, came to the rescue with £25 to help print the second number, which appeared in the spring of 1922.

ready for publication; and James Joyce jumped to the conclusion that his American publisher might regard himself as at liberty to pirate the book—if it was ever completed. The meeting in London went better. Harriet, in spite of a warning letter from Paris, took a more sanguine view. She saw that Mr Huebsch had no intention of turning pirate; and, as he now represented the only chance she had of publishing *Ulysses* herself, by importing sheets from him, she did everything she could to encourage him. She lent him her copy of the first fourteen episodes and received from him before they parted a strong indication that he would publish the book as it stood. She started collecting orders for her own edition and, by the new year 1921, had a hundred and fifty.

John Quinn was not successful in getting the trial of the editors of *The Little Review* postponed. It came on in February but, when two of the three judges found incomprehensible the offending passages from *Nausikaa* read to them, it was postponed for a week to enable them all to read the whole episode. At the next sitting the judges were apparently satisfied by John Quinn, who was rather reluctantly defending the editors, that the offending passages would revolt but not contaminate. They felt impelled, however, to find for the Society for the Suppression of Vice.

James Joyce, meantime, was writing and rewriting the *Circe* episode, sitting at one stage in an unheated room, wrapped in two borrowed blankets, his head muffled in a shawl lent by Mrs Pound, and unburdening himself frequently to Harriet: more eye trouble, neuralgia; fruitless flat hunting; the dim prospects of getting *Exiles* performed; the difficulties of following the fortunes of *Ulysses* in *The Little Review*, not having been vouchsafed a copy of the issues as they appeared. Flashes of humour, enormously relished by Harriet, lightened the gloom. For instance: 'I have not heard lately . . . from the Swedish translator of [*A Portrait*] who proposed, by the way, to omit the philosophical and free passages. The Spanish translator possibly may wish to retain these and omit the rest and a combination of both versions would suffice for the central European if he or she could read both those languages.'[29]

Harriet followed each advance or reverse and did what she could, in her dry way, to encourage him. But her market for the second edition of *A Portrait* remained sluggish and, judged by sales, Wyndham Lewis was her most successful author. As a result, there was still some money in the Development Fund and she used it to produce

27 John Rodker in about 1916

28 The *Ulysses* slip issued by John Rodker

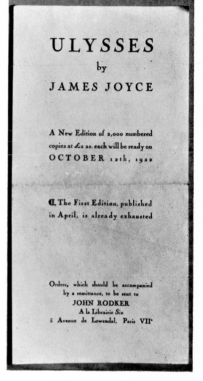

ULYSSES
by
JAMES JOYCE

A New Edition of 2,000 numbered
copies at £2 2s. each will be ready on
OCTOBER 12th, 1922

¶ The First Edition, published
in April, is already exhausted

Orders, which should be accompanied
by a remittance, to be sent to
JOHN RODKER
A la Librairie Six
5 Avenue de Lowendal, Paris VII*

29 Iris Barry as Praxitella, by Wyndham Lewis—detail

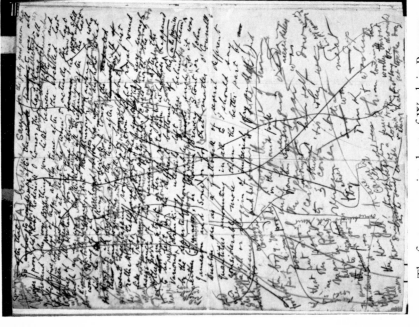

31 James Joyce's letter from Bognor, 7th August 1923

30 The first manuscript sheet of Work in Progress

Cock and Harlequin: notes concerning music by Jean Cocteau: 'Translated by Rollo H. Myers. With a portrait of the author and two monograms by Pablo Picasso'.[30] It is a beautiful little book, printed with great elegance by the Pelican Press, the only fine printer she had ever used. This was the last of the books paid for by Egoist Press funds, but not the last of the imprint. Edward Storer had offered to pay the printing costs of his poems *Terra Italica*, and Harriet had agreed to publish them. It was now her intention to save her own resources for James Joyce, but she was very willing to publish subsidized books. It was not long before several others were added to her list, financed by her new friend Bryher.*

Harriet and Bryher, although they met rarely, were on terms of genuine friendship; Harriet had always been drawn to people who had come to terms with life in an independent way. In the spring, when Bryher came to London with her husband, the young American poet Robert McAlmon, he too became a friend. Harriet liked him at once, and recommended him warmly to James Joyce when he went on to Paris.

Bryher, who did not feel at ease in his 'crowd' of Paris expatriates and suffered from being the only abstainer at their long-drawn-out drinking evenings, stayed on in London for a while, and she and Harriet had time to discuss plans. She particularly admired American poetry and recommended, first, an Egoist edition of Marianne Moore's *Poems*, financed by herself.

At Seldom Seen, things were not going smoothly. Dora had enjoyed a 'wonderful' autumn: 'a crystal globe flushed with ever[y] kind of soft but penetrating coloured light'.[31] But as winter approached, her mood changed. Only Miss Allsop remained and, worried by Dora's habit of staying indoors all day, disconcerted her by peering through the window to see what she was doing. It was not only 'the loneliness but the heavy labour', when the weather broke, that made Dora dread the winter. She decided to stick it out but, mewed up in her tiny cottage, was beset by anxiety over her health and her work.

* Bryher was the pseudonym of Winifred Ellerman, and the name she had taken legally after publishing her first book. She had detached herself from her wealthy family and, after sharing Hilda Doolittle's flat, had gone with her to America, where she met many of the American poets and made a 'marriage of convenience' with Robert McAlmon, the tenth child of an itinerant minister. He was eager to visit Europe, and she was happy to share her very good income for the sake of a marital status which liberated her from the conventions that, as a young single woman, she had found unendurable.

'Scarcely one day in three is a good working day owing to my head—which I now believe is incurable,' she told Harriet. 'I get so depressed with things at times that I wonder whatever it is which prevents me from being content with some steady useful humdrum labour, & I have to beat about to find my authority for attempting anything different, & I find it in my great need to state problems clearly even if this results in stating their difficulties clearly.'[32]

Over her health, Dora would seek no help or advice. Her work was another matter. She was consulting her brother Ewart, an engineer and inventor, about her 'electric (by analogy that is) theory of our experience of substance',[33] though she knew he was not in sympathy with this or with any other of her 'scientific' theories; and to Harriet she looked to carry out all sorts of odd jobs, mostly of a more practical kind.

Harriet could not resist her pleas and helped to keep her going by reading and making abstracts from the work of the idealist philosopher William McTaggart; by supplying her with books and by groping through and commenting upon the manuscripts, sometimes barely legible, that Dora sent her. Edna Hicks,* the 'postman' who delivered letters at Seldom Seen and had made friends with Dora, did some of her typing—she had learned to type for this purpose—but Harriet often made the first copy. The completion of the book was still nowhere in sight, and Dora, although she recognized the fact that she was asking a great deal of Harriet, could not reduce her demands. On the contrary, they seemed to be increasing. 'I am a tremendous tax on your energies,' she wrote, 'so tremendous that it is no use apologising for it. What about settling in London? That would be one solution.'[34]

It was a solution that would have made Harriet her permanent, and perhaps almost full-time, personal assistant. That was out of the question: she had other things to do. Another solution was that she should move, for at least a good part of the year, to Seldom Seen. Exactly when, and how, this possibility was discussed is not known; the letters must have been of the highly personal kind that Harriet always destroyed. She was not attracted by the idea of living primitively or of giving up the life she had made for herself in London. She was beginning to feel disturbed, also, by some of the wilder flights of Dora's 'analogical' reasoning. A letter on hallucinations raised a protest from her, and Dora made a kind of retraction: 'I did not mean to

* Later, Mrs Cox.

say that dreams hallucinations & the rest had to be regarded as *proofs* as to the nature of substance but merely that they acted as instruments of release for the mind in its otherwise almost hopelessly fixed tendency to regard the habitual as the inevitable. That is, without in any way constituting proof in themselves, they nevertheless gave the mind a significant clue which otherwise it is very unlikely it could have got wind of. But more anon. . . .!!!'[35]

Harriet had now learned the verdict on the *Little Review* case. Ezra Pound, occupied with plans for moving to the Continent, had not passed it on at once, but at last she heard from Ben Huebsch, who broke the news and explained that, much to his regret, he could not now publish *Ulysses* without excisions. He felt, again, that it would be 'simpler for Mr Joyce' if he gave his decision through Harriet—and perhaps it was simpler for him himself!

James Joyce, too, had only just heard the result of the trial—from a chance cutting from a New York paper. He had then bribed a porter at an American bank to let him look up the files of all the papers they had. '. . . the trial took place on February 21, it seems. Since that time no person in New York has sent me a word of information on the subject,' he expostulated to Harriet.[36] It was not a good moment for her to break to him Ben Huebsch's decision but she did so at once and tried to soften the blow by dwelling on the longer-term possibilities of publication in America and her own unaltered determination to publish in England.

An hour after receiving her letter, he cabled to New York to withdraw *Ulysses*. The next day, in despair, he looked in at Shakespeare and Company's bookshop and library, then housed in an old laundry near the Odéon, a habit he had acquired in the nine months since he first met, a few days after his arrival, its diminutive, bird-like owner, Sylvia Beach, an American passionately in love with books and with Paris. She had taken him, as she had taken other expatriate writers, under her wing and felt for him in his latest disappointment. 'My book will never come out now,' he told her, as he sat beside her desk, sighing deeply. It had already occurred to her that she, wholly inexperienced though she was, might undertake the colossal task.[37] The next moment, one she remembered ever afterwards with emotion, it was settled: *Ulysses* would be published by Shakespeare and Company.[38]

Sylvia Beach, having no idea what her next step should be, went round to the rue de l'Odéon, to her close friend Adrienne Monnier, who suggested using her own printer, Maurice Darantiere* in Dijon, and helped her work out a plan which was put to James Joyce when he called the next day.† He wrote at once, and in 'the highest pitch of nervousness' to Harriet:

. . . The proposal is to publish here in October an edition (complete) of . . . 1000 copies . . . They offer me 66% of the net profit. . . . The actual printing will begin as soon as the number of orders covers approximately the cost of printing. . . .

This does not cover the English edition but I think it would be to your advantage if that were amalgamated with the Paris one. . . . As for American sales a great number of Americans are in passing and they are likely to become a fixed colony here. I could not think of entering into a correspondence with Mr Quinn and Mr Huebsch . . . after seven years' hard labour and in the present exasperated state of my nerves.

There followed a frenzied appeal for money. He had been counting on an advance (of $1,000) on publication in America and could not accept that nothing would be forthcoming: 'I need absolutely an advance such as Mr Quinn suggested upon the book. . . If you can think of any way by which a partial arrangement of this kind can be made immediately, pending a clearing up of the matter by correspondence, I mean or suggest through *Shakespeare and Co* here, I shall be infinitely relieved. . . . Perhaps a guarantee of some kind on sales or orders in England would do. . . .'[39]

This letter was sent on to Harriet at Whitby, where she was looking forward to three weeks' walking on the Yorkshire moors. Campbell Hone had lately been appointed Rector and he was to hold the living for ten years.‡ A letter from Sylvia Beach, who was not unknown to

* In spelling his name, he appears not to have used an accent.

† Adrienne Monnier, who came from French peasant stock, had been running for some years in the rue de l'Odéon, on the *rive gauche*, a bookshop and library *La Maison des Amis des Livres*, already an established literary centre where members of her circle—among them Jules Romains, Valery Larbaud and André Gide—gave readings from their manuscripts.

‡ There is a story of Campbell Hone, bound for an important diocesan conference at York, reaching Whitby station just as his train was drawing away. The next moment, however, it stopped, shunted back to the station and stopped again. So he boarded his missed train, a little puzzled by its behaviour until he remembered that one of his churchwardens was the station master.

Harriet, was forwarded also. (A few days after meeting James Joyce for the first time the summer before, she had ordered as many Egoist publications as she could have for £1 and Harriet had offered to supply her with books at 'one third off the English net price and post free' because of the adverse rate of exchange.)[40]

It was a relief that Miss Beach had turned publisher and Harriet wrote at once to welcome the news and to try to get clearer what was now proposed about an English edition:

. . . I am very glad to hear that you are to take over the American publication of *Ulysses* as the New York publishers are so much upset over the question of prosecution and as Mr Joyce has been so greatly worried by their indecision. On my return I will send you names of American people and shops who want the book.

I am not clear from your letter whether Mr Joyce wishes to have only one edition of the book, to include this country as well as America, or whether you will send sheets for a separate English edition as would have been done by the American publisher—but I shall doubtless hear about this before long either from you or from Mr Joyce.[41]

But by the next day she had decided not to wait on Paris. She was perhaps not attracted by the idea of an 'amalgamated' edition but at any rate she saw in fresh arrangements for an English edition the chance of meeting James Joyce's urgent and disturbing appeal for help. She drew up, then and there, a new contract of her own making and posted it that day to Paris. Under it, he would receive 25 per cent of the English edition until expenses had been covered, when he would receive 90 per cent of the profits. In the meantime he would receive—if he agreed to these terms—an immediate advance of £200.*

He did agree—by telegram—and Harriet cut short her visit to return to London to get off the money and to give time to the other things that now had to be done. His 'greatly worried' state had made her anxious, perhaps a little flustered, on his account. The arrival of the two latest episodes, *Circe* and *Eumeus*, brought her some relief, however, as she could detect in them no signs of his fatigue. And it was a relief, too, to discuss with Shakespeare and Company the proposed Paris and Egoist editions. Might she have seven hundred and

* It is hardly necessary to say that the money was Harriet Weaver's own.

fifty to one thousand copies of Miss Beach's prospectus? She would send it to *Egoist* subscribers and Irish and American bookshops with a slip that all applications should be sent direct and immediately to Paris. What discount should shops get? They had been expecting an ordinary edition and she herself had no experience of limited editions. Miss Beach explained that booksellers made a practice of buying copies of such editions to sell later at double or treble the original price and that 10 per cent was quite enough for them. Harriet agreed, but pressed for 15 per cent for wholesalers, who could not cash in. Would Miss Weaver accept a presentation copy? Would Miss Beach think of circulating with her prospectus a leaflet of reviews of *A Portrait*? Mr Joyce would almost certainly want this.[42]

When the arrangements for the two editions were reasonably clear, Harriet felt ready for her one disagreeable task—breaking to J. B. Pinker the news of her unilateral action in cancelling the contract of May 1920, and of the new contract, which made no provision for any fee for him. She wrote at length, with emphasis on Mr Joyce's tiredness and nervous exhaustion when he was trying to finish the book. 'I made the suggestion to him on account of his worried state and great need of money; but for which need I should have proposed a larger share of the profits (if any) for the Egoist than 10 per cent.'[43]

James Joyce, at any rate, could now relax. He had been tided over; *Ulysses* was going to be published after all; the amount of writing left to do was no longer overwhelming; and Paris, at first unkind, had suddenly become human. Valery Larbaud had lent him his flat for the summer and was 'raving mad' over the book, which he thought 'as great and comprehensive and human as Rabelais'.[44]

Harriet's own social life continued on its even keel, irrespective of her private preoccupations. She entertained, in a modest way, the friends whose courage and enterprise she admired. At this period she invited Iris Barry once a week for dinner and talk—and a hot bath— and she still had Helen Saunders to tea from time to time. Helen always enjoyed meeting 'Josephine', though she never felt she could be 'on very intimate terms' with a friend who 'could rarely be persuaded to talk about herself': Josephine's interest was 'in other people', and particularly, she observed, in the next generation.[45]

It was true that Harriet loved young people and felt at ease with them; she accepted their confidences with understanding and sympathy and the fact that confidences were not exchanged was no bar to intimacy. But perhaps it would be truer to say that what she loved

in young people was the same thing that she valued in older friends—
the sense that a life of independent, creative action was still open before them. James Joyce and Dora Marsden had this appeal for her, and
it was all the stronger because she never ceased to feel rebuked by their
courage in cutting themselves off from conventional life. Helen
Saunders and Iris Barry also belonged to this company.

Another visitor, of a different sort, was a young man, Beaumont
Wadsworth. He had sent Harriet some of his writing and had received kindly comment. He was asked to coffee one evening and later
recorded his impressions:

I was a shop-assistant at William Whiteleys when I visited her, and
she seemed rather surprised that I was reading a highbrow like Joyce.
As a matter of fact I jumped right from the world of Arnold Bennett,
who had been my idol, into the world of Joyce and Wyndham Lewis.

[Two] other guests were at Miss Weaver's flat that evening. Miss
Storm Jameson, the young novelist, the spirit of youth wrapped in a
decorative long dark blue cloak, and a young man named Pender. . . .
Like myself, Pender had no literary passport to this rarefied 'Egoist'
world. We had been invited because of our known admiration for
Joyce and the other writers of Miss Weaver's stable. So it was natural
that we talked of Joyce, Pound, Lewis and Eliot.[46]

He was particularly struck by the contrast between his hostess's 'wild'
writers and the atmosphere she herself created of modest simplicity
and calm.

There was another contrast, too, though it was known only to
herself. She was battling in her own mind with her disinclination to
yield to further claims from Dora. Could she bring herself to embark
on the close collaboration that she now so obviously desired? All her
instincts were against making any change now, when she was becoming more and more convinced of James Joyce's genius and less
and less of Dora's. Besides, if she gave herself to Dora's book, what
would happen to The Egoist Press? These were solid arguments; and
yet, it was still difficult for her to grudge anything to a friend in need.

As she struggled, alone, to find a way out of this conflict she saw
herself—as James Joyce had recently seen himself—trying to round a
storm cape. In the event, she did not move house and Dora did not
come to London. Harriet set about feeling her way towards a compromise arrangement, and in the meantime protected Dora against

inroads on her income by making a loan to her brother Ewart Marsden, through the Egoist Account, to help him directly with the development of his inventions.

She was still conscience-stricken about her 'weakness' in making a compromise, when she learned, in a roundabout way, that some of James Joyce's difficulties were brought about by a weakness she did not share.

Wyndham Lewis and Robert McAlmon had got to know James Joyce quite well. Wyndham Lewis had been going to and fro between London and Paris a good deal for a year or more and had made a drawing of him—besides one of Harriet; Robert McAlmon, on the strength of Harriet's introduction, had quickly got on to convivial terms. Though their company was not as rewarding as Frank Budgen's, James Joyce liked them both and whenever they were in Paris saw a lot of them—usually in the evenings, when he did not work and liked to entertain. Through this *va et vient* Harriet learnt, in a moment of casual talk, that Mr Joyce's ordinary mode of life was quite other than she had imagined it to be. Anything that Ezra Pound said, on returning from Paris the previous summer, could hardly have prepared her for what she now learnt. As Frank Budgen has pointed out, 'Joyce was very capable of suiting his conduct to any situation he was faced with. The less Ulyssean he if he wasn't';[47] and at Sirmione and later in Paris, Ezra Pound was left with the impression (among others) that he was like a dour Aberdeen minister.

When Wyndham Lewis called on Harriet in May, he let fall—in his rather brash way—that James Joyce entertained lavishly and that it was fairly usual for him to end the evenings—'uproarious allnight sittings (and dancings)'—very drunk.[48]

This news was shattering. Harriet's whole nature and upbringing revolted against overindulgence in drink; and she was acutely aware, from first-hand experience as a social worker, of the wrecking and waste caused by it, the wrecking of the happiness and health and prospects of the drinkers themselves and of their spouses and children. Drink, she had been brought up to believe, was one of the great evils; and to that dictum she held still. Besides, she was frightened of drunken people.

Harriet felt constrained to write to Mr Joyce: it would not do to pass over what she had learned. She told him what Mr Lewis had told her and went on to explain, almost apologetically, what she thought about drink—a great evil—and how much disturbed she was to learn that he allowed it to get the better of him. But this sudden plunge into the personal and ethical she seems to have found rather embarrassing and, perhaps for this reason or out of politeness, she ended the letter on another, less controversial subject: her own interest in the figure five.

He, in turn, was shattered. He had been caught out by his habit of running his life in insulated departments and of assuming that each could be kept indefinitely separate from the next; he had overlooked the fact that little more than the Channel now separated him from Miss Weaver. The last thing he would have wished was that she, of all people, should have received an impression of him that was both unflattering and not stage-managed by himself. And now she was up in arms. What was to be done?

In sudden panic, he sent her letter to London, to Frank Budgen, and asked his advice how he might reply.* His best course, his friend suggested, was to play the whole thing down: he should dwell on his sense of release after years of labour on the book, now nearly completed, and his need to relax just for a while—Wyndham Lewis' visit had made him realize that the moment had come.

On 24th June 1921, James Joyce sat down in Valery Larbaud's luxurious flat to send his reply.† His idea of 'playing the whole thing down' took the form of suggesting that no report about him had any solid foundation and thus of discrediting Wyndham Lewis' report. His remarkable effusion is given as published (except for a digression about current difficulties with *Exiles* and the 'six or seven people' who were supposed to be translating *Dubliners* in different parts of France):

Dear Miss Weaver:
    ... ‡ A nice collection could be made of legends about me. Here are some. My family in Dublin believe that I enriched myself in Switzerland during the war by espionage work for one or both com-

---

* This letter from Harriet Weaver to James Joyce has not survived. Frank Budgen's recollection of it, which rings true, is given here. He returned the letter by registered post, at James Joyce's urgent command. (And when he was in Paris some time afterwards, James Joyce borrowed his wallet at the end of a convivial party, to raise money for the bill. In the wallet he noticed his own letter to Frank Budgen pleading for advice, and removed it.)

† To be precise, it seems that James Joyce's letter of 24th June 1921 was his reply to Harriet Weaver's letter about his overdrinking. The number of excisions made by her before its publication (in the first volume of *Letters*) reinforce this assumption.

‡ Harriet Weaver's ellipses.

batants. Triestines, seeing me emerge from my relative's house occupied by my furniture for about twenty minutes every day and walk to the same spot, the G.P.O., and back (I was writing *Nausikaa* and *The Oxen of the Sun* in a dreadful atmosphere) circulated the rumour, now firmly believed, that I am a cocaine victim. The general rumour in Dublin was (till the prospectus of *Ulysses* stopped it) that I could write no more, had broken down and was dying in New York. A man from Liverpool told me he had heard that I was the owner of several cinema theatres all over Switzerland. In America there appear to be or have been two versions: one that I was an austere mixture of the Dalai Lama and sir Rabindrath Tagore. Mr Pound described me as a dour Aberdeen minister. Mr Lewis told me he was told that I was a crazy fellow who always carried four watches and rarely spoke except to ask my neighbour what o'clock it was. Mr Yeats seemed to have described me to Mr Pound as a kind of Dick Swiveller. What the numerous (and useless) people to whom I have been introduced here think I don't know. My habit of addressing people I have just met for the first time as 'Monsieur' earned for me the reputation of a *tout petit bourgeois* while others consider what I intend for politeness as most offensive. . . .* One woman here originated the rumour that I am extremely lazy and will never do or finish anything. (I calculate that I must have spent nearly 20,000 hours in writing *Ulysses*.) A batch of people in Zurich persuaded themselves that I was gradually going mad and actually endeavoured to induce me to enter a sanatorium where a certain Doctor Jung (the Swiss Tweedledum who is not to be confused with the Viennese Tweedledee, Dr Freud) amuses himself at the expense (in every sense of the word) of ladies and gentlemen who are troubled with bees in their bonnets.

I mention all these views not to speak about myself but to show you how conflicting they all are. The truth probably is that I am a quite commonplace person undeserving of so much imaginative painting. There is a further opinion that I am a crafty simulating and dissimulating Ulysses-like type, a 'jejune jesuit', selfish and cynical. There is some truth in this, I suppose: but it is by no means all of me (nor was it of Ulysses) and it has been my habit to apply this alleged quality to safeguard my poor creations. . . .*

Mr Lewis was very agreeable, in spite of my deplorable ignorance

* Harriet Weaver's ellipses.

of his art, even offering to instruct me in the art of the Chinese of which I know as much as the man in the moon. He told me he finds life in London very depressing. There is a curious kind of honour-code among men which obliges them to assist one another and not hinder the free action of one another and remain together for mutual protection with the result that very often they wake up the next morning sitting in the same ditch.

This letter begins to remind me of a preface by Mr George Bernard Shaw. It does not seem to be a reply to your letter after all. . . .* You have already one proof of my intense stupidity. Here now is an example of my emptiness. I have not read a work of literature for several years. My head is full of pebbles and rubbish and broken matches and lots of glass picked up 'most everywhere'. The task I set myself technically in writing a book from eighteen different points of view and in as many styles, all apparently unknown or undiscovered by my fellow tradesmen, that and the nature of the legend chosen would be enough to upset anyone's mental balance. I want to finish the book and try to settle my entangled material affairs definitely one way or the other (somebody here said of me: 'They call him a poet. He appears to be interested chiefly in mattresses'). And, in fact, I was. After that I want a good long rest in which to forget *Ulysses* completely.

I forgot to tell you another thing. I don't even know Greek though I am spoken of as erudite. My father wanted me to take Greek as third language, my mother German and my friends Irish. Result, I took Italian. I spoke or used to speak modern Greek not too badly (I speak four or five languages fluently enough) and have spent a great deal of time with Greeks of all kinds from noblemen down to onion-sellers, chiefly the latter. I am superstitious about them. They bring me luck.

I now end this long rambling shambling speech, having said nothing of the darker aspects of my detestable character. I suppose the law should now take its course with me because it must now seem to you a waste of rope to accomplish the dissolution of a person who has now dissolved visibly and possesses scarcely as much 'pendibility' as an uninhabited dressinggown.[49]

To hide, to vanish behind a cloud of rumours was his object. He was not prepared to allow Miss Weaver—or indeed anyone except

* Harriet Weaver's ellipses.

his wife—to know him except on terms agreeable to himself. But the very length of the letter betrays his anxiety to restore her confidence in him. Nor was this all. He asked Robert McAlmon to write in his defence.

Robert McAlmon, more kindly than Wyndham Lewis, and not without understanding of a sort of Harriet's point of view, wrote, he hoped persuasively, that Mr Joyce 'drank, but in moderation' and assured her that 'so gentle a type' became 'merely released with drink'. He never failed, moreover, to 'hold his drink properly and as a gentleman'. There was some truth in these pleas, as Harriet was to discover later. But, at the time, she probably dismissed them because Robert McAlmon himself drank too much. So, when he followed up his letter with a visit, he saw that she had not been won over, though she agreed, in nervous monosyllables, that if Mr Joyce were 'working and well' that was what mattered most.[50] No doubt, Harriet was 'consuming her own smoke'.

Robert McAlmon also had a message for her from Sylvia Beach. Subscriptions for *Ulysses* were beginning to flag and she was much agitated as some people were refusing to subscribe because, they said, they would prefer to wait for the (many times) cheaper English edition.* Would Miss Weaver consider urgently what could be done?

This was the first evidence Harriet had of what was to become Sylvia Beach's frequent alarm over the financial quagmire into which she feared *Ulysses* might lead her. She was 'much concerned' and hastened to put things right. She would 'cross off *Ulysses* (or the price at any rate)' from the Egoist publications leaflet and notify everyone on her own list that her edition was postponed 'indefinitely' or, if Miss Beach preferred, for two years, or three years, or any length of time. And she would mention the Paris edition on the bookwrappers she was having printed of the third edition of *A Portrait of the Artist*.†[51] A few days later, while staying at Castle Park, where she was to

---

* Havelock Ellis, for example, wrote that the price, 150 frs, was rather beyond him. He would prefer to wait for The Egoist Press edition—though he would consider buying Miss Beach's if she would buy his six *Studies*. (Havelock Ellis to Sylvia Beach, 11th July 1921. Princeton)

† Harriet Weaver was pleased with the appearance of the third edition of *A Portrait*: 'a better looking volume than the poorly produced second edition'. (To Sylvia Beach, 27th August 1921) She had imported sheets for it from Ben Huebsch but many of the corrections made by James Joyce included in her second edition were not included in the (revised) text from New York. (*James Joyce's Manuscripts & Letters at the University of Buffalo*, by Peter Spielberg. University of Buffalo, 1962)

remain for several weeks, she was relieved to hear that Miss Beach thought, or hoped, that the 'postponed indefinitely' would make the matter right.[52]

The visit to Frodsham was comforting—being met at the station by her aunts' old coachman in the landau, sitting with her aunts and reading to them, calling on old friends and visiting Hannah, her old nurse, who had married in middle age and returned to her native town. Best of all, the visit gave her time and peace in which to consider what best to do as regards Mr Joyce. By the time she returned to London towards the end of August she evidently had resolved that his mode of life must not stand in the way of her continuing to help him.

He had, perhaps, done something to encourage her in making this decision by suggesting, in a letter that reached her at Frodsham, that The Egoist Press should become his sole publisher in England: 'I think it would be well if *Ulysses* makes my name to unify my publishers.'[53] This was not a proposition that she could refuse. She accepted it, but with some diffidence. The Egoist Press were not in a position to advertise books and generally to push them, as were regular publishers. He, however, was content to leave things entirely to her.[54]

Harriet went first to see Elkin Mathews about *Chamber Music*. She was not surprised to find him reluctant to sever his connection with the author, now very different in standing from the unknown poet whose lyrics he had published fourteen years before. But she persuaded him finally to transfer to her the copyright and moulds for £15 on the understanding that he would keep the three hundred copies he had still in stock. Grant Richards, encouraged by her offer to pay him £150 in three instalments, proved ready to transfer the copyright of *Dubliners* and *Exiles*. By the middle of October, the copyright of the three books was in her hands. As stocks of *Exiles* were low, she realized that an Egoist edition would be needed very shortly.

The negotiations coincided with another eye attack that threatened James Joyce early in September 1921. He was 'far too nervous from illness and overwork to attend to business of any kind' and though, as he told Harriet, he recognized that Mr Pinker was 'nominally (except for *Ulysses*)' his agent and might have to be associated with the drawing up of the agreements, he hoped nobody except her herself would write to him 'on that or any other subject'.[55] Harriet fell in with this and was no doubt a good deal gratified. But it was the last straw for

J. B. Pinker. When the transfers to The Egoist Press were completed, he announced that he would never again deal with Mr Joyce through her.

There had been no opportunity, since May, of presenting her annual accounts. The annual general meeting was finally fixed for 6th October but had to be deferred because there was no quorum. When it took place, on 13th October, the minutes show an attendance of only two—Miss Marsden and Miss Weaver—and the fact that Harriet has not recorded the place of meeting suggests that she and Dora, as they had done once before, had conducted their business from a distance.

The accounts Harriet 'presented' on this occasion showed much the usual picture. Both Wyndham Lewis' books had now sold over six hundred and Ezra Pound's *Quia Pauper Amavi* led the rest with sales of one hundred and fifty-five. Her new publications, *Cock and Harlequin*, *Terra Italica* and the periodical *Tyro*, had not done much so far, but they had been issued only shortly before the accounts were made up. The second *Poets' Translation Series* was 'in the red' and the final four numbers, though announced, were never to appear.

Since May, Harriet had brought out Marianne Moore's *Poems* and *Hymen*, by H. D. Bryher, who paid the whole cost of printing the *Poems*, subscribed for three hundred copies of *Hymen* and arranged for a bulk purchase of sheets for sale in America.

All the publishing was going smoothly, thanks, in part, to Bryher's support; and she was also getting on well with correcting for James Joyce, as they came in, batches of proofs of *Ulysses*. But her worries about him had not been diminished by further glimpses of the way he conducted his life. He seemed to be as prodigal of his eyesight and his health as he was of money—at one stage, he told her, he was working sixteen hours a day. This seemed madness. Surely no rational being would be so unwise? Or perhaps his friends had failed him? Perhaps she had failed him? It was the duty of friends to speak their mind, to give advice, when occasion demanded. And Mr Joyce, scarcely more than six months after receiving her 'advance on royalties' of £200, was again out of funds. It was all very surprising and difficult. And one of the difficulties, though Harriet could not recognize it, was that she was judging another by herself. She was a rational person. He was not. Yet, once her loyalty had been given, to whatever cause or person, she was incapable of withdrawing it.

10

MISS WEAVER'S *ULYSSES*

In December 1921, The Egoist Press published, at his expense, Robert McAlmon's poems *Explorations*, the last book on Harriet's general list. The Press existed thereafter for the purpose of publishing James Joyce—and in the hope of publishing Dora Marsden.

The coming edition of *Exiles* was in proof and only awaited the author's corrections. It was Harriet's larger commitments to him that daunted her. A photograph he had just sent her reminded her of a description of his appearance in an Italian review—a lean figure and stooping head making an outline in the form of a question mark. The question mark was looming large. His last plea for money would have to be met. But how? And the prospect of publishing *Ulysses* was at once attractive and frightening. She was sometimes depressed, and hoped he would be able to get to London in the spring to judge what reception the English edition would be likely to receive. At other times she felt more sanguine: public opinion was perhaps becoming more favourable. Joseph Hone, regarded by him as one of the villains of the 'curious history' of Maunsel's failure to publish *Dubliners*, had written, she noticed, an article that gave evidence of a change of attitude that she had never expected.

Harriet had now seen all the episodes of *Ulysses*. She was spellbound by *Circe*, though she would say of it only that it interested her very much. *Ithaca* she found less difficult than *Oxen of the Sun*, which seemed to demand more knowledge than she had of the Roman Catholic Church and of Homer's *Odyssey*; and the 'unschooled' style of *Eumeus* she found refreshing. Her comments on *Penelope* seemed to have pleased him; and she must have been pleased by his remark that the episode's name, by a 'strange coincidence', was her own: Penelope, the weaver.* [1]

Paris, meantime, was the epicentre of Ulyssean activity. James Joyce had resolved that the book should be published on his birthday, a date still too early for the printers. But by the most frantic efforts they managed to put two copies on the night train to Paris on 1st February 1922 and some more a few days later. On 12th February, Harriet received an inscribed, deluxe, copy and found it was numbered '1'. She felt honoured indeed, she told Miss Beach, and added: 'What an immense volume the book has made! . . . I possess no other book on such beautiful paper. . . . Mr Joyce told me how your shop had been beseiged by clamorous buyers . . . when two copies, and no more, had arrived.† It must have been a most distracting state of affairs. . . .'[2]

Harriet then took a hand by selling in London copies of the 'cheap edition', at three guineas; but in mid-March, when she learnt that it was fully subscribed, she switched to the deluxe copies, at five and seven guineas. Three of these she at once sold secretly to the new manager of Bumpus, who was unable to order any further copies from Paris as his partner objected to having the book on the premises.[3] His objection was more complex than she imagined. She had understood—or misunderstood—Mr Pinker to say that only publishers' premises could be raided by policemen in search of obscene books, and that the booksellers, and she herself, ran no risk. Lighter in heart, as she walked from bookshop to bookshop, she was able to make up her mind what to do about James Joyce's need for a larger private income. She decided to settle on him a further £1,500.[4] The income would enable him to have holidays and rests—provided by a private 'Invalid Aid Association'!

Reviews began to appear just as she was trying to get up courage to announce the book to her family. Fortunately, the first, by Sisley Huddleston in the *Observer*, was highly appreciative: '. . . Mr Joyce is a man of genius. . . . Here is erudition transfigured by imagination

---

* This unwitting 'reference' to Harriet Weaver appears to be the only reference to her of any sort in James Joyce's works.

† Two copies of the cheap edition ordered by Harriet Weaver, one for herself and one for Dora Marsden, arrived a week later. Her own copy, which proved defective (sixteen pages were missing and sixteen duplicated) was promptly borrowed by Wyndham Lewis and could not be sent to be rectified until he returned it—in October.

32 The Joyce family in 1924

33 Harriet, photographed by Man Ray, in 1924

. . . [the] *monologue intérieur* is, I imagine . . . the vilest, according to ordinary standards, in all literature. And yet its very obscurity is somehow beautiful and wrings the soul to pity. . . .'⁵

The next review to appear was of a rather different order: 'an absurd article', in the *Sporting Times*, 'Otherwise known as the *Pink 'Un*—Largest Circulation of any Sporting Weekly in the World', a journal not likely to be seen by her family. When the cutting arrived, she went to the editorial offices for more copies. There she found that the front page had printed across it in big black capitals: SCANDAL OF JAMES JOYCE'S ULYSSES and that the article had been 'honoured with a large notice on a placard', with similar wording. She carried off some copies of this also, for Paris, glad that 'the wonderful thing was not lost to us all';⁶ though she realized that the article illustrated 'the tone' likely to be adopted in any prosecution of The Egoist Press edition:

. . . As the readers of the PINK 'UN know, I have dealt appreciatively with many unconventional books in these pages; but I have no stomach for 'Ulysses' . . . James Joyce is a writer of talent, but . . . he has ruled out all the elementary decencies of life and dwells appreciatively on things that sniggering louts of schoolboys guffaw about. . . .⁷

Sylvia Beach and James Joyce, who declared that the *Sporting Times*' reputation was worse than his own, were pleased with this left-handed publicity and later had themselves photographed sitting beneath the placard, pinned up on the wall at Shakespeare and Company, by then installed at 12 rue de l'Odéon.

Although there were few reviews at first, Harriet was inclined to discount the author's suspicion that the book was being boycotted and was amused when he wrote:

. . . One person who is supposed to be reviewing the book (and has read it all) and wants to be strictly accurate, asks me whether the Christian name of Mrs Bloom is Milly or Molly. Another American 'critic' who wanted to interview me (I declined) told me he had read the book with great interest but that he could not understand why Bloom came into it. I explained to him why and he [was] surprised and disappointed for he thought Stephen was *Ulysses*. He had heard some talk of Penelope and asked me who she was. This also I told him but did not convince him entirely because he said rather doubtfully 'But is Penelope a really Irish name?' . . .[8]

Dora asked, 'What has happened to Ulysses? Has the storm burst or is the author to be destroyed by silence?'[9] She had seen no reviews and, indeed, was not reading anything outside her own subject. She was, however, extending her 'analogical' arguments drawn from the exact sciences and asked Harriet to send her books and papers on 'the Generation of Life . . . the relation of the atomic weights of the chemical elements to the complexity of their atomic structure' and 'any really recent matter on the structure of the atom'.[10] Because of some criticism from Harriet that she had 'evaded & burked' 'the question of stimulus', she had recently 'revised the whole scheme of exposition' to give emphasis to 'the nature of life & sensation' but hoped to have the first of her volumes ready by the summer and the second, to include the 'Nature of Mind', by October.[11] She was in buoyant mood.

When Harriet arrived for a fortnight's visit in April, however, she found these hopes had been abandoned and she stayed on beyond the fortnight because she was needed—by Mrs Marsden, hampered by arthritis, for practical help, and by Dora for intellectual support and emotional solace.

The prime purpose of Harriet's visit was to put to Dora and her mother a plan for giving them both a little more space and comfort and for providing accommodation for herself when she visited them. This was the way in which she had rounded her 'storm cape': her solitary struggle had led her to the conclusion that she must stand by Dora while she was still writing her book. The Marsdens needed a permanent home and, in spite of the hard winters, Glencoin had become their home. Harriet's solution was for the Marsdens to take over, permanently, two adjacent cottages at Seldom Seen and to rent a third for herself when she came on a visit. Dora was pleased with the proposal and decided to knock down a wall in one cottage so that the sitting-room would have two windows, one looking up and the other down the hillside and there would be more room for her books. There was only one flaw: Dora wanted her friend to stay all the year round. Harriet, however, held to her decision. She could not and would not leave London. But before returning south she promised to pay a much longer visit later in the year.

By the time she returned to London, the Egoist *Exiles* and *Dubliners* had been delivered by the binders and needed her attention.* Better still, it looked as though she would soon be able to publish *Ulysses*. Another outstanding review, this time by Middleton Murry, could not fail, she felt, to influence opinion for the better. '. . . the work of an intensely serious man . . . indisputably the mind of an artist, abnormally sensitive to the secret individuality of emotions and things . . .' he had written, in a long article in *The Nation and Athenaeum*.[12] And Miss Beach's edition, she had just heard from her, was almost, though not quite, fully subscribed.[13] It was already settled that the Egoist edition was to be printed from plates made from the type for the Paris edition and James Joyce planned to be in London at the end of May to discuss details—though, as usual, he was agreeable to anything she might propose. The only immediate trouble was the text. Darentiere, the printer, had done an heroic job but it was still riddled with misprints—'an average of one to half a dozen typographical errors per page', as Sylvia Beach put it. [14] Harriet had made a list of those she had noticed and was now asked by James Joyce 'to put them in' and so leave him 'free for the correction of the text only'. He wanted to make some changes and additions, though the prospects of getting Darentiere to co-operate were, according to him, poor: 'Heartrending telegrams mean nothing to him. He will reply (about some totally different matter) three days later and in conclusion beg you to deign to accept the assurance of his most perfect consideration'.[15]

Harriet was looking forward intensely to meeting James Joyce and freed herself from as much work as possible before he came. A review of the year's publishing showed that she had put in nearly £450, but some of her donations were intended as loans and were paid back later on. These loans were mainly needed by the Joyce account—for the copyrights, moulds and binding of *Dubliners*, for printing *Exiles*, and for sheets and binding of the third edition of *A Portrait*—but the repayments to Harriet were made out of the main account, to which she had given rather more than necessary. She was certainly succeeding in her aim of giving all she could, directly or indirectly, to James Joyce.

Her work on the accounts was interrupted by news from Paris that James Joyce had a severe eye attack in his 'good' eye—and would be prevented from coming to London for some time. The news was a

* For economy, Harriet Weaver imported sheets from Ben Huebsch for this edition of *Dubliners*. (To John J. Slocum, 25th February 1947)

shock as well as a disappointment. But when Sylvia Beach's running reports implied that the iritis was getting no worse, Harriet decided that he was probably well enough to be sent, through her, the latest press cuttings about *Ulysses*, including a diatribe in the *Sunday Express* by its editor James Douglas. 'What will he say and do when it is published in England?' Harriet asked.[16] 'I took them at once to Mr Joyce,' Miss Beach replied, 'and read them to him. . . . He gets very much depressed and bored lying in bed and Douglas' article quite made him forget the pain in his eyes for the moment but he seems to be somewhat too excited at present. I think it is good for him to have something to think of that takes him out of himself however. The doctor says that his eyes are better. . . .'[17]

Harriet was much relieved. But three days later, before lunch on Friday, 9th June, and two minutes before she left the Egoist office in Robert Street for the day,* she was handed a telegram:

consultation this morning doctors unexpectedly advise operation other eye Joyce reluctant as this means closure his career please telephone Sydney Schiff 18 Cambridge Square Hyde Park W 2 whom I am wiring Sylvia Beach.[18]

Harriet was thunderstruck. She had understood that the operation in Zurich had been successful. Now it seemed that it had not and 'the other eye', the left eye, was threatened. She at once telephoned Sydney Schiff. He had met James Joyce several times in Paris and had taken a kindly interest in his difficulties. But he was puzzled by the telegram he had had. It ended:

is it possible to send doctor Thompson immediately to Paris wire urgent reply every minute important.[19]

He knew nothing of this specialist—and neither did Harriet.† However, they got on to his consulting rooms in Harley Street and, on learning—hardly to their surprise—that he could not see them at once, they sent a joint wire to Miss Beach. They 'strongly advised immediately consulting and relying on the best Paris opinion, as

* Harriet Weaver worked at the office only in the mornings.

† George Thompson, MB, CM, FRCS England, a Scot trained at the universities of Edinburgh and Paris and at the London Hospital, was an ophthalmic surgeon of standing.

English doctors were always reluctant to interfere in such cases'.[20] Then Mr Thompson (as he should be called, as an ophthalmic surgeon) said he could see them after lunch. Harriet hastily scribbled down some notes 'Mr Joyce's illnesses as known to me 1922' and took them with her to Harley Street. Mr Thompson agreed to fly to Paris at the weekend and to operate, if necessary. But at nine o'clock next morning Harriet had another wire reporting that their advice had been taken and that another leading Paris specialist, in fact Sylvia Beach's own American oculist, Dr Louis Borsch, had been brought in and had decided to postpone operating for the moment.[21] Harriet took the telegram to Mr Thompson and by half-past ten had relayed his advice to Sylvia Beach by airmail, and the gist by telegram. He did not operate when the eye was greatly congested and inflamed but tried to reduce the congestion by leeching and by purgatives. Bad teeth could start an attack of iritis.

She had to wait until the Tuesday for more news, when a long airmail letter, written on the Sunday, arrived. The wait had been very trying. Dr Borsch, it appeared, had decided on treatment very much like that advised by Mr Thompson and Mr Joyce seemed to be suffering a little less. If an operation was avoided, he would like to go to London 'to consult the best specialist there'. But his former specialist, Dr Morax, thought the operation inevitable. Miss Beach ended:

This is a long letter dear Miss Weaver and with my ignorance of these technical things I do not succeed in making them very clear. But Mr Joyce is so anxious for you to know all about this matter. He is deeply grateful for all you have done and regrets all the trouble he has been putting you to. He wishes to thank Mr Schiff for his kindness also. These have been very anxious days and it [is] terrible to see Mr Joyce's despair at the thought that he is threatened with the loss of his eyesight and of how much depends [on] the outcome of all this.[22]

Harriet wrote to Kearsley, her doctor brother, whose judgment she trusted, to find out about Mr Thompson's reputation and to ask for the names of other leading London eye specialists; and, after showing Sylvia Beach's letter to Sydney Schiff, relayed to her his suggestion that 'it would be well for Mr Joyce to consult a good doctor when he comes to London as general health appears to have much to do with causing these eye attacks'.[23] Two days later, she wrote again to Sylvia Beach to report her brother's answers and went on:

Mr Schiff says he thinks Mr Joyce's mode of life in Paris very unhealthy; he thinks he ought to leave Paris for good and live in some quieter and healthier place following a strict regime—in order that the danger of the recurrence of these attacks might be reduced to a minimum. But I gather that Mr Joyce does not wish to leave. . . .[24]

Then another telegram arrived:

continued slight progress doctor still optimistic Ulysees [sic] sold out.[25]

And a fortnight later Sylvia Beach reported that Mr Joyce was really beginning to recover: 'he was feeling so much better yesterday when I called to see him and was talking cheerfully and eating 2 mutton chops.'[26]

The crisis was over but it affected Harriet deeply and lastingly. Dread of James Joyce going blind was now always with her.

A more immediate consequence of the crisis was that Sylvia Beach confided some of her other worries. She agreed to a large extent with Sydney Schiff: the Joyce family should live in a place where they had 'plenty of room to spread out' and where he could have perfect quiet for his work—he was 'such a terribly nervous, sensitive man'.[27] 'I think that plenty of sleep, food, work and outdoor exercise and perhaps to see one's family as little as possible is the only way to be healthy,' she wrote.[28] Yet for months he had been sharing a noisy room in a maison meublée with his wife and daughter and had been obliged to go out for all meals. He insisted, however, on remaining in the Odéon quarter where she saw no possibility of finding other accommodation. Perhaps London would be less difficult? Mr Schiff thought so. And—a problem even more delicate—Mr Joyce was so entirely absorbed in his work that he was unable to consider the needs of his family. What did Miss Weaver, 'Mr Joyce's best friend', consider should be done?[29]

Harriet had to explain that she was 'at a complete loss as to a solution'; and could 'only worry to no purpose'.[30] Sylvia Beach, flurried, said it was 'very dreadful' of her to have written.[31] But Harriet reassured her. 'I have wished not to intrude in Mr Joyce's private affairs but it seems necessary to do so now.'[32]

This conclusion marks a turning point of profound significance in her relations with James Joyce. But, in the meantime, she could share in Sylvia Beach's jubilation over the price, £22, paid for the last three copies of *Ulysses* sold by the Egoist office; and could exchange views with her on the latest press notices. As the tension eased, she began to think once more about her own edition.

Miss Beach suggested that Harriet should make her own arrangements directly with the printer, Maurice Darentiere, and advised her to write in English (which he knew well) as he was apt to be 'evasive and slippery' in French. He still had the 'empreintes'—impressions—of her own edition, and she assumed that they would be used by The Egoist Press.[33] Harriet, whose first concern was to restore Mr Joyce's own text, was interested above all in discussing 'the question of corrections'.[34] But she was not yet ready to open the discussion, for a reason she did not reveal.

She was being pressed by Dora, whose militant spirit had been roused by the attacks on the book, to bring out, quickly, an 'ordinary' edition of *Ulysses*. This proposal raised doubts in Harriet's mind about whether she correctly understood the law governing the seizure of books. Could she safely assume that the Egoist office would be the only place where copies could be seized? And would it be a protection, if a prosecution was brought, to distribute the stock among agents with their own premises? When she got back to London in May, she asked the Egoist's solicitor (now Mr Arnold Carter) and he told her it was not so: a prosecuted book could be seized from any premises whatever (including any shop) where it was kept for sale or distribution. But a private edition would be less vulnerable to police action because it would show that the publisher's intent was to make a limited distribution only. On learning all this, she suggested to Dora a private edition—subject to Mr Joyce's approval—in order to lessen the risk of prosecution, with possible heavy financial loss.[35]

The risk of prosecution had, now, in Harriet's view, become much greater since the publication of Mr Douglas' article. He denounced *Ulysses* as 'the most infamously obscene book' in all literature; and he denounced it as blasphemous. 'Mr Joyce is a rebel against the social morality of Europe'; and a choice must be made between 'the devil's disciples and the disciples of God'. This was 'a battle that must be fought to a clean finish . . .'. And so on, and so on, column inch after column inch.[36] Harriet was quite sure that Mr Douglas would feel bound to have an ordinary edition sent to the police.

Dora, however, dismissed out of hand Harriet's case for a private edition. If 'the unpleasant-minded old ladies who do the reviewing in respectable journals' and who were 'doing themselves well in the way of imagining unsavoury stinks' were going to take a firm line, the two of them would have to take one still firmer and force these people to make them into martyrs. As a first step, would Harriet draft a letter to H. G. Wells, seeking his support?[37]

Harriet would not. But Dora was adamant. If the next edition had to be a private one, then Shakespeare and Company were well set to bring it out and should do so. 'All *we* can add to what Miss Beach has already done is to sponsor the claim that *Ulysses* is the kind of book which not only ought to be written but ought to be pressed upon the public for perusal. That is what the difference between a public & a private edition amounts to. . . .'[38]

Harriet's reply was forthright and factual. The machinery for publishing a private edition was now no more in existence in Paris than it was in London: Miss Beach had made special arrangements for *one* edition and one only; and an English edition to follow Miss Beach's had already been announced by The Egoist Press.[39] But Dora's stonewalling turned her thoughts once more to America.

Was there now perhaps some slight chance of *Ulysses* appearing without excisions in the United States? One or two publishers besides Mr Huebsch had shown some interest. And a Mr Samuel Roth, of whom she knew nothing except that he said he was editor of *Two Worlds* (or prospective editor, for she gathered no issue had yet appeared) had written making an offer. He would publish *Ulysses* entire—in a single issue, together with a play, a short story, verse and reviews—and would pay the author. How this issue was to be produced was not clear, unless the print was 'the size of a needle's head'; nor 'how any financial results were to accrue at the price of a dollar and a half'.[40] Still, even though this proposition was itself unpromising, it did suggest that, somewhere in the States, a publisher might be found. John Quinn, however, to whom Harriet now appealed, was emphatically of the opinion that there was not the slightest hope of finding one.[41]

At this point, Dora announced an ambitious plan to come to London, when she could free herself from her work, to mount a campaign to defend a public edition and, at the next inevitable stage, to vindicate it in court. Harriet freely confessed that, if their edition were a public one, this new proposal would be 'a very great relief'. Her 'feeling of nervousness' or, more likely, 'cowardice' about a public edition arose partly from her consciousness that, with Dora up in the north and absorbed in her book, she herself would have 'the whole affair of the prosecution' on her 'own unaided hands', a prospect from which she shrank. But with Dora in London, 'the chances of a favourable verdict would be immensely increased'.[42]

Harriet was, however, still not altogether happy: for one thing, it was difficult to know when Dora could free herself. She turned for help, this time, to Miss Beach. Would it be 'possible and convenient' for her to bring out another edition of her own? Or would Mr Joyce be content to wait till the new year?[43]

Sylvia Beach apparently felt that she would rather answer verbally. At any rate, she sent a message about her 'position' through her assistant, Myrsine Moschos, who visited London early in August. In the light of subsequent events, it must be assumed that she told Harriet that James Joyce was anxious to press on but that she herself was disinclined to undertake the heavy task of another edition.*

While Harriet was trying to brace herself to face the fact that a second edition of *Ulysses*, whether private or public, would have to be published, if it were published at all, by The Egoist Press, James Joyce announced his imminent arrival in London. Though he was not yet cured—the dressing of his eye every morning still took him an hour—his oculist had agreed to his having a holiday on the south coast. On 17th August, he and his wife arrived at the Euston Hotel, en route for the coast.

The meeting long awaited by Harriet had come at last. And her expectations were more than fulfilled. Mr Joyce—Stephen Dedalus now a grown man—had charm, wit, great dignity and an old-world manner a little like her father's. His soft voice, very Irish, his slow, persuasive way of talking, were haunting; and an unexpected waywardness, thought it hinted at another side to his character, was engaging.

James Joyce certainly wanted to impress her favourably and he certainly succeeded—handsomely. And the sudden relapse that set

---

* Some thirty-five years later, Sylvia Beach recalled in her autobiography being 'somewhat surprised at this precipitate second [first Egoist] edition'. (*Shakespeare and Company*, p. 104) But her correspondence with Harriet Weaver during the summer of 1922 must in fact have prepared her for it.

in almost immediately after his arrival only deepened the impression he had made: it enabled her to see with her own eyes the wretchedness of his affliction and his patience and good humour under it.

The journey or the weather, or both, affected him so badly that he had an attack of conjunctivitis. Most days he spent contemplating, with half an eye, the brass knobs of his hotel bed;[44] and consulting specialists. As Mr Thompson and other oculists Harriet had shortlisted, with Kearsley's help, were all away on holiday, she was soon caught up in shortlisting new ones, and then in accompanying Mr Joyce to appointments, to which he chose always to go by taxi, never by bus. He tipped the drivers lavishly, she noticed.* [45] The first oculist consulted wanted to operate at once but two others advised against an operation and this advice was taken.† Getting to the south coast was now out of the question. James Joyce wrote the holiday off as 'a complete fiasco'.[46]

He and his wife did, however, get as far as Harriet's flat and it was there, perhaps, when she had settled him in the armchair with its back to the windows, that she was able to tell him the latest development in her negotiations about an Egoist edition of *Ulysses*: Miss Marsden, still determined on a public or ordinary edition, had just let her know that it would be some time before she could free herself from her work to come to London to launch the book, and it could not be published until the following April at the earliest.[47]

James Joyce's despair must have gone to her heart. He had been depressed enough at her news that booksellers were currently asking up to £50 for a second-hand copy of Miss Beach's edition.[48] He must have been appalled beyond measure at the thought of waiting for eight months, and very likely more, before a second edition was out.

Harriet made up her mind to make one more attempt to persuade Dora to agree to a private edition. And, this time, she succeeded. Within a week, she had worked out a plan that would enable the book to be published immediately and would also, she hoped, reduce to a minimum the risks of police action.

---

* James Joyce told his aunt Josephine Murray that he spent 'about £200' during his stay in London—that is, in thirty-three days. (*Letters* I, 194)

† One oculist was a Mr James, another was a Mr Tibbles, who applied leeches to reduce the conjunctivitis. The name amused James Joyce because of the then well-known 'Tibbles' Vi Cocoa'. (To Richard Ellmann, 15th November 1953) An eminent dentist (Mr Cyril Henry) was also consulted and insisted on an X-ray. (To Sylvia Beach, 7th September 1922)

She asked John Rodker, now living in London and running a small publishing venture for limited editions, whether he would act as agent to The Egoist Press, working from Paris, and whether he would go over there the moment detailed plans had been laid. He agreed. A day or two later, he had borrowed an office from a friend in Paris; and arranged to go there the next weekend and on to Dijon to see the printer about a contract. It was to be for a uniform edition of two thousand copies at £2 2s. 0d. each.[49]

James Joyce, consulted at every stage, may have recommended bringing in John Rodker.* He certainly suggested inserting press notices of *Ulysses* in every copy of the Egoist edition and Harriet was already going through them and making a selection when she wrote to Miss Beach to bring her up-to-date. By then, James Joyce was, not surprisingly, 'better in himself';[50] and before he and his wife returned to Paris, on 18th September, there was time to talk of subjects other than *Ulysses* and dental decay and glaucoma. Harriet ventured to ask him what he would write next. 'I think,' he replied, 'that I will write a history of the world.'

To commiserate with him on his wretched 'holiday', she sent him a couplet based on an old nursery rhyme:

> *The king of France, when he laid down his pen,*
> *Crossed the sea—and crossed it back again.*

However reluctant she had been to 'intrude' in his 'private affairs', there was now no going back: James Joyce's relapse had drawn her in, irretrievably. And, unhappily, Harriet's capacity for mothering was matched by his dislike of being mothered—as she might have guessed from his books.

Meanwhile, work on The Egoist Press *Ulysses* claimed her. The decision to get it out as soon as possible meant, to her regret, that no misprints, not even the worst, could be corrected. A list of errata was the most that could be managed. The decision meant also that someone had to be found at once to go over with John Rodker to get off the copies when they arrived from Dijon, while he concentrated on office work.

Harriet was delighted when Iris Barry agreed to go.† Her work as

---

* John Rodker had made a proposal, in some respects similar to the current one, when he first met James Joyce in Paris two years before. See page 173.

† As Harriet Weaver did not want the *Ulysses* account to incur extra expense, the

a secretary in a firm in Bond Street had just come to an end, because the firm had gone out of business. She was very glad of the Paris job and had liked John Rodker ever since she had first met him during the war, when he had just been released from prison as a conscientious objector and had joined the supper parties in Soho and the readings by candlelight at W. B. Yeats' flat.[51]

John Rodker had undertaken to be responsible for all dealings with the printer, for holding the bulk stocks, for supplying the Egoist office and Miss Beach, and for handling all other orders. For this work, he was given a 'commission' of £250 and was entitled to charge his expenses—travel, postage, freight—to The Egoist Press.

The room put at his disposal was in his friend's bookshop, A La Librarie Six, in the Avenue de Lowendal, between the Invalides and the Ecole Militaire. Here he would do the office work. He hired a room on the ground floor of the old Hôtel de Verneuil, over a mile away, behind the Quai Voltaire, in which Iris Barry would do her work of packing and despatching the copies.[52] Then he had printed, in a stylish manner, a slip announcing the edition, and asking that remittances accompany orders. He gave his Avenue de Lowendal address, but, perhaps because of the rush, omitted to mention that the new edition was being undertaken by The Egoist Press. This was an unfortunate omission, as Miss Beach and others were complaining that the position had not been made clear. It was, however, undoubtedly made in error and not by intention. John Rodker, as Iris Barry saw, considered himself, and was, 'a devoted agent' of Miss Weaver.[53]

Sylvia Beach, on hearing of Harriet's decision to commission him, had offered to be 'Paris agent', a proposal welcomed by them both.[54] The arrangement was, on the face of it, very suitable. Although Sylvia Beach had not wanted to bring out a second edition—*Ulysses* had kept her away from her bookshop work and, to her distress, had by this time been included in catalogues of erotica—she still felt that it was in a sense *her* book. Harriet was glad to meet her wish to be formally associated with the Egoist Press edition and, as she made clear, saw no reason why she and her agent-in-charge with a voice in policy-making, John Rodker, should not work out between themselves the details of their collaboration.[55] But Sylvia Beach then

arrangement was a personal one, between friends. Iris Barry's salary is not shown in the Egoist books, and Harriet Weaver evidently felt that she preferred to pay it herself.

repudiated her own suggestion, put off, perhaps, by the gossip in literary circles in Paris about the oddity of the arrangements for the edition.*

John Rodker, meantime, had brought things on so rapidly that he was able to fix a day, Thursday, 12th October 1922, for the delivery of copies to the Hôtel de Verneuil. He and Iris Barry would cross over to Paris on the preceding Sunday or Monday.[56] By the beginning of October also, Harriet had had printed four thousand copies of her leaflet of reviews, four closely-printed pages on honey-coloured paper. The thirty-four extracts, headed by Valery Larbaud in *La Nouvelle Revue Française*, Ezra Pound in the *Mercure de France*, Arnold Bennett in *The Outlook* and Middleton Murry in *The Nation*, she had selected and marshalled in accordance with James Joyce's wishes.†

Maurice Darentiere, firmly handled by John Rodker, delivered the copies on time—two thousand numbered copies printed on white laid paper for the edition proper; and a hundred unnumbered copies.‡ The title page bore the unusual legend: *Published for The Egoist Press,*

* There was, in any case, one hard fact in the way of Harriet Weaver's willingness to give Sylvia Beach a satisfying part in promoting the edition and, at the same time, a useful share of the profits. The main market was to the trade, but the main profits depended on sales at the full price to private customers.

† In the shaping of one review, Harriet Weaver had had a hand. In the summer of 1922, she asked Ford Madox Hueffer whether he would write an article on *Ulysses* for an English paper (not knowing then that he had already written on it for *The Yale Review*). He told her he was afraid that English papers would boycott him as much as they would Mr Joyce—he had in fact given up writing for them and was confining himself to America. But he approached *The English Review* and when his offer was accepted, she put in a plea for composure regarding the book. He met James Joyce in Paris a few weeks later, and 'apologised in a way for his article' which he explained, was written at Miss Weaver's dictation. 'I am glad you have taken to writing the favourable criticisms,' James Joyce wrote to her. Harriet Weaver had, indeed, gone one farther: she had put an extract from the review in her leaflet before the review was published—in the issue for December 1922. The extract reads:

One feels admiration that is almost reverence for the incredible labours of this incredible genius. . . . No writer after today will be able to neglect *Ulysses* . . . an 'adult', a European work . . . austere and composed . . . a book of profound knowledge and of profound renderings of humanity. (To Sylvia Beach, 7th July 1922; from James Joyce, 25th November 1922)

‡ The *Ulysses* accounts kept by Harriet Weaver give a total of 2,600 copies for both Egoist editions; and references in letters establish that the hundred unnumbered copies were printed for the first Egoist edition. See, for example, her letter to Sylvia Beach of 5th November 1922.

London by John Rodker, Paris 1922. The next page bore the message: 'The publishers apologize for typographical errors a list of which is appended'. This list, compiled by Harriet, of some two hundred *Errata*, was laid in. At the Hôtel de Verneuil, Iris Barry, surrounded by 'piles of blue Ulysses, brown paper, labels, string', set to work at the big table, almost the only piece of furniture in the room, wrapping up the copies 'one by one and trundling them in small lots to the Post Office'.[57]

Orders came rushing in and, four days later, the edition had been subscribed. Harriet was sorry she had not decided on a larger one but was greatly relieved that it was going so quickly.[58] She sent a telegram to Mr Joyce, recuperating at Nice, and followed it up with a happy letter and an advance of £120.

This royalty was the first she charged to the *Ulysses* account. Although her own sales in London had started slowly, and provided only a meagre credit balance, she could rely on money coming in from Paris; and she must have felt that the successful start should be celebrated with the author in a practical way. He thanked her briefly. Bad weather had pursued him to the south and rain and windstorms had affected his eyes. His letter, dictated to his daughter, was signed 'James Job Joyce'.

Towards the end of October, John Rodker crossed over to London for discussions with Harriet. Getting copies into the United States was, as she realized, the only really difficult problem: Miss Beach, indeed, had had to smuggle some in from Canada. John Rodker, she learned to her amusement, had found a first mate of an American ship willing to smuggle through a large number of copies; and he hoped the American bookshops would receive theirs if a scheme he had concocted with the wholesale booksellers, William Jackson, worked out. They had offices in the same place as himself—Tooks Court—and had agreed to strip the copies into sections and to conceal each section inside a newspaper to be sent as such in the ordinary way as second class mail—the *Manchester Guardian*, perhaps, or the *Morning Post*, or *The Times*. The sections would be rebound on arrival. He believed this scheme would be pulled off.* But he thought the outlook for individual orders which could not be smuggled was

---

* In 1954, John Rodker gave his recollections of the sale of the first Egoist edition of *Ulysses* to Richard Ellmann. (Ellmann, p. 521, footnote) He did so, however, more than thirty years after the event and many years after his own papers were lost in an aerial bombardment of Paris in the Second World War. It is difficult to reconcile

not bright. The first lot to go off from the Hôtel Verneuil, not more than a hundred, had got through; but the chances of those bringing up the rear slipping through the defences of the United States Post Office were dim. The risk, in his view, was so large that he could not recommend accepting all the American orders, though, if accepted, the whole edition would be disposed of.

Harriet trusted his judgment and agreed to hold over a number for disposal elsewhere. '. . . you had better send on immediately to Miss Barry any inquiries from bookshops', she suggested to Miss Beach, after telling her of the decision, 'as you want to keep your own copies for selling at full price. I can sympathize with enterprises run on a very small margin such being not unknown to me! . . .'[59]

Apart from these difficulties about American orders, everything had worked out very well. Harriet must have underwritten the printing bill herself but orders, with remittances, had come in so fast that John Rodker was able to pay the printer out of the proceeds and had also started a series of payments to The Egoist Press. He handed over £250 when he came for the discussions with Harriet and two days later she passed on the whole sum to James Joyce, as an advance on royalties. The pound had strengthened meanwhile, and he was pleased to see that she had played the exchange to his advantage.[60]

Except for an order for twenty-five copies, which she asked John Rodker to supply direct, Harriet herself dealt with the London orders. She had her stock sent over to a mailing agency and drew on it as the orders came in so as to have only a few copies at the office. James Joyce thought she ought not to keep any there. Harriet did not agree but lessened the risk by holding some at her flat, hidden away in her capacious Victorian wardrobe. 'Shops used to send for the book discreetly' and, to avoid posting them, she often delivered copies herself, and had seen them 'put away out of sight under the counter with some haste!'[61]

In the eighteen months during which Harriet sold copies, the possibility of a police raid was always present.* Her perceptive sister-

the figures he recalls (eight hundred taken by Jacksons and 'hundreds' by the first mate) with other known figures of sales and they have, therefore, not been quoted. His remark, as recorded, that Jacksons cut their copies 'into pieces and sent them over to America wrapped in newspaper' for rebinding there has been interpreted as given above. The stripping of the books into sections would have been a simple operation to a bookbinder—and there was one at Tooks Court.

* A 'solitary detective' was observed by Harriet Weaver keeping watch—perhaps

in-law Muriel Weaver detected in her some nervous strain. But Harriet may also have felt grateful for an opportunity to put her courage to the test.

There never was a raid, and another danger she feared—a family quarrel over *Ulysses*—also failed to materialize. Her brothers and sisters and sisters-in-law and brother-in-law had realized by this time what sort of a book it was—or what sort of a book they would undoubtedly find it. But they were not going to quarrel with her over it. Indeed, one or two of them, Campbell Hone and Alfred certainly, later went so far as to read it or some of it. They remained astonished that Harriet should seriously consider it literature and not disgusting rubbish; and even decades later Campbell Hone wrung his hands and exclaimed: 'How could she? How could she? An enigma! An enigma!'[62] It was not until the next generation had grown up that Harriet was able to discuss Mr Joyce's works with members of her family.

Dora's viewpoint, too, though very different from the family's, was also very different from Harriet's. She was much more interested in fighting for *Ulysses* than in reading it; and, when Harriet did not take her advice to invite a public outcry, longed only to get back to her work, from which 'frequent inundations of relatives' had also distracted her. Once her house-move to the double cottage was over, however, she took 'stern measures to ensure peace and quiet'.[63] But in the peace and quiet she came to the conclusion that what she had written was not entirely to her liking and she began 'to revise from the beginning'. Harriet must have felt the drafting would never be over; but Dora still hoped to publish, within the foreseeable future, if she omitted the volume on *Mind* and issued the two on *The Nature of the Philosophic Enquiry* and *The Nature of Life*. She was not really happy about this, however, as the 'three make a whole'.[64]

She was happier putting the finishing touches to 4 and 5 Seldom Seen. Her long and narrow sitting-room was rather dark and needed colour. Could Harriet bring with her, on her coming journey north, four candle shades, one lamp shade and about four yards of scarlet drill for window blinds, among other 'frivolous merchandise'? And 'if the lampshade could have a fringe: it would be very nice. At present, the lamp is wearing the fringe from my jumper!'[65]

James Joyce, meanwhile, had been peppering Harriet with ideas for

outside her office—a few weeks after the book came out. (From James Joyce, 8th November 1922) publicizing *Ulysses*. He wanted a revision of the Extracts from Press Notices, long before her stock was exhausted. Extracts from about a dozen of the very latest reviews, some full of praise, some the reverse, must be added, and more emphasis given to the French reviews: 'the longrange gun from Paris' was the most effective.[66] Harriet was quite ready to act on this suggestion, if only because it amused her to learn what James Joyce wanted in it, and why.

After much correspondence, a thousand copies, on pale pink paper, were issued early in December with extracts from forty-seven periodicals: twenty English, thirteen American, nine French, two Italian, two Irish and one Scottish. Valery Larbaud headed the new list, as he did the first, but was now followed by Edmond Jaloux, who had spoken of the book as 'au-dessus de tout éloge'.* Ezra Pound's article in the *Mercure de France* now stood third. These were followed by the heavy English artillery, led by Arnold Bennett, and including, at James Joyce's express wish, the Irish critic, Shane Leslie. In an article in *The Quarterly*, which Harriet thought 'unintentionally' very useful,[67] he thundered against *Ulysses* as 'an assault upon Divine Decency as well as on human intelligence'; and reported that it had been received in Dublin with 'jocular contempt'—a report contradicted later in the list of extracts by another Irishman who proclaimed that it had been 'received with enthusiasm'.†[68] As James Joyce impressed on Harriet, 'all is fair in literature and war'.[69]

Although a number of critics and reviewers had already been sent, or had got hold of, a copy of the first edition, Harriet had decided that, without duplicating anything done by Miss Beach, she might need up to a hundred complimentary copies; and the unnumbered copies were printed for this purpose. Later, she sold some of them, after her other stock had run out; but she probably used most of them as free copies for the press and for writers for whose help she or James Joyce was grateful. H. G. Wells, for his work in helping to launch *A Portrait* and Arnold Bennett and Middleton Murry, whose articles on *Ulysses* were the most distinguished of the English reviews, and Iris Barry, for her labours at the Hôtel de Verneuil, were among those who received a free copy.‡ And at the author's request, Professor

---

* Edmond Jaloux, a French author and critic of distinction, later wrote on *Ulysses* in the *Revue de France*.

† The writer of this article was W. K. Magee—'John Eglinton', who had been librarian of the National Library of Ireland and had known James Joyce in his student days.

‡ The first numbered copy, inscribed by the author, went to Sylvia Beach.

George Saintsbury was among those to receive a press copy. 'I am old-fashioned enough to admire him,' James Joyce told her, 'though he may not return the compliment. He is however quite capable of flinging the tome back through your window, especially if the 1922 vintage has not matured to his liking.'* [70] The Professor refrained from windowbreaking but refused to review the book or to comment on it privately. The *Times Literary Supplement* also refused a review, though T. S. Eliot, at Harriet's instance, offered to write it. Little more remained to be done about reviews—except when James Joyce himself came up with some new proposal.

He had satisfied himself, before he left London, that Harriet was prepared to follow up her first edition with a second, as soon as it was called for; and had written, while he was working on the *Errata* list: 'The lines cancelled in red pencil . . . are to stand. They are not misprints, but beauties of my style hitherto undreamt of. The red cross at the top is not a signal to posterity to cease fire. It means that the paging is wrong. . . .† A revised proof should be sent to you which you could keep so that as soon as the second edition is out the printers could start to alter the plates for a third edition. . . .'[71] † He was already eager to press on with this 'third' edition and on his way south broke his journey at Dijon and got an estimate for corrections from Maurice Darentiere, 'about 1 franc per "opération" (agreeable word) that is, change of letter or line'.[72] The work could begin at once, if Harriet approved. At Nice, he started going through the text, making his 'additions' in a child's blue exercise book.[73] When he had reached page 258, he sent the cahier to her for checking and forwarding to Dijon.‡ [74]

Harriet checked the list, found a few slips—mostly references to pages or lines—and typed it out. But the corrections for pages 259 to 735 did not follow because of more eye trouble; and her plan to publish a second Egoist edition of *Ulysses*, with a fully revised text, foundered.

There was, however, much else to give her mind to. James Joyce, to her disappointment, as she had hoped he would winter in Nice, returned to Paris in mid-November. He unburdened himself about

---

* Professor George Saintsbury, the distinguished literary scholar, was also famous for his *Cellar Book*.

† Harriet Weaver's ellipses.

‡ James Joyce, in his accompanying letter, dictated to Lucia, speaks of having reached page 290.

the situation there—in a sixteen-hundred-word letter. Miss Beach, it appeared, was still in a state of distress at some of the reactions to *Ulysses* and in a huff because she felt she had been kept in the dark about the second and the proposed third edition. James Joyce gave it as his opinion that her criticism on this score was directed mainly at John Rodker and he thought this unfair. 'Mr Rodker . . . I fancy, has enough to do at present putting the King beaver off the track and ought not to be troubled.'* And as for himself, he had told Miss Beach, he 'knew very little at first hand' as his only correspondence with John Rodker had been about a parcel of collars; and with Harriet about royalties.[75] This defence of himself, as Harriet cannot have failed to notice, was hardly based on the facts—at least as far as they concerned herself. But she probably guessed that Sylvia Beach's criticism was aimed mainly at James Joyce: it was from him that she would have expected and wanted to hear everything. And she guessed perhaps that James Joyce guessed this too. In the previous few weeks he had, in fact, given Sylvia Beach almost no news at all.

Miss Beach had also written to him, in strong terms, of a 'boycott' by booksellers and bibliophiles who, she said, complained that the Egoist edition had been got up to look like the first, thus, according to them, turning hers into a 'dishonourable fraud'; and they threatened to bring her up before a French court. This complaint had no real foundation, as James Joyce was able to demonstrate and as Harriet must have known. The Egoist edition differed in size and weight from the Paris edition and proclaimed itself the second edition in two places. Nor was there any sign of an angry attitude towards it among booksellers, he reported, after sending out his son with two young friends to make 'oblique enquiries'.† Nevertheless, he was thoroughly upset:

* A King beaver, according to James Joyce, is what the English called an Irish constabularyman with red whiskers riding a red bicycle. He was evidently privy to John Rodker's schemes for smuggling copies of *Ulysses* to their purchasers.

† Though nothing came of Sylvia Beach's reported threat by Paris booksellers to sue her, she seems to have felt, to the end of her days, that the Egoist edition did transgress the rules and place her own edition in jeopardy. See *Shakespeare and Company*, p. 105. But the reasons she gives there for the transgression are first, the appearance of this Egoist edition 'a few months after the first', and second 'that the booksellers had not been given enough time to get rid of their stock of the original limited edition before another one was announced'. Neither is relevant to the question of alleged 'fraud'.

For many reasons, my own health and peace, the decorum of correspondence, even for the sake of the writers themselves I wish such
letters as the one I received were not written. They neither provoke
the rupture which they probably do not intend and which I certainly
would do everything to avoid in the case of those who have befriended me in time of trouble nor do they evoke any new element
into the case since you cannot get a possibly non-existent periwinkle
out of his shell with a pin which has no point on it. Possibly the fault
is partly mine. I, my eye, my needs and my troublesome book are
always there. There is no feast or celebration or meeting of shareholders but at the fatal hour I appear at the door in dubious habili-
ments, with impedimenta of baggage, a mute expectant family, a
patch over one eye howling dismally for aid.[76]

Harriet's dislike of storms, whether meteorological or personal,
dictated her reaction to this outbreak. She declined to be drawn
into it, and, by confining her next letters to Paris to severely
practical matters—questions about review copies and so on—succeeded in keeping clear. She had, in any case, other claims on her
attention.

Dora had reiterated her need for help and company and Harriet
had promised to go to Glencoin for three months as early as she
could in December. She decided to let her flat while she was away.
Helen Saunders, who had given her some help in the spring, was prepared to look after the office and, as they both knew she was not good
at accounts, Harriet had to get them 'as straight as possible' before
leaving.[77] This work was interrupted by the return to London of John
Rodker. He needed to consult her rather urgently.

Though the copies of *Ulysses* stowed away on board ship and the
copies, posted in sections wrapped in newspapers, had been successfully smuggled into America, the later copies sent off by Iris Barry
had run into trouble, as he had feared. Altogether, about four hundred copies for subscribers in the States had been intercepted. Harriet
was not surprised—she had just heard from Mr Quinn that only two
of his five copies had reached him.

Subscribers could not be let down, and she decided, without hesitation, to reprint. It was a welcome opportunity to put right some of
the misprints. She could deal with the *Errata*, now corrected by the
author, and she had hoped to include his corrections of the text, as
far as they went. But Mr Darentiere refused to accept an incomplete

set. This disappointment explains why the edition was only five hundred. It was intended mainly as a replacement, and the extra hundred represented the farthest she would go with a text that had not been revised by the author.*

To make these decisions was one thing; to devise means of getting copies to American subscribers was another. The best prospect was to adopt a stratagem pioneered by Shakespeare and Company: smuggling the books through Canada, where *Ulysses* was not 'banned'.[78] Miss Beach's official smuggler was the painter Barnet Braverman, a friend of Ernest Hemingway's, who worked from Windsor, Ontario. He had crossed the border by ferry, day after day, with a copy of *Ulysses* tucked into the top of his trousers; and had thus imported the forty copies entrusted to him.[79] John Rodker agreed to go over to the States and see what could be done on a much larger scale. He and Harriet decided, evidently, that it was safest not to consign the books direct from Dijon, but to hold them in London until, as Harriet darkly observed to Sylvia Beach, she had finished 'settling up affairs with Mr Rodker'.[80]

Their plan in train, Harriet turned to other troubles, not Dora's this time but her own family's. Aunt Emily was failing. For some little time a member of the younger generation had been needed at Castle Park and Harriet had now been called on.[81] It was a request she could not refuse. Her two old aunts had lived together all their lives and her Aunt Harriet, eighty-one and the elder by two years, needed her support.

Harriet arrived at Frodsham in mid-December 1922 to find Aunt Emily's condition had worsened. She had little time to herself, with a large household and a sick room to supervise, but she managed to send James Joyce for Christmas some more royalties—£100, making a total of £650—and a personal present of a pocket sized Donne with a binding in the Greek national colours, chosen by him for the binding of *Ulysses*. She felt, however, that as he had had so much illness that year, blue and white had hardly proved lucky colours. And she dreaded for him the heavy dental operation and another eye operation in prospect. But his Christmas letter to her was buoyant and ended with thanks for all her kindness in London and best wishes for 'a happy and quiet Christmas' after all the trouble '*Ulysses II*' had

---

* Maurice Darentiere went to work at once. He completed making the corrections by 6th December, by which date Harriet Weaver had also paid for them—750.95 francs, or £11 12s. 2d., as shown in her *Ulysses* accounts.

213

given her.[82] He also sent her *The Book of Kells*, a present that delighted her.*

Christmas was quiet but not happy: Aunt Emily was sinking and died on 4th January. Harriet saw that she must stay on to comfort her 'solitary old aunt, left desolate by her sister's death'.[83]

The two Harriets had always been good friends, though the elder had remained a faithful and untiring supporter of the Church of England in its most evangelical form. Miss Wright, small and wiry, had been amused, not alarmed by her namesake's tomboy exploits as a child and perhaps shared in some degree the longing for freedom that they betokened.† And years later, when her namesake, then aged thirty-seven, ventured—again, no doubt, in the cause of freedom— to tax her for some suspected pretence, Miss Wright could reply aimiably: 'You are a *naughty* little thing for calling me a Hypocritical Jesuit! I am astonished. *If* I am, it is because I have been instructed in those ways by my dear Niece Harriet. . . .'[84]

The dear niece, now engaged in exploits about which not a word could be uttered, remained for two months. After her stricken aunt had retired to bed shortly after dinner, Harriet would return to the drawing room, open wider one of the windows, pull a shawl over her shoulders and get down to her own ploys.‡ With other papers, she had brought her account books with her and hoped as usual to keep them up to date. But she found that Helen, though keeping conscientious records of payments into the bank, was not making a note of what the money was for. She could not attribute receipts to individual titles and so marked them simply 'banked on account'. When she got back to London she would have to try to sort out, for the title accounts, exactly how much had been received for each book and how many copies sold.

---

* *The Book of Kells* reproduced in facsimile some of the original and had a commentary by Sir Edward O'Sullivan. It was published in London by The Studio.

† Some years before, Harriet and Emily Wright, already elderly, were staying at an hotel one summer and had brought with them, as usual, their personal maid. Harriet Wright, on hearing that the maid was going on a coach trip on her day off, decided to join her, but swore her to secrecy: Miss Emily might not approve. The great day came. She made some excuse to her sister for not wishing to join her on their afternoon drive, stole out of the hotel with the maid, and sat with her in the front seat of the coach, next the driver. Such an adventure! A trip in a public vehicle! She enjoyed it hugely—until spotted by Emily returning from her drive in the landau.

‡ The bedrooms at Castle Park were lit by gaslight, which Harriet Weaver found too dim to work by. Electric lighting had, however, been installed downstairs.

Keeping in touch with all Joyce affairs, and especially with progress in replacing the lost copies of *Ulysses*, was more straightforward. Towards the end of January, John Rodker reported that her first edition was now entirely disposed of except for twenty-five mutilated copies which were being rebound; and that the new edition of five hundred was ready, paid for and on its way to London. She asked him to send a copy to Paris, so that further checking for corrections could be done from the amended text. John Rodker also sent another £150 on account. [85] This Harriet sent on at once to James Joyce, believing—mistakenly—that he had already undergone the two operations; and, for once, ended her letter on a more personal note which reveals, incidentally, how serious a student of *Ulysses* she had become:

... When in London you gave me a sample of your obedience. Now observe mine. You directed or commanded or advised or suggested that I should set aside Rabelais and read the Odyssey, neglected as it has been during all the years of my life.* I did not do so. I continued the Rabelais in any odd time I had between September 15th and December 15th—but these volumes have not come away with me. With me has come—not to mention a bulky blue telephone directory†—the copy of the *Odyssey* bought when you were in London and having had more free time during the last week, I completed a first reading of it last night. I am glad you issued the command though I am not sorry to have delayed obedience until now. . . .[86]

This peaceful mood was shattered a few weeks later, just as Harriet was setting off for Glencoin, by news from John Rodker that the entire consignment of five hundred copies of the new edition had been seized by the Customs at Folkestone. She waited until her return to Gloucester Place to discover more than these bare facts;[87] but asked him in the meantime to consult the Egoist's solicitor, Arnold Carter.[88]

Unknown to them—either then or, apparently, later—a copy of *Ulysses*, presumably of the first Egoist edition, sent by air from Paris to London, had been seized by the Customs at Croydon Airport on 22nd December.[89] H.M. Customs and Excise headquarters,

* Valery Larbaud compared *Ulysses* to Rabelais and to the *Odyssey*, a comparison for which James Joyce had been hoping.

† James Douglas, in his article in the *Sunday Express*, had likened *Ulysses'* bulk to that of the London Telephone Directory, then in one unwieldy volume.

no doubt made aware of the book by reviews in the English press, and already clear what they thought about it, consulted the Home Office, in accordance with their normal routine; and the Home Office, in turn, sought the advice of the Director of Public Prosecutions. His advice, that the book was prima facie obscene, was duly passed back to Customs and Excise, who decided that they would be justified in seizing any further copies.* [90] All ports were alerted. When the Egoist consignment sailed into Folkestone, it sailed into the arms of the law.

Harriet, evidently convinced that she herself could do nothing to help John Rodker, did not hurry back to London. She kept to her plans and went to Dora for a week;† and then on to Whitby for a longer stay at the Rectory to see the Hones and their new baby, Robin. She was not much good at baby talk, but she had already been recognized by the Hone girls, Katharine and Margaret, as the aunt who gave them at Christmas the book that was to prove the favourite of the year.

Her own favourite of the year greeted her return to London: John Rodker had sent her by post a sample copy of the seized edition and this had got through.‡ But this wonderful piece of luck hardly compensated for the unnerving news that John Rodker now gave her.

Under Sections 207 and 208 of the Customs Consolidation Act, 1876, goods seized as prohibited, like her consignment at Folkestone, were forfeit unless the owner claimed, within a prescribed period of seizure, that the goods were not liable to forfeiture. If she wished to claim that the consignment was not liable, Customs would then take condemnation proceedings in a Court of Law, and the issue would be determined by the Court. It would, however, rest with Customs to prove that *Ulysses* was obscene, not with The Egoist Press to prove that it was not.

---

* Action was taken under Section 42 of the Customs Consolidation Act 1876 (still extant) which prohibits inter alia the importation of indecent or obscene prints, paintings, photographs, books, cards, lithographs or other engravings, or any other indecent or obscene articles.

  † Dora Marsden's letters for this period have not survived and it is therefore not possible to say whether she knew about the smuggling plans.

  ‡ Harriet Weaver later sent this copy to Sylvia Beach to sell at 'a fancy price' to help James Joyce. John Rodker bought it and it is now at Yale University Library. John Rodker carried out Harriet Weaver's instructions to send a copy to James Joyce. This copy is now at the State University of New York at Buffalo. These two copies are the only known survivors of the Egoist second edition.

Harriet decided not to claim. Her decision is hardly surprising. She had always shrunk from the idea of appearing in Court in defence of *Ulysses*, whether or not she was likely to win her case; Arnold Carter's opinion on her succeeding in her claim can scarcely have been encouraging; and—perhaps most convincing argument of all—as a consequence of the seizure, there was now little or no chance of smuggling into the States. Her reply given, Customs proceeded to the next stage: the destruction of the books by burning.*

This major calamity brought with it day-to-day embarrassments. The practice of making deliveries by hand to under-the-counter booksellers had never been easy; and it was more difficult now that the book was officially classed as pornographic.

A more personal question, and one needing thought, was what to do with the bequest Harriet had learned was to come to her from the estate of Emily Wright. The bequest, she was told, would yield an income in the region of £500 to £600 a year. She had no need of it herself, any more than she had needed the £100 a year her aunts had given her in 1920. The precedent she had established then she decided to follow now. Mr Joyce had, not long before, described his prospects as murky; and indeed, it was hard to see how they could be anything other than murky with *Ulysses* 'banned' in most of the English speaking world. When the bequest eventually reached her, she would ask Fred Monro to invest the money in London for him.

Any reservations she had about what Sidney Schiff called James Joyce's 'mode of life' had now been thrust aside by more important considerations. The unknown young man in Trieste whose genius she had recognized years before was now acclaimed;† and, at forty-one, still had perhaps three decades or more of working years ahead. He needed peace, space in which to work, a more settled life. But

* H.M. Customs and Excise have no record of claim by The Egoist Press against forfeiture and (though their files for this period are no longer complete) consider that it may be assumed that no claim was made. No other evidence contradicts this assumption. Destruction by burning was Customs' normal practice at this time, and, though there is no record of the method employed, burning can be presumed. Whatever the method employed, Customs made a thorough job of the *Ulysses* consignment.

† The acclaim was no longer confined to literary circles. On returning to Paris in September 1922, James Joyce wrote: 'I shall have to take my meals in some other quarter as both yesterday and the day before persons have come over to me after long scrutiny and asked if I am the great etc etc who wrote the etc etc and requested the pleasure of shaking my hand—an art for which I have very little talent'.

post-war Paris, the only place where he wished to live, was likely to remain expensive. Almost more important, in Harriet's view, was the need to regain his health and to ward off eye attacks. If he went blind, might he not cease to write? Her own marvellous physique and perfect eyesight, and her corresponding tendency to be anxious on other people's behalf, made her sensitive to his woes.

Harriet had had far more practice in leading a detached life, than in developing and controlling relationships with individuals. She was vulnerable; and her vulnerability is reflected in the impression she gives of becoming a captive of her personal relationships with Dora Marsden and with James Joyce. And her weakness in withstanding undue claims on her friendship was matched by their inability to cease making them.

Meanwhile, her growing friendship with James Joyce delighted her, though it had one drawback: he was still, in a sense, too clear-sighted. She felt that he, like grey-eyed Athene, both saw and did not see—both saw and did not see her. Long before she met him she seems to have been made uncomfortable by his eyes and, for example, was disturbed by remarks about them by others—by Ezra Pound, on studying a photograph, that they seemed 'pathological'; or by a writer in an Italian journal who had spoken of 'gli acutissimi occhi'—his intensely observant gaze.* This sense of being scrutinized, sized up, by unseeing eyes, accorded ill with her natural preference to go her way unseen.

Her pleasure must, however, have been intense when, shortly after she made her decision about her aunt's bequest, James Joyce wrote to her in the north to tell her that he had made a start on the 'history of the world':

. . . Yesterday I wrote two pages—the first I have written since the final *Yes* of *Ulysses*. Having found a pen, with some difficulty I copied them out in a large handwriting on a double sheet of foolscap so that I could read them. . . .†[91]

---

* Sylvia Beach conveys much the same idea when she says James Joyce 'could see as well as anyone when he wanted to'. (*Shakespeare and Company*, p. 122)

† The two pages, a sketch of King Roderick O'Conor, were eventually used in 1938 and appear, redrafted and with other matter, at the end of Part II section 3 of *Finnegans Wake*. James Joyce had not started from scratch. From early in 1922, and perhaps longer, he had been collecting ideas, phrases and words in a notebook now known as *Scribbledehobble* and at Buffalo.

He promised her the sheet of foolscap.

It was the invalid rather than the writer with whom she was most concerned on her return to London. The operations, postponed from January, were performed in April: two for the removal of seventeen decayed teeth, and after an interval, a sphincterectomy on the 'good' (left) eye, not so good since the acute attack the previous summer.* Harriet, who had been steeling herself against this critical moment, sent £100 for royalties two days before Dr Borsch operated, and another £100 two days afterwards—bringing the total at that point to £1,000.[92]

She was sorry not to be 'on the spot at the time of the operations';[93] but she could at least do something to ease Mr Joyce's mind and so help his recovery. She followed up the second £100 with a hint that something larger would follow—when her aunt's estate had been wound up. She was not specific—she did not wish to burden him with figures—but said enough to show him that his prospects were not wholly dark.

For the time being, earnings from *Ulysses* were enough to keep the wolf from any ordinary door, and the prospects for the next few months, with money coming in from sales already made, were quite good. But Harriet was beginning to see, and to accept without disquiet, that James Joyce's expenditure never waited upon his income; and, to protect his peace of mind, she wanted him to know well in advance that, when his present source of income dried up, there would be another.

In the latter half of April, Harriet analysed the receipts banked by Helen Saunders and in most cases managed to arrive at the number of copies sold. But her running record for *Ulysses* she did not keep up to date, as instalments were still coming in and she did not, or could not, give a figure for the sales they represented. The remaining stocks, mainly unnumbered copies, were now in London; and she decided to put up the price to £3 3s. od.[94]

At the close of the financial year in May, she was able to make an assessment of her position and prospects. *Prufrock*, sold out in the previous year, had a balance in the account. She gave £2 10s. od. to Ezra Pound, to complete repayment of his loan, £6 to T. S. Eliot as a royalty payment; and she made a note that The Egoist Press had taken 18s. 8d. profit.† T. S. Eliot's royalties now amounted to

* An operation to release the tension in the muscle surrounding the eyelid.
† As this is the only unsubsidized Egoist book which made a profit, it is sad that the

£10 10s. od. It was not a great sum, but he had at least benefited from his publisher's policy of giving a generous allowance of press and complimentary copies.*

Of her other publications, H.D.'s *Hymen* had fared best: it had sold nearly two hundred. *Terra Italica, Explorations,* and Marianne Moore's *Poems* had done very poorly. In between came the *Dialogues of Fontenelle,* the *Poets' Translations,* and, in spite of the success of *Ulysses, Exiles, Dubliners* and the third edition of *A Portrait.*† Indeed, James Joyce's royalties on all three of these books amounted, during the year, only to £60 odd.

A review of stock brought home to her that there were only four books for which she could reasonably have some hope both for herself and for their authors if she continued to sell them for another five years: *A Portrait* (about four hundred on hand); *Quia Pauper Amavi* (about two hundred and eighty-three); *The Caliph's Design* (about one hundred and fifty); and *Tarr* (about one hundred and ninety). As things turned out, however, The Egoist Press had only one more year to live.

real profit was less than Harriet Weaver thought. The Egoist Press had put in 15s. 11d., mainly in the form of books given to Ezra Pound as part repayment of his loan, so that the profit on *Prufrock* was really 2s. 9d.

* The last copy of *Prufrock* that was sold, out of an edition of five hundred, brought the record of sales to three hundred and seventy-five. In the hundred and twenty-five that are not accounted for, some should probably be set against bad debts; but most of them must have been used either as press or as author's copies.

† *Chamber Music* was unlikely to add much to James Joyce's royalties; and, for the time being, while she was completing arrangements for The Egoist Press edition, Harriet Weaver bought some copies from Elkin Mathews and sold them more or less at cost price.

II

CLOSING DOWN

In June 1923, James Joyce was well enough to travel and decided to have a holiday, postponed from the previous year, on the south coast. His wife and his sixteen-year-old daughter Lucia came with him; and his son George, who was studying singing in Paris, stayed behind, charged with the task of finding a new flat.* The lease of the furnished flat in the Avenue Charles Fouquet was running out, and the family possessions were already packed up in 'ten cases of books and manuscripts, three sacks of newspapers, four trunks, four valises, three hat-boxes etc.'.[1]

Harriet, determined that the holiday should not be spoiled by anxieties about money, sent royalties of £200 shortly before the family set out. She also made the arrangements for a short stay in London, where Nora's youngest sister Kathleen Barnacle was joining the party, and going on with them to Bognor in Sussex. She had a long journey from Galway and, as she was unused to travel, had to be met at Euston station. So the family were installed nearby at the Belgrave Hotel, which was convenient also for the British Museum.†

Harriet and Nora—with little in common beyond a dislike of cooking and thunder, and an exceptional capacity for loyalty—had already laid the foundations of an enduring friendship; but Harriet

---

* George Joyce (two years older than Lucia) was known as Giorgio in the family and was so called by Harriet Weaver. On this account, he will be referred to as Giorgio, though he has for long preferred to be known as George.

† The hotel was modest and may have been chosen because James Joyce, who had not yet seen his sister-in-law, was uncertain if she was presentable; but he very soon discovered that Kathleen Barnacle had a splendid carriage, good looks, charm and dignity.

and Lucia were meeting for the first time. Harriet noticed that she spoke English remarkably well, considering that Italian was her first language and her schooling had been in Italian, German and French. She obviously had her father's keen ear; she looked a little like him, too, and talked in rather the same way, although with a slight Italian accent. There were times when she acted unpredictably, but Harriet interpreted this as the 'absentmindedness' her father had mentioned. Allowances had to be made, after all, because of her unsettled childhood, moving from place to place and from school to school.

She and her brother had to be taken to school by force, when they were first in Zurich; James Joyce, with a child on either hand, had dragged them forward while they fiercely dragged back.[2] Later, during three years in France, she had had only eighteen months' education, interrupted because, when her parents went to Nice, she was too young—and too useful as her father's amanuensis—to be left at school in Paris. Each change was disturbing, and her parents' love and concern did not protect her from the repeated shock of losing playmates and schoolfriends. James and Nora Joyce could indulge their children, but they could not give them the kind of attention that a child needs. Their devotion to one another, and James Joyce's devotion to his work, too often came first.

Harriet was sorry for Lucia and wished something could be done, even now, about her education. She did not take to London, where she had no friends; and neither she nor her mother could find their way about.[3] Harriet arranged outings and treats, and willingly made double journeys to fetch them from the hotel and see them safely back. But the weather was hot and thundery, which none of them liked, and the visit as a whole was not a great success. Lucia enjoyed the 'delicious' teas they all had together, but she was too shy of Miss Weaver to feel at ease.

James Joyce himself had trouble with his new French dental plates, and went to the dentist twice.* [4] But his general health, and his eyesight, showed a distinct improvement.[5] He got from Harriet a list of public libraries and worked hard on the notes he had brought with him. He was also taken to see the tiny Egoist office and discussed with Harriet the preparation of her new edition of *Chamber Music*. It was urgently needed, as the Elkin Mathews edition was sold out, and she had been waiting to learn 'Mr Joyce's wishes'.[6] He had completed a

* The dentist was probably Mr Henry, consulted the year before.

revision, using more 'daring' punctuation and forming new com-
posites of single words.[7] Now, they agreed on the format: 'a bulkier
volume than the thin second edition . . . bound in dark green cloth
(uniform with the other three) and priced at 3/-'.[8]

They also spoke, as his later letters show, about his current work on
the 'universal history'. Harriet was eager to hear; and he, anxious to
please her, was also happy to confide. In his imagination, protean
forms were coming to life and speaking a language of their own.
Ulysses, the book of the day, was well known to Harriet; this was her
first acquaintance with the night book, the dream of Finn Mac-
Cumbal, legendary hero and wise man, 'lying in death beside the
river Liffey and watching the history of Ireland and the world—past
and future—flow through his mind like flotsam on the river of life'.[9]
His twentieth-century avatar was the publican, Humphrey Chimpden
Earwicker, father of 'the eternal, unholy family', created to act out
the eternal human themes of love and strife.

James Joyce gave Harriet an outline of his general conception, and
some useful shorthand references. 'H.C.E.' was the central character
(in one of his many manifestations) and 'Mamalujo' stood for 'those
four fellows': Matthew, Mark, Luke and John.[10] But he did not reveal
the title; it was still a secret confided only to Nora. He wanted to see,
later on, if Harriet could guess that the death and resurrection of
mankind (and of Tim Finnegan, the ballad hero, who rose from his
coffin when he smelt whiskey) had presented him with the double
pun *Finnegans Wake*.

Harriet was not inclined to comment on the book at such an early
stage; she simply undertook to type out anything he wrote while he
was at Bognor. She had another subject she wished to bring up before
he left London on 29th June. In order to sort out the money matter
she had touched on when he was laid up and instruct Fred Monro to
draft the transfer of Aunt Emily's bequest, she had to find out how his
finances stood. She had now become attached to his family, as well
as to himself, and intended to make her gift in a form calculated to
serve the family interests.

Money troubles were discussed, but the gift was not mentioned,
perhaps because she was overtaken by shyness, perhaps because she
found him in an irritable mood, caught up in the considered policy of
enlarging on his own bleak prospects.[11] From Bognor, he apologized
for his 'ill-temper'.[12] His intention was, as Richard Ellmann says, to
meet the English Protestant middle-class with adequate decorum.[13]

But it proved a strain; and Harriet, revered because she had singled him out to receive her attention and sympathy as well as her money, was fated to suffer when he lapsed from the high standard of politeness that he wished to attain in all his dealings with her.

Her main objective, to set his affairs in order, remained unchanged. He soon learned, from her or from her lawyers, the size of the gift that was coming to him. His acknowledgment is among the letters that she did not release for publication. But he naturally gave the good news to other friends who had some interest in his financial entanglements. Among them was Sylvia Beach:

... You will be glad to hear that Miss Weaver made over to me a couple of days ago the very great gift of another £12,000 (twelve thousand pounds) equivalent at today's exchange rate of 936,000 frs. This throws some light on the situation. In view of benefactions of various proveniences [sic] it ought to be pointed out that the sum for which the entire MS of *Ulysses* was acquired is equivalent to the interest *for 6 weeks* on the total sum (£21,000) made over to me by her. . . .*[14]

Harriet was criticized later for giving an extravagant man a lump sum which had a 'bad effect on the whole family'.†[15] But at the time she sized things up differently. Her gift was intended to provide an assured family income; and the income, more than doubled by Aunt Emily's bequest, was not excessive for James Joyce's needs as a semi-invalid, a family man and a writer of great achievement and promise. His children were unlikely to be independent for some years; the cost of medical and ophthalmic treatment was almost certain to be heavy; and there was no prospect of a continuing income from *Ulysses*, now that it was 'banned' in England and America, and Sylvia Beach was reluctant to re-issue it in France.

The income Harriet had provided, calculated at 5 per cent, was about £1,050 gross or (since even a genius, silent, cunning and in exile, is liable for tax) £850 nett.‡ This represents, in the currency of

---

* The MS of *Ulysses* had recently been sold in America by John Quinn for a sum James Joyce considered ludicrously small and a slight to himself.

† This passage was omitted in the 1966 edition of Mary Colum's *Life and the Dream*.

‡ James Joyce, a little later, put his private income at 'not quite £1000 a year' and his income from royalties at about £60. (Both figures presumably gross) (To Stanislaus Joyce, 8th January 1927. *Letters* III, 149)

1969, a nett income of about £2,500, which would not seem exorbitant to any professional man who was obliged to pay for doctors, medicine and his children's education.

The suggestion made, long after the event, that Harriet should have kept her capital and given James Joyce a yearly income, was presumably considered by Harriet at the time. But, aware of the risks, she preferred to make over the capital, with certain safeguards. She was not interested in having Mr Joyce as her pensioner; she wished to see him a free man. Her own freedom, too, was involved. She was still living on 'usury'—her own word for unearned income—and her sense of guilt had not abated. But she gave herself some relief by passing on the inheritance; and gained some compensation for her disappointment in herself as a writer by passing it on to the writer she admired above all.

She could not, however, do more than relieve her guilt. The 'genuine freedom' she sought demanded complete independence from inherited money. But her private means protected her other freedoms —independence of thought and of expression—and for this reason her inner conflict could never be logically solved. Because she had not been trained to earn an independent living, it would have been no solution to give away all that she had.

There is a curious affinity here between James Joyce and Harriet: neither of them liked keeping money. They both preferred to get rid of it, although in very different ways and for very different reasons. Freedom, to James Joyce, meant freedom to live the life he chose, and to remain dependent on others. Even before he left Ireland in 1904, he had announced that 'he should be supported at the expense of the State' because he was 'capable of enjoying life'.[16] He was also inclined to dependence because of his frail constitution; and had assumed that he was frail long before his health or his eyesight deteriorated. When Yeats told him that only in William Morris, a man of robust physique, had he 'felt the joy of life to be so keen', the young James Joyce had replied with a laugh: 'I am afraid that my physique cannot by any stretch of the imagination be described as robust'.[17] His sense of vocation as a writer further justified his right to live at someone else's expense. His remark to Sylvia Beach that Harriet's gift threw 'some light on the situation' was facetious in manner but serious in substance. He was saying, in effect, that here was the support appropriate to his destiny.

Other people were sceptical about his vocation; and so he saw himself also as an innocent and helpless creature pursued by enemies, a hunted deer. And this image acquired a cruel twist because he desired the hunt and fled to ground where he stood at a disadvantage, court-ing betrayal in order to test himself—as well as those in pursuit.* It was a concept that influenced him in many ways, and certainly helped to make him a spendthrift. Behind the handsome instinct to be open-handed was a real desire to become, and remain, insolvent. The 'murky' appearance of his financial prospects usually correspon-ded with reality, but he often described them, as he evidently did to Harriet, with visionary fervour. These were afflictions he sought and, indeed, engineered.

It is hardly likely that Harriet had any inkling of this mephisto-phelian-messianic drama, concerned with the conflict between Betrayer and Betrayed. She was a rationalist, imbued with the un-conscious optimism of the liberal reformer. If Mr Joyce's mode of life was bad for his health, or if he found it difficult to manage his money, a little determination to do the sensible thing, and proper encouragement from his friends, should eventually put things to rights. It was fortunate that, when this reasoning proved to be faulty, she was able to draw on another source of strength: her genuine, though not unlimited, taste for the eccentric.

Meanwhile, the eccentric Mr Joyce was grateful, and his gratitude was of the enduring kind. While writing *Ulysses*, he had told Wynd-ham Lewis that 'he, his wife, and his children would have been on the streets had it not been for the kindness of this benefactress'.[18] Now, he decided to send her, as he finished with them, all the manuscripts, typescripts and proofs of his new work.

The money from Emily Wright's estate was some time in transit through the lawyers' offices. Harriet reverted to her other role, and began doing the chores. James Joyce, eager to see his first page in type, sent her from Bognor a single hand-written sheet.† [19]

The first lines that Harriet read and typed ran:

So anyhow after that to wind up that long to be chronicled get together day, the anniversary of his first holy communion, after that same barbecue beanfeast was all over poor old hospitable King

* Richard Ellmann traces the image of the hunted deer back to the essay-story written in 1904 and rejected by the journal *Dana*. (Ellmann, pp. 151/152)

† Sixteen years later, the completed series of manuscripts, typescripts and proofs weighed fifty-four pounds.

CLOSING DOWN

Roderick O'Conor, the paramount chief polemarch and last pre-electric King of all Ireland. . . .[20]

On and on it went, not a full stop to be seen, to the point where His Most Exuberant Majesty licked up:

whatever surplus rotgut sorra much was left by the lazy lousers of malt-knights and beerchurls in the different bottoms of the various different replenquished drinking utensils left there behind them on the premises by the departed honourable homegoers. . . .*[21]

By the time she had typed her way to the end of this piece, Harriet, perhaps to her surprise, had rather taken to Roderick O'Conor, Rex, his midnight thirst notwithstanding. The next day, she received from Bognor two 'scattered passages', as different from each other as they were from the first. St Kevin, in his alb of cloth of gold, had at least some features she could recognize; but Tristran and Isseult were entirely new and startling:

that handsome brineburnt sixfooter Gaelic, rugger and soccer champion and the dinkum belle of Lucalizod quite charming in her ocean-blue brocade and an overdress of net darned with gold well in advance of the latest fashion exhibits bunnyhugged scrumptiously . . . with sinister dexterity he alternately rightandlefthandled fore and aft on and offside her pulpable rugby and association bulbs. . . .† [22]

As she typed the pieces, moving gingerly from word to word, from line to line of his spidery script, Harriet must have asked herself what Mr Joyce could be intending. What sort of history was this, of what sort of world? Ten days later came 'a piece describing the conversion of S. Patrick by Ireland'.[23] It was even more puzzling. History, if history it was, had been inverted, time turned inside out. Bishop Berkeley, surely, lived many centuries after St Patrick? And why pidgin English? She could make nothing of it. The first sentence began:

Bymby topside joss pidgin fella Berkeley, archdruid of Irish chin-chinjoss, in the his heptachromatic sevenhued septicoloured roranyell-

---

* See *Finnegans Wake*, II, 380–81.   † See *Finnegans Wake*, II, 384.

greeblindigan mantle finish he show along the his mister guest
Patrick. . . .* [24]

On 15th August, when the family returned to London for two
nights before leaving for Paris, a telegram for James Joyce arrived at
Gloucester Place. It was an offer from Miss Lewisohn, owner (with
her sister) of a New York theatre, to produce *Exiles*. Harriet thought
it a serious offer (as it proved to be) and, when she failed to reach
him by telephone, she sent him a copy of the telegram by post. Next
day, they agreed a draft contract, and she typed it out.

No one had succeeded in finding a flat for him in Paris and Harriet,
before she gave him his copy of the draft, made him promise he
would not attempt to work in the darkness and discomfort of a hotel
room. A week later, installed in the Victoria Palace, he had broken
his promise and 'began drafting other parts in spite of the heat, noise,
confusion and suffocation'.[25] The wild hunt through the Paris jungle
of stampeding omnibuses and 'taxielephants' failed to produce the
miracle of a flat, and the family stayed more than a year in the
'caravanserai peopled by American loudspeakers', where he had to
do his work on the green suitcase he had bought in Bognor.[26]

The hotel was in his favourite arrondissement and more comfortable than the maison meublée of earlier days. But his room was dark,
as Harriet had feared, and the darkness did affect his eyes. Dr Borsch
thought another operation would be necessary, although not at
once.[27] More encouraging news came from John Quinn who, when
they met in the autumn, found him 'a new man physically'.[28] And
James Joyce himself was well pleased when his dentist agreed to
make a new set of plates free. 'With this one,' he wrote, 'I can neithef
sing, laugh, shave nor (what is more important to my style or
writing) yawn.'[29]

After *Chamber Music* came out at the end of August, Harriet had
more leisure to reflect on the 'pieces' she had typed, and she made
some considered comments. He was sorry that Patrick and Berkeley
were 'unsuccessful in explaining themselves' and gave his own
explanation: 'The answer, I suppose is that given by Paddy Dignam's
apparition: metempsychosis. Or perhaps the theory of history so well
set forth (after Hegel and Giambattista Vico) by the four eminent
annalists who are even now treading the typepress in sorrow will ex-

* See *Finnegans Wake*, IV, 611.

plain part of my meaning. I work as much as I can because these are not fragments but active elements and when they are more and a little older they will begin to fuse of themselves'.* [30]

Sylvia Beach, meanwhile, spurred on by a visit from an American member of the Joyce circle, William Bird, a journalist, who hoped to secure *Ulysses* for his new Three Mountains Press, had announced that she wanted to bring out the next edition herself; and had only been waiting for the author to suggest it. 'I did not do so,' he told Harriet, 'because I was not sure of her attitude and also because I did not know what my proposal might entail for her.'[31] Harriet heard also from Sylvia and said, in reply, that she was 'interested' in the plan for a cheap Paris edition, specifically not for export. She had no objection, and expected Miss Marsden to agree. Then she went on to talk about the text, always her first interest: the corrections made for 'the disastrous supplementary edition of 500' were taken from the *Errata* slip, but 'Mr Joyce's additional corrections were not made', because the work had been interrupted by illness and Mr Darentiere did not wish to use an incomplete list. Harriet promised to look out her own copy for Sylvia and, in a diffident manner, gave a strong recommendation: 'It would be well for them to be made before a new edition is printed I should think'.[32]

Dora agreed at once that an ordinary edition would be a good thing, but as Harriet was coming to stay within a fortnight, she wanted to defer the formal decision until they had talked it over. Sylvia was content to wait, and Harriet wrote next from Glencoin:

Dear Miss Beach,

I arrived here on Monday to find Miss Marsden poorly. She is better today and we have talked over the suggestion for a new (ordinary) edition of *Ulysses*. . . Miss Marsden agrees with me that it will be quite the best thing if you will do this and at any time that is convenient to you and to Mr. Joyce. We think it had better be called a *fourth* edition in order to give a high curiosity value to the single copy of the small edition of 500 printed in December 1922 to replace

---

* Harriet Weaver's comments have not come to light but are revealed, by implication, in James Joyce's replies. This is the first of his letters in a long and unique series, extending over many years and comparable only with that to Frank Budgen on *Ulysses*. Harriet, at first merely puzzled, came increasingly to doubt the wisdom of this new enterprise, while he, perpetually in need of her approbation, plied her with 'pieces' and begged for her comments.

those lost in transit to the U.S.A. (or, rather, burnt in the New York
Post Office, as I hear now from Mr. Quinn).* I hope to sell this one
copy sometime or other at a fancy price for Mr. Joyce.†
I return on Saturday to [Frodsham] and must take this down the
mountain side to the distant pillar box before early dark comes on.

With kindest regards

Yours sincerely

Harriet Weaver.[33]

In the long, dark evenings on their mountainside, Harriet and Dora
had many problems to discuss. The return of *Ulysses* to its first publisher was not the only intimation that the good days of The Egoist
Press were over. But no general decision was made. Harriet's time
was limited. She was paying Dora another visit in February, from
Frodsham, where she was staying from December to March to keep
her aunt company through the winter.

She took with her to Frodsham the corrections she wanted to see
in the new edition of *Ulysses* and typed a new list, so that it would be
easy for Sylvia to take her advice. On five quarto pages she set out Mr
Joyce's 'additions', the half-dozen corrections that the printers had
failed to transfer from the *Errata* slip, and a few further corrections of
misprints she had found in the supplementary edition. She worked
fast, and sent the new list to Sylvia early in December, with another
reminder: 'If you decide to have the corrections made before printing
the new edition Mr Darentiere should have the new list to work from
and be asked to destroy, or send to you, the list sent to him by me a
year ago'.[34]

Sylvia was grateful; since James Joyce had not been able to complete his revision, these pages supplied her with all the known corrections. She responded to Harriet's kindness by buying ten copies of the
Egoist *Ulysses*. Harriet was left with only three copies unsold, and
decided to reserve them for enquiries in London, now that *Ulysses*
had left that port of call and returned to France.‡

The spring of 1924 was a turning point in Harriet's life. Her most

* Many years later, after the removal of the ban on *Ulysses* in the United States,
copies with numbers corresponding to those lost came on the secondhand book
market in New York.

† Harriet Weaver had forgotten that she had asked for a copy to be sent to James Joyce.

‡ Sylvia Beach published the next eight authorized editions. Her last edition
appeared in 1930.

important—and most successful—author had moved on, and the other writers on her list were ready to move too.* She had done what she set out to do: helped them through the first, difficult stages of a literary career. But she had not been able to launch the first of the writers who looked to her for support—Dora Marsden.

Dora had never appeared on the Egoist list because, year after year, she had failed to finish her book. Now, her health was deteriorating and she no longer had frequent, if fleeting, visits from Grace Jardine, who was acquiring a bookshop in Manchester. Grace had reached the conclusion that Dora's book would never be fit for publication. Harriet, too, was beginning to have doubts. Yet she still felt that Dora needed to complete it, and decided that she must help her. She could not ignore the evident need of an old friend who was ill, frustrated and solitary.

These personal motives certainly influenced Harriet when, later on in the winter, she and her fellow directors took the logical decision to close down The Egoist Press. For the last ten years, daily visits to the office had occupied much of her time, and she now planned to spend more than half the year out of London, at Frodsham and Glencoin, and to sub-let her flat.

At Glencoin, she rented number 6 Seldom Seen, next door to the double-cottage where Dora lived with her mother. There she did all her own cooking and chores, and worked regularly on Dora's book. It was an austere life. Although she was devoted to the Marsdens and loved the beauty of Ullswater, she was more at home in London and missed the conveniences of her own flat. Moreover, though she still admired Dora's historical and analytical work, she was finding it difficult to follow—or approve—her excursions into theology.

Yet she kept to the decision to stand by her friend, aware that she was taking on a long job with very uncertain prospects.† She wrote about them to James Joyce, who remarked that the tone of her letter was 'very discouraged'.[35] She sent him also her comments on his latest pieces, the 'description of Shem-Ham-Cain-Egan etc and his penmanship, Anna Livia's visit and collaboration and delivery of the memorial by Shawn the post'.[36] Although she had allowed herself to write a discouraged letter, she was not yet ready to admit that his recent writing, like Dora's, had given her some anxiety. When he

* Richard Aldington had bought back, for £5, the remainders of *Images*: 220 bound copies and 480 sheets. He later passed them on to Allen & Unwin.

† In the event, the new arrangements were in force until 1931.

sent her the next mixed bundle, he made the suggestion, not entirely ironical, that 'the nightman sketch I send may produce by allopathy a mood of contentment'. His own situation seemed 'hopeless' but he was working on.[37]

The bundle included a piece previously omitted, a revised page, and a fresh batch of typescript to follow the earlier instalment of Part I, vii, which ran from 'Let us now . . .' to 'Shem the Penman'. Harriet read the first few lines, and then came upon the horrific description of Shem's 'bodily getup':

an eighth of an eye, the whole of a nose, one arm, fortytwo hairs off his crown, eighteen to his mock lip, a quintet from his chin, the wrong shoulder higher than the right, all ears, not a foot to stand on, a handful of thumbs, a blind stomach, a deaf heart, a loose liver, two fifths of two buttocks, a stone and a half . . .* [38]

In her reply, Harriet revealed some hint of her real feelings, and James Joyce told Robert McAlmon, 'I don't think she likes the tone of my last effusions'.[39] He was particularly eager that the next piece should please her. It was, he explained, 'a chattering dialogue across the river by two washerwomen who as night falls become a tree and a stone. . . . The stream is quite brown, rich in salmon, very devious, shallow . . .'. Now he was drained of energy by 'work, worry, bad light, general circumstances and the rest'.[40]

It was a letter to touch her sympathies and it introduced a passage that gave her flawless pleasure:

O tell me all about Anna Livia! I want to hear all about Anna Livia. Well, you know Anna Livia? Yes, of course, we all know Anna Livia. Tell me all. Tell me now. You'll die when you hear. Well, you know, when the old chap went and did what you know. Yes, I know, go on. Wash away and don't be dabbling. Tuck up your sleeves and loosen your talktapes. Or whatever it was they try to make out he tried to do in the Phoenix park. He's an awful old rep. Look at the shirt of him! Look at the dirt of it! He has all my water black on me. And it steeping and stuping since this time last week. What was it he did at all? It was put in the papers what he did. But time will tell. I know it will. Time and tide will wash for no man. O, the old old rep! What age is he at all at all? . . .† [41]

* See *Finnegans Wake*, I, 169. † See *Finnegans Wake*, I, 196.

Harriet must have been relieved, as well as delighted, to find that she could still be a whole-hearted admirer. James Joyce, apprehensive, awaited her verdict impatiently for over a week. He wrote again: 'I hope none of the MS was lost. The first words are 'O tell me' the last 'waters of. Night' . . . . You did not say if you liked the piece?'[42]

Her letter was on its way, and he wrote next to say he was very glad that she did like it. Valery Larbaud (who had praised the effusions that Harriet did not care for) was 'in a trance' about Anna Livia.[43] But he himself was depressed. A lamp had been taken away from his room in the hotel and he foresaw that Shaun was going to give him 'a very great deal of trouble'. Meanwhile, he felt it would amuse Harriet to see the signs he was using for his chief characters, and he wrote them out on the back of his letter:

m   (Earwicker, H C E by moving letter round)
△   Anna Livia
[Shem-Cain
∧   Shaun
S   Snake
P   S. Patrick
T   Tristan
⊥   Isolde
X   Mamalujo
▢   This stands for the title but I do not wish to say it yet until the book has written more of itself.[44]

Harriet was now back in London, winding up the affairs of The Egoist Press. On Mr Joyce's behalf, she approached Jonathan Cape. He had been with Duckworth as a young man, and had signed the letter rejecting *A Portrait*. But now, with a publishing house of his own, he agreed to take over, for £130, the publishing rights and stock of the four titles still on the Egoist list.

The stock was delivered, and payment made, by the end of April. Harriet noted in her ledger that the sum fixed was 'the amount of the deficit on *Dubliners*, *Exiles* and *Chamber Music*'; and it gave her some satisfaction to show these three titles in credit. But the actual cash was passed on at once to the author.

Apart from this payment, his royalties were small: in round figures £24 from *Dubliners*, £11 from *Exiles*, and £4 from *Chamber Music*. He had earned more from the three editions of *A Portrait*,

but hardly a princely sum: £201 less Mr Pinker's commission.*
Nonetheless, he regretted the change to a new publisher and felt
'mistrustful' of Harriet's successor.[45] Cape had contracted to give
15 per cent on a new edition of *A Portrait*, and as Miss Weaver and
Miss Beach had both given better percentages, this seemed 'rather
low'.† [46]

The terms were certainly poor compared with Harriet's arrangements for *Ulysses*. The Egoist earnings, in round figures, were
£2,608 gross and £1,637 nett, out of which Joyce received 'royalties' of £1,636! In addition, he had the 'advances' which Harriet did
not put through the accounts.

Her gift of capital was not made until May, when the executors
finished their work on Aunt Emily's estate. During April James
Joyce, awaiting the proceeds of Harriet's sale to Cape and a royalty
cheque for the New York performance of *Exiles*, ran out of money.‡
He had been borrowing from Robert McAlmon and Sylvia Beach,
and finally asked Harriet for 'an advance of some kind in the circumstances'.[47] His circumstances were indeed wretched, as she knew from
his recent letters. While waiting for his next eye operations, postponed until the fine weather came, he had been 'working ten hours a
day in semi-dark' and was suffering from 'a secretion in the con-
junctiva'.[48] Dr Borsch had forbidden him to read at all for several
days and insisted that he must limit his work to half or a third.

Soon after she received this letter, signed James Job, Harriet asked
Fred Monro to send him an advance of £100. She was no longer his
publisher but still his good friend. She remained also his literary aide;
and here she was beset by anxiety. In the past, she had been supported
through all the trials of publishing *A Portrait* and *Ulysses* by her deep
and unquestioning love for the books. Now, through the difficult task
of reading Work in Progress, she was burdened by lack of faith. Was

* See Appendix.

† James Joyce had other reasons for feeling mistrustful of publishers and printers.
On 11th July, he wrote to Harriet Weaver: 'Mr Cape and his printers gave me trouble.
They set the book with perverted commas and I insisted on their removal by the
sergeant-at-arms. Then they underlined passages which they thought undesirable.
But as you see from the enclosed: they were and, behold, they are not . . .'.

‡ On 19th April he was without funds of any kind and sent a note by hand to
Sylvia Beach '. . . I would be very glad if you could manage to advance me another
500 francs. I sincerely hope, if things finally straighten out, that this is the last time I
shall have to bother you. If you have it please put it in an envelope and give it to
Lucia . . .'. (Buffalo)

it even conceivable that she would ever understand and approve of it as the author would wish?

She had at least found a good home for his copyrights; and she had made some progress, too, in disposing of the other Egoist titles. She wrote to remind Sylvia to order any that she wanted soon, before they were 'scattered to the winds'. The smaller books were no particular problem. H.D.'s *Hymen*, with the larger part of the edition exported to America in sheets, was sold out; while Robert McAlmon's *Explorations* and Edward Storer's *Terra Italica* had been handed back to the authors, who had both paid their own printing costs. The other books, including two by Ezra Pound and two by Wyndham Lewis, were not yet placed. The remainders, stacked in Harriet's minute office, were a challenge of considerable bulk. So were the periodicals —mainly *Egoist*s and *Tyros*. Harriet sent Sylvia samples of those she might find interesting. Only one issue of *The Egoist* was sold out, and one other Harriet reserved for 'some special purpose'.[49] It was the issue of 15th January 1914 where she had first made the acquaintance of James Joyce by reading his *Curious History*.

Sylvia had enquired about Harriet's own prospects, and Harriet allowed herself, for once, to make a personal statement: 'I shall be both sorry and glad to give up the Egoist Press. It has done its chief work, I think; and too much capital would be required for expansion into a flourishing publishing company'.[50] Her publishing business (apart from the special arrangements for James Joyce) had not cost her very much, compared with the cost of the journal.* But she was certainly right in thinking a flourishing business could not be established unless she increased her backing. Meanwhile, her personal income, in real terms, had dropped since the war and the obligations she put first were to James Joyce and Dora Marsden.

Sylvia had evidently written very warmly about Harriet's services to literature and her goodness to men of letters. Harriet never welcomed any sign of recognition but on this occasion she was not altogether displeased, merely embarrassed:

I feel very flattered by a request for my photograph! I have no recent one but if I should happen to acquire any within a reasonable time I will send you one if you still want to have it. I have been looking all round for the halo you spoke of but can't catch a sight of such an uncomfortable thing anywhere.[51]

* See Appendix.

By the end of May, James Joyce had worked himself to a standstill. The weather was very hot and the hotel courtyard, with all windows flung open, echoed with talk, shouts and laughter. After four days of it, he had decided to stop work. He stored his books and summoned Sylvia Beach to take away his manuscripts and notebooks. He felt he was losing his memory, vision and power of attention, and he had not even been able to copy out Shawn, 'a postman travelling backwards in the night through the events already narrated . . . a *via crucis* of 14 stations . . . a barrel rolling down the river Liffey'.[52]

Since all temptation to work had been removed, he had time to spare to sit for Patrick Tuohy, the Irish painter who had done a successful portrait of his father. He asked Harriet if she would like to see the new work; the artist was taking it to Dublin for exhibition, when it was finished, and would gladly break his journey in London.

In spite of rest and distraction, he was very depressed, and Nora was in a weak state of nerves. 'I believe,' he told Harriet, 'the operation will cause her more pain than it will cause me. I do not know what to do. I will speak to Dr Borsch tonight. As soon as it is decided I will let you know. What will happen after I do not know.' He longed to get away from the hotel, and have a study of his own, but it was useless to leave until they had found another place. He concluded by saying he would trouble her no longer with his 'eternal worries', but go out for 'some fresh air laden with tar, benzine, noise, dust etc— all *gratis*'.[53]

Harriet wrote to commiserate. She hoped to hear from him soon, as she knew Dr Borsch had intended to operate in May. But when June came, she had still heard nothing and wrote to Sylvia to ask how the operation had gone, and to enquire after Mrs Joyce's state of nerves. As Mr Joyce had promised to report Dr Borsch's decision at once, she was afraid she must have annoyed or hurt him by a 'hasty' letter she had sent him.*[54]

He had in fact written that day, to thank her for a kind letter. He was still awaiting the operation, a second iridectomy, and when it was performed, Harriet was kept posted by Lucia. Dr Borsch, when he had done the operation, said that he expected it to prove a success, and Harriet wrote to tell the patient how very glad she felt. By this time, she had seen the new portrait and had not liked it very much. Mr Tuohy, on his way to Dublin, had brought it to her flat on Whitsun Saturday, and had seen and liked—as a caricature—Wyndham

* The 'hasty' letter has not come to light.

236

Lewis's drawing of James Joyce, recently given her by the sitter and now framed and hung above her desk.

Harriet's desk, where she had poured over Joyce's enigmatic fiction, and written philosophy summaries for Dora, was now invaded by a new subject. Dora, in pursuit of scientific evidence for her metaphysical theories, had taken up astronomy, with the object of showing that the forces of gravity and magnetism were the same thing, under different names. She hoped to prove it by relating sun-spot cycles to the movements of the planets, and to the magnetic disturbances affecting weather on earth; and had enlisted Harriet to make the required abstracts and tabulations.

The weather, the sky, and the heavenly bodies already had an important place in Harriet's imagination. She was excited by the prospect of studying systematically the movements she had watched in the night sky, and the work had a technical appeal too: she always enjoyed doing simple arithmetic. For Dora, this work was a side-line, a skirmishing attack on the theories of Einstein; but for Harriet it was an introduction to studies that were to occupy her mind and time for many years to come. Meanwhile, it distracted her from nagging anxiety about James Joyce's health.

He was back at the hotel, but in a higher room with more light, and seventeen days after the operation he was able to write to Harriet at length. Although Dr Borsch was hopeful, he himself was depressed because there was practically no improvement in his vision and, as the eye was still kept bandaged, he had to depend on the other. This made reading difficult, and work was hardly possible in the grey Paris light. But he could get about, his appetite was good, and he was even glad the operation had been done—if only to ensure against the risk of another attack of iritis developing into glaucoma.

He was told he looked well. But whenever he had to lie down with his eyes closed he saw 'a cinemagraph' of memories he had almost forgotten: 'The long drudgery and disappointment in Trieste (I scarcely ate anything, taught until late every night and bought one suit of clothes in nine years, but the Irish literary movement has finally had its attention called to my existence) and then the labour of *Ulysses* must have undermined my strength. I was poisoned in more ways than one'.[55]

Even the gift of 'hortensias, white and blue, dyed', on Bloom's day, 16th June, roused his self-distrust. 'I have to convince myself that I wrote that book. I used to be able to talk intelligently about it. If I ever try to explain to people now what I am supposed to be writing I see stupefaction freezing them into silence.'[56]

Harriet could take little pleasure in the fact that others besides herself were stupefied by Work in Progress. If they were right, then he was wasting his time. But the letter was not altogether discouraging. She could well appreciate his gallant efforts at memory training —five hundred lines of The Lady of the Lake got by heart and repeated without a mistake—and she was delighted that he had managed to write her one of his long letters. That in itself was a good sign.

Her work on sunspots had now become very absorbing. Dora's intuitions were supported so far by the correlations, over short periods of time, between sunspots and planetary positions.* Harriet drew up an elaborate chart, and sent it to Dora, with notes. Dora, 'delighted to hear of this observed action of the earth', urged her to go and 'play' with a model of the planetary orbits at the Royal Astronomical Society. She need only 'work the balls through the complete cycle of their revolutions' and all would be made plain.[57]

They both felt they were on the verge of discovery. Harriet, excited by some new insight, sent off a telegram; and Dora was writing to her at least three times a week, and had put aside two unfinished volumes in order to start a third, Space, Time and Gravitation. Harriet's work was to appear, as an appendix, under her own name.

Harriet, though still insisting she was not an original writer, liked the idea of seeing herself in print as a research worker. T. S. Eliot, who was taking over her office for his magazine The Criterion, had given her some encouragement, and showed a definite interest in the book. Dora, however, made difficulties. She thought she might, perhaps, let him have the book, but she intended to ask for an unusually high royalty, thirty-three and one-third; and she had decided to withhold her name, as she felt paralysed by personal involvement. 'Your piece of research,' she told Harriet crisply, 'would therefore also need to be anonymous. . . .'[58]

As the book was only just started, Harriet's disappointment was not

---

* Dr A. J. Meadows, Department of Astronomy, University of Leicester, asked to comment on Dora Marsden's sunspot theory, said that 'rather similar theories had been put forward during the 19th Century' and that, although the correlation always seemed to break down over periods of the order of a century, 'the idea of such a correlation—in a much modified form—has recently been revived in the United States'. (Librarian, Royal Astronomical Society to Jane Lidderdale, 20th January 1967)

acute. Her enthusiasm for the research was unabated. But there were other urgent demands on her time: the practical tasks, and the legal formalities, of winding up her company. The work kept her tied to London, and to her desk, and she had to cut down her weekend visits to Mary and Annie at Guildford, to Alfred and Muriel in Buckinghamshire. She found time in July, however, to organize and to preside over a family gathering—a dinner party at the Empire Exhibition, Wembley, for her three brothers and three sisters and three 'in-laws' and five connections of the family.* 'It is heroic,' wrote Dora two days before, 'to gather together fourteen members of one's own family all unprotected by the softening sentiment of Xmas.'[59]

The occasion evidently gave Harriet great pleasure; and James Joyce, now recuperating at St Malo with his wife and children, enjoyed her lively account of it: 'I have reached nearly the end of the Wembley dinner party. The tangential relationships, the spiral progressions and the presence of the absent remind me of something which perhaps I wrote or ought to have written.'[60]

In the first half of July there had been two very hot days, and Harriet had dreaded tidying her office in the thundery weather that always made her uneasy and out of sorts. But cooler weather came and she was able to get on with the job of sorting and listing her stock. She also arranged, with considerable difficulty, a series of company meetings—only to learn from the Egoist solicitor that formal liquidation was unnecesssarily expensive and troublesome. All that was wanted was to satisfy Somerset House that the 'company is not still trading'.[61] So she scratched out the resolution passed at the first meeting, and tore up the minutes of the second.[62]

Dora had commented: 'Peace to the ashes of "The Egoist Limited" '.[63] But it was only in a metaphysical sense that the Egoist was consumed; in the office, its material existence was still manifest. Although Harriet had dispatched more than nine hundred books to Jonathan Cape, at least one thousand seven hundred remained; and there were more than three thousand *Poets' Translations*, besides other pamphlets. In addition, Harriet had underestimated her stock of *Egoists*.

She made up a number of sets to be stored in her flat, and was still

* Edward Weaver married Ela Monro, whose sister Edith married Percy Hone, whose brother Campbell married Maude Weaver. And the Monros and Hones were distant cousins.

able to offer Sylvia about a hundred copies. Richard Aldington's *Images* went, ultimately, to Allen & Unwin. The *Tyros* went back to Wyndham Lewis, and with them, as no publisher had yet come forward, the remainders (about three hundred) of *Tarr* and *The Caliph's Design*. And finally, T. S. Eliot, who had helped her throughout, although as she could see he was as usual overworked and tired, agreed to take delivery, on the spot, of Marianne Moore's *Poems*, Jean Cocteau's *Cock and Harlequin*, Ezra Pound's two books, *Fontenelle* and *Quia Pauper Amavi*, and the *Poets' Translations*.

It was convenient that the pamphlets, and over one thousand two hundred books, could pass to new owners without moving. On Monday, 11th August, Harriet was ready to make her final dispositions. She told Sylvia 'I am closing my office this week'. She enclosed her printed list, annotated to show where all the books were now lodged: with individual authors, Jonathan Cape, Allen & Unwin or *The Criterion*.

Harriet was not apt to ponder on her own achievement; nor was she inclined to waste time on regrets. But she allowed herself to mark this critical moment in her life. On the list she sent Sylvia, against the imprint of The Egoist Press, she wrote one word—closed.

PART III

1924—1941

Q

12

SELDOM SEEN

HARRIET had certainly enjoyed her responsibility for a group of young writers and felt some sense of loss when the burden was laid down. She was not left long, however, with any empty spaces in her life. She had no office work, and was able to travel more, but her time was increasingly occupied by the interests—and troubles—of her friends.

In August 1924, when the Joyces were on holiday in Brittany, she received some snapshots. Evidently, he was overworking again: he lacked the look of 'sea-dazed blankness' that she considered the hallmark of a successful holiday. Holidays, according to her family tradition, ought to be regarded as cures; and she had hoped his recovery would be speeded up by the windfall she had just given him: £550 that came to her when Aunt Emily's estate was finally wound up.[1] She put the blame on the weather—wet, windy and cold. When he should have been basking on the sea-shore, he must have been writing indoors, or taking cheerless walks to the public library.

James Joyce's reply to her condolences was not very consoling:

. . . I am sorry my cyclopeyed face has that worried look. Really I have got some rest and a good deal of sea air. But it is true I have been thinking how and how and how can I and can it—all about the fusion of the two parts of the book—while my one bedazzled eye searched the sea like Cain—Shem—Tristan—Patrick from his lighthouse in Boulogne. I hope the solution will presently appear. At least I have never found anything in any other way than sitting with my mouth open picturesquely.[2]

The photographs had shocked her, and he now confirmed the impression they had made with another image of pathos. 'I have goloshes, a tarpaulin raincoat, a hood, an umbrella and a pair of yellow spectacles—so won't the Londoners, standing beside the park wall out oĵ the shower's way, be delighted to see me groping by!'³

He was coming to London, to see Jonathan Cape and to get legal advice about establishing British citizenship for Giorgio, who had just had call-up papers for the Italian army. The rain should have kept off, he felt, until he reached England. He arrived, with his family, in the middle of September. Harriet was looking forward to hearing his explanations of his latest 'pieces', but this pleasure was deferred for another meeting arranged, unexpectedly, to take place in Paris. Bryher, Robert McAlmon and Hilda Doolittle were just going there for a week, on their way from London to Switzerland, and asked Harriet to come with them.

Robert McAlmon had felt for some time that Miss Weaver should be rescued from her shyness. In 1921, when he took on himself the task of interpreting James Joyce to her, he had been concerned to remove the barriers; and had succeeded better than most of her literary friends. Although at first she had answered, looking into space, with 'a short-gasped "yes" or "no" ', she had in the end made a confession: 'she feared she had never faced life with sufficient courage to know reality' and she had always been afraid of 'people who drank'.⁴

The invitation to Paris, three years later, was given on the spur of the moment, and Harriet had no reason to suspect a missionary motive. She feared only that she might be 'in the way'. But she was eager to meet Miss Beach; her own work for Dora was in abeyance, after the zeal and excitement of the previous months; and a few remaining odd jobs for The Egoist Press could wait. For once, she could do what she liked with her time; and she decided to accept.

The McAlmons understood her diffidence but they cannot have known that the thought of setting out at once was a challenge in itself. A trip abroad was an everyday affair to them. To Harriet, any journey—even at home—was a hazardous undertaking. Not only the train she was taking, but every train, both ways, had to be listed; and the list stowed where it could be consulted at a moment's notice. Then clothes, shoes, rugs and assorted impedimenta had to be thoughtfully selected, ranged in the order in which they would be needed (or might be needed in an emergency) and packed in reverse order for instant unpacking. These were precautions she could take. Other habitual precautions were of no avail. In England, she always travelled with a Post Office Savings Bank book as well as a cheque book, in case she needed emergency money between three and six o'clock, when post offices were still open after the banks were closed. Now, this reassurance was denied her; and she was venturing across the Channel, for the first time, without a single relation to give her support.

The McAlmons, firm in their intention to help her 'know reality' and get over her fear of the 'less high-minded pastimes' of writers and artists, started the trip, in advance, by taking her out to a London Music Hall. She appeared to be 'highly entertained' particularly by Norah Bayes' rowdy song 'No-one ever loved like Samson and Delilah'.* [5]

The next morning, when Harriet dressed for the journey, she fastened round her waist, over her petticoat, a leather belt. Attached to it was a pocket, closed with a snap fastener, in which she had placed her reserves of Treasury notes and franc notes. Two leather straps, suspended from the belt, met in a V just above the hem of her petticoat, and held there another, smaller pocket where she had placed her tickets. She had always taken (and never gave up) these prudent precautions against the loss or theft of her handbag.

She had also the prudent habit of getting to the station at least half an hour before the train started. The McAlmon party, as they made their way down the continental platform at Victoria, saw a neat figure, in a lightweight, tailor-made coat and skirt—just right for the journey—which gave no hint of the contraption beneath it. This was their dear friend Josephine. Even Robert McAlmon, whose sympathy for her was penetrating and active, had no way of knowing all the barriers that prevented her being one of a crowd. He himself enjoyed the idea of a 'crowd' (artistic, literary, convivial) and wanted his friends to join.

In Paris, he planned a party to the fashionable cabaret run by Bricktop, the red-headed '100 per cent American Negro with a trigger-Irish temper' for whom Cole Porter wrote *Miss Otis Regrets*. Harriet might have seen there two or three reigning monarchs, and any number of Bricktop's famous friends (two of her admirers were

---

* Harriet Weaver was never unnerved by the subject of sex, as she was by the subject of drink. Later on, when some of her young friends dissolved their marriages, she listened to their troubles with tolerance and sympathy; and when she took her young niece Rosamond to *The Beggar's Opera*, her comment on the ladies of the town was calm and dry—'Not really a good way of life to follow'.

Evelyn Waugh and Lord Beaverbrook).[6] But this challenge she was
spared, as the party broke up over dinner at l'Avenue where, among
others, William Bird, the sculptor Thelma Wood and novelist Djuna
Barnes had joined them. Robert McAlmon described, much later,
how and why the evening failed, but for once his understanding of
Harriet was a little at fault:

. . . Throughout the meal everything went charmingly. Several were
newly acquainted with each other and Miss Weaver's obvious dignity
and reserve dominated the affair. However, Hilda Doolittle, who had
known Miss Weaver for years, urged with me that she should have
at least one glass of wine. The rest drank more generously. By the
time dinner was over Miss Weaver may have sipped half a glass of
wine, and Ezra Pound arrived.

Ezra had left England some years before and not seen Miss Weaver
since, but surely he recalled that she was reticent. Ezra doesn't drink
to an extent that one can mention. He seemed gay as he entered,
however, so that he may have had an extra cognac or so. In any case
he greeted us all jubilantly, and suddenly turned to Miss Weaver
saying, "Why, Harriet, this is the first time I've ever seen you drunk".
His eagle eye had spotted her half-filled wine-glass.

Hilda gasped and her eyes caught mine, and we both let out a gasp
of laughter, and both turned scarlet upon seeing Miss Weaver. She
sat back as though struck. Later Hilda and I agreed that she thought
she did look drunk because of that thimblefull of wine. The party was
dumb with consternation. Ezra realised that his comedy had not gone
over and sat down, self-conscious and fidgety, looking at Djuna and
at H.D., at Bill Bird and at me, hoping that some one of us could
rescue the situation.

Djuna did best. She saw that Miss Weaver wasn't going to recover
through a wittily made remark or even a short and earnest explanation that it was a joke. She asked her quietly if she wished to leave.
It was past ten, and Miss Weaver did want to leave. Hilda saw her to
her hotel, across the square, and returned, explaining that Harriet
thought her very brave to venture again into that scene.[7]

Robert McAlmon called on Miss Weaver next morning and took
her for a long walk on the right bank, with a stop at Fouquet's for
coffee. She did not seem to believe his version of the incident, but he
went on arguing 'that Ezra was to a good extent a thwarted comedian;

he hadn't been intoxicated, he was a self-conscious and shy individual and had made an awkward remark to cover his entry into the party which seemed gay'. At last, as they reached her hotel, she said: 'I am sure you are right. If you will give me [his] address I will call on him at tea-time. I have always admired his work and must not let my prejudices get the better of me.'[8]

Harriet certainly lacked the experience to distinguish between merriment and alcoholism, and probably thought the party drunker than it really was. The same mistake seems to have been made, with less excuse, by Robert McAlmon, who knew that Bryher never drank and that H.D. was always (like Ezra Pound) very abstemious. To this extent, he embroidered his story, and he also made one startling slip; it was inconceivable that Ezra Pound, clumsy as he was, would address Miss Weaver as Harriet.*

Bryher, in a more sober account, has confirmed that everyone was dismayed by 'Josephine's' stiff and utter disapproval of the misdirected joke, but that she took the incident less seriously when several people had told her that there was 'certainly no malice connected with it'. 'All of us had simply wanted to make her feel that she belonged to the group that was interested in Joyce.'[9]

So Ezra Pound was forgiven, for friendship's sake, and no one guessed that Harriet had in fact been struggling with a private nightmare. She had promised to visit the Joyces when they came home, and she feared she might have to live through the appalling experience of seeing Mr Joyce the worse for drink. She had tried to steel herself, in imagination, and her friends' vain efforts to evoke a spirit of gaiety, had brought home to her how ill-armed she was in fact.

Within a few days, she was writing to thank the McAlmons for 'having pressed me to come to Paris in your party'.[10] By that time, she was pleasantly settled in a small hotel, 151 Rue de Rennes, just off the Boulevard Montparnasse; and she had met and made friends with Sylvia Beach. The address she had written so often on parcels of books—Shakespeare and Company, 12 rue de l'Odéon—now took on material form as a bookshop and library set in a narrow street, with a tiny office behind and a tiny flat above. Miss Beach herself was diminutive and sparkling with energy. She provided a centre, a club, and 'American Express' services for left-bank writers, and looked after their needs with unflagging spirit. Harriet could appreciate the

* When Robert McAlmon's autobiography came out, neither Harriet Weaver nor James Joyce (for different reasons) liked it.

friendly, unpretentious atmosphere, and there was special pleasure in
seeing the fifth edition of *Ulysses* on the shelves, and on the wall a
trophy she had sent Sylvia herself—the 'scandal' poster of the *Sporting
Times*.

She learned that Sylvia's background was not unlike her own. She
had been brought up strictly and, except for a few months' schooling,
had been educated privately. Through her late teens she had lived in
the civilized setting of a large Colonial-style manse (rather like Cedar
Lawn) in the university town of Princeton, where her father was
minister of the First Presbyterian Church. There were striking
differences too. Harriet had been led into publishing by one thing
following another; Sylvia had wanted a bookshop ever since she
acquired in childhood a voracious appetite for reading. She had no
private means, but her family, unlike Harriet's, approved her longing
to strike out. It was her mother's savings that gave her a start, and
her sisters Holly and Cyprian came to Paris whenever they could and
gave a hand. Because the bookshop was her living, she intended to
make money.* But her generosity often thwarted her ambition.

Within a very few days, Sylvia persuaded Harriet (who had failed
to find a suitable photograph for her) to sit for her friend Man Ray,
once a Dadaist painter and now producing imaginative work 'with a
camera instead of a brush'.[11] The studies he made, at two sittings, are
quite unlike any other photographs of Harriet. They are interpretative
pictures, not studio portraits; and they were taken, moreover, in the
short period when she wore her hair in a bob. It was a touching
attempt to be in fashion and feel less old, but her family did not care
for it.

Harriet saw a good deal of Miss Beach and their talk ranged from
literary news and plans to the personal troubles of Mr Joyce. Miss
Beach introduced her, too, to interesting people; the beautiful Mina
Loy, who supported herself and her children by making lampshades
and wrote poetry—praised by Mr Eliot in *The Egoist*—whenever she
had time; the editors of *The Little Review*, Margaret Anderson and
Jane Heap, who were now publishing their journal from Paris; and
above all, Adrienne Monnier, whose bookshop was just across the
road. For some reason she never explained, Harriet took a dislike to
the *Little Review* editors; but she had already two good reasons for

* Sylvia Beach, writing to Holly Beach on 23rd April 1921, had rejoiced in the
prospect of making some money on *Ulysses* 'not only for Mr Joyce but also for me'.
(Princeton)

being well disposed towards Mademoiselle Monnier. She was Miss Beach's great friend, and had lately published, in the first number of her literary review *Commerce*, translations of passages from *Ulysses*. Harriet entertained her new friends at a restaurant near her hotel and, whenever she could, went for walks—through the Luxembourg gardens on her way from her hotel to Miss Beach, down little streets babbling with village gossip and along the banks of Mr Joyce's Anna Sequana.

The Joyces returned to Paris with good news: with the help of Monro Saw & Co., Giorgio's right to British citizenship had been established and he was free to go on with his training as a singer. He was often at the flat when Harriet visited his parents but Lucia rarely appeared. She felt uneasy with her father's friends and she was frightened of Miss Weaver, so 'distinguished' and so 'very well dressed'. 'I used to avoid her,' she recalls, 'and run out when she came.'[12]

For Harriet and James Joyce, the absorbing subject was Vico's *Principi di una Scienza Nuova*, which had greatly influenced his recent pieces. He gave Harriet a copy, inscribed 'Ad Harriet Weaver questo libricciano in segno di sua grande riconoscenza James Joyce Parigi li 17 8bre 1924'.* She had no time in Paris to set to work on it so she put it aside until she got home; and heard first Mr Joyce's exposition of history's recurring cycles and of the arcane wisdom contained in language and in myth.

She and Miss Beach were both invited to the flat to hear his latest pieces: the first watch of Shaun, falling asleep in 'nonland' among 'objects nonviewable'; and the second watch, where Jaunty Jaun loosens his 'bruised brogues'.[13] For Harriet, the reading was a test of her understanding; for James Joyce, the first of a series of tests given ambiguously to her and to himself.

'Hark!' he said, and then came the tolling heartbeats of sleep. 'Tolv two elf kater. . .'

Harriet did not fail the test, but she evidently gave Mr Joyce the impression that she still needed, and would welcome, any guidance he felt disposed to offer. She had already taken, in imagination, another test; and had reconciled herself to the idea that he sometimes drank. Now she faced the ordeal of seeing him drinking. Since he was a convivial, not an obsessive drinker—and was careful about whom he

* The book is now in the James Joyce collection at the National Book League, London.

was drinking with—she cannot possibly have seen him incapacitated, merely cheerful.* The trivial signs of reaction to alcohol were enough to upset her, but not enough to weaken the ties of friendship.†

Her introduction to reality was extended, just before she left, by the first scenes of a literary squabble. One of the assistant editors of *Commerce*, Léon-Paul Fargue, was ganging up with the backer, the American-born Princesse di Bassiano (backer also of *The Criterion*) against the publisher, Adrienne Monnier, who apparently had the support of the other assistant editor, James Joyce's friend and admirer Valery Larbaud. James Joyce was confided in by both factions and wrote to tell Harriet, after she got home, that Larbaud had changed sides. He had been 'denounced by Miss Monnier' and 'warned not to walk, run or creep through the rue de l'Odéon'.[14]

This was a mode of life that was strange to Harriet, but her interest and sympathy were engaged. She was sorry to leave Paris. It had been 'a very great pleasure' to meet Miss Beach, and she was conscious that some barriers had been broken down: 'now I have been over once, another trip will not seem quite such a terrible undertaking!'[15]

No doubt she felt she had made some friends; but it would not have occurred to her that she had made a deep impression. Sylvia Beach had noticed particularly how 'tenderhearted' she was— 'Almost weeps if anyone even stubs their toe'—and had written to tell her mother that they got on 'like a house afire';[16] while Robert McAlmon had privately decided to dedicate to her his *Contact Collection of Contemporary Writers*, where he was using works by a number of her friends and contributors.‡

In London, she was in a 'distracted rush' with her 'head in a whirl'. She had to clear up her flat for a four-months let, but she had undertaken first to help her brother Kearsley, who was not very well, to move house. She spent four days in Guildford, with Mary and Annie,

* James Joyce had some notable drinking bouts with, among others, Frank Budgen and Wyndham Lewis. But Arthur Power, who knew him well at this period (conversation with Jane Lidderdale, 17th June 1967) never saw him 'the worse for drink'.

† Richard Ellmann says she was 'greatly' upset and appears to assume that she would have seen James Joyce obviously intoxicated. Harriet Weaver saw Richard Ellmann's MS in draft, and the fact that she did not correct the passage does not mean that she agreed with it. She avoided commenting on any references to herself.

‡ Djuna Barnes, Bryher, Mary Butts, Norman Douglas, Havelock Ellis, Ford Madox Ford, Wallace Gould, Ernest Hemingway, Marsden Hartley, H.D., John Harriman, James Joyce, Mina Loy, Robert McAlmon, Ezra Pound, Dorothy Richardson, May Sinclair, Edith Sitwell, Gertrude Stein and William Carlos Williams.

settling him in to the house he had built for himself, called by their father's name—Poynton. Back in London, she tidied and sorted; made up two sets of files of *The Egoist* that Bryher had ordered as presents for Sylvia Beach and Jane Heap; wrote to Miss Beach to remind her to secure the best set, complete and 'less soiled', and signed the first number—for 1st July 1914—that appeared under her own editorship; posted, with some new press cuttings, a copy of *Penguin Island* she had promised Mr Joyce; and read it before sending it off.

She heard twice from Mr Joyce before she left for the north. Work was going well, and a week after 'one of the partitions gave way' the tunnelling parties were 'hammering on all sides'.[17] But he was threatened with another operation, this time for cataract. Here was bad news, but Harriet, who had found glaucoma very mysterious— even after she had read a treatise on the subject—could not but feel that there was some advantage in having an affliction that surgeons were competent to remedy.

At the end of November, she went to Seldom Seen. There, too, she had work to do, including the domestic chores she was spared at home. The outdoor jobs suited her; in a cheerful spirit (except when she was drenched with rain) she drew water, fetched the groceries, gathered sticks and collected bark and chips where timber had been felled. Cooking, less congenial, she restricted to once or twice a week, when she boiled half-a-dozen eggs, a stew of meat and root vege- tables, and a large dish of prunes. It was a monotonous diet; fresh vegetables were not to be had in winter. But Harriet's austere objec- tive was to keep out the cold with hot, or warmed-up, meals; and to waste not a moment of time on it.

By this time, Dora had a large collection of books, and Harriet always brought another load with her, some for her own department of the work and some for Dora's. But Dora's field was in a constant state of expansion, and she soon needed more. Harriet wrote to order from Miss Beach Duheim's *La Théorie Physique* and *Le Système du Monde*, and to ask also if she could track down some old periodicals.[18] Dora was still seeking, in science and mathematics, support for her metaphysical theories.

Harriet's interest in these subjects was more direct. She enjoyed reading about matters of fact and making orderly abstracts, but she sometimes suffered when it came to discussing them with Dora. Dora was quick to 'fly off the handle' and once, after arguing over the angles at the base of isosceles triangles, she was not on speaking terms with Harriet. Harriet, however, remained a non-combatant and peace was restored in the morning.[19]

About them lay the hills and lakes, and Harriet's walks abroad, with the help of the guide book, brought her a reminder of the jokes she had with Mr Joyce about the ubiquitous St Patrick. A roadside well at Patterdale (originally Patrick's Dale, with a church dedicated to St Patrick) was known as the place where he baptized his converts and was still called by his name. This was at the head of the lake; Sir Tristram, the guide book told her, occupied a fortress downstream. She was pleased with her discovery and left for Frodsham, just before Christmas, in a cheerful mood.

It was very pleasant to be in a comfortable house, with proper meals appearing at regular intervals. Here, too, she saw around her the scenes of childhood, and she saw them shining in a new light. Across the Marsh, she could follow the course of the river Weaver—un-romantic, unadventurous, her own kin—and reflect on the endless cycles of evaporation and rainfall, and the Weaver moving in rhythm with the great rivers of the world, and with the all-containing river, Anna Livia Plurabelle.

She had Vico's book with her and set herself to the exacting but rewarding task of puzzling it out. Mr Joyce's Christmas present was another book, Victor Bérard's *L'Odyssée Poésie Homérique*. It was a new book, just out, and beautifully printed, a virtue she had learned to appreciate. But her pleasure was flawed by bad news. His cataract had been removed but the result, so far, had been only 'splendid sights for a minute or so' and the alarming threat of 'an electric cure when the broken window of my soul can stand more shocks'.[20] A week later, he reported a conversation with his doctor:

Dr B.: How is our eye?

J.J.:   *Semper idem.*

Dr B.: (business) Not to me. I have still a fortnight.

J.J.:   Ten days, doctor. You still think you'll win.

Dr B.: Sure I'll win.

J.J.:   (baffled, beaten, vanquished, overcome, pulverised) smiles broadly.

Dr B.: You'll see all right.

J.J.:   It is an obstinate eye, doctor, no?

Dr B.: No fellow is any good if he's not obstinate.

J.J.:   (checkmated, silenced, overpowered) smiles broadly: And
        when do you think you can prescribe for the lenses?
Dr B.: Three weeks or a month after.
    I don't know what he means. But he ought to be the ambassador
for the two Americas. . . .[21]

    James Joyce's dramatizations of his suffering were intended to pro-
duce the most poignant effects on himself as well as on others. Harriet,
had she not been so very tender-hearted, might have felt that there
were rather too many of them, particularly as she herself had been
taught to suffer in silence. But she was never deceived into thinking
that only the silent suffer, and she honoured the reality behind the
appearance—James Joyce's extraordinary courage and firmness of
will. He was by no means overpowered. He had ordered for her a
book of spirit talks with Oscar Wilde, revised the watches of Shaun
and was sending them to her, and had taken the trouble to send her,
in advance, notes on the new text. He was eager for her approval and
had seen the risks of submitting, unexplained, to her judgment. She
must know 'a few things' first: the Irish Alphabet; the dualist philosophy of Bruno Nolano; one or two points of Danish grammar and
syntax; and the 'words expressing nightmares 'from Greek, German,
Irish, Japanese, Italian and Assyrian. 'I speak the latter language,' he
observed, 'very fluently and have several nice volumes of it in the
kitchen printed on jampots. Most coastal towns in Ireland (E) are
Danish. The good old fellows were often wreckers. In ancient Dublin
there was a ceremony similar to that of the Doge wedding the
Adriatic sea.'[22]
    Harriet moved back to Seldom Seen in January. She could not
disappoint Dora, and she promised her aunt to make up for the short
visit by coming again in April, instead of going back to London. One
of the days at Frodsham had been taken up by a shopping expedition
in Chester, where she had ordered a house-warming present for
Kearsley, whose pride and pleasure in the new house had been a
delight to see. The present was meant as a surprise, and a bit of a
mystery; and Kearsley wrote to thank in the same spirit. Two large
boxes, attributed only to Messrs Jones of Chester, had arrived, containing 'a very beautiful and appropriate READING LAMP' and 'a
well-made shade in excellent and green taste'. He had asked himself
who the offender could be. Then, as the Weaver family always enjoyed parodies, he went on: 'As, jury-like, I sift the evidence, and as

you stand for trial at the bar, I come irresistably to the verdict that you are GUILTY.' The sentence was 'that you be summarily, and at the same time greatly and violently thanked for this unprovoked crime'; and invited to come and stay.[23]

Harriet, meanwhile, was writing a whole series of thank-you letters to Miss Beach, who not only sent the books she wanted, but also released her assistant to transcribe articles from the library files of rare technical journals; and then had to be reminded to charge for time as well as costs. One of her parcels had a touch of black comedy: the book of spirit talks, with a medium James Joyce had described as a Dublin professor's daughter, included a message that Oscar Wilde did not like *Ulysses*.

It was during February 1925 that Harriet received from Mr Joyce the last letter, for five months, to be written in his normal hand. A series of new troubles forced him to write large, in broad black pencil, or to dictate. Dr Borsch wanted to do a further operation, described as slight, and unknowingly proposed to do it on his patient's birthday. This was unacceptable, unfortunately as things turned out. He developed conjunctivitis, and then episcleritis, and had to spend about ten days at the Clinique des Yeux in the rue du Cherche Midi. Harriet heard of this set-back first from Lucia and then from Mr Joyce himself, in a letter dictated to an obliging but inexperienced scribe:

je me trouve ici depuis 8 jours le trouble dans mon oeuil persiste main l'on m'assure que ce n'est pas l'Iris et quil n'y aura pas de consequence . . . la douleur est parfois intolerable. . . On a donne la 1er de ma piece a New-York jai recu un télegrame d'un ami qui me disait quel a ete bien acceuillie je conte que se sera un succès destame. . . . Je vous dicts ma lettre par Raymond le fils de mon infirmiere il a dix ans il est bien gentil. . . *[24]

Harriet's comment was given in a postscript to a letter she had written, but not posted, to Miss Beach. She hoped that Dr Borsch,

* I have been here for eight days. The trouble in my eye remains but I am assured that it is not the iris and that there will be no ill consequences . . . the pain is sometimes intolerable. . . My play has had its first night in New York. I have received a cable from a friend who reports that it was well received. I believe it will be a succès d'estime. . . . I am dictating this to Raymond my nurse's son. He is ten and is very kind. . .

whose prognoses were sometimes aimed only at calming his 'highly nervous patient', was to be trusted this time. Because of heavy snow, she had put off the two-mile trudge to the post office and general store, so long as there was anything to eat at Seldom Seen, if only potatoes and bread.[25]

James Joyce, meanwhile, was experiencing the mockery of a *succès d'estime*. *Exiles*, a play with 'neither a motor car nor a telephone in it' had not been a great success.[26] * He sent a programme and a few notices, and Harriet, passing them on to Miss Beach when the play's short run was ended, observed that it evidently needed 'a very special cast'.[27]

All Mr Joyce's letters included bulletins on his health. The crisis was over; he had revised a text—in the dark; he had been 'near unreason' but morphia had relieved the pain; he could not see a word of print; Dr Borsch was certain that the next operation would restore his sight; his teeth were to be X-rayed; he was making *vocalizzi* at the piano and doing exercises with his son's elastic stretcher; the X-ray had shown a splinter of tooth in the gum; its removal had been postponed because there was more trouble in his right eye; he was on a starvation diet and, if he walked the eight or ten kilometres a day prescribed, he would apply for the legion of honour.[28]

Harriet had half-promised Miss Beach to pay her a visit in April, when she could have travelled, as before, with the McAlmons. But she still had to complete her 'curtailed' Christmas visit to her aunt, and she had a good deal to do in London when she got possession of her flat at the end of the month. Meanwhile, the obligation to relieve Dora's loneliness in winter had been succeeded by the obligation, in summer, to protect her from hordes of visitors. 'Nevertheless,' she told Miss Beach, 'I would like to try to dash over to Paris for a week . . . after May 4th.'[29] She could travel then with Mary and Annie, who were to pass through Paris on their way farther afield.

Mr Joyce, now recovering from dentistry, and awaiting the seventh of his eye operations, was working, in spite of it all, on a script he was getting ready for *The Criterion*, Anna Livia's Mamafesta;† [30] and going to the clinic every morning.[31] Harriet saw it was unlikely he would have much time to spare for her, but if she was going to Paris at all that year she had to go at once, before she settled in the north for her summer term of work.

* *Exiles* had a run of forty-one performances.
† An early version of *Finnegans Wake*, I, 5.

She went for one week. She stayed for three, at a simple little hotel in the Place de la Sorbonne. She began to feel at home in Paris, where everyone welcomed her and showed her 'so much kindness'. This was Miss Beach's circle and it was Miss Beach herself who showed kindness in 'an enormously large and overflowing measure'.[32] After only eight months' acquaintance, she was addressing Miss Beach as Sylvia, and gave her the right to use her own pseudonym Josephine.

During her visit, Sylvia was deeply involved in preparations for a new periodical, to be launched on 1st June by Adrienne Monnier: *Le Navire d'Argent*, Revue Mensuelle de Littérature et de Culture Générale. Its maiden voyage was to be graced by several names Harriet knew. Valery Larbaud, now restored to favour, was contributing the first article, on Paris; and Sylvia and Adrienne had collaborated in a translation:

> *Allons alors, vous et moi,*
> *Quand le soir est étendu contre le ciel*
> *Comme un patient anesthésié sur une table. . .*

T. S. Eliot, in the person of Alfred J. Prufrock, was singing his love-song, in French.

Mr Joyce, though still very blind, was not always immobilized in clinics. He had news for Harriet. Mr Samuel Roth, who had amazed her in 1922 by proposing to publish *Ulysses* entire in a single issue of his journal *Two Worlds*, had now committed an act of piracy. His latest issue carried unauthorized pieces—possibly the first of many—from Work in Progress. This was a professional reverse; but the family fortunes were on the mend. At long last, they were moving into an unfurnished flat (2 Square Robiac, rue de Grenelle, not far from the indispensable Sylvia Beach) where they had some prospect of making, as Harriet had always hoped, a proper and permanent home.* Meanwhile, she saw something of the appalling upheavals that attended a Joyce family déménagement and, when she called on Mrs Joyce in the new flat, found it still only half-furnished.[33] She went home with her growing concern for the family strongly reinforced.†

* It was permanent until the spring of 1931.
† With some reason. The upholstered chairs arrived four months later—and were taken back to be stuffed. 'I never do that when I supply prose to the public,' said James Joyce. 'All stuffing done on the premises.'

Harriet spent a rushed three weeks in London, mainly seeing the relations she felt she had somewhat neglected, fifteen of them in all.[34] She visited, among others, her elder sisters and Kearsley, who had the distinction of *not* disapproving her short hair; but nonetheless, she was starting to let it grow.

She saw Bryher, too, though not Robert, and collected the Joyce record that Sylvia had given her and had entrusted to them.* The McAlmons were enduring, as best they could, 'family life' with the Ellermans, while their own flat in Sloane Street was being converted.[35] Harriet saw no reason to be wounded by Robert's absence, but the reason he gave to Sylvia made her feel sad when she heard of it later: 'Bryher saw Miss Weaver. I thought I wouldn't as we seem to strike social paralysis into each other now. She always made me conscious that she was shy, and I thought I had to help out. But now I've become conscious that she knows I DO DRINK and am frightened to think that I frighten her.'[36]

At Seldom Seen, Robert's *Contact Collection of Contemporary Writers* was waiting for her, the dedication on the third page, and with it the first issue of Adrienne Monnier's new venture, *Le Navire d'Argent*. Harriet sent warm congratulations to the 'enterprising *directrice*', and made a shy comment on the dedication to herself: 'The third page of the printed matter surprised me very much'.[37] †

Harriet stayed with Dora for the rest of the year, except for a short break at Gloucester Place in the autumn and a brief visit to the Hones. The 'summer hordes' of walkers and day visitors, and boisterous families of young children in the Seldom Seen cottages, drove all peace from the hillside; and indoors, until it was at least eighty in the shade, Dora kept her fire going. The choice between unbearable noise and unbearable heat was very hard for Harriet to make.[38]

Sylvia wrote regularly, and long letters from Mr Joyce arrived about every other week. Another operation was hanging over him, and meanwhile he was having a holiday in Normandy, but not enjoying himself:

---

* James Joyce's reading of John F. Taylor's speech in the *Eolus* episode of *Ulysses*. Harriet Weaver had asked that it be sent over by hand, to avoid any risk of breakage in the post.

† At James Joyce's suggestion, another copy for Harriet had been put in Sylvia's hands, for her to collect the contributors' signatures as and when they presented themselves in her shop. This turned out a longer job than anyone expected. Gertrude Stein wrote the final signature in 1939.

Rouen is the rainiest place getting
Inside all impermeables, wetting
Damp marrow in drenched bones.
Midwinter soused us coming over Le Mans
Our inn at Niort was the Grape of Burgundy
But the winepress of the Lord thundered over that grape of Burgundy
And we left it in a hurgundy.
(Hurry up, Joyce, it's time!)[39]

T. S. Eliot's *Waste Land* had been transformed into 'Clinic', the last destination. But 'liffle Anna countrymouse' was keeping him awake at night, and Shaun's fourth watch was unfinished.[40] He went back to Paris, and then put off the operation, in order to get Shaun off his mind first. In any case, he said, 'None of the operations has been very successful yet.'[41]

Anna Livia meanwhile, in an early manifestation, had been accepted for a new London Review, *The Calendar of Modern Letters*. But the editor, unable to 'cope with the crude forces of convention' in the human shape of his printers, was obliged to return to Mr Joyce, with great regret, the 'masterly example of his genius'.[42] Adrienne Monnier lost no time in diverting Anna Livia to *Le Navire d'Argent*; and Harriet, who had bitter experience of these crude forces, much admired the speed and neatness of the operation.[43]

Harriet had just made a flying visit to London, to 'spring-clean' the flat for a new let. Dora, inspired with the idea that her first two volumes must go to a publisher in January, when Harriet went south again to see the first London production of *Exiles*, had been most reluctant to spare her. But she showed concern when Harriet chose a return date that was going to involve her in difficulties of a formidable sort, even for Seldom Seen: 'Are you aware that there will be *no moon*. Do you think that it will be safe stumbling up the hill in the dark?'[44]

The reviews of Anna Livia that came, in due course, to Glencoin, were further proof to Harriet that there were other people, like herself, who found the new work difficult; and the 'new press opinions' Mr Joyce sent her—gathered from conversation, of course—were of the same tone: 'All Greek to us', 'unfortunately I can't read it', 'is it a puzzle?' . . . and so on.[45] But Dora was keeping her very hard at work, and her immediate worry was how to meet, or indeed get anywhere near, the supposed completion date. 'Miss Marsden,' she told

Sylvia, 'wants it finished much sooner than I thought she did. I go off on Thursday—my bag weighted with books!—to my old aunt for Christmas.'[46]

Mr Joyce's Christmas present awaited her at Castle Park: Hans Andersen's fairy tales. It was a subtle choice. Harriet had never read them, as fairy tales were banned by her mother, who disapproved of all fiction. The only stories she regarded with unreserved favour were out of the Bible. They were, of course, true.

Harriet had decided long ago that the Bible was largely fiction, but while rejecting the faith she had retained some of the underlying habits of mind. She remained acutely aware of a gulf between true and not-true. Nowadays, when literature, science and linguistics are often concerned with probabilities and thresholds, and regular church-goers are allowed to treat theology as metaphor, the service of truth requires other disciplines. Harriet's principles were formed in another century and she carried with her, in revolt, the logic she learnt at her mother's knee.

Here lay an unexplored trouble. She could understand that Work in Progress had many interlocking themes; but it still disturbed her that the events in it seemed to take place both inside and outside the single night of Earwicker's dream and, even more strangely, inside yet outside his limited mind.* The author's copious notes helped over particulars, but not in general. It seemed a defect that his text, unlike the great books that spoke to her directly, had to be teased out round a set of clues before the message was—in some degree—disclosed. And she saw it going on for ever. His peace of mind, which her efforts as publisher and patron had failed to secure, seemed to require a sacrifice of her integrity. Her mounting perplexity, which in the end forced her to speak, was hard to bear alone.

It would have been very pleasant to concentrate on fairy tales over the Christmas holidays. But even when James Joyce's troubles were off her mind, Dora's demands pursued her. She was working at high pressure and was apt to want all sorts of information by return of post; and she regarded Harriet's growing collection of quotations and paraphrases, showing how the concepts of space and time had changed over the centuries, as source material for her book.

Harriet remained an obliging research assistant. But the pangs of

* Harriet Weaver could never adopt the solution, chosen by Edmund Wilson and others, that *Finnegans Wake* 'was' a dream—'preposterous'. (To Bjørn Rasmussen, 9th March 1961)

conscience that haunted her reading of Work in Progress began to afflict also her collaboration with Dora. She found herself disapproving of the use made of her researches to support Dora's recent theory that Time and Space represented, and perhaps *were*, a male and female principle.

In January 1926, Harriet went to London direct from Castle Park; Dora's manuscript was not ready for collection. As her flat was let, she stayed at the Belgrave, the small hotel where the Joyces had lodged in 1923, and went to work at the British Museum. The hotel had thirty-two bedrooms and no lift. 'But why are you not going to the Euston Hotel?' Mr Joyce wrote. '732 rooms, 2 wings, liveried porters, chatty meteorologist in the lift, whispering lounge, English breakfast, vitellusit, Danish bacon, Irish eggs, American sugar, French milk, Canadian marmalade, Scotch porridge, New Zealand butter, Dutch toast. . . .'[47]

When she had finished her work, she moved over to Paris where she had some further research to do in the Bibliothèque Nationale, and arrived in time for Mr Joyce's birthday celebrations. No doubt she kept to herself any embarrassment the party may have caused her; and he kept from her a pressing embarrassment of his own. 'Can you solve this problem?' he asked Sylvia. 'I have 700 francs . . . do you know how I could get at once 60 or 7000 [francs] . . . I do not want Miss Weaver to know how I am while she is here and to get the money from the solicitors would involve telling her. . . .'[48]

Her birthday present to him was Wyndham Lewis's sketch of herself in 1921. In a teasing mood, he proclaimed that it must be hung at Shakespeare and Company. In fact, he kept it himself, but months later she was still pleading with Sylvia to 'put it in the darkest corner you can find, or up the chimney or behind one of your double rows of books or under the doormat'.[49]

Her next engagement was a visit—the first for months—to Mary and Annie at Westwick. She was fond of them both, particularly of Annie, who, like herself, had been denied her wish to go to a university. After a few days of pleasant, sisterly companionship, she returned to London for the first performance there of *Exiles*. None of her friends came over from Paris. Sylvia was busy as always and Mr Joyce was still feeling too ill and helpless.[50] But she had the agreeable company of Mr Wyndham Lewis. They were delighted to see that the theatre was nearly full and equally delighted that the audience obviously appreciated the play. There was, however, an awkward moment at the end of Act I when the husband, testing his strategy of giving away what he loves in order to save it, discusses with his wife —and fails to deplore—the assignation she has made with his friend. The woman in the seat next Harriet rose, muttered 'I call this collusion', and walked out.[51]

Harriet's appetite was more robust. On the following afternoon, she attended the second of the two performances. The next day, a telegram summoned her to Westwick: Annie had had a stroke.

She found her sister 'in a very critical condition'. Her left side was affected and it seemed 'there was a danger of the mischief spreading and affecting her brain and speech'.[52] The shock gave Harriet several sleepless nights, but she was happy to be with Annie. The household needed her and the patient, like others in the old Cedar Lawn days, was solaced by her gentle, reassuring presence. The mischief did not spread and by April, although her left hand never fully recovered, Annie was able 'to walk a step or two with help'.[53]

Dora was very sympathetic about Harriet's family troubles and realized that she was likely to be needed at home. She realized, too, that her own constant worry over work could be cured by completing some part of it. She decided to concentrate on her first two volumes and to postpone 'all the historical work'. 'This decision,' she told Harriet, 'will have the very desirable effect of freeing *you* from any immediate urgency about the collection of material for your *Symposium on S & T plus the Atom.*'[54]

Later on, when Annie was rather better, Harriet offered to come for a flying visit. But Dora, though happy to take a few days off if Harriet felt she needed a change, was feeling, temporarily, very independent: 'It certainly seems a long journey for so short a stay.'[55] Besides, Seldom Seen was apt to be crowded for Easter. Six children and a dog, with attendant adults, had already arrived. They had no time-pieces, and it was fortunate that Dora's clock, which went fast and could not be re-set, had worked itself round to near-enough the right time. She had forestalled enquiries by winding the strike.

It was a cheerful, witty letter; and ten days later Dora asked Harriet to tell her sister that the change of plan, forced on them by her stroke, had worked out for good. Then she made a suggestion:

Perhaps you will feel disappointed not to finish the 'Symposium' now that it has gone so far. . . . Would you like to go on with the work *as an independent* work to be brought out by yourself as a book?

Certainly, it is getting very bulky for an *Appendix*. If you would, I am quite agreeable & would give you all the help I could. I should of course have to dip into it for all the bits on *S & T* which I require. . . . I think you would make a very interesting and valuable collection. . . . My advice is: *Do it*.[56]

Harriet, who had given up long ago her fragile ambitions as a writer, was delighted to think that she could nonetheless bring out a book of her own. When Maude came to Westwick to give her some time off, she spent ten days in London working in the London Library and the British Museum Reading Room. It was a glorious spring that year, but she did not grudge sitting indoors. When she had polished off some odd jobs for Dora, she turned with renewed pleasure to her own subject.

Bryher and Robert McAlmon were in London and she visited them in their new flat. She had heard from Sylvia that Robert was worried by her 'disapproval' and hastened to give him proof that he had imagined it all. Evidently much relieved, he was 'very nice and very friendly'. He presented Harriet with 'a copy of Miss Gertrude Stein's huge volume'; and had the tact not to ask her to read it 'line by line from start to finish'.[57]

James Joyce had spent the spring revising Shaun's four watches. They were packed tight with composite references, among them traces of some grist that Harriet brought to the mill. She had tracked down in London an Elizabethan song-book—John Dowland's—that he wanted for Giorgio. He loved hearing Giorgio sing these songs, and they still echo through the fourth watch of Shaun.* Harriet would dearly have liked to share his hope that something he had written might 'bear some comparison with *Come silent night* for instance'.[58] But she must have understood better the ironic comment made by Stanislaus Joyce. 'My brother,' Mr Joyce reported, 'says that having done the longest day in literature I am now conjuring up the darkest night.'[59]

Towards the end of May, when she had been back at Westwick for a month, he wrote to ask where he should send the typescript. He had rather the same anxious attitude to illness as Harriet's and had taken a most sympathetic interest in Annie's convalescence. He knew that Harriet was soon leaving for Castle Park and Glencoin. Although

---

* 'night by silentsailing night . . . deeply, now evencalm lay sleeping;' *Finnegans Wake*, p. 556.

Mary and Annie had felt at times that Dora was making use of their sister, they respected her own wish to spend time on her own work and with her own friends.

Mr Joyce was most anxious that his text should go to the right address; he was also very eager to have her comments on the interaction between the four sections.[60] Before it was dispatched, and while it was on its way, he sent her the questions he wanted her to answer—and a formidable list of books she should be reading. 'I shall be waiting to hear how you like it—if you like it. While reading it could you make a complete list of words misspelt. Some, of course, are intentional, most, but there must be others overlooked by my dim sight. Will you let me know whether the "plot" begins to emerge from it all?'[61]

This letter and the typescript reached Harriet at Castle Park. It was evident that he no longer took her approval for granted and she did show signs of rebellion on one point: she was not equipped to classify misspellings by choice and by chance. She had, however, after three years of diligent work, gained a considerable insight into the shifting reflections and echoes that held together the structure he now called a plot. She could trace links forwards and backwards and eddies 'riprippling' in all directions; and comment on them with some assurance, without giving pain to herself, or to him.

She had brought with her the precious recording from *Ulysses*, read by the author, and took it on to Glencoin, where other records, mainly instrumental, and a gramophone she had ordered—the first she had ever owned—had arrived safely. She and Dora stayed up late listening to 'Mr Joyce's record' and *Molly Brannigan* over and over again.[62] They had been asked to make notes on how Mr Joyce's voice sounded; and it was an easy thing to do because everyone thoroughly enjoyed the new 'implement', as Harriet called it. Although it was rather late in life for her to realize the hope of educating her ear, she was glad to have introduced, into this strenuous community, a little entertainment. Even Dora was sometimes distracted from her work, and Mrs Marsden was delighted to have a change from the rigours of housekeeping. She had read in the popular press that James Joyce was a devoted family man, and she decided she liked him next-best after the Prince of Wales.

Another cheering event was the arrival of 'an amusing, naughty but bewitching kitten'. But that, Harriet observed, completed 'the sum of our diversions'.[63] She had imagined that her round of invalid visits was ended, but now Dora was ill too, with constant attacks of 'biliousness'. Harriet had, however, escaped the thunderstorm over the southern counties, when one of the Westwick chimneys was brought down by lightning. Mr Joyce expressed his concern for Annie: 'a dreadful experience for an immobilised person!'; and added an ambiguous note of hope: 'Sometimes a shock like that does good and in any case a visitation of that kind rarely recurs'.[64]

At the end of September, he suddenly had the 'funny idea' that she might care to revive an ancient practice and 'order' a piece from him. He gave her an example:

Dear Sir. I should like to have an oil painting of Mr Tristan carving raw pork for Cornish countrymen or anicebust of Herr Ham contemplating his cold shoulder. . . .[65]

Harriet was amused, pleased and by no means stumped by this strange order for an order. St Patrick and Sir Tristram between them had interested her in local antiquities, and she was able to produce at once a local pamphlet describing and illustrating a weird monument in the churchyard at Penrith, reputed to be the grave of a prehistoric giant.* With it, she sent her order:

To Messrs Jacques le Joyeux, Giacomo Jakob, Skeumas Sheehy and whole Company:
Sirs: Kindly supply the undersigned with one full length grave account of his esteemed Highness Rhaggrick O'Hoggnor's Hogg Tomb† as per photos enclosed and oblige
Yours faithfully
Henriette Véavère‡

She then permitted herself a sad little confession: 'But what I would really like is to place an order well in advance when another book is under contemplation'.[66]

Three days later, on Monday, 4th October 1926, a telegram came from Mary. Their brother Kearsley was dead. A letter from Alfred arrived next morning. Kearsley had died from the shock of an

* Pamphlet by the Reverend James Cropper, Vicar of St Andrew's, Penrith.
† The four side-stones of the 'grave' are, in fact, tenth-century 'hogg-back' tombs. In design, they derive from Scandinavian heathen 'shrine' tombs—no doubt one of the reasons why Harriet Weaver chose the pamphlet for her 'order'.
‡ Sylvia Beach had taught Harriet Weaver to recognize herself under this name in Paris.

emergency operation for peritonitis and if he had lived 'his life would have been intolerable'.[67] Her brothers and sisters understood that Harriet might not be able to get to the funeral; it was a long journey, and Miss Marsden might be too ill to be left. They had, also, a feeling that could not be expressed: they wanted to spare Harriet expense. They had come to the conclusion that she was not as well off as she should be.

Harriet did not go to the funeral, much as she loved her rather crusty, disappointed-bachelor brother, who had enjoyed for so short a time the house he had wanted all his life. Maude wrote:

Mary . . . is going to write in a day or two—she sends you so much love. . . . It is a fearful blow, & it all seems rather pathetic, which adds to it. . . . Mary is all right—better than I expected—hardly breaking down except very occasionally & then she seems able to pull herself together at once—she got through yesterday all right though it was an awful strain. . . .[68]

Harriet had meant to come south early in the winter, and advanced her plans when she heard that she was an executor, in order to get to Westwick while Alfred, the other executor, was still staying there. Mary and Annie, who was not so well, longed to have her with them. 'We are all,' said Mary, 'sorrowing together.'[69]

Mr Joyce, who knew what it was to lose a brother, wrote in sympathy: 'I am much distressed. . . . You will have a very gloomy return to your sister [Annie]. I hope her case will not be aggravated by the death of her brother and that your family will be spared any of these dreadful troubles for a long time to come'. It was not the moment for 'news and articles and gossip', so his letter was unusually short. But he mentioned that he had set to work on her order. 'I know it is no more than a game but it is a game I have learned to play in my own way. Children may just as well play as not. The ogre will come in any case.'[70]

Harriet knew how grief and loss may be contained within the familiar order of duty and affection. She was not yet acquainted with the ogre that visits the waste lands where human ties have lost their meaning. Her life for the next two months was spent in a way that yielded some satisfaction. She divided her time between Guildford, where Annie was slowly getting better, and London, where she could do some work and live, between lettings, in her own flat.

She was there in November, when Mr Joyce reverted to his custom of keeping her up to date with his affairs. He had stupefied himself with work on her 'esteemed order' and had been recuperating for three days, on a sofa, reading *Gentlemen Prefer Blondes*. He had decided to put her piece in the place of honour 'namely the first pages of the book', and could send 'page 1, if the customer so desires', as a sample. At this point, he had to explain that the book ends in the middle of the sentence where it begins; and then concluded:

P.S. *Re* sample vide above. Reply will oblige
respeakfolly yours
M.M. Inkpen & Paperasses
(Writers to the Signet)[71]

Customer did desire a sample, and it came a week later, described as 'prosepiece ordered in sample form. Also key to same':

brings us back to
Howth Castle & Environs. Sir Tristram, violer d'amores, had passencore rearrived. . . [72]

Harriet's order had pleased him. The unusual, ambivalent figure of her 'giant', or 'hero king', had the right mythological overtones. Here was yet another manifestation of Finnegan/Earwicker; even the shape of his gravestone was like Earwicker's sign ⊔ recumbent. Harriet, on her side, was happy to have given an inspiring order and happy to have a piece done specially for her. In addition (as the notes in the key were rather longer than the text) she felt reasonably sure she understood it. The idea of a book making a circle appealed to her; it was like a serpent with its tail in its mouth, she thought. But without 'a comprehensive key and glossary' 'the poor hapless reader' would lose 'a very great deal' of his intention. 'Would it,' she asked, 'be utterly against the grain, your convictions and principles to publish (when the day comes), along with an ordinary edition also an annotated edition (at double or treble price, say?). I throw this out as a mere suggestion.'[73]

The 'mere suggestion', which followed fast upon more fundamental criticism from Ezra Pound, who could get no 'inkling' of the purpose of the book, was too much for James Joyce. He took to his sofa. When he recovered, he wrote to say that she would probably like the piece better than the sample. He reminded her that 'One great part of human existence is passed in a state which cannot be rendered sensible by the use of wideawake language, cutanddry grammar and goahead plot'.[74]

This cogent saying was hard for Harriet; she had always liked lucidity. His next communication was much easier:

Madam i ave today finished the draft No 2 in nice MS of peece of prose yʳ rispected O/ to me which i will now give 1 coat of french polish to same which will turn out A 1 as desired. . . [75]

Harriet loved joining in this sort of fun. She replied: 'Congratulate you on smartness of execution of order solicited, given and received a bare two months ago, days on sofa not excluded'. She asked that 'one firstclass beauful phrase' ('When all vegetation is covered by the flood there are no eyebrows on the face of the Waterworld') be shifted from the key to the text;[76] and was assured by return 'insertion desired duly made'.* [77]

Although Sylvia was pressing her to go to Paris again, Harriet felt she should stick to her original plans, and went back to Castle Park in the middle of December. So she did not hear James Joyce reading her piece to a small group of invited friends. Among them were three new American friends, Eugene and Maria Jolas and Elliot Paul, the associate editor of a new review the Jolases were planning: *transition*, an international quarterly for Creative Experiment. The reading was a success. Eugene Jolas had a special interest because he was developing a philosophy of language which implied a revolution in the use of words; and it was arranged that Work in Progress should be published serially in *transition*, beginning at the beginning with the new piece.

It was a pity that Harriet, who did not readily interpret spelling as sound, missed hearing the reading, as it would have conveyed directly some of the answers she was left to puzzle out. James Joyce, when he sent her the piece, hoped that she too would like it, but her efforts to be encouraging, yet truthful, failed to carry conviction. She was, however, wholeheartedly in sympathy with him over his persistent troubles with Mr Samuel Roth—'that rogue', as she called him. His journal, published in America where the copyright was not protected, was still running unauthorized instalments of *Ulysses*. Sylvia

---

* In Harriet Weaver's piece (*Finnegans Wake*, p. 12) the spelling is 'whaterwelter'. The word 'waterworld' appears on p. 367. The 'firstclass beauful phrase' did not survive.

Beach was organizing a protest from authors all over the world, and Harriet gave her, with Christmas wishes, her own views on the subject. 'I hope very much that all your great activity in the matter is, or soon will be proving effective in getting this scandalous piracy put an end to and also that—as you hope—*Ulysses* will benefit by the advertisement. . . .'[78]

Dora was one of the signatories. But when Harriet joined her again after Christmas—scrambling up the glen under a waning moon—she found Dora very withdrawn, uninterested in Harriet or her friends. Harriet was still asked to order books and hunt up quotations, but most of her working time was spent listening and saying yes. Any other comments were resented. The nights—and the days too—were dark; and even the kitten, now grown into a cat, was no longer very amusing. Harriet examined her conscience. She could not bring herself to speak freely to Dora; she had equivocated with Mr Joyce; and he had now presented her with a new moral problem. He wanted to realize a little capital. This she had provided for but she now felt uneasy lest it proved the thin end of a very big wedge.

Worry—on top of cold and discomfort—gave her an unprecedented attack of neuralgia. Then she instructed Fred Monro to sell, made the decision to be (though not at once) more open about Work in Progress; and took a little comfort from the fact that Mr Joyce had at least acted on one piece of advice she had lately given:

As the ceasework order was followed so promptly I feel encouraged to 'try my hand at it again' and give another and different order—but also for eyes and health's sake. As its subject matter is, however, not such as to present any very strong appeal to you (unless perhaps on the minus side of the line) and is indeed, as we read, an 'ungrateful' one, I shall await your express permission to mention it. . . . And perhaps when the present book is finished you will see fit to lend ear to several of your older friends (E.P. to be included in the number): but the time to talk of that matter is not yet.[79]

The gentleness of her manner did not soften the blow. James Joyce, desperate to shield his creative energy against threats from all sides, answered at once: 'I conclude you did not like the piece I did? . . . It is possible Pound is right, but I cannot go back.'[80]

Harriet could not go back either. She had to make at least one attempt to explain herself:

Some of your work I like enormously—as I am sure you know—especially the more straightforward and character-analytical parts and the (to me) beautifully expressed ghost-parts (for instance the sentence in Shaun about the date and the ghostmark and the one about the waterworld's face before you, as I think, distorted it—though I confess it couldn't otherwise have been inserted where it was); but I am made in such a way that I do not care much for the output from your Wholesale Safety Pun Factory nor for the darkness and the unintelligibilities of your deliberately-entangled language system. It seems to me you are wasting your genius.

She had to say it. But she feared the cruel effect and took refuge in polite disclaimers:

. . . I daresay I am wrong and in any case you will go on with what you are doing, so why thus stupidly say anything to discourage you? I hope I shall not do so again.[81]

From now on, this self-denying ordinance exerted its baleful influence on both of Harriet's friendships. She felt that she could hardly open her mouth without causing unhappiness.

The embarrassments of daily life at Seldom Seen were particularly acute. James Joyce could sometimes recognize that others besides Ulysses and himself had storm capes to round. But Dora's self-absorption was more complete; and Harriet's doubts about Dora had more substance. James Joyce might be misguided, but he had produced two important works. Dora had failed to produce a single book, and her whole conceptual system seemed to be a rope of sand.

In fact, after years of collaboration, they were left with very little common ground. Harriet had long ago lost her faith and had been well suited by a rational habit of thought. Dora had moved in the opposite direction and had turned her mind—the clear mind Harriet had so much loved—to an unorthodox form of Christianity. 'The Holy Ghost,' Harriet observed, 'was a female deity to whom she used to pray and who, she believed, intervened on her behalf.'[82]

Harriet had suffered in the past because there was no bridge between her humanism and the orthodox beliefs of her family. Now she saw another chasm opening before her in a friendship that had been as close as a family tie. There was no easy way of deciding what she ought to do.

13

SPACE AND TIME

HARRIET's habit of withdrawing from argument had helped her over difficult moments with Dora. But the magic formula 'I daresay I am wrong' failed to work with Mr Joyce. Her approval was particularly important to him, and he was appalled to find it lacking at a time when other friends, too, were making open criticisms. Discouragement brought on a collapse. He stayed miserably in bed for several days, worrying about Miss Weaver and about his other once-faithful reader, Ezra Pound.

When he felt better, and had been assured by Robert McAlmon that he was certainly not mad, he began to ask himself if Pound's judgment could be trusted. Pound's latest 'discovery' was Ralph Cheever Dunning, whose work he praised extravagantly; but surely these verses were not poetry at all? And if Pound were wrong, then he himself might be right. He sent Miss Weaver a poem of Dunning's, *Rococo*, and asked her for an opinion.[1] He was anxious to have her support for his own views, in spite of her recent strictures; and she was able to respond, this time, exactly as he would have wished.

The subject of *Rococo* is a crime of passion. The Duke's wife Simona is neglected, because 'her hips were slender, And lacked of flesh his grosser lusts to bolden'; and falls in love with a scholar. The lovers are surprised by the Duke, and then:

> . . . *he choked and drew his dagger snarling*
> *And all his bulk was shaken like a feather*
> *And made towards Simona dumb and gnarling,*
> *But then her lover smote his face and felled him.* . . .

270

Once he is down, Simona joins in. She holds the Duke by the hair while the scholar slits his throat; and then insults the corpse. Retainers haul him off for torture, leaving Simona

> *to wail and hover*
> *Outside the door, save that there came to twit her*
> *The dead duke's brother, bitter-lipped to sadness. . . .*

Harriet wrote to say that this poem was rubbish; but meanwhile Mr Joyce was deeper in trouble. As Arthur Symons had suggested that he might publish a small collection of his own poems, he had rashly shown two of them to Ezra Pound and had been told that they were not worth reprinting. This seemed to mean that they must be 'worse than Mr Dunning's drivel which Pound defends as if it were Verlaine'.[2]

James Joyce, describing the incident to Harriet, was so disturbed that he addressed her as 'Miss Marsden' and left his first sentence unfinished. Harriet could share his distress and was disappointed that he felt he could not pursue the idea of publication. Even when he changed his mind, the first humiliation still rankled, and he gave the collection the humble title *Pomes Penyeach*.

He had been encouraged, he told Harriet, by two pleasant compliments. The American poet Archibald Macleish, on a visit to Paris, had read the poems and given them warm praise, and the London P.E.N. club had 'invited James the Punman to be guest of honour at a dinner'. He had accepted the invitation because 'many English writers signed the protest'.[3]

James Joyce was in London only briefly and Harriet was at Seldom Seen. There, the tedium and the rigours of life had lately been marked by a horrible event. The cat, now nubile, had her first brood of kittens; and it fell to Harriet, tender-hearted as she was, to drown and bury them. Nobody else could do it.

But a new and amusing quiz-game, proposed by James Joyce gave her something cheerful to think about. He asked her to guess the secret title of his book. Like all good gamesmen, he wanted to win; and Harriet thoroughly enjoyed pitting her wits against his. Since the title exploited several ambiguities, with 'wake' as a noun or a verb (active or imperative) and with Finnegan as a name or an abstraction ('a resurrection' suggested by '*fin* again'), and the fourth part ended where the first began, he could readily produce a series of puzzling clues. For some months, they made their moves in turn:

Mr Joyce: I am making an engine with only one wheel. No spokes of course. The wheel is a perfect square. . . .[4]

Miss Weaver: *A wheeling square. . . . Squaring the wheel. . . .*

Mr Joyce: (After commending her good guess) The title is very simple and as commonplace as can be . . . it is in two words.[5]

Miss Weaver: (recalling that one times one is one) *One squared.*

Mr Joyce: (pleased by a suggestion he can use for a 'math' lesson) The title . . . is much more commonplace . . . ought to be fairly plain from the reading of ⊔ . The sign in this form means HCE interred in the landscape.[6]

Miss Weaver: (who has noticed word-play on 'Dublin' and 'doubling') *Dublin Ale* . . . (after further thought and more hesitantly) . . . *Ireland's Eye* . . . *Dublin Bay* . . . *Phoenix Park.* . . .

Mr Joyce: As to 'Phoenix'. The Irish was *fiunishgue* = clear water from a well of bright water there.[7]

Miss Weaver: *Finn MacCool* . . . *Finn's Town* . . . *Finn's City.* . . .[8]

At this point, James Joyce called off the game; his opponent was almost home. He had other reasons, too, for losing interest. It was pleasant to have his ideas taken up with enthusiasm but, when he himself moved on, he was apt to feel suddenly vexed because other people were working them to death. Harriet's thoroughness, so useful to him in general, was on these occasions a disadvantage. Even if he had taken great pains to rouse and maintain her interest—as he did about his health—he was not always pleased when he evoked a wholehearted response. He sometimes felt trapped in the sympathy that she was so ready to express.

While the quiz was in progress, he was borrowing, as usual, from Sylvia Beach: his income from investments was never enough, though large enough, now (thanks to Harriet) to make his demands on the till a constant irritation to Sylvia, who had become a victim of migraine. One note he sent round to her was headed 'To be read when your headache is gone', but the fact remained that he was unable to pay a bill that had to be paid at once; and Sylvia, though by now heartily sick of his endless appeals for rescue, felt bound to yield when he threatened 'to let the bailiffs in and watch them walk off with the furniture and animals in the ark'.[9]

A little later, Harriet heard from him directly that he hoped to raise money for a holiday on the Dutch coast by selling his copy of *Dubliners* 1912, the only copy that survived when Maunsel destroyed the edition. This plan was only half successful; he failed to sell the book but he managed to have the holiday. He felt he could not go on writing—Sidney Schiff was 'among the latest to express dislike' of Work in Progress—and he was even playing with the fantastic idea of getting someone else to complete his book 'on the lines indicated'.[10] He went on 'But who is the person? There is no such absurd person as could replace me except the incorrigible god of sleep. . . .'

In spite of misunderstandings, their correspondence sometimes had a playful note. Here James Joyce picked up a recent remark of Harriet's that he was 'incorrigibly absurd', though he seemed so solemn about it all. Yet she could not take lightly the prospect of a ghost writer. When he said he had asked Miss Beach to sound out James Stephens, the plan still seemed foolish. James Joyce had not liked James Stephens' *The Crock of Gold*, and the magical reasons he gave for the choice—that the two Jameses, Joyce and Stephens, were born on the same day—did not help to recommend it. Although she was not an admirer of Work in Progress, Harriet felt she must encourage him to go on writing it himself, and she hoped that he would feel less in need of a collaborator after he had had his holiday. This was the attitude she adopted whenever the idea was mentioned, as it was off and on over the next two years.

Meanwhile, he wanted her to do some work for him: check the text of the three instalments already published in *transition* and read the proofs of the coming instalment and check them against the MS corrections in his son's handwriting and the proof corrections in his own.[11] This was a task Harriet could discharge, ably and willingly; but it did strengthen her conviction that this kind of writing was not to her taste and that any kind of involvement with it was a mistake.

She was thoroughly pleased, however, by Mr Joyce's happy thought that the Reverend James Cropper, who had written the pamphlet on her 'Giant's Tomb', might like to see the piece it had inspired.[12] But when she sent him a copy, it was returned marked 'gone away'. She was somewhat out of touch with local church news; he had been gone for sixteen years.

As the summer of 1927 advanced, James Joyce's money troubles mounted until, in July, when he had some bills he must settle within a week, he asked Harriet to arrange for £100 of his capital to be disinvested. He had put off raising the subject as long as he could, per-haps because, conflicting with the impulse to treat capital as income, was a sense that this particular capital symbolized his value in her eyes. Nonetheless, from this time on, he drew on his capital con-tinually, slicing off £100 or so more and more frequently.

She took his latest request at face value. Although she was out of London—and stock is not sold over the counter—he received the cheque on the seventh day. But it did little to raise his spirits. His letter of thanks was dejected: things were going from bad to worse. He had already told her that his unique copy of *Dubliners* (given to Archibald MacLeish to dispose of in America) was still unsold, that he must wait several weeks for any royalties on Sylvia Beach's ninth edition of *Ulysses*, and that people all over the world were 'ridiculing and attacking' his pieces.[13] Now, the 'pirate' Samuel Roth, appealing for subscriptions to a 'Samuel Roth defence fund', had described him as a 'renegade Jew' who had behind him an 'organisation and vast funds'.[14]

A present came with this letter, number 2 of a special edition of *Pomes Penyeach*, initialled not signed, because a signature on such a 'poor effort would look too ridiculous'.[15] He acknowledged her letter of thanks in the same shrinking spirit: 'I am glad you got the booklet and did not dislike it'.[16] This is no proof that her letter lacked warmth. It was a moment when he saw hostility all round him, and with some reason. He had sent copies to several other friends, and only Miss Weaver had taken the trouble to say thank you.

The attacks on his prose were, in general, paralysing. But the 'best' attack, launched by his old friend Wyndham Lewis in *Time and Western Man*, proved stimulating rather than depressing. Wyndham Lewis had spoken with particular scorn of his small middle-class world and shabby-genteel manners, and these taunts roused him. He told Harriet he had something in hand that would poke fun at Mr Lewis 'in his know-all profoundly impressive role'.* It was a welcome opportunity for action, yet it did little to relieve his sense of helpless suffering: 'I am more and more aware of the indignant hostility shown to my experiment in interpreting "the dark night of the soul"....'[17]

Harriet was distressed by his unhappiness; and more distressed when he told her that she herself was one of the most depressing in-

---

* Shaun's lecture, *transition* February 1928.

fluences round him. She had, in fact, yielded to his persuasion and given him a comment on his latest piece; she had said—he indignantly reported to Miss Beach—that she was 'wallowing in its verbiage'. He may not have quoted her exactly, but the sentiment is one that any writer would resent; and it was exactly what she felt. As she could not in honesty withdraw it, the only consolation she could offer was, as usual, the thought that she was a stupid critic and he should not pay any attention to what she said.

As in the past, the theme that haunted one great friendship was re-appearing in another. James Joyce, like Dora Marsden, feared and courted persecution, and defended himself (as Dora did in her own way) by appealing to Harriet's conscience and reducing her self-esteem. He punished Harriet for the comments he had begged her to make; and Dora still refused to hear any comment at all. At Glencoin, Harriet was doing her best to show interest in Dora's book without any reference to its content; but it is not surprising that she worked mainly on her own symposium, which had 'swollen to a size far beyond the original intention'.[18]

In the autumn, she made a short round of visits—to Greenhalldoor Palace (as James Joyce called 74 Gloucester Place), to her sisters at Westwick, and to her aunt at Castle Park. While she was with her aunt, in November, she confided in Sylvia about her mixed feelings towards Work in Progress:

. . . It must be a great pleasure to him that you [like it]. It is a grief to me that I am unable so far to be enthusiastic about it. At present I very much prefer his plainer writing. Perhaps I shall get really to like his new style in time and it would be a great help towards this, I am sure, if I could share the pleasure and advantage of hearing the pieces read by himself as they are written, for they seem to be essentially oral. Magnificent reader as he is, he would render them in the rhythms and with the emphasis he intended them to have and this would tend to lessen the obscurity. I suppose I ought to be content if the obscurity clears itself in part, but I like to see behind every word and phrase, as far as possible, and to know why it was written—and for this a great deal of time is (to me at least) necessary and I have not that now. When writing to Mr. Joyce I try now to say all I can in praise of the pieces and nothing against them but I find it difficult as I have the feeling all the time that his genius and his immense labours are being to some extent wasted in producing what appears to me to be—to put it baldly—a curiosity of literature. I daresay I am wrong (*you* certainly believe so) but I cannot help it—and I have neither the art nor the ability to lie adroitly in order to please him. But it distresses me to hurt him and I wish he would not always so insistently ask me how I like the pieces. I *do* like immensely the ending of *Anna Livia* and have told him so. . . .[19]

In the new year 1928, Harriet was still preoccupied with this problem. It seemed that Mr Joyce's peace of mind could never be restored so long as she was in any way associated with his current work; and that the only hope of avoiding a break with the Joyce family, as dear to her now as her own, lay in establishing her right to keep her thoughts to herself. She decided she must persuade him to stop asking her opinion, and convince him at the same time that he could always depend, whatever he wrote, on her support and regard.

She had failed to explain herself in writing, and she felt she must talk to him. She went to Paris from Castle Park on 19th January 1928, giving as her reason for the sudden visit her work at the Bibliothèque Nationale and her distress at hearing of a recent intestinal attack, alarmingly like Kearsley's. As events proved, Harriet had by chance hit on the correct diagnosis.

She found him feeling better, and saw that he was touched and pleased when she told him he could count on her as long as he lived.[20] But she could not persuade him that he ought to stop discussing his writing with her. Instead, he pressed her to come often to the flat, so that he could explain the structure of his book and take her through the pieces one by one. It was a strenuous fortnight's course and Harriet's gift for listening served her well. She began to feel more warmly towards Work in Progress than she had ever thought was possible.[21]

James Joyce's buoyant mood owed much, no doubt, to the fact that she had given practical evidence of her regard by undertaking to put him in funds again herself, and had thus enabled him to renew the lease of his flat. The new understanding between them, though precarious, had made them both happier.

At his birthday party, where Mrs Joyce was as usual 'a delightful, natural and unpretentious hostess',[22] Helen Nutting, Myron Nutting's wife, was deeply impressed by Harriet's 'quality', and afterwards made a long entry in her diary. It affords a rare glimpse of Harriet in the Joycean setting:

Miss Weaver sitting on the sofa with Bob McAlmon beside her* . . .
Adrienne Monnier filled a chair near her, whiter, more blue-eyed and
golden than ever, immense and shapeless. She is a gourmet and looks
it. Bright and talkative, trying to keep the conversation going. Power
came in, with a beautiful violet-red silk handkerchief peeping from
his pocket and a sumptuous English silk tie of violet and red checks, a
fine subdued harmony. . . . Lucia, Mrs. Antheil, and Kitten sat on the
sofa. Lucia's face is fine and thoughtful this winter, Kitten handsome
and plump, and Mrs Antheil small and dark, in a *robe de style*, elegant
and discreet.†

While George Antheil played old English music, James Joyce and
Robert McAlmon 'danced quietly in the back parlour', improvizing
on Greek and negro themes. 'Mais regardez donc ce Joyce,' exclaimed
the golden Adrienne, 'c'est le satyre sur un vase grecque!' Then
McAlmon sang several songs, omitting the ribald verses, and James
Joyce sang several ballads. Helen Nutting asked him for 'Oh, the
brown and the yellow ale' and he sang it beautifully. 'More beautifully,' she wrote, 'than I have ever heard him, his voice charged with
feeling. . . . Tenderness, melancholy, bitterness.'

Harriet was no connoisseur of beautiful singing, but she could
appreciate the feeling and spirit of the performance. It was followed
by more singing, with champagne and dancing. Although she could
not take part, there was nothing awkward about her composure; and
Helen Nutting saw it as a highly individual, but not alien, note in the
festivity:

. . . everything was gay, stiffness melted. Only Miss Weaver kept her
calm and stillness. . . . Joyce's silence comes, I think, from a profound
weariness of spirit, but Miss Weaver's is like the stillness of a stone, a
quality.

Miss Weaver's visit seems to have dispelled some of the clouds, and
made JJ more at rest as to the cares of living.[23]

* The McAlmons were now divorced and Bryher had married again. Harriet had
already met her second husband.
† Arthur Power, the Irish writer, had met James Joyce in 1921 and become a friend.
Mrs Antheil was the Russian wife of the composer, a protégé of Sylvia Beach. In
the spring of 1928 Harriet gave £5 towards a fund to provide for his convalescence
after an illness. Kitten was a young friend of the Nuttings. Sylvia Beach, strangely
enough, is not mentioned.

SPACE AND TIME

After the party, Harriet still had a week in Paris and was caught up in burning discussions about the prospects of copyrighting Work in Progress in America; of improving the copyright position there; and of punishing Samuel Roth. She was also present—'luckily for me', James Joyce observed—at a heated scene involving the translators who were now at work on the French edition of *Ulysses*. Stuart Gilbert, lately retired from the British Colonial Service, had joined Auguste Morel and Valery Larbaud (currently at loggerheads with his publisher Adrienne Monnier), and the three translators could not agree about who had the last say.

A more enjoyable entertainment was a rehearsal at the Empire theatre, where Lucia danced as a wild vine in a 'ballet Faunesque'. Lucia was a promising dancer and, after two years' training, she was more grown-up and felt more at home with her parents' distinguished friend. She was delighted to hear from her mother that Miss Weaver had said she danced very well.[24] Indeed, Harriet hoped that dancing would give her a career and prospects of an independent life.

When Harriet left Paris, she took with her a present, a reminder of Mr Joyce's birthday and of the peace of mind that she had been able to secure for him. It was a copy of the latest edition of *Ulysses*, inscribed:

à H.W.
      Pour Ulysse IX
L.B. lugubriously still treads the press of pain
But J.J's joyicity is on the jig again
And he'll highkick every abelboobied humballoon he cain
      As he goes jubiling along.
                               ·ſſ*

      Souvenir de la Chandeleur 1928
      Paris

He added, as he so often did, a footnote:

* These capital jokes represent the dancer kicking the balloons of imposture back into the heaven of deception.

The air was cleared between himself and Miss Weaver and when she was back at Glencoin, after a brief visit to Westwick, she had two letters confirming the new dispensation. 'I am very glad you came to

278

Paris,' he said first, 'for at least I know where I stand.'[25] In his next letter, though he was still suffering from cramps and nervous exhaustion, he added: 'There is a great difference in the state of my mind since your visit so the spasms are only physical.'[26]

She enjoyed his next piece, the legend of 'the Ondt and the Gracehoper', where he launched the second wave of his attack on, among others, Wyndham Lewis. It was more cheerful than usual, and reminded her of the dedication in her new book:

The Gracehoper was always jigging a jog, hoppy on akkant of his joyicity, (he had a partnerpair of findlestilts to supplant him) or if not he was always making ungraceful overtures to Floh and Luse and Bienie and Vespatilla to play pupa-pupa and pulicy-pulicy and to commence insects with him even if only in chaste, . . . [27]

It is impossible to know what Harriet made of the idea of committing incest in jest, but she was able to convey that she approved of the legend as a whole, and had worked out for herself a number of references, among them, that the 'weltall Ondt in his windhome' was Mr Lewis. Nonetheless, he sent her later a long glossary and followed it up, when the second watch of Shaun came out in the summer number of *transition*, with 'a few shafts of moonlight on the duskier bits'.[28] Under his guidance, she enjoyed the pieces more and more; and her relations with him were more stable, more tranquil and more rewarding than they had ever been.

Her relations with Dora had not changed for the better. For a while, she had been well suited by Dora's edict that her book was not to be discussed, but the prohibition had now become an inconvenience. Dora had had the sensible idea of submitting her manuscript to Professor Alexander, the distinguished philosopher who had taught her at Manchester University;* and Harriet had been condemned, through the early spring when a heavy cold was making her feel wretched, to prepare a tidy text without taking any interest in what it was saying. She was allowed to send some sections to Helen Saunders for re-typing, but this was the only concession Dora felt able to make.

* Professor Samuel Alexander came to England from Australia in 1878, and at Oxford got a first in Greats. He became a fellow of Lincoln, and then went to Manchester University. His books are mainly on moral philosophy, but one publication, *Space, Time and Deity* (1920) was of special interest to Dora Marsden. In 1930 he was appointed to the Order of Merit.

Dora was much encouraged by the Professor's reply to her first letter: he agreed to read any parts of her book she cared to send him, although not 'within any prescribed short time'.[29] When she and Harriet had worked hard for a month, she forwarded volume 1, and caused great alarm by saying she would send volumes 2 and 3 as soon as they were ready. He had seen that one volume would take him a very long time. 'Pray *therefore do not send me any more,*' he cried, 'until I write about this and ask for more. It will only lie about and look at me reproachfully.' He was a slow reader but he knew already that Dora should be discouraged from building on false hopes. 'As for your MS,' he went on, 'you had better let it lie untouched for a good time. Things look different later on. Lock it up.'[30]

Dora did no such thing. Anxiety about his verdict made her write 'at greater pressure than ever'.[31] Harriet, though she was anxious too, got on well with her own work, and in April she had a short break. She was invited to spend a week-end with the Hones, who were having a holiday on the far side of the Helvellyn ridge, and as the weather was bright, though cold, she arranged to walk over from Glenridding across the pass. Soon after, Maude Hone made a return visit (her first, and her last) to Glencoin; and she did not like what she saw. She had never approved of her sister spending so much time there, at Miss Marsden's disposal, and she realized now that Harriet's life must be even harder than she feared. She was the only able-bodied person about the place; Mrs Marsden had become very arthritic and Dora, who had put on a lot of weight, hardly stirred from her book-lined room.

The two sisters kept their thoughts to themselves. Maude understood that nothing she could say would alter her sister's determination to see Dora's work through to the end; and Harriet was as usual disinclined to mediate between her family and her friends.

Professor Alexander, though a very busy man, was taking a great deal of trouble over his ex-pupil's work, and wrote to her in May. His letter, a model of its kind, reveals him as a kind and honest man, who did not want to discourage a gifted but wayward writer but felt it was his duty to speak his mind: 'I am going to ask you to reconsider'.[32]

Although he appreciated the book's originality—and the mass of knowledge the author had acquired astonished him—he emphatically did not think she should try to publish it 'in its present form'. It was really two books, a philosophical statement and a history of philosophy and opinion; and even the philosophical sections—where he was sometimes in sympathy with her—read like a statement of a 'happy idea', uncritically presented and obviously not tested 'over a range of philosophical data'. He felt very strongly about this, but described himself, gently, as 'troubled'. He treated more severely her habit of laying down the law to specialists in other disciplines:

You urge that geometry must be entirely revised, and do not appear to know that the mathematicians (cf Whitehead) are doing so all the time and have done so a long time back . . . I am horrified when I read your refusal to accept the physicists' identification of electricity and magnetism. Do you really know enough of the subject to put them right? . . . Some of your statements about the history of Greek philosophy I think you should check with the help of some learned person. . . .[33]

Professor Alexander's comments give a very fair picture of the book. Dora had not, as he implied, worked hastily; but she had worked blindly. Her repeated re-writing did not amount to revisions in the ordinary sense; she was simply re-arranging, again and again, the intuitions of a very isolated mind. He concluded by urging her, again, not to publish; though he did remark that if she could bring herself up to date with recent philosophical studies, she might then be able to produce a short statement of her own.

Dora could not make use of the professor's advice. Since she sent off the text, her thoughts had been running ahead to the time when her book would give the world a new philosophy and a new religion; and her sense of mission (unlike James Joyce's—who had no mission at all) made her impervious to criticism. She even toyed with the idea of using some of his remarks, adapted of course, to publicize her book. He had said, among other things, that the way she treated the proofs of God's existence was 'very interesting indeed'.

Harriet, already out of sympathy with Dora's 'heretical gnosticism' (as Professor Alexander called it) had to agree, privately, that her inspirational method led her into errors of fact. But she still wanted to believe that Dora was a genius, of some kind; and there was one very good reason for seeking publication. Dora, now writing frantically, was never going to rest until her book was out.

For the time being, Harriet was not allowed to discuss this problem. Instead, during the summer, Dora wrote to Margaret Storm

Jameson, who had been working for a London publisher, to ask her help. Storm Jameson started the campaign at once. She was soon obliged to ask Dora not to send her any more long explanations of what the book was about, and not to rush up to London to help her sell it. Later on, when it had been rejected by several publishers, and she realized that Dora was losing confidence in her, she defended herself: 'Do believe that I am making both the nature and the magnitude of the work clear'.[34] They both regretted that The Egoist Press was no more, since now there was 'nothing to be done, but go beating at the door of the commercial firms'.[35]

At times, when Dora proposed some unworkable plan, Storm Jameson urged her to consult Miss Weaver. But Dora was in no mood to treat Harriet as a colleague; and Harriet, who greatly admired Miss Jameson's willing and efficient discharge of a very difficult task, avoided any kind of interference. Then, suddenly, the situation changed. Dora and Harriet quarrelled, openly and fiercely.

Once the barriers were down, everything that had rankled, perhaps for years, was thrown in. Dora was furious because Harriet was not, and had never been, totally committed to her interests; and Harriet was frightened, as well as enraged, by Dora's ruthlessness. She told her some home truths, among them that James Joyce's work was at least as good as hers.

Dora, outraged by the very thought of making any comparison, wrote indignantly to Storm Jameson. Harriet, too, had a confidante. Mr Joyce had lately asked for news of Dora, and for once the traditional Weaver reserve gave way. She told him how wretched her life had been lately, under storm-clouds that had been piling up for years. She wrote two days later to Sylvia, to tell her that she might ask to see this letter. Confession had relieved her, yet she did not want Sylvia to think she was concerned only with herself. 'To try to cheer him up a little,' she said, 'I told him what a help his friendship and belief in me had been to me.'[36]

By this time, the skies had cleared: Harriet had agreed to revive The Egoist Press and finance, herself, publication of The Definition of the Godhead. In the serene, harmonious atmosphere, she was able to enjoy Mr Joyce's merry description of the book as a mine of treasures for himself. 'If I had sufficient energy,' he said, 'I should be as restless as a small boy outside a pantry thinking of all the nice little bits I could pilfer with no loss to her. . . .'[37]

It was pleasant to joke, but the practical difficulties remained. Dora, though still working hard on her second volume, had decided to manage personally the publication of the first. She had chosen a printer recommended by her brother, Charles Birchall of Liverpool, and was planning to arrange distribution with the help of one of her sisters, due to arrive soon on a visit from America. Meanwhile, she was writing round to people who might help her to secure good reviews.

Harriet was not consulted over the decisions; but she had to help carry them out. Under Dora's supervision, she wrote a long letter to T. S. Eliot, recommending the book as 'an intellectual rehabilitation of Christian theology without the loss of a single dogma'; but she mainly worked as a typist or a messenger, as a letter to Sylvia reveals:

I have been so very busy lately . . . fearfully rushed some days. On Monday I ran most of the two miles to the village to catch the post, accomplishing the journey in a little under 20 minutes! Not bad for a person of my old age!* The rush is on account of negotiating with printers for the production of Miss Marsden's book. The Egoist Press has been called to life again to be the official publisher. At present it has no address but this one. . . . It is a wonderful book. I shall send you a copy whenever it comes out. If it goes well, the other volumes (which are nearly finished) will also be published soon.[38]

It was now the middle of October. In September, Sylvia had proposed a trip to some peaceful part of France; and Harriet had regretfully replied, 'Someday, someday'.[39] It was only a dream. She had too much to do in England and, when she was released, there was too much to do in Paris.

The Joyce family had received another blow: Mrs Joyce had been operated on for a suspected cancer. Because she was frightened, and because James Joyce hated any separation from his wife, he insisted on sleeping at the clinic. He himself, his friend Stuart Gilbert, and Sylvia Beach plied Harriet with bulletins. Sylvia, though still plagued with headaches, was still an admirable correspondent. She had also become, with Adrienne Monnier, joint owner of a motor-car, and it was she who drove the Joyces home. She knew the prognosis, withheld from them, that if the cancer spread nothing more could be done. Harriet, sworn to secrecy, replied in great agitation:

* Fifty-five.

283

. . . I will certainly say nothing whatever to Mr Joyce of such a possibility. I am sure it is far far better that he should know nothing whatever about it, but that he should believe that the trouble was completely cured, once and for all. If it does come, it would be far far better for the truth to dawn upon him gradually and not a moment before it was necessary. Does Giorgio know of the possibility? I hope not.[40]

The patient responded well to radium, and once she was home, with Giorgio very attentive to his mother and his father, the Joyces were 'a happy family again'. Harriet, who had a great affection for Mrs Joyce and was well aware how much her husband depended on her, was wonderfully relieved.[41] She turned her attention to Dora's affairs.

The book was in print. Twenty-eight review copies were sent out, and a select list of influential people were given complimentary copies. Bertrand Russell, who was on the list, decided instantly that he was not a proper person to commend the book.[42] He must have reached this conclusion as soon as he caught sight of the dedication:

To
THE GREAT NAME
HUSHED AMONG US FOR SO LONG
of
HER,
HEAVEN,
THE MIGHTY MOTHER
of
ALL

Harriet, too, was sceptical of this sort of thing—and she probably had not seen it until it was in print. But it was a triumph to have got the book out at all, and she was eager to know what her friends thought of it. 'After a very great push,' she told Sylvia, 'Miss Marsden's book came out on Saturday . . . I shall be much interested (so will Miss Marsden) to know how you like it. . . . Publishing from a mountainside and without an address has many difficulties! We have had to borrow the printers' addresses.'* Her own 'two outgrown

* Charles Birchall had a London office, so that Harriet Weaver was able to give the book, and its successor, the imprint: 'London. The Egoist Press'.

appendices' were 'grandly announced on the back of the book jacket':
A history of the Concept of Space and *A history of the Concept of Time*,
both sub-titled 600 B.C.–A.D. 1928. These subjects, Harriet remarked,
would 'certainly amuse Mr Joyce and I daresay you too'.[43]

Dora had announced three forthcoming books. The first, *The
Mystery of Time*, she hoped to have ready by Easter, but she was
having a holiday over Christmas; she and her mother were going on
a long visit to her married sister, Eleanor Dyson, in Preston. Harriet,
who had put off her move to Frodsham so as to leave on the same day,
commented to Sylvia: 'We were very rushed for several days beforehand, Miss Marsden going through papers of nine years' accumulation and taking away all her books'.[44]

At Frodsham, she found her aunt very forgetful, and unable to read
or write after recent eye-trouble, but all the more sweet and gentle
because she was helpless. It was a pleasure to look after her, a pleasure
interrupted by various duties. Harriet, in spite of her own doubts,
was most anxious that Sylvia should think well of Dora's book, and
warmly recommended it:

... The book certainly, as you can see from your first glance, represents an enormous labour and I think Miss Marsden is a great genius.
Her grasp of her subject in its entirety is most profound and her
learning amazing. Review copies were sent out at the beginning of
the month and she is eagerly awaiting the first reviews. . . . It is very
nice of you to say you would like a copy for your library, with the
bill. I will pass on the order which has to go via Miss Marsden who
has the invoice book. . . .[45]

The first review, in *The New Age* of 27th December 1928, ridi-
culed the book, for its subject-matter and for its 'execrable' prose.
The reviewer allowed there were one or two phrases which almost
made it worth reading but added that it was, 'alas', the first of a series,
published very appropriately by The Egoist Press. Harriet did not
pass on these comments to Dora, but she typed out for her the somewhat bewildered remarks made by Alfred, Maude and Mary when
they thanked for their complimentary copies. Alfred cautiously
observed that he was 'totally unqualified to pose as critic' and hoped
the reviews would be good; Maude said that Campbell, who had
read more of it than she had, was impressed by the 'marvellous knowledge and range of study' which was only to be expected from 'the

train loads of books'; and Mary simply did not know what to say: 'I could really only sit and *gasp* at the stupendous knowledge and vast learning *and* the terrific work . . . it is really overpowering'.[46]

Mr Joyce's Christmas present to Harriet was a leather-bound copy, number 165 of a special edition, of Benjamin Constant's *Adolphe*.* In his letter, he warned her, rather light-heartedly, that he was going to need more money. Harriet was not disturbed by this news; she had expected it. She had promised to see him through whatever happened; and she knew, though he did not, that Mrs Joyce was threatened with a 'much more serious' operation.† Through the first weeks of 1929, she and Sylvia shared their almost frantic alarm. At first, the doctors put off telling Mr Joyce of the 'terrible alternative' that could be avoided only by permitting them to operate; and they finally gave Sylvia the painful errand of bidding Mr Joyce and Giorgio to come and see them. Harriet, when she heard of this, dashed off a reply by return of post. The news was 'indeed terrible', and she felt distracted because she dared not write to Mr Joyce until she knew what he had been told, and because a letter from Sylvia might not reach Glencoin until after she had left for a short visit to her sisters. 'Then,' she said, 'I want to get over to Paris if only for quite a short visit. My mind is rather incoherent today but that is what I have succeeded in planning . . . I meant, would you telegraph the date of the operation, if it is fixed. . . .'[47]

Harriet's plans were arranged, as she thought, so that she could be useful to Mrs Joyce in the 'long weary period' after the operation.[48] In the meantime, she looked forward to a short break at Westwick. But there, she found both her sisters laid up in bed, Mary with a strained knee and Annie with neuritis in her right arm—the good arm that she could not afford to have permanently affected. To top it all, Harriet herself had a bad cold. So she stayed on with the invalids, and travelled up to London by day to look after Dora's business.

Restored to health, she arrived in Paris on 30th January and went to the Belmont, near the Etoile and convenient for the clinic at Neuilly. But it turned out that Mr Joyce had not yet brought himself

* Harriet Weaver was interested to find that she could not agree with Rebecca West's criticism of it, in her recent book *The Strange Necessity*—but perhaps her confidence in Rebecca West's judgment had been shaken by a witty remark in the same book that the creator of that sentimental hero, Stephen Dedalus, had 'given him eyelashes an inch long'!
† A hysterectomy.

to sanction the operation; it was deferred until 5th February. To cheer up his wife, who looked to Harriet very frail and was feeling intensely nervous, he had his birthday party as usual. Harriet stayed on for nearly two months and, when the operation was over, she spent a great deal of her time with Mrs Joyce, providing the unexacting company that invalids had always valued.

Members of the Joyce circle, who thought of Miss Weaver as distant not only in manner but also in space, a powerful influence from the other side of the Channel, may have been surprised to see her in this new role—and disturbed, too, if they saw it as their own.

When Harriet went back to London at the end of March, her tenant had gone and she was able to settle for a while in her own flat, and get on with her symposium, which she hoped to bring out in the following year, 1930. Dora and her mother had decided to move back to Glencoin. But Harriet's plans were not affected. She hoped to be allowed to read Dora's current book before it was printed, but as Dora was still reluctant to discuss it there seemed no hurry to join her in the north.

In general, the change had done Dora good. She was in a calmer and more hopeful mood. 'No review has appeared as yet,' she wrote, 'but I am, somehow, much more cheerful about the matter than I was some time ago. Though I cannot set out my reasons for the feeling I *have* the feeling that the book will, quite speedily, make itself felt.'[49]

Her second, and her last, review had in fact appeared.[50] It was a serious analysis of her 'Trinitarian metaphysic', with a very fair summing up: 'Her constructive work, so far as it has yet proceeded, depends on a belief in the vision of immediate truth bestowed on the primitive "mythopoeic" mind which many may hesitate to accept; but her knowledge of philosophy is thoroughly adequate and her critical powers considerable'.

Unhappily, this review had no effect on sales. A few bookshops had taken copies on sale or return, and all of them, one by one, returned. Dora and Harriet, meanwhile, had drawn up a list of eminent people —dons, bishops, writers and editors—who might conceivably promote the book, and seventy-five presentation copies were distributed in the first half of 1929. But again, no sales. It was left to Grace Jardine, in her Manchester bookshop, to score a small success. She sold four copies during the year.

It was a melancholy period, but Harriet, in London, was having a real break from the embarrassments of publishing books she had never read; and she had some cheerful company. Edith Walker came to stay. Harriet and Edith had always kept in touch, since the days when Harriet, working for the Charity Organization Society, had got her her first training; but there were long periods when they could not meet. Edith had worked during and after the war as an auxiliary nurse; and was now training to be a qualified nurse. Whenever Harriet's flat was unlet she was invited to stay there for the one week-end a month when she was off duty; and once, when she arrived in London exhausted by a night journey sitting-up, Harriet had given her a splendid surprise: 'There on the platform stood Miss Weaver' ready to carry her off for a good meal at Gloucester Place.[51]

It was in the same spirit that Harriet, when she returned from Paris and heard that Edith was ill, went to fetch her from Margate. When a friend she had been nursing died, she had a breakdown and she was still very depressed. But her six weeks' stay at Gloucester Place restored the zest for life, quick wits, courage and sense of fun that Harriet had always liked. Harriet's respect and affection for her increased, and the old relationship between a well-disposed senior and a deserving junior was transformed into a friendship between equals, with an understanding, sensitive yet bracing, of each other's qualities and frustrations.

Sometimes Harriet read aloud—Greek legends and Mark Twain's *Joan of Arc*, chosen as a reminder of another's suffering. They walked and talked and, above all, laughed. Edith's wise brown eyes often looked sad, but her bushy eyebrows had an appealing 'George Robey' buoyancy; and, unlike most of Harriet's friends, she was a born comedian. When she had no money for a new hat, she made a good game of cutting round the brim of her old one, and hitching it up to give a fashionable effect; and she could play for laughs when the brim fell over her nose in the middle of the street.[52]

Edith went back to work in good order at the beginning of August and Harriet, also more cheerful, went for a week to Torquay where Mr Joyce, who had long dreamed of a holiday in the West Country, was at the end of a long stay, with his family, at the Imperial Hotel. Harriet had asked him to find her humbler lodgings but he had, perhaps intentionally, failed and she had to resign herself to unaccustomed grandeur.[53] It was some consolation, perhaps, that he had negotiated a reduction of the rates.

She was sorry to miss seeing Giorgio, who had gone back to Paris by the time she came, but pleased to hear a good account of his début as a singer. Lucia was not so well placed, as she feared she was not strong enough to make a career as a dancer; and Mrs Joyce, still very weak, was subject to fits of weeping which Lucia attributed, in retrospect, to worry on her account.

Harriet spent much of her time keeping them company, as Mr Joyce had a routine of his own. As she had already heard, he had felt encouraged to keep on writing by James Stephens' response to the suggestion that he should play ghost,* and he spent most mornings collecting material for Part II from a mixed bag of technical journals and comics. In the afternoons, he lay on the beach.

But he found time for one expedition with Harriet, to Kent's Cavern, a mile up the coast. The cavern's five large chambers, and the surrounding labyrinth of smaller caves, were all hung with stalactites. The deposits of prehistoric life, eleven feet thick, went back half a million years; and, they learned with amusement, had been an embarrassment to nineteenth-century archeologists, who had to show respect for the orthodox Christian view that the word was created in 4004 B.C.

In September, she was back in Dora's orbit. Dora, who had worked well through the summer, had rather rashly decided that her next two volumes were to come out, two months later, in November 1929. Harriet, at her request, arranged everything with the printer, Captain Birchall; only to find, when she got back to Glencoin at the end of the month, that the second volume of the two was not going to be ready until 1930. Captain Birchall, fortunately, was prepared to print one volume at the rate he had asked for two. When Harriet wrote to Sylvia at the end of October, she was quite looking forward to a short period of hard but rewarding work on the publication before she settled down to her own work on space and time.

She began her letter, as she so often felt obliged to do, by commiserating with her correspondent's recent calamities, Sylvia's 'poor crushed finger. . . . And Miss Monnier's wretched tooth!' Next she thanked for the *Revue des deux Mondes* which Sylvia had sent her, and for various other reviews she was going to send. And then she talked about her own affairs:

. . . Miss Marsden has been working at great pressure over final cor-

---

* James Stephens had told him roundly that he could finish the book and had praised *Anna Livia* as 'the greatest prose ever written'.

rections to the typescript of her next book. A first instalment is to go to the printers on Monday. I am to have the pleasure of reading it before it goes—when the clean copy emerges from the typist's hands. I have not read any of it as yet. . . .

The country here is at its most beautiful moment, arrayed in its autumn gorgeousness. . . . The pity is it is all over so soon.

With very much love

Yours affectionately

Josephine[54]

As Harriet/Josephine observed, the weather always breaks in the end. At Seldom Seen, the whole climate was turning grim. Dora, in a moment of weakness she regretted, had asked her to deal with the printer, but she was now determined to control all the arrangements. Harriet was finding it impossible to keep track of what was going on. She typed the letters that Dora dictated, but she did not see the hand-written notes, often unsigned, that gave other instructions. The text was dispatched, behind schedule, in blocks; printing was delayed; the compositors could not always read the copy; and Dora was upset when they made a bad guess, or when the proofs, like her copy, arrived late.

Behind these practical difficulties lay a conflict that Harriet and Dora had avoided, by mutual consent, for many years. Dora's assertive mysticism and Harriet's rational humanism could not be reconciled; and Harriet could not accept that Dora, who had certainly had some visionary experiences, was thereby divinely appointed to reveal the truth to the world.

Soon after she arrived at Frodsham for her usual Christmas visit, she had an angry letter from Dora, who complained that 'The Captain' ignored all she told him and took notice only of Harriet. '*That*, I suppose,' she said, 'is because you are the firm's bank reference!' As Managing Director of the firm, Dora 'refused any longer to condone the villainous vulgarity of this situation'.[55]

She also sent Harriet, for typing, an equally fiery letter to Captain Birchall, accusing him of negligence, explaining that Harriet's authority was 'quite intermittent', and instructing him to address all correspondence to the Managing Director of The Egoist Press. Harriet had a good deal of sympathy for the Captain, as well as for herself. He had kept his head under a flurry of telegrams and scribbled notes, and his latest crime—failure to produce on request three Hebrew characters—was not very heinous. She typed Dora's letter, but she sent back with it a 'milder and shorter' draft of her own; and she also took up, as Dora had now raised it, the harassing question of their 'relative positions':

Personally, considering how dependent the Egoist Press is at the moment on the Captain's good will, I think it would be a mistake to send the distinctly 'huffed' No. 1. But just as you like, of course. Only I, poor worm, must turn and assert myself so far as to decline to sign it . . . surely it is *I* who have occupied the subordinate position. . . .[56]

She was a director too, she observed, and she should at least have been shown the 'advertisement' that had now appeared on the cover of the book. 'But isn't it a pity,' she concluded, 'at Christmas time to have unpleasantness of any kind? . . . I very much hope you will decide not to send letter No. 1. With much love, Josephine.'

Dora scorned the advice, which she attributed to a fit of temper, and wrote Harriet several harsh letters, charging her with 'unconscious cruelty', 'triumphant self-righteousness' and a total lack of womanly sympathy. Unmindful of the pain she gave, she turned the knife in the wound by asking Harriet for typed copies of all the letters in the series and, when she apologized for causing 'upset and worry' immediately went on to cause more. She explained that divine messengers had always had to go into solitude before announcing their message, and that she had made a mistake in letting Harriet 'inside her straining mind':

. . . I thought you, though silent, were sympathetic. But how far from the truth I was you yourself know . . . I am not upbraiding you, I am merely pointing out that, standing by as you have been doing, during the last ten years, at a very strange phenomenon, you have completely failed to understand *what* you were standing by . . . now, even if you wished to discuss my books with me, I don't think I could do it. It is too late.[57]

There was nothing new in the prohibition. Only a few days had passed since Harriet, in the middle of reading the book, for the first time, in proof, had offered Mr Joyce a copy and recommended it in a manner well-judged to excite his magpie instincts. She was in a more serious mood when she wrote to Dora. 'I think it would perhaps be well,' she said, 'on account of the recurring crises in our personal relations, to set down as best I can, probably incoherently and all too badly, my point of view, which I don't think you quite grasp.'[58] She explained that responsibilities without authority put her in a real dilemma; she should know, beforehand, what she was sending to the printer. Then she made an effort to establish that the quarrels which hurt them both had arisen from legitimate differences of opinion which she, for one, believed should be accepted calmly:

. . . I admire enormously the great power and enormous fertility of your mind and am quite sympathetic (though you do not now think so) on the score of your vast and most enormous labours; it is the *direction* in which they are applied that sometimes seems to me not so fortunate. Your brain is so exceedingly fertile that it can, so it seems to me, find overwhelming evidence for any idea that takes hold of you, evidence so dazzlingly overwhelming as to blind you to contrary views. That seems to me to be a pitfall to which genius is specially exposed. I have observed it in you often in small things and I think I see it now, to some extent, in larger (as a part of your work, that is).[59]

The subject of Dora's visions was yet more delicate. But Harriet, once she had decided to speak out, spoke boldly. She distrusted revelations which did not 'seek and submit themselves to reason'. She was not, emphatically, questioning Dora's good faith, but she herself believed that inspiration uncontrolled by reason weakened the intellect of those who were asked (or ordered) to put their faith in it. Dora had promised a reasoned explanation in her fourth book, but Harriet was 'not very hopeful' of conversion. At this point, she used the face-saving phrase, 'perhaps I am wrong'; and straightway told Dora what she really thought of her:

Perhaps I am wrong in thinking that you yourself have seemed to me to demand absolute submission to your own views and to become antagonised unless it is yielded to you. . . .

She seems to have been right. Her next point, made in the course of attacking Dora's 'unsound science', has not yet, at least, been disproved by events: 'Your "living" atom seems to me now a physical impossibility, inasmuch as the breaking up of the atom . . . would release an incomparably greater amount of energy than living creatures display'. Finally, she remonstrated against the theory of an evolutionary élite: 'Give humanity a fair chance and trust it, I would say. It has never yet had a fair chance, never had good conditions, never had equality of conditions. Why should there not be a whole human race of supermen instead of only a sect?'[60]

Dora replied by raking over a long list of past offences. Twenty years ago, she said, she had exhausted herself in efforts to overcome Harriet's taciturnity, and her bones still ached to think of it.[61] Harriet, when this last blow fell, took it with splendid self-control and wrote a magnanimous reply:

I feel in myself a combative desire to make a long string of replies to your last letter but I have a deeper desire for peace . . . I still send much love to the big side of you, which is still liked and loved by what I hope you will recognize as the better side of your wellwisher

Josephine[62]

She was and remained a well-wisher, not only in words but in deeds. Dora's two books had cost her, in money alone, over £500, and virtually no money had come in. By January, they both knew that the second, like the first, was a failure. Meanwhile, Dora had used up some of her capital and had very little to live on. She tried to repay Harriet by giving her the copyright of her first book, and for a while considered taking up her old profession of teaching. But Harriet knew that her health was far too frail and, after giving her a small loan to tide her over, seems to have provided later some kind of regular subsidy. Dora's rage against her had no bearing on the general principle that help must be given to a friend who is in trouble.

Throughout the disastrous winter, Harriet's practice of keeping her life in compartments brought her some returns. Tranquillity was reigning in the other departments, and she enjoyed it. At Castle Park, her aunt, now eighty-eight, had been finding the days very long until Harriet produced the 'wonderful and exciting event' of installing a gramophone with records of a 'suitable nature'. The old-world household was even more delighted when Mr Joyce sent them his new record, of *Anna Livia*. It gave great pleasure, not only to Harriet but also, she told Sylvia, to her aunt's 'faithful housemaid-attendant, a simple, almost illiterate creature. After hearing it twice she said, quite spontaneously, "I like the Oirish one best". Her mother was a washerwoman, and I think she feels the humanity of it'.[63]

When she went back to Glencoin at the end of January, the cold was so intense that she dressed every morning under the bedclothes. The ice round the water pipe had to be hacked away before any water could flow, and all the household jobs took 'hours and hours'. She tried to think of her blessings—the good health and good eyesight that had been denied to most of her friends, and the beauty of the glen, sparkling with frost and snow.[64] But even when the jobs were done, and she was working 'tooth and nail' on her symposiums, she was still in an icy draught and two hundred miles from a library! She longed for April, when the tenant was vacating her flat, and she could go back and work in London.

She found time, as always, to keep an eye on cuttings, and was particularly pleased to see a friendly article on *Ulysses* in the *Sunday Referee*, written by her old colleague Richard Aldington.[65] Mr Joyce himself did not write until the spring, but she heard from Sylvia that he was busy revising *Haveth Childers Everywhere* and had also taken up an unexpected role as promoter of a struggling artist, the Irish tenor John Sullivan. When he wrote at last, in March, he told Harriet that his protégé had 'incomparably the greatest human voice he had ever heard'.[66] He had been 'working incessantly' on his behalf, 'telephoning, writing, interviewing, newspaper hunting, theatre-going, entertaining and being entertained'. Some of his friends thought he had gone 'somewhat soft in the head', but he was clearly enjoying his experience of the unfamiliar aspect of patronage. Unhappily, it seemed to be linked with a reverse in his own work, linked in turn with the temporary suspension of *transition* in the previous November and the loss of an incentive to produce regular contributions. When the 'frightful job' of revising them for publication came to an end, he felt 'a sudden kind of drop' and in 'this frame of mind . . . first heard Sullivan singing'.

He very much wanted Harriet to notice that he, too, was a patron; and she, though she had no interest in opera, or indeed in Sullivan, responded to such effect that bulletins on progress were sent her for many years. She was more nearly concerned with Mr Joyce's stratagems for reserving the copyright of Work in Progress in the United States, and here Sylvia's interests were involved as well as his. Publication in America was required to secure the copyright, and Sylvia 'naturally' felt that she should be given the licence to print, in France, a book that she had been helping him to write, over a stretch of years.

This was a sinister warning of trouble to come. Another warning, that 'living in Paris meant continual sacrifice of capital', was not altogether a surprise; and she was glad to learn that, as Dr Borsch had died, Mr Joyce had been thinking of consulting a Swiss specialist, Dr Alfred Vogt, who had a brilliant reputation for achieving results with very difficult cases.

All these items of news were on familiar topics. The big news was that Mr and Mrs Joyce wanted to get married. In the past, Mr Joyce had postulated, for the sake of appearances, a wedding in Trieste; but he had now discovered that, as a British subject, he could secure advantages for his family from his estate, by establishing 'domicile' and getting married, properly, in England.[67] He asked Harriet to find out from Fred how he should proceed.

Fred had become pretty seasoned against shocks from his old friend Harriet. This one almost floored him. But he felt it was his professional duty as well as his desire to help her; and he rose to the challenge.[68] At the end of April, she went to Paris, to the Belmont again, to convey his advice to the bridegroom.

She found his affairs under a new dispensation. Not long ago, he had mentioned seven people at work on his behalf, and he generally had the help of quite a large team. Now, one section of his life, the personal and literary correspondence, was under the capable management of Paul Léon, writer, lawyer, philosopher and sociologist, who had emigrated from Russia and settled in Paris. He was James Joyce's 'seeing eye'.* Harriet took a great liking to him and his charming wife Lucie. And she could appreciate his diligence.

In 1930, when Harriet first met him, he was already beginning to do anything and everything. He loved Joyce for his 'exquise douceur liée à une infinie comprehension';[69] and he gradually devoted himself to daily discussions of literary work and business, and to correcting proofs as well as writing letters. He did a great deal for Harriet too. He became a good friend, and a prodigal correspondent; and she was always happy to hear news of Mr Joyce from the man who stood by him so faithfully.

* Lucie Léon was his 'seeing eye' on occasion also, and the expression is hers. For example, she went with James Joyce to a film—*Extase*, in which Hedy Lamarr runs around the countryside 'perfectly beautiful and quite nude'—when her husband could not be persuaded to go because he thought he would be bored. (*Story of a Friendship*, by Lucie Noel (the name, an anagram of Léon, under which she writes). New York. Gotham Book Mart, 1950, p. 19)

Sylvia's attitude was very different. Mr Léon had taken over some of the jobs she was accustomed to do, and although (particularly since the Wall Street crash and the consequent decline in her business) she had found it hard to meet Mr Joyce's demands on her time, energy and petty cash, she was not happy to have the demands reduced when she was also losing her status as publisher of *Ulysses* and would-be publisher of *Work in Progress*. Moreover, she was beginning to suspect that Harriet, who had no interest in either money or prestige, could never appreciate her difficulties and might even add to them. Sylvia was one of those who had some doubts of Harriet's wisdom in leading Mr Joyce to think that money was always forthcoming in need and she had concluded, correctly, that she could not count on her support if a reliable American publisher offered him a good contract for *Work in Progress*. Whether or not she expressed her feelings to Harriet, it was at this point that some of the warmth went out of their relations.

During the visit, Harriet was more concerned with the Joyce family. It was satisfactory to learn, at the last minute, that Mr Joyce was prepared to defer his marriage until after he had consulted Dr Vogt, and although he was determined to stay in Paris for an appearance by John Sullivan, the consultation was to take place soon. But she came back to London very much worried about Lucia who was evidently not at all well. Her parents were disturbed about her too, but had not taken her to a doctor, and it was an added worry that no one knew what was wrong.

Harriet got back to Gloucester Place in May. Edith again came to stay once a month for her off-duty week-end and they became regular, and eager, playgoers, at the Old Vic and Sadler's Wells. Harriet's own domestic life, throughout the summer and autumn, was delightfully comfortable and peaceful. She was in her own place and doing her work; and she had a good friend in whose company she spent many happy days.

14

THE DARK SIDE OF FRIENDSHIP

AFTER her spring visit to Seldom Seen in February 1930, Harriet decided to stay away for a while. The difficulties between her and Dora had been contained in the context of a joint publishing venture, but this context no longer seemed real.

The failure of the second volume of Dora's opus was even more disturbing than the first. The complimentary copies sent out—as before, a very large number—had fallen on stony ground, and the few copies taken by bookshops, on sale or return, were coming back to stock rather the worse for wear. For this reason, it was decided to discontinue the arrangements for 'sale or return'. The booksellers, however, took this to mean that the book was now available only for free distribution.

The practical effect of this misunderstanding was insignificant; the moral effect was violent. Dora suffered a personal disaster from which she never recovered. Her sense of existence in this world had always depended on a faith in her mission, as a writer with a message to deliver; and when her mission failed, she retreated more and more into the visionary world which cut her off from human society. Her withdrawal was masked for the next few years by the assumption that she was still engaged on creative work;* though, on and off, in occasional poignant flashes of insight, she knew that her work was finished; and there were occasional moments when she recognized the truth courageously and even cheerfully.

When the disaster came, however, only Dora's mother, her

* *Time and the Homo-centric Universe*, *The Immemorial Cross* and *The Constitution of Knowledge*.

'dearest friend and lifelong companion', could bring her solace.* Harriet could not. It was some time since Dora had announced how much she regretted allowing her to trespass on her solitude; and Harriet decided the time had come to take her at her word. Her retirement, though inevitably accompanied by more 'plain speech', was achieved without any formal break.† Dora professed herself willing to criticize drafts on *Space* and *Time*; and Harriet persuaded her that she was still willing—whatever Dora thought of her abilities as a collaborator—to look up references and make extracts in the London libraries.

In the event, she often had to put her own work aside when some urgent query arrived from Seldom Seen, as she did also when Fred Monro raised questions bearing on the prospective Joyce marriage and on domicile in England. What, for instance, was the nationality given for passports from Trieste to Switzerland, from Switzerland to Trieste and from Trieste to Paris? Harriet, acting as unofficial agent for him and his client, passed on the questions and relayed the answers.

By the time the Joyces arrived in July on a long-planned visit to England, most of the questions were answered.‡ Harriet was relieved to see Mr Joyce looking a good deal better than he had been in Paris; and was thankful that the operation (on his left eye, for a tertiary cataract—his ninth) performed by Dr Vogt in April, had done so much for him. He was busy pursuing people likely to help in getting John Sullivan an engagement at Covent Garden and she saw him only in glimpses: once when he and his wife, both looking rather tired, were leaving for their holiday destination, Llandudno, and again when they passed through London on their way to Paris and she gave him a loan to finance the journey.[1]

By the autumn, he was fit enough to make a new start on Work in Progress, in spite of a nasty accident when driving in a taxi in Paris, which gave Harriet, at one remove, a horrid moment, though no

* From the dedication to *The Mysteries of Christianity*. London. The Egoist Press, 1930.

† For some months after February 1930, all Dora Marsden's letters were 'personal' and so were destroyed by Harriet Weaver.

‡ Harriet Weaver was probably secretly rather relieved than otherwise that the Joyces were held up over their visit and arrived too late to take her to the opera *Romeo et Juliette*, as arranged when she was in Paris, though she had done what she could to prepare herself for it by getting the libretto weeks beforehand. (Postcard to Sylvia Beach, 15th May 1930)

THE DARK SIDE OF FRIENDSHIP

bones were broken and his eyes were not harmed. '. . . I began to write the 2nd part on Sunday last—but with what labour! It is always like that when I start a fresh bout,' he wrote in October;[2] and a little later sent his draft, the first chapter of Part II, minus the last page. It began:

Chuffy was a nangel then and his soard fleshed light like likening. Fools top! Singty i sangty meeky loose, defendy nouse in prayley boos. Make a shine on the curst. Emene.[3]

Puzzling out a draft had, over the years, gradually become a genuine pleasure to Harriet and, though she had had no practice on a new piece for eighteen months, she was able to understand and enjoy some of the wordplay in this one. But the structure she found difficult and so she was grateful when, the day before he left for Zurich with the prospect of another operation before him, James Joyce dictated a letter explaining it, and sent also the last page. The piece had come out 'like drops of blood' but he thought it 'the gayest and lightest thing' he had done, in spite of 'a dreadful amount of worry'. The scheme was

the game we used to call Angels and Devils or colours. The Angels, girls, are grouped behind the Angel, Shawn, and the Devil has to come over three times and ask for a colour. If the colour he asks for has been chosen by any girl she has to run and he tries to catch her. As far as I have written he has come twice and been twice baffled. The piece is full of rhythms taken from English singing games. When first baffled vindictively he thinks of publishing blackmail stuff about his father, mother etc etc etc. . . . When he is baffled a second time the girl angels sing a hymn of liberation around Shawn. The page enclosed is still another version of a beautiful sentence from Edgar Quinet [who] says that the wild flowers on the ruins of Carthage, Numancia etc have survived the political rises and falls of Empires. In this case the wild flowers are the lilts of children. Note especially the treatment of the double rainbow in which the iritic colours are first normal and then reversed. . . .[4]

Harriet looked at the piece again, with new eyes. She was not, however, entirely convinced that it showed no signs of worry. One passage seemed to suggest the reverse: '. . . What's my muffinstuffin-

299

aches for thease times? To weat: Breath and bother and whatarcurss. Then breath more bother and more whatarcurss. Then no breath no bother but worrworrums. And Shim shallave shome'.[5]

This piece, compound of gaiety and suffering, was the last piece of new drafting that James Joyce sent Harriet. Except for some further work on Part II, and for redrafting at the proof stage, he had finished Work in Progress.

Why was it that from the first, from King Roderick O'Conor's piece onwards, he wanted to know what she thought—often showed impatience to know what she thought—of his latest draft? One reason must no doubt have been the obvious one: it was she who, having recognized his genius, had singled him out for help and support. Another may have been the plain fact that she was English. Except for Stuart Gilbert, who did not meet him till 1927, no member of his Paris circle was English. His experiments in language were not in their languages—French, Spanish, Russian or even American English; and Stuart Gilbert, a shrewd judge, came to the conclusion that the other members of the circle liked the idea of breaking up the language; and that James Joyce, who could expect an unbiased judgment only from Miss Weaver, got from her, in a roundabout way, the answers he needed.[6] Frank Budgen has expressed a rather similar view: that James Joyce needed someone who represented Justice to him—someone dedicated, with an unswerving sense of duty; and that this person would have to be English.[7] English Harriet certainly was, to the bone. And, as she said of herself, she had neither the art nor the ability to lie adroitly in order to please. Above all else, it must have been her sincerity that appealed to him.

But with James Joyce nothing was simple. Harriet's sincerity was also her undoing, because he needed and always desperately hoped for a favourable judgment from her. The pains he took, particularly during her visit to Paris in 1928, to win her over were, however, unavailing. Though she was able, after that visit, to appreciate better what he was endeavouring to do, she could not give him her whole-hearted support; and she knew that he knew that she could not. She had no illusions about the significance of her failure to do so and gradually came to feel that his disappointment in her was the cause of the increasing coolness he showed her from this time on.

Harriet had no reason to seek any other cause for his coolness. But, in fact, their friendship had always been at risk. Her role as judge was difficult enough, and so was her role as financier. She had also felt a personal responsibility for looking after his health, and had acted on it. This is the natural concern of a mother. He had fled from his mother, from Mother Ireland and from Mother Church; but the inescapable mother appeared again in the person of his benefactress. Her 'alms' supported him; her frown disturbed or irritated him.

Harriet, unaware of the risks inherent in mothering him, continued doggedly to concern herself with every aspect of his and his family's wellbeing. Lucia's health was giving the Joyces great anxiety. She had hoped that their visit to Zurich, on which they did not take their daughter, would at least give them a rest. But they were back within a week, the next operation postponed because bad weather had affected the eye. Shortly after their return, Giorgio married Helen Fleischman, *née* Kastor, an American living in Paris on private means, whom he had known for some years. The wedding precipitated another financial crisis.

'Things are in a bad mess here on account the the [sic] banco-political scandal and my royalty reserve dropped with a bang just when wedding, Xmas and New Year announced themselves so that I have to realise another £100 immediately and would be greatly convenienced if M and S could advance me half of it the moment they enetter [sic] their office after the Yuletine [sic] alltoobrief respite from me,' James Joyce wrote on a typewriter, his 'new toy'.[8]

Harriet, at Castle Park, for a visit of six weeks, did as she was bid but was not altogether sorry when Fred Monro reacted strongly. The capital realized now amounted to £2,000, he pointed out. Mr Joyce should make an effort to live within his income. She relayed Fred's admonition to Paris and hoped, now there were fewer family responsibilities, that expenditure would be less.

There was no answer for seven weeks. Then, at intervals between mid-February and mid-March 1931, Harriet received a four-part letter of immense length.[9] He was unsettled, restless, worried and once more penniless. He was now acting on his decision (of which Harriet already knew) to give up the flat in the Square Robiac and, in the process of choosing mementoes to give to friends, had found 'some rubbish' 'in a sack, that lay in the house that Joyce leaves'— early drafts of sections of Work in Progress, which he was sending to Gloucester Place. But, in spite of the upheavals, he was trying to conclude section 1 of Part II. 'Personally the only thing that encourages me is my belief that what I have written up to the present is a good deal better than any other first draft I made.' He was also trying to secure that 'the facts and dates were correct' in a biography being written of him;* and was presiding over the final stages of translating *Anna Livia Plurabelle* into French.† 'I think it must be one of the masterpieces of translation.' Adrienne Monnier was arranging a séance for 26th March at which it was to be read. If the séance was successful it would probably break the back of the English resistance to Work in Progress; if it were a failure, it might 'celebrate the close' of his Paris career. He planned to go to London shortly after the reading but did not wish to stay for long. For one thing, he was sure that the tinted glasses he wore in the street would give Londoners the impression that he had committed some crime and was trying to sneak around in disguise. 'However I deserve all this on account of my iniquities,' he added—an oblique reference, perhaps, to Fred Monro's broadside. On the other hand, he felt he could not go to Zurich for another operation in his 'unsettled state'. 'So to conclude I shall probably go into a small furnished flat in London and then perhaps go to Zurich . . . and then perhaps go somewhere else and then perhaps come back to Paris. . . . I hope you will let me hear from you what you think of this bewildering situation.'

Harriet failed to see anything bewildering in the situation. If, as Dr Vogt had expected, his eye was ready for operation, Mr Joyce ought to go first to Zurich. To come to London first and only for a short stay would be pointless: he would be paying for a London flat while in Zurich and would not, she imagined, be staying long enough to satisfy the requirements for the earning of domicile.

An invitation from Mademoiselle Monnier to attend the séance, backed by another from Sylvia, Harriet decided to accept. She was keenly interested in the translation and hoped there would be an opportunity some time during her stay for pointing out the importance of putting Zurich before London. There were, however, two distinct difficulties about going: 'lack of Parisianish clothing (though no lack of antedeluvian English garments)'—as she lamented to Sylvia; and shortage of money.[10] Her real income—largely from

* The biography was being written by Herbert Gorman.

† The translation of *Anna Livia Plurabelle* had been begun months before by Samuel Beckett and a young French friend. He had then had to leave for Ireland and it had been continued by Eugene Jolas, Paul Léon and Ivan Goll, a poet whom James Joyce had first met in Zurich. A complete overhaul of their translation had then been undertaken by James Joyce with Paul Léon and another friend, Philippe Soupault, who had translated Blake into French. The revised draft then went to Adrienne Monnier and, once more, to Eugene Jolas for final comment.

fixed-interest stock—had been much reduced by inflation and no longer stretched to an occasional extravagance. So she 'braved' Fred Monro, who did not approve of her making away with stock any more than he approved of a certain other client doing so, and got him to sell enough to finance ten days at the Belmont,[11] and to enable her to help out James Joyce, if he were still penniless.

Adrienne Monnier, as only the French know how, had worked up an elaborate and elegant programme for the evening at her Maison des Amis des Livres.* Harriet found it difficult to follow all the 'riviérantes ondes de, couretcourantes ondes' d'Anna Livie, as the translation was read. But she appreciated the value of the event, at a time when Work in Progress was progressing so slowly that interest in it was flagging; and was moved by the occasion itself. In her own country, there was nothing resembling the French tradition of paying homage to creative artists.

Unfortunately, Robert McAlmon, a reluctant guest at an occasion foreign to him also, thought it altogether too solemn and reacted by raising his hands for a second in a gesture of prayer. At this Edouard Dujardin rushed across the room and slapped him in the face.† His wife had large ankles and he thought the gesture was one of mock horror at them. Sylvia, observing that Harriet had frozen into tight-lipped disapproval at this untoward behaviour, coaxed her back into her usual gentle mood—a kindness that did not go unnoticed by Robert McAlmon. He reminded her a little later, how she had 'helped to keep Miss Weaver humanly understanding at moments when she was going Britishly and Quakerishly quavery'.[12]

The little fracas at the Maison des Amis des Livres was not the only jolt that Harriet received. There were, apparently, no funds for moving the remaining furniture from the Joyces' flat, nor, indeed, for anything else. She lent £160 to tide things over. A far worse jolt was Mr Joyce's announcement that he had decided to go to London as soon as possible to establish domicile. He felt his marriage more urgent now that he had a daughter-in-law as well as his wife and children to consider; and he was determined not to put it off any longer.

* The programme opened with a speech by Adrienne Monnier on James Joyce's influence in France. Then followed an address by Philippe Soupault on the work of translation, and James Joyce's record of *Anna Livia* in English; and finally Adrienne Monnier read the French translation.

† According to James Joyce, Edouard Dujardin, in his novel *Les Lauriers sont coupés*, was the first to develop the interior monologue.

Harriet thought this madness—his eyes were far more important than his marital status—but could not speak her mind to any of his friends for fear of betraying his confidence. Members of his circle, such as Maria Jolas or Moune Gilbert, who met her at the flat, would have found her looking and behaving as she always looked and behaved in the presence of her host: 'so timid',[13] 'so humble, sitting on the edge of her chair and confining herself to a deferential "Yes" and "No, Mr Joyce", when addressed by him'.[14] This was not, of course, a pose: it reflected Harriet's own estimate of her standing relative to his. But it gave a false impression. She was capable of saying 'Boo' to a goose.

On returning to Gloucester Place, there was nothing for it but to do what she could against the family's arrival, and to get some final information from Fred about establishing domicile. As neither James nor Nora nor Lucia Joyce wanted to settle in London, they were glad to learn that domicile could be established merely by a solemn declaration of intention.

They were delayed five days in Calais by bad weather and Lucia went down with stomach trouble when they got to their hotel, the Belgravia, Grosvenor Gardens. It was more expensive than those Harriet recommended. By the middle of May 1931, they had moved into a 'dreary little' flat in a Victorian terrace house near Kensington Gardens, 28B Campden Grove, for which they bought 'some still drearier necessary pieces of furniture'.[15] None of them liked it, Nora Joyce because the kitchen was so cramped and because she regretted her Paris flat and was convinced London would never suit her husband; he, because 'the grove was inhabited by mummies' and should be called 'Campden Grave'; Lucia, because she was desperately unhappy about the need for a marriage ceremony. Indeed, in the middle of the summer she returned precipitately to Paris to stay with her brother and his wife.

Harriet did what she could to smooth their path: arranged about fire insurance, found out the terms for subscribing to libraries, arranged an immediate cash advance.

The marriage ceremony took place at Kensington Register Office at 28 Marloes Road, on Saturday, 4th July, by licence.* This pro-

---

* On learning of the Trieste 'marriage', the Registrar refused to officiate and insisted that he could do so only if the pair first obtained a divorce. But Fred Monro, who had put in a lot of preparatory work, and had come armed with law books, was able to persuade him that the 'marriage' could not be regarded as valid in English law.

cedure had been carefully chosen as it required only one clear day's notice. But on the Friday, the journalists who regularly scan the list in the Notice Book spotted the name James Joyce. The next day, when the wedding pair emerged, several press photographers moved into action. The bridegroom tried to brush aside their enquiries with vague words about the ceremony being necessary 'for testamentary reasons'; and later fled to Robert Lynd's house in Hampstead, to escape further attention. When he wrote angrily to Harriet about the miscarriage, she hurried off to the public library, round the corner in Marylebone Road, to look through the papers—and found a horrid photograph on the front page of the *Evening Standard*. Though sorry for his discomfiture, Harriet was also highly amused by his efforts to 'cover up'.

A little later, when he was instructing Fred Monro about the drawing up of his will, he asked her whether she would be his Literary Executrix. She was much touched and agreed to serve, though she did not expect she would ever do so: he was, after all, her junior by more than five years.

The relevant clause of the will—clause 2—embodied further evidence of James Joyce's sense of indebtedness to her:

I leave all my manuscripts to Harriet Shaw Weaver and direct that she shall have sole decision in all literary matters relating to my writings published and unpublished.

Harriet's immediate activities on his behalf were more varied. They included writing letters for him; lending him more money; watching over negotiations for a contract with Faber and Faber and with Ben Huebsch for *Work in Progress*; and lending Faber some pages of the manuscript to set up in different types. James Joyce wanted the type to be 'extremely clear so that the readers may never make a mistake about a letter'; and, eventually, was 'nearly satisfied' with one of eleven types in which the pages were printed.[16] He was trying to find a publisher for Ezra Pound's *Cantos* and she had T. S. Eliot to tea to ask his advice about an offer from America to bring them out.* When a story he had not written appeared in the *Frankfurter Zeitung* under

* Later in the year, when Harriet Weaver was less pressed for time, she did something she had long wanted to do: to ask T. S. Eliot whether he would sign the books of his she had. When he agreed to do so, she wrote: 'I feel much honoured and am venturing to take you at your word and to send these five. I had always meant to ask

his name, James Joyce was up in arms and wanted to prosecute the paper for forgery. Unmollified by the paper's apology and explanation that 'James' had been inadvertently substituted for 'Michael', he enlisted Harriet's help in establishing whether there was a writer of this name. The British Museum Catalogue she found not very helpful: there was only one entry under this name, a book entitled *An Exposure of the Haunts of Infamy and Dens of Vice in Bombay*, published in 1854. But she discovered soon afterwards that there was another Michael Joyce—a young writer at the start of his career—and so reported. Still unmollified, James Joyce still wanted to prosecute—and was eventually dissuaded only when Fred Monro convinced him that his reputation would suffer more than his purse would gain.

This incident was not the only occasion when James Joyce showed signs of increasing tension; and it was perhaps as well that work on the symposiums still claimed a great deal of Harriet's time and that the Joyces had invitations in which she was not included, such as the luncheon party given for him by the chairman of Putnams, with Desmond MacCarthy and Harold Nicolson among the guests.* As she put it later, he was 'in an irritated state of mind' throughout his stay, though, as she realized, not without cause. Lucia's health was far from improving; *Ulysses* had not found a publisher in America (though the climate of opinion there had changed for the better) and the royalties, certain to be large, were tantalizingly as far off as ever.

Perhaps it was his old weakness for tempting fortune—for courting betrayal—that drove him, in defiance, to greater and greater extravagance; and Harriet may have noticed him giving the waiter a five pound tip when he and Nora took her to Kettner's for her birthday.[17] He was certainly drinking much more than was good for him—according to evidence she had extracted, over several years, from books and pamphlets. The Medical Research Council's report, *Alcohol: Its Action on the Human Organism*, seemed conclusive, par-

if you would sign Prufrock'; and added, '. . . please put the name untitled', in the hope—to be fulfilled—that the inscription would not be in quite the formal terms in which he invariably addressed her. (To T. S. Eliot, 13th October 1931)

* James Joyce, described by Harold Nicolson as 'so blind that he stares awry from one at a tangent, like a very thin owl', was hardly a success. Attempts to draw him into conversation began and ended with his replying 'with the gesture of a governess shutting the piano' that he was not in the very least interested—until a chance remark brought the talk round to something that concerned himself. (*Diaries and Letters of Harold Nicolson 1930-1939*, edited by Nigel Nicolson. London. Collins, 1966, pp. 83/84. New York. Atheneum, 1966)

ticularly as regards the effects on the digestive system; and the two bottles of wine usually drunk by Mr Joyce at dinner was far in excess of the pint prescribed by Black's Medical Dictionary as 'the utmost that even a large-sized, healthy hardworking man can daily dispose of without damage'.

Before he left London in the middle of September, she remonstrated with him; and she appealed to him always to start dinner with a glass of water and to drink another glass between each glass of wine. The remonstrance epitomized her conception of the responsibilities of friendship—and her inability to recognize that he could not admit the risk, however great, of drinking white wine when at the end of the day he needed its solace.

By the end of October, Harriet was at Castle Park, rather annoyed with Herbert Gorman for asking her, just as she was leaving London, to make a selection for him of Mr Joyce's letters to her. She could do nothing until her return. Her old aunt was 'very much confused, mixing up time and place hopelessly'; but was 'very sweet and gentle', more so than Harriet had ever known her to be. She thought it must be her aunt's 'true nature coming out, rid at last of the hard ultra-protestant poison with which she was infected in her youth and which narrowed her mind and whole outlook'.[18]

Ulysses, however, was soon competing for her attention. Sylvia had become apprehensive about the New York publishers who were now seriously considering bringing out *Ulysses*. They were, she believed, contemptuous of her standing; and, to bring home to them that she was not to be trifled with, she had named $25,000 as the sum she would require if she ceded her rights.* She unburdened herself to Harriet, who was glad to hear her side of the affair and was ready with sympathy. 'I understand your desire and determination to make all these men publishers recognise your rights and position as first (and most courageous and enterprising and hardworking) publisher of Mr Joyce's wonderful book,' she wrote, 'and I hope they will see this and make a really substantial offer so that a working arrangement can be come to as soon as possible.'[19] She knew, however, that she was unlikely to agree with Sylvia on what would constitute a working arrangement and perhaps to compensate for this and to assure her of

* Under a contract drawn up in December 1930, Sylvia Beach was entitled to receive compensation from any succeeding publisher in a sum to be named by her, if she and James Joyce agreed that, in his interests, she should abandon her rights. (*Shakespeare and Company*, p. 207)

her personal regard she invited her to stay, a little later on, at Gloucester Place.[20]

Harriet was staying at Castle Park for ten days only. She was coming back as usual for Christmas, but meantime she planned to spend five weeks at Glencoin, and was looking forward to her visit. She was taking a risk in rejoining Dora, after an absence of nineteen months, but she had at least grounds for hoping, from Dora's recent letter, that her attitude towards her had eased.

The place was just the same, beautiful and wild. But Dora had changed. Unlike Harriet, who had lost a little weight on purpose, Dora had become, for no apparent reason, startlingly thin.* But she seemed to have attained some kind of serenity: she was fond of her cat Sara, ironically interested in her neighbours, and prepared to look with a critical eye at Harriet's drafts.

They also managed to talk over some business. The Egoist Press had been revived, in October 1928, in a very casual way. No meetings had been held and no record kept. Now, on Friday, 27th November, Harriet and Dora held an official meeting. It was recorded that the firm now had two directors—Miss Marsden the Chairman and Miss Weaver the Secretary; that *The Mysteries of Christianity*, although boycotted by booksellers, was still on sale; that its price was to be raised from 10s. to 21s.; and that Miss Marsden's two books, and Miss Weaver's 'philosophical research' should be offered to 'an ordinary publisher viz. Faber and Faber'.[21]

The Egoist Press was closed down, for the second time. Harriet and Dora must have felt some relief. They both had confidence in Mr Eliot, who was now with Faber and Faber. He had always been a good friend, and, although Harriet had not yet put any definite suggestion to him, they were hopeful that he would look after their books when the right time came.

The visit went off well, but it was cut short when Harriet heard that her old aunt was failing, and she returned to Castle Park. A few days later, her aunt died. Harriet had thought she would live to a hundred as she had such a splendid constitution, so, to her, the end was 'very sudden'.[22] After the funeral, she returned with Mary and

---

* With Sylvia Beach's encouragement, Harriet had adopted a 'regime'. She expected it to simplify housekeeping at Glencoin, in spite of the winter shortage of the main ingredient—vegetables. James Joyce, when she told him about it, was not sympathetic. 'Raw vegetables', he said, 'were created by the Lord to be thrown at Covent Garden tenors'. (6th December 1931)

Annie to Westwick to stay with them until her flat was free again. Ahead lay the task of helping to dismantle the house and clear away the 'manifold accumulations' of seventy years.*

Soon after her arrival at Westwick, Harriet heard (through Padraic Colum) that James Joyce's father had died. Getting Fred to send £100 to Paris for the expenses of the illness and funeral was straightforward. Helping his 'prostration of mind', of which he wrote three weeks later, was a different matter: 'I am thinking of abandoning work altogether and leaving the thing unfinished with blanks. . . . Why go on writing about a place I did not dare to go to at such a moment. . . ? My father had an extraordinary affection for me. He was the silliest man I ever knew and yet cruelly shrewd. He thought and talked of me up to his last breath. I was very fond of him always, being a sinner myself, and even liked his faults. His dry (or rather wet) wit and his expression of face convulsed me often with laughter. . . . I got from him his portraits, a waistcoat, a good tenor voice, and an extravagant licentious disposition (out of which, however, the greater part of any talent I may have springs) but, apart from these, something else I cannot define. . . . I knew he was old. But I thought he would live longer. It is not his death that crushed me so much but self-accusation. . . .'† [23]

Harriet gently encouraged him to persevere with Work in Progress but felt unable to do more than touch lightly on his confession that self-accusation, not grief, was at the root of his despondency. This was not a problem into which she could enter because she was not aware of the irrational edge of his remorse. Quick to make accusations against his friends, he was subject also to a morbid impulse to accuse himself; and the habit had been taking a stronger hold as his daughter's condition worsened. Now, it was further encouraged by his father's death. He became obsessed by thoughts of his own shortcomings and hypersensitive to criticism, especially if it came from his patron and benefactress.

Her anxieties about his work, his love of drinking and his prodigality were already a kind of criticism and he was quick to conclude that she condemned him root and branch. He still saw her as the elective power who had confirmed his faith in his own genius, but he

* Among the 'manifold accumulations' was found a note-book in which Harriet's grandfather Edward Abbott Wright had recorded regularly the height and weight of his only son, Edward, who died as a schoolboy.

† Harriet Weaver's ellipses.

endowed her also with the attributes of a recording angel; and, as his sense of guilt towards Lucia deepened, he began to think that the angel was prejudiced against him.

Harriet had not learned, over the years, anything at all about the graceful art—or the wretched doom—of being a symbol; and this particular symbol would have been quite unacceptable. She knew she was Mr Joyce's inferior in every way and although she sometimes presumed to remonstrate with him, she never felt that their friendship gave her any rights.

Meanwhile, her sense of duty involved her in his family problems, and although she saw them very clearly her view was totally unlike his. She felt sure they could be mitigated, if not solved, by the application of common sense and the help and encouragement of friends. Mr Joyce's 'irritated state of mind' in London cast some doubt on her ability to help in an acceptable way. But her devotion to his welfare and, in spite of Work in Progress, her continuing conviction of his genius, made it impossible for her to do other than soldier on. As a friend, she would continue to do what she could for him; and, equally, she would continue to counsel prudence if she felt, as a friend, she ought to do so. But as the occasions when her counsel or help seemed called for increased, so her relations with him came under increasing stress.

How much under stress became manifest in the new year 1932, when Harriet told him she was celebrating his fiftieth birthday by cancelling his outstanding debt to her—incurred at intervals since her last visit to Paris. She also offered to help in letting his flat in Campden Grove for the period before their expected return in April and to lend or provide linen and other things. Otherwise, it was unlikely to find a tenant.

Harriet's letter arrived, as she intended, on James Joyce's birthday. That same day, Lucia threw a chair at her mother. She was seriously deranged and her brother took her to a *maison de santé*.[24] Her father, intensely grieved, was in no state to look objectively at Harriet's proposals. Whatever he may have thought about her offer to cancel the loans, he was incensed by the offer to find a tenant for the unlet flat. He refused it with an abruptness that reduced Harriet to a state of abject contrition. She felt she would never be able to forgive herself for what she now saw as blockheaded officiousness. She had been tactless at a moment when he needed all the sympathy she could give.

At this point, two fortunate events eased the tension. Padraic Colum persuaded Sylvia Beach that she was 'standing in the way of Joyce's interests' by holding out for compensation for the cession of rights in *Ulysses* and she thereupon renounced any further claim.[25] On 15th February, Helen Joyce gave birth to a son. Paul Léon sent Harriet the good news about *Ulysses* and a poem, *Ecce Puer*, written by James Joyce on the day he became a grandfather:

> *Of the dark past*
> *A boy is born.*
> *With joy and grief*
> *My heart is torn. . . .*

Harriet decided to go to Paris. She always considered that any mis-understandings and upsets were best put to rights by a talk rather than by letter; and the two happy events and the hint, in the sending of the poem, that she was no longer in complete disgrace, no doubt per-suaded her that the sooner she went the better. In any case, there was much to discuss, both pleasant and less pleasant.

Most pleasant was *Ulysses*. Now that there was no impediment in the way of concluding negotiations with an American firm, Harriet knew an offer from Random House to publish the book unabridged and unaltered, and on terms James Joyce had considered acceptable, would be clinched. This done, he would press for the publication of a regular, not private, edition in England, to appear before *Work in Progress*, already accepted by Faber. What English publisher would be willing to run the gauntlet? She wanted to discuss the whole question and to offer to help in any way she could.

Less pleasant, was yet another démarche from Fred Monro on the subject of disinvesting. Something would have to be said about it: James Joyce had been upset when Fred had recently expostulated: 'This can't go on'. But, as before, during the last stages of finishing a book, he was in a state of stress and had been spending wildly, perhaps because of his anxieties over Lucia.

Lucia's breakdown, least pleasant of all the subjects to discuss, was also more difficult than any other to write about and Harriet probably felt that a visit to Paris was imperative on this account alone. Her private hope, long held, that the girl would, some day, live an inde-pendent life and be enabled to fulfil her promise, now looked faint. But, as she realized, her own misgivings were as nothing compared with the anguish that the parents must be suffering and, as on previous occasions of illness in the family, she longed to be with them.

When Harriet went over to Paris for a short visit at the beginning of March, however, she found Lucia at home and in a tranquil mood.[26] The scene, indeed, had changed dramatically—and was to change again. Such changes were to prove characteristic of the illness, though Harriet was not in Paris long enough to witness them. Lucia, she found, was on the point of accepting a proposal from Alex Ponisovsky, Paul Léon's brother-in-law, though she apparently did not know him well. More curious still, it appeared that her recent attack on her mother had been precipitated by an irrational suspicion that her mother had broken up her friendship with Samuel Beckett, the young Irish writer whom Harriet had met on several occasions at the Joyce's flat.[27] It was all very puzzling.

The remission of Lucia's symptoms had, at least, given her parents some relief, though Harriet found them both in low spirits and her father suffering from some bilious trouble. She got through her discussions with him well enough, however, though she no longer felt, as she had in the past, a sense of easy and spontaneous friendship; and she welcomed his efforts to interest Lucia in some occupation. He had persuaded her to design initial letters for each of his thirteen poems in *Pomes Penyeach* and was already negotiating with publishers for a de luxe edition, with facsimile of his manuscript.*

Harriet fared less well in her talks with Sylvia. Indeed, for almost a year afterwards, they stopped writing to each other. Sylvia was, perhaps, in need of more sympathy than Harriet was able to give. She had been trying to reconcile herself to the consequences of her sudden and generous cession of the *Ulysses* rights but she had not altogether succeeded; she wanted her friends to show that they were on her side. Harriet, however, was much more on Mr Joyce's side than on hers and may well have made it a little too plain that it was his interests and the book's that she considered paramount.

When Harriet got back to London, she received from Dora her re-re-re-amended symposium draft, amended once more. She was relieved to learn (as she had two delicate missions to discharge for Mr Joyce) that Dora wanted a rest from collaboration. Dora had been spring-cleaning, papering her sitting-room, recently shattered by the chimney that had fallen into it, and rejoicing in the fact that the sun

* The poems were published by the Obelisk Press, Paris, in October 1932.

had risen, in spring brilliance, above the hill. Now she felt ready and eager for another spell of concentration on her own writing.[28] Later in the year, she sent Harriet a short note, to settle a trivial point about the builders of Liverpool Cathedral. 'After all,' she said, 'words are very queer things & the different values different people set on them lead to much misunderstanding.'[29]

Harriet was well aware of this sad fact. Dora herself, in the past, and Mr Joyce more recently, had given her some hard lessons. But it was a consolation that, even if he misinterpreted what she said to him, or took it amiss, there were still a great many useful things that she could do. One way or other, her attachment to him and his family had to be expressed.

15

DESPATCHES FROM MR LEON

THE first of the missions with which Harriet had been charged in Paris was—if possible—to placate Fred Monro. James Joyce had been upset by his remark that disinvestment 'could not go on' but was not sure what exactly was meant by it. Did he mean to insist on retrenchment? Harriet found, rather to her surprise, that he had not intended to comment on Mr Joyce's extravagance, only to remind him that the sale of stock always reduces income—a cogent point at a time when his earned income was small and *Ulysses* was 'banned' here and in America. Harriet, at her most diplomatic, assured him that disinvestment was resorted to only with reluctance and that Mr Joyce was keenly aware of the danger to which he had drawn attention. And so the matter rested—for a few months.

The second mission, not unconnected with the first, was to find out whether Faber and Faber would bring out an ordinary edition of *Ulysses*. She went to see Geoffrey Faber and he promised to discuss the idea with his board. While she was waiting to hear the result, T. S. Eliot, whose *Selected Essays* were just coming out, wrote to ask if he might, 'in recognition of her services to English letters', dedicate his book to her.* She was astounded, flattered, and very uncertain if she should accept a public compliment. But she had known Mr Eliot for

---

* T. S. Eliot's letter to Harriet Weaver asking for permission to dedicate has not come to light. The dedication reads: 'To Harriet Shaw Weaver/ in gratitude and in recognition of her services/ to English letters'. (*Selected Essays* by T. S. Eliot. London. Faber and Faber, 1932. New York. Harcourt, Brace & Co., 1932) The book was hailed (by *The Manchester Guardian*) as 'An event of importance . . . critical essays . . . hardly equalled in our time'; and (by James Agate) as a book 'of a quality to humiliate us all. It shows a mind of immense range, both imaginative and critical'.

a long time and the dedication would, in a sense, confirm her regard for him. So she wrote to say that she was 'deeply touched both by the very great honour' and by the terms in which it was couched. 'Though I feel,' she said, 'rather embarrassed and quite undeserving of such a tribute, it is yet a great pleasure to me humbly to accede to your most kind and most generously expressed wish.'[1]

Characteristically, she then went straight on to a subject other than herself. Might she call one day to discuss Miss Marsden's books? A fortnight later, when she went again to the Faber office in Russell Square, he told her his directors would certainly consider them and her own symposiums on space and time. But when their talk turned to *Ulysses*, he was not encouraging. Even if Random House, in America, were successful in defending an action, he felt sure that any English publisher would be prosecuted if he brought out a complete text. Harriet was left with the impression that he and the firm had been rather shaken by a recent successful prosecution of a young man sent to Wormwood Scrubs for six months merely for asking a printer whether he would print an obscene manuscript for private circulation only. And she was shaken when he pointed out that she herself might have landed in prison for even offering *Ulysses* to a printer.

Harriet, though she may well have thought that Mr Eliot and his fellow-directors were unduly apprehensive, had to accept their decision; and within a day or two she had other, unexpected, Joyce business to transact. The family were not coming back to Campden Grove because Lucia, who was being 'terribly difficult', had refused to return to London;[2] and her father was now eager to have Harriet's help. 'It would be very kind if you went to the agents (you may use the window pole to explain my point of view) and ask them to try to get it off my hands,' he wrote in the slapstick style that so often hid despair.[3] Harriet went off at once to the agents, Marsh and Parsons in Church Street, near the flat, and was not surprised to learn that prospective tenants who had seen it had all been put off by the lack of furniture and equipment.*

Lucia's condition was now deeply disturbing. After a party to celebrate her engagement to Alex Ponisovsky, she had gone into a catatonic stupor.[4] Her father, desperate for a cure, brought himself to seek medical advice. But Lucia did not respond to various physical treatments and, at the end of May, was taken, by a ruse, to a mental

---

* The flat was eventually let to an embassy chef.

home. Dr Maillard, who ran it, diagnosed her condition as 'hebephrenic psychosis with serious prognosis'.[5]

The diagnosis expressed Dr Maillard's view that Lucia was insane. It was not otherwise very enlightening to her anxious parents. The word hebephrenia meant either a form of insanity manifested at puberty or, more narrowly, a syndrome of bizarre actions and inappropriate moods which looked like a parody of familiar adolescent behaviour. Some doctors favoured the second meaning but it seems likely that Dr Maillard favoured the first. In either case, the diagnosis roused the spectre of schizophrenia, then generally known as dementia praecox; and (since the chemical control of schizophrenic conditions had not yet been developed) only a few doctors had any faith in any form of treatment. Most doctors had none.

Nora Joyce, already terrified by Lucia's attacks on herself and haunted by fear that she was mad, had no heart to dispute the doctor's verdict. James Joyce, who could not accept it, was determined to find a cure for his daughter's affliction and, as the doctors seemed to have little hope, took on himself the responsibility of choosing, or changing, her treatment. Since there was no specific treatment known, his impulse to try anything was understandable; and might even have proved fortunate.

But Lucia's predicament roused spectres in his own soul. In the past, he had thought of her as a gifted and beloved daughter with a mind very like his own; now, he saw her as a genius in his own image, distorted and frustrated by a world that conspired against his genius too. He felt very close to her because they were both victims; and then despaired because she was also his victim, sacrificed to his work and to his wanderings.* In moments of deepest despair, when his sense of guilt was almost unendurable, he insisted on faith and hope in a manner that betrayed his doubt. He feared that his friends were plotting to reassure him and begged them to tell him 'the facts'. Yet he could not admit any facts that challenged his articles of faith: his daughter was sane, and was getting better. As her condition grew worse, any attempt to speak openly became an act of treachery.

Harriet had never seen Lucia during an attack and had no useful information about her condition; and she could not know what lay behind James Joyce's gestures of love and grief. The complexity of

* Stanislaus Joyce also took the view that the Joyces' mode of life in Paris was the cause of Lucia's breakdown—and no doubt told his brother what he thought. (Mrs Stanislaus Joyce, in conversation with Jane Lidderdale, 21st November 1967)

his distress—and the effect on her relations with him—were not yet manifest. All she could do was to follow events with sympathy and offer comfort as occasion arose.

Dr Maillard's advice was that Lucia would do better at his clinic, away from her parents; and that she might, indeed, require to be isolated. All James Joyce's instincts revolted against such a possibility; and, in spite of having just resolved that she should have a more settled life, decided to take her away. As he was—at last—about to go to Zurich to see Dr Vogt, he decided Lucia should have a holiday nearby. Eugene and Maria Jolas, the editors of *transition*, who had become friends, were taking their family to Feldkirch, just over the border in Austria, and agreed to have Lucia with them if she were accompanied by a nurse. 'I smuggled Lucia and her nurse out of the clinic, through Paris and to Austria,' her father wrote. 'Whether my plan in double-crossing the 3 doctors succeeds or fails I shall be blamed—if it succeeds for having allowed her to go into the clinic, if if fails for having thwarted the doctors. . . .'[6]

As a doctor's daughter, Harriet was inclined to question the wisdom of this move though she sympathized with him in his revolt against the idea of isolation. Longer-standing anxieties were uppermost. What would Dr Vogt have to say about the neglected eyes? She had not long to wait. Paul Léon sent on an extract from a letter to him from the procrastinating patient. Dr Vogt thought it now too late to operate on the right eye. The cataract was total and complicated by secondary glaucoma and partial atrophy of the retina. The eye might, however, possibly be saved by two very difficult operations in succession. As it had been neglected, he was reluctant to touch the other.[7]

This report was a heavy blow to Harriet not only in itself but because of the effects she knew it would have on Mr Joyce's spirits—and on his wife's.

Then another blow fell. He wanted to sell £1,000 of stock. He was spending even more freely under the stress of Lucia's illness and, obviously, the search for a cure was going to be costly. His immediate need was, in fact, for a good deal less: cash to pay his hotel bill—the Carlton Elite was not cheap—so that he could join Lucia at Feldkirch, where she was working, at his suggestion, on more *lettrines*, this time a whole alphabet.

Harriet was prepared for some further selling, if only to finance Lucia's holiday, but not of £1,000. He was squandering his money as well as his eyesight. She told him roundly that he was throwing his money away. He reacted sharply and protested that this was not the case: he needed new false teeth, for instance, and money for a tombstone for his father:

... My father sent me a message by a friend in the curious roundabout delicate and allusive way he had in spite of all his loud elaborate curses (he is quoted on the jacket of an amusing book *Lars Porsena* or *The Future of Swearing*) that if I thought fit he would like a tombstone to be placed on his grave bearing the names of himself and my mother. He left the wording to me... Poor foolish man! It seems to me his voice has somehow got into my body or throat. Lately, more than ever—especially when I sigh.

Jolas sends good news from Feldkirch but I never know whether these letters are rigged or not. . . .[8]

Harriet was not deflected. She told him he needed only a quarter of the sum he asked; and had it sent him. This was her last major stand against his 'throwing his money away like a drunken sailor'. She had provoked and upset him too much. His peace of mind—the 'psychische Ruhe' his doctor said was a condition of saving his eyesight—must come first. She determined never again to oppose any request for the release of capital.

No longer a prisoner of the Carlton Elite, whose bill he could now pay, James Joyce went in the middle of August to join Lucia at Feldkirch where, much to Harriet's satisfaction, he returned once more to the first chapter of Part II of Work in Progress, spurred on, perhaps, by having a deadline to work to again: his draft of the rainbow-flower-girls-games episode was to be published in the next number of *transition*, now revived.

Lucia seemed to him (though not to Maria Jolas) well enough for another holiday with a nurse somewhere within easy reach of himself and his wife. After that, they would return to Paris and get a place where she could be with them. Though she had from time to time expressed a desire for an independent life, her mother was convinced that she did not really want to leave her parents yet.[9]

James Joyce wrote from Nice to bring Harriet up-to-date:

We are all here. Lucia and the nurse came over from Vence today. . . .

I saw Vogt again on Saturday. He injected I don't know what and I had to go back in 3 hours. It was a test for tension. The result was favourable and he then said he could wait (bad eye). . . . He says the capsule will shrink in about 1-1½ years and so leave him some space. . . . He . . . insists I am to come back to see him every 3 months during that 1-1½ yr. . . .

The Albatross Press (rival of Tauchnitz) has been bombarding me with phone calls, telegrams etc. . . . They want to take over Miss Beach's continental rights whether Cerf wins the U.S. case or not.* They would sell at ¼ her price but pay only half as much royalties. Of course the sales would be infinitely more numerous. . . .[10]

Sylvia Beach had accepted the offer by the time the Joyces returned to Paris towards the end of October. She had many reasons for choosing to stand down. Her relations with the author had been unhappy for several years; she was still smarting over the manner and outcome of the American negotiations; she was plagued by headaches; and she had other personal troubles. Besides, as she now claimed, she had never made any profit out of the book.

This seemed to Harriet very surprising, after Sylvia's earlier claim that cession of the American rights would mean a heavy loss to her. She had, perhaps, not kept separate accounts for *Ulysses* and her other stock, so that she was unable to pinpoint her losses and profits?† Harriet's own deep aversion from the whole subject of profits prevented her from dwelling on this Shakespearian mystery. Her prime concern was for the Joyces, though her own position was becoming increasingly difficult. During the whole year, James Joyce had been in a 'sour' mood, 'turned against everything English',[11] including, she suspected, herself.‡ As she understood very well, the mood arose primarily because he was 'harassed over Lucia'.

When the Joyces moved back to Paris, the harassment became more

---

* Bennett Cerf, of the Random House publishing company, New York, was inviting prosecution of his forthcoming edition of *Ulysses* but expected that the verdict would go in the book's favour.

† The state of Sylvia Beach's records, now at Princeton, appears to bear out Harriet Weaver's surmise.

‡ Harriet Weaver had sent James Joyce a book by Charles Duff—*James Joyce and the Plain Reader*—thinking he would be interested to see it; and she thought he would have been, 'had he not been out of temper'. Herbert Read wrote the preface, which T. S. Eliot sent her in draft, before publication. But James Joyce returned the book to her. (To Bjørn Rasmussen, 9th March 1961)

intense. Lucia claimed more and more of her father's time and energy, and Work in Progress took a poor second place. She had finished her alphabet. It was exquisite and her father hit on the idea of using it to illuminate an A.B.C. poem by Chaucer, in praise of the Madonna, beginning 'Almighty and almerciable queen'. He was asking everybody to help in finding a publisher, though Lucia meantime had switched to bookbinding.[12] 'The whole affair,' he told Harriet, 'continues to be a terrible strain and I am really a blind man walking in a fog. I do not know as much about illumination as I think I know about singing but S. was child's play in comparison with this. I wonder what kind of people you encounter for wherever I walk I tread on thistles of envy, suspicion, jealousy, hatred, and so on. . . .'[13]

The Joyces were in an hotel, vainly trying to find an unfurnished flat. The nurse had been dispensed with, all doctors were still being kept at arms length and Nora Joyce soon looked as though she would collapse under the strain of looking after her daughter.[14] So Myrsine Moschos, Sylvia Beach's kindly ex-assistant, was brought in to look after Lucia in the morning and a French girl took over in the afternoon.* Her father pretended to take her lightly. 'In fact,' he told Harriet, 'I am sure she tells a good few lies and does a fair amount of comedy but so do most girls in one way or another. I gave her 4000 frs out of my cheque to buy a fur coat as I think it will do her inferiority complex more good than a visit to a psycho-analyst. But it is all rather trying to me (who am very far from being a model myself) and I do wish I was settled in a home, sweet home with a piano to which I could sing *Come into the Garden, Maud* every evening at 6 p.m.'.[15] The fur coat, as a cure, was a failure. Lucia became increasingly restless. 'You will be rightly alarmed to hear,' her father wrote, 'that Lucia the other night expressed her intention of going over to stay with you ! ! !'[16]

There was more behind this intention than Harriet realized but in the meantime her attention was briefly deflected northwards by a Christmas letter from Dora—'quite an event', after some months without hearing from her. The letter revealed a number of changes; changes in Glencoin and changes in Dora's own mood.

When Harriet first visited Seldom Seen, it was a deserted settlement. Dora, a solitary eccentric, was the only kind of tenant the owner was likely to get. Recently, fashions had changed. Town

---

* Myrsine Moschos was Sylvia Beach's assistant for nine years from 1921.

people were now looking for week-end cottages. Inevitably, Dora felt her position was challenged, particularly by a family from Southport who were people 'after the Landlord's own heart, money, car, clothes, food, dog'.[17] A cat-lover, Dora disliked all dogs at Seldom Seen, particularly her landlord's latest retriever, a noisy animal which had been worrying her cat Sara.

From the Christmas letter, Harriet learned the 'dolorous' news that Sara was now dead. She had died in September, and for three months Dora had felt unable to write. Obviously, she had suffered a considerable shock; and Harriet, who had suffered when Wolf died, was well able to understand that the death of an animal is often like the death of a friend. Sara had been so close a friend that she had also become associated, in Dora's mind, with the ultimate success of her mission: 'I had so promised myself that, when my work was finished and began to be profitable, Sara should have her comforts & be cared for'.[18]

Although the cat had appeared too weak to move, she had disappeared. For three days, Dora had strained her eyes over the hills 'searching for some small black speck', and only then learned from a neighbour that Sara was lying on the fell, dead. She was buried with ceremony, on a grey day, near the gooseberry bush.[19]

The shock had a profound effect on Dora. She felt that in some sense she owed it to Sara to complete her mission. She made a vow to devote herself 'single-eyed to getting on with the series and finishing it'. This vow introduced the last in a long series of tragic efforts.

James Joyce, weighed down by his tragic efforts on behalf of his daughter, was, meanwhile, moving towards another crisis; and by the new year 1933 he was exhausted 'both physically and morally' and without funds.[20] He, Nora, Lucia and Myrsine Moschos were at last installed in a furnished flat—in the rue Galilée. But the worry had been too much for him. It was not from him that Harriet heard but from Paul Léon.

From this point onwards, indeed, it was largely through Paul Léon that Harriet was able to keep in touch: James Joyce himself wrote at increasingly rare intervals. It was a great comfort to Harriet, therefore, that she and Mr Léon found themselves very much of one mind on the most important matters: the need to encourage Mr Joyce to continue to work, to take enough rest, to look after his health and his eyes, and, above all, to have confidence in himself.

Paul Léon's new-year despatch was devoted to explaining why

selling more stock was unavoidable and to giving his views on how James Joyce was bearing up under the strain:

... He tries to react by working very hard, at least as much as he has the chance, but I have seen him suffering so deeply and with such disastrous effects on his strength that my impression is that he is sometimes at the end of his forces. ...* [21]

Harriet, true to her resolution of the previous summer not to oppose any further request to disinvest, telephoned Fred Monro at once. He expressed his disapproval, bluntly, and she was not disposed to argue. She bade him goodbye; put down the receiver; and wrote him a formal letter to convey his client's instructions.

The cash was despatched and duly received. Nevertheless, a few days later, James Joyce had a collapse. He was alarmed, naturally, and yet so fascinated by his own actions and reactions that he dictated a thousand-word account, for Harriet, of his 'long by others foreseen collapse' the moment he began to recover. It had started on the train from Rouen where he and Nora (who shared his love of opera) had been hearing John Sullivan in one of the very rare performances of *Sigurd*. 'Rouen was full of grippe and the theater [a] coughing booth.' Before the train was a quarter of an hour out of the station, James Joyce was 'in full collapse', convinced that he had fallen a victim of the epidemic. He had not done so; but, back at the rue Galilée, the collapse continued in another form apparently precipitated by a sudden decision, made at Rouen, to stop taking any sleeping pills— after having taken six every night for the past year. 'Then began a night of mild horrors including sleeplessness, hallucinations of the ear (how I deserve that) and sometimes of the eye too. ... But worst of all next morning while I was near the telephone in the corridor I got myself all up in a moment into a state of terrified alarm on account of something that was taking place, grabbed my overcoat and hat and got down into the snowing streets followed by the shivering Miss Moscos, the only at that hour fully clad female of my household and ten minutes afterwards I was standing before the partially shaved writer of the present Mr Paul Léon trying to tell him of the danger I was in.' Paul Léon endeavoured to get hold of James Joyce's doctor, failed, and so got hold in his own, Dr Debray. 'Dr Debray says I

* Paul Léon's letters are reproduced as written. His command of English was remarkable but not perfect.

must have three days of consecutive sleep. I have to remain at home for about a week . . . One good effect anyhow it seems to have had is to have produced an obvious amount of solicitude on the part of that subtile et barbare person—my daughter.'[22]

This account, ironically dismissed by James Joyce as 'on the whole' nice and cheerful, disturbed Harriet profoundly; and his need for and abuse of somniferents was a new worry for her. She decided to go over to Paris to judge for herself the state of the whole family and to see what, if anything, she could do to help. She travelled on 10th February 1933 and stayed at the Hôtel Galilée, just opposite the new flat. Nora Joyce had had a look at it, against her arrival, and thought she would prefer it to the Belmont.[23]

The visit seems to have been an almost unqualified failure, though it had been welcomed by everybody. Paul Léon had hoped she could persuade James Joyce to return to Zurich for the next appointment with Dr Vogt, now two months overdue, and make arrangements for Lucia that allowed her parents to get away without her and come back to a tolerable life at home; and James Joyce wanted to discuss things with her—including, no doubt, finance.

But Harriet, inadvertently, made a bad start. She had not realized how much readier he now was to misjudge his friends' motives and take offence. It did not occur to her that he might not wish her to listen to anyone other than himself. Her first step was to enquire about his situation from friends who shared her concern. Some, she found, agreed with her that he was drinking more than was good for him and that he was finding it almost impossible to bear the daily misery of seeing his daugher's sufferings.

Sylvia Beach, in spite of her recent coolness, was still Harriet's closest friend in Paris. They met and talked, thinking no harm. But James Joyce was outraged when he heard that Harriet had discussed him behind his back, worst of all with Miss Beach who, he said, had 'maltreated' him.*[24] Like many men with a habit of dependence on women, he had a wild terror of being trapped in their monstrous regiment. Their compassion, eagerly sought, wove a net round him, detested and feared whether or not it was meant for his own good.

He drew his own conclusions about what Harriet had heard. What-

---

* A low point in James Joyce's relations with the rue de l'Odéon had been reached in May 1932 when Adrienne Monnier had taken upon herself to write a letter to him saying, in short, that he asked too much of both herself and Sylvia Beach and that they could do no more than they did. (Ellmann, p. 664)

ever it was had warped her attitude towards him; he had already made up his mind that his friends, or ex-friends, were 'misconstruing' the 'facts'; and interpreted as a betrayal her well-meaning efforts to size things up objectively. Undoubtedly, she had made a tactical blunder, but her punishment was out of all proportion. When she came to talk to him she found him (in the understated terms the Weaver family favoured) 'very elusive'. In fact, he refused to discuss anything and met her enquiries with silence.[25]

The coolness between them was not lost on Lucia who, in 'a new Messianic phase', determined to reconcile her father and his benefactress.[26] She had grown very fond of Harriet and she felt deeply distressed. Paul Léon, saddened too, was at least able to tell her himself enough about finances and expenditure to enable her to make up her mind what was required on that score.

What was required, it seemed to her, was enough money to meet all foreseeable expenses in the next few months, until royalties began to flow steadily from the Albatross Press edition of *Ulysses*. She gave her blessing to further disinvestment and may also have given some help herself, for she abandoned at this time her plan to subsidize the publication of Dora's next books and her own symposiums.

On her return to Gloucester Place, Harriet had the satisfaction, though it was to prove a passing one, of learning from Paul Léon that Mr Joyce 'appreciates greatly that as a result of your kind intervention the material problem is at least for the next few months assured and that is one source of constant worry that is taken away from his mind'.[27] She could not tell Mr Joyce that she was glad: he had asked her—through Paul Léon—not to write to him.

The other problems still remained and, indeed, worsened. Lucia, in the course of new treatment hit on by her father, which included drinking seawater, had a relapse; and her father, another collapse because of comments that the treatment was only superficial and he was wrong in insisting on it.[28] 'Some kind soul' had also told him that 'he had ruined his eyes definitely and that Vogt would never agree to operate him again', as Paul Léon reported. He had a good deal of sympathy with Harriet's view that Mr Joyce's drinking had affected his digestive system. But Dr Debray, called in after this second collapse, and asked to consider this assumption, came emphatically to the conclusion that it was without foundation: the liver and 'digestive tube' were 'in perfect order'. Paul Léon himself remained convinced that Lucia's state of health was 'the root of the thing'. It was only her father who wanted to keep her at home and he still insisted that he alone could decide what ought to be done. But the strain was affecting him deeply. Since this second collapse, he varied 'from states of great irritation and impotent fury to sudden lacrimose fits'. Paul Léon went on:

Finally and to wind up I think the voyage to Zurich of prime necessity and if you could do something in this respect your interference would be a blessing. For I do think Mr Joyce belongs to his work and unless he is able to do it he will not get well. . . .

I am writing to you in this manner because I have the impression that you can do a lot by words and acts and it is this consideration which gives me the courage to write to you in this way and I have absolutely nothing but the most respectful thoughts.[29]

Paul Léon was evidently readier than Harriet to discount the failure of the February visit.* A month later came an even more alarming despatch—thirteen hundred words—and an even more urgent plea for help.

James Joyce had an attack of 'colitis' so acute that (Dr Debray being away) Dr Fontaine was called in. To their 'general astonishment', she found that there was 'absolutely nothing the matter with him at all' and attributed the spasms to 'a disequilibrium of the system of the sympathetic nerve'. But she insisted—as Dr Debray had done—that a rest cure was essential. Paul Léon described his state as 'listless disgust and apathy in connection with the most vital problems of his life and work. The latter is even not considered to-day and whenever I mention the subject Mr Joyce merely waves his hand in despair and resignation. . . '. Visiting Zurich seemed out of the question: there was no money left. He might contrive to stay on in the rue Galilée until the middle of June if he could realize another £100 immediately 'but afterwards he absolutely does not know what to do and his usual remark is "let everything go to pieces"'. Paul Léon, however, insisted that the visit to Zurich was 'a prime necessity' and that Mr Joyce would never get well or resume his work unless he went there.[30]

The day she received this letter, Harriet decided she must go over to Paris again.[31] She must see if she could not, after all, coax Mr Joyce into getting away. She arranged also, in spite of his disapproval, to

* With one unimportant exception, Harriet Weaver's letters to Paul Léon have not come to light.

see Sylvia. For her, there was something she could do that she knew would give pleasure. Sylvia had loved an earlier present of a 'Simonside shawl';* and wanted another for her sister. So Harriet took one with her from London.

She went at the beginning of May, just as soon as she could, and stayed again at the Galilée. James Joyce's changes of mood—almost as varied and unpredictable as those of his daughter—this time worked in Harriet's favour. He was neither 'irritated', nor 'sour', nor silent. He was friendly, ready to listen and to talk. He talked about a play, *Loire*, by André Obey, then on in Paris, which he thought would interest her as much as it interested him: the chief characters were the river Loire and her five tributary daughters. He gave her a copy of the play;[32] and he also got her to choose, from some sketches Frank Budgen had sent him, the one that pleased her best. He had decided to commission an oil painting from it for her birthday.[33]

Though Harriet stayed about ten days only, other, more important, matters seem somehow to have been settled also. This time, perhaps, she was better attuned to his predicament, not so set on cautioning prudence and restraint, and readier to show her compassion and her willingness to help him to achieve peace of mind. At any rate, James Joyce began to work again, or, at least, began reading the four watches of Shaun;[34] and, when an old friend from Switzerland, Carola Giedion-Welcker, arrived in Paris for a short stay and suggested his returning to Switzerland with her, he was ready to agree—though only on condition that Lucia went with them.[35]

'Mr Joyce and his family left Paris to-day at 2 p.m. for Zurich,' Paul Léon wrote. 'After all the worries this is I think a step forward and may I congratulate you on the fact that your stay here has not been in vain.'[36]

Harriet would have liked to stay on in Paris to see them off but was prevented from doing so by an engagement in Frodsham she particularly wanted to keep. Aunt Harriet Wright's surviving nephews and nieces had decided, as none of them wanted to live at Castle Park, to present it, as a memorial to her father and their grandfather, to the Runcorn Rural District Council. The house was to become the Council offices and the grounds were to be turned into a public park.

* Mary and Annie Weaver had discovered Simonside shawls, made in Cumberland, some years before, had liked them so much that they had since given thirty or forty as presents, including one to Harriet. It was this shawl that she used to wear in the drawing-room at Castle Park after her aunt had gone up to bed.

DESPATCHES FROM MR LEON

On Wednesday, 24th May, Harriet, Mary and Annie, Edward, Maude and Campbell, Alfred's son Anthony and cousins on the Wright side assembled for the first part of the official opening ceremony outside the main entrance to the house. With them were members and officials of the Rural Council and other bodies. On the 'platform' were the chairman and clerk of the Rural Council and Alfred who, as usual, had borne the brunt of the winding-up of a family estate.

After speeches by Major Ashton, the clerk, and Mr Walton, the chairman, Alfred was called on to declare the offices and grounds open. He sketched the history of Castle Park from the time when Hugh Lupus, a nephew of William the Conqueror, had built a castle on the site to block any advance by the Welsh. Although built to serve the owner's selfish ambition, it had been of 'real public service' and, Alfred concluded, 'It stood for protection and the well-being of the community and I believe that that spirit will still live on and again be made manifest in the high and responsible work of the Council as the local authority of the district'. The assembly then went into the house and gathered in the hall, where a commemorative plaque was unveiled; toured the 'premises' and grounds and finally returned to the lawn in front of the house, where tea was served.[37]

The transition from the stresses of the rue Galilée to the ordered procedures at Castle Park was typical of Harriet's continuous movement from one department of her life to another. She was now about to reactivate an old one which had lain dormant for a considerable time. Her absorption for the last twenty years in her literary protégés had been at the expense of her earlier interests in political philosophy and social reform. With the ceremony at Castle Park over and the Joyces—though with Lucia—in Zurich, Harriet began to give time to political and social problems that were increasingly claiming her attention.

In Italy, Benito Mussolini had created and consolidated a fascist state and, now, in Germany, Adolf Hitler had been appointed Chancellor and was demanding equality in armaments with France and the United Kingdom. In Spain, there were ugly signs that fascists were ready to break up any left-wing organization and frustrate all attempts at agrarian reform. At home, economic rights were at stake. The number of unemployed in the United Kingdom had more than doubled since world-wide unemployment had mounted after the Wall Street crash of 1929. In coalmining, about one worker in four

327

was unemployed, in cotton, one in two. But the weekly 'dole', barely adequate to tide over short periods without work, was totally inadequate over long periods. The blight of misery and poverty and stunted lives was everywhere.

Harriet, like many others who had private means, felt conscience-stricken. How could so vast and intractable a problem be tackled? Many felt that, whatever else needed to be done, aid on the spot was vital, and gave themselves to local schemes in the 'depressed areas'— South Wales, Lancashire, the Clyde, the North East. Harriet might well have joined them had she not been convinced by her training and experience in the East End that only through political action on a national scale could justice be done.

The British Labour Party, divided though it was after the formation of the coalition National Government formed in the financial crisis of 1931, yet seemed to her, with her long-standing socialist convictions, to offer the only hope of securing reforms on an appropriate scale, whether at home or abroad. Harriet accordingly joined it and went round to her local party office in Marylebone to offer her help with clerical work or canvassing. The office was in Daventry Street behind Edgware Road Underground Station, in a slum area, Lisson Grove, within a quarter of an hour's walk of Gloucester Place. It was a miserable little office—and a miserable little local party. Marylebone was a Conservative stronghold and Lisson Grove was the one Ward that returned Labour members to the borough council. But Harriet felt she had made the right decision.

There was little news of the Joyces during the summer; and that little probably from Paul Léon. James Joyce does not appear to have written at all and Harriet thought it best to keep her distance, although he had made known to Paul Léon that he was once again prepared to receive letters from her.[38] A holiday in August on the Merionethshire coast, with Alfred and Muriel and their children, and Maude and Campbell and their children, and Campbell's brother Henry and his wife and children, and Campbell's nephew Evelyn Hone, provided her with some distraction; and 'strenuous walks', in the Berwyn mountains, brought their usual solace.[39] But 'The Gap', the tacit agreement not to discuss with her family any interests uncongenial to them, prevented the comfort of unburdening herself.

Some comfort arrived, however, from another quarter. At the end of August, Harriet returned to Gloucester Place, and the day before her birthday, Frank Budgen, whom she had not yet met, rang up to ask whether he could bring Mr Joyce's present to her.[40] He arrived carrying the picture done from the sketch she had chosen. It was of the Liffey at Chapelizod, one of several scenes sketched by him on a recent visit to Dublin – his first. Harriet was delighted, and hung it in the place of honour, above the mantelpiece.*

Discouraging news of the Joyces came at the end of September—from Paul Léon. Lucia was worse. She had spent part of the summer at a clinic, Prangins, at Nyon, where the earlier diagnosis of schizo-phrenia was confirmed, and she was now back at the flat in the rue Galilée. Every time Paul Léon met her father, he said, 'some new origin of her condition has been discovered the only thing which does not vary is the fact that he is the culprit'.[41] And Mr Joyce, on returning to Paris, had collapsed with 'those terrible pains which have poisoned his existence during the last several years'. This time Dr Fontaine was away so Dr Debray had come and put the collapse down to 'nerves' caused by worry. But 'a certain relief has been brought . . . by the stay here of Mr Budgen who came with the proofs of his book through which Mr Joyce went with him and Mr Gilbert. It is a long time since I have seen Mr Joyce so interested in anything as he has been in this work making suggestions, remember-ing points, etc.'.

The rest of the letter was given to the ever-recurring subject of the 'material incertitude'. The £ was down; the $ was down. *Ulysses* was still failing to come to the Joyces' rescue. The Continental royalties were coming in too slowly and were paid quarterly, not monthly. Yet another English publisher had cried off; and the long-awaited trial of *Ulysses* in America, with its hoped-for result, had been postponed again. Harriet quite understood when Mr Léon ended by saying that Mr Joyce 'does not seem to wish to write at all when it is a question of repeating endlessly the same unconclusive story'.[42]

Ulysses was not to remain much longer in the doldrums in America. On 25th November, the case came on before Judge John M. Woolsey and on 6th December he delivered his judgment. He found the book a 'somewhat tragic but very powerful commentary on the inner lives of men and women'; but 'after long reflection' came to the conclusion

---

*As will be seen shortly, however, before a year was out, the picture was damaged beyond repair. Frank Budgen painted a replica, on a slightly larger canvas, which he liked better than the original. This was the second picture by him given to Harriet Weaver by James Joyce. The first, given a few years before, was of the Thames be-tween Kew and Richmond.

'that whilst in many places the effect of "Ulysses" on the reader undoubtedly is somewhat emetic, nowhere does it tend to be an aphro-
disiac. "Ulysses" may, therefore, be admitted into the United
States'.[43]

Meantime, Faber and Faber had begun, very gingerly, to take
soundings of public and official opinion in England. 'Not until we
are thoroughly acquainted with the case shall we be in a position to
conjecture in what way, if in any, proceedings against a new publication of the work in this country after more than ten years' lapse of
time, might be instituted,' Mr Eliot explained.[44] On 9th January
1934, Harriet went to see him at his request to tell him about her own
adventures in publishing *Ulysses*. But by then James Joyce had lost
patience.* He had received an offer to publish from The Bodley
Head and gave Faber five more days in which to make up their minds.
It was not long enough for them and *Ulysses* went to The Bodley
Head.

In spite of her disappointment that *Ulysses* had not gone to Faber,
Harriet could only rejoice that the book had at last a 'regular' English
publisher and was shortly to appear in a large edition in the United
States. At the same time, she had to recognize that this Ulyssean
break-through was not going to solve any immediate Joyce problems. Expenditure—and extravagancies—were mounting steadily;
the family was still without a home of their own where Mr Joyce
could work in proper comfort; and Dr Vogt's desire to operate in the
previous autumn had been passed over.

Moreover, Lucia had lately shown increasing signs of instability:
for example, she often slipped off on her own and returned only under
threat of being taken in charge by the police.[45] The strain on the
family was becoming intolerable and her father was being pressed by
Giorgio to place Lucia permanently in a clinic.[46] Harriet already
knew that a clinic—to judge by the cost of Prangins—might well cost
more than the Joyces' private income. She decided, perhaps rather
precipitately, that there was nothing for it but another visit to
Paris.

There she learned—presumably from Paul Léon—that Mr Joyce,
acutely distressed about Lucia and the pressure on him to send her
away, was again completely unapproachable. Discussions about Joyce
affairs appear to have been conducted wholly with Paul Léon and she

* Progress had, however, hardly been encouraged by James Joyce's refusal to answer
letters from the firm for six months. (From Paul Léon, 9th January 1934)

was not even invited to the birthday party on 2nd February.[47] It was, perhaps, just as well. At the party Lucia struck her mother; and was sent back by her father a day or two later to Prangins.[48]

Harriet was made welcome, however, at the rue de l'Odéon; and her letter to Sylvia, written from Gloucester Place on 7th February, the day after her return, is evidence of the extent to which life in Paris—as well as in England—had become departmentalized:

I had a good journey yesterday and an absolutely smooth crossing and reached Victoria punctually at 7 p.m. But O the fuss at the customs there! For some reason or other they were suspicious of me. Perhaps because I said I had nothing to declare. This evidently seemed to them too true to be good and so the official proceeded to examine my baggage minutely. An old stager of a black evening dress that I have had for six years was unrolled and only got through when a small tear where I had tripped on the skirt was discovered. Two quite ordinary dresses, a year old and which had been to Paris before, were microscopically examined—even after I had produced the bills for them from John Lewis of Oxford Street! But how was I to prove the bills were for *those* dresses? One of the bills had a charge for alterations. He lighted on that. Could I tell him *what* alterations had been done? Luckily I remembered that the shoulders had been lifted, so he had to be satisfied with that. Then a hat. When and where did I buy it? Then he rooted down to my shoes through a layer of un-frenchy underclothing! Finally, but still almost suspiciously, he let me off, rolling my dresses up again carefully—I can at least say that for him. . . . And another official . . . had meantime demanded to see my passport though it had already been examined at Dover. It has never before been examined at Victoria. And all this for a most harmless person returning to her native land. . . .

I hope Mademoiselle Monnier is feeling better today after her rest in bed yesterday and that she will soon get rid of her cold entirely. Please give her my love and my thanks—and my thanks also to your-self—for your combined hospitality to me which I much appreciated. I do hope you will succeed in keeping your own headaches under—by changes of cachet if that is the only way.

With much love

Yours affectionately

Josephine[49]

Harriet brought back from Paris, besides her luggage, a much heavier burden—the conviction that she had failed in her duty as a friend to convey to Mr Joyce the counsel and the comfort he needed at this dreadful time. She hoped, however, that he would now gradually become less overwrought and so, after holding her hand for a few weeks, she wrote. What she wanted to say was not new but, none the less, had to be said: he ought to go to see Dr Vogt and he ought to get his furniture out of store and move into a flat where he could work with all his books within arm's reach—including those left behind in London. She and many others had been waiting a long time now for the dawn to break at the end of Work in Progress. Above all else, whatever money troubles lay ahead, she would always do what she could to help him through them. It was an assurance of her continued backing, an assurance that, if he had to go on disinvesting, he could do so with ease of mind.[50]

Whether or not as a result of Harriet's intervention, the Joyces went to Zurich. (Two friends providentially turned up in April and invited them to join them on a motor tour to Switzerland.) And, on their return to Paris, they set about looking for an unfurnished flat and eventually found a nice five-roomed one at 7 rue Edmond Valentin, off Avenue Bosquet. Harriet was not told until July; but she did hear from James Joyce himself the good news that Dr Vogt had given him 'a new glass to see a trifle better', and would examine him again at the end of September. He went on:

I enclose a prospectus of a new fragment which should be out in a fortnight now.* Also a thing I wrote in the train partly returning from Z'ich. My son and his family sail for U.S. on 19 prox. My wife is very wound up about it as she fears they may stay over there if the $ falls. . . . By the way, my daughter-in-law had Cerf (Random House) to lunch on Saturday—he was here for half a day en route for half the world. Up to April 15 33,000 copies had been sold. He says the Irish catholic and puritan prohibitionists are furious. Hence the pressure on the U.S. govt at the eleventh hour to enter an appeal.† Now the fat is in the fire again. . . .[51]

* The fragment was *The Mime of Mick Nick and the Maggies*. The cover and the initial letter and tailpiece were designed by Lucia Joyce.

† The appeal was heard by the United States Circuit Court of Appeal, and on 8th August 1934, was lost.

Harriet took the letter with her when she went, a fortnight later, for a stay of several weeks at Seldom Seen; and she brought with her also the 'thing' written in the train, a poem *Epilogue to Ibsen's Ghosts*. Mr Joyce had apparently seen some similitude between himself and the dissolute Captain Alving. The poem ended:

> *Nay, more, were I not all I was,*
> *Weak, wanton, waster out and out,*
> *There would have been no world's applause*
> *And damn all to write home about.*

Harriet, happy to get a good long letter, was sorry that he was still suffering from strain and worry. She had not decided what more could be done to help him, when, on 30th May 1934, a telegram for her was brought up the fell from Glenridding.

There had been a fire at Gloucester Place. Harriet returned at once —to a scene of desolation.* There was a hole in her sitting-room floor and, as she picked her way round it and over the sodden, charred carpet, she took stock: the sofa, an armchair, her dining-table, the Georgian chest of drawers, totally ruined; the charming electric lamp Mrs Joyce had given her, perished; Mr Budgen's picture of the Liffey, very badly damaged. But Mr Lewis' portrait of Mr Joyce, was only a little discoloured at the base. She was relieved when she found that most of her precious first editions, kept in her glass-fronted bookcase, and her precious personal papers, kept in a deed box, had been spared. But many of her books had been burnt beyond retrieve, though some of the little octavo books, on an upper shelf, had come off better, including Monsieur Cocteau's *Le Secret Professionel*, with its nice inscription, 'à Madame Weaver avec ma reconnaissance fidèle' and a little heart drawn above his name. But the smoke had reached the foot of Mr Joyce's first Christmas present, *The Book of Kells*, and had blackened two presents from Mr Pound—his *Instigations* and his *Pavannes and Divisions*; and scores of others were drenched with water. She went through to her bedroom, and noticed that the green baize on the double door leading to it had been burnt off and that the destruction in her bedroom and in her spare room was scarcely less.

---

* A young man walking along the street noticed smoke belching from the house. He rushed to the nearest fire alarm signal post to call the brigade. His prompt action saved Harriet Weaver's flat from total destruction. The fire was caused by a fault in the electric wiring in the flat below hers.

She was specially sad when she saw that her beautiful brown silk umbrella was no more.

'My great fire', as Harriet called it, at her own place, her sheet anchor for twenty years, was a great shock. If the fire brigade had arrived a few minutes later, she would have lost everything she treasured, every book, every photograph, every letter. She went down to Westwick to collect her thoughts and remained there for three months while she went through the laborious task of having everything put to rights, from the recoppering of the hearth trivet upwards.

Westwick was still 'home' to her; its peace and stability a solace after the devastation at Gloucester Place. Better still, Harriet was able, for once, to share an event in her life with her dear Mary and Annie. Her 'great fire', unlike her literary and political interests, was something this side of The Gap, something that she could talk about freely, assured of their concern and sympathy.

16

'THE OGRE WILL COME'*

HARRIET had enjoyed working for the Marylebone Labour Party, and she had come to feel at home at the Social Evenings, where she had a part to play as the good listener in a highly articulate, dedicated group. Through the summer of 1934 at Westwick, cut off from this work, she was freer to read and to think; and her political attitudes began to change.

For more than thirty years, she had been content to express her passion for social justice in the form of personal service—service to downtrodden East Enders, to struggling writers and struggling friends, and latterly, to the political party which represented for her the cause of the underdog. It was a personal response to specific injustices, an attempt to rescue at least some of the individuals that society had wronged, and she had seen no reason to question the Fabian philosophy of gradual reform.

Now, however, she began to feel that gradualism could never secure individual rights; and when she looked around at the world in which she lived, her conclusions seemed to be confirmed. From Edith Walker, now sister-in-charge of a ward in a Poor Law hospital, she learned of miserably inadequate provision for the unmoneyed sick; and she read, almost daily, of fascist brutality on the Continent. Among these stories, one from Madrid was particularly horrifying. The sister of the fascist leader, Primo de Riviera, as she drove past a young girl, a known socialist, shot her dead with her revolver; and was never brought to justice.[1]

* 'I know [Work in Progress] is no more than a game but it is a game that I have learned to play in my own way. Children may just as well play as not. The ogre will come in any case.' (From James Joyce, 16th October 1926)

Mary and Annie, life-long Conservatives, did not share Harriet's outlook. But some of her younger relations were on her side and so was Edith Walker. James Joyce, a resolute neutral in politics, refused to take her seriously.* '. . . the newsboys,' he wrote, still in friendlier mood, 'keep careering round the streets shouting out about "L'Autriche".† I am afraid poor Mr Hitler-Missler will soon have few admirers in Europe apart from your nieces and my nephews, Masters W. Lewis and E. Pound.'‡ ²

James Joyce wrote from Belgium, where he and his wife were on holiday. Harriet expected him to return before long to Paris and to work. But her hopes were to be endlessly deferred. Instead of returning to Paris, they went south at the end of August to see Lucia, separated from them now for seven months, and to hear from her doctors at Nyon how she had got on. Lucia was worse and her father, distraught, took responsibility for her once more into his own hands. He was to remain away from Paris for a further five months, in the hope of finding a cure for her in Switzerland.

Harriet, by this time back at Gloucester Place, was absorbed in her reading and was giving an increasing amount of her time to party work. But she was gradually to be caught up again in these tragic Joyce family problems and, this time, with consequences for her that were cataclysmic. She had no intention of breaking her promise of support because he had been cool, but he was increasingly ready to interpret anything she did in the way of friendship as a sign, at best, of her lack of understanding, and, at worst, of treachery.

Frank Budgen was charged to call on her in London, to show her Lucia's alphabet, and she learned from him that Lucia was worse physically as well as mentally. As she seemed to be suffering from some kind of anaemia, Harriet at once sent off a book recommending grapes as a cure. James Joyce thought it useless and told her so.

'Thanks for the book calling my attention to the excellence of the juice of the grape,' he replied. 'The best seller who wrote it never had a more ardent disciple than I. But alas not even scraped carrots can

* James Joyce did, however, help several refugees from fascism.

† On 25th July 1934, when the Nazis attempted to seize power in Austria, they murdered the Social Christian Chancellor Engelbert Dollfuss.

‡ Harriet Weaver's nieces Rosemary Weaver and Margaret Hone were in Germany learning the language. After watching a tremendous Nazi parade, they had been attracted to the movement but, to their aunt's relief, were soon disillusioned. Wyndham Lewis was going through a phase of admiration of Hitler and Ezra Pound had become a dedicated supporter of fascist ideas in their Italianate form.

34 Castle Park, Frodsham

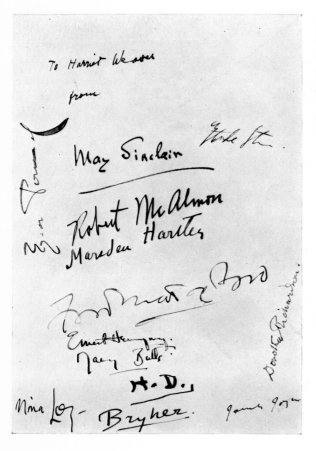

35 Inscriptions in Harriet's copy of Robert McAlmon's *Contact Collection of Contemporary Writers*, dedicated to her

37 Nora Joyce in 1935

36 T. S. Eliot in about 1932

solve the dreadful problem which for years has involved me and now confronts me under a bewildering aspect.'* ³ As the regime at Nyon had not helped Lucia, he had brought her to Zurich, to Burghölzli, the mental hospital there, to be seen by 'the best blood specialist in all Europe'. She was, in fact, suffering from leucocytosis, an excess of white corpuscles in the blood. He hoped, as so often before, that if this physical condition were cured, her mental condition would be cured also. 'The poor child is not a raving lunatic, just a poor child who tried to do too much, to understand too much. Her dependence on me is now absolute. . . '⁴

From Burghölzli, which terrified Lucia, her father, almost at his wits' end, decided to move her to Kusnacht near Zurich, where she could be seen by Dr Jung;† and he got Paul Léon to join him and to be at hand. His friend was 'overwhelmed' by the 'sadness' of the situation and, when he returned to Paris, he sent Harriet a poignant appraisal of it.

The psychiatrist at Burghölzli, Dr Binzwanger, considered that 'the variety and number of causes and complexes which agitated Miss Joyce's soul were so great that an improvement could not even be desired. Granted an improvement . . . every improvement would have as a result a recrudescence of the illness shortly afterwards. . . . The patient herself being able to live through many, many years. . . You can imagine what impression this diagnosis left on Mr Joyce'. But then Dr Jung, whom Paul Léon also saw, expressed 'a few words of hope' after seeing Lucia and to them her parents clung 'desperately'. Mr Joyce's 'dignity and gentleness' were moving; so was Lucia's 'desperate clinging' to her parents. But he hoped Miss Weaver would agree that, as the illness could last for twenty years, 'to allow him to live as they do now is simply to allow a suicide. . . . From day to day he should be told that he does not belong to himself that besides being a father, a husband even a human being he is a genius and has no right towards himself to sacrifice his work'. 'The object is to create in Mr Joyce a new energy and a new desire to live—this is unmistakeably our object and you can help immeasurably.'⁵

Harriet needed no convincing that Mr Joyce would not return to

* The reference to carrots is no doubt to the diet followed for a time by Harriet Weaver, about which she had been teased on an earlier occasion.

† Two years before, James Joyce had rejected advice (from Maria Jolas) to consult Dr Jung because of his general dislike of any form of depth psychology and his particular antipathy to Dr Jung, who had written critically of *Ulysses*.

Work in Progress as long as he was distracted by his daughter's tragedy. But she knew, if only from her experience of his mood on her last visit to Paris, that direct intervention was out of the question. Still, to take his mind off Lucia, she wrote to him at his Zurich hotel—again the Carlton Elite—to enquire about progress—or lack of it—in publishing *Ulysses* in England, now that the appeal in the United States against Justice Woolsey's favourable judgment had been lost. In Mr Joyce's view, as she knew, The Bodley Head had been making altogether too heavy weather of the whole business. Her enquiry elicited the news that he had decided, in exasperation, to 'break off' his contract but that 'now after some more weeks consultations of pro-cess-servers and policewomen [they] write saying that they will print and publish at once and that nothing on earth will prevent them from publishing what twelve years ago nothing on earth would have in-duced them to publish. I trust that the slow but steady advance of our depleted forces in this sector meets with Your Highness's approval'.[6]

But the rest of his long letter was devoted to Lucia. He and his wife had seen 'hundreds of examples of her clairvoyance'. 'Her in-tuitions are amazing.' He gave three examples, none of them very convincing to a mind like Harriet's. More important, as an indication of his state of mind, was his evident joy in having received from Lucia a letter (as usual in Italian) overflowing with affection. It ended '... if ever I should go away, it would be to a country which belongs in a way to you, isn't it true?'[7] She was coming to feel that she should go to Ireland to achieve the reconciliation she felt she was destined to bring about between him and the country which, she had been brought up to believe, had rejected him. To him, however, the expression of her love seemed a proof 'that the attempts made by more than one person to poison her mind against me have failed....'[8]

His Christmas letter was joyless:

... I don't think you can have any idea of what my position is. I am trying to work....* I am urged to go away but it is very risky. The idea is to efface myself, and also Jung or someone else to get contact with Lucia. I did for 7 months....† Result, almost irreparable. Lucia has no trust in anyone except me and she thinks nobody else under-stands a word of what she says. But she also profits by my indulgent character....

All the few friends we have here leave Zurich on 21 or 22. We shall

* Harriet Weaver's ellipses.   † Harriet Weaver's ellipses.

not have a soul to join us. Jolly after 30 years. And word comes from
U.S. that Giorgio and Helen are not coming back till summer, perhaps till etc. And to crown all I have yesterday and today the start of a
colitic attack. Yet what I am trying to write is the most absurdly
comic thing in the book. Eliot is dusting pews in an Anglo-Catholic
church round your corner.* Ask him to have an A-C mish-mash
mass said for the three Joyses. . . .⁹

Two batches of manuscript arrived for Christmas too, and brought
home to Harriet how little work had been done in the twelvemonth
since Lucia's condition had worsened so decisively. She thought Mr
Joyce heroic to write anything at all, let alone anything comic; but
she was becoming alarmed at his manifest determination to remain
near Lucia, despite the strain and despite the likelihood that Work in
Progress would never be finished.

It was in this despairing mood that Harriet heard from Paul Léon
that Mr Joyce had returned to Paris, to the new flat, long since re-
furbished and ready, and that he had brought Lucia with him.

Dr Jung had been able to do nothing for her. With his approval,
her father had removed her from Kusnacht and had installed her with
a nurse in the annexe of his hotel. Then Lucia, now in a calmer phase,
recalled an earlier wish for the company of her aunt Eileen, known
and loved since the early days in Trieste;† and in the middle of
January 1935 Eileen Schaurek arrived in Zurich. Lucia's nurse was
immediately dispensed with. A fortnight later, they all came back to
Paris and settled in the new flat at 7 rue Edmond Valentin.

Harriet, though she thought the Joyces were making a great mistake in keeping Lucia with them, dared not interfere. But when she
heard that Lucia had taken a dislike to Paris and wanted to come to
London, she saw a chance to retrieve the situation. She invited Lucia
and her aunt to come and visit her.

Lucia accepted with alacrity. One of the attractions was that Samuel
Beckett was in London; another was the prospect of fulfilling her
mission to reconcile her father and Miss Weaver.¹⁰ Her father agreed
to let her go; but not happily. He tried to hope that a short spell of

* 'Round your corner' is a mistake. T. S. Eliot had earlier in the year started to
attend St Stephen's (Anglo-Catholic) Church, Gloucester Road, Kensington—not
Gloucester Place, Marylebone.

† Lucia, at Kusnacht, told her father: 'Eileen is a bit loony. So am I, they say. I
think it would do me good to be with her'. (From James Joyce, 21st October 1934)

independence might do her good, yet at heart he remained convinced that he alone could control her and should be always on hand. His guilt and pride were, inevitably, visited on Harriet. If he were wrong to put Lucia in her care then it followed, in the logic of the psyche, that she was fated to betray the trust. In a sense, he was seeking betrayal, and there were many practical, as well as mythological reasons, for expecting things to go wrong. He had never doubted her sincerity—the quality above all that gave her a special standing in the hierarchies of his friends and helpers—and the dread of learning what she made of Lucia's condition was shot through with a bitter satisfaction. There was little chance that Miss Weaver, when she was with Lucia day in and day out, would respond to her as he did.

His feeling for Eileen Schaurek was at least as complex. He was irked by having some responsibility for a widowed sister; and he was not happy about Lucia's affection for her. Harriet, who had met Mrs Schaurek and knew something of her history, knew nothing of this background.* She had no reason to think that she might be laying herself open to the charge of intriguing with another suspect.

Eileen Schaurek had got some leave from her work at the Irish Sweepstake office so as to be with Lucia. Harriet could not very well put her up so she booked a room for her at a small hotel, the Mascot, round the corner in York Street. Lucia she would put in her little spare room, overlooking Gloucester Place.

On Thursday evening, 14th February 1935, Harriet went to Victoria Station to meet the train. For once, she was not feeling very well, as she had a sudden attack of shingles, perhaps brought on by nervousness lest her guest, who had made her poor aunt travel separately, might be uncontrollable or even violent? But on arrival, and for several days afterwards, Lucia did nothing to alarm her and, in fact, impressed her so favourably that Harriet thought it ridiculous to call her insane—and told her father so. True, Lucia seemed depressed, told Harriet she could not concentrate, and spoke to her aunt of buying a pistol. But when Eileen Schaurek, who seemed to Harriet very quick-

---

* Eileen Joyce, when a young woman of twenty, had joined her brother and his wife in Trieste, to help run their flat. Five years later, she married a Czech bank cashier, Frantisek Schaurek. He died suddenly in 1926, leaving her with three young children. She returned to Ireland and in 1935 was living half at Bray, on the coast twelve miles from Dublin, where her two daughters were installed, and half in Dublin, where her sister Eva was bringing up the third child, Patrick, and where she herself had a clerical job in the Sweepstake Office.

witted, suggested her buying two in case one should not work, Lucia laughed and slapped her on the back.[11] Lucia was also very amenable in following her latest regime, which included two tepid baths a day, prescribed by a Paris gland specialist her father consulted when he decided glands were her trouble;* and, on her first Sunday morning, she helped Harriet cover in various art papers some of the books blackened in the fire.

The only complication of the first week of the visit came from her father, who went into a state 'of almost complete collapse'. Paul Léon sent Harriet an urgent appeal 'to drop a line daily mentioning even the most trifling incidents so that he feels he is kept absolutely *au courant* of everything'.[12]

There were soon incidents rather more than trifling to report. Lucia began to show increasing signs of restlessness, perhaps precipitated by her aunt's announcement that she must spend a few days seeing to things in Dublin. It was not only that life would be duller without her aunt, who kept her amused and was always game to take her to the cinema, or fall in with any other plan, but also that she felt herself once more in the grip of her long-felt desire to go to Ireland. It was with difficulty that Harriet dissuaded her from accompanying her aunt. When they returned from Euston after seeing her off, Lucia was ill and spent the next day in bed.

The following morning, Lucia got up, as they had an appointment in Harley Street with a Dr John Joly, no doubt recommended to her father.† The consultation proved disturbing to Lucia. After he had talked to her, Dr Joly insisted on seeing Harriet alone. Lucia, banished to the waiting-room, soon decided the interview had gone on much too long. When they left, she was in an intractable frame of mind. She announced that she was going to Piccadilly and, furthermore, she was going by herself. Harriet reluctantly went back to Gloucester Place to await her return. She waited and waited and by the small hours was beside herself with worry. Next morning, in walked Lucia, quite unconcerned. She had slept, she said, somewhere in Gloucester Place—apparently in the open; and she made it plain that, as an adult woman, she was in no need of an escort and would be obliged if Miss Weaver would cease foisting her company on her.

---

* This specialist had diagnosed a deficiency in adrenalin secretion. (James Joyce to George Joyce, postscript to letter of 19th February 1935. *Letters*, III, p. 346)

† Dr John Joly was a distinguished urologist and a member of the Association Française de l'Urologie.

Lucia's mood had changed decisively. Out walking a few days later with her aunt, now back from Dublin, she jumped on a Green Line coach marked *Windsor*, a place she had wanted to see. Eileen Schaurek, quick-witted as ever, jumped in after her. At Windsor, Lucia announced her intention to stay there. Harriet, sitting by her telephone wondering what had happened now, was relieved when it rang and she heard Mrs Schaurek's voice. Could Miss Weaver collect some clothes for Lucia and herself and bring them down to Windsor?[13] She did so and, back in London, kept in constant touch with Eileen by telephone and later visited them.

Lucia was now determined to go to Ireland—either to Bray or to Galway—and told her father of her intention both by letter and by telephone. Eileen Schaurek, who wished in any case to return herself, was in two minds about taking her niece with her. She first wrote to seek her brother's approval and then sent a wire urging him to forbid the visit. But, as usual, he was prepared to listen only to his daughter. If she wanted to go to Ireland, whether to Bray or to Galway, 'all right'.[14] Eileen Schaurek decided to get away as soon as possible and, after Lucia had led her another dance, managed to take her to Bray the next day.

Harriet, meanwhile, tried to keep James Joyce *au courant* as she had done while Lucia was under her roof but, inevitably, failed to give him quite the same version of events as his sister did;[15] and was, thereupon, suspected of withholding or misrepresenting the facts. There had already been a sharp exchange between them about the Piccadilly escapade. James Joyce had accused her of boasting to him that she would be able to control Lucia during Eileen's absence and Harriet had roundly denied that she had made any such claim.

Altogether, the month had been a strain and she took the almost unprecedented step of going away for a few days' rest. She wanted to throw off her shingles and to be fit again quickly. The extracts Dora wanted her to use in her *Time* symposium had now arrived and were far longer than any Harriet had chosen from the works of other philosophers. The problem of scale needed thought.

It was hard for Harriet to believe that she had done anything to help Mr Joyce by having Lucia to stay. With the last manuscript for the instalment of Work in Progress in *transition*, Paul Léon sent her a report. Mr Joyce looked better but was constantly complaining of having 'not a morsel of strength left'. His morale was no better. 'Mr Joyce has an inner conviction that he has saved his daughter from

Schizzophrenia. . . . However this had developed a peculiar atmosphere here. Mr Joyce trusts one person alone, and this person is Lucia . . . naturally his attitude merely covers up a constant strain and anxiety, especially now since the departure for Ireland and the absence of your detailed news leaves him with but occasional communications from there. . . .'[16] Harriet was glad her detailed letters, or some of them, had been of some help, after all. That was a grain of comfort, thought it was to prove shortlived.

The rest of Paul Léon's letter was unrelieved melancholy. The new flat seemed to Mr Joyce too large without his children; he was 'suffering from solitude' and a 'sense of desertion'. 'I think it would be advisable if you were to write to him,' Paul Léon went on, 'or even to visit Paris to see him.' There was also 'the material question', as always: some expected royalties from Random House had not come in and the rent was due on 15th April. 'If,' he ended, 'you could write him a comforting letter on this score I believe you will greatly ease his present pre-occupation.'[17]

Paul Léon had failed to realize the crux of the situation: that Harriet, the well-trusted, was now also mistrusted. James Joyce, a few days later, thanking her belatedly and formally for 'kindness and hospitality', accused her of several crimes. He did not like her 'great sympathy' for his sister, nor her coldness towards his daughter. 'Possibly Lucia, not having been brought up as a slave and having neither Bolshevik nor Hitlerite tendencies, made a very bad impression on you and she certainly does not flatter. . . .'[18]

He had already hurt Harriet by accusations she could neither understand nor accept; and she had told him that she was hurt. She had tried also to convey to him her real feeling for Lucia, but she had not written effusively. She never did, as he very well knew. So it was bewildering to her that he had so grossly misinterpreted what she had said. It was true that, at the start of the visit, she had felt able to assure him that Lucia did not seem insane and now, she was less sure. But she had certainly not told him so. What could it be that he wanted? On her own rational level, no explanation offered.

In fact, as so often before, his wishes were in conflict. He was testing her loyalty and hardly knew if he wanted it proved—or disproved. He wanted her to put Lucia, 'a vessel of election', above himself—and to tell him that he came first. He wanted her to respond to his slightest wish—but he loathed her readiness to respond. He wanted to hear that he alone could sustain his family in their sufferings—and to hear that he must respect his longing, as a writer and creator, to be alone. 'Perhaps I shall survive,' he wrote, 'and perhaps the raving madness I write will survive and perhaps it is very funny. One thing is sure, however. *Je suis bien triste.*'[19]

Harriet was very sorry she had, obviously, expressed herself badly, and deeply sorry about his other worries. The latest blow was that Lucia's last letter to him had threatened suicide. Though he had decided to treat the threat as a bluff, as Harriet had heard from Paul Léon, he was agonizingly aware of the risks.[20] His distress might have persuaded her to pay the suggested visit to Paris, had she not another journey to make—northwards.[21]

Dora, while staying with her sister Eleanor, had fallen and broken her leg and had then contracted hypostatic pneumonia.[22] She had been moved to Liverpool Infirmary. Harriet went down to see her. Dora, in the big hospital bed, looked tinier, frailer and thinner than ever before. She was wretchedly sad and depressed at the thought that her work had been interrupted; and far too ill to talk about the symposium extracts or anything else.

Harriet came away heavy hearted. For some time, Dora had been working with enthusiasm and had been looking forward to a break in June, and 'the thrice-blessed joy of human fellowship'.[23] But her prospects were poor. It seemed unlikely that she would ever be strong enough to take up her work again, and Mrs Marsden was not expecting that she and Dora would return to Seldom Seen.

Back in London, Harriet's thoughts turned to Mr Joyce. What to do for the best? She wanted to write but did not want to provoke him by some unwitting tactlessness. She decided to ring up Mr Léon for the latest news. Next day, 1st May 1935, James Joyce heard she had telephoned. This roundabout, delicate approach touched him. He sat down and wrote her a long letter, in spite of the fact that his sight was very hazy 'after six hours proof correcting the other day'; and, as he wrote, the rehearsal of his miseries moved him to tears.

He was afflicted materially because some expected royalties from Holland had not arrived; and afflicted spiritually because, whatever he did or said, he found himself 'in a minority of one' and was listened to in silence. Exceptional singers, like exceptional writers, went unrecognized. Yet the Russian basso, Zaporoyetz, made Chaliapin sound like 'a cheap whistle'; and the 'tiresome footling little Anglican parson who afterwards became a prince of the only true church'—Newman—wrote incomparable English prose. His son

344

had prolonged his visit to America, but his musical career had not benefited. As an Irishman, he was expected to sing only popular, romantic, Irish songs; and in the course of a year, his earnings amounted to $35.

After this long preamble, on 'minor matters', James Joyce turned to the all-absorbing subject—the situation of his daughter and himself in an unenlightened world:

. . . I sleep like a log, eat like a hog and people say I have *une mine superbe*. But if they could see inside the watch they would use other words. I feel like an animal which has received four thunderous mallet strokes on the top of his skull. Yet in my letters to both my children and my daughter-in-law I keep up a tone of almost gay irresponsibility. . . .*

While I am glad in a way that Lucia is out of the dangers of Paris and especially of London, every ring at the doorbell gives me an electric shock as I never know what the postman or telegraph boy is going to bring in. And if it is bad news all the blame will fall on me.

Perhaps I was too hasty in thinking you meant to throw doubt on Lucia's words. . . .†

It was a sort of apology, but not quite a retraction. It seemed to him that everyone on earth, except himself, misunderstood his daughter, and misinterpreted her 'curious abbreviated language'. But her mind was 'as clear and unsparing as the lightning':

. . . she spoke to me about you and what you had done for me. She wanted through herself to establish a final link between the dissolute being who is writing these lines and your honourable self. Then she went on to Ireland with the same idea. Whatever she may have succeeded in doing with you she will do nothing over there. How well I know the eyes with which she will be regarded!

It was pleasant for Harriet to learn that she was valued by Lucia; but Mr Joyce's ironical tone showed that he was keeping his distance. He could credit his friends with their good deeds, but it was not in his power to accept the deeper consolations of friendship:

. . . now, though I have the faithful support of my wife and Léon's

* Harriet Weaver's ellipses.   † Harriet Weaver's ellipses.

345

loyal friendship and that of some others here to say nothing of your
own patience and sympathy there are moments and hours when I
have nothing in my heart but rage and despair, a blind man's rage
and despair.

He knew he could control Lucia when she was with him; yet
people said he was an evil influence. Was he inventing it all? Meanwhile, there was nothing for the children to come back to in Paris;
the city, like himself, was decayed.

At this point in his letter, he was interrupted by the arrival of the
post—a letter from Lucia, and another from an acquaintance, René
Bailly, whose Irish wife was also on a visit to Bray. He dared not
open them, he said, and prepared to take them both to Paul Léon.
Before he went, he asked Harriet a final question—and gave some
extraordinary instructions:

What I would like to know if you are writing to me is whether you
liked Lucia or not. . . . I do not like you to mention her in the same
breath with my cousin or sister or anybody else. If she should be so
mentioned it is I who am mad.[24]

Harriet took note of the instructions and answered the question:
she did indeed like Lucia. But though she tried to please, she failed.
'Ebbi una lettera dalla Weaver,' he told his daughter. 'Essa ti vuol
bene anche se si esprima male.' 'I had a letter from Miss Weaver. She
is fond of you though she expresses herself badly.'[25]

Black despair had descended on him and on Dora, and over
Europe storm clouds were gathering. On the day Harriet received
James Joyce's letter, a statement was made on behalf of the Government that experts had made progress towards producing satisfactory
gas masks at reasonable cost. Germany was raising an army of four
hundred and fifty thousand men. Italy was preparing for—undeclared
—war on Abyssinia. There were still over two million unemployed
at home. Harriet felt only contempt for the British government;*
and grieved for her friends. Dora's prospects were wretched and she
saw no way of relieving Mr Joyce's unhappiness.

But she was not without hope for, in the course of her political
reading, she had come, she believed, upon a great truth—the truth

* Stanley Baldwin was about to succeed Ramsay MacDonald as head of a Coalition
Government.

that universal social justice and universal peace were inevitable. The apocalyptic vision of Karl Marx had burst upon her. The freshness and unexpectedness of its impact were part of its strength. As she sat at her Egoist desk, the Russian Revolution had gone unheeded; and it was not until she opened the pages of *Das Kapital* nearly twenty years later that she became aware that there was such a thing as Marxism, so remote had been her life from politics.* [26]

Marxism means different things to different people. To Harriet it offered a glorious justification of her deepest instincts and longings. Its buoyant optimism was matched by her nineteenth-century liberal optimism; its rationalism (irrationalism to some) was matched by her own naturally rational turn of mind and her own devotion to the rational; its violence, by her out-and-out commitment to any cause or person that she chose to support, without possibility of retraction; and the identification of Marxism with new, insurgent forces was matched by her championing of the underdog in society and the pioneer in literature. Marx's labour theory of value had a particular appeal for her. She had always had a guilty conscience about the 'exploitation' of labour by capital. The theory provided a sanction for her abhorrence of 'usury'. Above all else, perhaps, Harriet responded to the Marxian *dicta* that a socialist state, the first objective, when equality was not yet possible, should be governed by the principle 'from each according to his ability, to each according to his work'; and that a communist state, the final objective, should be governed by the principle 'from each according to his ability, to each according to his needs'. Personal dedication to the needs of others, however passionate, was not enough, would never bring about a better world, a world in which the individual would find fulfilment. But Marxism offered a practical programme for the changes it promised.

Harriet, as a member of the middle class, was not alone in seeing communism as the answer to fascism, and want, and war. But at this stage, she continued merely to read quietly on her own and to do what she could for the local Labour Party, though more and more critical of it and of the Party at every level.

As the summer went on, however, she had to give her attention once more to the problem of Lucia, who was still at Bray—'un luogo magnifico pieno di fiori', 'a splendid place, full of flowers', she had

* In a letter to Sylvia Beach, for example, Harriet Weaver wrote in 1930: 'I see no books now except those I have to read in connection with my great compilations'. (25th February 1930)

told her father. [27] But her parents' hope that a more independent life, away from them, might help her was shortlived. Lucia became wilder and more and more restless and unpredictable in her movements. The days and nights that she had spent in Paris away from her family were the precursors of many similar escapades. Her letters home became fitful and, in the middle of May, ceased. For a time her father continued to believe that the experiment was turning out well but after some weeks with no letter from Lucia he felt he must make enquiries. For reasons that will appear shortly, he decided to ask for a report not from Eileen Schaurek but from his wife's uncle, Michael Healy, who for twenty-five years had been a loyal friend.

Michael Healy, now an old man, crossed Ireland from Galway and arrived at Bray on 25th June. He evidently found it difficult to discover or at any rate to convey what had been happening; but after James Joyce had besought him to write 'without paying any attention to what are called laws of polite reserve',[28] he wrote recommending Lucia's removal from Bray. James Joyce, disturbed, sent the letter to Gloucester Place. He thought of sending Miss Weaver over as an 'ambassadress' to investigate things more thoroughly, then changed his mind and decided on Mrs Jolas.[29]

In the meantime, Lucia, tired of Bray, decided she would like to go to Galway, or, as she wrote to Harriet, to England for a holiday.[30] Then she vanished. Eileen Schaurek, alarmed and overwrought, went to see Constantine Curran, a staunch friend of her brother's from his Dublin University College days. He had shown himself very willing to do anything to help on an earlier occasion and, besides, as Registrar of the Appeal Court, he could be very useful.* Very discreetly, when he had first been made aware of Lucia's presence in Ireland and of her escapades, he had alerted the Dublin guards (police) and made it plain to them that, if Miss Joyce was found wandering, nothing must be leaked to the press.[31] Now, he got a message to them that she could not be traced. On the sixth day after her flight from Bray, the guards found her, in Dublin. She asked to go to a nursing home and, after consulting her father by telephone, Constantine Curran found one for her that same day.[32]

Harriet meanwhile consulted Paris about Lucia's plea to her to arrange another holiday in England. This was a plea to which she wanted to respond, and not only for Lucia's sake: it seemed her last

---

* Constantine Curran later became Registrar of the Supreme Court.

chance of demonstrating, beyond a shadow of doubt, her loyalty and good faith.

Mr Joyce took up the idea but almost the next moment changed his mind. Miss Weaver, he had just learned, had been corresponding with his sister and, he believed, had been deceiving him. 'I am less keen on letting her [stay] with Miss Weaver,' he wrote to Giorgio and his wife, 'as it turns out that the latter has been for months past in collusion with Eileen "not to write this to Paris etc", keeping me in ignorance of all the sordid squalor of the case and of the warning of the authorities that their next step would be to commit her or intern her. I was told "she is getting on fine" and Miss Weaver, as with her other female charms, walked blue-eyed and prim-mouthed into my sister's booby-trap.'[33]

It is quite likely that Eileen Schaurek did write to Harriet. But whatever the facts that led to this baffling indictment, Harriet was commanded to cease to communicate with her, and was again in disgrace.

Paul Léon poured oil on the waters. After careful enquiries at the rue Edmond Valentin, he asked Harriet to renew her invitation to Lucia. He himself liked the idea and Mr Joyce seemed to agree. Any doubts she may still have felt, because her offer of hospitality had been received so coldly, must have been swept aside by the harrowing description that followed of Mr Joyce's black and utter despair. Mrs Jolas, whose 'embassy' in Ireland had coincided with Lucia's disappearance, had returned with a report that had had 'a disastrous effect' on Mr Joyce—sleepless nights, nightmares, hallucinations. But he was still determined to solve the 'spiritual problem' of his child's illness. 'There is not a moment, a gesture, a thought during the day or night which is not devoted some way or other to the solution of this problem.' He now trusted no one even with the everyday aspects of the problem; could not work and was obsessed by the thought that he had 'transmitted' to his daughter 'whatever sparkle of gift' he had himself; and that this sparkle had kindled 'fire and storm within her brain'. His remorse might yet drive him to the sacrificial act of abandoning his work for ever in the belief that, by punishing himself, he could make the required reparation. He could not see, what Paul Léon saw clearly, that there was 'no conflict between his work and his most real and deep affections'.

In any case, there was little left to be done on Work in Progress. The third part was already 'practically finished' when the news from

Ireland brought it to a standstill. Paul Léon thought the Epilogue could be written in six months or a year at most, while the rest of the book was printing. But, he lamented, how could they ensure the time, 'the gaiety, the security, the moral support necessary?'. This was not the only anxiety. Mr Joyce was insisting, against his advice, on selling the stock hardest hit in the slump; and proposed to give lessons when his money ran out. Meanwhile it would be a good thing if Miss Weaver came to Paris and talked to Mr or to Mrs Joyce:

. . . the part you play in their lives is so great that I think this alone could be entirely beneficial. They will never ask you to come, it is sure but if the suggestion would come from you they will gladly accept it. . . .[34]

It must have been plain to Harriet, on reading this letter, that however carefully she trod, she was hardly likely to come unscathed through another visit from Lucia. Nevertheless, she invited her to stay again at Gloucester Place; and, this time, she knew, or thought she knew, better what to expect. Constantine Curran, to whom she had written with Paul Léon's encouragement, had given her a full report on Lucia's condition.[35]

Harriet was soon undeceived. James Joyce, immediately after the invitation had gone out, made a sudden decision to have his daughter given a gland treatment in London. He still had great hopes of his latest theory about the cause of her illness. 'For more than a year,' he wrote to Mr and Mrs Curran, 'I have been harping on the subject of a glandular disturbance. Nobody seemed to listen. . . .'[36] Nevertheless, the gland specialist consulted in Paris in February had diagnosed a deficiency in adrenalin secretion, and so substantiated his own intuition. And now, just as Lucia was about to leave for London, he heard of a new gland treatment that seemed heavensent. A friend, while on board ship from Ireland on the way to Paris to see him, heard splendid things spoken of a Professor Ischlondsky who achieved miraculous cures with a bovine serum developed by him.* And, best

* Professor N. Ischlondsky was a man of varied interests, in clinical practice, teaching and in research. In his early years he had published, in Russian, on the gonad glands and the physiological chemistry of nutrition. In the thirties, he wrote on psychiatry and brain dynamics; and on regenerative gland treatment. A further example of his wide interests is a monograph, in German, on a new cage for small experimental animals. His later works are in English. (Derived from reference sources in the library of the Royal Society of Medicine)

of all, he lived in Paris.[37] Professor Ischlondsky, thereupon consulted, recommended a London doctor, Dr W. G. Macdonald, a friend of his who used his serum.*

James Joyce, through Paul Léon, asked Harriet to see Dr Macdonald; and she went to his consulting room off Harley Street. He undertook the case 'rather lightly', she thought; and, without even seeing the patient, decided on a course of twenty-five injections, to be given by himself.[38]

Harriet saw that she would have to have someone to help her. Who better than Edith Walker?† By good luck she was free and came at once to get the flat ready. Preparations had to include nailing all the windows so that they could not be opened wide. Edith agreed, at Harriet's suggestion, to wear ordinary clothes, not uniform, so as not to upset Lucia.

At the end of July, Mr and Mrs Curran brought Lucia over on the night boat, which got in to Holyhead at one o'clock in the morning. They feared she might refuse to leave Ireland but she was in a calm mood, pleased with her invitation to stay at Gloucester Place and looking forward to her visit. They met Harriet on the station platform and had a few minutes' talk before the train went. Constantine Curran, who had expected an imposing 'literary lady', was pleasantly surprised. 'A fine woman,' he thought, 'a charitable woman.'[39]

The next day, Dr Macdonald called and gave Lucia, after a violent struggle, the first injection. It was a bad start and he did not improve things by ordering Lucia, for the seven weeks of treatment, to keep to her bed. Harriet felt it best to make no complaint about having her flat turned into a nursing-home, but Lucia found it 'very irksome'.[40] It was an unusually hot summer.

Paul Léon sent two photographs of Mr Joyce, and one of Mrs Joyce, for Harriet to show the doctor; the popular books on gland treatment suggested that he would be interested in his patient's

* Dr W. G. Macdonald graduated at Aberdeen in 1908. He appears to have been neither a gland specialist nor a psychiatrist but a surgeon; and to have achieved only one publication of his own, an article on the pylorus (the opening from the stomach to the intestines) in *The Lancet* in 1921. He had been attracted by Professor Ischlondsky's work and regularly helped him by reading his manuscripts and preparing his illustrative material. (Ibid)

† Edith Walker had given up hospital nursing in protest at the conditions in the Poor Law institution in which she had been working; and had joined a Nurses Cooperative at Croydon.

parents. Lucia, too, had a letter—from her father: 'I am very glad that you have already started the cure of glands with Dr M. and I have almost the conviction that he will be for you what Vogt has been for me. That is to say the man who does his business and comes at the end of a series of "botchers". . . . Leave Ireland alone and the rest of the universe and think only of getting better. The cure is short and seems certain.'[41]

Hopes were riding high in Paris. James Joyce had had an assurance from Dr Macdonald that although Lucia would still have relapses, as she recovered, they would become shorter and less frequent.[42] He was in buoyant mood—and working four or five hours a day. 'Everything—all hopes—and eyes are turned on you and 74 Gloucester Place,' wrote Paul Léon, at midnight.[43]

Whatever Harriet's sins of omission earlier in the summer, she certainly made up for them now. She wrote almost daily, from the day of the first injection. And there was more to report than progress with the treatment. It was immediately apparent that Lucia, though sunburnt and apparently physically fit, was, in fact, decidedly out of condition. Still, as Paul Léon assured her, 'Mr Joyce seems to live from one [letter] to the other, and as after all the news they contain is on the whole satisfactory—be it the mere conscience that something positive is being done—he seems to me to feel better. He asked me to thank you for everything you were doing for Lucia'.[44]

But as injection followed injection and there was no sign of improvement, either in Lucia's physical or in her mental condition, Harriet and Edith became worried. She became more frequently unmanageable and violent. Harriet moved out of her bedroom, which looked on to the mews, and put Lucia there, as she had been throwing books out of her own bedroom window on to the street. One had hit a passer-by, who had complained.[45] Before the end of August, Harriet had to bring in a second nurse for the day and then a strong night nurse. Lucia threatened to go away—to Switzerland, to Ireland —and, very understandably, bore a grudge against her hostess for having invited her over on a visit and then kept her prisoner. The irony of the situation was not lost on Harriet, or on Edith. But it was plain to them that Lucia could not be kept much longer at the flat. Her behaviour—she would, for instance, sing to herself excitedly for long periods in any one of four languages—was too disturbing to the other residents. They were relieved when Dr Macdonald said that Lucia might go to the country to convalesce once the injections were over.[46]

38 Paul Léon with James Joyce, photographed by
Studio Lipnitzki, in 1936

39 Lucia Joyce at Loveland's Cottage. 'You look as if you did not care in the least about the *terrestrial globe*, absorbed as you are in your reading and swinging', her father wrote. 'If all the inhabitants of the above mentioned rolling ball were so peaceful!'

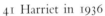

40 Edith Walker in 1934

41 Harriet in 1936

Harriet found a furnished bungalow with a pretty garden near Reigate in Surrey—Loveland's Cottage, Lower Kingswood. She and Edith and Lucia went down there, in the middle of September, with a Scottish nursing assistant, Mrs Middlemost, specially chosen for her splendid physique. She had also engaged a capable and understanding local woman as cook-housekeeper. The weather was still glorious and Lucia took to the hammock in the garden. She felt less of a prisoner and for a week was in a calmer frame of mind.[47]

Her improvement was shortlived, however. The speed, frequency and extremity of mood, from the babyish to the suicidal and the violent, increased. And trying to control the moods was not made easier by the absolute ban on sedatives of any kind imposed by Dr Macdonald. It was only by the greatest ingenuity and resourcefulness that disaster was avoided from hour to hour. Every evening, for example, Edith went out into the garden and turned off the gas at the main; and every morning, when she went in to Lucia, she saw that the poor girl had the gas 'turned on'. When Lucia went on hunger strike, Edith would get Mrs Middlemost to sing a Scottish song and dance a Highland fling and would pop in a mouthful of food when Lucia, amused, forgot for a moment her determination not to eat. On short walks along the lanes round the cottage, if Lucia's mood changed to a dangerous one, the help of the local grocer or A.A. man was enlisted. One or the other, on spotting them in difficulties, would give a helping hand and drive them all back to the cottage in his van.[48]

Under the plan she had worked out, Harriet remained a little apart, in the hope that this would help Lucia to feel that she had an ally in her. There were moments when the arrangement did not turn out well—Lucia once threw over her a tub of water in which some sheets had been put to soak—but on the whole it seems to have succeeded. Harriet, for instance, hired a car the day after Lucia had a bad attack of hysterics and took her for a drive without the nurses—a drive that Lucia remembered with pleasure decades later.[49] When not too disturbed, Lucia read a little, wrote letters, took snapshots with a camera given her by her father, and much to Harriet's delight, did some drawing.

In writing to Mr Joyce, Harriet still tried, in her dry way, and without arousing unnecessary alarm, to convey the facts about Lucia's condition. But for the first three months of Lucia's visit her reports seem to have left him with the impression that, in spite of everything, progress was indeed being made, because he always read them in the light of his conviction that treatment would be followed by convalescence and convalescence by recovery: Dr Macdonald had written to him also and had continued to be encouraging.[50]

In mid-October, delighted that his daughter was getting on so well, he suggested to her that she should go up to London to buy 'a nice fur coat'—an aid to recovery dear to his heart which he had provided on an earlier occasion.[51] Harriet had to tell him that Lucia was not yet fit enough to go to London and advised the postponement of the expedition.* It was perhaps this news that caused her father thereupon to abandon his optimism and to jump to the only other assumption open to him—that Lucia's convalescence was being bungled. Maria Jolas was sent over by him on a quick visit to report.

As November wore on, Harriet began to wonder how much longer Edith and Mrs Middlemost could keep going. Edith, particularly, who had borne the brunt, was very tired.† Then Dr Macdonald came down from London, perhaps at James Joyce's request. He had not seen much of his patient since she left London. Harriet found his attitude very confusing. Having examined Lucia, he began by saying that he considered she had improved but ended by saying that he proposed sending her to St Andrew's, Northampton, for blood tests. It was a mental hospital, where he sometimes sent patients. Edith, particularly, was relieved at this decision. She had not yet revealed to Harriet her growing suspicions about Lucia's physical ills. She had nursed patients with symptoms like hers and they were suffering from internal cancers.[52]

Dr Macdonald did not discuss his full diagnosis with Harriet. He went to Paris to discuss it with the patient's father. The patient's father wrote—in Italian—the day they met, 9th December, by airmail, to tell her about their conclusions—as he saw them:

---

* But Lucia Joyce did need a sensible coat. Harriet Weaver wrote to her mother to enlist her support; and she, in turn, wrote to her daughter: '. . . And what about your hair do keep it well brushed and I hope you will be able to find a warm coat in Reigate as apparently a tweed coat will be the more serviceable for the moment Miss Weaver thinks and I agree . . .'. (Nora Joyce to Lucia Joyce, postmark 24th October 1935. Lucia Joyce)

† One day, Edith Walker said: 'I must have two days' holiday. And when I come back Mrs Middlemost must have two days' holiday'. Lucia said: 'And when Mrs Middlemost comes back it's my turn for two days away from you both'. Edith replied: 'What about Miss Weaver?' 'She does not do anything, so she does not need a holiday,' said Lucia.

I have had today a long interview here . . . with Dr Macdonald. He has come from London expressly to see me and he makes an excellent impression on me. Where you are now, as I have suspected for a time, is not doing you any good. So he will go to see you and will propose a change and I fully approve of his idea. . . .

Dr Macdonald is more than optimistic. And I feel more than ever, my poor, dear and good Lucia, that the long night of your travails is drawing to an end and that the dawn is coming.[53]

A few days later, Harriet and Edith took Lucia to Northampton; and at the end of January 1936 they went to see her. Lucia was unhappy and Harriet sat with her for two hours. Then they went to see an assistant on the medical staff in the hope of hearing what the outlook was. As they seated themselves, he was called out of the room. One of Lucia's papers lay on the desk. Edith, glancing down, caught sight of the word '?carcinoma'; and, in an unthinking moment, told Harriet what she had seen. It was a possibility that had to be investigated, as the young doctor admitted when challenged but, since the suspicion was later proved to be unjustified, she ever afterwards regretted that she had spoken.

Harriet, too, had cause to regret what she did. In order to ensure that the news should be broken gently to Mr Joyce by word of mouth, she wrote to a mutual friend in Paris. It was cruel to be open with him, but she felt she must be open with someone who could talk to him.

The first result was a letter from Dr Macdonald, who had just made another visit to Paris. He wrote scathingly and condemned her for the fiendish torture she had needlessly inflicted on a suffering parent. He forbade her to visit Lucia again. As she gave Edith the letter, she looked as though she had been struck. Edith, outraged, defied medical etiquette and wrote to him to tell him what she thought of his letter and explained that it was all her fault. His reply, which she never forgot, she kept to herself. At least, she hoped, she had vindicated her dear, maligned 'Josephine'.[54]

Harriet heard next from Mr Joyce. His letter she showed to no one. She did not attempt to vindicate herself. She knew she had lost her head and, in her distress, had given him needless pain, had shattered the peace of mind that she desired for him above all else. Would she ever be forgiven?

17

COMRADE JOSEPHINE

AT her father's wish, Lucia was removed from St Andrew's Hospital at the end of February 1936 and brought back to Paris. Three weeks later, she was removed, in a straitjacket, to a sanatorium.[1] James Joyce had to recognize that the treatment, about which Dr Macdonald had been so encouraging, had done nothing, as yet, for his 'poor, dear and good Lucia'. And he could no longer ignore the implication of the reports he had received from Gloucester Place and from Loveland's Cottage: Miss Weaver, he felt, believed that Lucia had not benefited in any way from the treatment and that she was, after all, insane. Her unspoken verdict was as devastating as her doubts about Work in Progress, and for the same reason: he knew she could not compromise her conscience.

Harriet's attitude was, as usual, very different. Overwhelmed by her sense of failure, as a friend, to protect Mr Joyce from news that should never have reached him, she longed for forgiveness and the chance to restore better relations. She had no stomach for discord. She had no stomach for injustice either. While she knew that she had lost her head over the tentative diagnosis, she felt that she had kept it in looking after Lucia, that she had not failed her or her father in the appalling situation thrust upon her by Dr Macdonald's treatment. And she suspected that Dr Macdonald had been less than fair to her in his reports to Mr Joyce—that he was indirectly responsible for some of Mr Joyce's animosity towards her.

She decided to go over to Paris for the weekend and had almost fixed a date when a letter came from Sylvia announcing a visit to London. Whether on this or another account—some advice, perhaps, from Paul Léon—Harriet abandoned her plan and invited Sylvia to stay.*

The five-day visit was a success and did Harriet good—as the visit to Paris might not have done. Mr Eliot sent two tickets for *Murder in the Cathedral* (which Harriet had already seen, but was glad to see again); and she took Sylvia to *Romeo and Juliet* and accompanied her on some of her other expeditions—to the Zoo, the British Museum, the National Portrait Gallery and Rotten Row. The weather was fine; and Sylvia was at her gayest. 'I hope you got my postcard,' she wrote to her sister Holly, 'staying with my dear friend Josephine who is a regular duck . . . did you ever pass by her house, I wonder, and see the brass plate announcing that Elizabeth Barrett Browning lived there at one time. Well now it's Miss Weaver, just as remarkable a person, in her way, as E.B.'[2]

When Sylvia left, Harriet took to Mr Eliot, in Russell Square, a copy of her first Egoist edition of *Ulysses* that Sylvia had ruled was to be delivered 'personally into his own hands'.[3] Sylvia had told her that he had had two copies 'stolen' from his library and Harriet had insisted on giving him an extra copy she still had.† [4]

The visit to Paris abandoned, and with it the chance of achieving a reconciliation with Mr Joyce, Harriet turned, grimfaced, to the troubles of the world. She had been elected to the committee of the local Labour Party and was now free to attend meetings.‡

It seemed to her that nothing was going right either at home or, with the exception of Russia, abroad. Japan was pursuing an aggressive policy of aggrandisement in the Far East. In Spain, right-wing bankers and landowners were sabotaging the efforts of the left-wing government to bring in agrarian and other reforms. Germany was furiously rearming and had just reoccupied the Rhineland. Abyssinia, helpless before the Italian army, was about to capitulate. Great Britain, jealous of France and suspicious of Russia (now in the second year of the Stalinist 'purge trials') had refused to join the Franco-Soviet Pact of 1934 and, to Harriet's way of thinking, seemed to be rearming to defend not democracy but fascism. At home, the Coali-

---

* Harriet Weaver destroyed letters to her of this period from Paul Léon. He had a touching confidence in her diplomatic powers but, on this occasion, may have felt that a visit was not advisable.

† Sylvia Beach gave T. S. Eliot another copy of *Ulysses*, from her own stock.

‡ Exactly when Harriet Weaver was elected to the committee of the St Marylebone Labour Party is not known; but she was certainly a member by the spring of 1936.

tion government was proceeding, at a snail's pace, towards some social reforms; and, much to her disgust, was supported by the Trades Union Council and the right wing of the Labour Party, dismissed by her as mere 'reformists'.

Though Harriet remained for the rest of her days primarily a Marxian idealist, she did not stop short at theory and was helped by her wide reading and two recent books in particular to focus on the contemporary scene. Sidney and Beatrice Webb, eminent socialist reformers of the Fabian school and both now in their late seventies, had come out with a book, *Soviet Communism: A New Civilisation?** Their studies in Russia had brought them round to the Soviet view that the country was, indeed, on the road to communism and that the victory of world communism was inevitable. *The Times* had asked whether this was really the last word of these 'two great figures in the history of our English thought in their honoured age?'; but, for Harriet, the book came as a precious message of reassurance. The obverse of the rosy picture painted by the Webbs was one drawn by a young economist, John Strachey, whose recently published book, *The Nature of the Capitalist Crisis*, she also seized on.† A convinced Marxist, he argued that slumps were not accidents of the capitalist system but an inherent element of it; that capitalism led to fascism and fascism to war and to barbarism. The system could not be reformed. It must be swept away.

At the Labour Party meetings in the scruffy committee room in Daventry Street, Harriet, as might be expected, virtually never spoke but when she did, she spoke cogently and increasingly critically of the Labour Party line. A young graduate starting out on his professional career, who had recently been elected to the committee, noticed her with growing interest. Miss Weaver had a 'marvellously sweet manner' but behind it he sensed 'a good strong flame burning somewhere'.‡ [5]

He had recently become a communist and he and about half a dozen others had been assigned to the St Marylebone branch of the Labour Party to work as Labour Party members, without revealing

---

* In later editions of the book, the Webbs removed the question mark.

† John Strachey was Minister of Food 1946–50 and Secretary of State for War 1950–51.

‡ This young man worked closely with Harriet Weaver for two years but it was not until the war of 1939–45, when he met Halliday Lidderdale in Egypt, both of them then in the Services, that he learned of her literary interests.

358

their communist affiliations, and to do what they could to influence policy. He asked other members of the committee of longer standing who she was. He got the same answer from them all: 'Miss Weaver? I don't know anything about her, I'm afraid, except that she is always willing to do envelope addressing and that sort of thing'.

He was on the look-out for possible recruits and, having come to the conclusion that he had found a likely one who knew her Marx and voted in the right way on critical issues, he called one evening at Gloucester Place. The flat—newly carpeted and still as fresh as paint after refurbishing—looked, from his point of view, rather unpromising. But, as he seated himself in the chair offered him, his eye fell on the first Left Book Club publication, Maurice Thorez's *France Today and the People's Front* and he felt reassured.

'Do you think, Miss Weaver, that the Labour Party is going to get us anywhere?' he asked.

'I hardly think so, no.'

'Have you thought of joining the Communist Party?' Her look of 'obvious pleasure at being sought out' heralded her reply.[6]

Harriet's first duty on joining was to go to classes on Sundays, for three months, to study the *Communist Manifesto* and other literature, already, in fact, familiar to her. The classes were held conveniently near, in Upper Montagu Street at the basement flat of the local party leader, Jack Gaster, a solicitor. She felt happy in her decision but decided not to leave the Labour Party—and hid her C.P. membership card in a volume of her *Encyclopaedia Britannica*. Many others like her made the same decision, believing they would be less cut off and more useful as crypto-communists. Harriet had no twinge of conscience and her long experience of running her life in separate compartments must also have made the decision easier to carry out.

As a member of the Labour Party, however, she could not take part in the local C.P. group meetings nor be appointed to any official position. But, as almost the only member of the group free during the day, she did a certain amount of case work—interviewing tenants in Lisson Grove having trouble with their landlord, for instance—and before setting out would go round to Upper Montagu Street, descend the area steps, take the key of the door out of the milk bottle, its appointed hiding place, and let herself in to find the papers she needed.[7]

Harriet had never before been freer of commitments and gave herself with enthusiasm to her new work for both parties. It helped to

359

distract her from fruitless sorrowing over Dora and the Joyces. Dora, after many months in Liverpool Infirmary, had recovered from the pneumonia; but the depressions that had troubled her intermittently for so many years had become more severe. She had been moved, a fortnight before Harriet took Lucia to Northampton, to a hospital at Dumfries, across the Scottish border. There, her prospects of returning to the world gradually faded and, although she sometimes asked for stocks of paper, she never again took up consistent work on her philosophy. Harriet, no longer needed as a publisher, remained a staunch friend. From time to time, she made the long journey to see her, and she wrote to her regularly, to mark anniversaries, to give news of relations and old friends, and to confide her new political interests. These letters meant a great deal to Dora even though, living in the 'everlasting now' of hospital routine, she often did not answer for weeks or months.[8] Her ties with the outside world were few and she valued them increasingly.

The lines of communication with Paris were kept open by Paul Léon. He continued, most faithfully, to keep Harriet posted, though his news was uniformly melancholy. Mr Joyce's eyes had continued to trouble him 'off and on' and so had the 'colitis pains due to nerves'. He had an abscess on his back. He was exasperated by protracted delays over the English edition of *Ulysses*. His son, who had returned with his family from America, had thyroid gland trouble. An operation had been decided on. Lucia had had to be removed from the sanatorium because she had been violent and was now in a clinic at Ivry, on the outskirts of Paris, run by a Dr Achille Delmas. Her new consultant was Dr Agadjanian, a friend of Paul Léon. To everyone's surprise, he did not think she had dementia praecox and 'emphatically' maintained 'that there is something to be saved. In these circumstances Mr Joyce cannot change his attitude . . . that as long as there is hope or not even hope but possibility to keep Lucia away from interment he will do so. . . . Mr Joyce is resolved to make Lucia a present for her birthday in the form of publishing her alphabet with the Chaucer poem'.* He had worked out an elaborate scheme for financing the book, which would cost about 15,000 francs, and had 'even acquired a money box wherein to put occasional savings to cover parts of the money due. The key is in my possession'. He 'intends to place some fifty copies by subscription. Entrusting the subscriptions in France to

---

* Chaucer's alphabet-poem, which begins 'Almighty and almerciable queen'.

himself, in England to you, in America to Padraic Colum and in Switzerland to some friend of his'.[9]

The unexpected news that Mr Joyce was looking to her for help evidently touched Harriet. In any case, the scheme interested her, as she thought Lucia's *lettrines* 'exquisite'. She at once offered to pay half the cost of producing the book; and was rewarded by a letter from Mr Joyce himself. It was almost entirely devoted to a defence of the expensive birthday present and of his attitude to Lucia. 'My idea is not to persuade her that she is a Cézanne but that on her 29th birthday . . .* she may see something to persuade her that her whole past has not been a failure. . . .' He knew people blamed him for spending so much on trying to find a cure; and he knew he could put a stop to their criticism 'so cheaply and quietly by locking her up in an economical mental prison for the rest of her life'. But:

I will not do so as long as I see a single chance of hope for her recovery, nor blame her or punish her for the great crime she has committed in being a victim to one of the most elusive diseases known to men and unknown to medicine. And I imagine that if you were where she is and felt as she must you would perhaps feel some hope if you felt that you were neither abandoned nor forgotten. . . .[10]

He was more grateful than he allowed himself to appear: he sent Harriet Lucia's original *lettrines* for the alphabet.

He also assigned to her twenty-five copies 'to place on the British market' and drew up a list of people to whom the book was to be offered, though he thought that 'without strong moral and personal pressure being brought to bear' hardly any would be sold. He was, however, determined to break off relations with any of his acquaintances who did not subscribe.†

The printers managed to get one copy of the Chaucer ABC to Lucia for her birthday on 26th July. Before Harriet's copies arrived for 'the British market', General Franco had proclaimed his intention

---

* Harriet Weaver's ellipses.

† Paul Léon, devoted as he was, obviously thought this decision silly, particularly since the Joyces appeared to him to be living a life of almost complete isolation, as he told Harriet Weaver. They had quarrelled for trivial reasons with a number of their oldest Paris friends and were 'constantly and singly devoted to one idea: that of worrying about Lucia'. (From Paul Léon, 22nd May and 22nd August 1936) Some acquaintances who did not subscribe were, indeed, dropped. (Ellmann, p. 703)

'to liberate Spain from Marxism: at any price';[11] and had led a revolt of the army against the government, which, at that time, contained no communists. Civil war had broken out and help for the Spanish government became Harriet's chief preoccupation.*

Marylebone was in the vanguard of this movement. Comrade Weaver (later to be known and addressed as Comrade Josephine) was in the vanguard at Marylebone. Lists of subscribers were generally headed by £1 from her, the next largest sum often only half a crown squeezed out of a wage packet. She gave more help in other ways. Soon, dressed in a coat and skirt and a 'sensible' felt hat, worn very straight, she was marching with the Marylebone platoon through the streets of London in demonstrations for 'Arms for Spain'.

But even in the first flush of enthusiasm for this new cause, Harriet kept her family engagements. Her summer holiday was spent at Westwick, from which, in September, her niece Mercy was married.†　'Aunt Hat', acknowledged on all hands to be second to none at the job, packed her clothes for the honeymoon.[12]

Back at Gloucester Place, she wrote, with the blessing of the 'cell' at Upper Montagu Street, or at its instigation, the first of a series of letters to the Tory local newspaper, the *Marylebone Record and West London News*. A 'Political Article' in the issue for 31st October 1936 drew her fire. It looked forward to the early triumph of the rebels in Spain and praised the soundness of Great Britain's policy of non-intervention. Harriet wrote at length to expose the baseness of this policy. The Non-Intervention Committee, set up by the European powers, had never done the work it was set up to do. It had done nothing to prevent intervention on behalf of the insurgents and a

---

* Under a Non-Intervention Pact to which Russia and the western European powers were signatories, it was agreed that neither side should be supplied with arms. Germany and Italy, however, at once broke their word and sent aeroplanes, tanks, munitions and technical advisers to the rebels. The Spanish government was soon at a severe disadvantage. Opinion in England and France was divided whether to recognize openly the flouting of the Pact by the fascist powers by supplying arms to the government: to do so might lead to war. In England, however, there was a substantial body of opinion in favour of helping it by any means at their disposal. 'Arms for Spain' committees sprang up all over the country to collect money and food, to charter ships to run the fascist blockade and to send out volunteers to fight and to tend the wounded.

† Harriet Weaver's eldest brother, Edward, had died suddenly after a few days' illness at the beginning of June 1936. His wife (Ela) had died some years before and so his two younger daughters, Mercy and Elizabeth, went to live at Westwick— Mercy, because of her marriage, only for a few months.

great deal to prevent intervention on behalf of the government. The French had not honoured their written agreement to give arms to the government because they felt they could not do so unless Great Britain supported them, and Great Britain had failed to support them.[13]

Having let off this salvo, Harriet had to turn to a distressing report from Mr Léon. Mr Joyce had gone on a holiday to Denmark, which he had always wanted to visit, but on his return he had had a recurrence of the 'colitis' pain and his condition had deteriorated steadily. He was in 'a state of listless weakness'; and appeared to have had some sort of 'fit', though all the doctors consulted assured him that there was absolutely nothing the matter with him. 'Ever since he has returned from Copenhagen he has never been out, or hardly, sees almost nobody, and sits listlessly within his four walls. Just about five days ago he has started to prepare for publication a short new fragment to be issued in "Transition", hence the pages enclosed. I do not know what the effect will be as for the moment . . . he appears in the same and very bad shape and I really do not foresee what this will all end with.'[14]

Mr Joyce was clearly unwell and more than usually unhappy and, though the clinic at Ivry was not so expensive as some of the other places where Lucia had been, he needed, as Paul Léon had put it, to be 'financially saved'. Over half a million francs had been spent by now in the vain search for a cure;[15] and the holiday in Copenhagen had been snatched before his money was 'entirely swallowed up'.[16]

Harriet sensed that Paul Léon was hoping once more that she would come over to Paris; but she was much more diffident about 'intervention' there than she was about intervention in Spain. She had not seen Mr Joyce for nearly two years; she was still acutely conscious of her failings, and was still hurt. The prospects of any good coming of a visit seemed dim.

Nevertheless, Harriet wrote to Paul Léon and raised, very tentatively, the question of a visit. She was well aware that Mr Joyce needed to be 'financially saved': more than three-quarters of the capital he could draw on had been spent.

Paul Léon's answer, delayed by the need to take soundings at the rue Edmond Valentin, came a fortnight later:

You probably know my opinion about your coming here and that is, that I think it extremely good and I sincerely deplore the fact that you did not come all this time. Personal contact would have long ago dispelled little things which really mean nothing at all and should not be allowed to accumulate. . . . I think that you should come and the sooner you do it the better, as it will certainly help matters here and dispel grave worries which are darkening Mr Joyce's thoughts.

I am sure that he wants to see you and the more so that all he wants to tell you is hardly expressible otherwise than orally and because I am sure he would like to see you in his practically total estrangement from people.

His only comment has been that his situation is so black that he hardly thinks anybody would like to see him in the present state. . . .

But all this . . . seems to me to point to the direction of your arrival here in order to attempt to break this wall which events have erected around him. . . . For the moment he is working hard and I believe that the book will be ready within a year. But at the same time his physical strength is greatly taxed. He sleeps very little sometimes falling asleep as late as five or half-past five in the morning which undoubtedly is a great strain on his nerves . . . it might be that you will think I am a pessimist but anyhow I would not like in any way [to] deter you from coming as on the contrary I consider your coming here as essential. . . .

I see Mr Joyce only rarely now and sometimes he is quite silent for many hours. . . .[17]

Paul Léon's reply was probably what Harriet had expected and, despite her hesitations, wanted; though she probably thought him too optimistic in supposing that 'personal contact' would dispel 'little things which really mean nothing at all'. She always thought that personal contact was more likely to succeed than letter writing, certainly. But they were not 'little things' that divided her and Mr Joyce; and they were unlikely to be dispelled if he still wished to keep a distance between them and to question her goodwill towards him. But the letter seemed to suggest that Mr Joyce no longer felt quite so coolly towards her and that the visit would, perhaps, be worthwhile.

Harriet went to Paris, probably at the end of November. She returned on 8th December. Not a word, not a syllable survives to cast light on their meeting. But their relationship, though desperately strained, had remained intact: he needed reassurance now more than ever before; and she still believed in him and needed and wanted to make her belief manifest. She promised to tide him over until Work

364

in Progress was published; and he accepted this help from her, as he had accepted her help in the past, as the outward and visible sign of his inward and invisible 'grace'.

At a more superficial level, the meeting was undoubtedly fruitless: easy relations were not re-established. Perhaps that was impossible. They never met again.

After Christmas with Mary and Annie, Harriet, with a vehemence that was not unconnected with the visit to Paris, plunged into a year of almost uninterrupted work for local political campaigns; there, in contrast to her loneliness in her dealings with the rue Edmond Valentin, she had companionship.* Besides, Edith Walker, on a walk one weekend, had joyfully announced that she had recently become a communist and Harriet had confided her own allegiance. Unlike Edith, she was to remain a communist always; and her dedication to Marxist theory made her intolerant of half measures. Her old pragmatism of the Egoist days had given way to a doctrinaire approach to the political, social and economic problems of the day. The situation at home and abroad was seen strictly in terms of the class war, but the 'foreign side' was her chief interest.[18] Anthony Eden, the Foreign Secretary, became her bugbear and she made a detour rather than walk past his house.†

In her party work, as might be expected, Harriet had no desire for the limelight or even for a position of influence. She simply took on more and more jobs. One was selling copies of the *Daily Worker* every Saturday in the market in Church Street off the Edgware Road, or in Hyde Park, near 'Speakers' Corner'. The market was a pretty rough quarter. Comrade Josephine stood stolidly between the vegetable and fruit stalls calling out '*Daily Worker! Daily Worker!*' in her usual low voice and was entirely accepted by her customers, who saw through the cockney accents assumed for the occasion by some of her fellow vendors. At Hyde Park, the crowd was different. Once, two

* Harriet Weaver's letter to Sylvia Beach, on returning from Paris, is an example of her isolation in her dealings with James Joyce. She mentions only the crossing—'a bit choppier than she liked'—Sylvia's headaches and her kindness, in spite of them, in producing several meals, including 'a delicious chestnut confection'. (To Sylvia Beach, 9th November [not December] 1936)

† Anthony Eden seemed to Harriet Weaver especially open to criticism because he had, at an earlier stage, shown a good deal of courage and firmness in opposing Italian aggression in Africa but now expressed views indistinguishable from those of his extreme right-wing colleagues. He lived, at this time, near Gloucester Place in Fitzhardinge Street.

smartly-dressed women, noting Harriet's well-cut coat and skirt and 'good' shoes, murmured as they passed, 'Poor, deluded woman!'[19] Another job, which generally took the whole day, was delivering by hand notices of public meetings. More and more time was given to this as political activity in the borough mounted. In January 1937, for instance, the Marylebone Labour Party set up a Peace Council, linked to the nationwide campaign for a Popular or People's Front to oppose fascism in England and France.

Harriet marched in her first May Day demonstration this year, shoulder to shoulder with the other members of the Marylebone Labour Party, behind their banner and their band. The assembly point was on the Embankment at Charing Cross and they marched from there to Hyde Park, where a hundred thousand others were gathering, with their banners and their bands, to press for a People's Front. After speeches—from open carts—a bugle call sounded the climax and clenched fists were raised in assent to the resolution: 'to consolidate Labour power in London to pledge itself to the final triumph of peace, freedom and democracy and its solidarity with the workers of Spain in their resistance to aggression'.[20]

Altogether, Harriet had plenty to do, but, however active her life, she never neglected her personal correspondence with family and friends. At midsummer, for example, she always sent a special letter to Dora. It was when they were celebrating the summer solstice, sometime in the 1920's, that Dora, watching the sun go down behind the lakeland hills, had announced her expectation of seeing her books published.

Links with Paris were tenuous, though Harriet still subscribed to her press cutting service and so could follow the latest news about James Joyce's works. She was allowed to send Lucia a message for her birthday and her father, who was, at last, working 'extremely hard', got Paul Léon to write to thank her for it—it was 'greatly appreciated'.[21] Grace Jardine, a rare visitor, came to see her on her way north to her bookshop after a visit to Paris, where she had seen Sylvia;[22] and at the end of August Harriet herself went north to a farm at Beeswing, near Dumfries, so that she could see something of Dora. She had her birthday there and received for it from the left-wing members of the younger generation comradely greetings ending:

> For the HAT marx the place
> Where the engels embrace!

to which she replied in a jingle opening:

> *To her nephew and nieces*
> *The Old Hat at Dumfrieses*
> *Doffs itself in obeesance. . . .*[23]

On returning to London, Harriet found that there had been a pocket revolution in Daventry Street. The 'reformist' secretary and assistant secretary had resigned and the 'progressive' members, now in control, had put in new officers in sympathy with them. The local Labour Party was being run by her friends, the local crypto-communists.*

The triennial borough election, with polling day on 1st November, was ahead. It was decided to put up Labour candidates in all nine wards, though there was no hope of success in eight of them: only the Lisson Grove slum area was Labour. Harriet refused to stand as a candidate but flung herself into the election campaign with an enthusiasm and energy remembered ever afterwards by those who worked with her. Housing was the main issue: luxury flats were going up on sites that should have been bought by the borough for housing. Harriet delivered by hand more election addresses than anyone else and was tireless in climbing stairs, canvassing. She was 'fluent, neither patronising nor familiar, just herself'; and her companion in this work, thirty years her junior, envied her need to wear only a coat and skirt, while she herself had to wear a heavy coat to keep out the autumn chill.[24] To the new secretary of the local party, she seemed 'one of the few really good people' he had ever met, 'not lazy, spiteful or jealous'.[25]

Polling day was appallingly wet. Torrents of rain descended hour after hour. Dr Elizabeth Jacobs, a Labour borough councillor of long standing, was a candidate again on this occasion. Driving by one of the polling stations, she caught sight of a solitary figure, clad in a macintosh cape, taking the cards of Labour voters as they left the station. 'Miss Weaver!'† [26]

---

* The 'reformist' secretary and assistant secretary, had attempted to have removed from the electoral roll a left-wing member who, they believed, was not qualified to vote because she was not a resident of the borough. Their complaint was heard by the Town Clerk, who ruled against them. They had acted without the authority of the local party committee, and resigned.

† Though, as expected, no Labour candidate was returned for any other ward, all those for the Lisson Grove ward were returned with increased majorities.

Even for Christmas and New Year at Westwick, Harriet did not rest. She took with her, as she told Sylvia, who shared in some degree her left-wing views, 'a quantity of reading matter, first and foremost Koestler's *Spanish Testament*, published this month as the Left Book Club choice for December'.[27] His uncensored reports on the savagery, bigotry and lawlessness of Franco's Spanish followers and Italian and German mercenaries; and his account of his imprisonment—without trial—and condemnation to death (a sentence that, in the end, was not carried out) moved her profoundly. Here was irrefutable evidence of what was in store for Europe and the world if the fascist challenge were not met.

Paris, however, continued to prevent Harriet from becoming completely absorbed in the tragedies of Spain. Not all the news was depressing. Lucia had responded well to a different type of gland treatment; George had got back his voice and was singing again; and Mr Joyce was relieved, too, that the appearance, at last, of the Bodley Head's ordinary edition of *Ulysses* had not led to any trouble.[28] By Christmas, Paul Léon's part in helping forward Work in Progress 'seemed to be done'; but, he said, it was still taking 'five or six people to check the corrections, verify the additions and read the proofs. Himself, he does the composing part quite alone and from what I hear from Mrs Joyce, he works daily till about five in the morning'.[29] By the new year 1938, however, he had worked himself into a state of collapse complicated by a retinal congestion which, though it proved to be a passing condition, was so alarming that Paul Léon telephoned Gloucester Place. The collapse was brought on partly also by exasperation at the slowness of the English printers setting Work in Progress, as he reported on James Joyce's birthday:

. . . I sent the other day under Mr Joyce's dictation an extremely curt and frank letter to Mr Eliot. Of course Mr Eliot diplomatically retired from the scene and handed the pen to one of the partners, Mr Geoffrey Faber who sent a reply couched in very Baldwinian complicatedness . . . [Mr Joyce] spent yesterday and today in his bed where I found him this morning but this does not prejudice his state to night as from my observations the Irish temperament has some infinite resources which escape my comprehension. . . .

. . . both your cable and Mr Curran's were on the table beside his bed together with the usual six or seven others, prominent among them being that from a friend an obscure greek bankclerk without which the feast would not be complete. I have seen these now year after year and in view of the way in which his reputation as a great poet increases in the world it is surprising to find what a minute circle of friendships surrounds him. . . .[30]

For Harriet, the first half of 1938 was remarkable chiefly for its numerous protest marches. By now she had acquired a special responsibility towards them: that of bailing out any fellow marchers who were 'picked up' by the police.

A march which appealed to her very much was the culmination of a campaign by the Marylebone Labour Party against the letting of the borough's Seymour Hall, for two evening meetings, to the Anglo-German Kameradschaft, a fascist society. The view of the Conservative majority on the council was that as long as the society conducted their functions in a 'becoming manner' there was no reason to cancel the bookings: to do so would be to deny the society freedom of speech; and, secondly, that the letting of the hall as frequently as possible helped the ratepayers.[31]

Harriet moved into the attack with a letter to the *Marylebone Record*:

. . . As to the first plea [put forward by the Conservatives], we all want freedom of speech, and it is for that reason that it is necessary to protect this freedom by restraining the organisations which are out to destroy it. It is, in my opinion, an unfriendly act, a disservice to the German people, to lend any support whatever to the intimate and deadly foes of their own household—the German Nazi party; just as it is a disservice to the British people, an unpatriotic act, to encourage in any way whatever the British Union of Fascists. The second plea, that of making a few pounds to relieve the ratepayers, is unworthy of consideration in a case such as this.[32]

A few days later, on 20th February 1938, Hitler announced to the Reichstag 'a further understanding' with Austria—in fact, as anti-fascists feared, the first step in the subjugation of that country by the Nazis. The Kameradschaft were, none the less, allowed to hold their meetings. Harriet and her friends organized a demonstration march on 14th March, the day of the second meeting. A loudspeaker van toured the borough calling on supporters to join. The response was splendid: socialist, liberal and communist supporters, Co-operators, trade unionists and peace workers turned out in hundreds and marched, a United Front, through the borough and along Oxford Street, with banners flying. A deputation later waited on Mr Attlee (leader of the Labour Party) and Sir Archibald Sinclair (leader of the Liberals) at the House of Commons. The Seymour Hall was not let again to the Kameradschaft.[33]

The march on May Day, that year called 'Spain Day', came when Harriet was particularly busy helping the local Spanish Aid Committee to raise money for a fully equipped ambulance. According to the *Daily Herald*, it was the 'mightiest' May Day of them all;[34] and the Marylebone contingent was certainly the mightiest Marylebone had ever seen.[35] Thirty bands—a record—led over a hundred thousand marchers to Hyde Park, carrying the tricolour of the Republic and banners proclaiming 'Save Spain' and calling for the resignation of the Prime Minister and his Conservative, non-interventionist administration—'Chamberlain Must Go'. Harriet, marching with the Marylebone contingent, was disappointed that the speakers at the rally, among them Herbert Morrison, were all 'reformists', not revolutionaries. But she was glad of any means by which to show her solidarity with the oppressed Republic.

Another opportunity to do so came in July, when the second anniversary of Franco's uprising was marked by meetings and demonstrations throughout the country. Harriet, with Edith Walker marching with her, was among the ten thousand people who assembled in Trafalgar Square to raise money for the starving children of Spanish loyalists, to listen to speeches, and then to march to the Spanish Embassy in Belgrave Square.[36] Tension over Spain had risen sharply during the summer, partly because the British Government had refused to recognize a state of belligerency even when British ships had been bombed in Spanish waters by the rebels and their allies. The organizers of the march were determined to drive home as hard as they could their opposition to Mr Chamberlain's policy and had recruited a large number of volunteers at various points in the long column to lie down and stop the traffic when they reached Piccadilly. Comrade Josephine's job, to bail out the members of the Marylebone contingent who lay down and were taken into custody, kept her very busy indeed.[37]

Meantime, James Joyce's works were getting into political difficulties. 'The publication [of Work in Progress] in the opinion of many . . .' Paul Léon wrote in August, 'will lead to a general and very strong onslaught on the part of the younger generation of left and communist linkings which will seize the opportunity to launch the rampant accusation that Mr Joyce is in the service of capitalist art accessible only to the idle few and rich. On the other hand the German and Italian translations . . . of Anna Livia have been [held back because] . . . these countries have not interfered with [Mr Joyce's works] (Ulysses has not been included on the litterary holocaust staged in Berlin) but should an attempt be made to introduce the experiment he is making with the English language . . . it would immediately result in drastic measures . . . against all his litterary production as the leading bolshevist writer.'[38]

The idea that Work in Progress might fall foul of young communists must have seemed strange to Harriet, whose political convictions had hardened. She had become increasingly critical of the Labour Party and now felt that she could not longer march under its banner. The 'Munich crisis' of the autumn of 1938 gave her her pretext for declaring her allegiance to communism.

The inertia of the governments of Great Britain and France while Hitler annexed the Sudetenland—the first step in his plan to annex Czechoslovakia—appalled her.* She was equally appalled by the large measure of support given to the British government by the Labour Party. To her, the Labour leaders now seemed Mensheviks, agents of the bourgeoisie within the working class.

At a meeting of the Marylebone committee in Daventry Street,

---

* The annexation of Austria had been the first step in the realization of Hitler's declared objective—to unite all Germans in one Reich and to extend its frontiers eastwards, so as to give the 'Herrenvolk' 'Lebensraum'. The next step was the annexation of Czechoslovakia. The substantial German-speaking minority in the Sudetenland, bordering Germany, had some real grievances which gave him his opening. To ensure that voting in the autumn municipal elections went his way, he moved troops to the frontier and from that moment never looked back. Czechoslovakia's allies, France and Russia, believed, wrongly, that he was ready to fight. France was not prepared to move against him without Great Britain; but a request for support was refused in London, where the idea that Hitler might invade seemed hypothetical. Russia wanted something done through the League of Nations, put out feelers in London, and was also brushed off. Then, too late, the British government became alarmed and tried to wring some concessions from Hitler. On 29th September 1938, the Prime Minister, Neville Chamberlain, flew out to Munich to meet him. Hitler insisted on his terms—the handing over to Germany of the Sudetenland and its evacuation by Czechoslovakia by 10th October. He was, however, agreeable to signing a joint Agreement, proposed by Neville Chamberlain, symbolic of the desire of Great Britain and Germany never to go to war with one another again. The Prime Minister returned to England fully persuaded that the Agreement had secured 'peace in our time'.

Harriet announced her resignation and followed it with a speech which was admired both for its manner and its content. She demolished, one by one, the main planks in the Labour platform; she denounced the Labour leaders; and she made it clear, without being absolutely explicit, that the message of her resignation was: join the communists.[39]

The decision to break with the Labour Party seemed to Harriet unquestionably right and gave her great satisfaction. And she left a local Labour Party which was one of the smallest in London, in spite of its recent 'progressive' leadership, for a local Communist Party which was one of the largest and most active. She was soon on its committee and attending meetings at Jack Gaster's new flat, on the corner of Baker Street and Paddington Street, two minutes' walk from her own, or in an upstairs room in a pub nearby, the Westmoreland Arms. She also took on official jobs such as the collection of party dues.[40] Jack Gaster had married Moira, a daughter of Robert Lynd, to whose house in Hampstead James Joyce had fled after his marriage in 1931. Moira, too, was a devoted worker for the communist cause and became a great friend.

Harriet's happy arrival at this new milestone coincided with James Joyce's exhausted arrival at another, the completion of Work in Progress. In December 1938, Paul Léon reported that the book 'for all practical purposes' was finished. In fact, he said, it was finished on 13th November. Then 'some 1,000 pages of proofs' had to be 'completely read and corrected'. Shortly afterwards, the Léons were about to lunch 'when the door bell rang and at the door stood Mr Joyce accompanied by a taxicab-driver'. He had 'suffered a sudden collapse' in a 'lonely part near the Bois de Boulogne'; had asked a passer-by to call a cab; and had driven to the Léons in order not to distress his wife. 'The collapse, happily, did not last—but of course he cannot take his attention from his work.' Paul Léon then went on, in a passage that moved Harriet greatly:

. . . The thousands or more correctly the hundreds of thousand words of [Work in Progress] having passed through my machine I can easily understand how any person who is concerned with the grave social, political and economic problems of this oppressive period will be painfully affected by its colossal triviality, its accumulation of words, meaningless, I suppose, for the ordinary intelligent reader of today. For I cannot see anywhere the slightest attempt in it to face or still less to solve these pressing problems. But it is impossible to deny that he has acted according to his conscience and that he has actually consumed almost all his substance, physical and spiritual, moral and material in the writing of a book likely to be received with derision by his ill-wishers and with pained displeasure by his friends. And in this attitude he has remained true to himself. . . .

Mrs Joyce . . . told me that he was in a state of exhaustion over the closing pages of the book which he had written in a state of extreme tension. It deals with the mixing of the fresh water of the Liffy and the salt water of the Irish sea at the Dublin estuary![41]

The meeting of the waters at dawn brought the book to an end— and its beginning. It was a dawn that Harriet had long awaited. But she knew that the sun would never rise again on her friendship with Mr Joyce, and was grateful for the solace of unremitting work for the party. 'As for me,' she wrote to Sylvia at the end of the year, 'I have been more and more absorbed in political questions since I last saw you and for the last 12 months completely absorbed in work for a People's Front in this country. . . . The feeling . . . seems to be very much turning that way but it is divided and the chiefs of the Labour Party will *not* yet give a lead and concentrate on the first objective— the getting rid of Mr Chamberlain and his gang—as France needs to get rid of M. Daladier and *his* gang. . . . I am going down for Christmas and two boxing days to my sisters at Guildford who still cling tenaciously to the political faith they were born in and who tell me with no mincing of words that they consider I have become absolutely idiotic in my old age!'[42]

The two 'gangs' had, in fact, at last recognized that Hitler was out to conquer Europe and had further proof of his intentions when, in March 1939, he invaded what was left of Czechoslovakia and incorporated it in the Reich. Guarantees to Poland and, later, to Greece and Roumania and a Treaty with Turkey were Great Britain's eleventh-hour effort to warn him that his next act of aggression would be met by force. But the German army was now ready for action. War was inevitable.

Russia, obviously vulnerable ever since the occupation of the Sudetenland and suffering from the loss of five thousand Service officers in Stalin's purges, became Harriet's chief political concern. Her readiness to defend Soviet foreign policy and Soviet attempts, however superficially illogical or however repugnant to English thought, to put Marxist ideals into practice, became absolute. Something of her attitude can be glimpsed in her comments on an essay by Paul Valéry, *Fluctuations sur la Liberté*, one of a collection entitled *La France veut la Liberté*, Sylvia's Christmas present.[43] 'I want to argue with him at times. Which is all to the good, I suppose, showing freedom of mind!' Harriet wrote. 'Or perhaps only hidebound unfreedom of fixed ideas! Anyway, when he says (second paragraph, page 25) that all politics presupposes an idea of *man* he seems to me entirely to overlook class conflict and to forget that in the present so-called "democracies" a powerful clique possessed of the money bags gets hold of the state machine and runs it in the interest of its own class which it represents to itself as "man". . . .'* [44]

With the 'state machines' at last preparing to fight Hitler and with the prospect of Russia as an ally, Harriet felt impelled to do what she could, in a practical way, to help; and she volunteered to become an Air Raid Warden, one of two thousand needed in the borough, though the prospect of war and of air raids unnerved her.

While undergoing her course of training—eighteen lectures and demonstrations on how to deal with incendiary bombs, work stirrup pumps, fit gas masks, take precautions against blast—Paul Léon kept her informed about the final stages in publishing *Work in Progress*— or *Finnegans Wake*: James Joyce allowed the publishers to learn the title only when they reached the binding stage.†

Paul Léon's letter to Harriet of 10th March 1939, his last to her, is brief. She was to expect the arrival of eight parcels he had made up from a huge bundle of proofs that had been discovered in the course of dismantling the flat in the rue Edmond Valentin. (Nora Joyce had made it 'really cosy and charming';[45] but it had always been too large without Lucia and it was now far beyond their means.) The eight parcels, symbol of the indestructibility of her now cheerless friendship with James Joyce, came also as a fitting close to her always cordial relations with Paul Léon.

* Paul Valéry's thesis was that individual freedom was so much hedged about by law, justice and other restrictions of civilized societies as to become a mere figment. This passage (the first of two to which Harriet Weaver took exception) reads: 'Toute politique, même la plus grossière, suppose une idée de l'homme, car il s'agit de disposer de lui, de s'en servir, et même de le servir'. (Every political theme, however crude, presupposes some concept of man, since it involves doing something with him, making use of him, and, even, doing something for him.)

† Faber and Faber managed to get to the author, for his birthday, one bound copy, though not in a stiff cover. The English and American editions were eventually published on 4th May 1939.

His own colossal work on Work in Progress was finished, and his correspondence with Miss Weaver finished with it, as if the completion of the work had been the only tie between them. Yet the letters they wrote to each other had a meaning, for both, independent of the practical purpose they served. He, engaged on a most difficult task and in a difficult situation, evidently needed, besides help and advice, the release of thinking aloud to a sympathetic listener; and she, estranged against her will from a family she loved, had a measure of happiness in following their lives with all the concern she still felt for them, but could not express directly.

By the summer, Harriet was a trained warden and took part, in June, in an elaborate Air Raid Precautions exercise, with mock 'incidents'. But most of her time was given to the local C.P., in particular to helping to get support for their plan to provide, in steel-lined underground tunnels, bombproof shelter for all the ninety-two thousand inhabitants of Marylebone. The official plans, in which small surface shelters and shored-up basements figured largely (estimated to cost some £250,000) the Party considered totally inadequate.[46]

Now that *Finnegans Wake* was out, James Joyce no longer needed the isolation he had sought while finishing it. He wrote twice in the summer and Harriet sent him some cuttings. Of the scores of reviews, few showed any understanding or appreciation. Some thought the book an elaborate joke. But she knew that, as usual, Mr Joyce would want to see every one. His second letter was almost in the old vein— gossip and news and letting off steam. He had refused to authorize publication of Herbert Gorman's biography before approving the text, in typescript and in proof, and had had to send him 'three very long cables' and a letter before winning his point.[47]

The exchange of letters was a brief interlude in Harriet's preoccupation with Europe. In August, there came, like a thunderbolt, the German-Soviet Pact of non-aggression. Most people were at first incredulous and stunned and then outraged. Not so Harriet. Her faith in Russia's long-term objectives and, therefore, in her short-term decisions, remained unquestioning, though an occasional shakiness in the voice showed with what emotion she held it.[48] She stood by Russia even when, after Hitler had marched on Poland and Great Britain had honoured her guarantee, Russia pronounced Great Britain's war against Germany 'imperialistic' and ordered all communists in the country so to regard it: Great Britain was playing the fascist game and had gone to war to see how much of Europe she could seize for herself. Harriet remained a warden nevertheless, although at sixty-three she was not obliged to do war work. She had been assigned to one of the three A.R.P. posts in Crawford Street, which runs along the flank of 101 Gloucester Place; and, when on night duty, waiting for an air raid alarm, her tin hat and gas mask beside her, always insisted on lying in the bunk nearest the door. It was the draughtiest.[49]

Few alarms occurred during the 'phoney' war that lasted until August 1940, when Hitler turned his attention to 'thrashing' England. Until then, when off duty, Harriet's life went on much as usual, though with some changes. She invited Edith Walker, who had been drafted to a first aid post in Stepney, to stay at Gloucester Place. The arrangement suited them both: they kept up each other's courage, and shared the chores. The tenants had now to cater for themselves as best they could in kitchenless flats and with food rationed.

The only major disposition that Harriet felt it necessary to make to put herself on a war footing, was to send to safer places all the papers she most valued. Mr. Joyce's letters and some other documents she sent, in a deed box, to Yorkshire, where Campbell Hone, now Bishop of Wakefield, was installed in the large and solid episcopal residence. The fifty-four pounds of manuscripts, typescripts and proofs of *Finnegans Wake* she divided into two. The bulk went, in a deed box, to the vaults of her bank, and the rest, with her Egoist account books and her Joyce magazine articles and newspaper cuttings, to Mary and Annie.[50] Her only major difficulty was trying to see in the black-out. Once, in Oxford Street, she walked across the path of an oncoming taxi. The cabby braked violently, leaned out and yelled, 'Why don't you look where yer going, you silly bitch?' Harriet was affronted—until she told the story to Edith, who laughed aloud, and then she did too.

James Joyce found getting about the blacked-out streets of Paris almost impossible; and he and his family had been altogether more disorganized by the war than had Harriet. Lucia, who was no better, was moved with Dr Delmas' other patients to Pornichet, on the Brittany coast. Nora Joyce, in constant dread of air raids, and irked by wartime restrictions, decided that keeping house was too difficult. She and her husband abandoned their new, smaller flat and every-thing in it—the lease was not up for nine months—and moved to an hotel. For Christmas 1939, they went to Saint-Gérand-le-Puy, Allier, near Vichy, in central France, to which Maria Jolas had moved her bilingual school. Stephen, at his grandfather's suggestion, had recently joined it. His mother could no longer look after him. She had been having breakdowns, and was in hospital.[51]

James Joyce decided to stay on in Allier, where Nora could, at least, be tolerably certain there would be no air raids, though she remained, none the less, in a state of alarm. He himself was too much taken up with family and other problems to care very much where he was. He believed the outlook for his daughter-in-law hopeless. He wanted to have Lucia transferred to a local hospital, a complex undertaking in which Paul Léon's help would have been invaluable. But he had quarrelled with his friend.* It was proving increasingly difficult to get money from England or even from not-yet-belligerent America. The war, he believed, was preventing *Finnegans Wake* from receiving the attention it deserved. It would, in any case, like all wars, achieve nothing—a view diametrically opposed to that of Harriet.

It was in a state of stress, therefore, that he wrote to her in March. Herbert Gorman's biography of him was out, at last, but apparently unobtainable on the Continent. Would she, if she could, find a copy in London and send it to Mrs Barnacle, his mother-in-law? 'It will give her great pleasure to have it.'†[52] This was his pretext for writing. He went on, however, to give intimate details of the illness of his daughter-in-law, probably merely to unburden himself. But the subject was an unfortunate one. Harriet had been—still was—a scapegoat for his sense of guilt over his daughter's derangement. It was unlikely that she would come unscathed through any exchange about his daughter-in-law. When she expressed sympathy, as she thought in her usual manner, he construed her remarks as evidence of improper curiosity.‡

This was too much. She had held her tongue for too long, she felt. He had accused her, at the height of his distress over Lucia, of having long been poisoned against him. The converse was true: it was he

* The marriage of George and Helen Joyce had run into difficulties even before her breakdown. Paul Léon had shown greater sympathy for her than for him and it was on this account that James Joyce quarrelled with him. The friendship was, however, patched up later. (Ellmann, p. 741)

† Harriet Weaver was unable to find a copy of the biography for Mrs Barnacle, who died on 15th November that year. The Joyces received the bare news of her death before they left France. (From George Joyce, 27th December 1941)

‡ Harriet Weaver later destroyed the letter giving details of the illness of Helen Joyce and also James Joyce's following letter. (To John J. Slocum, 27th August 1948)

who was poisoned in his attitude towards her. She wrote, scathingly, to tell him so.

The distance that she felt this outburst put between them seemed to Harriet to be infinitely widened when Hitler, having occupied Denmark and Norway, swung westwards through the Netherlands and Belgium into France. By the end of June, the whole of northern France and the west coast was occupied by the Germans, in accordance with the terms of surrender agreed to by a new French Government headed by Marshal Pétain. As so often before, she failed to have the courage of her convictions. She was soon contrite about her outburst and could not reconcile herself to the fact that there was nothing she could do, until the war was over, to mend matters.*

Hitler, however, left her little time to grieve. In August, the Battle of Britain began, first over the south coast and then over London. In September, came the first of many mass attacks. Raids continued night after night uninterruptedly into November, when the Battle was over and Hitler's great offensive had been repelled. With raids lighter and intermittent, Harriet was able to make up some sleep. Like most other wardens, she had put in many hours of extra duty helping to deal with 'incidents' near her post. Fortunately none of them was major; Marylebone was far enough from the City and the docks, the main targets, to get off more lightly. Even so, the months had been a strain and she had had to steel herself to remain in London.

In the middle of December, to Harriet's intense surprise, Fred Monro wrote to say that the firm had had a cable from Mr Joyce—from Switzerland. It appeared that he, with his wife, son and grandson, had reached Lausanne from France and had immediately wired for funds. Fred had sent £50 by wire and on 18th December had an acknowledgment from Zurich, which he enclosed: 'Arrived today fifty received wire air mail address seven Dolderthal Zurich inform Harriet Weaver hope both safe and well'.[53] Harriet dashed off a letter by air mail.[54] Perhaps he had not taken her outburst as hardly as she imagined? At any rate, she could assure him that she was safe and well and welcome the news of their flight from France.

* After the fall of France, communication even with 'unoccupied France' became difficult and uncertain. Monro Saw & Co. prevailed on the Irish High Commissioner to transmit to the Irish Minister at Vichy, for James Joyce (still a British subject) a small monthly remittance—of £30—sanctioned by the Bank of England. Harriet Weaver wrote, in very formal terms, to tell him of the arrangement. This letter got through. (To James Joyce, 14th October 1940. Jolas)

COMRADE JOSEPHINE

A week later, Harriet received a cable appealing frantically for her help: 'Two urgent telegrams Monro unanswered please investigate need three hundred maintenance family debts arrears transfer Lucia Switzerland send Yule greetings kindest regards James Joyce Pension Delphin.'[55] The cable, held up by routine censorship and the Christmas holidays, had taken several days to reach her. She telephoned Fred Monro.

The sense of relief that the Joyces were in Zurich was enormous. It was a relief, too, of a kind that those who lived through the 'blitz' will remember, that the nights continued to be a little less noisy. When, a fortnight later, Edith had a night off duty, Harriet felt more at ease than she had for a long time. On the Monday morning, 13th January 1941, she laid breakfast and turned on the wireless so that Edith could listen to the BBC eight o'clock news while she returned to her bedroom to tidy it. She left open the door leading into the sitting-room and listened herself with one ear.[56]

'This is the B.B.C. . . . and this is . . . reading it . . . The Moscow radio broadcast last night a strong denial . . . that German troops had moved or are moving into Bulgaria, with the knowledge and consent of the Russian Government . . . the Bulgarian Prime Minister, Dr Filoff . . . Bulgaria's determination to defend . . . Bulgaria must always be prepared . . . doomed to slavery. James Joyce, the Irish author . . . in hospital in Zurich after an operation. He would have been fifty-nine next month. Joyce was the most powerful . . . '

Harriet went into the sitting-room.

'Did he say Mr Joyce was dead?'

'Yes.'

'. . . unintelligible to the average reader, and its frankness caused it to be banned in this country for many years. Earlier works include "Portrait of the Artist as a Young Man" and "Dubliners"; a group of pungently realistic short stories. Joyce had lived in Paris for many years, and for some time he fought against rapidly failing eyesight. Because of this, he used to dress in white, saying that it was soothing to his eyes. He had an excellent tenor voice and singing was his chief recreation.'[57]

That was the end of the news and Harriet switched off. They sat down to breakfast. She looked stunned and murmured at intervals, 'But there was no hint of illness. . . . What can have happened?'* [58]

* James Joyce, like Kearsley Weaver, died of peritonitis.

It was only later on in the day that she began to collect her thoughts. The funeral. Would Mrs Joyce be able to pay for it? Probably not, almost certainly not. She would pay for it herself. The £250 she was about to send to Mr Joyce must be sent to Mrs Joyce.⁵⁹ Fred would see to the proving of the Will, of course. And she was now Literary Executrix. Or perhaps only when Fred obtained Probate? She must ask him about that.

From Mr Joyce's Will, her thoughts went on to her own. She had left all the manuscripts and typescripts and proofs of *Finnegans Wake* to him. She had been intending to ask him to what library he would like them left if she survived him.⁶⁰ Now it was she who would have to make the choice. And, with air raids still continuing, she ought to make it soon.

Fred managed to get the money to Zurich, and Harriet was glad to have the cable that came ten days after the funeral: 'Money received many thanks your wonderful help in our great sorrow kindest regards Nora Joyce.'⁶¹

But Fred could hardly help her to make up her mind about *Finnegans Wake*, and Harriet decided to consult Mr Eliot. She rang up Faber and Faber to make an appointment to see him, only to be told that he was living in Surrey and coming up on Wednesdays only. Harriet wrote to tell him: 'I have the British Museum in mind and should be glad to hear your views as to this. . . . I hope you are well and in a spot where you are not too harried by raids and alarms'.⁶²

T. S. Eliot was ill and dictated a letter at the end of January while 'still not up to correspondence'. He suggested she should come down to see him and asked whether she had considered Dublin.⁶³ Harriet replied:

. . . I did think of one of the Dublin libraries for Mr Joyce's manuscripts. It was because the British Museum would be more accessible to the greater number of writers and students who might in the future like to examine them that I inclined to it rather than to Dublin which, as you say, might be considered to have the first claim to them. However . . . I think it would certainly be a help if you would very kindly, when able to do so, consult, as you suggest, some of your Irish friends privately and in a tentative way and without mentioning my name. . . .⁶⁴

In the middle of February, Harriet managed to get away to Guild-

380

ford and arranged to go over from there to have tea with Mr Eliot, at
Shamley Wood. As her nephew Tony Weaver and his Russian wife,
Alla, were living at Rushett Common, on the way there, she lunched
with them first; and they walked over to Shamley with her after-
wards. Tony and his aunt could no longer talk politics, as he was now
a pacifist, but, as always, they had a great deal else to talk about.* At
Shamley Green, Harriet took out the map that Mr Eliot had drawn
for her so that she could find her way up the steep hill to his house—
a hill which, she said, she did not 'in the least mind . . . taken slowly'.[65]
Only at the gate did she say that 'the friend' she was visiting was Mr
Eliot, and of the purpose of the visit she said nothing.[66]
   Harriet walked back to Rushett Common after tea. She had almost
decided on Ireland but now needed to establish that there was a suitable library there. Mr Curran, it seemed to her, would be able to
advise her about this. His letter, as she expected, was most helpful.
After dismissing the claims of other Dublin libraries, he went on:

There remains the National Library and I have no hesitation in
recommending it alone. It is a modern and admirably managed
library of first rate standing with the same privileges . . . as the British
Museum or the Advocates Library. . . . It has a valuable and growing
MSS department particularly in regard to modern literature in Ireland, i.e. from the 18th century . . . I am entirely of T. S. Eliot's
opinion that every serious student of Joyce must come to Dublin.
Joyce is inseparable from Dublin. . . . There is further Joyce's personal
association with the National Library. I know his seat in it . . . I can't
go near the place without thinking of him. This library makes a
chapter of Ulysses. . . . Anyway the National Library is, to my mind,
the natural destination of these MSS if you remain with your present
intention and so far as I can honestly and fairly interpret the mind of
our dead friend it would be his desire.[67]

   Harriet needed little persuasion. She had come to feel strongly that
Finnegans Wake should go to Ireland, that, in a sense, Mr Joyce should
return there; and she had confidence in Mr Curran's advice. The

* Anthony Weaver had become a pacifist at the fall of Barcelona to Franco because he did not see that the Republicans could ever attain their objectives by military
means. At his Conscientious Objectors Tribunal, he had defended his position so well
that he had been granted exemption from military service on the condition that he
continued to teach—which, in fact, was what he wanted to do.

bequest to Mr Joyce was revoked and the bequest to the National Library of Ireland, Dublin, took its place.[68]

The nights began to get noisier again shortly after Harriet's return to Gloucester Place. Edith pleaded with her to leave London as there was nothing to hold her there except her political work, which she could continue almost anywhere else. But Harriet thought she would be a coward to move and stayed on. In the middle of March, however, raids became heavy again. One night, when Harriet was on duty at her A.R.P. post, Edith, off duty, and lying on the sofa at the flat, heard bombs falling. She put on her tin hat and went round the corner to offer help at the post. 'Josephine' was farther up the street, where some fire bombs had fallen, in a chain of people passing up buckets of water and sand to throw on the blaze.

As Edith watched, she heard someone say 'Now the corner house has gone'. She felt it must be number 101 and went back to find out. The roof was ablaze. She rushed upstairs and found the caretaker fumbling with a small and useless fire extinguisher. He had lost his nerve and was incapably drunk. She rushed into the street and found a young soldier, a captain, and a second man willing to help. They found the fire had reached the flat above Harriet's and the staircase to it was already catching. Edith poured a bucket of water over herself before passing more bucketfuls to the two men, working with stirrup pumps at the head of the staircase. By four o'clock in the morning, they had managed to put the fire out. Harriet's flat and those below were saved.*

Edith returned to Crawford Street and stood by until there was a pause in the fire fighting. But Harriet glanced up and noticed the drenched, diminutive figure, with a pitch-black face.

'Where have you been? Look at you!'

Edith's news decided her, on the spot, to leave London.[69] A few weeks later, Edith had joined her brother at Harrow and Harriet was installed in a boarding house in the place she had chosen as her refuge —Oxford.

---

* The soldier slipped away before Edith Walker had time to ask him who he was. The other young man stayed to talk long enough for her to discover his name and address. He lived in York Street, nearby. Harriet Weaver later went to see him and gave him a gold wristwatch as a mark of her gratitude for his help in saving the house.

PART IV

1941—1961

18

OXFORD

HARRIET's decision to live in Oxford proved a happy one. Oxford had been, and remained, free of air raids; Maude and Campbell were going to live there when he retired as Bishop of Wakefield; several friends of the old Hampstead days had already moved there; and Helen Saunders went down every fortnight or three weeks to be with her mother and sister, who lived in North Oxford, where Victorian dons had built themselves large houses in large gardens.

But Oxford was already overcrowded with evacuees—Londoners who had been bombed out, Civil Servants in departments that had been moved there. The boarding house in which Harriet managed to find a room she did not like at all; and, after two months' vain search for better quarters, she decided to go on a round of visits and to return in the autumn in the hope of finding a small flat. Fortunately, before she left, Helen discovered her predicament and asked her mother to invite 'Josephine' to stay on her return, so that she could at least be comfortable while she flat-hunted. Helen was no more intimate with her than she had ever been, but she was 'very fond' of her, had a deep regard for her 'unique personality' and did not want her to return to poky quarters.[1]

On her return in October, Harriet went to stay with Mrs Saunders, at 4 Rawlinson Road—and remained for fifteen and a half years. She stayed on as a paying guest and proved such an 'ideal lodger' that her room was put at her disposal to make her own.[2] It was a large, square room with a long bay window looking south over the flowering trees of the road. Harriet put into it most of her things from her sitting-room at Gloucester Place and arranged them as she had had them there. Then she bought a divan bed, tucked it against the wall opposite the window and covered it with a turkey-red cotton bed-

385

spread made from some curtains from Castle Park. She took her meals with the Saunders but sat in her own room and sometimes gave people tea there.

Mrs Saunders, for whom Harriet came to have a deep affection, was a delightful and lively octogenarian and keen gardener.* She had known Oxford since she was a girl and remembered Matthew Arnold there. She had been living for twenty years at Rawlinson Road with her elder daughter, Ethel, and still had two resident servants. Harriet's unlooked-for arrival was a blessing: the spare room might otherwise have been commandeered for billeting.

But there was one snag. Though Helen did not know (and never discovered) that 'Josephine' was a member of the Communist Party, she did know that she was 'immensely interested in Communist theory and practice' and 'enjoyed the company and friendship of enthusiastic young Communists in London'.[3] But Helen realized that her mother and sister would not brook for one moment any overt work at the house for the left wing. Harriet therefore promised not to talk politics with them and to hold no meetings under their roof. In the event, they turned a blind eye to the occasional 'caller' she smuggled in and the arrangement worked well—except sometimes at breakfast. Mrs Saunders breakfasted in her room; Harriet and Miss Saunders, a staunch and active Conservative, at one end of the long table in the dining-room, each embattled behind her favourite morning paper. Both of them found it hard to remain silent when outraged by the doings of the rival camp and occasionally spoke out.

Harriet joined the local Communist Party, the Oxford City Branch, and was soon elected to the committee. The Branch had only about a hundred paid-up members, of whom half came from, and eventually returned to, London. Almost all of them were wage-earners and there was no one on the committee to match the intellectuals and middle-class idealists of the Marylebone Branch.† Later, she met

* Mrs Saunders was a Paley, and a descendant of William Paley, archdeacon of Carlisle, whose *Evidences of Christianity*, published in 1794, made him famous. She had married Alfred Robert Henry Saunders, seventh child of the Dean of Peterborough, a member of one of the families that had promoted the Great Western Railway.

† In the whole membership of the Oxford City Branch there were only two people of her generation and kind, both women. One was Mrs Winifred Carritt, the widow of the philosopher E. F. Carritt of Merton; the other a member of a distinguished Cheshire family. They were known as 'the three old ladies' of the branch and became great friends.

and made friends with some members of the university Communist Club but devoted herself wholly to the 'proletarian' City Branch. She took no part in the local Labour Party activities: double membership was no longer permitted by the C.P. headquarters.

As before in Marylebone, Harriet aspired above all to be useful; she did not seek to be influential. She distributed leaflets and later on became Minutes Secretary. This was work she was used to. Another job she took on was quite new. The branch had a book shop in Hythe Bridge Street, between the canal and the railway, a dismal spot. There she spent two hours, at least, every day from Monday to Friday; and on Saturday she took a thermos and sandwiches and minded the shop all day. It served the whole of the South Midland area, and business was thriving. The sales of communist literature, it was claimed, exceeded Labour Party sales throughout the country.[4]

Harriet greatly enjoyed her work in the shop and relished her good luck in being able to live in Oxford the kind of life that she preferred: Victorian comforts and conventions at home, work with and for underdogs away from it. And at Hythe Bridge Street she was assured of the anonymity that she had enjoyed in Marylebone—or almost so. One day into the shop came Phyllis Ford, her rival in tennis of the Hampstead days, now Lady Floud and living not far from Oxford.* She wanted a book for her left-wing son, Bernard (later a Labour Member of Parliament). What should she see the other side of the counter but someone who looked exactly like Harriet Weaver, looking exactly as she did at Cedar Lawn. And it *was* Harriet![5]

The Soviet-German Non-Aggression Pact had allowed the Germans to subjugate the west without fear of attack from the east; and had allowed Russia a little breathing space in which to prepare her defences. But by the summer of 1941 Hitler was ready to attack and on 22nd June advanced along a one-thousand-five-hundred mile front from the Arctic to the Black Sea. Great Britain became an ally overnight; and Harriet and all her comrades were transformed overnight from collaborators in an imperialist war to fellow-workers with the peoples of the Soviet Union in the supreme fight against fascism.

Harriet had followed the steps taken by Russia, beginning with the subjugation of Finland, to protect herself against the expected German

---

* Phyllis Ford had married in 1909 Francis Floud, a Civil Servant who later held a number of important posts. He was High Commissioner in Canada from 1934 to 1938 and at this time was chairman of or serving on several national arbitration boards. They both went later to Rawlinson Road and were shown the *Wake* MS.

invasion and had considered them justified, in the circumstances; and she welcomed Winston Churchill's assertion, in his broadcast to the nation on the night of 22nd June: 'The Russian danger is our danger'; and his promise of help. Within a week, a British Mission had flown to Moscow. But until help arrived, Russia had to fight on alone. By the middle of August, the streets of Leningrad were barricaded; by the middle of October, the Soviet government and the diplomatic corps had moved to Kuibyshev, three hundred miles to the east of Moscow, on which fourteen thousand German tanks were converging. As the winter wore on, few people dared to think that Russia could much longer withstand the German offensive. But Harriet never doubted for one moment that they would. 'Oh no! They will never surrender. Oh no!' she said, at tea with friends at Woodstock.* She spoke with such vehemence that all eyes were turned in her direction.

Russia's entry into the war brought one blessing, though not immediately: the reappearance of the *Daily Worker*. In January 1941, a week after James Joyce's death, the *Daily Worker* had been suppressed. It had been faithfully following the Moscow lead and had consistently denounced the government for entering the war to make profits for capitalists and to further the country's imperialist ends. The Home Secretary, after holding his hand for several months, had suppressed it.[6] Harriet had thought this action against the only 'independent' workers' paper monstrous.

The *Daily Worker*, short of funds, now appealed for help. Harriet sent their People's Press Fighting Fund a 'guarantee' of £5 a month, and frequently sent further gifts later on. She followed their struggle 'with the freshness and sincerity' that Barbara Niven, the inspired and untiring Secretary to the Fund, 'came deeply to love in her'.[7]

Harriet also took on the job of delivering copies of the paper once a week to party members in Jericho, a cluster of mean, terraced houses, abutting on the canal, built mainly for bargees. It was not a large newspaper round—perhaps twenty at the beginning and fewer later. She undertook it all the years she was at Oxford and did not feel it incongruous, so her customers did not either. To other members of the branch, the weekly trudge would have seemed a form of martyrdom but to Harriet it did not. 'They are all so nice,' she insisted to Christopher Hill, a left-wing don, who became Master of Balliol.

* Norah and William Lidderdale.

Later he, and his wife Bridget, got to know Harriet well and he was one of the few people who saw her both at Rawlinson Road and in the party. He was struck by the difference in her attitude in her two 'separate lives'. At Rawlinson Road, she seemed 'almost school-girlish' in her efforts to conceal her political activities, even getting all party letters to her sent in plain envelopes; but on her Jericho round she was frank and serene.[8]

Another weekly round was walking up and down Rawlinson Road at night on A.R.P. duty—or Civil Defence duty, as it was called later. Harriet gained a reputation with the senior warden for 'a nice sense of humour', though nothing amusing or even untoward ever happened, with the exception of Helen Saunders' meeting one night a hedgehog on his after-dinner stroll.[9]

A great deal of Harriet's time was spent at her desk. She returned, for a time, to her work on her *Time* symposium, dropped since the outbreak of the Spanish Civil War.[10] Dora, whose creative power (unlike James Joyce's) had proved shortlived, had now recovered in a new and gentler form the old urge to inspire her friend. She wrote encouragingly. She was pleased, too, that five chapters of her own, on *Time and the Ego-centric Universe*, were to be included. But she did not feel able to give any practical advice; and as Harriet had few university contacts she might have been in difficulties had not an undergraduate frequenter of the bookshop, Iris Murdoch, then a budding philosopher, come to her rescue.* She introduced a young graduate, Wolfgang von Leyden, who was writing a thesis on Time.[11] Harriet consulted him two or three times and was glad of the help he gave her. But soon 'burning political questions seemed so much more urgent' and she put the symposium to one side.[12]

These questions were not allowed, however, to interfere with her work as Literary Executrix and—a further, and unexpected, responsibility—as Administrator, with Fred Monro, of the Estate of James Joyce.† This new responsibility, which included the execution of copyright agreements and the collection of royalties, was to grow

---

* Iris Murdoch, then at Somerville College, went down in 1942 with a first in Greats.

† Under his Will, James Joyce appointed his wife as Executrix or alternatively the Public Trustee. Nora Joyce, in Zurich, did not feel able to prove the Will and the Public Trustee declined to do so. Eventually, Nora Joyce appointed Harriet Weaver and F. R. D'O. Monro as her 'attorneys'; and, in February 1942, a grant of Letters of Administration was made in favour of them.

from small beginnings. It was not one, however, that could be exercised formally for a considerable time. When the Administrators attempted to prove the Will, questions were raised by the Probate Registry about the validity of the deceased's English domicile. They led to long and intricate negotiations with the Bank of England. Until the Will was proved, none of the royalties, nothing in the Estate, could be touched.[13]

Fred, as anxious as Harriet to give what help they could to Mrs Joyce, sought and received permission from the Exchange Control Authorities to send her what Harriet later described to Ben Huebsch as 'monthly advances on a modest scale'. The 'advances' were, in fact, gifts from Harriet. Towards the end of the war, the negotiations were concluded and it was possible, at last, to send money from the Estate. As royalties had accumulated, though not by any means greatly, Harriet and Fred decided to 'increase the monthly remittances to some extent'.* [14] But as the income from royalties was still modest and the income from capital was only £175 a year, Harriet's worries over Mrs Joyce were by no means at an end.†

But the new responsibilities—the Literary Executorship and the attorneyship with Fred—though they were to prove heavy, proved also a solace. They helped her to forget the painful last years of her friendship with James Joyce and carried her back, in a Vico-Joycean cycle, to the situation in which she found herself before they met. It was with his works that she was concerned then, and with his works that she was concerned again now. She had known nothing then of the tortuosities of his character and what her concern for him and his family would entail for her. As she turned to her new tasks, the bitter memories began to fade.

Herbert Gorman's biography probably helped in this process. By the time Harriet settled in Oxford, it was at last on sale. She bought it, read it and annotated it, page by page. He had, in fact, painted an

* A little help came also from America. Maria Jolas, who returned there in the autumn of 1940, organized a 'Joyce Memorial Fund', which sent 'an occasional $100' to Zurich. (From George Joyce, 27th December 1941)

† Some idea of the income from royalties can be deduced from the fact that the capitalized value of royalties, for the purposes of the Estate, was only £1,000; and the only capital left by James Joyce was the £5,000 War Loan which Harriet Weaver gave him in 1919 and put into the hands of the Public Trustee. In 1932, James Joyce accepted an offer of a bonus to holders of the stock willing to accept 3½ per cent instead of 5 per cent, thus losing £75 a year thereafter for the sake of an immediate cash advantage.

'academy' portrait of a man and writer innocent of any serious failure of character or judgment. But to Harriet, who knew that it had been checked by James Joyce in typescript and in proof, it was, simply, the authorized version of his life. She followed it, step by step, from Ireland to Trieste, to Zurich, to Paris, almost as a mediaeval pilgrim would have made his way across Europe to the shrine of St James at Compostella; and marked in the margin the addresses she remembered so vividly. Kreuzstrasse, Seefeldstrasse, yes; rue de l'Assomption, Hotel Victoria Palace, 2 Square Robiac, yes; rue Galilée, rue Edmond Valentin, yes.* His intemperance, his feckless-ness, his injustices to her, were slowly eclipsed by his genius, his courage and his wit.

Harriet turned to her new tasks with all the devotion of which she was capable. Her policy as Literary Executrix was simple: to do what Mr Joyce would have done.† She did not accept a publisher or a translator until she had assured herself that they were of good standing and that the translation would not be done hastily. She tried to arrange for the books, in whatever language, to come out in the order written; and, for Mrs Joyce's sake, stood out for the best possible terms. She sometimes made, and occasionally proposed, concessions on secondary issues, but she never lost sight of her main objectives. She never allowed herself to be hustled; and it was only when she was quite satisfied that a proposition was acceptable that she was prepared to go on to the stage of having an agreement drawn up, to be signed by her and by Fred Monro, as Administrators.

As time went on, and the number of applications increased, another virtue came into its own. When any new proposal came in, she was always able to marshall the facts that bore on it—often without referring to her files. Her mind seemed to work like a computer; and she could always be relied on to answer letters by return of post. In short, she brought to her work a combination of qualities at once unusual and formidable.

Needless to say, while the war lasted, few publishers in any part of

* Harriet Weaver noted down only three criticism of Herbert Gorman's biography of James Joyce: that he made 'no mention of the English residence in 1931'; was 'a bit mixed as to English visits'; and that it was not Ezra Pound who introduced Sylvia Beach to James Joyce. Herbert Gorman was also incorrect about the dates of her gifts. But she made no comment on these inaccuracies or on any of the few references to herself.

† Under James Joyce's Will, Harriet Weaver had 'sole decision in all literary matters relating to his writings published and unpublished'.

the world were in a position to apply for any new rights. But the very first application with which Harriet had to deal must have given her peculiar pleasure. It was from the Bodley Head, who wanted to exercise an option to publish a cheap edition of *Ulysses*. This was just what James Joyce had urged on her in 1920. Neither were his two other English publishers inactive: Faber put in to publish *Introducing James Joyce*, a selection made by Mr Eliot himself; and Jonathan Cape, to publish *Stephen Hero*.*

Harriet's first experience of dealing with applications from abroad is illustrated by two examples from the surviving papers. In 1943, she and Fred Monro signed an agreement with Señor Santiago Rueda for an edition of two thousand five hundred copies of *Ulysses* in Spanish. This licence was exclusive and appears to have given Harriet a good deal of satisfaction. Perhaps she saw it as an outflanking of General Franco?† The same year, she also decided to enter into negotiations with Livario do Globo (Barcellos Bertaso & Cia), Rio Grande do Sul, Brazil for a translation of *Ulysses* into Portuguese. Harriet felt at a disadvantage in dealing with a part of the world about which she knew nothing but was reassured when she realized that Livario do Globo's agent, Miss Placzek, was as anxious as she was that 'the translation should be the best possible', and later she held her up as a model.[15]

During the last four war years, therefore, Harriet was able to give the lion's share of her time to the book shop and to her other C.P. activities. But, as usual, family and friends were not neglected. She could not have people to stay—and, on this account, missed Gloucester Place acutely—but she got away herself quite frequently, even though travelling, with blacked-out stations and blacked-out trains, was more nerve-racking than ever. Once, towards the end of the war, she made an especially difficult journey to a remote spot, Swynnerton, in Staffordshire, twenty miles from the nearest station, where Edith

* The surviving half of a first draft of what later became *A Portrait of the Artist as a Young Man*. A littler later, an American firm, New Directions, was granted a similar right to publish *Stephen Hero*.

† This application came through Maria Jolas, to whom it was forwarded by Curtis Brown, New York agents. James Joyce made her his literary attorney for the U.S.A. in August, 1940, before she sailed for America. Harriet Weaver wrote to her on 16th April 1942: 'It is difficult for me to judge from here as to the merits of the person making the application. . . . I think it well to empower you to go into the matter. . . . I do this with all the more sense of the rightness of the action in that Mr Joyce . . . appointed you his literary attorney for the U.S.A. . . .'

Walker was looking after the health of a thousand girls at a hostel near a powder-filling factory. Edith was at a loss how 'Josephine' could reach her, until she hit on the idea of getting her chemist in Stafford, who delivered medicines to the hostel every day, to give her a lift. Harriet, on arrival at the hostel, insisted on eating in the main dining-hall—'five hundred girls and a terrible noise'.[16] But this was a glimpse she could not otherwise have had of members of the proletariat employed in vital war work. Edith could not see it in quite the same terms: she had ceased to be a communist when Russia signed the Non-Aggression Pact with Germany.

In 1946, when the war was over, Harriet went to see Dora at Dumfries and made the first of fifteen annual summer visits of a fort-night or so to Cliftonville, Margate, where Edith had a minute cottage, one of a row just off the coast road. Walking was their chief pleasure; and in the afternoon Edith would settle her friend in a chair on the front—in the hollow 'Oval' if it were windy—run over to Godwin Cottages and return with tea on a tray, teapot, bread and butter and all.[17]

Victory over the fascist powers was celebrated by Harriet with a donation of £500 to the *Daily Worker* 'in memory of all those who have fallen in the struggle for peace and socialism'. The money was to be used to equip the canteen in their new premises in Farringdon Road, Finsbury.[18]

As for herself, she felt justified, now, in giving a little less time to politics and a little more time to her own 'exacting research work' on the symposium on *Time*. She put aside, for the 'year or so' she needed to complete it, her other symposium, on *Space*.[19] She was determined to finish the work, though it had become somewhat of an imposition and she sometimes regretted that her notes and her drafts had not perished in her 'great fire' of 1934.

Her work for the party was now done mainly at the lunch-time meetings for workers at Morris Motors and the Radiator and Pressed Steel works, some of them held in the open, some at Johnson's Café. She enjoyed selling the *Daily Worker* and party pamphlets at these meetings. She did not enjoy carrying out a new policy at the book shop of selling sex novels and crime magazines in order to make more money; and she gave the shop less of her time. She had opposed this decision in committee and had found an ally in Comrade Mick Leahy, an Irish tailor who, between spells of illness, had worked with her in the shop during the war. She remained grateful for his support, and later on helped him over financially when he went into hospital. She got him a book to read, too, *Ireland Her Own*, whose author, T. A. Jackson, she recommended as a Marxist. She must have some reason or other, Mick Leahy decided, for liking the Irish.[20]

More and more of her time had, however, to be given to the literary executorship. The number of applications for new rights that came in once the war was over increased rapidly. This took her by surprise. She thought 'the circulation of the various books' had 'doubtless passed its peak'.[21] She had concluded that James Joyce's works would appeal only to the small public it had reached in the Egoist days; but she was delighted to find she was wrong.

Two early post-war applications from abroad that pleased her were from the Italian firm, Mondadori, for Italian translation rights in *Ulysses* and *Stephen Hero*; and from a firm in Tel Aviv, Am Oved, for a Hebrew translation of *Dubliners*. 'I think it would be interesting to have a Hebrew translation of "Dubliners" so long as it was competently done,' she wrote to Fred, '(not that we could judge as to that!)'.[22]

This was one of the last letters she addressed to Fred Monro, as head of Monro Saw & Co. He was to continue as an Administrator until 1951 but was now in the process of handing over Joyce affairs at the office to his son Lionel, an enthusiastic cricketer like himself, who had joined the firm twenty years before and returned to it in 1946 after active service in the army. Letters from the firm no longer began 'Dear Harriet', but 'Dear Cousin Harriet'. The Monros had been neighbours of the Weavers in Hampstead and Lionel had known her since the Cedar Lawn days.

Fred Monro had been Harriet's solicitor for more than thirty years. However much he disagreed with her at times, he was fond of her and, in his own fashion, understood her need to help her chosen underdogs, come what may. In particular, he had dealt shrewdly and with good humour, in spite of occasional expostulations, with James Joyce's importunate demands for instant disinvestment, the legal intricacies of the marriage in 1931, that gave him a 'terrific time', and the many complications following James Joyce's death—and in spite of suspecting that he looked on him, 'with some amusement, as a rather stupid business man'.[23]

It was with Lionel Monro that Harriet corresponded about other applications that came in at this period. One example may be given of her handling of them. She lowered to £25 the advance on royalties

to be paid on *A Portrait* by Mortensen, in Norway, because the country
was 'small and rather poor'; and extended the time limit for publication so as not to rush the translator.[24] While this straightforward
agreement was going through, she heard of an ambitious plan,
launched by Librairie Gallimard, to translate *Finnegans Wake* into
French. She told Lionel:

. . . I feel that a very special point should be made as to the work
being put into the hands of only the very best translator or translators obtainable. No translation of this book has yet been attempted
in any language, except for an isolated chapter in an early form which
was published in a French journal in 1925 or 1926. . . .
   I think Faber & Faber might be asked to go into this side of the
matter carefully and report.[25]

   Librairie Gallimard were proposing to appoint as translator-in-
chief Philippe Soupault and as his assistants MM Queneau, Eugene
Jolas, Stuart Gilbert and Samuel Beckett. Harriet was 'thoroughly
well satisfied' and did not think 'a better team could have been got
together'. 'I think it would be a mistake to hurry the translators,' she
told Lionel, 'better to give them as long a time as they think they will
need.'[26] (In the event, this plan was shelved; and André de Bouchet
began working on translations of some fragments. Harriet was not at
all put out when, years later, she heard they were still unfinished.)[27]
   As might be expected, some applications fell through, others had
to be turned down. Ulyse, a Rumanian publisher, wanted to bring
out *A Portrait* and *Stephen Hero* but had to cry off even though Harriet
offered to reduce the advance on royalties from £30 to £15: the
country was in an 'impoverished state', as she realized. An enquiry on
behalf of an Argentine firm to acquire world rights in a Spanish
translation of *A Portrait* looked promising. But Harriet remembered
that the Biblioteca Nueva, Madrid, had produced the work in 1926.
On enquiry, she found that, though their documents had been lost in
the Civil War, the firm claimed world rights, and she and Lionel
were agreed that the Argentine offer could not, in the circumstances,
be proceeded with.[28]
   Complications such as this, however, were as nothing compared
with those generated by the war in Europe and the controls introduced when it was over. There was, first of all, the problem of finding
out how firms had fared and, if Exchange Control regulations

allowed, of gathering in any accumulated royalties. Some firms had difficulty in making returns of sales because their records were lost or destroyed. The Albatross Press, for instance, had some of its stock and records in Leipzig bombed and took three years to make a return because Leipzig was in the Russian Zone—later East Germany—and contact had become almost impossible.[29] Some royalties could be collected only by the Custodian of Enemy Property and the money received was blocked and could not, for the time being, be transferred to London. Meantime, the Bank of England ruled that the transfer of royalties to Switzerland must stop, which meant that Mrs Joyce would have to reside in England. The Bank's attitude, which distressed Harriet very much, was reversed only in 1947, after Mrs Joyce had sent a medical certificate pronouncing the arthritis, with which she was now increasingly troubled, too much advanced to allow her to travel.

Trying to ensure that the works did not go out of print, or if they had gone out of print, that they were reissued as soon as possible, was not easy. England and much of Europe was suffering from a shortage of paper. Harriet kept a critical eye on the whole scene. Jonathan Cape, for instance, lamented that it was not possible to keep all their Joyce titles in print. As soon as they reprinted one, it was sold out; and, because of Board of Trade restrictions, it might be a matter of many months before they were able to reprint again.[30] The Bodley Head, in despair, and with *Ulysses* out of print, decided to reprint in Holland, which was better off for paper. Harriet felt that foreign proof-readers might not be equal to this task but was reassured when she learned that the Dutch printers were using a photographic process and working on an earlier Bodley Head edition.[31] Piracy was an occasional nuisance during the war but not after.*

Granting new rights had its own set of problems. It was difficult to know, for one thing, to which body to apply for advice on the standing of an unknown firm. The Foreign Office, the British Council or the Central Office of Information? And, under the Trading with the Enemy Act, no contract could be entered into with any publisher in the areas to which the Act applied. Any German publisher, for example, had to apply to the Control Office for Germany and Austria to obtain permission even to open up negotiations for an agreement with the Administrators.

* *Dubliners* and *A Portrait* were published in Danish, *Dubliners* also in French—and *Anna Livia Plurabelle* in German!

Moreover, new rights could not be granted while any doubt remained about rights already granted; and when the Administrators enquired about the continental contracts, handled by Paul Léon after Sylvia Beach withdrew, they learned, to Harriet's deep distress, that he was dead: he had been murdered by the Nazis in 1942, because he was a Jew.

'In the later years at any rate,' Harriet said, 'Mr Léon was Mr Joyce's staunchest and most loyal and devoted and understanding friend.'[32] In those 'later years', too, he had been a great support to her. And now thanks to him, the contracts were safe.

Paul Léon had left occupied France for a time and, with his wife, had joined the Joyces and the Jolases at St-Gérand-le-Puy. Lucie Léon returned to Paris in the summer of 1940 and he in September, against the advice of his friends. When he heard that the Joyces' landlord was selling the contents of their abandoned flat to recoup arrears of rent, he rescued some books and papers and bought others, and the pictures, at an auction held (illegally) by the landlord. He deposited the pictures and some of the papers, including the contracts, with a Paris lawyer employed by James Joyce, Maître Charles Gervais, and other papers, under a fifty-year seal, with the Irish Ambassador, with instructions for their transfer to the National Library of Ireland should he not survive the war.[33]

The Administrators failed to recover the contracts at once, because Maître Gervais was preoccupied with other post-war problems and Harriet turned her attention to other work: work for the first volume of *Letters of James Joyce* and work on enquiries from Joyce scholars and enthusiasts.

The suggestion that James Joyce's letters should be published was first put to Harriet early in 1945 by the American publishers New Directions. She and Fred both like the idea and agreed to it in principle, if Mrs Joyce consented and they found a responsible editor.[34] The same year, The Viking Press put forward the same proposition and was eventually given the contract because Mrs Joyce, on being consulted by the Administrators, proved 'anxious to have Mr Huebsch'.*[35]

Ben Huebsch wrote to Harriet suggesting that she should be 'co-editor with Mrs Jolas' of the proposed volume.[36] Harriet declined,

---

* Ben Huebsch was now with The Viking Press, founded in 1925 by Harold Guinzburg and George Oppenheimer. The Press had taken over his one-man publishing house shortly afterwards.

because she was working on her *Time* symposium and because, in her opinion, Mrs Jolas

will know much better than I the people with whom Mr Joyce had correspondence. Moreover . . . it will take me a good while to go through and make selections from the correspondence I had with Mr Joyce, dating from the time when *The Egoist* first published his Portrait in serial form. . . .[37]

From this point on, however, Harriet was inevitably caught up in all the discussions and negotiations about the book, which was eventually published in 1957—when plans were already afoot for a second volume.

Ben Huebsch came over in the summer of 1946 for a meeting with the Administrators at the offices of Monro Saw, for which he arrived late, being unused to the slowness of London traffic.[38] As Maria Jolas felt unable to take on the editorship single-handed or even to share it,[39] they discussed other possible names—Stuart Gilbert, Padraic Colum, Samuel Beckett, Harry Levin. A little later, though they decided no approach should be made to him as yet, they agreed on Stuart Gilbert. His *James Joyce's Ulysses, A Study* was outstanding; and he had been a friend of the author's since first meeting him in 1927, a qualification to which Harriet attached importance. She decided to ask Faber and Faber to be the English publishers for much the same reason—'because Mr Eliot was a friend of Mr Joyce and the personal touch is desirable'.[40] When they said they were 'most interested' and that Mr Eliot approved the proposal that Mr Gilbert be asked to be the editor, she was delighted.[41]

Nothing further could be done, however, until Mrs Joyce gave her consent to the publication of her husband's letters. Though they ranked as 'writings', and Harriet therefore had 'sole decision' regarding them, she felt that, in this matter, she must carry Mrs Joyce with her. But over the previous year she had written more than once to Zurich and had had no answer. Mrs Joyce had never cared for letter writing and was now less inclined than ever for it because her arthritis had affected her shoulder and hand.

After Ben Huebsch's visit, another attempt was made to get a reply and, this time, it was successful. A friend of Mrs Joyce, Miss Evelyn Cotton, wrote on her behalf and enclosed a note:

Zurich, August 31, 1946.

re. Letters of James Joyce.

I consent to the publication of my husband's letters and give full
authority to Miss Harriet Weaver to make all the arrangements she
considers best and most advantageous.

Nora Joyce

Miss Cotton added, however, that Mrs Joyce wished to see the letters
before they were published in case there was 'something she would
rather not have appear in print'.* [42]

The reply came just after Harriet's birthday, 1st September, when
'a feeling of surprise came over her as she realized that the anniversary
had made her one with the several members of her family who were
septuagenarians'. Yet she felt, as always, that she 'still belonged to the
younger generation'.[43] Dora hoped that she would continue to do so.
'Somehow', she wrote, 'the inner "ego" of us seems to remain age-
less'.[44] By then, Harriet had settled down to the last stage of her work
on her 'history of the concept of time' and to her other Oxford
pursuits. And life was now even fuller.

Campbell Hone had retired as Bishop of Wakefield and he and his
wife had bought a house, 2 Belbroughton Road, only a few minutes'
walk from Harriet. From now on, Harriet was in constant touch
with them, generally had tea with them once a week, and saw
Katharine and Margaret, both now married, and their children, and
Robin, whenever they were there.† But having so near her a sister
and brother-in-law who did not share her political views and had
never warmed to her literary activities was not altogether straight-

* Miss Cotton, still a resident in Zurich in 1968, met the Joyce family there in 1918,
when acting with the English Players. In December 1940, when the Joyces, with their
son and grandson, arrived in Zurich from France, James Joyce rang her up. She was
flattered that he remembered her, called on them and invited them to tea. After his
death, she called on Nora Joyce and tried to help her 'through that difficult time'.
They became friends. After the war, Miss Cotton offered to write letters for her.
(Evelyn Cotton to Jane Lidderdale, 10th April 1968)

† Much to his pleasure, Campbell Hone, on retiring to Oxford, was made an
Honorary Fellow of his old college, Wadham, where he had been a contemporary of
a brilliant group of undergraduates, among them C. B. Fry, John Simon (later Sir
John and then Lord Simon) and F. E. Smith, later Lord Birkenhead; and where he
was joined, in his last year, by Fred Monro. He embarked on an active life in retirement which was to include, among other things, writing the life of Dr John Radcliffe
(1652–1714), a benefactor of the university. The Life was published by Faber and
Faber in 1950.

forward. 'The Gap', that had separated Harriet from her family since the Cedar Lawn days when she became too left-wing for them and could not reconcile herself to their opposition, yawned visibly. But they all decided to ignore it and Harriet continued to live her two, separate, lives—though not always entirely successfully. One day, Maude—the Bishop's wife—was standing in front of a tailor's long glass having a skirt lengthened by 'a little man' recommended to her: the post-war 'New Look' demanded a longer line. Suddenly there floated up to her the words 'How's Josephine?'. The tailor was Comrade Mick Leahy.

By the end of the year, Harriet's symposium on *Time* was, at last, ready to be shown to a publisher.[45] She had marshalled the views 'of outstanding philosophers from the time of the Greeks onwards—first in chronological order and then classified'.[46] It was a typescript of over a thousand pages. In the middle of February 1947, she took it to the Secretary to the Oxford University Press, though not very hopefully. He had already told her that his Delegates preferred to publish fresh theories or fresh criticism rather than a re-ordering of existing materials;[47] and she was not surprised when they turned it down.

Still, she 'cherished a faint hope', as she told him, that Mr Eliot would 'use his influence with the co-directors of his firm' or would make some other suggestion.[48] But Mr Eliot, when he returned in the summer from America, had also to disappoint her:

> . . . I am afraid that the reasons which prevent us from considering this book are imperative. We could not expect that such a work would have a very large sale, although it might go on for many years, and while it may well be a book which would add distinction to our list, we are now obliged to be very parsimonious in our outlay of paper. . . . I am very sorry about this and hope you may find some other publisher in a different position.[49]

Harriet thought Mr Eliot's reply 'considerate and kind'. She 'regretted' his board's decision but 'could understand the reasons for it'.[50] The paper shortage was proving as tiresome to her as a compiler as it was to her as Literary Executrix. She put the symposium one one side and decided not to go on, for the moment, to that on *Space*. In any case, there were now other things to be attended to.

At the end of February 1947, there came the first of what was to prove an unending series of enquiries from Joyce scholars and en-

42 The 1936 May Day rally assembling on the Embankment

43 Annie Weaver
at Westwick

44 Mrs. A. R. H.
Saunders in about
1951

thusiasts: John Slocum, at Padraic Colum's suggestion, wrote to her from New York to tell her about a plan to publish an exhaustive bibliography and to enlist her help. He and his collaborator intended to include all James Joyce's 'book and serial publications in all languages' and did not expect to complete the work (on which a start had been made before the war) for at least two years.[51] 'My dear Miss Weaver,' he began and went on:

   . . . There are certain details concerning your publication of Joyce between the years 1914 and 1923 (?) that only you can provide us with. Without these facts, we feel that our bibliography would be as inadequate as those Joyce bibliographies that have been published in the last ten years. . . .[52]

There followed questions on The Egoist Press editions of *A Portrait*, *Dubliners*, *Chamber Music*, *Exiles* and *Ulysses*.

   This enterprise appealed strongly to Harriet. She sent at once the figures for *A Portrait* and *Ulysses*, both of which she 'remembered well', together with a thousand-word resumé of the history of publishing these works, with generous references to the part played by 'Miss Marsden', 'the late Mr H. G. Wells', John Rodker and others. She promised to send the figures for the other titles when she got out her account books, still in store at Guildford, on her next visit there.[53]

   'I cannot tell you how pleased my colleague and I were to receive your two interesting and informative letters,' John Slocum wrote in May. 'I only wish that other editors and publishers were as helpful to us as you and Mr Huebsch. . . . Grant Richards has sent us an irritated postcard in which he says he is too sick and too old to discuss Joyce. . . .'[54] Harriet sent next a complete list of 'translations of books published with authority from Mr Joyce', because he had been encountering difficulties in collecting the particulars he needed. So began a correspondence that ended only with the publication of the bibliography in 1953;* and her work in answering other such enquiries that ended only with her death.

   As Harriet was completing the list of translations, Robin Hone returned from a holiday in France, with important messages for his Aunt Hat, who had been worrying about Sylvia and had asked him to try to look her up. She had attempted to get news of her during

* *A Bibliography of James Joyce, 1882–1941* by John J. Slocum and Herbert Cahoon. Yale University Press, 1953. London. Rupert Hart-Davis, 1953.

the war through the American Embassy, but had failed; and a friend who had gone over to Paris in 1946 had failed to find her.* Robin reported that he had found her, in her old flat; that she had had six months at a concentration camp during the war; and that Ernest Hemingway, working with the Resistance, had helped her. (Urged on by Sylvia, he had, in fact, helped to free the rue de l'Odéon of the last German snipers as the Allies moved into Paris.)[55] Sylvia had given Robin a 'sumptuous' tea and had sent an invitation to Harriet 'three times repeated' to pay her a visit.

It was a great relief, after so long and anxious a wait, to know that Sylvia had survived the war. Harriet wrote at once, and at length, to bring her up to date, but typed the letter because she now had the family failing of a shaky hand and Sylvia would probably 'curse' her if she wrote in her 'own foul fist'. She had given up her London flat . . . she had joined the Communist Party and was very interested in 'the spectacular growth of communism in France. . . . Do you remember how we tried to attend a great socialist meeting addressed by M. Blum in December 1936 and couldn't get anywhere near the entrance on account of the vast crowds? . . . Did you really and truly and sincerely and honestly . . . mean [to invite me to stay]? If so, I should love to come for a week, though I do feel very hesitant. . . .' Food in Paris could mostly be bought only on the black market, she believed; and travel restrictions were formidable.[56]

But Sylvia reassured her and, by the beginning of June, the trip was fixed up. 'Hurray!' wrote Harriet, in high spirits:

. . . It is sweet of you to say you will meet me. I shall be wearing a black hat and coat and a 10½ years older face which you might fail to recognise at first! It will be lovely to stay with you at your flat, ever so much nicer than staying at a hotel. The lack of a bath does not appal me in the least. I was months and months without such a thing when living at Glencoin where there was not even a tap or a sink.

I am interested to hear that you have your library housed upstairs in your flat; also that you are busy translating a French book into English and finishing your history of Shakespeare & Co.† You must dispatch me out-of-doors on my own whenever you want to get on with your work quietly. . . .[57]

* At this time, Sylvia Beach was in the Channel Islands. She wrote to Harriet Weaver from there, to Gloucester Place, and had the letter returned 'Gone away'.
† The French book was *Un Barbare en Asie* by Henri Michaux.

Harriet stayed not for a week but for a crowded fortnight, though Paris was not its old self without the Joyces: Mrs Joyce sent a message, through Miss Cotton, that she felt 'terribly grieved' she could not be there 'to receive' her.[58] Harriet wanted not only to see the remaining members of the old circle but also to have talks with them about the proposed volume of letters, to find out what she could about what works in French were, or were not, in print, and to make another effort to get hold of the missing contracts.

Lucie Léon armed her with a letter to Maître Gervais: '. . . je vous prie cher Maître de bien vouloir faciliter l'accès à ces papiers à Miss Weaver pour qu'elle puisse prendre les renseignements necessaires à ce sujet.'[59] But he protested that so many of the papers deposited with him by various clients before the invasion were unlabelled and he could not search for the contracts yet. (He eventually found and returned them eighteen months later.) Adrienne Monnier, still living in the rue de l'Odéon, also gave Harriet a warm welcome—and succeeded in persuading her to call her by her Christian name. Maria Jolas, back from the United States, took her to see Lucia, again at Ivry. They found her 'sweet and Ophelia-like', as Maria Jolas put it.[60] Harriet thought she looked thin;[61] and later sent her some food from a parcel from America.* Sylvia, who thought Stuart Gilbert a good choice as editor of the letters, had him and his wife to dinner one night and sat him next to Harriet whom he had met before the war but did not know well. He had thought of her simply as 'like Cordelia—not a publicity seeker, as most do-gooders are'.[62] He was amused and pleased when she turned to him and whispered, 'Mr Gilbert, I think I ought to tell you I am a communist'.[63]

Harriet was worried by Sylvia's worn looks and wondered if she were not being 'too forgetful of the inner woman', in spite of food parcels from Bryher.[64] But Sylvia did not spare herself and insisted on eating at the rue de l'Odéon every day, queuing for food and cooking all the meals herself—restaurants were 'terribly dear'. She also did all the telephoning for Harriet's many appointments. 'I certny was busy,' she told her sister Holly.[65] Harriet was touched. 'I appreciated it all so very much,' she wrote on her return, 'though my tongue is not much use to me.'[66]

At Rawlinson Road, there awaited her a searching test of her

* After the war, many people in America sent parcels of food to friends in England and on the Continent. As the parcels mostly contained rationed foods and unobtainable luxuries, they were much appreciated.

judgment as Literary Executrix: a proposal from a New York film agency who wanted to acquire, for a substantial sum, the American film rights of *Ulysses*. It took Harriet very little time to make up her mind what to do. She wrote to Lionel Monro to impress on him 'the necessity for ensuring the suitability and capability of the script writer—that he should be concerned with the artistic rather than the sensational possibilities of the work, and the same with the Film Company'.[67] She herself also made a number of painstaking enquiries and eventually turned the proposal down. She had no regrets.*

Meantime, she wrote to T. S. Eliot to tell him about her enquiries in Paris and elsewhere for sources of James Joyce letters. He had said that he was very much in the dark about this;[68] and Faber and The Viking Press had been wondering whether enough letters would be found to make a worthwhile volume. Besides the Paris friends, Harriet had been in touch with Claud Sykes, a friend of James Joyce from his Zurich days, and others, and was now able to reel off the names of a dozen people who might be willing to lend letters likely to be of interest. This was a promising start and the two publishers a little later agreed that they should both 'with all due diligence' set about to collect letters.[69]

Though it remained doubtful for some time whether enough letters would be found, Harriet made a start on her own collection, now with her again in its deed box. She began to sort it and select from it letters she would be prepared to see published in whole or in part, and to type them in triplicate.[70]

There was, however, as she saw, no need to press on. Some visits could be fitted in: to Edith at Margate, to Muriel and Alfred in Sussex—though he could no longer be a companion on walks on the Downs, as he had heart trouble; to Mary and Annie, and, at the end of the year, to her niece Rosemary—'a favourite niece', as she told Sylvia—who, with her husband, Geoffrey Cockle, had acquired a small farm which they were 'running very efficiently, raising a herd of tuberculin-tested Jersey cows—beautiful creatures'.[71]

It was while she was with Mary and Annie that Harriet reached an

---

* Harriet Weaver did not live to see a film of *Ulysses*, though several other proposals were put to her. One, from Stuart Gilbert, in 1948, 'appealed' to her, though it came to nothing. He wrote: 'In my opinion ULYSSES, if filmed, should be treated as Joyce wished it to be treated—with a film technique corresponding, mutatis mutandis, to the techniques of the writing, pictorial replacing verbal patterns. . . .' (From Stuart Gilbert, 12th June 1948)

important decision. It was to lead to the first of a number of gifts, over the next decade, of books and papers of one kind and another amassed since the Egoist days. She had learned that John Slocum had for years been collecting 'manuscripts, first editions, critical essays, translations, letters, etc., by or about Mr Joyce, with the idea of eventually turning them over to a deserving university library which could make them the basis of a really adequate research collection'.[72]

Here, it seemed to her, was a splendid opportunity for finding a home for some of her papers stored at Westwick. Mary was now an octogenarian and Annie, though younger, was beginning to fail. (She could no longer prune the roses in the rose garden she had designed years before and planted herself.) The 'deserving university library' eventually chosen for the collection would, however, almost certainly be in the United States. This presented some difficulty to Harriet. America would not have been her first choice. Mr Joyce belonged to Dublin, or, at least, to Europe, if he belonged anywhere in particular; and American foreign policy was, to her mind, wholly misguided. What, for instance, was the U.S. Navy doing in the Eastern Mediterranean? There was no Russian fleet in the Gulf of Mexico. On the other hand, her main objective was to make her own material accessible to students, and interest in Mr Joyce was undoubtedly stronger in America than on her side of the Atlantic.

Harriet sent John Slocum a list of magazine articles she had at Westwick and told him that, 'as she was growing old', she would be 'happy to present them' to be used for the purpose he spoke of, if he would care to have any of them, though she did not 'altogether like parting with them':

What of the innumerable press-cuttings I have? Would it be of any use to send these? They date from the days of the first publication of A PORTRAIT OF THE ARTIST. . . .[73]

John Slocum accepted both offers: and at Christmas, when Harriet was at Westwick again, she began parcelling up the collection for despatch by book post, for which there were no 'tiresome' forms to be filled in.[74] But as the maximum weight allowed was four pounds, Harriet had to make up fourteen parcels, each of which she numbered in the lower left-hand corner, for checking off on arrival.[75] Another five parcels went off from Oxford, after her return in the new year 1948.

'I cannot tell you what an exciting experience it was to open and to go through the contents,' John Slocum wrote, when the first eight had come:

the *Pink Un* with its wonderful poster; the articles by Bennett, Middleton Murray [sic], Aldington and all the wit and wisdom and stupidity of Joycean criticism gathered in one place instead of scattered through the infinite corridors of public libraries. . . . I cannot thank you enough for your kindness. . . .[76]

When the eighteenth parcel had arrived he wrote again:

. . . It is undoubtedly the most remarkable batch of Joycean criticism that has ever been gathered together and one that could not possibly be duplicated again. . . .* [77]

Harriet's collection, not listed as such, is now in the Eileen and John J. Slocum collection at Yale University. In giving it away then, she had acted with foresight, for his second letter of thanks arrived when she was again at Westwick: her beloved Annie had had a fall; and her visits to her old aunts at Castle Park a quarter of a century before were now being repeated, though in a more poignant form.

It was a poignant experience, too, transcribing her letters from James Joyce. She had reached the last decade, the 1930's, and relived those years. He had written less and less frequently then and few of the letters lent themselves to publication. Still, she decided to add a few more. 'But the gaps were there, alas,' she exclaimed.[78] She had 'agenbite of inwit' about her 'lack of sympathetic, imaginative understanding both of his work . . . and of his utterly overwrought condition in those years'.[79]

The handling and re-reading of his letters led to a decision to undertake a task which she felt she 'owed' to him: the sorting and tabulating of the manuscripts, typescripts and proofs of *Finnegans Wake*. They had arrived in no particular order and were often sent by the person who had been helping with the typing. Sometimes, especially towards the end, disconnected loose papers, that had been forgotten or mislaid, had been bundled in.[80] His incomparable gift to her must be passed on in good order.

The work of sorting and tabulating (fitted in as her other commit-

* The collection soon proved its worth. Richard Kain and Ellsworth Mason were already working on it by April 1948. Harriet Weaver was very pleased.

ments allowed) was completed in two years with the help for a time (unpaid) of a young Joyce bibliographer, Crawford Collins. Meantime, rather against her will, Harriet gradually found herself involved in the collecting of Joyce letters, though 'from the outset' she had not wanted to undertake 'any responsibility'.[81] John Slocum turned out to have a considerable number and sent her photostats of some and a microfilm of others—to Frank Budgen, Ezra Pound, Grant Richards, St John Gogarty. She undertook to get the microfilmed letters typed but, in the end, typed them herself. As she was 'very ignorant' about 'implements for interpreting a microfilm', she did not find it very easy working at the Bodleian's 'not too well lighted' machine. Deciphering the handwriting was a slow business. The letters to Grant Richards and Ezra Pound nearly defeated her.[82]

There was also much correspondence about other letters. Constantine Curran, for instance, reported he was going through his, and his daughter (Elizabeth) was typing them; to her alone could he confide letters with passages he regarded as confidential.[83] Stanislaus Joyce was not able to help. Harriet wrote to him hoping he might be able to provide some letters from the earlier days, which Mr Eliot thought 'would probably be the most interesting'. But Mrs Joyce, she told him, wanted 'to rule out any further ones dealing mainly with the family financial difficulties which she thinks were gone into fully enough in the biography'.[84] Stanislaus Joyce, however, had sent to Herbert Gorman copies of all the letters he could find of the kind that they wanted.* [85]

In the middle of this work of collecting letters, Stuart Gilbert was offered the editorship, and said he would accept it, if enough letters could be brought together. 'Of course I feel greatly honoured by this proposal,' he wrote to Harriet, 'and, if I undertake the work, shall do my best to present Joyce both as he was in life and as he would have wished to be presented posthumously—in his case these are not, I think, incompatibles, as they would be in so many cases'.[86]

Though troubled that the letters to her would be 'rather disproportionate in number' unless some more were found to other people,

---

* Stanislaus Joyce went on to say: 'I do not like Mr Gorman's portrait, although it seems to have had the benediction of the sitter. It has many inaccuracies and even absurdities. . . . As for the financial censorship. My brother was an agnostic in politics, but he called himself a socialist. He never lost sight of the financial problem. Are his own grappling[s] with it (before you came to the rescue) of no importance?' (From Stanislaus Joyce, 7th March 1948)

Harriet now felt more hopeful that the volume of letters would, one day, be published;* [87] and she was encouraged when, a few months later, Peter du Sautoy (to whom T. S. Eliot had handed over much of his work on the letters) told her that some others had been found in Ireland by Patricia Hutchins, who was working there on her first book—*James Joyce's Dublin*.† Shortly afterwards, Harriet discussed with her, at Rawlinson Road, the idea that she might look for letters not only in Ireland but in Great Britain and on the Continent.‡ [88] Faber agreed to pay her fares; and Harriet was soon following closely her 'indefatigable' and fruitful investigations.

During the winter, Harriet drove on steadily with the sorting of the *Finnegans Wake* manuscripts, though she thought she was 'unspeakably slow'.[89] She started on Part I and then went on to Part III, as she knew it best and hoped that the experience gained in going through it would help her when she came to Part II: most sections of it would be 'teasers', she foresaw, as the manuscript was in 'a very confused state' and there were many loose pages that had 'the appearance of hieroglyphics'.[90]

To the Saunders, she seemed a tremendously hard worker: she never took time off for rest or recreation 'even after the mid-day meal'. They used to find her, if they had occasion to look in, tapping away at her machine or snowed under with MSS, wrapped in jerseys, shawl and rug and with the minimum of fire burning, to save their gas. 'In spite of repeated protests from the family this practice continued.'[91]

Harriet brought to the work of 'sorting and tabulating' a mind much less troubled about *Finnegans Wake* than it had ever been.

* Of the six hundred and ninety letters sent a little later to Stuart Gilbert by Faber, a hundred and forty-four were from James Joyce to Harriet Weaver and there were others from Ben Huebsch to her. (Stuart Gilbert to Peter du Sautoy, 18th September 1950. Faber)

† Patricia Hutchins came from a County Cork family of English origin in the seventeenth century. She had married a young Belfast poet, Robert Greacen, but wrote under her maiden name. When working in the National Library, Dublin, on *James Joyce's Dublin* (London. Grey Walls Press, 1950) she had come across some Joyce letters and wrote to Faber about copyright. They put her in touch with Harriet Weaver and also with John Slocum, then in Dublin buying up letters. He had clues to others in Ireland that he had not been able to follow up, and she followed them up herself.

‡ Robert Greacen went with his wife to Rawlinson Road. When they had been left for a moment by Harriet Weaver in her room, he characteristically inspected the bookcase. 'Good heavens, fancy the Left Book Club *here*!'

Study of some of the books and essays on it had helped her to feel more at home with it—to understand better both its structure and language; and she was glad she had bequeathed the manuscripts to the city where Mr Joyce was born. It seemed appropriate that he, 'having set forth from Ireland and made a circular Vico life's journey, should in the end return, by proxy of his great last book, to the city whence he set forth and which was at the base of all his writings'.[92]

Sylvia came on a long-promised visit for twelve days in May 1949. Harriet found lodgings for her with a Mrs Bird at 12 St John's Street. 'I think you will find,' she wrote to Sylvia, 'that she makes no charge for B. and B. It is her way of conducting business.'[93] But she warned her that Oxford would be very crowded as it would be Eights Week. 'Well,' replied Sylvia, 'how I shall enjoy it! And if its a trifle rowdy, . . . why all the better! I shall go whooping up and down myself so as not to make a false note.'[94]

Because of the early season, Sylvia came too late to see the flowering trees at their best, but she delighted in the colleges and the college gardens; and it gave Harriet particular pleasure to see her joy when she caught her first sight of Woodstock and Blenheim.[95] Sylvia also saw some of the *Finnegans Wake* manuscripts, shown to her—as to all visitors—with a kind of reverence; and she got a glimpse of Harriet at her literary executorship work, taking her first, deliberate steps towards sizing up an application from Edwin R. Armstrong, of New York, who seemed to be in a hurry, to put on a stage production of the *Wake*.[96]

Sylvia returned to London by coach with Helen Saunders and plied her with questions about 'the to her strange anomaly of H.S.W.'s quiet and gentle personality and her championship of communism and Joyce's "Ulysses" '. Helen told her that the explanation lay, she thought, in her 'intense feeling for the under-dog' and her 'very free-thinking and independent mind'.[97]

Later in the summer, Harriet had a visit from W. R. Rodgers, who was devising a broadcast on James Joyce and had put to her the alarming proposal that she should record some recollections. He came down to Oxford to persuade her to agree. At their first meeting, Harriet stonewalled steadily. 'Bertie' Rodgers tried various openings as they sat at a small table in her room.

'And what was Ezra Pound like, Miss Weaver?' he asked in his gentle, Irish voice. She did not answer but looked down at the table and, with a finger, traced an outline across and along the grain.

'Mr Pound was like that.'

'In Trieste, now, Joyce used to go to the Easter church celebrations, didn't he?'

'Yes, but only to watch the black beetles.' There was a flicker of a smile and then silence.[98]

Still, Bertie Rodgers persevered and, after another visit, Harriet came to feel that she might record something, if she could write it out first and then read out what she had written. 'I think he is very clever,' she wrote to Patricia Hutchins, 'in his gentle but persistent way of working on people until he gradually gets them to do what he wants!'[99]

This was an amusing episode in a sad summer. Alfred, her last surviving brother, died in July in spite of all that Muriel had done for so long to stave off another heart attack; and Annie, who had been going downhill since the beginning of the year, was finding the hot summer exhausting. Harriet, who had been taking turns with Maude and their niece Rosamond in staying at Westwick, went for a fortnight in August and found Mary overwrought and 'pathetically glad' to see her.[100] Annie, 'patient and heroic', became 'weaker and weaker, until, early in the morning of September 5th, she died in peaceful unconsciousness'.[101] Harriet stayed on after the funeral until Maude could relieve her. She had to get away to Paris—Sylvia had again insisted on putting her up—for talks with several people who wanted to see her or whom she wanted to see, among them Mrs Joyce: though grievously crippled, she had come to Paris for an important event.

The manuscripts, books and pictures rescued from the Joyces' flat by Paul Léon had now been retrieved from storage. Maria Jolas was organizing an exhibition and sale of them, to raise money for Nora Joyce. To add to the interest of the exhibition, other things were being lent by Nora Joyce and by friends; and Harriet herself was lending four large galley proofs from *transition* of the second watch of Shaun (Jaunty Jaun . . .), her own inscribed copy of her first edition of *A Portrait* and three other books.

Harriet wanted to see the exhibition and particularly a notebook of James Joyce's, found among the retrieved papers, in which he had put down some highly illuminating comments on and stage directions for *Exiles*: an exciting discovery. Maria Jolas had sent her a rough, first typescript and had suggested that the notes should be published. Harriet thought them 'extremely interesting'; but, as she had always thought *Exiles* 'had something of autobiography in it', she wanted to discuss the question of publication with Mrs Joyce before making up her mind.[102] Other items on her agenda were a talk with the French radio people, who wanted to put on *Exiles* in French, and an application from Gallimard to publish it.[103] But, above all, she wanted to see Mrs Joyce.

Once in Paris, she was so busy that the excursions that Sylvia had planned—to the confluence of the Seine and the Marne and to other places—had to be abandoned. She worked on the *Exiles* notebook with Maria Jolas until, thanks to Stuart Gilbert's help with some indecipherable Latin, the typescript was, they thought 'word-perfect'. Ben Huebsch turned out to be in Paris, and already knew about the notebook. He wanted to publish it with a new edition of the play.[104] He put to Harriet also some ideas he had for a 'biographical framework' for the volume of letters: he thought the number of letters so far brought together would not justify publication.[105] The French radio asked her to speak for three or four minutes on publishing *A Portrait* and *Ulysses*.* [106] Harriet was immensely interested in everything she saw at the La Hune Gallery, where the exhibition was taking shape against a background of huge 'blown-up' photographs from Patricia Hutchins' book. But, in spite of working night and day, Maria Jolas had to postpone the 'vernissage' from 8th to 25th October. This was a disappointment. Harriet had to return before then to be with Mary and to get through a backlog of political work. (A general election was looming ahead.) She was only represented on the opening day—by Wyndham Lewis' drawing.[107]

Another disappointment, a severe one, was suffered in her talks with Nora Joyce, though they started happily enough. During the thirteen years since they had met, Nora Joyce had sent a cable to Harriet on her birthday; and Harriet, besides birthday greetings, had sent to Zurich one of the Administrators' copies of each new edition as it appeared. (Nora Joyce was glad to have them and gave some away as presents.) Through Evelyn Cotton, they had corresponded, most amicably, about current problems. Now, Harriet wanted to consult her about the *Exiles* notebook and to bring her up to date with the latest developments, particularly in collecting letters. Nora Joyce 'seemed ready to agree to anything' until Harriet moved on to the subject of the *Finnegans Wake* manuscripts.[108]

* Harriet Weaver wrote out on large sheets of blotting paper what she intended to say in her broadcast, presumably so that she could read her text easily in the studio.

Two years before, Nora Joyce had been 'extremely upset' to read, in a cutting from the *Irish Independent* sent her from Galway, that her husband's letters to Paul Léon and 'documents relating to the affairs of Joyce during the period 1934–1940' had been given by Paul Léon to the National Library of Ireland.[109] She considered the wishes of the family should have been consulted and that, as Ireland had 'never appreciated' her husband, the library would not have been her choice. Harriet, asked 'to take the matter in hand', had replied that it was impossible for her to do anything. But, having learned what Mrs Joyce felt, she decided she must set out in detail the steps leading up to her decision to bequeath the manuscripts of *Finnegans Wake* to Ireland. It had not occurred to her, she wrote to Miss Cotton, that this might be 'displeasing' to Mrs Joyce.[110]

... In favour of Dublin I was also influenced by the fact that of all the obituary notices of Mr Joyce that I had seen at that time the Dublin notices were far the best. *The Times* had a very poor article and the Times Literary Supplement a disgracefully obtuse article. Considering all these things I decided to bequeath the MSS to the National Library of Ireland and I made a codicil to my will to that effect. But if Mrs Joyce strongly disapproves of this I could alter it. I should not, however, like to leave the MSS to any institution in America, which country has, to my mind, become unbearably aggressive since President Rooseveld's [sic] lamentable death.[111]

Mrs Joyce 'would not dream of suggesting to you what you should do with the manuscript in your possession', Miss Cotton had reported. 'She has now got reconciled to the thought that the letters & manuscripts should be in the National Library of Ireland; it is probably the best place for them.'[112]

Nora Joyce, however, had been causing discreet enquiries to be made whether her husband's body could not be brought by the Eire Government to Dublin. While his grave remained in Zurich, she felt she must remain there, though the climate was bad for her. But she was prepared to leave if her proposal were accepted. Harriet had thought there was not much hope—Mr Joyce had antagonized the Irish priests and other Irishmen;* and the proposal had come to nothing.

* James Joyce had described them to her (and, she suspected, to others) as 'barbarians armed with crucifixes'. (To John J. Slocum, 8th October 1948)

Nora Joyce had been bitterly disappointed and, unknown to Harriet, was now absolutely opposed to the idea of her husband's manuscripts going to Ireland. When Harriet mentioned her work on sorting the *Finnegans Wake* material for its eventual transfer to the National Library, she found her 'without a good word to say for the Irish' and 'strongly averse' to the bequest. She returned to England badly shaken by 'Mrs Joyce's bombshell'.[113]

ST LUKE'S SUMMER

HARRIET had 'set her heart' on giving the *Finnegans Wake* manuscripts to the National Library of Ireland and did not want to yield to Mrs Joyce's views.[1] For the time being, therefore, she let the matter rest; and, as soon as she had settled down after two visits to Mary, she gave herself to her party work.

The Oxford City Branch membership, much reduced by the return to London of evacuee comrades and by some losses to Labour, was now composed of a small band of loyalists. Harriet and the other members of the branch committee were fast friends; and with Ernie Keeling, the District Secretary of the South Midlands communist area, and with Isabel (Betty) Cooper, the branch treasurer, she was on specially close terms.*

The committee looked to Harriet for help and advice, especially in a crisis. During the day, when they were all at work, she could be relied on to move into the breach if, for example, 'squatters' backed by the branch were suddenly threatened with eviction. She had also, long since, become their chief adviser on finance. She never questioned headquarters policy but always insisted that the branch should keep within its means in carrying it out. Ernie Keeling, the main fundraiser, was sometimes a little too optimistic. He had a great regard for 'Josephine's discipline' and recognized as 'a reproof' her turning of a loan into a donation.[2]

---

* Ernie Keeling and Betty Cooper had both been rather puzzled on first meeting Harriet Weaver. They could not place her. 'Rather staid.' 'The mother of a member, perhaps?' She was making tea in Hythe Bridge Street, in the hut behind the bookshop where the local leftwingers had a 'hop' on Saturday nights. (Interview with Isabel Cooper, 26th January 1962)

Clement Attlee's Labour Government, returned to power in 1945 with a majority of one hundred and eighty-six, had run its term; and, in February 1950, it declared a general election. The Communist Party headquarters decided to fight the Oxford constituency for the first time and put in Ernie as their candidate. The party was as bitterly opposed as ever to what it regarded as Labour's halfmeasures at home and misguided policies abroad. It offered the country a bold programme of reform: end the wage freeze; build four hundred thousand houses a year; build health centres and more hospitals; raise the old age pension to £2 a week; raise the school leaving age to sixteen; give women equal pay; extend the nationalization of industry and cut compensation drastically; ban the bomb; make a peace pact with the USSR; trade with Russia and her allies and with China; end the Atlantic alliance with the United States.[3]

Ernie's chances from the first were not very brilliant. Quintin Hogg, Conservative, had held the seat since 1938; Lady Pakenham, Labour, was the wife of the Minister of Aviation in the outgoing government.* Even the Liberal candidate, D. Tweddle, could count on some solid support. But Ernie was undeterred—and so was Harriet. She threw herself into the campaign and trudged for hours each day putting election addresses through 'thousands and thousands' of letter boxes—there was an electorate of seventy thousand. Ernie, who thought her ten years younger than she was, was alarmed to see her 'not too steady on her feet' in the frosty weather. He held her up as an example in his election speeches to factory workers: 'If Comrade Josephine can do it, you can do it!'[4]

There were some rather hectic meetings at the traditional place for open-air gatherings, the Martyrs' Memorial in St Giles. Undergraduates from St John's College, overlooking the Memorial, threw firebrands and buckets of soot from their windows. Harriet stood her ground, went on handing out leaflets and seemed 'quite unintimidated'.[5] But the results of the campaign were not difficult to foresee. Quintin Hogg was returned again; and, out of a total of fifty-eight thousand, seven hundred and eleven votes cast, four hundred and ninety-four went to Ernie.[6]

To Harriet, the results were 'somewhat disappointing' but not surprising. 'The whole of the Press (except the *Daily Worker*) and the BBC,' she told friends, 'are vehemently anti-communist and un-

* Frank Pakenham, now Lord Longford.

scrupulous in what they say and the lies they tell.'[7] To the party, 'the BBC allotted only 8½ minutes' and 'would not soil its pages' by naming it![8]

The BBC, however, earned one good mark. The James Joyce programme, first broadcast on 13th February, pleased her; and she listened to the two repeats. She wrote to Bertie Rodgers to congratulate him. But about her own part in it, she was not at all proud. She had proved, indeed, a lamentably poor broadcaster. 'Your letter cheered me up,' she wrote to Tony Weaver, 'as my own contribution (much cut down because what I had written turned out not to be in keeping with the conversational tone of the broadcast . . .) sounded to me very feeble. . . . Mr Rodgers said it would have been easy to give an academic and merely adulatory picture but . . . he wanted it to be a vivid and balanced whole and I think he succeeded. I was glad he had also cut out some very lame replies to some more questions he had shot at me without warning.'[9]

After the election, Harriet turned once more to the sorting and tabulating of the *Finnegans Wake* manuscript and had it 'practically finished' by the beginning of May,[10] when she was caught up in a plan, originated by Patricia Hutchins, to have a Joyce exhibition at the Institute of Contemporary Arts, then in Dover Street. Maria ſolas was sending over the collection shown in Paris and Patricia was in the process of bringing together over a hundred new items.[11]

As well as the galleys and the books she had lent in the autumn, Harriet agreed to send her copy of *The Transatlantic Review* for April 1924, in which appeared the first published episode of Work in Progress—*Mamalujo*; and, after great heart searchings, and making the condition that it must be displayed in a glass case with a stout lock, her most treasured single manuscript. 'I think,' she wrote to Patricia, 'I will bring myself to lend what I believe is the very earliest bit of F.W. to have been written, in the spring of 1923. A sketch of King Roderick O'Conor, great old toper. It is a very big sheet, very much worked over by Mr Joyce, and more or less coming to pieces.'[12]

During May 1950, she wrote almost daily and sent draft captions which Patricia found 'excellent'.[13] When, in the middle of June, the show was being mounted, she went up to London to help label and arrange some of the exhibits. But the ICA officers, like everyone else outside her own literary circle, knew nothing of her connection with James Joyce; and they would not have invited her to their dinner party with T. S. Eliot the night before the opening, had

45 Fred Monro, in his robes as Master of the
Drapers Company, in about 1937

46 Harriet, drawn by Wyndham Lewis in about
1921

47 James Joyce by Wyndham Lewis—the drawing
presented by Harriet to the National Gallery of
Ireland

To
Harriet Weaver
in token of gratitude
James Joyce

Paris
13 February 1922

ULYSSES

I give this first copy of _Ulysses_ to
the National Library of Ireland
after thirty years
Harriet Weaver

Oxford
s. Patrick's Day 1952

48 The fly-leaf of the first copy of _Ulysses_

not Patricia asked them to do so, and stood down herself to make it possible.[14]

On the opening day, with the gallery filled to overflowing with a throng of enthusiasts, Harriet looked, and was, very happy. To the editor of the review *Nine*,* who had sought, unsuccessfully, to interview her, she had written: '. . . If by chance you looked in [at the exhibition] and were to see an antiquated figure in a dark blue dress, with or without a black coat over it, and wearing a small dark blue hat with a bunch of white flowers on the front of it, it would almost certainly be me and you could safely accost it'.[15] He was privileged. Harriet, as might be expected, gave the other visitors to the exhibition no more chance than she had given the ICA officers of discovering who 'the antiquated figure' was.†

Meanwhile, Patricia Hutchins had learned from Harriet that Mrs Joyce did not want the *Finnegans Wake* manuscripts to go to Ireland. With Harriet's approval, she suggested to the High Commissioner, John Dulanty, that if the Irish government wanted the manuscripts, they should make their wishes known. As a result of an informal approach to him, Sean MacBride‡ wrote to Nora Joyce expressing the desire, which he felt sure was shared by his colleagues in the government, that the manuscripts should go to the National Library. They were proud, he wrote, that James Joyce, 'one of the greatest Europeans of his time, was also a son of Ireland'.[16]

Nora Joyce was not prepared to listen to his plea because the Irish government had not offered to bring her husband's body to Dublin. She did not reply to him but sent his letter, without a covering note, to Harriet. Giorgio addressed the envelope for her.[17] Harriet, knowing

---

* Peter Russell.

† The exhibition could be put on, of course, only because no firm bidder had yet come forward to buy the books and manuscripts rescued from the Joyces' flat, which Mrs Joyce hoped to sell as one collection. Now, she was in serious need of money to pay for treatment for her arthritis. (Cortisone, new and expensive, had given her miraculous relief at first, but had left her worse than before.) Her income from American royalties did not meet her needs; and there was not much left of the other royalties after Lucia's fees at Ivry were paid. When Harriet Weaver heard of Mrs Joyce's plight, she sought, and received, permission from the Bank of England to send £300 to Zurich. The University of Buffalo (as it then was) bought the collection a month later—for $10,000. But the £300 from London tided Mrs Joyce over until the negotiations were completed and the money from Buffalo arrived. (To Maria Jolas, 5th June 1950 and 1st July 1950)

‡ Sean MacBride was then Minister for External Affairs.

a letter to Zurich was unlikely to be answered, sent Maria Jolas a copy of Mr MacBride's letter and asked her to find out, on her next visit to the Joyces, whether Mrs Joyce was still 'adamant as to the National Library of Ireland'.* [18] Maria Jolas got to Zurich at the end of July and had a conversation lasting several hours with Mrs Joyce and Giorgio about the manuscripts. It ended with Mrs Joyce declaring that whatever Miss Weaver's decision, she would abide by it. But, as Maria Jolas wrote, the Irish 'must indeed be very dull-witted if they imagine that the irony of it all escaped' Mrs Joyce.[19]

Harriet was now free to do as she chose; and she chose, for the time being, to do nothing, because she felt that Mrs Joyce probably regretted her generous withdrawal; and because Harvard had now been added to her short list. She needed time to make up her mind. Harvard had been suggested by John Slocum, though he realized that she might think it a 'preposterous suggestion' because of her disapproval of American politics and policies. Harriet had not turned down his 'preposterous suggestion' out of hand but had told him:

... Yes, I do intensely dislike and mistrust the present political set-up in the U.S.A. but no more than I dislike and mistrust the present political leaders in this country, whether they go under the name of Labour or Tory. So that Harvard and the British Museum would really run neck and neck in that way as far as I am concerned. ...[20]

After the Joyce exhibition, therefore, Harriet returned to her work on the *Wake* manuscripts. She finished typing fair copies of her notes and of her 'tabulated lists' by the beginning of August; and then got away on a round of visits ending up at Westwick, where she had 'some great games of croquet' with a greatniece.[21]

By then, Stuart Gilbert had written more than once to say that he wanted to have 'some long discussions about the volume of letters'.[22] 'I do wish you would come over here,' he had written, 'as I would like to be able to talk over with you my many problems ...'.[23] In spite of appeals through the press for letters, the number collected was still not as large as the publishers would have liked; and Ben Huebsch had elaborated to Stuart Gilbert his proposal for a 'biographical framework': 'I suggest dealing with Joyce, his work and

* Maria Jolas was keeping in touch with Nora and George Joyce by going to Zurich from time to time and by telephoning between visits. This was the only way in which she felt, she could be 'of any real use or comfort'. (From Maria Jolas, 3rd April 1950. Copy Jolas)

his relations with acquaintances and friends in a series of chapters, each of which will relate to one of his important books; . . . a sort of setting of the scene,—yet the appropriate letters would follow interrupted by running commentary; or to put it differently, your commentary might be interrupted by letters. . . .'[24] Stuart Gilbert, in an appeal to Harriet, protested that he could 'hardly write a sort of new Life of Joyce—after Gorman's "definitive" biography. I have no first-hand knowledge of the subject previous to about 1927'.[25] 'Mr Huebsch's exigencies are alarming.'[26]

Harriet asked Sylvia if she would put her up as a paying guest. If not, she could go to a pension de famille she had heard of: 'I beg you to agree to this suggestion, as a good friend should, without hesitation'.[27] 'What's all that about a pension de famille?' Sylvia replied:

If, knowing all the drawbacks of this dump and the faults of its owner, you are willing to come to it, then not another word about anywhere else but chez Sylvia—just let me know when to expect you, only the sooner the better. . . .* I would be terribly upset and it might even mean a feud between us, who are such old friends, if you stayed with anybody else in Paris. . . .[28]

Harriet crossed on 21st September 1950, for what she expected to be a few days' visit; and Sylvia, knowing how bad a sleeper she was, and that she preferred the noises of the courtyard—'baby crying, dog howling, housepainters assembling in the early dawn etc'—to the street sounds on the front, put her in her 'dumproom' on the court.[29] To save herself cooking, this time, she took Harriet every day at noon to 'a little place behind the Odéon theatre called "Au Pommier Normand" where you get quite a nice meal. . . . Three generations of Normandy apple-ites serve you—Granny, Momma and a small girl of perhaps 7 or 8 at most'.[30]

Unfortunately, Stuart Gilbert, whom Harriet had expected to return to Paris before her own arrival, was held up in Switzerland for over a month by talks with his publishers. Harriet stayed on, as she had a compelling reason for wishing to see him; and she felt that this was likely to be her last visit to Paris. But the long wait was irksome. Sylvia wanted to get on with her memoirs; Harriet wanted to get back to Oxford. She filled in the time seeing acquaintances, mending

* Adrienne Monnier was giving up her library and flat because she was ill; and was shortly joining Sylvia Beach at 12 rue de l'Odéon.

sheets for Sylvia and making an eyeshade, to help her headaches, out of stout brown paper and elastic.*

When Stuart Gilbert at last returned at the end of October, Harriet spent two long afternoons with him, fortified by his wife's cakes and jam.[31] In looking over the six hundred and ninety letters he had been sent by Faber, he had been struck by two groups of them. 'In the Budgen letters,' he had written to Peter du Sautoy, 'are many valuable comments on the progress and structure of ULYSSES. These are cheerful letters, in a rather Rabelaisian vein, and show Joyce *en pantoufles*. The letters to Miss Weaver, different in tone, are even more interesting; they give glimpses of Joyce's daily life, his hopes, fears and ailments, and will be indispensable to students of FINNEGANS WAKE, on the genesis, meaning and method of which they throw much light. . . .'[32] But Miss Weaver had cut out some passages in the letters to her; and he had asked her whether these omissions were really necessary.

Harriet had stayed on in order to explain to him in person why she had made them. Her main ground, she said, was her respect for family privacy. But her abiding desire to attract the least possible attention to herself and to avoid hurting people's feelings (she had blue-pencilled the references to the Irish as 'barbarians armed with crucifixes', for instance) also entered in. Stuart Gilbert, when he had heard her argument, assured her that he would comply in all cases with her wishes.[33]

This delicate matter settled, they turned to the possibilities of collecting more letters for the volume: neither of them wanted to pad it out with other material. Harriet promised to have translated some more letters to Lucia; to choose some more to herself from the earlier years; to make a string of enquiries of other owners,† and to provide some notes on the Egoist days.‡

* The eyeshade, showing signs of much use, is among Sylvia Beach's papers at Princeton.

† Ben Huebsch wrote, at Harriet Weaver's request, to Dorothy Pound to enquire whether her husband had any letters. She replied that she was unable to get at papers until her husband was freed from St Elizabeth's Hospital, Washington, where he had then been for nearly ten years. (In 1945 he had been indicted for treason on the ground that his broadcasts from Italy had given 'aid and comfort' to an enemy country; but he had not been tried as he had been found unfit to plead.) Dorothy Pound went on to say that she was sick of the false statements about her husband made in the American press and noted that The Viking Press advertised in those same papers. (Mrs Ezra Pound to The Viking Press, 25th December 1950. Copy Weaver)

‡ Harriet Weaver's six pages of notes on *The Egoist* and The Egoist Press were sent

She felt like 'sinking through the floor with nymphant shame' at all the trouble she had given Sylvia.[34] But she had had the talks with Stuart Gilbert; and she also, quite unexpectedly, had a talk with Giorgio, whom she had not met since 1936. He was in Paris for discussions about the final stage of the sale of the collection to the University of Buffalo.

Harriet seized the opportunity to broach the subject of the 'disposition', as she called it, of the *Finnegans Wake* manuscripts. Nora Joyce, in recent messages, had reiterated that the decision lay wholly with her; and Harriet hoped to hear from Giorgio that his mother was now reconciled to Dublin. He quickly undeceived her: both his mother and he himself were 'still utterly hostile to Dublin'. Harriet thought this attitude 'quite prejudiced';[35] but she sounded him out on an alternative choice and found that they would approve of the British Museum.[36]

Giorgio also said that his mother was very ill and that the outlook was poor.[37] Harriet decided it would be wrong to ask her to change her views; and felt 'driven' to decide against Dublin. It was a hard conclusion and she could not bring herself to choose another library at once.

It was an embarrassing conclusion, too. She had told John Slocum, in 1948, of her bequest to the National Library in Dublin and had fallen in with his plea that he be allowed to tell the Director about it. He had not done so but had told another Joyce enthusiast, Quentin Keynes, who had broken the good news.[38] She and the Director, Dr R. J. Hayes, had then corresponded about the complexity and state of the manuscripts and she had informed him that it was her intention to present them as soon as she had them ready.

By the end of the year, Nora Joyce's condition had worsened considerably and the prognosis was almost hopeless: high blood pressure and uraemia had set in. She was moved to a clinic, the Paracelsus. While Harriet was conducting a three-cornered correspondence with Mrs Jolas, who made a flying visit to Zurich in the middle of January 1951, and with Lionel, about the best way to finance fees, another crisis blew up. Ivry could no longer keep Lucia.

Under a scheme for the reorganizing of mental hospitals, Lucia (with other long-stay patients) was to be sent to the provinces, where she could scarcely ever be visited. It was an intolerable idea.[39] Giorgio,

to Stuart Gilbert a fortnight later. (To Stuart Gilbert, 9th November 1950. Copy, Weaver) unable to leave his mother, asked Maria Jolas to find out whether Lucia could go to St Andrew's, Northampton, where, he believed, she had been well looked after fifteen years before;[40] and Harriet and Lionel welcomed the proposal because residence in England would do away with the endless applications to the Bank of England for francs to pay fees.

By the middle of March, to everyone's relief, St Andrew's had accepted Lucia. Harriet went to see her at once, although an hour's visit meant a day's cross-country journeying; and then went regularly every week until Lucia was transferred to the hospital's 'ladies' house' in North Wales, where she remained for the next seven years, except for summer holidays at Northampton. Lucia was still very ill and her mood varied from visit to visit. Sometimes she was very depressed, sometimes inclined to be violent; and a nurse had to remain in the room.* [41]

Lucia was still at Northampton, fortunately, at the beginning of April. On the eve of her weekly journey, on Tuesday, 10th April 1951, Harriet had a telegram from Zurich: 'Mother died this morning'.[42] She was in doubt whether to tell Lucia and wanted to consult the doctor at the hospital. But she was not able to see him and, as Lucia asked about her mother, she broke the news to her. Lucia had spoken of her father on every visit but this was the first time she had spoken of her mother. Harriet thought this strange. Perhaps she was, after all, clairvoyant? But Lucia took the news 'calmly' and asked, twice, for her mother's photograph.[43]

'Poor Mrs Joyce,' Harriet wrote to Maria Jolas, 'how she has suffered these last years, and especially these last months of dreadful illness. I imagine that even Giorgio could not have wished her to linger on in that miserably wretched state, much as he will grieve to part with her. I am so glad to have seen her when she was staying with you in Paris 18 months ago. What a wonderful friend you have been to her.'[44]

The sadness of Mrs Joyce's last years and death touched Harriet deeply and made her feel all the more strongly that she must 'fall in' with her wish that the manuscripts should not go to Ireland. But to what library should they go? She felt she needed advice, and asked

* Shortly after Lucia's arrival in England, Harriet Weaver was appointed her Receiver (guardian) under the Court of Protection. Until 1958, she could visit Lucia only during the summer, as North Wales was too far away. At other times, she kept in touch by letter.

Patricia Hutchins whether she could suggest someone without an axe to grind.

Patricia Hutchins was already collecting material for her next book, *James Joyce's World*, and had been plying Harriet with questions, particularly about *The Egoist*.* She had been the first student of Joyce in England to seek her out and had become a great admirer. Harriet's enthusiasm, 'unlimited patience and resourcefulness' had won her gratitude and she was very ready to help. In June, she took Harriet to the British Museum and introduced to her George D. Painter of the Department of Printed Books, whom she had already met in the course of collecting letters. He regarded James Joyce as one of the three greatest writers of the twentieth century: only Proust and Gide could stand with him. *Finnegans Wake* he considered by far the greatest of James Joyce's books.

Perhaps it was her consciousness of the importance of the decision with which she was faced that made Harriet rather more reserved than usual. At any rate, George Painter, as he looked up at her—he was not as tall as she was—felt deeply impressed by her air of gentle and gentlewomanly austerity.[45] It was very hot, so they went out on to the steps of the museum, where they could sit and get some air.

George Painter knew nothing of the history of her difficulties, only that she wanted advice on libraries to which the manuscripts might suitably be given. He decided that the best thing to do was to approach the problem quite objectively—not to press the museum's claim in any way. He started with Ireland, and Joyce's physical links with Dublin, the setting of all his books. The National Library of Ireland would be the right choice there. . . . France had made Joyce welcome as no other country had done and the Bibliothèque Nationale was one of the great libraries of the world. . . . Though he thought it would not remain so for long, American Joyce scholarship was still ahead of British, and Buffalo, with its large Joyce collection, ought to be considered. . . . The Bodleian would suit her own connection with Oxford, and the rebel and exile Shelley would be a worthy companion. . . . But the British Museum was the seat of English literature and English was the language in which Joyce wrote.

---

* *James Joyce's World*, London, Methuen, 1957, has a chapter, 'London (The Literary Background) 1914–1919', for which Harriet Weaver provided much material. She always asked Patricia Hutchins, 'with a little laugh', to withdraw whatever was said about her help to James Joyce; but later, in order not to disappoint her, always let her put it in, slightly redrafted. (Notes by Patricia Hutchins, March 1969)

That night, Harriet despatched to George Painter a note to say that she had decided on an outright and immediate gift to the Museum; and the next day, before returning to Oxford, she went to the Department of Manuscripts to arrange for collection from Rawlinson Road.

Then came the disagreeable task of breaking the news to Dr Hayes, a task made a little less disagreeable, however, by her realization that she could do something to soften the blow to his hopes—and to her own. When she had explained her decision, and expressed her deep regret, she went on:

I did not discuss with Mrs Joyce the disposal of the manuscript of *A Portrait of the Artist as a Young Man* which Mr Joyce gave me a long time ago. I should like to give this to the National Library of Ireland if you would care to have it. It is really a fair copy made for the typist and without corrections. . . . I should also be pleased to give you for the library—and I think Lucia Joyce would be pleased too—the wonderful illuminated initial letters she made (urged on by her father) for the Chaucer A.B.C. I do not know how I could get these to you, not liking to trust them to the post. Would it be possible, I wonder, for the conveyance to be arranged through the Irish Embassy in London if I were to deposit them there one day? . . .* [46]

Dr Hayes gratefully accepted the two gifts and went on: 'We know and appreciate here the wonderful support you gave for so many years to Mr Joyce's work and Ireland is under a very great debt to you for all that'.[47] His disappointment about *Finnegans Wake* was, understandably, keen: 'The Joyce family seem determined that we shall have as little as possible, why I do not know. We have Shaw and Yeats material and have always purchased any Joyce items that we could. . . . You must do, of course, whatever you think best . . . but if you still feel you must give them to [the British Museum] I must say that I think it is the next best place to deposit them. I wonder what would Joyce himself have wished?'[48]

The day he wrote, Wednesday, 27th June 1951, Julian Brown and Godfrey Davis, two members of the Department of Manuscripts, arrived at Rawlinson Road to collect the gift.† Harriet inspired them

* In 1951, with a change in her relationship with the Commonwealth, Ireland was represented in London by an Ambassador, not, as formerly, by a High Commissioner.

† Julian Brown was later appointed Professor of Palaeography at King's College, University of London.

both with 'some awe'. After 'a very good tea, on small tables', when Julian Brown felt that his feet were growing larger and larger, to the point where they were about to knock his table over, their hostess announced that she had revoked the codicil to her Will in favour of the N.L.I. and handed over the parcelled-up manuscripts. Her synopsis, twenty-one pages long, and prepared by her for the presentation, was with them.*[49] For good measure, she had added also a number of translations of *Ulysses* and other works not in the library and a complete set of *The New Freewoman* and of *The Egoist*, which, she had been surprised to find, the library lacked also.[†]

A few days later, Harriet went up to London again to keep the engagement, made for her by Dr Hayes, with the Irish Ambassador, F. H. Boland. She brought with her Patricia Hutchins, who carried the rather heavy package containing the fair copy of *A Portrait* and Lucia's *lettrines*.[50] The Ambassador had always thought of her as 'a well-to-do patroness of James Joyce's work' and his impression, when she was announced, was of someone 'rather demure and unobtrusive', in attitude 'rather business-like and purposeful'.[51] Harriet, never anxious for formalities or praise, no doubt wanted the presentation over as quickly as possible and listened, motionless, to his expression of thanks for her 'munificent benefaction'.[52]

The presentation made, Harriet seemed to regard the occasion as ended but at this point Mr Boland began to talk about James Joyce and her face lighted up. He had been, he told her, at the same schools—at Clongowes and at Belvedere—and, when at the Irish Embassy in Paris in 1932–34, had met him frequently: 'Joyce was always prepared to listen to Dubliners born and bred like myself!'[53] Harriet was delighted and thereupon announced that she wanted to give the portrait by Wyndham Lewis to the National Gallery of Ireland but did not know how to get it there. When Mr Boland undertook to send it with the other gifts, she asked Dr Hayes to ring up the Curator to tell him to expect it.[54] And she returned to London the next week and handed it over.[‡]

* Harriet Weaver sent a copy of this synopsis to John Slocum, who thought it had been prepared especially for him and Herbert Cahoon. When, in 1953, she saw this stated in their *James Joyce Bibliography* she was a good deal put out.

† In October 1951, Harriet Weaver presented to the British Museum, as an additional gift, the galley and page proofs of *The Egoist* instalments of *A Portrait of the Artist as a Young Man* with the deleted passages added at the time, to make a complete text; and with corrections in James Joyce's hand.

‡ Harriet Weaver brought with her, as well, a copy of the Chaucer ABC, to keep Lucia Joyce's *lettrines* company at the National Library.

This additional gift to Dublin was followed, a little later and with as little ceremony, by another. In a further effort to make amends to the National Library, Harriet gave it her No 1 copy of the very first edition of *Ulysses*—again via the Embassy, because she was so nervous of the post.[55] James Joyce had inscribed it to her at the head of the fly-leaf 'in token of gratitude'. At the foot, she inscribed it herself: 'I give this first copy of *Ulysses* to the National Library of Ireland after thirty years'; and dated the gift 'St Patrick's day 1952'. The gift delighted Dr Hayes.

Harriet was in her element. That same March, she walked to the Bodleian carrying in her open-top bag (without which she rarely went out) the copy of her first edition of *A Portrait* in which she had added, for her second edition, all the hundreds of corrections, mostly of punctuation, sent her by James Joyce; and, learning that they would like to have it, she left it there. The gift was made, perhaps, as a mark of gratitude for the many hours she had spent at the Bodleian working on her symposium and deciphering microfilmed letters for Stuart Gilbert.

A start had been made in putting her affairs in order; and Harriet's own natural selflessness and her sense of James Joyce's greatness had combined to dictate how it should be done. Now, in her seventy-sixth year, she decided that her remaining literary treasures must also be transferred from her own, private, ownership to public owner-ship.

Her collection of James Joyce books, nearly forty inscribed by him, and a number of rare books about him and rare periodicals containing his work, such as the *Ulysses* issues of *The Little Review*, presented at first rather a problem. She did not want the collection dispersed, as she believed it would be if given to a library. She wanted students to see, read and handle the books as part of a permanent collection. She was rather stuck for a suitable legatee until a young Wadham friend of Campbell's, J. B. Bamborough, a Joyce enthusiast,* suggested the National Book League.[56] The League welcomed her offer and readily undertook to observe the conditions she proposed to lay down—among others, that the books should not be lent.†

---

* Then a fellow of Wadham and Tutor in English, later appointed Principal of Linacre College.

† On learning that the National Book League had little money, Harriet Weaver decided to make an additional bequest to it of £50 for the purchase of a glass-fronted bookcase for the protection and display of the collection, when the time came.

Forty-six leaves of notes on the last seven episodes of *Ulysses*, bundled in with the last batch of *Finnegans Wake* manuscripts sent from Paris in 1938, she decided to bequeath to the British Museum.* The most personal and most precious of her treasures, James Joyce's letters to her, she decided to bequeath to it also.

The choice of the museum was a natural one. After a series of visits, to watch the work of preparing the manuscripts for inclusion in its collection, she became attached to the place. Julian Brown, whom Harriet thought 'a very scholarly young man', had been given the task of getting the manuscripts ready for binding. He soon realized that she had made it a comparatively easy one: everything was 'in excellent order, the various instalments of each section identified and briefly labelled'. His only changes were made 'with the object of adjusting her arrangement, here and there, to fit in with the Department's accepted method of arranging papers and cataloguing them. There was next to no real work left to be done, apart from the normal checking', though, even so, it took nearly a year. An odd sheet turned out to be misplaced, and there were about two dozen sheets that she had failed to place at all.[57] These sheets, 'a batch of jumbled pages', had arrived 'at the very last', when the Joyces were moving out of the rue Edmond Valentin.[58] Some were identified before binding by George Painter; and those that baffled even him were later identified by Matthew Hodgart (then librarian of Pembroke College, Cambridge), one of the first scholars to work on the manuscripts.

Julian Brown, who met Harriet about half a dozen times when she came to the museum to see the progress he had made, 'never lost the feeling that she was, without making the least effort in that direction, a formidably superior person'. Having been misled, before he met her, by George Painter, he went for several years under the delusion that she was American and was astonished, in the end, to be told she was not. He had met a number of New England ladies of her generation; and it seemed to him that she and T. S. Eliot, whom he had also met, had a great deal in common 'in the matter of extreme quietness and extremely fine discrimination in all things. . . . Being quiet, courteous, serious and good, she seemed to take for granted the same virtues in anybody she spoke to'; and that, he supposed, was why she

* A little later, Walton Litz worked on these notes in Oxford, when writing his thesis. After he had published an article on them (in the review of the Modern Languages Association of America) Harriet Weaver decided, in July 1958, to give them to the museum straight away.

'didn't think it necessary to use many words' and never had to speak for long. He looked forward to her visits and soon came 'to feel fondness for her as well'.[59]

When at last, in the summer of 1952, the manuscripts (with her synopsis) were bound in their nineteen volumes, Harriet made another visit and 'was surprised and a little upset to find that the donor's name appeared on the binding'.[60] This jarring note, however, did not spoil the happiness of the visits to the department, not least the happiness of getting to know more members of a new generation of admirers of James Joyce and to share their interest. At the end of his year's work, Julian Brown 'never got over a sense of fraudulence' when she, 'of all people', asked him what he thought of *Finnegans Wake*, as though his opinion was as valuable as her own. For a moment, he hesitated to tell her that he had found it one of the funniest books he had ever read. But he need not have worried. She was 'obviously delighted' to find he shared one of the pleasures she said the book gave her.[61]

Harriet's own understanding and appreciation of the book had, indeed, steadily matured as she went through James Joyce's letters to her and sorted the *Wake* manuscripts. Although she was still, perhaps, unready to acclaim it James Joyce's greatest work, she was now at home with it and had much greater insight into his objectives and methods. Writing a little later to J. S. Atherton, the English Joycean then working on his *Books at the Wake*, she said:

> My view is that Mr Joyce did not intend the book to be looked upon as the dream of any one character, but that he regarded the dream form with its shiftings and changes and chances as a convenient device, allowing the freest scope to introduce any material he wished —and suited to a night-piece.[62]

Her gradual, hard-won appreciation of the book brought her, in her last decade, much satisfaction.

Links with a new generation of students of James Joyce, some young enough to be her grandchildren, multiplied during the nineteen-fifties, as his full stature and the immense possibilities for research offered by his works were increasingly recognized, though these links were broken for several months from the autumn of 1952 when Harriet was at Westwick to be with Mary, who had suddenly become senile and distressed in mind.

After Mary was moved to a nursing home near Oxford (where she died a few months later), Harriet returned to Rawlinson Road and gradually found herself the centre of a changing constellation of students who wrote to her or sought her out. If they turned up with their wives and families, they were all made equally welcome and their children's names were added, in a hand grown even shakier, to her address book.

The help she gave Walton Litz, who came over in the van of American scholars, is typical. He was at Merton, reading for a D. Phil.; his thesis the art of James Joyce.* Two days after he had called on her and plied her with questions, particularly about *Finnegans Wake*, she typed and sent him, unasked, about twenty pages of extracts from letters, carefully chosen to help his work. They were exactly what he needed.[63] This was how another new friendship began.

Then Richard Ellmann, in England and at the beginning of his years of work on his great biography of James Joyce, asked whether he might come to see her. Harriet replied, rather stiffly, that she would not care to give an 'interview' of any kind—he had not, in fact, suggested any such thing—nor did she feel prepared 'to authorise the book in any way, as Mr Joyce authorised Mr Gorman's biography'; but that she would agree to see him 'in a quite informal way'.[64] She was soon disarmed and answering streams of questions on this subject and on that, as best she could. Where were James Joyce's letters to his father? Was there a Dublin Shem and Shaun? When did *Finnegans Wake* begin to gather in his mind? What oculists did he consult in London in 1922?[65]

The following summer, 1954, she had visits from Joseph Prescott and Richard Kain, two American scholars she had not met before, and Richard Ellmann came again, several times, equipped with a dictaphone, an 'intriguing instrument' to Harriet.[66] He sat at her table, going through Joyce letters and dictating extracts. As he got to know her better, he came to admire her very much; and he felt (as he wrote later) that she 'lived like some Jamesian epitome of feminine intelligence and sympathy'.†

* In his preface to *The Art of James Joyce*, Walton Litz says he 'owed the greatest debt of all' to Harriet Weaver. (New York and London. Oxford University Press, 1964)

† (Preface to Volumes II and III of *Letters of James Joyce*, p. xxviii) Richard Ellmann and the publishers dedicated their part in that edition to Harriet Weaver's memory:

The mounting interest in the works of James Joyce, and in the man himself, kept Harriet chained to her desk for longer hours than ever before. She was still, of course, Literary Executrix and, though she would have preferred to have been relieved of the responsibility, still an Administrator of the Joyce Estate. After his mother's death, Giorgio Joyce reappointed her to administer it, with Lionel Monro as Fred Monro's successor; Giorgio and Lucia now divided the income from royalties between them, as provided under their father's Will.

The post-war restrictions that had hampered publishers, in England and on the Continent, had gradually disappeared. The steadily rising demand for the books was being met. Royalties rose. The number of languages into which the works were translated continued to rise and to present new problems. Royalties from Serbo-Croat translations, for example, could be paid only into the Yugo-Slav National Bank, where they were blocked. But Harriet decided to accept this rather than to risk a possible piracy.[67] On the texts of new editions in English, she kept a proof-reader's eye as sharp as it had ever been. No one but she, for example, noticed that a new edition of *Ulysses* had been printed (by an oversight, while the managing director of the firm was away ill) not from its immediate predecessor, in which there were a number of errors, but from their first edition, in which there were twice as many. She sent the firm a four-page list of *errata*: had a slip, checked by her, put into all the unsold copies; and arranged that, when the time came, the text of the next edition be submitted to her before publication.[68] All illustrations she scrutinized closely, too, with Helen Saunders at her side to help her make up her mind. Most of Robin Jacques' illustrations for Jonathan Cape's new edition of *A Portrait* she liked very much, but not the frontispiece. He had made the 'chief figure' 'too stolid, insensitive, heavy-jowled and policemanlike—in fact the typical policeman'.[69] Only when the drawing was resubmitted, with the 'jowliness' removed, did she pass it for publication.[70]

The same close scrutiny was given to drafts based on Joyce texts: Harriet returned for revision, more than once, a stage adaptation of *Ulysses* where, among other things, Molly and Milly were mixed up and Stephen was given—eighteen times—words originally spoken by his father.[71] Most of the drafts, however, earned her approval and it was an added pleasure when authors came to discuss their ideas with

'Her generosity, her literary judgment, her intelligence and tact, establish her among the true patrons of English letters. . . .'

her. She particularly enjoyed a visit from Donald Jonson and Clifford Williams to talk over their plans for adapting *A Portrait* and *Stephen Hero* as a play,* because she saw at once that they were anxious to give 'as faithful a rendering as they could of the character and mind of Stephen Dedalus'.[72]

By the mid-fifties, applications for permission to quote took up a lot of time and often gave rise to delicate issues. The Administrators' policy was to allow serious students to quote what they wanted to quote, for a suitable fee; though Harriet always wanted to satisfy herself, before coming to a final decision, that the proposed publication would lead readers back to the original work. But Ben Huebsch thought her 'soft hearted' in her handling of these applications—and was not alone in his opinion.[73] He was against encouraging 'scholarly works' that might be inaccurate and do harm.[74]

The issue came to a head when David Hayman, a young American Joycean, applied for permission to bring together and publish the earliest drafts of *Finnegans Wake*.[75] A rather similar proposal, to publish the first 'fair copies', had already been turned down,† on the ground, as Harriet recalled, 'that it might very likely lead to the substitution by prospective new readers of the outline of the book itself to the detriment of the sale of the latter and also to the detriment of the readers themselves'.[76] But David Hayman's proposal did not seem to her, or to Faber, open to this criticism. She decided to approve it, if The Viking Press could be persuaded to agree. And they did agree.‡ Though her generous policy towards the younger generation bent on 'scholarly works' was clearly tinged with sentiment, it was, in the event, justified. She was 'soft-hearted' but not soft-headed. The younger generation did not let her down.

The first full list of James Joyce's book reviews and other critical writings, published in John Slocum's and Herbert Cahoon's *Bibliography*, generated a crop of applications to use the same material. Harriet found it 'rather awkward' adjudicating between them. She disliked disappointing any serious student but her first concern was to be scrupulously just.

* Later produced by the BBC.

† The proposal was discussed at a meeting at the British Museum, attended by Harriet Weaver, Peter du Sautoy (for Faber), Lionel Monro, Julian Brown and George Painter.

‡ *A First-Draft Version of Finnegans Wake* was published by the Texas University Press in 1963 and by Faber and Faber the same year.

In August 1954, while she was considering the rival bids, Stanislaus Joyce arrived in England with a party of students from Trieste, his first visit for nearly thirty years. Harriet went to London to see him. She had never met him before and never met him again. In the course of their long talk, he told her that his journey had been 'a great strain —very crowded, so much so that he had had to stand in the corridor a great deal of the way'; and soon after he arrived he had had 'an unpleasant attack which a doctor he consulted attributed to the heart'.[77] Harriet was worried by his state of health. She was also, for a moment, rather taken aback when she learned of his long-cherished hope of publishing his own annotated edition of the critical writings. He let fall that he had not known that his list of them was to be included in the *Bibliography*. 'I alone,' he added, 'had a complete list of the book reviews my brother wrote in Dublin. As I always believed in him, I had kept them from the beginning'.[78] Harriet was wondering how it was going to be possible to reconcile Mr Stanislaus Joyce's family claims with the fact that he had entered the lists rather late, when he told her that he was asking the American scholar, Ellsworth Mason, to be his collaborator. As Ellsworth Mason had been the first to put in an application, her problem was happily solved.*

A very different problem confronted Harriet soon after her meeting with Stanislaus Joyce: that of 'the Fleischmann letters'. Some months before he left Zurich in 1919, James Joyce had caught sight of a beautiful young woman at the door of her house. She reminded him strongly of the girl he had seen paddling with her skirt tucked up, the 'wild angel' who had called him 'to recreate life out of life' and whose 'image had passed into his soul for ever'.[79] The coincidence affected him deeply. In the following months, he watched Marthe Fleischmann from his window, talked to her if they met in the street; and, on his birthday, took her briefly to the studio in which Frank Budgen was working. There, much to his friend's amusement, he staged a candlelit ceremony to celebrate Candlemas—and the discovery of a model, beautiful and what's more lame, for his own 'Nausikaa'.

He also wrote her four letters. In 1948, when she was ill and had lost her money, she sold them to the Professor of English in Zurich University, Heinrich Straumann. Their existence became known. Both Faber and The Viking Press came to the conclusion that their

---

* Stanislaus Joyce died a few months later and his full plans were never realized. But he edited, with Ellsworth Mason, *The Early Joyce: The Book Reviews, 1902–1903*. Colorado Springs, Mamalujo Press, 1955.

49 Muriel Weaver in the drawing-room at
Castle End

50 Lucia Joyce's sketch of Harriet,
2nd October 1961

51 Sylvia Beach and Harriet, at the *Paris in the Twenties* exhibition, in 1960

omission from the volume of letters would be more damaging to the author's reputation than their inclusion in it. Harriet agreed. As T. S. Eliot pointed out to her, there appeared to be nothing in the least scandalous about the affair and the letters themselves were 'of a touching simplicity'.[80] But Giorgio (whom Harriet and Lionel Monro felt they should, in this instance, carry with them), after giving his consent, withdrew it. Harriet urged on him the wisdom of 'early and responsible publication' and the unwisdom of suppression, which might arouse just the sort of suspicions that he would not like.[81]

Before he had time to reply, Harriet heard from Stuart Gilbert, who turned out to be absolutely opposed to publication: '. . . Joyce . . . had, as you know, a strong family feeling, deep love for his wife and a rare sense of personal dignity. Indeed I can't help feeling I would be playing false to a friendship whose memory I cherish if I connived at the "broadcasting" of these letters. . . . It is not a question of Victorian propriety (which means little to me and meant little to Joyce) but one of loyalty and deference to what our dead friend would probably have wished had he foreseen this discovery at Zurich'.[82]

Stuart Gilbert's plea made Harriet waver. 'I am now in a state of perplexity,' she wrote to T. S. Eliot, 'feeling I did not allow sufficient weight, as Mr Gilbert most loyally has done, to what Mr Joyce himself would be likely to have wished. . . . You will think me a most exasperating person for this vacillation. . . . It is perhaps too late for me to withdraw now but I think Mr Gilbert's views should be seriously considered.'[83]

T. S. Eliot was, indeed, upset and annoyed—though he did not tell Harriet so.[84] Ben Huebsch was brought in to try to persuade Stuart Gilbert to change his mind and shot off to Paris a long and able re-capitulation of the case for publication, including the argument that suppression might tempt somebody to 'create spurious letters for publication or sale.[85] No denial would ever catch up with such a fake'. He did not succeed. Then Stephen Joyce, to whom Harriet had allowed Stuart Gilbert to show the letters, wrote to her in consternation at the idea of publication; and insisted that his most wonderful and understanding 'Nonno', a proud family man, would have been against it.[86] As Giorgio was still adamant in refusing his assent, Harriet had to conclude that the very strong wishes of the son and the grandson must be allowed to prevail.*

* The four letters, with an introductory note by Professor Straumann, were eventually published in 1966 in *Letters of James Joyce*, Volume II.

The repercussions of her decision were still a subject of correspondence between London, New York, Paris and Zurich when, in the spring of 1955, Stuart Gilbert announced the completion 'at last' of the volume of letters; and, in May, the typescript arrived for Harriet's scrutiny. It took her a fortnight to go through and to type her comments for Faber, with copies for Stuart Gilbert and Ben Huebsch. The Introduction seemed to her 'good', though she 'figured in it a bit too much' for her liking;[87] and a quoted remark of Ezra Pound's that 'Miss Weaver *is* The Egoist . . . and Miss Marsden only the titular editor' she asked to have deleted because it was 'not true'.[88] Then Peter du Sautoy brought down Ben Huebsch, now on the point of retirement, and they all lunched at the Mitre to review progress. Harriet produced a photograph of the Joyce family in 1924 which, they all agreed, would make a splendid frontispiece.

Maude and Campbell had by now had so many glimpses of Harriet's comings and goings as Literary Executrix that they came to the conclusion that she ought to publish her recollections of her Egoist days, and urged her to do so. Campbell even went so far as to enlist in this cause his Wadham friend, John Bamborough. But Harriet refused. She was, in any case, 'toiling at typing' something else—her symposium on *Time*. She had despaired of finding a publisher and was now cutting down her thousand pages to under two hundred. This meant leaving out the five chapters salvaged from Dora's unpublished book *Time and the Homo-centric Universe*.

Harriet felt she must do something about them before she became 'totally senile'.[89] That prospect had haunted her since Mary's last sad months, although she was still as clear-headed as ever, and indeed, until the end of her life, showed signs of age only by occasional verbal slips. 'Don't listen to what I say,' she would exclaim, 'listen to what I mean.'[90] So it was with some sense of urgency that, as no publisher would consider extracts from an unfinished book, she arranged for Dora's five chapters to be printed by the Holywell Press. For the cover, she chose black on yellow—night and day—because she liked it so much, and the production turned out well.* It was a satisfaction to send out complimentary copies to university libraries, and a few review copies to the press. She was delighted also that the university bookshops, Blackwell's and Parker's, and Foyle's and Harrods in London, took some copies to sell.[91]

* *The Philosophy of Time* by Dora Marsden. Oxford. The Holywell Press, 1955. 34 pages.

By the end of 1955, Harriet had finished pruning her symposium on *Time* and bound the twenty-seven sections, with a preface, index and bibliography, in seven manila folders. These she deposited in the Oxford Philosophy Library in Merton Street, though with little hope that her work would ever be consulted except by 'some misguided research student once in a hundred years'.* [92] As for her other, long-neglected, symposium on *Space*, that would, as she told Sylvia, 'probably find its destiny in the waste paper basket'.[93] And there, indeed, it ended up shortly afterwards. So ended the work begun, at Dora's instigation, more than three decades before, but which, over the years, had gradually lost its appeal.

The year 1955, one of almost unrelieved desk work, ended with a jolt. Mrs Saunders, now ninety-five, was beginning to fail, though she still gardened occasionally; and Helen and her sister told Harriet that they would not be keeping on the house after their mother died. The news was a shock and Harriet did not know what to do. She was too old, in her eightieth year, to take a flat, even if she could afford it; and she could not reconcile herself to going into a residential home, where she could have around her only a very few of her own things and hardly any of her books.

Muriel, Alfred's widow, proposed a solution. She had moved to a house, Castle End, on the outskirts of Saffron Walden, in Essex, to be near her daughter's farm. Would Harriet come to live with her? Harriet went down, in April 1956, for a longish visit (the galleys of the volume of letters catching up with her there) to see whether the idea would work. Though Muriel's drawing-room was lined with books, they had been Alfred's: she herself was unbookish to a degree. But, since Harold's death in 1905, when they had walked over Hampstead Heath together day after day in silence, she had been one of the very few people in whom Harriet sometimes confided. Harriet knew that Muriel was fond of her and that, in some curious way, she understood her.

'Since you were here I have thought a lot about it,' Muriel wrote after the visit. 'About being a noose round my neck, we have each to get older and perhaps feebler in some way or another but I feel you will be patient with me & I should love to be able to care for you. If the noose got too tight round either of our necks, then something surely could be arranged to slacken it. I should thoroughly *hate* you

* In twelve years, one student, at least, did.

435

to live anywhere by yourself, glorious though you may think complete freedom would be. . . . But I know . . . what you would be losing by not living in Oxford.'[94] Harriet, after a good deal of deliberation, decided to accept; and a little later, when Mrs Saunders fell and broke her thigh, she was thankful the decision had been made.

After a spell in hospital, when the bone was pinned—dismissed by her as 'an interesting experience'—Mrs Saunders returned to Rawlinson Road little the worse, though not able to walk. Harriet felt, however, that she ought to make a start on preparing for the move to Saffron Walden by doing something about her books, which had gradually overflowed into three other rooms, one of them on the floor above hers.

She had, some time before, decided to turn into a gift her bequest to the National Book League of her 'James Joyce collection'. Now, as part of the work of weeding out, she made up her mind to make the gift as soon as possible; and, after her usual visit to Edith at Margate, began putting the collection together.

Parting with them was not easy: they were among her most personal possessions. Indeed, the inscriptions epitomize the author's relations with her:

> 1917—To an unknown and generous friend in gratitude for
> a munificent gift
> 1924—To Harriet Weaver his guest today
> 1926—ad Enrichetta Weaver omaggio riconoscente dello
> scritore
> 1934—To Harriet Weaver publisher of the first English
> edition [of *Ulysses*] this first American edition after
> twelve years
> 1937—With the compliments of James Joyce [A typed slip][95]

Most of the books given to her as presents she had already said she would give also, an idea suggested by Joseph Prescott, when working in London on *Ulysses*.[96] These too she brought together; but, after handling them again, felt she could not part with them all—yet. She put aside the first present, *The Book of Kells*, and the last two, those for 1936 and 1937.

In the middle of this work, a physical and emotional strain, Sylvia wrote—from Connecticut. Adrienne Monnier had died the previous summer, at 12 rue de l'Odéon, after a long and distressing illness; and

Sylvia had gone to stay with her sister Holly and to discuss with her New York publishers her now almost completed memoirs. Harriet invited her, for the two nights of her stop-over in London at the end of October, to stay at the club in Cavendish Square she had joined when appointments in London began to multiply. It had proved most useful, though 'full of old fogeys'. Sylvia, who arrived for breakfast, agreed: they ate in 'a dining room full of sweet low voiced ladies with rheumatism and rather protruding teeth'.[97]

The two friends were delighted to meet again, though a jarring note was struck when Sylvia showed Harriet what she had written about the first Egoist edition of *Ulysses*; Sylvia saw that she was 'quite upset' by a particular passage and decided to 'skip it' as 'darned petty'.[98] But the writing of her memoirs had revived old resentments about what, to her mind, had seemed precipitate and ill-considered arrangements for an edition to follow her own first before it 'had even reached all the subscribers'.[99] When Sylvia left to fly on to Paris, however, they had forgotten their differences. Harriet had been to see Lionel Monro about the Joyce copyright material Sylvia wanted to use and they had agreed not to charge her; 'all their little matters' were settled 'very amicably'.[100]

Larger, and more immediate, matters were occupying Harriet's mind. Hungary, a Soviet satellite, was showing signs of a return to fascism—or so it seemed to her. Imre Nagy, a former Prime Minister, recently condemned for 'rightist deviationism' but now 'rehabilitated' and again in power, had promised a programme of 'democratisation'. He had the country solidly behind him. But an ousted opponent, Gerö, appealed to Russia for help and Soviet troops were already fighting widespread insurrection. For Harriet, the rightness of the Soviet cause was put beyond question when—on the day she returned to Oxford—Cardinal Mindszenty, the Hungarian Primate, to her the personification of all that was retrograde, was released by Imre Nagy from eight years' detention and was reported as saying: 'We shall start all over again'. Fighting throughout the country became more savage; and on Saturday, 4th November 1956 Budapest was bombed from the air.

The next day, Harriet and a small group of comrades were at an open-air meeting in St Giles when they were joined by a young man from the *Daily Worker*. He told them the news had just come through that at least ten thousand Hungarian workers had been killed. The dead had not been counted. Harriet, motionless and silent, 'withdrew into herself'. It was plain to Mick Leahy that she 'did not like the news at all'. Yet, when he met her again a few days later, and Soviet tanks were patrolling a prostrate Hungary, she had, somehow, convinced herself that Russia had done right. 'Against fascism, one must use violence. There must be no going back,' she said;[101] and the resignation from the party, then and there, of many of her friends, though it saddened her, did not make her change her mind.

Harriet's ideas on *Finnegans Wake* had developed steadily. Her political ideas had become fixed. She was as doctrinaire, in her way, as the evangelicals from whose influence she had sought to escape in her youth: her own need for absolutes had proved as inescapable as theirs.

The day after the news from Hungary, Mrs Saunders, who had been keeping much the same and having great jokes with her doctor, suddenly became very ill indeed;[102] two days later the gift to the National Book League was collected by two young women members of the staff with a van—'something of a wrench' to Harriet;[103] and four days later Mrs Saunders, to whom she was devoted, died. After the funeral, Harriet tried to steel herself against the day when the house would be given up, by going on with the sorting of her books. She plodded upstairs and down, building piles for throwing away, for giving away, for Saffron Walden. But she was already over-strained. She had a severe heart attack.

Mrs Saunders' doctor (Harriet had never had one of her own) sent her to bed and kept her there for four weeks. Helen, who had been helping to nurse her mother, now nursed Harriet. Miss Saunders lent a hand whenever she could; Maude looked in every day and Campbell very often. For Harriet, it was 'so strange to be ill'; and, of course, she hated being 'a nuisance'. But she was a rewarding patient: in the week before Christmas, the 'jitterings' stopped; and on Christmas day she was allowed downstairs to make the two-minute drive, chauffered by Robin, to the Hones for tea.[104]

No one awaited bulletins more eagerly than Patricia Hutchins. With the help of her husband, Robert Greacen, she had organized a commemorative dinner, to be held in the Kensington Restaurant in Church Street, near the Joyces' ill-fated flat and Ezra Pound's haunts, for the thirty-fifth anniversary of the publication of *Ulysses* and for what would have been the seventy-fifth birthday of James Joyce, 2nd February 1957.

Harriet had liked the idea and had agreed to come as a guest of honour; and T. S. Eliot and Stephen Spender had accepted invitations to be guests of honour also. But, unknown to Harriet, lest she took fright, she was to be the toast of the evening. Admirers of James Joyce were being gathered together to pay her tribute not only for her encouragement of him and of other authors but also for the great help she had given to Joyce students all over the world; and T. S. Eliot had told Patricia Hutchins that he wanted to speak his own 'praise and gratitude to her'.[105]

In the weeks after Christmas, however, Harriet made slower progress. She had still to breakfast in bed and to rest between lunch and tea. It did not seem possible that she would be fit enough to attend. But she was, just. On the morning of the dinner, in her god-daughter's flat on Campden Hill, she noticed in 'Today's Arrangements' in *The Times*, propped up on her bed table (the *Daily Worker* having thoughtlessly not been provided): 'The Archbishop of Canterbury consecrates . . . . Enthronement of the Bishop of Ely. . . . James Joyce commemorative dinner . . .'. 'This is going to be quite an occasion, is it?' she asked, a little puzzled. And when the news was broken to her that Stephen Spender had flu, and that Mr Eliot would not be there either —as he explained to her afterwards, he had just married and had gone into hiding in an attempt (not altogether successful) to avoid the press on returning from the honeymoon—she grasped only slowly that she would now be the sole guest of honour.

For the dinner, Harriet dressed from head to foot in black and coaxed the collar of her dress half an inch higher up her neck with the aid of a safety-pin-like gold brooch. She was adamant that her shawl must be black also. For a woman of her age, any colour would be 'quite unsuitable'. There was a moment of anxiety, on arriving at the restaurant because, after two months' seclusion, she found the sudden babble of talk and the milling faces confusing. But once Peter du Sautoy, who was presiding, had placed her on his right in the middle of the open E in which the long tables were arranged, she was serene, or, as she told him, 'much less terrified' than she 'had every right to feel in the absence of Mr Eliot, thanks to his very kind support and the friendliness of everyone'.[106] Between the candles, appropriate for Candlemas, she glimpsed Matthew Hodgart, John Bamborough, Lionel Monro, Tony and Alla, Patricia and Robert, her god-daughter; and on Mr du Sautoy's left was Mr Joyce's nephew Paddy, Eileen Schaurek's son, representing the family. Some faces she did not know—Osbert Lancaster . . . Anthony Powell.

The meal over, telegrams from T. S. Eliot and Ben Huebsch were read out and Peter du Sautoy, by now a staunch admirer, spoke movingly about her achievements: the whole English-speaking world was in her debt. When Patricia Hutchins had proposed and Matthew Hodgart had seconded the toast, Harriet, like a black swan, rose to reply. 'I will say,' she said, 'only what Mr. Joyce said on a previous occasion: thank you.'* The evening ended with Allan McClelland, the Irish actor, reading, with enormous verve and to everyone's delight, passages from the *Cyclops* episode of *Ulysses*.†

Harriet, for once, was content not to efface herself and was touched by the tribute that had been paid her, though the dinner had, perhaps, been something of an ordeal. The next day, however, she was more at ease and amused herself writing in the margin of the notes—and compliments—about her in the printed dinner programmes: 'False, dear Mr Pound', 'Many grains of salt required'; and sending copies to nieces. Then, in the evening, at her invitation, Paddy, and his fiancée, called on her. His Irish voice and his long head were evocative. The talk turned to his uncle's parties in Paris. All at once, Harriet rose from the sofa and steadied herself for a moment on the arm. Then she pulled out her black dress to either side and gave a three-second imitation of Mr Joyce pulling out his trousers as though they were a skirt and doing his imitation of an Irishwoman dancing a jig.

---

* 'Thank you' was James Joyce's reply when, on 5th April 1927, he was the guest of honour at the PEN Club dinner, presided over by John Drinkwater.

† Allan McClelland was then working on his play *Bloomsday*, based on *Ulysses*.

20

CASTLE END

'I was a little busy in London,' was all Harriet would say, on her return to Oxford, in answer to enquiries from Christopher and Bridget Hill. They had seen the notices in the press about the dinner and would have liked to hear more.* But, as she seemed a little embarrassed, they changed the subject. When could she come to their house for a farewell party? They wanted to gather together all her communist friends, whether still party members or not, to say good-bye. They were all going to miss her very much when she left.

The farewell, in March 1957, was marked by a presentation. As a last-minute surprise and token of affection, they all signed their names in a book of photographs of Oxford.[1] Harriet knew she was going to miss them very much too. With Maude and her family they had made up her Oxford circle. At Saffron Walden, she was going to be cut off from them; and she felt—though, as it turned out, wrongly—that Joyce students could hardly be expected to find their way to a small market town down a branch line in rural Essex. Only Matthew Hodgart, at Cambridge, would be anywhere near. On the other hand, the house itself, Castle End, now had an unforeseen advantage: her bedroom would be on the ground floor.

The warmth of her welcome from Muriel and from Rosemary and her husband and their two boisterous little boys, Tim and Jamie, when they came over from their farm to greet her, meant much. A few days later, when her furniture arrived and Frank Budgen's paint-ing of the Liffey was hung in the usual place of honour over the

* The *Manchester Guardian* had an appreciative notice of the commemorative dinner but described Harriet Weaver as 'easily recognizable as the daughter of a long line of leading evangelical laymen'. (The *Manchester Guardian*, 3rd February 1957)

mantelpiece, her room became her own. She soon settled into a comfortable routine with breakfast in her room and two short walks every day across the common or to post letters, often accompanied by Muriel, who shared the Weaver passion for fresh air; and when the weather was mild enough, she waged war on dandelions in the garden.

Waging war on capitalism could be done, now, only vicariously. Saffron Walden offered no opportunities for her own brand of political action. But Harriet kept in constant touch with all the doings of the Oxford City Branch, down to the latest jumble sale; and continued to support (as well as to read) the *Daily Worker*. Barbara Niven, the Secretary of its People's Press Fighting Fund, had become a friend since they had met at a conference in Oxford, and—a rare honour now occasionally accorded to members of the younger generation— had been invited to call her Harriet. They saw little of one another thereafter but exchanged greetings every month, when Harriet sent her 'guarantee' to the Fund. The letters she wrote (like those of other supporters) were not kept; but those she received give something of the quality of the relationship: 'How clearly you see things! A very heartwarming piece of perspicacity . . .'; and (of special help one month) 'Harriet, that was lovely of you and ever so like you'.[2] With Angela Tuckett, the Manager and Assistant Editor of *Labour Monthly*, she continued a correspondence already of eight years' standing; and her words, 'always so apt and to the point', were often quoted, anonymously, in the column about readers, much to her amusement.[3]

Though Muriel had good daily help in the house and in the kitchen, Harriet insisted on making her own bed and dusting her own room, an operation that always included dusting the back of each picture; and on Saturdays, despite Muriel's protests, sometimes marked her independence by 'turning it out' herself. Muriel protested also at the hours she spent at her desk and, when Harriet admitted that she must delegate some of the work, urged her to do it quickly. In the evenings, at least, Harriet joined her in the drawing-room. She sat on the sofa, away from the fire, with a book or sewing, trying to keep awake so as to be sure of sleep during the night.[4]

This peaceful round was interrupted by a plea for her help as an Administrator of the James Joyce Estate. She responded to it, as she had to a long line of others, with her usual objectivity. But, unlike these others, it had unforeseen consequences for her. Joseph Prescott wrote from Paris to ask her, if she were sufficiently recovered, to meet him in London on 'a matter of grave importance'. She had no idea what this was until a letter from Sylvia arrived a few days later.[5]

Sylvia had always allowed students to consult and to make extracts from the manuscripts James Joyce had given her; and Joseph Prescott, who had worked on them at intervals from 1954, had returned from the United States, with his wife and daughter, for a final session at the rue de l'Odéon. 'They have such family affection and such a kind way with everybody—they are wonderful,' Sylvia had written at Christmas. 'I work on my job in the kitchen, but once in a while there's a tap on the door and there's Joe showing me something on Joyce he wants me to see. . . . He is a really good fellow.'[6]

Sylvia had put aside her memoirs in order to finish the 'job' of cataloguing her precious collection of Joyce manuscripts and letters, which she hoped to sell to an American university library. She was now seventy and wanted security for her old age. But, then, a London bookseller she had consulted warned her that the prior publication of any 'item' would halve its selling price.[7] She did not ask herself whether this advice was, or was not, correct; but concluded on the spot that her open-handed attitude to students had seriously prejudiced her chances of getting the best price, of providing for the future. She told Joseph Prescott that he must cease work. Her decision was a bitter disappointment to him and he reacted sharply. But Sylvia was now seriously alarmed. She flew to Switzerland to ask Bryher's advice. Bryher told her to forget about her collection till she had finished her memoirs. Sylvia did not take her advice but returned to Paris and sought out an old American friend, Jackson Mathews, to ask his. He advised her to urge that no one should be permitted to publish any of her Joyce material. Sylvia wrote in this sense;[8] then changed her mind and sent Harriet, instead, a detailed account of the whole position, as she saw it, in the hope that it would explain itself.[9]

Harriet, now aware of the matter Joseph Prescott wanted to discuss, agreed to meet him, though she was not, in fact, well enough to do so; and, on the day, finding she had 'no brains whatever' during their talk, asked him 'to write in detail'.[10] His work on the evolution of the text of *Ulysses*, begun twenty years before, had been brought to a standstill, at an advanced stage, by his sudden banishment from the rue de l'Odéon. He wanted to establish with the Administrators 'priority of application' against the time when Miss Beach's papers could be studied again—when they had been acquired, as he expected, by an American university library.[11] Harriet came to the conclusion that, as far as she could judge, his case was a good one;[12] and, when Lionel Monro, at first inclined to take Miss Beach's part, came round to the same view, the 'priority of application' was accepted.

Harriet prefaced the announcement of the decision to her old friend by expressions of sympathy in the breakdown of what had seemed a happy friendship. But she had little patience with Sylvia's anxieties about money, which she thought exaggerated, and her announcement of the decision was forthright. She saw 'no harm' in Mr Prescott's proposal, 'seeing that he has done a lot of work on the subject over a number of years—but you will not be interested as to that . . .'.[13]

Sylvia (as she declared to her sister Holly) was 'as mad as could be'. Miss Weaver had brought to an end 'a friendship of about thirty-seven years duration';[14] she was 'so easily persuaded to foolishness by the creatures who flock around her'; and ought no longer to handle 'the Joyce business'.[15] Sylvia's distress was clearly heightened by her unfamiliarity with the principles governing her own rights as owner of manuscripts and those governing the Administrators', as owners of the copyright. Even a year later, she was taking legal advice on her 'case' against the Administrators.[16]

A quarrel was the last thing Harriet wanted and it was some time before she realized that Sylvia had taken the decision so much to heart. Her own mood was one of increasing detachment. Stuart Gilbert's *Letters of James Joyce* was about to appear and an advance copy had arrived.* The letters to her, so long hers alone, were to be broadcast throughout the English-speaking world. As she held the book in her hands and looked back over the years, one figure only stood in the long perspective, that of Mr Joyce; and for publication day, 24th May 1957, she went up and stayed at her club, where she could count on the anonymity that seemed appropriate for the occasion.

A few days later, her god-daughter, to whom she had given a copy of the *Letters*, lunched with her. 'They are a revelation, Aunt Hat,' she said. 'What a marvellous friend you must have been. Always ready to do anything asked of you, always there!' Shaking from head to foot, Harriet burst out, 'I did nothing, *nothing*!' The exclamation seemed to spring less from her usual desire for self-effacement than from a recognition, an acceptance, that what she had done she

* *Letters of James Joyce*, edited by Stuart Gilbert. London. Faber and Faber, 1957. Published in America at the same time by The Viking Press.

had had to do: it was to Mr Joyce that she had had to give that money, he had needed it and he had had to spend it 'like a drunken sailor' to give the world *Ulysses* and *Finnegans Wake*.

It was self-effacement, however, rather than this deep sense of reconciliation with the past, that seemed uppermost in Harriet's bearing at two London events that followed the publication of the *Letters*. On 28th May, the National Book League staged a little ceremony in its noble Georgian house in Albemarle Street for the formal acceptance of the 'James Joyce Collection', which was on view for the first time. Flanked by Muriel, Tony and Alla Weaver, her god-daughter and Patricia Hutchins, Harriet sat, a little tight-lipped, in the second row of chairs, having spurned the first. Robert Frost, a contributor to *The Egoist* long ago, was to have spoken but, over-tired by his London visit, could not come. Percy Muir, the critic, who took his place, spoke of the donor of the collection as 'the person who made Joyce's life as a writer possible—the "unknown and generous friend" to whom the first edition of *Chamber Music* in the collection was inscribed. . . . She had been an entirely undemanding patron . . .'.[17] Harriet had not foreseen 'the fuss' that would be made;[18] and was surprised—even put out—by the half column given to the event in *The Times*'.

The second of the 'crushes', as she called them, was a symposium arranged by the Institute of Contemporary Arts for 18th June to bring together some of the recipients and readers of the *Letters*. Harriet, the chief recipient, agreed to attend on condition she could remain quite 'mum'; and, this time, spurned even the second row. She decided to sit at the back, and to have with her, for her support, her niece Margaret Bruce Lockhart. Peter du Sautoy was in the chair; Allan McClelland read some of the letters; and Patricia, whose travels in search of letters Harriet had followed with so much interest, was among the speakers.[19]

The work as Literary Executrix, and as an Administrator with Lionel Monro of the Estate, was still very demanding. But Harriet had found, at last, a way of reducing the burden. After consulting the Society of Authors, in 1950, on a copyright question, she had realized how useful they could be; and, the following year, had become a member in her two Joyce capacities. The discovery that the Society administered a number of literary estates, including George Bernard Shaw's, eventually led to a decision to ask them to act on behalf of the Joyce Estate; and they had agreed to do so.

Miss Anne Munro-Kerr was in charge of this side of the Society's work; and Harriet now went to see her, to conclude the arrangements worked out by Lionel Monro.[20] The Society would conduct all formal correspondence with publishers and applications for copyright permissions, draw up agreements and collect royalties and fees, and thus take the brunt of the desk work. But the main features of the old dispensation were preserved. The Administrators were to remain owners of the copyright; and 'sole decision in all literary matters' relating to James Joyce's writings 'published and unpublished' would still rest with Harriet. All new questions of policy would be referred to her, as Literary Executrix, or to her and Lionel Monro, as Administrators.

Largely because of the massive bulk of files to be transferred to the Society and to be sorted, to conform with their filing system, it was not until the beginning of 1958 that the pressure of work on Harriet began to slacken. When the arrangement eventually got under way, it went very well. Harriet found Miss Munro-Kerr 'very pleasant and helpful' and most efficient in gathering in all the mounting royalties;[21] and she was impressed by Harriet's 'clearheadedness' and quickness in seizing on the main issues.[22]

Meantime, buoyed up by the prospect of the relief that was in sight, Harriet was irked only by one or two importunate requests for copyright permission from America, which made her feel rather 'short'.[23] She was pleased by a good contract for *A Portrait* in Polish; by enquiries from France and from Germany about possible translations of the *Letters*; and by further progress in planning a second volume, decided upon after Richard Ellmann discovered that Stanislaus Joyce had kept some hundred and fifty letters to Nora Joyce and to himself, many of them of the greatest interest.

Richard Ellmann had been appointed editor—Stuart Gilbert did not wish to take on the work—and Harriet had told him 'there is no one with a greater right than yourself to undertake the task—or who would do it better'.[24] The only question was how soon he could begin. She was relieved when he arranged things so that, instead of starting two years later, he could start in the 'fall'. He had nearly finished his biography and, in August 1958, sent the thirty-seven chapters for Harriet's scrutiny.

She was then making a round of visits and it was a little time before she finished reading the draft and could write: 'You have made Mr Joyce a very living and human figure. I like your Introduction particularly: its sympathetic understanding of your protagonist in his manifold moods and with his two most deeply rooted passions: his work and his family'.[25]

Rounds of visits were still a feature of Harriet's life and were still made regularly. One visit in 1957 was to her niece Mercy in Wiltshire. While she was there, the Russians launched their first satellite and she told her greatniece, Sarah-Jane, then aged five, that there would probably be a real 'Man in the Moon' by the time she was twenty—a prediction that has been fulfilled.[26] On another round, she made the long journey down to Devon, to see her eldest niece Rosamond, her children and the first of her grandchildren: Harriet was now a great-greataunt.

These visits to members of the younger generation had always been a deep pleasure; and so, now, were her visits to Oxford. Harriet missed her old life there and made a point of getting back every six months or so, the 'hithering and thithering' like that of the 'twenties and 'thirties to and from the north, to and from Paris. In Oxford in the autumn of 1958, staying with Maude and Campbell, she saw Ernie Keeling, who had been seriously ill for a long time, and dropped a hint to Betty Cooper, still the branch treasurer, that she could be counted on to go on contributing to a comrade's fund for him if he was unable to find suitable light work. (He became a porter at Exeter College a little later.) Mick Leahy she saw too and was pleased when he told her that some Shop Steward friends, to whom he passed on the copy of the *Labour Monthly* that she sent him after reading it herself, were coming round to its point of view.

Christopher and Bridget Hill, who like everyone else looked forward to her visits, invited her, as usual, to tea. But, this time, much to their surprise, they found themselves the object of one of her rare, split-second flashes of fury. As they were awaiting her, they saw her pass their gate. Harriet had, in fact, as she explained afterwards, merely walked on to get a glimpse of her dear 4 Rawlinson Road before joining them. When she arrived a few minutes later, the Hills teased her for missing the house. 'Of course I knew it!' she retorted, scathingly.[27] They had touched unwittingly on her hidden fear of becoming—or being—senile.

In London, in May 1959, before a visit to Edith at Margate, Harriet went to the first night of Marjorie Barkentin's *Ulysses in Nighttown* at the Arts Theatre, and took with her Tony, Alla and her goddaughter. Zero Mostel, who played Bloom, she thought a 'marvellous' actor, 'a great artist'; and the whole production she thought excellent. She watched, radiant, and determined to see another performance—but the play had been taken to the Continent by the time she tried for a seat.[28]

Harriet's visit to Lucia that autumn was a particularly happy one. Lucia, who had been transferred from North Wales to Northampton, was now much better: new treatment had made 'an enormous difference'.[29] She was writing letters to old friends, going to dances and, in short, though not 'cured', had taken on a new lease of life. She welcomed Harriet with affection, presented her with an amusing red felt dachshund she had made for her birthday and took her for a walk in the grounds.*

Visits away were matched by visits from nieces and nephews and their children and, to her surprise, from Joyce scholars, some newly graduated and some of an older generation, Joseph Prescott, Walton Litz and David Hayman among them. Matthew Hodgart brought over Clive Hart, the Australian scholar, then working at Cambridge, who wished simply to meet her, not to ply her with questions. They came for tea, presided over by Muriel. Clive Hart's first impression, like that of so many before him, was of Harriet's capacity to be still, 'both inside and out. She sat very straight in her chair, a little wispy, but very alert. . . . For some reason Matthew was very nervous, sitting on the edge of his chair and crumbling fruit cake with his fingers'—not the first of Harriet's visitors to find Edwardian drawing-room tea a little nerve-racking, though Clive Hart wondered whether the cake crumbling was not occasioned 'by dismay at any gaucheries committed' by himself.

After tea, Harriet said: 'Do come and see some books,' and carried them off to her room, where she showed them some recent Joyce criticism and some of her few remaining Joyce treasures, which she handled 'not with reverence—that would be far too strong and dramatic a word—but with a very unusual sort of careful movement of the fingers. It sounds idiotic,' Clive Hart recalled, 'but it was almost like a caress.'[30]

J. S. Atherton, who had corresponded with Harriet for some years

---

* A few months later, Lucia Joyce wrote a short essay entitled *The Real Life of James Joyce*. It was rather disjointed, but there was humour in it, and she had interesting things to say, particularly about the origin of the rainbow girls in *Finnegans Wake*. Harriet Weaver typed it for her, after making a special visit to Northampton to check some words in Italian she could not read.

on *Finnegans Wake* and the Joyce family, came twice. On his second visit, they talked, among other things, about the theory he was putting forward (in *The Books at the Wake*) that James Joyce held that the original sin was creation. Harriet was at first prepared to go only as far as saying 'There may be something in what you say'. But when he went on to argue that there was autobiographical support for this in the *Wake*, she agreed and then recalled an incident of which Nora Joyce had told her.

'Lucia had been unusually exasperating and Mrs Joyce had been driven to make use of what she called "an unfortunate expression". Lucia had shouted "And who made me one?" She then refused to speak to her mother for several days and would say nothing to her father except the same thing. Presumably what Lucia kept asking her father was "Who made me a bastard?" It certainly upset Mr Joyce considerably,' Harriet went on, 'and I think it was one of the reasons for his going through a ceremony of marriage—although he always insisted that he and Mrs Joyce were married soon after their arrival in Europe.'[31]

Dora had not written to Harriet—or to anyone else—for some years but shortly after Harriet's move to Castle End she began to write again and, in her Christmas 1958 letter, said that she had been inspired to write one last 'cosmo-historical book. . . . It constitutes the promised *Book of Truth*, which is Heaven's Covenant with Creation'.[32] The book, her '*magnum opus*', had appended to it two autobiographical chapters—to prove her 'bona fides'. Soon she was asking for help in finding a typist. Harriet suggested that her brother Ewart might secure one in Liverpool and added that if she herself were not eighty-three, and if she did not find her writing illegible, she might possibly offer to type it herself.[33] It was an unfortunate aside. Dora seized on the idea, assured 'Josephine' that the manuscript was entirely legible and went on: 'Now Deity has enabled you to help me with such spectacular help & in so many ways during an almost *full half century* that it seems probable that she will help you to complete the full fifty years. . . . You were not your own. *You were a dedicated being.* . . .' She ended by asking her to consider her letter 'carefully & prayerfully'.[34]

Posterity would agree that Miss Weaver/Josephine was 'not her own'. But she had grown firmer with others in old age. Although she was sorry to blight Dora's hopes after inadvertently raising them, she had to do it. Her reply was a firm 'No'. She could not 'pray over the matter. . . . It must be over sixty years since I prayed to any being whom I could regard as divine'. She was very sorry but she could not undertake the typing: '. . . the whole thing would be an inferno'. (Her eyes were now apt to smart in the bright light she needed for writing. She thought she was getting a cataract.) And she repudiated equally firmly Dora's assumption that her help had been divinely ordained: '. . . if it was your Deity who arranged my dedication from before birth . . . she will have to shoulder a not too enviable operation: the encompassing of the death at the age of 14 of my uncle Edward Henry Wright, a healthy and merry boy, in order that his father, my grandfather should not leave the bulk of his fortune to him. . . .'[35]

Harriet's relatively active life was brought to an abrupt stop by an accident in mid-November 1959. She tripped outside her room and fell heavily on her left side. Muriel was with her at once and managed to get her up from the floor and into bed. Harriet was badly bruised and shaken but, worse still, her heart was affected. She was too ill to be nursed at Castle End, even with the help of friends Muriel recruited for the nights; and a few days later she was taken by ambulance to a nursing home in Cambridge. Maude came. But, to everyone's astonishment, Harriet rallied and was well enough to return before Christmas, to be 'pampered by breakfast in bed' and generally cossetted by Muriel who, she exclaimed, was 'marvellously kind and good'.[36] Harriet was, indeed, still very much an invalid—she was not able, for example, even to go on reading Richard Ellmann's biography, now published, 'because of the sheer physical weight of it'.[37]

One good came of the illness, however. It helped Sylvia Beach to feel less coldly. When Harriet was in the nursing home, she was too ill to write her Christmas letter and asked Maude to do so: she had not wanted to quarrel with Sylvia and, as she had continued to write at Christmas in spite of the breach, she wanted to do so now. Maude wrote and ended '. . . my Sister . . . was reading your book [*Shakespeare and Company*, in its American edition, published in 1959] for the second time & asks me to say how much she enjoys it—as it is so well & gaily written & is so interesting'.[38]

Sylvia thought 'Josephine' must have had a stroke; and, yielding to the claims of old friendship, wrote to her and sent a little book with pictures of the windows of Chartres cathedral. Harriet was delighted with the little book and even more delighted with the letter. In the new year, when she herself could again hold a pen, she wrote at length and dwelt particularly on *Shakespeare and Company*. 'I couldn't discover any trace of the agony you went through, forcing yourself to concentrate on the writing of it in spite of splitting headaches so much of the time. . . . And it is such a *live* book. You write so vividly —and charitably!' She added compliments about Sylvia's long-ago appointment to the Legion of Honour and the recent conferment on her of a doctorate of letters at the University of Buffalo, to which her collection had been given by an anonymous, and generous, donor.[39] Sylvia, convinced from the start that Harriet had wanted to break with her, came to the conclusion that she was now 'ready to be on the same friendly footing again poor thing . . .'.[40] At any rate, the breach was healed well enough to enable them, a few months later, to meet.

Sylvia was arranging, at the United States Embassy in London, an exhibition she had put on in Paris the year before, of 'Souvenirs from Shakespeare and Company', *Paris in the Twenties*. At Harriet's suggestion, the National Book League lent several new exhibits from her James Joyce collection.

Harriet was feeling very much better, though she was still subject to fits of giddiness. In June, she went up to London a few days before the opening so as to visit Lucia at Northampton (the journey from Saffron Walden was too difficult); and Barbara Niven, at the *Daily Worker* offices; and to have Sylvia to dinner at her club on Bloomsday, 16th June. 'I couldn't bear to keep up ill feelings,' Sylvia wrote the next day to Holly. ' "Pax Nobis" as Father used to say';[41] and at the opening of the exhibition she seemed to overflow with affection as she greeted her old friend.

After the opening, when it was impossible to see the exhibits, Harriet went twice to *Paris in the Twenties* and wrote to Sylvia to congratulate her and to tell her how much she had enjoyed it.[42] What pleased her most, however, was the warmth that had at last returned to their relationship. Perhaps as a symbol of this, she sent Sylvia for Christmas, which she herself was spending with Maude and Campbell, a Glen Cree 'shawl-wrap, light in weight and very warm'. She had found it in a Saffron Walden wool shop down an 'out of the way street' suggested by Muriel. '. . . they were nearly sold out', she wrote. 'There was no choice in fact between one in the old suffragette colours of mauve, green and white and a pale gray one and when the shopkeeper said that gray was fashionable in Paris just now I decided that of course that would be the one for you!'[43] It was 'a delightful surprize' to Sylvia. 'It's so beautiful and unusual looking,' she wrote, 'and the only thing this can be compared with is the one you gave me long ago, with that mountain design, you will remember. You brought another for Adrienne and she never could do without it, every night in bed, she used to have it around her shoulders and her back, and always took it to Savoie in the summer. I still have mine. . . . But . . . I can economize on coal this winter, now that you have provided me with a mohair stove'.[44] There their correspondence ended—on the sort of domestic note that had always been congenial.

Coaxing Dora to write again had not proved possible. She had ceased to write to anyone. And now came the news that she had died on 13th December 1960, St Lucia's day, of a sudden heart attack.[45] Harriet could feel only relief that the end had come for her poor friend but she was saddened at the thought that she had denied her last plea for help.

When the Reverend James Dyson, Dora's kindly brother-in-law, told Harriet that the family was uncertain what to do about the 'Magnum Opus', still in manuscript, she offered to read it and let him know what she thought about it. As she feared, Dora's last work was not publishable: it bore too many signs of her long illness. But, as though driven by Dora's ghost, she typed out the two almost indecipherable chapters of autobiography; and, when she returned them and the other fourteen chapters to Mr Dyson, she expressed the hope that the family would preserve them.[46]

Dora's death might of itself have turned Harriet's thoughts back to the old days. But in the new year 1961, there came a letter in an unknown hand that was to lead to a correspondence ranging over the years to 1912. The letter was from Bjørn Rasmussen, the Danish film critic and historian and Joyce enthusiast. He was in hospital recovering from a serious pulmonary illness, had just read Richard Ellmann's biography and had been moved to write by what he had learned. It was a 'thrill', he said, to address the 'Dear Miss Weaver' to whom James Joyce had written. Harriet laughed with Muriel about this and protested to him that she was 'a very unpretentious person'.[47] But she was touched, too, and was soon engaged in a correspondence that ended only with her own last illness. She was in a mood for reminiscing and, as always, pleased to indulge an invalid. Little, unexpected sidelights were thrown on some of the subjects he raised. For example, in defending Stanislaus Joyce's attitude towards his brother, she told him that he used to send her a postcard from Trieste signed by all the friends he collected every year to celebrate 'Bloomsday'.[48] And, with Dora in her thoughts, she dwelt on the odd parallelism between her and her other chief protégé: '. . . you speak of Molly Bloom having been called the all-time-female principle (I don't myself think she is big enough for that, but that is by the way) and that the Church Fathers sometimes imagined the Holy Ghost as a female element in the Trinity, and that Mr Joyce when asked by a Danish critic what he thought of this replied "could be, could be". My friend Miss Marsden . . . held that the world had gone wrong because of the "shedding of a God", the Great Almighty Mother Space: the Magnetic Ocean . . .'.[49]

In the spring and summer there was another string of visits from Joyceans, including two specially enjoyable ones from Richard Ellmann. In May, he came down with Peter du Sautoy and his wife.* They wanted to have a talk about what letters to Nora Joyce should be included in the next volume, on which Richard Ellmann had by now done a good deal of work. Many were highly intimate, so that the subject of the talk was, as Harriet put it, 'not altogether straightforward'. In July he came again, this time with his wife and three young children, who, until then, had been only names in her address book. Stephen, the eldest, particularly delighted her by getting through three helpings of a pudding he found to his liking.[50] But most days were given to the quiet Castle End round (broken from time to time by the noisy incursions of Rosemary's two boys, who liked to seek her out). Her favourite job in the garden now was teasing weeds from the tangle of roots of the hedge that skirted the drive, for which she would sit on a camp stool placed by Muriel at the exact angle that would prevent the sun troubling her eyes.

Harriet tired easily since her fall and was ready enough to be cossetted. At the end of September, however, after a visit from Donald Gallup from Yale, who was working on his Ezra Pound bibliography, she went off on a short round of visits. She particularly wanted to go, though Muriel, who knew she had had some disturbed nights, did not think her well enough. From her god-daughter's flat on Campden Hill, she saw some London friends, including Patricia Hutchins, who gave her tea in her house, 10 Church Walk, where Ezra Pound had lived for a time in the *Egoist* days. After tea,

* Mollie du Sautoy was the daughter of Harriet Weaver's tennis-playing friend of the Cedar Lawn days, Phyllis Ford, who married Francis Floud (pronounced Flood). She and her twin brother were born during a heavy thunderstorm. 'The rains descended and the Flouds came,' said the Weavers, misquoting Genesis.

she insisted on walking back up the hill—perhaps to catch a glimpse of the Joyces' old flat in Campden Grove?

Next morning, before going to Northampton, she wrapped in tissue paper and tied with pink ribbon a watercolour paintbox she had bought for Lucia. The neat bow completed, she gazed long and sadly at the packet, as though it epitomized for her the unfulfilled promise of Mr Joyce's daughter.

The welcome at Northampton in the afternoon changed her mood. The two were soon seated on a sofa, talking about old times, Harriet allowing herself to be sketched as they talked. Suddenly, Lucia recalled her long stay at Gloucester Place and at the Surrey bungalow in 1935.

'And you were in love with Dr Macdonald?' she asked.

'Oh, no, no, no!' Harriet's face lit up with delight at the absurdity.

'Then Dr Macdonald was in love with you?' Harriet's laughing disclaimer was without bitterness.

But at Campden Hill that evening she sat in silence, gazing across the room as though across the years. Lucia's chance remark seemed, somehow, to have stirred up a lurking fear that, when all was said and done, she had failed her friends. At last, she spoke, though at long intervals, and hardly heeding the no doubt pointless words of reassurance and comfort of her god-daughter. 'I never heard again from Dora Marsden, after I wrote to her to say I could not type her last book. . . . But I always admired her analytical mind. . . . In the last years, my relations with Mr Joyce were cooler, on account of my inability to grapple with *Finnegans Wake*. . . . Yes, he was very dependent on what others thought of him. . . . Lucia once said that he thought me "avaricious". . . .'

Next day, Harriet went down to Bournemouth for three nights with Maude's elder girl, Katharine Mills, and her family. The sun shone and the remorse of the day before was forgotten. They walked along the beach—'. . . seaspawn and seawrack, the nearing tide . . .'— towards the Purbecks the first day, towards the Isle of Wight the second. Not to be outdone, Harriet went as far as a breakwater reached on a recent visit by Campbell, three years her senior; and, after tea, sat with her greatniece Rosemary while she did her homework and afterwards helped her to make a necklace with beads she had brought her as a present. She had again, and for the last time, the deep pleasure of joining in the life of a family she loved.

Tony's wife, Alla, met her on her return to London, escorted her from Waterloo to Liverpool Street station and put her in her train. Harriet looked, and was, tired and, when she reached Castle End, her heart was racing. It was soon clear that, this time, she was going to slip away. On Saturday morning, 14th October, a week after her return, she lost consciousness; and a few hours later, with Muriel bending over her, both hands on the pillow, she died. 'Beside the rivering waters of, hitherandthithering waters of. Night!'

The funeral was held at the Oxford Crematorium because Campbell, although he was not well, wanted to take the service. As the three generations of relatives were gathering to go into the chapel, he came out of the robing room, his episcopal sleeves billowing in the wind, and walked across to them. 'We have decided against the Lesson we had for Kearsley,' he said. 'There is only one that is right for her—I Corinthians 13. She loved and she was not puffed up.' His words were echoed in Paris. When Samuel Beckett heard the news, he told Sylvia 'I . . . shall think of her when I think of goodness'.[51]

Appendix

THE FINANCIAL HISTORY OF
THE NEW FREEWOMAN, EGOIST
AND EGOIST PRESS

BETWEEN 1913 and 1925, Harriet Weaver spent just over £3,000 on publishing, about two-thirds of it on the periodical and one-third on books. This analysis shows how the money was laid out and how her authors fared. It is based on her records, which present a fascinating picture of a small enterprise run on a shoe-string and throw light on her own attitude to the causes she supported.

SOURCES

New Freewoman/Egoist 'Day Book', giving receipts and expenditure, and transfers between the deposit and current account, from February 1913 to September 1920, continued to September 1925 in a little notebook stuck inside the cover. Balances are shown at the end of each financial year and a few small discrepancies with the bank book (now missing) are noted.

New Freewoman/Egoist Minute Book, recording directors' and shareholders' meetings from 1913 to 1924.

Prufrock accounts, May 1920 to February 1922; a penny notebook, with receipts, expenditure, and transfers of lump sums (such as £2 10s. od.) to the current account.

James Joyce title accounts: *A Portrait*, 3 editions, and *Ulysses*, in one book, from February 1917 to August 1925.

Penny notebook, with notes on *Portrait* distribution.

APPENDIX

Ledger pages of title accounts, complete except as shown:

        Portrait 3, *Dubliners*, *Exiles*, *Ulysses*
        Chamber Music (credits missing)
        Prufock, *Fontenelle* (debits missing), *Quia Pauper Amavi*
        Images, *Tarr*, *The Caliph's Design*
        Terra Italica (credits missing), *Explorations* (debits missing)

No pages have survived for *Hymen*, *Cock and Harlequin*, Marianne Moore s *Poems* or *Tyro*; and no entries were made for *Portrait* 1, or for *Portrait* 2 up to 1920, as these accounts were kept separately by Harriet. The first series of *Poets' Translations*, and André Spire's poems, *Et j'ai voulu la Paix*, were also kept separately, presumably by Richard Aldington.

Ledger pages showing *New Freewoman/Egoist* subscriptions, and sales of back numbers, from June 1915 to May 1919.

Annual statements of accounts for years ending 31st May 1914, and 1919–24.

Address Book of shareholders and subscribers (actual and potential).

Notes on disposal of stock, and lists of remainders.

NOTES ON SOURCES

The sources are incomplete, but all the Egoist publications are accounted for, somehow, except the reprints of 1916/17. After 1918, a few small sums came into the current account from *Poets' Translations*, series 1 (presumably they had covered their costs at last) but there is no record before 1918; and nothing at all is known about the fate of André Spire's poems.

The *Portrait* account has survived and, though it was at first managed independently, the independence was never total. Harriet sometimes noted in the Day Book (in pencil now partly rubbed out) that advances to James Joyce were drawn on Egoist cheques and 'equalized' by donations. After October 1920, when she started paying some of the *Portrait* receipts into the Egoist account, the payments offset by donations are entered in ink, but she sometimes made a note: 'not to go through the account', or simply 'not to be entered'.

Harriet was fond of doing arithmetic and kept her accounts carefully. But they are not easy to read. Her conflicting intentions to subsidize promising writers, and yet to show that their books paid their way, were sometimes expressed in riddles. Other riddles cropped up because, when cash taken at Oakley House was used to pay bills, she recorded it in the Day Book as a small marginal sum; and later on, she used the same method for other transactions, often with weird effects. In October 1921, James Joyce was sent a cheque, representing some royalties on *Portrait* 2 and a mysterious £14 'due from Grant Richards' (who does not seem to have paid it). This debit was equalized by three separate entries: a donation 'towards' the royalties, an in-payment marked 'H.S.W. owing on *Portrait* 2, *Exiles* and *Dubliners*', and a small credit appearing in a marginal sum as receipts for *Cock and Harlequin* set against royalties paid to the translator! Harriet herself evidently found her accounts hard to cross-check or summarize, as they do not always match exactly with the annual statements.

Her agreements with authors (apart from James Joyce) are not well documented, but it is on record that she paid a 20 per cent royalty on *Cock and Harlequin*, and published other books on a profit-sharing basis, with 25 per cent as the share of The Egoist Press. This was the arrangement with Edward Storer, who paid his own printing bill, and it seems to have been followed with the books later subsidized by Bryher. The unsubsidized books generally made a loss, so there was nothing to share. But if there was any surplus she always liked to interpret any agreement she had made in an undemanding fashion. On *Prufrock*, the only unsubsidized book that made a profit, the author received ten guineas and the publisher two and ninepence.

METHOD OF ANALYSIS

As Harriet was most particular about giving credit where credit was due, we assume that all unattributed donations came from her; and that she paid the initial costs of *Portrait* 1 and 2. These floats, and some other loans, were recovered later, and are not shown in the tables. Ezra Pound's smaller loans, also omitted from the tables, are shown in the notes.

From 1917 to 1920, Harriet's donations were ear-marked either for the James Joyce account, or for the Development Fund which financed other titles, or for the General Fund which financed the journal and all the office overheads. But when the journal died, the two Funds merged, and the loans Harriet made to the James Joyce account were paid back out of money she had donated to the other accounts. So we have attributed her donations, throughout, to the account where the money was in fact spent.

The Day Book is the only record for some titles, and it supplements the records in the surviving ledger pages and title accounts. So we have combined information from all sources, and arranged it under three heads:

Table 1. The financial History of *The New Freewoman*, *The Egoist* and The Egoist Press, with James Joyce titles included throughout.

Table 2. James Joyce titles: earnings, donations, royalties and other costs; and numbers of copies distributed.

Table 3. Other titles: earnings, donations, royalties and other costs; and numbers of copies distributed.

These summaries are arranged to show Harriet's work and achievements as editor and as publisher.

TABLE I

NEW FREEWOMAN / EGOIST / EGOIST PRESS: FINANCIAL HISTORY

Totals corrected to the nearest £. Items adjusted by not more than a £

	NF/EGOIST 1913 to May 1916	EGOIST/EGOIST PRESS Year to May				EGOIST PRESS Year to May				to Aug.	TOTALS
		1917	1918	1919	1920	1921	1922	1923	1924	1925	
RECEIPTS											
Unearned											
HSW Shares (£200) and Donations:											
NF/Egoist	868	251	342	234	185	68					1,948
JJ Titles	50		17			238	312	137	140		894
Other Titles			194								194
											—3,036
Other Sources, Shares (£159) and Donations:											
NF/Egoist	192		12								204
Other Titles						81	105				186
											— 390
Bank interest on deposits	4		5	5	4	5	4	1		1	29
	1,114	**251**	**570**	**239**	**189**	**392**	**421**	**138**	**140**	**1**	**3,455**
Earned											
NF/Egoist	418	46	60	57	26	2	1	1	1	7	619
JJ Titles		75	57	41	47	46	78	2,208	811	11	3,374
Other Titles			7	98	206	100	112	74	31	9	637
											—4,630
	1,532	**372**	**694**	**435**	**468**	**540**	**612**	**2,421**	**983**	**28**	**8,085**
EXPENDITURE											
NF/Egoist	1,442	306	349	260	198	50	48	64	66	16	2,799
JJ Titles: Fees and royalties	50	25	23	20	30	239	193	1,063	904		2,547
Other costs		83	110	26		10	370	1,094	28		1,721
											—4,268
Other Titles:											
Royalties					5	2	3	14	20	6	50
Other costs			27	183	322	126	244	32	2	32	968
											—1,018
	1,492	**414**	**509**	**489**	**555**	**427**	**858**	**2,267**	**1,020**	**54**	**8,085**

APPENDIX

NOTES ON TABLE 1

Receipts are shown in three sections: Harriet's contributions, other contributions, and earnings. Each section is sub-divided into *New Freewoman/Egoist*/Egoist Press (which includes all the publishing overheads), James Joyce titles, and other titles. Expenditure is similarly subdivided, with James Joyce's fees, advances and royalties distinguished from the other costs. This arrangement shows what Harriet put in and where it was used; and what went out each year as payments to James Joyce. His agent took a commission on the *Portrait* royalties, but not on the rest; and it is interesting that the royalty income, in the two years ending May 1924, reached quite a useful sum for those days.

3-plus years   The three years before Harriet went into book publishing are here
to May 1916   combined; but there is one point of interest in the annual figures.
        Dora Marsden's greatest success was in selling subscriptions before, and just after, the paper first came out; and its largest circulation was in the first six months—about 400 copies of each issue, two-thirds by subscription. Then it went into a long decline, with a sharp drop in November 1916 when the long-term subscriptions ran out; and the circulation never rose again above 200.

It was the same story with 'capital'. After the initial sale of shares, only £33 (including £10 from Amy Lowell) was raised from outside sources. Harriet took up the burden, and started putting in donations, in round sums, comfortably but not extravagantly in advance of demand. It is quite likely that she paid also, in 1916, for the reprints of *Poets' Translations* and André Spire's poems, but the cost is not known.

Her £50 donation to James Joyce, made in the spring of 1916, was for the serial rights of *A Portrait*. She used *Egoist* cheques, out of politeness, for the two instalments, and has left a ghostly record of them in the Day Book.

Year to   During the year, the sale of back numbers carrying James Joyce's 'tale'
May 1917   exceeded the sale of current copies at least once. It was a good sign. *A*
        Portrait, published in February 1917, recovered two-thirds of the outgoings by the end of May. As the account was not then combined, as it is here, with the *Egoist*/Egoist Press account, Harriet carried the deficit herself, and seems also to have felt uneasy about keeping for herself any proceeds from sales. For some months, she handed them over, as they came in, to *The Egoist*; topping them up, when required, with further donations.

Year to   *A Portrait* 1 sold out in October 1917, with a deficit of £17 (included
May 1918   here in Harriet's donation to the James Joyce account). She provided
        another float, in the spring of 1918, for *A Portrait* 2, and wrote off the deficit, as before, in 1923.

In August 1917, she decided to provide working capital for publishing other books; and did so by opening a Development Fund with a donation of £285. She also made a special grant to the General Fund, which carried all the office expenses, rent and salaries. Ezra Pound gave £12 to it, towards T. S. Eliot's salary of £36 a year. He also made a loan (not shown here) towards the expenses of *Prufrock*.

It was not long before Harriet had to produce more money for the General Fund; but she had been over-generous to the Development Fund. The title accounts (as shown here) needed only £194.

460

APPENDIX

Year to May 1919	There were only seven issues of the paper this year, and the price was raised, in January 1919, from 6d. to 9d. This saved Harriet some money, but did nothing to rescue the paper.
Year to May 1920	Ezra Pound, whose *Prufrock* loan had been in part repaid, waived the rest, so that T. S. Eliot could get a royalty. He made another loan, £10, to *Quia Pauper Amavi*. *The Egoist* came out three times. The last, and final, issue was in December 1919.
Year to May 1921	Edward Storer was paid 75 per cent of the takings on *Terra Italica*. The donations to 'other titles' are: £50 for *Tyro*, from Sydney Schiff; £31 for Marianne Moore's *Poems*, from Bryher. Harriet sent James Joyce £225 advance on *Ulysses* (recorded as 'not to be entered').
Year to May 1922	The donations to 'other titles' are: £25 for *Tyro*, from Edward Wadsworth; £50 for *Explorations*, and £30 for *Hymen*, from Bryher. She also arranged for sheets to be sold in America. The proceeds, £35, are credited here to earnings.
Year to May 1923	The *Prufrock* account was closed; and Ezra Pound was, after all, repaid the rest of his £5 loan—£3 10s. 0d. in cash and 15s. worth of books. The loan on *Quia Pauper Amavi* was repaid too.

It was a great year for The Egoist Press; and for Harriet. *Ulysses* earned over £2,000, and she was able to pass on over £1,000 to James Joyce. As John Rodker deducted his commission (£250) and his printing costs and expenses (£690) before remitting his takings, Harriet entered only the net figure in her accounts. Here we give the gross figure, and include the £940 in the costs.

Year to May 1924	In spite of losses and seizures, *Ulysses* did well. This year, James Joyce drew from it £636, making with his other royalties £674. Harriet evidently thought this too sharp a decline from the previous year. She added £130, from the sale of remainders to Capes, and a so-called 'loan' of £100 (both included here).

When she had disposed of her stock, to Cape and others, she still had debts to collect, and the books were not closed until 1925.

TABLE 2

JAMES JOYCE TITLES

	PRINTED	DISTRIBUTED Remain-dered	Credi-ted	Rcvd.	Fees/Royal-ties	Other costs	TOTAL spent	Loss/Profit
NUMBERS OF COPIES *Approximations marked**				**RECEIPTS/EXPENDITURE:** *Totals corrected to the nearest £. Items adjusted by not more than a £*				
A. IN TITLE ACCOUNTS				£	£	£	£	£
A Portrait of the Artist as a Young Man, Ed. 1, 12th Feb. 1917								
U.S. Sheets, bound U.K.	750	none	644	123	48	92	140	—17
Ed. 2, 2nd March 1918								
Printed U.K.	1,000	*1	903	167	74	138	212	—45
Ed. 3, August 1921								
U.S. Sheets, bound U.K.	1,000	130	851	228	79	152	231	—3
		131		518	201	382	583	—65
Ulysses, 12th October 1922 Printed France. Includes 'extra 500 copies and 100 unnumbered copies, i.e. 2,600 copies in all'.								
HSW, Ledger	2,600	none	*1,615	2,608	1,636	971	2,607	+1
Dubliners, April 1922								
U.S. Sheets, bound U.K.	500	171	308	67	24	93	117	—50
unbound	500	500						
Exiles, Spring 1922								
U.S. Sheets, bound U.K.	500	283	190	34	11	80	91	—57
unbound	500	500						
Chamber Music, Elkin Mathews	80							
Egoist Ed. August 1923		394	*174	17	6	30	36	—19
Printed U.K.	500							
Remainders to Capes: Sheets		1,000						
Bound		979		130				+130
				3,374	1,878	1,556	3,434	—60
B. SUPPLEMENTARY ITEMS								
Proceeds of remainders to JJ					130		130	—130
A Portrait, for serial rights				50	50		50	
Ulysses, for advances and 'loans'				465	475		475	—10
Dubliners/Exiles, for copyrights				150		150	150	
'Due from Grant Richards'				14	14		14	
Chamber Music, for copyrights and moulds (not used)				15		15	15	
Losses written off				200				+200
				4,268	2,547	1,721	4,268	

APPENDIX

NOTES ON TABLE 2

This summary is arranged to show the position as Harriet liked to see it, and as it actually was. The items in section A illustrate her preferences: she recorded losses on *A Portrait* but disguised the later losses in various ways, by paying some royalties and other costs through the General Fund, and by entering the proceeds from remainders, (suitably divided to put the titles in credit) without mentioning that the whole sum had immediately been passed on to James Joyce. In the end, she spent on the James Joyce list as a whole £894 more than the books had earned; and these expenses were met either by direct donations, or by diverting money—sometimes almost invisibly—from the other accounts. In either case, it was Harriet's money—shown here in Section B.

The numbers shown here for remainders include the sample copies given to Cape in advance. They are not on the invoice Cape receipted, but Harriet listed them separately. She did not show any remainders of *Portrait 2*, but she found a few copies (possibly damaged) when she was tidying up. Besides giving one to Cape, she sent an unspecified number to Sylvia Beach.

The numbers sold of *A Portrait*, *Dubliners* and *Exiles* are from Harriet's records. The figure for *Chamber Music* includes the 80 copies bought from Elkin Mathews for re-sale, while the Egoist edition was in preparation; the receipts were not kept separately. The figure for *Ulysses* is uncertain, as there is no record of the numbers represented by John Rodker's remittances. Our figure is based on an estimated selling price, allowing for some trade discounts. On the assumption that about 900 were seized (500 at Folkestone and about 400 in America) it leaves about 85 unaccounted for, which is not unreasonable.

The only record of free copies is 39 of *Portrait 2*. Harriet must have sent out press and complimentary copies of other titles; and there may well have been some damaged copies, or copies that were sold and never paid for. She did have some bad debts; and although some of the damaged copies of *Ulysses* were salvaged, it is possible that others were damaged beyond repair.

TABLE 3

OTHER TITLES

	NUMBER OF COPIES *Approximations marked**				RECEIPTS/EXPENDITURE: *Totals corrected to the nearest £. Items adjusted by not more than a £*				
	PRINTED	DISTRIBUTED			Rcvd.	Royalties	Other costs	TOTAL spent	Loss/Profit
		Free	Remaindered	Credited					
					£	£	£	£	£
Poets' Translations Series 1 Winter 1915/16			*475		4				
Series 2 1919 ... 1920	*4,850		2,979		140		172	172	—28
T. S. Eliot *Prufrock* Summer 1917	500		0	357	24	10	14	24	
Ezra Pound *Dialogues of Fontenelle* Autumn 1917	600	90	333	121	7		13	13	—6
Quia Pauper Amavi Autumn 1919 Ordinary	500	68	271	148	46		71	71	—25
Special	100	11	47	29					
Jean Cocteau *Cock and Harlequin* Winter 1920/21	750	61	399	192	29	7	63	70	—41
Marianne Moore *Poems* Summer 1921	500	110	268	98	42	9	31	40	+ 2
Remainders 1924 to Books			1,318						
Criterion Pamphlets			*3,454						
Wyndham Lewis *Tarr* Summer 1918	1,000	87	*165	729	145		167	167	—22
The Caliph's Design Autumn 1919	1,000	121	*84	707	79		81	81	—2
Richard Aldington *Images* Autumn 1919 Bound	500		220	176	29		49	49	—20
Sheets	500		485						
H.D. *Hymen* Bound	300		0	224	54	17	71	88	+1
Autumn 1921 Sheets	825				35				
Robert McAlmon *Explorations* Winter 1921 Bound	300	133	100	*35	54	3	49	52	+2
Sheets	200								
Edward Storer *Terra Italica* Winter 1921/22			13	*32	4	4		4	
Tyro 1 and 2	2,000		430		131		161	161	—30
					823	50	942	992	—169
Publicity, storage etc								25	—25
Donation to Development Fund, HSW					194				+194
					1,017			1,017	

464

APPENDIX

NOTES ON TABLE 3

Harriet kept careful records of copies sold, and also wrote down her final count for most titles. A figure for *Terra Italica* is missing, and we have done our own count, from the Day Book. We have done the same for *Explorations*, because Harriet's record of 60 sold does not agree with the earnings of £5 (combined in the table with Bryher's £50 subsidy).

We have used her figures for remainders, where they survive, although she noted that they were 'rather too high'. They are complete for stocks to *The Criterion* except for *Poets' Translations* series 1. As *The Criterion* passed on 460 to Faber (and Faber later sold 37) we picked on the arbitrary figure of 475. The size of the series 2 edition is also uncertain because a number of copies were damaged, at least 200 but perhaps more.

The size of the edition of *Terra Italica* is not known, and it looks as if Edward Storer kept most of it for private circulation. It is probable also that Wyndham Lewis kept most of *Tyro*. It is not possible to work out how many copies Harriet had, or sold. She did, however, note the remainders. She also noted that she had 200 copies on hand of André Spire's *Et j'ai voulu la Paix*, the only Egoist book that, for lack of information, does not appear on the table.

The subsidies for *Tyro*, *Hymen*, *Explorations* and Marianne Moore's *Poems* have already been listed (Notes on Table 1, 1921 and 1922). They are all straightforward, except for *Hymen*. Harriet recorded that Bryher 'bought' 300 copies; but the proceeds suggest that she paid for them, and left them in Harriet's hands. So we have classified this, in Table 1, as a donation, not earnings.

Apart from stocks given to *The Criterion*, and remainders sold to Richard Aldington (and later passed on to Allen & Unwin) all the remainders shown were given back to their authors.

Harriet's publishing venture was modest; but any publisher would be proud to have had, on a small list, first editions of writers who were then little known—James Joyce, T. S. Eliot, Ezra Pound, Jean Cocteau, Marianne Moore, Wyndham Lewis and Richard Aldington. As Ezra Pound observed, Harriet Weaver never turned away anything good.

SOURCES

A. Sources of quotations from Harriet Weaver's letters
Letters to:

Sylvia Beach	The Beach Collection at Princeton University Library, with one exception which is noted.
Peter du Sautoy	Faber and Faber.
T. S. Eliot	Mrs T. S. Eliot.
The Director of the National Library of Ireland (then Dr R. J. Hayes)	The National Library of Ireland.
Grace Jardine	Miss Elaine Dyson, with the papers left by Dora Marsden.
James Joyce	Cornell University Library, with some exceptions which are noted.
Dora Marsden	The Dyson Collection.
F. R. D'O. Monro and F. Lionel Monro	The Society of Authors.
Other people	The recipients, unless otherwise noted.

B. Sources of quotations from letters to Harriet Weaver
Letters from:

James Joyce	*Letters of James Joyce*—the first collection, now known as Volume I, edited by Stuart Gilbert; Volumes II and III edited by Richard Ellmann. (Volume I published in London by Faber and Faber and in New York by The Viking Press in 1957; Volumes II and III published by the same firms in 1966) Described as *Letters*.
Ezra Pound	Unpublished letters, the Executors of the Estate of Harriet Shaw Weaver (described as Weaver); published letters, sources noted.
John Slocum	(copies) The Eileen and John Slocum Collection at Yale University Library (described as Yale).

SOURCES

Other people   Unpublished letters, the Executors unless otherwise noted; published letters, sources noted.

C. SOURCES OF QUOTATIONS FROM OTHER PAPERS

The *New Freewoman/Egoist*
Egoist Press Minute Book
and Accounts and other
papers of The New Free-
woman Ltd. and The
Egoist Ltd.   The Executors (described as Weaver)
Letters to Dora Marsden   The Dyson Collection
Letters to Jane Lidderdale   Jane Lidderdale.
Other letters   Sources noted.

D. NOTES ON SOURCES AND REFERENCES

When the text has been taken from a published source, the publication is given as the source.

Page references are to English editions, unless otherwise noted.

The sources listed in A, B and C are not repeated in the references, except for some particular reason.

Letters to and from Harriet Weaver omit her name.

Brackets indicate a source of information, not of a quotation.

'Ellmann' is short for *James Joyce* by Richard Ellmann, published by the Oxford University Press, New York, in 1959.

'Buffalo' is short for the Lockwood Memorial Library, State University of New York at Buffalo.

Chapter 1

EARLY YEARS

1   To Sylvia Beach, 17th December 1950.
2   *The Chester Courant*, 29th April 1891.
3   To B. W. Huebsch, 6th January 1960. Copy, Lidderdale.
4   *The Weaver's Web*. Recollections by Frederic P. Weaver. Typescript. 1909. J. H. Weaver.
5   Weaver.
6   Lady Floud to Jane Lidderdale, 21st January 1962.
7   (Christ Church, Hampstead, Annual Reports 1897–1902)

Chapter 2

SOCIAL WORK

1   (*Canon Barnett: his life, work and friends*, by his wife. London. John Murray, 1918)
2   From Eleanor Davies-Colley, 16th March 1900.
3   Invalid Children's Aid Association, Annual Reports, 1900–1905.

SOURCES

4   Ibid.
5   Whitechapel Committee of the Charity Organization Society, Annual Reports, 1905–1913)
6   Interviews with Lady Floud, Mrs C. P. Barlow (*née* May), F. R. D'O. Monro, on various dates in 1962.
7   (Miss W. Adair-Roberts, in conversation with Jane Lidderdale, 10th March 1962)
8   Mrs Campbell Hone (Maude Weaver), in conversation with Jane Lidderdale, 2nd December 1961.
9   (Mrs Alfred Weaver (Muriel Adair Roberts), in conversation with Jane Lidderdale, 13th December 1961)
10 Mrs S. Snow (Rosamond Weaver), to Jane Lidderdale, 1st February 1962. Lidderdale.
11 Interview with F. R. D'O. Monro, 2nd August 1962.
12 To Alice Davies, 18th April 1961. Copy, Weaver.
13 From Edith Monro, 16th and 20th October 1905.
14 From B. Davies-Colley, 7th April 1909.
15 Interview with F. R. D'O. Monro, 2nd August 1962.
16 (Anthony Weaver to Jane Lidderdale, 22nd January 1963)
17 To Jane Lidderdale, 1st June 1954.
18 (*The South London Hospital for Women and Children*, Anon. Published privately. 1958)
19 *South London Press*, 5th July 1913.
20 *The Freewoman*, Editorial of 20th August 1912.
21 *The Freewoman*, Editorial of 12th September 1912.
22 *The Freewoman*, Editorial of 23rd November 1911.
23 *The Freewoman*, 22nd August 1912.
24 *The Freewoman*, 20th June 1912.
25 Rebecca West to Dora Marsden, undated. Written soon after 13th June 1912.
26 *The Freewoman*, 1st August 1912.

Chapter 3

'THE SPIRIT OF FREEDOM'

1   To Bjørn Rasmussen, 28th March 1961.
2   Emmeline Pethick Lawrence to Dora Marsden, 6th October 1909.
3   Margaret W. Nevinson, Acting Secretary of the Women's Freedom League, to Dora Marsden, 13th February 1911.
4   Rebecca West to Dora Marsden. Undated, written soon after 13th June 1912.
5   Presumably written to Dora Marsden, winter 1911/12. Quoted in *The New Freewoman* publicity.
6   Emmeline Pethick Lawrence to Dora Marsden, 22nd December 1910.
7   Constance Tite, Treasurer of the Women's Freedom League, to Dora Marsden, 26th April 1911.
8   Grace Jardine, in conversation with Mary Nicholson, 30th May 1967.
9   Rebecca West to Dora Marsden, undated, att. winter 1912/13.

468

10 Ibid.

11 Rebecca West to Dora Marsden, also undated, att. winter 1912/13.

12 Ibid.

13 Ibid.

14 From Dora Marsden, undated, att. early February 1913.

15 *The Suffragette*, by Sylvia Pankhurst. New York. Sturgis & Walton Company, 1911. London. Gay & Hancock Ltd., 1911, p. 367.

16 (Rebecca West to Dora Marsden, undated, att. spring 1913)

17 Circular headed 'The New Freewoman', undated.

18 Rebecca West to Dora Marsden, undated, att. spring 1913.

19 Rebecca West to Dora Marsden, undated, att. spring 1913.

20 From Dora Marsden, 10th March 1913.

21 Circular headed 'The New Freewoman', undated.

22 A. G. Fifield to Edwin Herrin, 6th May 1913. Dyson.

23 A. G. Fifield to Dora Marsden, 9th May 1913.

24 *The Freewoman*, 12th September 1913.

25 A. G. Fifield to Dora Marsden, 16th May 1913.

26 (From Dora Marsden, 15th May 1913)

27 From Dora Marsden, 20th May 1913.

28 Dora Marsden to Edwin Herrin, 5th May 1913. Dyson.

29 F. C. Charles to Grace Jardine, 11th June 1913. Dyson.

30 Rebecca West to Dora Marsden, undated, att. early June 1913.

31 From Dora Marsden, undated, att. 17th June 1913.

32 From Grace Jardine, 18th June 1913.

Chapter 4

The New Freewoman

1 Rebecca West to Jane Lidderdale, 29th January 1967.

2 Ezra Pound to Dora Marsden, undated, att. July 1913.

3 Ibid.

4 From Ezra Pound, undated, att. July 1913. First page missing, but probably to Rebecca West. Dyson.

5 Ezra Pound to Dora Marsden, undated, att. July 1913.

6 To Grace Jardine, 1st August 1913.

7 To Dora Marsden, 24th July 1913.

8 Ibid.

9 To Dora Marsden, 6th August 1913.

10 To Dora Marsden, 12th August 1913.

11 Ezra Pound to Dora Marsden, undated, att. August 1913.

12 Ezra Pound to Amy Lowell, 13th August 1913. *The Letters of Ezra Pound 1907–1941*. Edited by D. D. Paige. New York. Harcourt, Brace & World, Inc., 1950. London. Faber, 1951, p. 58.

13 Rebecca West to Dora Marsden, undated, att. August 1913.

14 From Dora Marsden, 19th November 1913.

15 To Dora Marsden, 12th August 1913.

16 Ibid.
17 To Dora Marsden, 8th September 1913.
18 To Dora Marsden, 3 September 1913.
19 Minute Book.
20 To Dora Marsden, 31st August 1913.
21 Ezra Pound to Jane Lidderdale, 12th July 1962.
22 From Eleanor Davies-Colley, 22nd December 1914.
23 To Dora Marsden, 15th September 1913.
24 To Dora Marsden, 28th September 1913.
25 Ezra Pound to Dora Marsden, undated, att. Sept./Oct. 1913.
26 From Rebecca West, undated, att. October 1913. Dyson.
27 From Dora Marsden, 16th November 1913.
28 From Dora Marsden, 19th November 1913.
29 To Grace Jardine, 8th December 1913.
30 Minute Book.
31 Bessie Heyes to Harriet Weaver, enclosed in Harriet Weaver's letter to Grace Jardine, 8th December 1913. Dyson.
32 To Grace Jardine, 13th December 1913.
33 (To Dora Marsden, 1st January 1914)
34 From Dora Marsden, 4th January 1914.

Chapter 5

EDITOR OF *The Egoist*

1 (*The Egoist*, 1st October 1919)
2 D. H. Lawrence to Ezra Pound, 26th December 1913. Dyson.
3 Ezra Pound to James Joyce, 15th December 1913. *Letters of James Joyce*, II. Edited by Richard Ellmann. London. Faber, 1966, p. 326. New York. Viking Press, 1966.
4 Ezra Pound to James Joyce, 17th–19th January 1914. *Letters* II, 327.
5 Ezra Pound to Amy Lowell, 23rd February 1914. *The Letters of Ezra Pound*, p. 70.
6 Ibid.
7 Minute Book.
8 From Dora Marsden, 19th March 1914.
9 From Dora Marsden, 31st March 1916.
10 From Dora Marsden, 3rd April 1914.
11 Ibid.
12 *The Egoist*, 15th April 1914.
13 Mrs Geoffrey Cockle (Rosemary Weaver), to Jane Lidderdale, 1st February 1962.
14 Storm Jameson to Jane Lidderdale, 21st April 1964.
15 Ibid.
16 *The Egoist*, 1st June, 1914.
17 To Dora Marsden, 1st July 1914.
18 Ibid.
19 From Ezra Pound, annotated by Harriet Weaver 'July 1914'.

20 To Dora Marsden, 1st July 1914.

21 (To James Joyce, 17th September 1917)

22 (To James Joyce, 6th September 1915)

23 From Dora Marsden, 15th July 1914.

24 From Dora Marsden, 19th July 1914.

25 Ibid.

26 To Grace Jardine, 22nd July 1914.

27 Annotated by Harriet Weaver 'August 1914' but acknowledged by Dora Marsden on 30th July. Copy, Weaver.

28 From Dora Marsden, 30th July 1914.

29 *The Egoist*, 1st January 1916.

30 To Dora Marsden, 5th August 1914.

31 *The Egoist*, 1st September 1914.

32 Ibid.

33 From Ezra Pound, 1st September 1914.

34 *The Egoist*, 15th September 1914.

35 From Dora Marsden, 16th September 1914.

36 From Ezra Pound, 12th October 1914. *The Letters of Ezra Pound*, p. 83.

37 *The New Freewoman*, 1st October 1913.

38 *The Egoist*, 2nd November 1914.

39 From James Joyce, 11th November 1914.

40 From Dora Marsden, 30th November 1914.

41 (To James Joyce, 28th July 1915)

42 To Truscotts, 7th December 1914. Copy, Weaver.

43 *The Egoist*, 1st January 1915.

44 From Grace Jardine, 23rd February 1915.

45 *The Egoist*, March 1915.

46 James Joyce to Grant Richards, 3rd July 1914. *Letters* II, 335.

47 (From James Joyce to Grant Richards, late January 1915 *Letters* II, 336)

48 (From James Joyce, 5th March 1915)

49 (From James Joyce, 25th March 1915)

50 (To James Joyce, 7th July 1915)

51 From Mrs Campbell Hone, 13th June 1915.

52 (From James Joyce, 30th June 1915)

53 (To James Joyce, 7th July 1915)

54 From James Joyce, 12th July 1915.

55 From James Joyce, 24th July 1915.

56 To James Joyce, 28th July 1915.

57 *The Egoist*, August 1915.

58 (To James Joyce, 6th September 1916)

59 From James Joyce, 10th and 28th August 1916.

60 (To J. B. Pinker, 5th August 1915. Yale)

61 To James Joyce, 24th September 1915.

62 From Dora Marsden, undated. Annotated by Harriet Weaver '? October 1915'.

63 Information from Hansard, and from *War on Great Cities*, by Frank Morison. London. Faber, 1937, pp. 84/93.

64 From Dora Marsden, undated, annotated by Harriet Weaver 'October 1915'.

SOURCES

Chapter 6

PUBLISHING *A Portrait*

1 Ezra Pound to Jane Lidderdale, 12th July 1962.
2 (*James Joyce*, by Richard Ellmann. New York. Oxford University Press, 1959, p. 413)
3 To James Joyce, 30th November 1915.
4 From James Joyce, 6th December 1915.
5 James Joyce to J. B. Pinker, 6th December 1915.
6 From Dora Marsden, 6th January 1916.
7 *The Egoist*, January 1916.
8 From Dora Marsden, 6th January 1916.
9 From Dora Marsden, 12th January 1916.
10 Harriet Weaver's comment, quoted in Dora Marsden's letter to her of 12th January 1916.
11 To B. W. Huebsch, 30th July 1917. MS Private.
12 (Ezra Pound to James Joyce, 31st January 1916. *Pound/Joyce*, edited and with a commentary by Forrest Read. New York. New Directions, 1967. London. Faber, 1968, p. 65)
13 From Ezra Pound, undated, annotated by Harriet Weaver 'Late 1915 or early 1916'.
14 To James Joyce, 14th January 1916.
15 From James Joyce, 22nd January 1916.
16 To James Joyce, 28 January 1916.
17 *Blasting and Bombardiering*, by Wyndham Lewis. London. Eyre and Spottiswoode, 1937, p. 254.
18 Ellmann, pp. 416/417.
19 From Dora Marsden, 6th February 1916.
20 From The Complete Press, 9th February 1916.
21 *The Egoist*, March 1916.
22 Ezra Pound to John Quinn, 26th February 1916. New York Public Library.
23 From James Joyce, 10th March 1916.
24 (Ibid)
25 Ezra Pound to Kate Buss, 9th March 1916. *The Letters of Ezra Pound*, p. 119.
26 Ibid.
27 From Ezra Pound, 17th March 1916. Ibid., p. 122
28 From Billing and Sons, 13th March 1916.
29 (To James Joyce, 25 March 1916)
30 (To James Joyce, 3rd March 1916; and 25th March 1916)
31 To James Joyce, 25 March 1916.
32 (*A Portrait* agreement. Weaver)
33 From Ezra Pound, 30th March 1916. *The Letters of Ezra Pound*, p. 124.
34 Ezra Pound to Margaret Anderson, c. May 1917. *The Letters of Ezra Pound*, p. 165.
35 From Dora Marsden, 31st March 1916.
36 Notes on Harriet Weaver, by Helen Saunders, 24th February 1962.

37 From Dora Marsden, 31st March 1916. Weaver.

38 To Ezra Pound, draft, 3rd April 1916. Weaver.

39 *The Egoist*, April 1916.

40 From Dora Marsden, annotated by Harriet Weaver 'April 1916'.

41 From Ezra Pound, 4th April 1916. His dots.

42 From James Joyce, 31st March, 1916.

43 To E. Byrne Hackett, 31st March 1916. *Letters of James Joyce*, I. Edited by Stuart Gilbert. London. Faber, 1957, p. 90. New York. Viking Press, 1957.

44 From E. Byrne Hackett, 4th May 1916.

45 (From Brendon & Son of Plymouth, 6th April 1916; The Garden City Press, 4th May 1916; and Hazel, Watson & Viney, 11th May 1916)

46 From The Complete Press, 15th May 1916.

47 To E. Byrne Hackett, 26th May 1916. Copy, Weaver.

48 From B. W. Huebsch, 2nd June 1916.

49 From B. W. Huebsch, 16th June 1916. *Letters* I, 91.

50 To B. W. Huebsch, 28th June 1916. MS Private.

51 To James Joyce, 28th June 1916.

52 (From Ezra Pound, 12th July 1916. *The Letters of Ezra Pound*, p. 135)

53 To B. W. Huebsch, 24th July 1916. *Letters* I, 92.

54 To B. W. Huebsch, 19th August 1916. MS Private.

55 To John J. Slocum, 25th February 1947.

56 From James Joyce, 1st July 1916.

57 From B. W. Huebsch, 25th August 1916. *Letters* I, 93.

58 To B. W. Huebsch, 6th September 1916. MS Private.

59 Cable to B. W. Huebsch, 7th September 1916. MS Private.

60 To James Joyce, 7th September 1916.

61 From James Joyce, 16th September 1916.

62 Ibid.

63 Ibid.

64 From Dora Marsden, annotated by Harriet Weaver 'September or October 1916'.

65 From E. Byrne Hackett, 4th October 1916.

66 From B. W. Huebsch, 9th October 1916. Copy, MS Private.

67 To B. W. Huebsch, 25th October 1916. MS Private.

68 From James Joyce, 10th October 1916.

69 Notes enclosed with the letter from James Joyce, 30th October 1916.

70 From B. W. Huebsch, 6th January 1917. Copy, MS Private.

71 To James Joyce, undated, but written on 25th October 1916.

72 From Ezra Pound, 14th November 1916. *The Letters of Ezra Pound*, p. 151.

73 From Ezra Pound, 22nd January 1917. *The Letters of Ezra Pound*, p. 155.

74 From H. G. Wells, postmark 25th January 1917.

75 Postcard from H. G. Wells, postmark 2nd February 1917.

76 From James Joyce, 14th January 1917.

77 To James Joyce, 26th January 1917.

78 To James Joyce, 7th February 1917.

79 Iris Barry, in *The Bookman*, October 1931, p. 167. The description of T. S. Eliot is from the same source.

SOURCES

80 Ezra Pound to John Drummond, 30th May 1934. *The Letters of Ezra Pound*, pp. 343/344.

Chapter 7

MORE PUBLISHING

1 From Ezra Pound, 6th February 1917.
2 From Dora Marsden, undated, but about mid-February 1917.
3 From Dora Marsden, undated, but about mid-February 1917.
4 From Dora Marsden, 2 March 1917.
5 (From Dora Marsden, 1st February 1917)
6 Ibid.
7 From Ezra Pound, 6th February 1917.
8 (From James Joyce, 30th October 1916)
9 To James Joyce, 26th February 1917.
10 Slack Monro Saw & Co. to James Joyce, 22nd February 1917. *Letters* II, 389.
11 Inscriptions in books now at the National Book League, London.
12 From James Joyce, 7th March 1917.
13 (To James Joyce, 2nd March 1917)
14 The *Times Literary Supplement*, 1st March 1917, pp. 103/104.
15 From Dora Marsden, 2nd March 1917.
16 From B. W. Huebsch, 23rd February 1917. *Letters* II, 389.
17 (To James Joyce, 29th April 1917)
18 From James Joyce, 22nd April 1917.
19 From Dora Marsden, 9th May 1917.
20 From Dora Marsden, 7th May 1917.
21 (To James Joyce, 24th March 1917)
22 (To James Joyce, 16th March 1917)
23 To James Joyce, 24th March 1917.
24 (To B. W. Huebsch, 14th March 1917. *Letters* II, 391)
25 (From B. W. Huebsch, 2nd April 1917. Copy, MS Private)
26 (To B. W. Huebsch, 18th April 1917. MS Private)
27 From Dora Marsden, 29th April 1917.
28 (From Dora Marsden, 6th May 1917)
29 From Dora Marsden, 16th May 1917.
30 From Dora Marsden, 9th May 1917.
31 From Hilda Doolittle (Mrs Richard Aldington), undated, annotated by Harriet Weaver 'May 1917'.
32 From B. W. Huebsch, 14th May 1917. Copy, MS Private.
33 (To James Joyce, 12th May 1917)
34 (To B. W. Huebsch, 18th April 1917. MS Private)
35 To B. W. Huebsch, 6th June 1917. MS Private.
36 To James Joyce, 31st May 1917.
37 To James Joyce, 18th July 1917.
38 From James Joyce, 13th June 1917.
39 Ibid.
40 To James Joyce, 29th June 1917.

41 From James Joyce, 7th July 1917.
42 From B. W. Huebsch, 17th July 1917. Copy, MS Private.
43 From James Joyce, 18th July 1917.
44 To James Joyce, 31st July 1917.
45 (To James Joyce, 17th August 1917)
46 Pike's Fine Art Press to The Egoist Press, 16th August 1917.
47 To James Joyce, 17th August 1917.
48 From B. W. Huebsch, 31st August 1917. Copy, MS Private.
49 (From Nora Joyce, 28th August 1917. *Letters* I, 107)
50 From Dora Marsden, 17th August 1917.
51 To Sylvia Beach, 12th January 1957.
52 (To James Joyce, 17th September 1917)
53 From James Joyce, 1st July 1916.
54 From James Joyce, 18th July 1917.
55 (To James Joyce, 17th August 1917)
56 (To James Joyce, 6th September 1917)
57 From Edmund Gosse, 14th September 1917.
58 To Edward Marsh, 11th September 1917. *Letters* II, 407.
59 (*Edward Marsh*, by Christopher Hassell. London. Longmans, Green, & Co., 199, p. 433. New York. Harcourt, Brace & World, Inc.)
60 (*The Egoist*, February 1918)
61 To Sylvia Beach, 27th August 1921 and 12th January 1957.
62 From B. W. Huebsch, 9th April 1918. Copy, MS Private.

Chapter 8

EDITOR OR PUBLISHER?

1   From James Joyce, 10th October 1916, and 8th November 1916.
2   To James Joyce, 6th September 1917.
3   To James Joyce, 8th March 1918.
4   Ibid.
5   From James Joyce, 20th March 1918.
6   From Dora Marsden, 10th April 1918.
7   *Beginning Again*, by Leonard Woolf. An Autobiography of the years 1911 to 1918. London. Hogarth Press, 1964, p. 246. New York. Harcourt, Brace & World, Inc., 1964.
8   Op. cit., pp. 246/247.
9   From Virginia Woolf, 17th May 1918.
10 From B. W. Huebsch, 22nd March and 7th June 1918. Copies, MS Private.
11 From James Joyce, 18th May 1918.
12 To James Joyce, 19th June 1918.
13 (Ibid)
14 From Dora Marsden, 6th August 1918.
15 From Dora Marsden, 30th October 1918.
16 From Dora Marsden, 4th December 1918.
17 To Sylvia Beach, 2nd March 1955.

18 (From James Joyce, 25th February 1919)
19 From James Joyce, 25 February 1919.
20 Interview with F. R. D'O. Monro, 2nd August 1962.
21 Notes on Harriet Weaver by Lucia Joyce, February 1967.
22 Ellmann, p. 470.
23 Frank Budgen, in conversation with Jane Lidderdale, 11th August 1966.
24 (Ellmann, p. 494)
25 Monro Saw & Co. to James Joyce, 3rd June 1919. *Letters* II, 443.
26 Monro Saw & Co. to James Joyce, 24th June 1919. *Letters* II, 444/445.
27 To James Joyce, 6th July 1919.
28 From James Joyce, 20th July 1919.
29 From James Joyce, 6th August 1919.
30 *James Joyce and the Making of Ulysses*, by Frank Budgen. Bloomington. Indiana University Press. 1961, pp. 133/134.
31 From James Joyce, 20th July 1919.
32 From James Joyce, 6th August 1919.
33 To Maria Jolas, 25th August 1949.
34 To James Joyce, 17th August 1919.
35 To James Joyce, 2nd November 1919.
36 To James Joyce, 18th December 1919.
37 James Joyce to Frank Budgen, 3rd January 1920. *Letters* I, 135.
38 To James Joyce, 28th January 1920.
39 To James Joyce, 18th December 1919.
40 From James Joyce, 6th January 1920.
41 To James Joyce, 28th January 1920.

Chapter 9

Storm Capes

1 *My Thirty Years' War*, by Margaret Anderson. New York. Covici, Friede, 1930. London. Alfred A. Knopf, 1930, p. 175.
2 (From James Joyce, 25th February 1920)
3 (B. L. Reid to Jane Lidderdale, 10th April 1967)
4 To James Joyce, 7th November 1919.
5 Ellmann, p. 489.
6 James Joyce to J. B. Pinker, 13th March 1920. *Letters* II, 462.
7 Mrs W. G. Q. Mills (Katharine Hone), to Jane Lidderdale, 5th March 1962.
8 (Mrs Geoffrey Cockle to Jane Lidderdale, 3rd January 1962)
9 To Bjørn Rasmussen, 28th March 1961.
10 *The Definition of the Godhead* by Dora Marsden. London. The Egoist Press, 1928, p. 27.
11 From James Joyce, 12th March 1920.
12 To James Joyce, 25th May 1920.
13 (Copy of the *Ulysses* contract signed by James Joyce. University of Texas Library)
14 To James Joyce, 25th May 1920.

SOURCES

15 To J. Schwartz, 23rd August 1948. University of Texas Library.
16 To Sylvia Beach, 21st March 1950.
17 (To James Joyce, 25th May 1920)
18 James Joyce to Frank Budgen, 13th March 1920. *Letters* I, 138.
19 Ellmann, p. 490.
20 From James Joyce, 20th July 1919.
21 From James Joyce, 16th August 1920.
22 Ellmann, p. 490/491.
23 From James Joyce, 12th July 1920.
24 (*The Letters of Ezra Pound*, p. 220)
25 *The Letters of Ezra Pound*, p. 216.
26 From James Joyce, 16th August 1920.
27 From Dora Marsden, 12th November 1920.
28 *James Joyce*, by Herbert Gorman. New York. Rinehart, 1940. London. The Bodley Head, 1941, p. 274.
29 From James Joyce, 9th December 1920.
30 Title page.
31 From Dora Marsden, 12th November 1920.
32 From Dora Marsden, 21st March 1921.
33 Ibid.
34 Ibid.
35 Postcard from Dora Marsden, 8th April 1921.
36 From James Joyce, 3rd April 1921.
37 (Sylvia Beach to Mrs Sylvester Beach, 1st April 1921. Princeton)
38 *Shakespeare and Company*, by Sylvia Beach. New York. Harcourt, Brace & World, Inc. London. Faber, 1960, p. 57.
39 From James Joyce, 10th April 1921.
40 To Sylvia Beach, 29th July 1920.
41 To Sylvia Beach, 12th April 1921.
42 (To Sylvia Beach, 21st and 27th April, 7th, 12th and 24th May 1921)
43 To J. B. Pinker, 9th May 1921. Copied (by Sylvia Beach) from *The New Colophon*, New York, September 1949. Princeton.
44 From James Joyce, 1st March 1921.
45 Notes by Helen Saunders.
46 P. Beaumont Wadsworth to Jane Lidderdale, 21st April 1964, with a transcript of his article, *My Visits with James Joyce*, written for *The James Joyce Quarterly* 1964.
47 Frank Budgen to Jane Lidderdale, 13th September 1966.
48 James Joyce to Frank Budgen. Undated but evidently written at the end of May 1921. *Letters of James Joyce*, III. Edited by Richard Ellmann. London. Faber, 1966, p. 42. New York. Viking Press, 1966.
49 From James Joyce, 24th June 1921.
50 *Being Geniuses Together*, by Robert McAlmon. London. Secker and Warburg, 1938, p. 42. New York. Doubleday, 1968.
51 (To Sylvia Beach, 8th July 1921)
52 To Sylvia Beach, 19th July 1921.
53 From James Joyce, 7th August 1921.

54 (From James Joyce, 30th August 1921)
55 From James Joyce, 9th September 1921.

Chapter 10

MISS WEAVER'S *Ulysses*

1 From James Joyce, 8th February 1922.
2 To Sylvia Beach, 16th February 1922.
3 (To Sylvia Beach, 11th April 1922)
4 (James Joyce to Stanislaus Joyce, 20th March 1922. *Letters* III, 61)
5 The *Observer*, 5th March 1922
6 To Sylvia Beach, 4th and 11th April 1922.
7 The *Sporting Times*, 1st April 1922.
8 From James Joyce, 10th April 1922.
9 From Dora Marsden, 13th March 1922.
10 Ibid.
11 Ibid.
12 *The Nation and Athenaeum*, April 1922.
13 (To Sylvia Beach, 20th May 1922)
14 *Shakespeare and Company*, p. 94.
15 From James Joyce, 16th May 1922.
16 To Sylvia Beach, 1st June 1922.
17 From Sylvia Beach, 6th June 1922.
18 Telegram from Sylvia Beach, 9th June 1922.
19 Telegram from Sylvia Beach to Sydney Schiff, 9th June 1922.
20 Copy of telegram from Harriet Weaver and Sydney Schiff to Sylvia Beach, 9th June 1922.
21 (Telegram from Sylvia Beach 9th June 1922)
22 From Sylvia Beach, 11th June 1922.
23 To Sylvia Beach, 13th June 1922.
24 To Sylvia Beach, 15th June 1922.
25 Telegram from Sylvia Beach, 15th June 1922.
26 Postcard from Sylvia Beach, 15th July 1922.
27 From Sylvia Beach, 18th June 1922.
28 From Sylvia Beach, 9th July 1922.
29 From Sylvia Beach, 18th June 1922.
30 To Sylvia Beach, 24th June 1922.
31 From Sylvia Beach, 26th June 1922.
32 To Sylvia Beach, 1st July 1922.
33 From Sylvia Beach, 26th June 1922.
34 To Sylvia Beach, 1st July 1922.
35 To Sylvia Beach, 22nd July 1922.
36 *Beauty—and the Beast*, by James Douglas. *Sunday Express*, 28th May 1922.
37 From Dora Marsden, 7th June 1922.
38 From Dora Marsden, 7th July 1922.
39 Summarized in Harriet Weaver's letter to Sylvia Beach, 22nd July 1922.

SOURCES

40 To Sylvia Beach, 22nd July 1922.
41 (From John Quinn, 27th July 1922. Copy, New York Public Library)
42 To Sylvia Beach, 22nd July 1922.
43 Ibid.
44 Footnote 4, *Letters*, I, 186.
45 (Ellmann, p. 551)
46 James Joyce to Sylvia Beach, 29th August 1922. Buffalo.
47 (Ibid)
48 (Ibid)
49 To Sylvia Beach, 7th September 1922.
50 Ibid.
51 (Iris Barry to Jane Lidderdale, postmark 5th December 1966)
52 (Ibid)
53 Ibid.
54 To Sylvia Beach, 19th September 1922.
55 (Ibid)
56 To Sylvia Beach, 4th October 1922.
57 Iris Barry to Jane Lidderdale, postmark 5th December 1966, and 31st August
    1967.
58 (To Sylvia Beach, 17th October 1922)
59 To Sylvia Beach, 1st November 1922.
60 (From James Joyce, 8th November 1922)
61 To John J. Slocum, 25th February 1947.
62 Campbell Hone, in conversation with Jane Lidderdale, December 1961.
63 To Sylvia Beach, 22nd July 1922.
64 From Dora Marsden, 9th October 1922.
65 Ibid.
66 From James Joyce, 22nd October 1922.
67 Postcard to Sylvia Beach, 25th October 1922.
68 John Eglinton in *The Dial*, New York.
69 From James Joyce, 28th September 1922.
70 From James Joyce, 17th November 1922.
71 From James Joyce, 28th September 1922.
72 From James Joyce, 17th October 1922.
73 Weaver.
74 From James Joyce, 3rd November 1922.
75 From James Joyce, 17th November 1922.
76 Ibid.
77 To Sylvia Beach, 22nd November 1922.
78 (To Kate Buss, 7th February 1924. University of Indiana)
79 (Barnet G. Braverman to Sylvia Beach, 16th January 1923. Princeton)
80 To Sylvia Beach, 27th November 1922.
81 (Ibid)
82 From James Joyce, 22nd December 1922.
83 To Sylvia Beach, 14th February 1923.
84 From Harriet Wright, 29th October 1913.
85 (To James Joyce, 30th January 1923. National Library of Ireland)

86 Ibid.
87 (To Sylvia Beach, 23rd March 1923)
88 (*Ulysses* accounts)
89 (Information from the Home Office, 7th December 1966)
90 (Information from the Commissioners of Customs and Excise, 16th December
    1966)
91 From James Joyce, 11th March 1923.
92 (*Ulysses* accounts)
93 To Sylvia Beach, 4th May 1923.
94 (To Sylvia Beach, 1st May 1923)

Chapter 11

CLOSING DOWN

1   From James Joyce, 10th June 1923.
2   (Lucia Joyce, in conversation with Jane Lidderdale)
3   (To Bjørn Rasmussen, 28th March 1961)
4   (James Joyce to Sylvia Beach, 12th July 1923. Buffalo)
5   To Sylvia Beach, 28th July 1923.
6   To Sylvia Beach, 14th June 1923.
7   W. Y. Tindall to Jane Lidderdale, 12th February 1968.
8   To Sylvia Beach, 31st August 1923.
9   Ellmann, p. 557.
10 (For example, James Joyce's letter of 9th October 1923)
11 (James Joyce to Sylvia Beach, 20th July 1923. Buffalo)
12 From James Joyce, 5th July 1923.
13 *Letters* II, Introduction, p. xlvii.
14 James Joyce to Sylvia Beach, 12th July 1923. Buffalo.
15 *Life and the Dream*, by Mary Colum. New York. Macmillan, 1947, p. 385.
16 *The Dublin Diary of Stanislaus Joyce*, edited by G. H. Healey. London. Faber,
    1958, p. 30. Cornell University Press, 1958.
17 *My Brother's Keeper*, by Stanislaus Joyce. London. Faber, 1958, p. 196. New York.
    Viking Press, 1958.
18 *Rude Assignment*, by Wyndham Lewis. London. Hutchinson, 1950, pp. 105/6.
19 (From James Joyce, 19th July 1923)
20 British Museum.
21 Ibid.
22 Ibid.
23 From James Joyce, 2nd August 1923.
24 British Museum.
25 From James Joyce, 23rd August 1923.
26 From James Joyce, 17th October 1923.
27 (To Sylvia Beach, 8th September 1923)
28 From John Quinn, 30th October 1923. Copy, New York Public Library.
29 From James Joyce, 17th December 1923.
30 From James Joyce, 9th October 1923.

31 From James Joyce, 2nd November 1923.
32 To Sylvia Beach, 5th November 1923.
33 To Sylvia Beach, 28th November 1923.
34 To Sylvia Beach, 6th December 1923.
35 From James Joyce, 8th February 1924.
36 From James Joyce, 16th January 1924.
37 From James Joyce, 8th February 1924.
38 British Museum.
39 James Joyce to Robert McAlmon, ? 18th February 1924. *Letters* III, 88.
40 From James Joyce, 7th March 1924.
41 British Museum.
42 From James Joyce, 15th March 1924.
43 From James Joyce, 24th March 1924.
44 Ibid.
45 From James Joyce, 6th April 1924.
46 James Joyce to Ford Madox Ford, 8th April 1924. *Letters* III, 93.
47 James Joyce to Sylvia Beach, 19th April 1924. Buffalo.
48 From James Joyce, 6th April 1924.
49 To Sylvia Beach, 20th May 1924.
50 Ibid.
51 Ibid.
52 From James Joyce, 24th May 1924.
53 Ibid.
54 To Sylvia Beach, 2nd June 1924.
55 From James Joyce, 27th June 1924.
56 Ibid.
57 From Dora Marsden, 7th July 1924.
58 Ibid.
59 Ibid.
60 From James Joyce, 30th July 1924.
61 Handwritten note by Harriet Weaver. Weaver.
62 Minute Book.
63 From Dora Marsden, 21st July 1924.

Chapter 12

SELDOM SEEN

1 (James Joyce to Sylvia Beach, 12th July 1924. Buffalo)
2 From James Joyce, 16th August 1924.
3 Ibid.
4 *Being Geniuses Together*, p. 42.
5 Op. cit., p. 54.
6 (*The Times*, 17th February 1969)
7 *Being Geniuses Together*, pp. 54/56.
8 Op. cit., pp. 54/56.
9 Bryher to Jane Lidderdale, 29th September 1963.

SOURCES

10 To Bryher, 9th October 1924.
11 *The Heart to Artemis*, by Bryher. New York. Harcourt, Brace & World, Inc. 1962. London. Collins, 1963, p. 215.
12 Notes by Lucia Joyce.
13 (From James Joyce to Sylvia Beach, 16th October 1924. Buffalo)
14 From James Joyce, 9th November 1924.
15 To Sylvia Beach, 12th November 1924.
16 Sylvia Beach to Mrs Sylvester Beach, 4th November 1924. Princeton.
17 From James Joyce, 9th & 16th November 1924.
18 (To Sylvia Beach, 16th December 1924)
19 (Ewart Marsden, in conversation with Jane Lidderdale, 25th June 1962)
20 From James Joyce, 23rd December 1924.
21 From James Joyce, 1st January 1925.
22 Ibid.
23 From Kearsley Weaver, 2nd February 1925.
24 From James Joyce, 23rd February 1925.
25 To Sylvia Beach, 20th February 1925; and postscript, 24th February 1925.
26 From James Joyce, 26th February 1925.
27 To Sylvia Beach, 11th April 1925.
28 From James Joyce, 26th February, 7th March and 25th March 1925.
29 To Sylvia Beach, 11th April 1925.
30 (From James Joyce, 11th April 1925)
31 From James Joyce, 25th April 1925
32 To Sylvia Beach, 22nd June 1925.
33 (Ibid)
34 (Ibid)
35 Ibid.
36 Robert MacAlmon to Sylvia Beach, 1st July [1925]. Princeton.
37 To Sylvia Beach, 22nd June 1925.
38 (Ibid)
39 From James Joyce, 15th August 1925.
40 From James Joyce, 29th August 1925.
41 From James Joyce, 27th September 1925.
42 From Edgell Richwood, editor of *The Calendar*, to Sylvia Beach, 3rd October [1925]. Princeton.
43 (To Sylvia Beach, 17th October 1925)
44 From Dora Marsden, 7th October 1925.
45 From James Joyce, 5th November 1925.
46 To Sylvia Beach, 15th December 1925.
47 From James Joyce, 20th January 1926.
48 From James Joyce to Sylvia Beach, 29th January 1926. Buffalo.
49 To Sylvia Beach, 5th April 1926.
50 (From James Joyce, 20th January 1926)
51 Ellmann, p. 587.
52 To Sylvia Beach, 5th April 1926.
53 Ibid.
54 From Dora Marsden, 22nd March 1926.

55   From Dora Marsden, 1st April 1926.
56   Ibid.
57   To Sylvia Beach, 14th June 1926.
58   From James Joyce, 5th March 1926.
59   From James Joyce, 17th April 1926.
60   (From James Joyce, 21st May 1926)
61   From James Joyce, 7th June 1926.
62   To Sylvia Beach, 14th June 1926.
63   To Sylvia Beach, 13th August 1926.
64   From James Joyce, 29th August 1926.
65   From James Joyce, 24th September 1926.
66   Ellmann, p. 594.
67   From Alfred Weaver, 3rd October 1926.
68   From Mrs Campbell Hone, 7th October 1926.
69   From Mary Weaver, 9th October 1926.
70   From James Joyce, 16th October 1926.
71   From James Joyce, 8th November 1926.
72   From James Joyce, 15th November 1926.
73   Ellmann, p. 596.
74   From James Joyce, 24th November 1926.
75   From James Joyce, 29th November 1926.
76   To James Joyce, 3rd December 1926.
77   From James Joyce, 5th December 1926.
78   To Sylvia Beach, 21st December 1926.
79   Ellmann, p. 602.
80   From James Joyce, 1st February 1927.
81   Ellmann, p. 602/603.
82   To Bjørn Rasmussen, 28th March 1961.

Chapter 13

SPACE AND TIME

1   *Rococo*, by Ralph Cheever Dunning. Paris. Edward W. Titus at the sign of the
     Black Manikin. 1926.
2   From James Joyce, 18th February 1927.
3   From James Joyce, 16th March 1927.
4   Postcard from James Joyce, 16th April 1927.
5   From James Joyce, 12th May 1927.
6   From James Joyce, 31st May 1927.
7   From James Joyce, 14th August 1927.
8   For Harriet Weaver's moves see Ellmann pp. 609/610.
9   James Joyce to Sylvia Beach, 27th March 1927. Buffalo
10   From James Joyce, 12th May 1927.
11   (From James Joyce, 20th May 1927)
12   (From James Joyce, 31st May 1927)
13   From James Joyce, 3rd July 1927.

14 From James Joyce, 10th July 1927.

15 Ibid.

16 From James Joyce, 26th July 1927.

17 From James Joyce, 14th August 1927.

18 To Sylvia Beach, 20th November 1927.

19 Ibid.

20 (Ellmann, p. 612)

21 (Ellmann, p. 611)

22 Arthur Power, in conversation with Jane Lidderdale, 17th June 1967.

23 Ellmann, pp. 611/612.

24 (Notes on Harriet Weaver by Lucia Joyce)

25 From James Joyce, 15th February 1928.

26 From James Joyce, 8th April 1928.

27 British Museum. In revised form, *Finnegans Wake*, p. 414.

28 From James Joyce, 30th June 1928.

29 Samuel Alexander to Dora Marsden, 28th February 1928.

30 Samuel Alexander to Dora Marsden, 20th March 1928.

31 To Sylvia Beach, 22nd March 1928.

32 Samuel Alexander to Dora Marsden, 5th May 1928.

33 Ibid.

34 Storm Jameson to Dora Marsden, 12th September 1928.

35 Storm Jameson to Dora Marsden, 26th September 1928.

36 To Sylvia Beach, 1st October 1928.

37 From James Joyce, 23rd October 1928.

38 To Sylvia Beach, 18th October 1928.

39 To Sylvia Beach, 29th September [not August] 1928.

40 To Sylvia Beach, 18th November 1928.

41 To Sylvia Beach, 25th November 1928.

42 Bertrand Russell (later Lord Russell) to Storm Jameson, 6th December 1928. Dyson.

43 To Sylvia Beach, 4th December 1928.

44 To Sylvia Beach, 20th December 1928.

45 Ibid.

46 Dyson.

47 To Sylvia Beach, 14th January 1929.

48 To Sylvia Beach, 21st January 1929.

49 From Dora Marsden, 9th March 1929.

50 The *Times Literary Supplement*, 7th February 1929, p. 102

51 Edith Walker to Jane Lidderdale, 8th June 1962.

52 (Edith Walker to Jane Lidderdale, 21st November 1966)

53 (From James Joyce, 16th July 1929)

54 To Sylvia Beach, 31st October 1929.

55 From Dora Marsden, 20th December 1929. Copy made by Harriet Weaver. Dyson.

56 To Dora Marsden, 21st December 1929.

57 From Dora Marsden, third page, undated, of a copy typed by Harriet Weaver. Dyson.

58 To Dora Marsden, 31st December 1929.
59 Ibid.
60 Ibid.
61 (From Dora Marsden, 3rd January 1930)
62 To Dora Marsden, 8th January 1930.
63 To Sylvia Beach, 20th January 1930.
64 To Sylvia Beach, 25th February 1930.
65 (To Sylvia Beach, 5th March 1930)
66 From James Joyce, 18th March 1930.
67 (Ellmann, pp. 635/636)
68 Interview with F. R. D'O. Monro, 2nd August 1962.
69 *An Appreciation of James Joyce*, by Paul Léon. *Poésie*, 1942.

Chapter 14

The Dark Side of Friendship

1   (From James Joyce, 6th September 1930)
2   From James Joyce, 22nd October 1930.
3   British Museum.
4   From James Joyce, 22nd November 1930.
5   British Museum.
6   Stuart Gilbert, in conversation with Jane Lidderdale, 3rd December 1962.
7   Frank Budgen, in conversation with Jane Lidderdale, 17th May 1962.
8   From James Joyce, 22nd December 1930.
9   From James Joyce, 16th, 18th February and 4th, 11th March 1931.
10 To Sylvia Beach, 15th March 1931.
11 Ibid.
12 Robert McAlmon to Sylvia Beach, 17th February 1932. Princeton.
13 Maria Jolas, in conversation with Jane Lidderdale, 25th November 1967.
14 Mrs Stuart Gilbert, in conversation with Jane Lidderdale, 2nd February 1966.
15 From *Miss Sylvia Beach* by T. S. Eliot, in the special number of the *Mercure de France* devoted to her. August-September 1963.
16 To Sylvia Beach, 17th September 1931; and from T. S. Eliot, 11th September 1931. Copy, Eliot.
17 (Ellmann, p. 652)
18 To Sylvia Beach, 6th November 1931.
19 Ibid.
20 (To Sylvia Beach, 28th December 1931)
21 Minute book.
22 To Sylvia Beach, 28th December 1931.
23 From James Joyce, 17th January 1932.
24 (Ellmann, p. 659)
25 *Shakespeare and Company*, p. 208.
26 (Ellmann, p. 663)
27 (Ellmann, p. 661/662)
28 (From Dora Marsden, 8th March 1932)
29 From Dora Marsden, 9th May 1932.

SOURCES

Chapter 15

DESPATCHES FROM MR LÉON

1 To T. S. Eliot, 5th April 1932.
2 From James Joyce, 20th April 1932.
3 Ibid.
4 (Ellmann, p. 663)
5 Ellmann, p. 664.
6 From James Joyce, 10th July 1932.
7 (Copy of an extract from a letter from James Joyce to Paul Léon, presumably made by the latter, 12th July 1932. *Letters* III, 248)
8 From James Joyce, 22nd July 1932.
9 (From James Joyce, 6th August 1932)
10 From James Joyce, 22nd September 1932.
11 To Bjørn Rasmussen, 9th March 1961.
12 (Ellmann, p. 674)
13 From James Joyce, 25th November 1932.
14 From James Joyce, 11th November 1932.
15 Ibid.
16 From James Joyce, 25th November 1932.
17 From Dora Marsden, 22nd December 1932.
18 Ibid.
19 Ibid.
20 From Paul Léon, 7th [not 4th] January 1933. *Letters* III, 268.
21 Ibid.
22 From James Joyce, 18th January 1933.
23 (From Myrsine Moschos, 29th January 1933. *Letters* I, 334)
24 (From Paul Léon, 17th and 23rd March 1933. *Letters* III, 270 and 272/275)
25 Ibid.
26 Ellmann, p. 675.
27 From Paul Léon, 17th March 1933. *Letters* III, 270.
28 From Paul Léon, 23rd March 1933. *Letters* III, 273.
29 From Paul Léon, 23rd March 1933. *Letters* III, 272/275.
30 From Paul Léon, 25th April 1933. *Letters* III, 276/278.
31 (To Sylvia Beach, 26th April 1933)
32 Paul Léon to Frank Budgen, 7th May 1933. *Letters* III, 279)
33 (Ibid)
34 (From Paul Léon, 22nd May 1933)
35 (Ibid)
36 From Paul Léon, 22nd May 1933.
37 The *Guardian*, 26th May 1933, p. 14.
38 (From Paul Léon, 22nd May 1933)
39 Postcard to Sylvia Beach, 22nd August 1933.
40 (James Joyce to Frank Budgen, 28th August 1933. *Letters* III, 283)
41 From Paul Léon, 23rd September 1933. *Letters* III, 287.
42 Ibid.

43 From the judgment reprinted in the first edition of *Ulysses* published by Random House, New York, in February 1934.

44 From T. S. Eliot to Monro Saw & Co., 28th November 1933. *Letters* III, 293.

45 (Ellmann, p. 679)

46 (From Paul Léon, 9th January 1934)

47 To Maria Jolas, 2nd February 1955)

48 (Ellmann, p. 679)

49 To Sylvia Beach, 7th February 1934.

50 (Ellmann, p. 680)

51 From James Joyce, 24th April 1934.

Chapter 16

'THE OGRE WILL COME'

1 (*Spanish Testament*, by Arthur Koestler. London. Gollancz, 1937, p. 54. New York, Macmillan, 1937)

2 From James Joyce, 28th July 1934.

3 From James Joyce, 22nd September 1934.

4 Ibid.

5 From Paul Léon, 2nd October 1934.

6 From James Joyce, 21st October 1934.

7 Ellmann, p. 589.

8 From James Joyce, 21st October 1934.

9 From James Joyce, 17th December 1934.

10 (Ellmann, pp. 693/694)

11 (Ellmann, p. 694)

12 From Paul Léon, 21st February 1935.

13 (Ellmann, p. 694)

14 James Joyce to Eileen Schaurek, 13th March 1935. *Letters* III, 349.

15 Ibid.

16 From Paul Léon, 28th March 1935.

17 Ibid.

18 From James Joyce, 7th April 1935.

19 Ibid.

20 (Postscript, written some days later, to Paul Léon's letter of 28th March 1935)

21 (From James Joyce, 7th April 1935)

22 (Edith Walker in conversation with Jane Lidderdale, 9th September 1963)

23 From Dora Marsden, 9th March 1935.

24 From James Joyce, 1st May 1935.

25 James Joyce to Lucia Joyce in Italian, [9th] May 1935. *Letters* III, 355.

26 A remark made at the time by Harriet Weaver to Norah Lidderdale (*née* Adair Roberts), a lifelong friend.

27 Postscript, in Italian, to a missing letter from James Joyce to George Joyce, about 10th April 1935. *Letters* III, 353.

28 James Joyce to Michael Healy, 28th June 1935. *Letters* I, 372.

29 (James Joyce to George Joyce, in Italian, 10th July 1935. *Letters* III, 364)

30 (James Joyce to Lucia Joyce, in Italian, [?] July 1935. *Letters* I, 377)
31 Constantine Curran, in conversation with Jane Lidderdale, 16th June 1967.
32 (James Joyce to Michael Healy, [13th July 1935]. *Letters* III, 368)
33 James Joyce to George and Helen Joyce, 16th July 1935. *Letters* III, 369.
34 From Paul Léon, 19th July 1935.
35 Constantine Curran, in conversation with Jane Lidderdale, 19th June 1967.
36 James Joyce to Mr and Mrs Constantine Curran, 31st July 1935. *Letters* I, 378.
37 Maria Jolas in conversation with Jane Lidderdale, 25th November 1967.
38 To Richard Ellmann, 23rd November 1958.
39 Constantine Curran, in conversation with Jane Lidderdale, 16th June 1967.
40 To Richard Ellmann, 23rd November 1958.
41 James Joyce to Lucia Joyce, [?] July 1935. Original, in Italian, apparently destroyed. Translated by Lucia Joyce for Harriet Weaver. *Letters* I, 377.
42 (James Joyce to George Joyce, in Italian, 13th August 1935. *Letters* III, 372)
43 From Paul Léon, 29th July 1935.
44 From Paul Léon, [? 4th] August 1935.
45 Edith Walker, in conversation with Jane Lidderdale, 17th August 1967.
46 Ibid.
47 Ibid.
48 Ibid.
49 Lucia Joyce, in conversation with Jane Lidderdale.
50 Edith Walker, in conversation with Jane Lidderdale, 17th August 1967.
51 From James Joyce, 11th October 1935. *Letters* I, 385.
52 Edith Walker, in conversation with Jane Lidderdale, 17th August 1967.
53 James Joyce to Lucia Joyce, in Italian, 9th December 1935. Lucia Joyce.
54 (Edith Walker, in conversation with Jane Lidderdale, 17th August 1967)

Chapter 17

COMRADE JOSEPHINE

1 (Ellmann, p. 699)
2 Sylvia Beach to Holly Beach Dennis, 2nd April 1936. Princeton.
3 To Sylvia Beach, 22nd March 1936. Princeton.
4 (Sylvia Beach to T. S. Eliot, 21st March 1936. Copy, Princeton)
5 Interview with an ex-member of the Communist Party who wished to remain anonymous.
6 Ibid.
7 (Notes on Harriet Weaver by Maire Gaster, 20th September 1967)
8 From Dora Marsden, 2nd August 1939.
9 From Paul Léon, 8th May 1936.
10 From James Joyce, 9th June 1936.
11 Quoted by *Labour Monthly*, September 1936, a periodical edited by Palme Dutt, to which Harriet Weaver was already subscribing. It was Marxist in outlook.
12 (Mrs J. Olivier (Mercy Weaver) to Jane Lidderdale, 4th October 1967)
13 (To the *Marylebone Record and West London News*, 2nd November 1936)
14 From Paul Léon, 3rd November 1936.

SOURCES

15 (From Paul Léon, 22nd May 1936)
16 From Paul Léon, 12th July 1936.
17 From Paul Léon, 18th November 1936.
18 To Sylvia Beach, 9th July 1937.
19 Interview with Helen Roeder, then a communist, 25th February 1962.
20 The *Daily Herald*, 1st May 1937.
21 From Paul Léon, 4th August 1937.
22 (To Sylvia Beach, 9th July 1937)
23 Weaver.
24 Lucile Hyneman, in conversation with Jane Lidderdale, 28th July 1964.
25 Geoffrey de Ste Croix, in conversation with Jane Lidderdale, 17th February 1962.
26 Dr Elizabeth Jacobs, in conversation with Jane Lidderdale, 18th September 1967.
27 To Sylvia Beach, 22nd December 1937.
28 From Paul Léon, 7th October 1937.
29 From Paul Léon, 18th December 1937.
30 From Paul Léon, 2nd February 1938.
31 (The *Marylebone Record*, 12th February 1938)
32 To the *Marylebone Record*, 26th February 1938.
33 (Geoffrey de Ste Croix, in conversation with Jane Lidderdale, 17th February 1962)
34 (The *Daily Herald*, 2nd May 1938)
35 (The *Marylebone Record*, 30th April 1938)
36 (The *Daily Herald*, 18th July 1938)
37 (Maire Gaster to Jane Lidderdale, 20th September 1967)
38 From Paul Léon, 17th August 1938.
39 (A. T. K. Grant, then a member of the Marylebone Labour Party Committee, to Jane Lidderdale, 1st April 1963)
40 (Maire Gaster to Jane Lidderdale, 20th September 1967)
41 From Paul Léon, 16th December 1938.
42 To Sylvia Beach, 20th December 1938.
43 *La France veut la Liberté*. Essays by Paul Valéry and others. Paris. Librairie Plon, 1938.
44 To Sylvia Beach, 15th January 1939.
45 From Paul Léon, 19th July 1935.
46 (The *Marylebone Record*, passim, April–June 1939)
47 From James Joyce, 19th June 1939.
48 (Notes on Harriet Weaver by Halliday Lidderdale, 1963)
49 Edith Walker, in conversation with Jane Lidderdale, 2nd May 1962.
50 (To T. S. Eliot, 17th January 1941)
51 (Ellmann, pp. 741/743)
52 From James Joyce, 22nd March 1940.
53 Copy, Weaver.
54 (Note by Harriet Weaver on her copy of the cable of 18th December 1940 from James Joyce)
55 Weaver.

SOURCES

56 (Edith Walker to Jane Lidderdale, 19th October 1966)
57 Extracts from the BBC 8 a.m. news bulletin, 13th January 1941.
58 (Edith Walker to Jane Lidderdale, 19th October 1966)
59 (From F. R. D'O. Monro, 20th March 1944)
60 (To T. S. Eliot, 17th January 1941)
61 Cable from Nora Joyce, 23rd January 1941.
62 To T. S. Eliot, 17th January 1941.
63 (To T. S. Eliot, 31st January 1941)
64 Ibid.
65 To T. S. Eliot, 5th February 1941.
66 Anthony Weaver, in conversation with Jane Lidderdale, 6th January 1968.
67 Quoted by Harriet Weaver in a letter to Evelyn Cotton, 29th August, 1947.
   Copy, Weaver. (Constantine Curran's letter to her has not survived.)
68 (To Dr R. J. Hayes, Director, National Library of Ireland, 22nd June 1951)
69 Edith Walker, in conversation with Jane Lidderdale, 2nd May 1962.

Chapter 18

OXFORD

1 Helen Saunders to Jane Lidderdale, [?] February 1962.
2 Notes by Helen Saunders.
3 Ibid.
4 Interview with Mick Leahy, 28th January 1963.
5 Notes on Harriet Weaver by Lady Floud, 1962.
6 (Hansard, 28th January 1941, column 518)
7 Barbara Niven to Jane Lidderdale, 12th December 1962.
8 Christopher and Bridget Hill, in conversation with Jane Lidderdale, 13th March
   1963.
9 Notes by Helen Saunders.
10 (To Sylvia Beach, 25th May 1947)
11 (W. von Leyden to Jane Lidderdale, 21st November 1967)
12 To Sylvia Beach, 25th May 1947.
13 (To B. W. Huebsch, 30th December 1945.)
14 Ibid.
15 To Lionel Monro, 27th September 1947.
16 Edith Walker to Jane Lidderdale, 31st December 1961.
17 Edith Walker in conversation with Jane Lidderdale, 17th August 1967.
18 Barbara Niven to Jane Lidderdale, 12th December 1962.
19 To B. W. Huebsch, 30th December 1945..
20 Interview with Mick Leahy, 29th January 1963.
21 To B. W. Huebsch, 30th December 1945.
22 To F. R. D'O. Monro, 1st January 1946.
23 Interview with F. R. D'O. Monro, 2nd August 1962.
24 To Lionel Monro, 29th May 1946.
25 To Lionel Monro, 4th July 1946.
26 To Lionel Monro, 15th July 1946.

27 (Peter du Sautoy to Lionel Monro, 3rd November 1955. Society of Authors)
28 (To Lionel Monro, 6th June 1947)
29 (The Albatross Ltd. to Monro Saw & Co., 7th March 1948 and 31st May 1949. Society of Authors)
30 (Jonathan Cape to Monro Saw & Co., 12th December 1946. Society of Authors)
31 (The Bodley Head to Monro Saw & Co., 8th October 1947. Society of Authors)
32 To John J. Slocum, 27th August 1948.
33 (Ellmann, footnote, pp. 746/747)
34 (To B. W. Huebsch, 30th December 1945. Huebsch)
35 Lionel Monro to James Laughlin, New Directions, 6th December 1946. Copy, Society of Authors.
36 From B. W. Huebsch, 20th December 1945.
37 To B. W. Huebsch, 30th December 1945.
38 (Note of meeting by Harriet Weaver, 25th July 1946. Weaver)
39 (Maria Jolas to Jane Lidderdale, 23rd April 1969)
40 To Lionel Monro, 19th July 1947.
41 Faber and Faber to Monro Saw & Co., 18th December 1946. Copy, Faber.
42 Evelyn Cotton to Monro Saw & Co., 2nd September 1946. Society of Authors.
43 From Dora Marsden, 14th September 1946.
44 Ibid.
45 (To the Secretary, The Clarendon Press, 30th January 1947. Copy, Weaver)
46 To the Secretary, The Clarendon Press, 5th February 1947. Copy, Weaver.
47 From the Secretary, The Clarendon Press, 4th February 1947.
48 To the Secretary, The Clarendon Press, 2nd March 1947. Copy, Weaver.
49 From T. S. Eliot, 4th July 1947.
50 To T. S. Eliot, 8th July 1947.
51 From John J. Slocum, 17th May 1947.
52 From John J. Slocum, 13th February 1947.
53 To John J. Slocum, 25th February 1947.
54 From John J. Slocum, 17th May 1947.
55 (Shakespeare and Company, p. 224)
56 To Sylvia Beach, 25th May 1947.
57 To Sylvia Beach, 5th June 1947.
58 From Evelyn Cotton, 18th June 1947.
59 Lucie Léon to Maître Charles Gervais, 30th June 1947. Princeton.
60 From Maria Jolas, 3rd January 1948.
61 (To John J. Slocum, 11th July 1948)
62 Stuart Gilbert, in conversation with Jane Lidderdale, 3rd December 1962.
63 Ibid.
64 To Sylvia Beach, 7th July and 16th December 1947.
65 Sylvia Beach to Holly Beach Dennis, 2nd August 1947. Princeton.
66 To Sylvia Beach, 7th July 1947.
67 Ibid.
68 (To T. S. Eliot, 12th July 1947. Faber)
69 To B. W. Huebsch, 18th February 1948.
70 (To Evelyn Cotton, 28th September 1947. Copy, Weaver)
71 To Sylvia Beach, 16th December 1947.

72 John J. Slocum to Monro Saw & Co., 5th July 1947, copied to Harriet Weaver. Yale.
73 To John J. Slocum, 25th October 1947.
74 To John J. Slocum, 4th January 1948.
75 To John J. Slocum, 9th December 1947.
76 From John J. Slocum, 15th January 1948.
77 From John J. Slocum, 30th January 1948.
78 To John J. Slocum, 27th August 1948.
79 Ibid.
80 (To David Hayman, 15th April 1959)
81 To Peter du Sautoy, 8th March 1948.
82 To Peter du Sautoy, 18th October 1948; and to John J. Slocum, 8th October 1948.
83 (From Constantine Curran, 24th October 1948)
84 (To Stanislaus Joyce, 21st January 1948. Copy, Weaver)
85 (From Stanislaus Joyce, 7th March 1948)
86 From Stuart Gilbert, 12th June 1948.
87 To Peter du Sautoy, 4th February 1949.
88 (Notes on Harriet Weaver by Patricia Hutchins, October 1962 and March 1969)
89 To John J. Slocum, 10th February 1950.
90 Ibid.
91 Notes by Helen Saunders.
92 To John J. Slocum, 14th December 1949.
93 To Sylvia Beach, 31st March 1949.
94 From Sylvia Beach, 2nd April 1949.
95 (From Sylvia Beach, 2nd November 1949)
96 (Sylvia Beach to Holly Beach Dennis, 25th May 1949. Princeton)
97 Notes by Helen Saunders.
98 Interview with W. R. Rodgers, 16th November 1967.
99 To Patricia Hutchins, 5th August 1949.
100 To Sylvia Beach, 21st August 1949.
101 To Sylvia Beach, 13th September 1949.
102 To Maria Jolas, 25th August 1949.
103 (To Lionel Monro, 16th October 1949)
104 (Ibid)
105 To John J. Slocum, 1st November 1949.
106 (Text of broadcast, annotated by Sylvia Beach. Princeton)
107 (From Sylvia Beach, 2nd November 1949)
108 To John J. Slocum, 1st November 1949.
109 The *Irish Independent*, 21st August 1947.
110 To Evelyn Cotton, 29th August 1947. Copy, Weaver.
111 Ibid.
112 From Evelyn Cotton, 25th September 1947.
113 To John J. Slocum, 1st November and 14th December 1949.

SOURCES

Chapter 19

St Luke's Summer

1 To John J. Slocum, 14th December 1949.
2 Interview with Ernie Keeling, 28th January 1962.
3 (Summary of the leader by Harry Pollitt, Secretary of the Communist Party, in the *Daily Worker* on the eve of the poll, 22nd February 1950)
4 Interview with Ernie Keeling, 28th January 1962.
5 Ibid.
6 (*Morning Star* Library)
7 To Sylvia Beach, 27th February 1950.
8 To Patricia Hutchins, 22nd February 1950.
9 To Anthony Weaver, 19th February 1950.
10 To John J. Slocum, 3rd May 1950.
11 (Patricia Hutchins to Jane Lidderdale, 24th March 1969)
12 To Patricia Hutchins, 29th May 1950.
13 Notes by Patricia Hutchins.
14 Patricia Hutchins to Jane Lidderdale, 24th March 1969.
15 To Peter Russell, 11th June 1950. Buffalo.
16 From Sean MacBride to Nora Joyce, 12th June 1950. Copy made by Harriet Weaver. Maria Jolas.
17 (To Maria Jolas, 21st June 1950)
18 To Maria Jolas, 28th July 1950.
19 From Maria Jolas, 31st July 1950. Copy, Jolas.
20 To John J. Slocum, 14th December 1949.
21 To Sylvia Beach, 10th September 1950.
22 Ibid.
23 From Stuart Gilbert, 8th May 1950.
24 B. W. Huebsch to Stuart Gilbert, 10th February 1950. Copied to Harriet Weaver.
25 From Stuart Gilbert, 8th May 1950.
26 From Stuart Gilbert, 10th July 1950.
27 To Sylvia Beach, 10th September 1950.
28 From Sylvia Beach, 13th September 1950.
29 Sylvia Beach to Holly Beach Dennis, 9th November 1950. Princeton.
30 Sylvia Beach to Holly Beach Dennis, 10th October 1950. Princeton.
31 (To Stuart Gilbert, 9th November 1950. Copy, Weaver)
32 Stuart Gilbert to Peter du Sautoy, 18th September 1950. Faber.
33 Stuart Gilbert to Jane Lidderdale, 26th March 1968.
34 To Sylvia Beach, 28th October, 1950.
35 To Dr R. J. Hayes, 30th June 1951.
36 (To John J. Slocum, 15th October 1950)
37 (To John J. Slocum, 12th October 1950)
38 (To Dr R. J. Hayes, 30th June 1949)
39 Maria Jolas in conversation with Jane Lidderdale, 25th November 1967.
40 George Joyce in conversation with Jane Lidderdale, 22nd June 1967.

41 (To T. S. Eliot, 7th July 1960. Eliot)
42 Cable from George Joyce, 10th April 1951.
43 To Maria Jolas, 14th April 1951.
44 Ibid.
45 George D. Painter to Jane Lidderdale, 17th March 1969.
46 To Dr R. J. Hayes, 22nd June 1951.
47 From Dr R. J. Hayes, 27th June 1951. Copy, National Library of Ireland.
48 Ibid.
49 (To Matthew Hodgart, 13th January 1957)
50 (To Dr R. J. Hayes, 4th July 1951)
51 F. H. Boland to Jane Lidderdale, 10th April 1967.
52 Ibid.
53 Ibid.
54 (To Dr R. J. Hayes, 8th July 1951)
55 (To Dr R. J. Hayes, 4th July 1951)
56 (To Peter du Sautoy, 1st June 1957; and to J. B. Bamborough, 4th June 1957)
57 Julian Brown to Jane Lidderdale, 3rd March 1968.
58 To Matthew Hodgart, 13th January 1957.
59 Julian Brown to Jane Lidderdale, 3rd March 1968.
60 Ibid.
61 Ibid.
62 To J. S. Atherton, 30th August 1954.
63 Interview with A. Walton Litz, 22nd October 1965.
64 To Richard Ellmann, 29th April 1953.
65 (To Richard Ellmann, 15th November 1953)
66 To Richard Ellmann, 10th July 1954.
67 (To Lionel Monro, 15th January 1956)
68 (To Lionel Monro, 23rd February 1956)
69 To Lionel Monro, 21st July 1956.
70 To Lionel Monro, 3rd August 1956.
71 (To Lionel Monro, 15th October 1953, et seq.)
72 To Lionel Monro, 30th August 1954.
73 (From Joseph Prescott, 1st August 1957. Society of Authors)
74 (To Lionel Monro, 19th July 1956)
75 (David Hayman to Monro Pennefather & Co., 11th June 1956. Society of Authors)
76 To Lionel Monro, 23rd June 1956.
77 To Sylvia Beach, 4th July 1955.
78 Quoted in a letter to Lionel Monro, 24th October 1954.
79 *A Portrait of the Artist as a Young Man.*
80 From T. S. Eliot, 29th September 1953.
81 (To George Joyce, 10th October 1954. Copy, Weaver)
82 From Stuart Gilbert, 8th October 1954.
83 To T. S. Eliot, 24th October 1954.
84 (Charles Monteith to Peter du Sautoy, 25th October 1954. Faber)
85 B. W. Huebsch to Stuart Gilbert, copied to Harriet Weaver, 3rd November 1954. Copy, Weaver.

86 (From Stephen Joyce, 17th December 1954)
87 To Peter du Sautoy, 12th July 1955.
88 To Peter du Sautoy, 23rd July 1955.
89 To Sylvia Beach, 10th December 1955.
90 Notes by Helen Saunders.
91 (To Anthony Weaver, 30th December 1955)
92 To Sylvia Beach, 19th June 1955.
93 Ibid.
94 From Muriel Weaver, 31st May 1956.
95 Inscriptions in books in the James Joyce Collection, National Book League.
96 (Harriet Weaver's *Notes for my Executors*, 21st February 1955)
97 Sylvia Beach to Holly Beach Dennis, 29th October 1956. Princeton.
98 Sylvia Beach to Holly Beach Dennis, 1st November 1956. Princeton.
99 Ibid.
100 Sylvia Beach to Holly Beach Dennis, 29th October 1956. Princeton.
101 Interview with Mick Leahy, 29th January 1963.
102 (To Sylvia Beach, 8th November 1956)
103 To Jane Lidderdale, 12th November 1956.
104 To Sylvia Beach, 23rd December 1956.
105 T. S. Eliot to Patricia Hutchins, 12th November 1956.
106 To Peter du Sautoy, 19th February 1957.

Chapter 20

CASTLE END

1 Christopher and Bridget Hill, in conversation with Jane Lidderdale, 13th March 1962.
2 From Barbara Niven. Undated but postmarked 1960 and 1961.
3 Angela Tuckett to Muriel Weaver, 17th October 1961. Lidderdale.
4 Notes on Harriet Weaver by Muriel Weaver 1962.
5 (To Lionel Monro, 30th April 1957)
6 From Sylvia Beach, 13th December 1956.
7 (Diary of Sylvia Beach, 4th March 1957. Princeton)
8 (Diary of Sylvia Beach, 8th April 1957. Princeton)
9 (From Sylvia Beach, 9th April 1957)
10 To Lionel Monro, 30th April 1957.
11 (From Joseph Prescott, 25th April 1957. Society of Authors)
12 (To Lionel Monro, 3rd July 1957)
13 To Sylvia Beach, 28th April 1957. Copy, Weaver.
14 Sylvia Beach to Holly Beach Dennis, 18th December 1957. Princeton.
15 Sylvia Beach to Holly Beach Dennis, 25th November 1957. Princeton.
16 Sylvia Beach to Holly Beach Dennis, 13th July 1958. Princeton.
17 *The Times*, 29th May 1957.
18 To Mrs J. Olivier, 30th May 1957.
19 ICA *Bulletin* 77, June 1957.

20 To Peter du Sautoy, 16th June 1957.
21 To Peter du Sautoy, 6th January 1960.
22 Anne Munro-Kerr in conversation with Jane Lidderdale, 17th October 1967.
23 To Lionel Monro, 12th September 1957.
24 To Richard Ellmann, 4th December 1956.
25 To Richard Ellmann, 23rd November 1958.
26 Mrs J. Olivier to Jane Lidderdale, 4th October 1967.
27 Christopher and Bridget Hill, in conversation with Jane Lidderdale, 13th March 1962.
28 (To Bjørn Rasmussen, 28th March 1960)
29 To Sylvia Beach, 2nd October 1960.
30 Clive Hart to Jane Lidderdale, 11th October 1967.
31 J. S. Atherton to Jane Lidderdale, 5th February 1968.
32 From Dora Marsden, 20th December 1958.
33 To Dora Marsden, 8th July 1959. Copy, Weaver.
34 From Dora Marsden, 19th July 1959.
35 To Dora Marsden, 29th July 1959. Copy, Weaver.
36 To Sylvia Beach, 2nd January 1960.
37 To Richard Ellmann, 30th December 1959.
38 Mrs Campbell Hone to Sylvia Beach, 2nd December 1959. Princeton.
39 To Sylvia Beach, 2nd January 1960.
40 Sylvia Beach to Holly Beach Dennis, 15th March 1960. Princeton.
41 Sylvia Beach to Holly Beach Dennis, 17th June 1960. Princeton.
42 (To Sylvia Beach, 8th July 1960)
43 To Sylvia Beach, 3rd December 1960.
44 From Sylvia Beach, 6th December 1960.
45 From the Reverend James Dyson, 14th December 1960.
46 Note by the Reverend James Dyson, undated. Dyson.
47 To Bjørn Rasmussen, 28th March 1961.
48 To Bjørn Rasmussen, 1st August 1961.
49 To Bjørn Rasmussen, 28th March 1961.
50 (To Bjørn Rasmussen, 1st August 1961)
51 Samuel Beckett to Sylvia Beach, 22nd October 1961. Princeton.

INDEX

INDEX

INDEX

INDEX

INDEX

Morning Post, 49, 206
Morrison, Herbert, 370
Morris, William, 225
Mortensens Forlag (Oslo), 395
Moschos, Myrsine, 201, 320, 321, 322
Mostel, Zero, 447
Muir, Percy, 445
Munro-Kerr, Anne, 446
Murdoch, Iris, 389
Murray, Josephine (Mrs William Murray), 130n.
Myers, Rollo H., 177

Nation and Athenaeum, The, 130, 136, 195, 205
National Book League, 426, 438, 445, 451
National Gallery of Ireland, 425
National Library of Ireland, 381, 382, 397, 412–14, 417, 418, 421, 423–6
Navire d'Argent, Le, 256–8
New Age, The, 285
New Directions, 392n., 397
New Freewoman, The, 56–81, 425; accounts, see Appendix
New Freewoman, Ltd, The, 87, 91, 109
New Hospital, 44
Nicolson, Harold, 306
Nine, 417
Niven, Barbara, 388, 442, 451
Norman, Charles, Ezra Pound, 67n.
Nouvelle Revue Française, 205
Nutting, Helen, 276, 277
Nutting, Myron, 276

Obey, André, Loire, 326
Observer, The, 192
Olivier, Mercy (Mrs J. Olivier, formerly Weaver), 362, 447
Olivier, Sarah-Jane, 447

Oxford Philosophy Library, 435
Oxford University Press, 400
Outlook, The, 205

Painter, George D., 423, 424, 427, 431n.
Pakenham, Lady, 415
Paris in the Twenties (exhibition), 451
Partridge and Cooper, Ltd, 91, 103
Path, The, 65
Paul, Elliot, 267
Pelican Press, 173–4, 177
Pentland, Mr, 114, 122, 155
Perceval, Spencer, 144
Percival, Hannah, 23, 27, 189
Percy, Lord, 49
Pethick Lawrence, Emmeline, 53, 54
Picasso, Pablo, 177
Pike's Fine Art Press, 140–2
Pinker, J. B., 102, 104, 109, 114, 116–18, 122–7, 129, 139, 141, 147, 168, 170, 171, 189, 190, 192, 234
Placzek, Miss, 392
Poetry, Chicago, 71
Poets' Translation Series, 103–4, 106, 109n., 111, 151, 157, 163, 172, 175, 190, 220, 239, 240
Ponisovsky, Alex, 312, 315
Pound, Dorothy, 119, 176, 420n.
Pound, Ezra, 66–80, 82–3, 86–8, 91, 92, 95, 97, 98, 100, 104, 106, 108, 111, 112, 113–21, 124, 128, 129, 133, 134, 136, 137–8, 139, 140, 143, 144, 146, 150, 154, 156, 158, 160, 161, 163, 172, 173, 179, 184, 186, 190, 205, 209, 218, 219, 220, 235, 240, 246–7, 250n., 266, 268, 270, 271, 305, 333, 407, 434
Powell, Anthony, 439
Power, Arthur, 250n., 277
Prescott, Joseph, 429, 436, 442–4, 448

INDEX

INDEX

EXTRACTS FROM SOME PRESS NOTICES

OF

A Portrait of the Artist as a Young Man.

By JAMES JOYCE.

THE EGOIST PRESS : LONDON : 1916 : 23, Adelphi Terrace House, 2, Robert Street, W.C. 2.

Price 6/- net : by post, 6/4.

Mr. Ezra Pound in **THE EGOIST:** James Joyce produces the nearest thing to Flaubertian prose that we have now in English . . . . his novel will remain a permanent part of English literature. . . . Apart from Mr. Joyce's realism is the style: hard, clear cut with no waste of words.

Mr. H. G. Wells in **THE NATION:** It is a book to buy and read and lock up, but it is not a book to miss. Its claim to be literature is as good as the claim of the last book of *Gulliver's Travels.* . . . Like Swift and another living Irish writer Mr. Joyce has a cloacal obsession. . . . Like some of the best novels in the world it is the story of an education. It is by far the most living and convincing picture that exists of an Irish catholic upbringing. . . . The technique is startling. . . One conversation in this book is a superb success. I write with all due deliberation that Sterne himself could not have done it better. . . . The interest of the book depends entirely on its quintessential and unfailing reality. One believes in Stephen Dedalus as one believes in few characters in fiction. . . . A most memorable novel.

Mr. Ernest Boyd in **NEW IRELAND:** . . . A pessimistic realist. . . . With a frankness and veracity as appalling as they are impressive he sets forth the relentless chronicle of a soul stifled by material and intellectual squalor. . . . An uncompromising confession. . . . A process whose analysis becomes, at the hands of Mr. Joyce, a truly amazing piece of personal and social dissection.

Mr. Solomon Eagle in **THE NEW STATESMAN:** All writing London is talking about it. . . . Sheer undecorated unintensified truth. . . . We have never had a novel in the least degree resembling this one . . . . He is a realist of the first order. . . . His honesty is complete. It is even a little too complete. Mr. Joyce can never resist a dunghill. . . . He is a genuine realist. Spiritual passions are as powerful to him as physical passions. . . . His detachment as author is almost inhuman. . . . He never even shows by a quiver of the pen that anything distresses him. His prose instrument is a remarkable one. . . . His method varies with the subject matter, and never fails him. His dialogue is as close to the dialogue of life as anything I have ever come across, and his descriptive and narrative passages include at one pole sounding periods of classical prose and at the other disjointed and almost futuristic sentences. . . . The story had better be neglected by anyone who is easily disgusted. . . . Its greatest appeal is made to the practising artist in literature. What Mr. Joyce will do with his powers in the future it is impossible to conjecture.

Mr. John Sullivan in **THE NEW WITNESS:** A finished artist. . . . Mr. Joyce describes . . . with the air of a surgeon, as frank, as clean and as severe. . . . Each character is brilliantly sketched. . . . The most obvious thing about the book is its beauty. The descriptions, the images, the wonderful prose make this novel the most exquisite production of the younger school of novelists. The welding of splendid expression and truly significant matter makes it the most authentic contribution to English literature which has appeared for some time.